HOLLYWOOD
& the best of
LOS ANGELES

Robert & Phyllis White

HUNTER

Hunter Publishing, Inc.
130 Campus Drive
Edison, NJ 08818-7816
☎ 732-225-1900 / 800-255-0343 / Fax 732-417-1744
Web site: www.hunterpublishing.com
E-mail: comments@hunterpublishing.com

IN CANADA
Ulysses Travel Publications
4176 Saint-Denis, Montréal, Québec
Canada H2W 2M5
☎ 514-843-9882 ext. 2232 / fax 514-843-9448

IN THE UK
Windsor Books International
The Boundary, Wheatley Road
Garsington, Oxford OX44 9EJ England
☎ 01865-361122 / Fax 01865-361133

ISBN 1-58843-286-6
© 2002 Hunter Publishing, Inc.

Cover: *Legends of Hollywood Mural* (Gala/Superstock)
Maps by Toni Wheeler, © 2002 Hunter Publishing, Inc.
Index by Barber Indexing

4   3   2   1

Preface

Greetings from Hollywood! Wish you were here!

Well, actually, greetings from Acton. I don't quite understand someone's desire to "see stars," but you can see me at the Shambala Preserve one weekend each month. Just call and make a reservation for a special, one-of-a-kind "safari." No, we don't have a barn full of old birds, but we do have over 50 endangered big cats, and an African elephant to keep you amused.

I came back to Los Angeles to test for the lead in *The Birds*. The year escapes me... I couldn't imagine then what I was about to get into, but it's all Hollywood history now. It was the movies, in fact, that led me down the path I have followed all the days since then. After working with Alfred Hitchcock and Charlie Chaplin (and, yes, ladies, Rod Taylor, Sean Connery and Marlon Brando. How's that for name dropping?), I made a movie in Africa that explored the endangered future of the beautiful and majestic wild animal residents of that massive and proud continent. Not long after, we began a movie project of our own that led to the founding of Shambala Preserve. That was nearly 30 years ago!

But I'm supposed to write something about "seeing stars" in Los Angeles. I can't imagine what I can add to this well researched volume of Hollywood tidbits, though I do recall many years ago running into Ida Lupino and her husband Howard Duff shopping in an all-night market. They were glamorously dressed, obviously on the way home after one of those legendary Hollywood parties. They were feeling no pain, and pushed a shopping cart up and down aisles, loudly arguing about what the other was tossing into the cart. But I digress.

This book is fun. It reads especially well with a tub of buttery popcorn and a box of Good & Plenty. I read with interest that there are over 60,000 actors living in Los Angeles. How disconcerting. No wonder I can't get a job. Which reminds me... if you really want to see stars, go to the Hollywood unemployment office. And get in line. Music swells. Lights fade. THE END.

With love for the Wild Ones...

Tippi Hedren

About the Authors

Phyllis and Robert White have lived in Los Angeles most of their lives. Robert spent much of his childhood here, and went to Hollywood High and Los Angeles City College. He started writing scripts for the networks while at LACC. Phyllis, after attending the University of Minnesota and working for CBS in New York for several years, also ended up in Hollywood. As a couple they worked at most of the studios, writing many prime-time television shows as well as daytime soaps. They know the movie business and many of the people who work in it, and in Hollywood, from the inside.

These days, Phyllis and Robert write about travel. They have written feature articles for the travel sections of several dozen newspapers and magazines. Their previous book for Hunter Publishing was *Romantic Weekends: San Francisco and the Bay Area*. They presently live in Venice, a beach community 10 miles west of Hollywood.

About the Alive Guides

Reliable, detailed and personally researched by knowledgeable authors, the *Alive!* series was founded by Harriet and Arnold Greenberg.

This accomplished travel-writing team also operates a renowned bookstore, **The Complete Traveller**, at 199 Madison Avenue in New York City.

We Love to Get Mail

This book has been carefully researched to bring you current, accurate information. But no place is unchanging. We welcome your comments for future editions. Please write us at *Alive Guides*, c/o Hunter Publishing, 130 Campus Drive, Edison, NJ 08818, or e-mail your comments to comments@hunterpublishing.com. Due to the volume of mail we receive, we regret that we cannot personally reply to each letter or message, but your comments are greatly appreciated and will be read.

Acknowledgments

Writing a book like this is great fun; at least, if your passion in life is writing, it is. But the facts to be checked, and the half-remembered stories to be double-checked and the research to be done would make it a never-ending job if there weren't so many people willing to lend a hand.

We can't thank everyone we talked to, or who called us back with more information or sent us a clipping; that would take another book this size. But we would like to mention John Duel at the LA Convention & Visitors Bureau, and our screenwriter friends who made suggestions about individual chapters relating to their communities. We have special appreciation for the staff of the Marina del Rey Public Library, who were, once again, incredibly patient over a period of months as they located obscure research material for us. And, of course, Lorry King and Anne White, our Internet mentors.

Oscar sketched on napkin, May 11, 1927, at the founding banquet for the Academy of Motion Picture Arts & Sciences.

Dedication

To Ray Walston and our days on *My Favorite Martian*, belatedly.

Contents

Below the Foothills

Day-Trips

The Movies & More...

Index

Maps

Introduction

Life is never quite interesting enough, somehow. You people who come to the movies know that.
— Shirley Booth, *The Matchmaker*

When you come to Hollywood, of course you would like to see television and movie stars. The footprints at Grauman's Chinese Theatre and the rides at Universal Studios are well and good, and as close as most visitors get to show biz, but they are not going to reveal any actual celebrities in the flesh. Yet seeing stars is, with a little bit of luck, perfectly possible.

This book first took shape in our minds a few years ago, when we were working at the studios and, every once in a while, greeting friends and relatives from out of town. It almost always turned out that what they wanted to see and do was connected with Hollywood. Did we know any actors we could introduce them to? Could they tour a studio? Was there a movie they could see being shot?

Hollywood is as much a state of mind as it is a geographic entity.

It was easy for us to accommodate them. Bob grew up here, with time out spent elsewhere. His paper route, when he was a kid, started at the home of Billie Burke ("Glinda, the Good Witch," in *The Wizard of Oz*) and ended at that of silver screen siren Linda Darnell. He went to Hollywood High, and started selling scripts to the networks when he was at Los Angeles City College. Phyllis also ended up in Hollywood, writing scripts for the studios, after enduring Minnesota's winters while at the University of Minneapolis, then working at WBBN in Chicago, followed by a stretch at CBS in New York. One thing led to another, as it often does.

We soon realized that everyone who comes here from somewhere else feels the same way as those friends and relatives. While we can't drive each of you past the guard at the studio gate, we can tell you how to do it yourselves.

When those actors who live somewhere else return for a meeting at a studio or to attend the Academy Awards ceremony they tend to stay at one of a handful of hotels. The

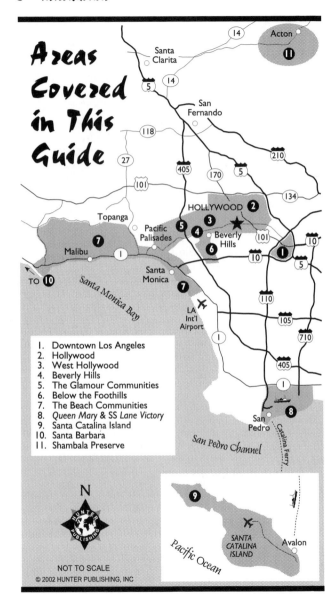

Areas Covered in This Guide

1. Downtown Los Angeles
2. Hollywood
3. West Hollywood
4. Beverly Hills
5. The Glamour Communities
6. Below the Foothills
7. The Beach Communities
8. *Queen Mary* & SS *Lane Victory*
9. Santa Catalina Island
10. Santa Barbara
11. Shambala Preserve

N

NOT TO SCALE
© 2002 HUNTER PUBLISHING, INC

idea is to stay at the same place yourself, or perhaps at least to have lunch or dinner there.

The same goes for restaurants and shopping. While new places to dine constantly appear, are hot for a while and then fade away, there are certain restaurants where the high-profile folk have been eating for years. You might splurge on at least one meal. Going shopping? You are not likely to see many celebrities at Kmart, but we will tell you where they do go.

How To Use This Book

If the name of a hotel is preceded by two stars, as in ★★ Chateau Marmont, You know it is the kind of place where you just might bump into a well-known actor in the elevator; if it has one star, like ★ Hollywood Roosevelt, you won't see any celebrities there, but it means the place has so much movie history it's well worth seeing, or even staying there yourself. If it is starless it is simply recommended as a place to stay, usually because it is handy to other things you will want to see, or to public transportation.

The same goes for restaurants, as in ★★ Patina for celebrity-watching, ★ Formosa for the good old days, and Alejo's for good food, moderately priced.

In many of the hotel and restaurant listings we mention the names of stars that we know have been seen there. Some places, however, are very protective of their celebrity guests' privacy and ask us not to use names. We respect that and do not list them, unless the names have already been mentioned in some other printed source.

The book is organized primarily by area; it covers *Downtown Los Angeles*, *Hollywood*, *West Hollywood*, *Beverly Hills*, *The Glamour Communities*, *Below the Foothills*, *The Beach Communities*, and *Day-Trips*; there is a map in each section keyed to the points of interest we mention.

If you would like to see the process of filming television shows and movies you will find out how to do that in the chapter titled *The Movies & More*, under *Going on Location* (page 547) and *TV Show Tickets* (page 549).

Several studios have tours you can join, most of them surprisingly inexpensive. A few are really very informative and provide good chances to run into working actors as you explore the studios. You will find this information in the *Studio Tours* section (page 543).

☞ DID YOU KNOW?

People who work in films and television say we work in "the industry." All those who do not work in the industry are called "civilians."

It is possible for non-film people to attend most film festivals and some awards ceremonies as guests; at others you have to stand outside to see the stars as they arrive. These events are all listed under *Film Festivals* (see page 557), with the needed information and contact numbers.

The section on *Where Stars Are Buried* (page 566) lists cemeteries where you can find graves of famous stars. There are even tours available.

Meeting the Stars

Finally, we want to talk about what to do when you find yourself in the company of a star. Years ago a friend Phyllis had gone to college with came into town with a gaggle of small Brownies in tow. We were working at Universal Studios at the time and arranged to do our part by showing the kids around the lot, ending with lunch at the executive commissary. But before we went in to the dining room we told them, "The actors eat here so they won't be bothered. Don't ask them for their autographs or tell them how much you like their movies. Promise?" Eight or 10 small heads nodded solemnly. We took them inside, led the way to a large table, looked around – no one was following us. All the Brownies were standing in a small crowd next to a table where Gene Barry (of *Bat Masterson* and *Burke's Law* fame) was sitting. As promised, they weren't asking for his autograph or saying a word, but all those big, round eyes silently watched every bite he took.

Sometimes, and in some places, it is appropriate to ask for an autograph, but we suggest that if you are in a restaurant and see your favorite star, remember that he or she is there expecting to eat in peace. Other than that, if you have a few days to spend here and really want to see stars, don't worry, you probably will.

UNIVERSAL STUDIOS' ETIQUETTE TIPS ON MEETING A CELEBRITY

◆ Don't interrupt a celebrity who is eating. The worst time to approach a star to talk to or take a photo of them is when they have food in their mouths.

◆ Adrienne Barbeau recalls the time she and a friend were having lunch in a restaurant and a stranger simply pulled up a chair and sat down as if to join them. Wait until, and if, you are asked.

◆ Stars are protective of their children. Do not try to engage their kids in any way. Do not touch a celebrity's child. Think how you would feel if strangers went after your kids. Photograph a celebrity's children only with permission (but do not expect to get it).

◆ Do not imitate their characters for them. Even if you just know they'll think it's funny or clever.

◆ Do not ask them if their hair, good looks or jewels are fake or borrowed.

◆ Don't say, "You were my favorite star when I was a very young child."

◆ Do not ask for home address or phone numbers, and don't supply yours unless you are asked.

◆ Do not ask them how much money they are making. This is always bad form, but it is a complete conversation-stopper with a celebrity.

- ◆ Do not comment on the size or shape of their physical features. How would you like it? This is not just a famous icon; this is, after all, a human being.

- ◆ Do not ask whom they are dating. Similarly, do not ask about the latest gossip, which can be one of the worst things in a celebrity's life. To you it is just intrigue; to them it is often painful and embarrassing.

▥ FILM GLOSSARY

Negative Pickup – A contract with a major studio that guarantees to distribute a movie to be produced by an independent company; the deal based on the cost of completing the picture and producing a negative. The contract is used as collateral for the producer to borrow production funds from a bank.

Geology & Geography

On a really clear day (don't smirk, we have some) you can see all the mountains that surround Los Angeles. With your back to the ocean, looking east, from left to right you'll see the Santa Monica Mountains; the higher Santa Susana Mountains behind them; and the San Gabriel Mountains with Mt. San Antonio their highest peak. The San Bernardino range is farther east; it's usually snow-capped from December to April and is a mecca for local skiers. San Gorgonio is the biggest, farthest peak in that range (with more snow that stays longer), flanking the San Gorgonio Pass to the desert; from there, the San Jacinto Range is to the south, with Palm Springs on the other side.

The Los Angeles County coastline, stretching from Malibu to Long Beach, is 76 miles long.

The Coastal Mountain Range runs northwest to southeast from Point Mugu, in Ventura County, past Malibu to Santa Monica, leaving the Pacific Coast Highway (California Route 1) squeezed between the steep slopes and the ocean. South of the mountains it is generally flat. But at the southern end of the Coastal range there is a spur that goes eastward. The south end of the range and the spur are locally called the Santa Monica Mountains. The easternmost portion, to their end at Los Feliz and the Los Angeles River, are the Hollywood Hills.

Present-day Los Angeles, of which Hollywood is a part, is many things. Within the city limits are beaches, deserts, canyons and mountains. From its northern border, the city extends 70 miles south, across a flood plain to San Pedro and the Port of Los Angeles. The altitude of the plain ranges from nine feet below sea level at Wilmington to 10,080 feet above sea level atop Mt. San Antonio. The San Fernando Valley is north of Los Angeles, behind and parallel to the Coastal Range, and is separated from Hollywood by the Hollywood Hills. The northwest side of the valley is walled in by the Santa Susana Mountains.

Hollywood is eight miles west of downtown Los Angeles and 12 miles east of the Pacific coast.

☞ DID YOU KNOW?

Happy thought for the day: most of the tens of thousands of buildings and homes on the alluvial soil south and southeast of downtown Los Angeles are built on the flood plain below the mountains. A little thing like that never stopped Los Angeles' land developers.

AN EYE-OPENING DRIVE

From its beginning at Cahuenga Boulevard (alongside the Hollywood Freeway in Cahuenga Pass), Mulholland Drive runs 43 miles west along the ridge of the mountains to their end at Point Mugu. A scenic drive nonpareil.

Los Angeles covers an area as large as Rhode Island.

History

Long Ago & Far Away

Rocks found here have been dated back 1.7 billion years. More recently, the land on which Los Angeles sits used to be in mainland Mexico. That was 25 million years ago, give or take a millennium, but that pesky San Andreas fault has been moving us north ever since. There was a time when the volcanoes were active. The geologists say the mountains rose about 15 million years ago, lifting up all this land, which used to be underwater.

Jump forward to practically modern times, a mere 10,000 years ago, to the Ice Age. The area around here was not the desert it is today (the desert is still here, merely hidden under all that cement), but had plenty of rain and was lush with tall trees, grasses and bushes. Perfect for the animals driven south by the ice: the mammoth, giant ground sloth, dire wolf, saber-toothed tiger and other things with big teeth and grumpy attitudes.

Brea *is a Spanish word meaning "tar."* You can see them all at **La Brea Tar Pits** at Wilshire Boulevard east of La Brea Avenue: the pools of thick, sticky tar are covered with water; when the animals went to drink they were caught and entombed.

The First Settlers

The latest evidence indicates that the area's first settlers came across the Bering Strait around 15,000 years ago when there was a land bridge from Asia. The group that worked its way south and settled along the coast in Southern California were called the Chumash; they spoke the Shoshonean language. The indians who lived inland called themselves the Yang-na; they founded their main village, also called Yang-na, on the west side of the river, about where present-day Los Angeles is. They were later called the Gabrielenos by the Spanish.

📖 HISTORIC NOTE

Juan Rodriquez Cabrillo began the recorded history of California when he landed at San Diego Bay in 1542.

The Europeans

The first Europeans to see the area were led by a Spanish army captain, Gaspar de Portolá, in 1769; they came by sea to San Diego and marched north. Because the priests with the expedition were Franciscans, they stopped and celebrated the jubilee of Our Lady of the Angels Church of Porciúncula, a small town in Italy. Then they camped on the banks of a river that Portolá named *El Río de Nuestra Señora de Los Angeles*.

Two years later, Father Junípero Serra arrived and founded Mission San Gabriel Arcangel a few miles east. And that was the end of the Indians' freedom and the beginning of their enslavement. Few Gabrielenos are alive today, and only a few thousand descendants of the Chumash are left.

California was owned by Spain until 1821, when the Mexicans revolted and threw out the Spaniards. Mexico secularized the Missions in 1833.

☞ DID YOU KNOW?

Present-day update: with luck, the remaining Chumash Indians will become millionaires – in California the Indian tribes are now the only ones legally allowed to open gambling casinos.

The Americans

Americans had been filtering into California throughout the Spanish and Mexican periods. Most of the ones who stuck around were deserters from ships that called here; a few, mostly trappers, made it overland. But they couldn't own land or do business if they weren't Catholic. Most converted to Catholicism, married beautiful daughters of rich *Californios* and ended up owning vast ranches. Oddly, in all of history, there is no record of an American marrying a poor or homely *California*.

You can visit Campo de Cahuenga in North Hollywood, where Frémont and Pico signed the peace treaty.

In the 1840s Commodore Robert F. Stockton, with a couple of US Navy ships, landed Marines in San Pedro. Captain Archibald Gillespie was left in charge of the town of Los Angeles and the commodore sailed away. But the Angelenos chased the occupiers off in the Battle of the Old Woman's Gun. The local people had a four-pound brass field piece that had been hidden by an old woman during the American's invasion. It was ancient, but proved to be enough. But, in the 1847 Battle of Cahuenga Pass, Andrés Pico, a leader of the *Californios*, surrendered to John Charles Frémont, an American adventurer and freebooter who had been given a field appointment as a "major" in the US Navy. Los Angeles was American from then on.

Men, and a few women, poured in from all over the world after gold was discovered in Northern California, but the newcomers were predominately Americans from the East. The *Californios*, who'd had little contact with the outside world, were used to a lush, easygoing life, where nothing was thought of spending huge amounts to throw a fiesta and inviting the families of surrounding ranches. Many

Americans, on the other hand, turned out to be hard-headed, practical and sharp in a business deal.

THE OAK OF THE GOLDEN DREAM

Gold was discovered just outside Los Angeles in 1842, six years before the famous find at Sutter's Mill up north. A ranchero named Francisco Lopéz was searching for stray horses in San Feliciano Cañon, a few miles from Newhall, north of the Mission San Fernando. He stopped in the shade of an oak tree to dig up some wild onions and saw shining golden flakes on the roots. Enough gold was found to send a quantity back to the mint in Philadelphia, but the lode itself was shallow. Everyone, though, knew the story of The Oak of the Golden Dream.

Over the next several decades, droughts caused a series of bad years, and owners of vast ranches found themselves needing money. In addition to their financial problems, squatters tried to claim the land for themselves, and the ranchers' land titles were being disputed by the newcomers in the American courts. Some of these titles went back more than a century but the boundaries were casually laid out: *"From the oak tree on the hill to the bend in the river... "* One way or another, by the turn of the century little of Los Angeles, or Southern California, remained in the original owners' hands.

The End of the 19th Century

When the Civil War started in 1861, the people of Los Angeles voted fairly solidly for the South, but the bulk of California's population was in the northern part of the state, which voted for the North. California remained loyal to the Union. After the war, local land developers advertised heavily in the East, with extravagant claims for the climate and the vast amounts of fruit the land would raise. When the transcontinental tracks laid by both the Southern Pacific and the Santa Fe railroads reached Los Angeles, a rate war dropped passenger fares from the

Los Angeles' population in 1881 was 11,183; nine years later it was 102,489.

Midwest from $125 to as low as $1. The area's population soared.

Oil was discovered. The land from around Azusa to Ontario became one vast vineyard. Beyond that, orange groves stretched all the way to Riverside. The motion picture business arrived in force in 1912.

Climate

The rain in Spain stays mainly in the plain.
– From the musical *My Fair Lady*.

Air Quality

Local land developers have always relied on our climate to lure homesteaders. Millions of badly colored postcards have been mailed East, almost always with a picture of an orange grove in the foreground and a snow-capped mountain nearby. Another popular card featured a slender woman wearing a one-piece bathing suit and white bathing cap cavorting on a beach in the never-ending sunshine.

Someone joked that the haze was a combination of smoke and fog and called it smog.

Actually, the area really looked that way until World War II. After the war it all became just too big, too sprawling. There were too many cars, and too many oil refineries; there was a sort of haze in the air so you couldn't see the mountains. We thought at first it was just a temporary condition. But instead of going away it got worse.

The mountain ranges – the Santa Monica Mountains, Hollywood Hills and San Gabriel Mountains – create a basin around the flood plain. The ocean breeze blows inland all day long and pushes the auto fumes, ozone and particulates of soot and dust ahead of it and north into the San Fernando Valley (there is a natural pass where the Los Angeles River curves around Los Feliz). An inversion layer forms on top of the pollution and keeps the smog from blowing away until nightfall, when the wind direction reverses and blows it all out to sea.

The people who live on Catalina Island have been smirking as they sit there, 20 miles offshore, avoiding the whole mess.

For years there was a lot of talk and no action, but eventually the consequences had to be faced. Scrubbers are now required in smokestacks and catalytic converters in every automobile engine. Los Angeles has the toughest clean-air regulations in the country, but even with that we have still had the worst air in the country year after year. Finally, it is getting better. There are more days when you can see the mountains. We're sorry to say the vineyards and orange groves are gone for good, but that slender woman's granddaughter is back on the beach, although her one-piece bathing suit has shrunk to barely a thong.

In general, the weather in the basin has the dry summer and moderate winter rainfall of a Mediterranean climate. The main complaint about the climate from those who move here from elsewhere is the lack of four distinct seasons. Most of the year it is sunny and warm, with gentle ocean breezes. There is fog along the coast in the spring, and lots of dry heat in summer.

Rainfall & Temperatures

You needn't worry too much about rain. California is prone to periods of drought that come in seven-year cycles (we are expecting one any year now). When you are here, instead of being handed an umbrella you are more likely to be told not to ask for a glass of water with your meal. The average annual rainfall is 15 inches, with an average of 34 rainy days each year.

Despite the monthly averages given below, Los Angeles almost always has at least three kinds of climate going on at the same time. In July it may be 82° in downtown Los Angeles, where the official temps are taken, but out at the beach there's a fog, and it is in the chilly 50s. Meanwhile, over the hills in the San Fernando Valley, the temperature may be headed toward 100°, and the hum of air conditioners is heard throughout the land. The annual average temperature is 66° F, with approximately 292 sunny or partly sunny days each year.

Local saying: Hollywood has only two kinds of weather – perfect and unusual.

AVERAGE TEMPERATURES (HIGH/LOW)
JANUARY . . . . 66° / 48° F
FEBRUARY . . . . 67° / 50° F
MARCH . . . . 69° / 51° F
APRIL . . . . 71° / 54° F
MAY . . . . 73° / 56° F
JUNE. . . . . 77° / 60° F
JULY . . . . 82° / 63° F
AUGUST. . . . . 83° / 64° F
SEPTEMBER . . . . 82° / 63° F
OCTOBER . . . . 78° / 59° F
NOVEMBER. . . . . 73° / 53° F
DECEMBER . . . . 68° / 49° F

The Dreaded Santa Ana Wind

There used to be a certain period of the year when we would get Santa Ana winds, but since *El Niño* and *La Niña* have changed our weather patterns there is no predicting them. If you are watching the telly and the forecaster says there is an area of high pressure over the deserts to the northeast and a low pressure zone offshore, you will know what to expect.

The wind comes down across the Mojave Desert, raising the temperature of the already hot air, and speeds through the mountain passes into our basin. Everything gets very dry, the thermometer may rise 10° or so and the air becomes startlingly clear. If you are out at the beach you can see that all the smog has been pushed out to sea and is simply a dirty cloud on the horizon.

📖 NOTABLE QUOTES

In his novel *Red Wind*, Raymond Chandler wrote a line that has been quoted often: "It was one of those hot dry Santa Anas that come down through the mountain passes... meek little wives feel the edge of the carving knife and study their husbands' necks."

Environment

When you fly into Los Angeles from the East, everything on the ground from about 40 miles out looks like a continuous carpet of houses and buildings. It is especially striking at night, when all the lights are on. Since we usually think of the environment in terms of nature, like forests and fields, it certainly doesn't look as if there is any of that left here.

Oddly, there is more nature and wildlife in Hollywood and the rest of Los Angeles than in any other major city in the country. A wide, excellent beach tens of miles long is our western border. Several mountain ranges have large untouched areas, covered with cactus and chaparral. Most of that stretches from Hollywood to Malibu.

Wildlife

One morning I shot an elephant in my pajamas. How he got in my pajamas I don't know.

– Groucho Marx, *Animal Crackers*

Friends who live in Whitely Heights, in the middle of Hollywood, recently saw a **deer** in their yard. A few years ago we were driving the San Diego Freeway with its usual eight-lane stream of fast, noisy traffic going in two directions over Sepulveda Pass and saw a small deer not 50 feet from the highway. Several times while driving in the hills on Mulholland Drive at night we have seen a big dog in the road ahead, not moving, staring steadily at us, and then realized it wasn't a dog, it was a **coyote**.

☞ **DID YOU KNOW?**

Coyotes have adapted exceedingly well to urban life. There are more of them in Hollywood than ever, as many a former owner of a cat or small dog can ruefully attest.

Anyone tramping about in Griffith Park, which is right next to Hollywood, or in Mandeville Canyon, with its multi-million-dollar mansions, should walk carefully and keep an eye out for **rattlesnakes** in the summer.

Birds

There are literally hundreds of species; some live here permanently, others stop over and stay for just the winter or summer. We have many varieties of **hummingbirds**. These tiny birds can hover in mid-air as they dip their long, slender beaks into a flower. The rubythroated hummingbird is fairly common. The loud birds that look like blue jays aren't; they are **scrub jays**. The little golf-ball-size birds you may see flitting from branch to branch in a eucalyptus tree are **titmice**; they are eating *lerp psyllids* (don't ask).

Hawks, which had disappeared from this region, have been saved from extinction by being raised in captivity and then relocated to nests on tall buildings throughout the area. Besides looking noble, they help thin out the pigeon over-population. Often, in the summer, one will see a flock of small, green **parrots** fluttering in a tree. If you think tropical parrots and parakeets are not indigenous to Hollywood, you're right. They have escaped from captivity and will live free for a while, but few survive the winter.

The small brown birds usually seen in flocks are not sparrows, but finches.

☞ **DID YOU KNOW?**

Mourning doves, so called for their sorrowful calls, are native and always come in pairs. The **pigeons** are non-native. Foolish Abbot Kinney imported a flock from Venice, Italy, when he created Venice, California.

Plants

Most of what we see growing in yards and parks has been imported, like the rest of us. Even the **cacti** come from farther east, where it grows naturally on the northern extensions of the Sonoran Desert. What was here before Europeans brought in interlopers was **coastal sagebrush**, **fennel**, **wild buckwheat** and other like varieties that existed in this climate without cultivation.

The predominant coastal sage, a low to medium height, three to five foot, gray-green, aromatic shrub, is still found on undisturbed low-lying land and lower slopes. At higher elevations is the **chaparral**: darker, less aromatic and taller at five to 10 feet.

Butterflies used to be everywhere, attracted at first by native plants like the sallow green **milkweed** and **deer weed**, and later by thousands of acres blanketed by orange groves; most are now gone for good. But more than 100 varieties of butterflies are still found in the greater Los Angeles area.

Oleanders are a large bush (they can also be trained to grow like a tree, as ours does) with long, narrow green leaves and a profusion of blossoms that can be white or pink. They grow in yards, public parks and along streets. They contain a chemical, *oleandrin*, which can be deadly.

Trees

Because this is basically an arid area, there aren't many dominant trees that are native. Up in the mountains (you can drive up into the Los Padres National Forest in an

The coral tree is Los Angeles' official tree as well as the California state tree.

hour from downtown Los Angeles) are **pines** and **spruce**. In the thousands of square miles of desert around here you will find mostly **yucca** and **creosote**, which is more of a bush. The **California oak**, of which there are several varieties, is the best known native tree.

Palm Trees

The tall, slender palms that sway at the tops as they line Beverly Hills streets are called Washingtonia robusta.

The only native palm is the **California fan palm** (*Washingtonia filifera*); it is found only in the desert, and is not often found even there. All the rest of those thousands of palms planted in rows in every neighborhood were put there during land booms, starting in the 1880s when Midwesterners arrived in Biblical throngs seeking the Garden of Eden in this new promised land. There were plenty of locals ready to dress up the environment to give them whatever they wanted. The advantages of palms are that they thrive in an arid climate, they can withstand extreme temperatures and they bend, rather than break, in strong winds. The disadvantages are that palms are a fire hazard; they ignite like a gas-soaked torch in the periodic fires that sweep whole areas. They are also a favorite home for rats and scorpions.

☞ DID YOU KNOW?

The palm trees you see are almost all imported from Africa, the Canary Islands, Japan, China, Mexico, Central and South America, the Mediterranean, and the Near East. Palm trees were imported as far back as 1769 when Junípero Serra planted a Moroccan date palm by the newly built San Diego Mission.

Eucalyptus

These tall trees have dull green, narrow pointed leaves, branches that usually don't spread out a great deal, and thick trunks with whitish or silvery bark that comes off in sheets. They all come from Australia. You will find them here and there, usually planted singly. Where they are in a long line you know there was once a farm there and the trees were planted as a windbreak.

WHOOPS!

The Santa Fe Railroad bought several square miles of land a few miles from the ocean and planted it thickly with thousands of eucalyptus, intending to use them as railroad ties. Too late, they discovered that eucalyptus is too soft and grows with a crooked grain, and therefore makes lousy railroad ties. Rancho Santa Fe, down the coast, is now a very shady place where millionaires, including Hollywood stars, go to retire.

Exotic Plants

Almost all the other hundreds of varieties of trees you see around the area are imported. A few of the more spectacular are the **banana trees** from Abyssinia, which don't bear fruit (the climate is wrong); the **jade trees** that are scarlet in the spring (there is a brilliant row down the middle of San Vicente Boulevard in Santa Monica); and the **jacaranda trees** from Brazil, which you will sometimes see planted on both sides of the street for a block or more in a residential neighborhood – the lavender flowers are unbelievable.

☞ DID YOU KNOW?

Most people think *jacaranda* is a Spanish word and pronounce the first syllable "ha"; actually, it is a Brazilian-Indian name and is pronounced with a hard "j", as in "jar": jah-ca-rahn-da.

HAVE YOU SEEN A CENTURY PLANT?

The drought-resistant Agave *americana* of the Southwest deserts is often seen in our area. It is a variety of cactus with long, gray-green, needle-tipped leaves, which radiate out from a low center; these leaves can be anywhere from one to eight feet in length. The plant grows slowly and flowers only rarely – once every century, it was thought; in reality it flowers once every 10 years or so. A single stalk springs from the center of the plant and grows 15 to 40 feet in a short time. It quickly flowers and then dies, leaving behind dozens of small, spiky new plants clustered around the bottom part of the parent.

Be careful – each triangular leaf has thorns on the sides and a vicious black needle. The century plant is a close cousin of Agave *tequilana*, which grows in Mexico, the source of the elixir so popular here: tequila.

Urban Parks

Los Angeles has the lowest square feet of park per inhabitant of any major US city, and what it lacks most are small neighborhood parks for kids to play in. What we do have are big spaces, mostly far from those kids.

Echo Park: This one's not so big, but there's a lake with boats. Many silent films were shot here.

MacArthur Park: The original name was Westlake Park; the name was changed during WWII and renamed for the general who faded away. There is a lake, with boats to paddle, but these days there are also an abundance of dope dealers plying their wares. Another place often filmed in days of yore, but not much lately.

Look for the statue of James Dean in Griffith Park; part of Rebel Without A Cause *was shot at the Observatory.*

Griffith Park: The largest urban park in the country, far bigger than New York's Central Park, with picnic areas, golf courses, a carousel and the Gene Autry Western Museum in the manicured area, and mountains and wild animals for the hikers and horseback riders to encounter (for more about this park see pages 164-175).

Santa Monica Mountains Conservancy: Private and government money is saving as much of these wild lands as possible. There are hiking trails and movie ranches where many pics are shot.

Palisades Park: This 1½-mile-long narrow strip of park along the edge of a bluff in Santa Monica is at the edge of the continent, as far as you can go.

Natural Disasters

We have had conversations with people visiting from the middle of the country who have said, "So many terrible things happen in this place, I don't know how you can live here." That from someone who has to dive into the tornado cellar every year.

Earthquakes

When the first European explorers arrived with Portolá, they got as far as the Santa Ana River, southeast of Los Angeles; they called it *Río de los Temblores* because that is where they experienced their first earthquake. The priest who was along, Fra Juan Crespi, wrote, "It lasted about half as long as an Ave Maria, and about 10 minutes later it was repeated."

They marched on. Crespi wrote again, "In the afternoon we felt another earthquake." The next day, "At ten in the morning the earth trembled. The shock was repeated with violence at one in the afternoon, and one hour afterwards." The following day they reached the river and the site of the future city. "Here we felt three consecutive earthquakes in the afternoon and night."

In 1812, an earthquake damaged the San Fernando Mission. According to Philip L. Fradkin's The Seven States of California, the Fort Tejon quake of 1857 "caused [the Los Angeles River] to leave its bed." There were good-sized quakes in 1860. The Long Beach quake of 1931 damaged many buildings and was felt extensively in Hollywood. We were living in Van Nuys in the San Fernando Valley during the 1971 quake. We are happy to report that, although the water came out of the pool in a tidal wave, there was no damage except for a startled, wet dog.

THE RICHTER SCALE

There are many small quakes, perhaps not every day, but it is not uncommon to feel a jolt. Unless you are extremely unlucky, in which case you should never get out of bed anyway, don't worry about it.

Earthquakes are measured by the Richter Scale, which was developed by Charles Richter of the California Institute of Technology. The scale starts at 0 and has no upper limit. On this scale, the earth's movement is measured in tenths of a percent. The scale does not ascend arithmetically; it has a logarithmic basis, and each whole number indicates a quake 10 times stronger than the previous whole number, with 31 times more energy. For instance, the 1994 Northridge quake, at 6.7, would be 10 times stronger than a quake measured at 5.7. If you experience a quake while you are in Hollywood, turn on the television or look in the paper the next day to see what you went through.

◆ 0.0 to 2.0 – Called microquakes, not usually felt by humans

◆ 2.1 to 2.9 – Won't rate even a line in the papers

◆ 3.0 to 3.4 – *Comme ci, comme ça*

◆ 3.5 to 3.9 – Definitely a small story on page 12 of the *Los Angeles Times*

◆ 4.0 to 4.9 – Story in the *Times*, plus 30 seconds on local TV

◆ 5.0 to 5.7 – Front page of the *Times*; live coverage of the result on TV

◆ 6.0 and up – *Times*: four to six pages; TV stations: hysteria

Introduction

The 1994 Northridge earthquake registered 6.8 and caused 61 deaths; the Maharashta, India quake six months earlier registered 6.4 and caused 9,748 deaths. The largest known shocks have had magnitudes in the 8.0 to 8.9 range.

Fires & Earthslides

We are discussing these together because one often causes the other. Within a month after the end of the spring rains, the green hills turn yellow and brown as the wild grass and brush dries up. Signs go up immediately on every road leading into the hills: "Extreme Fire Danger – No Smoking!" Summer sun bakes the chaparral for a few months, then in the fall the high winds start, along with a low moisture content in the air. When conditions are right (usually by Christmas), a spark can start a brush fire that quickly sweeps across mountains and through cañons that are almost impassible for fire equipment.

Famous for property losses and destruction of celebrities' homes was the fire that began in the Santa Monica Mountains on November 6, 1961. With a strong Santa Ana wind behind it, the fire roared through the canyons and over the steep slopes from Beverly Glen westward through Bel-Air; it jumped across the freeway at Sepulveda Canyon, raced through the Brentwood hills and joined another fire that had started in the Malibu mountains.

A big fire rating its own name, such as Malibu, Bel-Air, or Laguna, can be counted on at least every three to four years.

Close to 500 homes were burned; most were total losses, including those of Joe E. Brown, Zsa Zsa Gabor and Burt Lancaster. Whole blocks of homes were destroyed with only the chimneys and bits of plumbing left. The swimming pools, full of water, were untouched.

The Pacific Coast Highway, with heavy traffic every day, only two lanes in each direction and no other roads to take, is particularly prone to being closed because of landslides.

The fires typically consume most of the ground vegetation. In the spring following each fire, the city moves quickly to reseed the denuded hillsides with wild grasses – it is done by plane, from the air. If the seeds grow and the roots hold the soil together, all is well. If not, the first rain is likely to bring the hill down in a landslide.

Facts About LA

Size

County of Los Angeles	4,752 square miles
City of Los Angeles	467 square miles

Population

State of California	33.9 million
County of Los Angeles	9.5 million
City of Los Angeles	3.7 million

There are 88 incorporated cities in Los Angeles County, ranging from little Vernon, population 91, to big Los Angeles.

Tourism

In 1999, Los Angeles recorded 23.8 million overnight visitors. In 2000, the number of arrivals via air, train and ship totaled approximately 90 million.

By Air

Los Angeles International Airport (LAX) . 67,606,831
John Wayne Airport (Orange County) 7,772,801
Ontario International Airport 6,743,936
Burbank-Glendale-Pasadena Airport 4,748,742
Long Beach Airport 664,094

California's official state tartan (our legislators have nothing better to do) is that of the family of naturalist John Muir.

By Train

Amtrak, Union Station 1,300,000

By Cruise Ship

Port of Los Angeles 1,082,584

Beaches

Attendance at Los Angeles County beaches was 53.9 million people in 2000.

If Los Angeles County were a state it would rank eighth in population, behind Ohio and ahead of Michigan.

Leading Tourist Attractions

- ◆ **Universal Studios**, San Fernando Valley
- ◆ **Disneyland Anaheim**, 25 miles southeast of LA
- ◆ **Walk of Fame**, Hollywood
- ◆ **Rodeo Drive**, Beverly Hills
- ◆ **Venice Beach**, Venice
- ◆ **Grauman's Chinese Theatre**, Hollywood
- ◆ **Sunset Boulevard**, Hollywood to the beach
- ◆ **Santa Monica Beach/Pier**, just north of Venice
- ◆ **Knott's Berry Farm**, 20 miles southeast of downtown
- ◆ **Marina del Rey**, just south of Venice

Contemporary Hollywood

Greater Los Angeles is home to 7,000 screen and TV writers and 60,000 actors.

There have always been complaints about runaway production (shooting pictures far from Hollywood, either to achieve the reality of foreign locations or simply to take advantage of lower labor and production costs). Lately the complaints have become more anguished as runaway pics and TV series, especially to Canada, have multiplied. But Hollywood is still the leading supplier of entertainment to the world. There are still more studios here, more actors, writers, cameramen, grips and all the other skilled people it takes to make a motion picture (whether it's a good picture or a bad one, it takes the same number of people).

Films mean big bucks: the film and TV industry spent $31 billion in Los Angeles County last year, more than any other business.

☞ DID YOU KNOW?

One of life's little-known facts: Hollywood's nearest competitor in the production of movies is Bollywood, India's motion picture complex just north of Bombay, where more than 500 movies, mostly colorful romance-action extravaganzas, are produced yearly.

Telephone Area Codes

Because of its large population, Los Angeles County has several telephone area codes. You can tell what part of the county an address is in by its area code.

◆ **213** – Downtown Los Angeles

◆ **310** – West Los Angeles, Beverly Hills, Westwood, Century City, Culver City, Santa Monica, Malibu, Venice, Marina del Rey, Los Angeles International Airport (LAX), and south to San Pedro

◆ **323** – Hollywood, West Hollywood, Laurel Canyon

◆ **424** – Below LAX, south to San Pedro

Who Lives Here?

Here is how our information was unscientifically compiled. We've met some celebrities or worked with them during the years we were at the studios. And since we have been writing this book we have been calling friends who live in the various parts of town and asking, "Who lives in your neighborhood these days?" and we get answers like, "I bumped into so-and-so at the farmers' market last Sunday."

Everyone in Hollywood claims to be blasé about stars. It was the same when we were writing medical shows like *The Doctors* and *Medical Center*. We would call a doctor who was a specialist in our disease-of-the-week to authenticate some procedure. Without fail he or she would always start out, "Well, I never watch TV, but those medical shows are *so* inaccurate! Last week on *The Doctors*, that diagnosis was way off... " Blasé, but the information is always there.

Home Prices

Unfortunately, there is only one thing that stands between me and that property: the rightful owners.
– Harvey Korman, *Blazing Saddles*

As you mosey through the various communities, either on your own or on a tour bus, you might wonder what all these marvelous mansions cost. To give you an idea, we've included a sampling of median home prices for various communities (specific zip codes are indicated for some larger areas). Most stars' homes are between $1.5 and $4 million, though some mansions may be priced as high as $20 million.

MEDIAN HOME PRICES (YEAR 2000)

Bel-Air $715,000
Beverly Hills (90210) $1,236,000
Brentwood $851,000
Hollywood (90068) $513,000
Malibu $920,000
Marina del Rey $730,000
Pacific Palisades $885,000
Santa Monica (90402) $1,260,000
Studio City $450,000
Topanga $503,000
Venice $395,000
West Hollywood/LA (90069) $710,000
Westwood $805,000

Getting Here

Los Angeles International Airport

*L*os Angeles International Airport (LAX) is southwest of
Los Angeles and Hollywood, almost at the beach. Two
freeways are near at hand: one, the **San Diego Freeway**
(I-405), runs north and south to San Diego or San Francisco; the other, the **Santa Monica Freeway** (I-10) goes
east, toward downtown LA. The beach cities are nearby –
LAX is one of Marina del Rey and Venice are just a five-minute drive;
the busiest Hollywood is a half-hour to 45 minutes away. It is a fairly
airports in well organized airport; most of the distances spent walk-
the US. ing with luggage are not long. Hotels and restaurants
near the airport are listed in *The Beach Communities*
chapter, pages 368-372 and 376-378.

What to Expect

LAX has always been fairly friendly as big airports go. Of
course, after the events of September 11, 2001, it was a
mess, as were all the others. Many restrictions have been
dropped since then, but some remain as we go to press,

Los Angeles International Airport

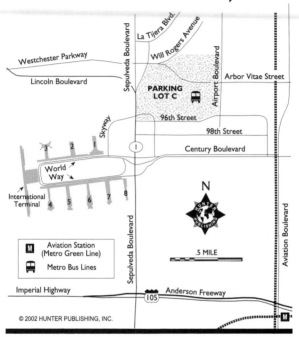

and look as if they will be with us for some time to come. Hope for the best, but be prepared. For more information, call LAX, ☎ 310-646-5252 or 888-544-9444; check their Web site at www.lawa.org; or contact your airline.

◆ **ID:** Passengers should have photo identification to present at airline check-in points.

◆ **Tickets:** If you have an electronic ticket you will need a printed confirmation or the passenger record locater number. Tickets, boarding passes and ID will be required at checkpoints and gates. Names on tickets and IDs must match.

◆ **Time:** Allow sufficient time for increased security. The new industry standard is two hours for a domestic flight and three for international.

◆ **Bags:** Curbside baggage check-in is available again for many (but not all) domestic flights, but not for international ones. If you can check your bags at the curb you may not have to stand in line at the airport ticket counter.

◆ **Carry-ons:** Take only one carry-on and one personal item, such as a handbag. Have identification tags on all carry-ons, which generally should measure less than 9x14x22 inches (this can vary by airline; check ahead of time). Remove batteries from electronic items, and do not wrap gifts.

◆ **Checkpoints:** Passengers and bags will be searched at random.

◆ **Prohibited items:** Items that may not be carried beyond the security checkpoint, either in carry-on bags or on your person, include knives, cutting instruments of any composition or description, spare blades, straight razors, metal scissors, corkscrews, baseball bats, golf clubs, ski poles and hockey sticks. It is wise to check with the airline or airport before your departure date to find out what is prohibited.

NATURE NOTES

The endangered **El Segundo Blue butterfly**, found at the end of the LAX runways on the land that slopes down to the beach, is the success story of the El Segundo Dunes. Because the butterfly thrives on coastal buckwheat, LAX installed a buckwheat nursery at the airport, and transplants the seedlings among the dunes. The rare butterflies emerge from their cocoons between June and August. More information is available at www.dune-prairie.org/projects/friends/animals/insects.html.

Other Airports

Burbank Airport is smallish, surrounded by homes and industries, yet it accommodates a large number of flights. It is closer to Downtown LA and Hollywood than LAX, without the large crowds. Among the airlines servicing this airport are American, Alaska Airlines, America West, Southwest, and United. 2627 Hollywood Way, Burbank, ☎ 818-840-8840, parking info 818-840-8837, www.burbankairport.com.

☞ *DID YOU KNOW?*

The P-38 fighter was mass-produced at the Burbank Airport during World War II.

John Wayne Airport south of LA is a very active one. Formerly the Orange County Airport, it was renamed in 1979 to honor the late movie star John Wayne, who lived in nearby in Newport Beach. It is not as handy to LA/Hollywood, unless your destination is along the south coast. It is serviced by most major airlines. 3160 Airway Avenue, Costa Mesa, ☎ 949-252-5171, www.ocair.com.

A nine-foot-tall bronze statue of "The Duke" stands in the terminal at the John Wayne Airport.

Ontario International Airport is smaller than LAX, but has shorter lines and usually less hassle. But it is farther from town, 35 miles east of Downtown LA. Ontario has 107 daily nonstop flights to 18 domestic cities and Mexico. 2900 E. Airport Drive, Ontario, ☎ 866-456-3900, www.lawa.org.

Long Beach Airport is the smallest and least-used of the area's airports. It's south of Downtown LA and Hollywood, midway between LAX and John Wayne airports. American, America West and JetBlue are among the airlines that service it. 4100 Donald Douglas Drive, Long Beach, ☎ 562-570-2600, www.lgb.org.

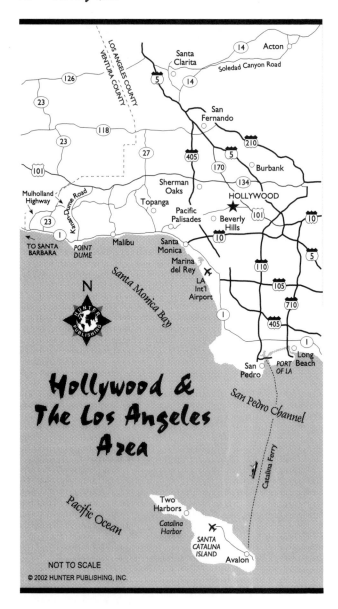

Hollywood &
The Los Angeles
Area

NOT TO SCALE
© 2002 HUNTER PUBLISHING, INC.

Getting Around

By Car

The building of freeways has enhanced Los Angeles' obsession with moving around only by car. Los Angeles has been called an autopia. Unfortunately, freeway speed is slowing year by year. It now averages 30 mph and it is estimated that in 10 years we will all be driving at 25 miles an hour. Here are some facts about Los Angeles' freeways.

◆ **Lane 1**, the fast lane, is next to the center divider; lanes are numbered outward.

◆ Most **potholes**, which are caused by trucks, are in the outside lanes.

◆ Patrolling of the freeways is the job of the **California Highway Patrol**, not the city police.

◆ **Sigalert** is a notice of an accident or anything that slows or stops traffic. The word is not short for signal, as it sounds; it was named for Lloyd Sigmon, who first broadcast traffic advisories from a plane over Los Angeles.

◆ **Slowdowns** are caused most often by rubberneckers gawking at another driver getting a ticket.

◆ **Telephones** along the side of the freeway are used by drivers to report a problem on the road. They have only one channel and are free.

◆ **Tow trucks** patrol the main freeways in the Los Angeles area. The drivers will fix a flat, supply gas or tow the car to the nearest garage. The service is free.

◆ **Traffic advisory** broadcasts on your car radio are notices of road repairs.

YOU SHOULD KNOW...

Throughout California, drivers and all passengers must wear seatbelts at all times when traveling in a car. Children under six years of age and under 60 pounds must be secured in a child safety seat.

Humorist Robert Benchley said, "Los Angeles is 72 suburbs in search of a city."

☞ DID YOU KNOW?

"Botts dots," the raised lane markers line California's roads by the millions, were invented by Elbert Botts, who gave his invention to the state free.

WATCH THOSE INTERCHANGES!

The Pasadena Freeway was completed in 1941 – the first in the nation.

Visitors are sometimes baffled by the freeways here: Angelenos typically refer to local freeways by name, not number – and then the names and numbers change. For example, the **Hollywood Freeway** is Highway 101 when you're in Los Angeles, but becomes CA 170 when it reaches the San Fernando Valley. The **Ventura Freeway**, which is CA 134 from Pasadena into LA, is suddenly Highway 101. The **Santa Monica Freeway** changes its name to the **San Bernardino Freeway** once it is east of Downtown and the LA River, but it is still I-10. I-5 is the **Golden State Freeway** until it gets Downtown; then it becomes first the **Santa Ana** and then the **San Diego Freeway** after it heads out of town to the southeast; and the faithful north-south **San Diego Freeway** (I-405) never actually arrives in San Diego (at least not until it merges with I-5).

⚠ WARNING!

The freeways that were built to speed up traffic are now often slow-moving or clogged. Give yourself plenty of time!

By Bus, Train & Subway

Los Angeles County Metropolitan Transportation Authority (MTA/Metro), ☎ 800-266-6883, www.mta.net, serves Greater Los Angeles, with 180 Metro Bus and

Introduction

LA's Freeways

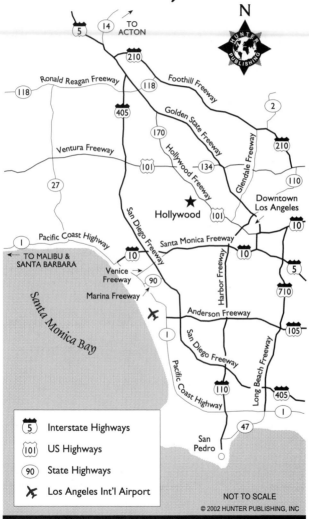

N

TO ACTON

Ronald Reagan Freeway

Foothill Freeway

Golden State Freeway

Ventura Freeway

Hollywood Freeway

Glendale Freeway

Hollywood

Downtown Los Angeles

Pacific Coast Highway

Santa Monica Freeway

San Diego Freeway

TO MALIBU & SANTA BARBARA

Venice Freeway

Marina Freeway

Harbor Freeway

Anderson Freeway

Santa Monica Bay

San Diego Freeway

Long Beach Freeway

Pacific Coast Highway

San Pedro

5	Interstate Highways
101	US Highways
90	State Highways
✈	Los Angeles Int'l Airport

NOT TO SCALE

© 2002 HUNTER PUBLISHING, INC

*Warning!
Jaywalking is
prohibited in
Los Angeles.
Violators are
ticketed and
fined.*

Metro Rail lines. Fares vary, with discounts for seniors and children.

Red Line – subway, downtown Los Angeles to Wilshire/Western, Hollywood, North Hollywood.

Blue Line – light rail trains between Downtown Los Angeles and Long Beach.

Green Line – light rail between Norwalk and Redondo Beach, stopping at LAX.

Metrolink – rail; ☎ 800-371-LINK (5465).

HOLIDAY TRANSPORTATION

The MTA traditionally offers free rides on buses from 9pm Christmas Eve and New Year's Eve to 5am Christmas Day and New Year's Day, and on the rail system from 9pm Christmas Eve and New Year's Eve to closing (generally at midnight). Metrolink trains do not run Christmas Day or New Year's Day.

By Taxi

*Taxis do not
cruise in Los
Angeles. They
wait at major
hotels and
respond to
phone calls.
Beware of un-
licensed, unin-
sured taxis.*

When leaving the airport you are required to take the next cab in the taxi line outside the terminal. In each chapter we list local cab companies and phone numbers so that you can contact them for your return trip to LAX. Flag drop is $1.90, plus $1.60 per mile. Following are sample taxi fares (without a tip) from Los Angeles International Airport. When traveling from the airport, add a $2.50 airport fee (the airport fee is not applicable when returning to LAX).

Beverly Hills $27
Hollywood $31
Downtown Los Angeles $35

By Shuttle

In the terminal, near the exit doors, you will see a bank of telephones with free, dedicated phone lines to each shuttle company; you can find out the fare to your destination and the arrival time of their next van. Or, skip the phones and walk outside to the traffic island marked "shuttles" and wait for the next one marked with your destination. You might end up sharing a van with several others; the driver may loop around the airport a few times, hoping to pick up a full load. You'll note that the fare to Beverly Hills is more expensive than the fare to Downtown; we have never understood the pricing, since the ride to Downtown is a longer trip. Shuttle operators include **Prime Time Shuttle**, ☎ 800-733-8267, www.primetimeshuttle.com; **Super Shuttle**, ☎ 310-782-6600 or 323-775-6600, www.supershuttle.com; and **X-Press**, ☎ 800-427-7483.

Average fares from the airport, without tip (there is no airport fee):

Beverly Hills. . . . . $22 first person, $9 each additional
Hollywood. . . . . $22 first person, $9 each additional
Downtown LA . . . . $13 per person

Best Places to Stay

Most of the places recommended here have been featured in numerous movies, such as the Regent Beverly Wilshire (*Pretty Woman*), or are the location of many star-studded events, à la Merv Griffin's Beverly Hilton, or are in a particularly good location. A few borderline exceptions are included because, to some film buffs, their unique historic significance relating to motion pictures may be enough to compensate for a lack of certain amenities.

Finding A Hotel

The City of Los Angeles is very spread out. Your choice of hotel is often dependent on your mode of transportation. If you are going to be driving a car here, you will need plenty of time to get from one place to another. Inadequate public transportation is a constant complaint, and it's the reason almost everyone who can afford to drives a car. Most of the large chains have hotels on or near Century Boulevard close by LAX, with free shuttle buses to and from the airport. This can be a good choice if you have a car, but not so

There are few inns or B&Bs in this area. The exception is the Venice Beach House (see page 401).

good if you are going to be dependent on public transportation.

MAKING HOTEL RESERVATIONS

To get the room you want and to avoid misunderstandings, make sure to take care of everything at the time you make the reservation.

◆ Reserve as early as possible; you are more likely to get the room you want.

◆ If you have floor or other location preferences, tell the reservation clerk. A room in the back, or over a garden, may be quieter. Higher floors may be less safe in case of fire; ground floor rooms are less protected from intruders.

◆ State the number of guests, including children, who will be staying in the room. Children often stay free or at reduced rates. Mention any special needs, such as cribs, cots, extra blankets.

◆ State smoking preferences. Do not ask for a non-smoking room unless you are sure no one will smoke. Just one cigarette could trigger a large surcharge.

◆ If someone in your party has a disability, ask exactly what a "disabled" or "handicapped" room means. Are there doors wide enough for a wheelchair? Is there a seat in the shower?

◆ Pay with a credit card, if possible, and ask if the hotel will guarantee your reservation; if you should be delayed in arriving, your room will still be waiting for you. However, if you don't arrive, you are still obligated to pay.

◆ If there is a change in plans, cancel your room as soon as possible to receive the maximum refund.

◆ A few hotels include a buffet or continental breakfast in the room rate. If they do, the listing will say so.

Accommodations Price Scale

We are not giving exact dollar amounts for room rates; they change too often. But to help you stay within your budget we use a scale to indicate rates from **Inexpensive** to **Deluxe**. The prices quoted are based on the cost of a double room, two people per room; they do not include any service charges or room taxes, which vary in Los Angeles County from city to city. Be sure to ask what additional charges apply when you make your reservation. If a hotel has a particularly wide range, with some rooms moderately priced and others in the expensive range, that is indicated in the listing.

ACCOMMODATIONS PRICE SCALE
Price scale is based on a standard room for two persons, per night.
Inexpensive . . . . less than $100
Moderate. . . . . $100-$200
Expensive . . . . $201-$300
Deluxe . . . . more than $300

Tip: Don't become victim to an alarm clock set by a previous guest. Check the clock radio before retiring.

 TIP

The Los Angeles area hosts many business travelers. Occupancy – and rates – tends to be lower on weekends.

Introduction

JUST FOR KIDS

If your kids are tired of being cooped up in a hotel room in the evenings and want something to do, try Storyline, a free service provided by the non-profit Screen Actors Guild Foundation. Call the number for your area and a professional actor will read a story to your child over the phone. The idea is to get children hooked on reading. In Hollywood, dial ☎ 323-374-2444; Downtown LA, ☎ 213-632-2300; West Hollywood, Beverly Hills and Santa Monica, ☎ 310-623-5777; San Fernando Valley, ☎ 818-239-3111. Storyline is also available in Las Vegas, Minneapolis and Phoenix, and on the Internet at www.bookpals.net, with sound and live scenes of the actors reading.

Best Places to Eat

Choosing A Restaurant

There are thousands of restaurants in the area between downtown Los Angeles and Malibu by way of Hollywood and Beverly Hills. We can name only a small percentage, so we have concentrated on those where celebrities go to eat, or that have strong connections to film, that you might recognize from movies or television series that were shot there. There are many perfectly good restaurants in the area that didn't make the cut where you will get a fine meal.

Food preferences are so personal and varied that we can't guarantee you will adore every meal in every restaurant we recommend. The majority of places listed are of high quality, though it is possible you are simply not a fan of a particular chef's style. We tell you of the few cases where the food is definitely not the main reason to visit a particular restaurant. Finally, we have tried to use the restaurateur's own description of his or her food, so if one place calls it continental, another calls it Mediterranean and the third nouvelle Euro and they all taste the same, well, that's the way the meatball bounces.

☞ DID YOU KNOW?

Though it comes as a shock to many European and Asian visitors, smoking is not permitted in restaurants, bars, theaters, museums or most other public buildings in Santa Monica or throughout California. You may smoke on the beaches, but please dispose of your cigarette properly so that some bare-footed beachgoer doesn't step on it.

Dining Price Scale

There is quite a price variation in Los Angeles restaurants, so to keep you on target we label them **Inexpensive** to **Very Expensive**. The prices quoted are for one meal, based on an entrée, soup or salad and coffee. Appetizer, dessert, wine and liquor are not included, because so many times they are not ordered. We do not include tax (which varies from one municipality to another) or tip (add 20% if you are a big tipper, 15% if you are or want to appear normal, 10% if you think tipping is immoral).

Don't forget, there is usually a valet parking attendant to tip.

As a general guideline, appetizers in most of the restaurants listed in this book will be priced from $6 to $12, desserts from $4 to $6, drinks from $5 up (martinis have reached $12 in some places), and wine is usually $4 to $9 a glass, with minimum bottle prices in the high $20s in some places, and much higher in others.

TIP

If you have never had Ethiopian cuisine, get to **Fairfax Avenue**, a block south of Olympic Boulevard, between La Brea and La Cienega boulevards, where a half-dozen Ethiopian and Eritrean restaurants are clustered. The food is delicious!

DINING PRICE SCALE
Pricing includes one entrée, with soup or salad and coffee.
Inexpensive . . . . .less than $20
Moderate. . . . . $20-$30
Expensive. $31-40
Very Expensive . . . . .more than $40

Other Arcane Matters

Making Reservations

Always reserve ahead, if possible. If you are going to be more than 10 or 15 minutes late, call and say so. And if your plans change completely, call and cancel your reservation. We realize that a lot of currently hot restaurants overbook shamelessly, but that is to protect themselves from the people who make reservations (sometimes at two or three restaurants) and never bother to cancel.

What can you do if you call and say you want a table for four on a Saturday night at 8:30 and are told that the only tables available that night are before six and after 10? There is one theory that you will find stars who have an early call at the studio the next morning dining in those restaurants at 6pm. We have never found that to be so. The obvious recourse is to simply try somewhere else.

One strategy is a gamble. You can go ahead and show up at the restaurant at 8:30pm without reservations and hope there have been cancellations.

⭐ **TIP**

At a restaurant with a show-biz clientele, psychology is all-important. You must walk up to the maître d's little podium with complete confidence that he/she will, of course, seat you as soon as something is available. If you are hesitant, or meek, or show any signs that you don't really expect to be seated, you won't be. But if you are turned away anyway, don't write us an irate letter. We said up front it is a gamble.

Dress & Undress

In Los Angeles, just as in the rest of the country, formality in dress has gone the way of the 3¢ postage stamp. You needn't worry that you won't be allowed in without a tie. But if you are going to an upscale place where other patrons will be dressed nicely, it's considerate to dress accordingly. Casual-stylish-chic is what to aim for. Clean and halfway decent will do.

Turning the Tables

Suppose you are just in town for a few days and want to see some celebrities while you are here. So you make a reservation at Ago or Spago Beverly Hills and, when the maître d' doesn't seat you next to a table full of stars, you complain loudly. This is definitely bad form. He doesn't know you, and what big pictures have you made lately?

On the other hand, if you are given what is obviously the lousiest table in the house you don't have to just settle for it. If you are seated next to the kitchen door, or by the bathroom door, or in front of the exit, or there is a draft on the back of your neck, the best policy is to politely ask if there is another table available. Indicate the empty table you would prefer. Maybe that one by the window with a view or that cozy booth really *is* reserved, but they will usually move you somewhere else, unless the table you have been given really is the only one available. In such a case we usually opt to wait in the bar for the next available table.

Those "A" Cards

The Los Angeles County Department of Health rates all restaurants, including hot dogs stands and fast food places. If there is an "A" card in the window the establishment passed their latest inspection with no problems. A "B" card indicates something was wrong, but not enough to close them down. A "C" card – well, we have never seen one; we assume the owners hide them. There have been times we have passed up places with B cards, figuring, "Why take a chance?" On the other hand, if there is no card in sight and it is supposed to be a high-class joint, you can figure the owner felt it was beneath him to have to show any card at all. Either that or he got a rating he is ashamed of. It happens.

Smoking

There is no smoking in any office, workplace, restaurant or bar in the state, unless you are seated outdoors, such as on an open patio. This sometimes annoys people from overseas, who mumble about the California health nuts. Tough.

Park Your Car?

Most restaurants offer valet parking. The charge can be anywhere from $2.50 to $5, plus a tip of $1 or $2. (Celebrities, because they are celebrities and highly paid, are expected to tip from $5 to $20, and often do.) If you have a

Lamborghini or a really sharp Rolls you can expect to see it parked right up front in the lot. Look for our Nissan SX2 somewhere back among the Hondas and Chevys.

Shopping

Would you be shocked if I put on something more comfortable?

– Jean Harlow, *Hell's Angels*

Malls

There are, of course, huge shopping malls that have become what we suppose the village green was like in days of yore, at least for the kids who now teem like lemmings in most of them: the place to hang out. For those who view shopping as a team sport, to be done only in crowds, here are the locations of the principal malls.

Beverly Center, 8500 Beverly Boulevard, at La Cienega. Barely in Los Angeles, almost surrounded by West Hollywood and Beverly Hills. ☎ 310-854-0070.

Century City Shopping Center, 10250 Santa Monica Boulevard, at Little Santa Monica and Avenue of the Stars. ☎ 310-277-3898.

Westside Pavilion Mall, 10800 Pico Boulevard at Westwood, West Los Angeles. ☎ 310-474-6255.

Santa Monica Place, on Broadway, at the south end of Santa Monica's Third Street Promenade. ☎ 310-394-1049.

The Galleria, San Fernando Valley, Ventura Boulevard and Cedros Avenue, Sherman Oaks. ☎ 818-382-4100.

Specialty Shopping

When people around the world think of Hollywood, they think glamorous, hip, funky, cool, with-it... and all that is to be found on four stretches of pavement. It is just a matter of strolling... and marveling.

In Hollywood, **Melrose Avenue**, from La Brea to west of Fairfax has funky little shops. This is where shopaholics head for far-out goods. What's created out of recyclables here today will hit the rest of the country next year. The celebrity-spotting ratio is higher west of Fairfax.

Beverly Hills' **Rodeo Drive**, from Little Santa Monica Boulevard to Wilshire, offers medium-size, upscale shops; it's the home of haute couture. A platinum American Express card will come in handy. On **Wilshire Boulevard**, from Camden Drive to Santa Monica Boulevard, a half-dozen *très*-expensive department stores line the south side of the boulevard.

In Santa Monica, shop along **Montana Avenue**, from 7th Street to about 20th. It's harder to walk here because the boutiques are scattered, but the hardware stores and bakeries long patronized by the neighborhood are steadily disappearing, as high-priced clothing stores able to pay higher rents move in. This trend is being accelerated by frequent mentions in print of the celebrities who shop here.

★ *TIP*

Even if you are not going to shop, you should know that most stars are avid shoppers. The four areas listed above are prime celebrity-spotting haunts.

A(te> Da>k

No lack of nightlife here! There are several hundred live theaters, probably more than you'll find anywhere else in the world. If you don't want to travel across town to one of the big houses, there are small, professional theaters in almost every community. And thousands of professional writers, directors and actors supply talent to those theaters.

Hollywood (meaning this entire area) never was a good nightclub town, and it still isn't if you define nightclub as a place where you can have drinks while you enjoy live music or a floor show. But it does have a very hot club scene, meaning DJs and dancing. Almost everyone who goes to the dozens of clubs is in their 20s, and conscious of the current dress trends. If you are a beautiful woman under 30, you will probably be ushered in with alacrity and without paying a cover charge. Otherwise, you will be hard put to get past the guards at the door unless you are a star, a producer or Hugh Hefner. But then, he always has six Bunnies with him.

If neither theater nor clubs tempt you, see the *Los Angeles Times* or one of the free weekly newspapers for listings of everything else going on, from circuses to museum events. And a long, leisurely dinner at a good restaurant is sometimes best of all.

Pronunciation

The Los Angeles area was owned first by Spain (aside from the indigenous Indians, of course), then by independent Mexico, and did not become part of the US until 1850; as a result, many place and street names are Hispanic. Land speculators, wanting newcomers to think it was all part of a romantic past, gave the streets names like Ranchero Lane and Ocotillo Drive, no matter how tacky a development might have been. Here's a guide to help visitors avoid gaffes over some of the trickier pronunciations.

A Spanish Accent

If a word ends in a vowel, stress the next-to-last syllable. It is AL-ta VIS-ta Avenue in Hollywood. Sepulveda, the name of an old land-grant family and of a boulevard that runs about a hundred miles, is pronounced Se-PUL-ve-da because there was originally an accent over the u. Alvarado Avenue, named after another founding family, had no accent mark and is pronounced Al-va-RA-do. A double "ll," as in Ocotillo, is pronounced like "y": Oc-o-TEE-yo. Cañon Drive in Beverly Hills has the Spanish spelling, but is pronounced exactly the same as Canyon Drive in Hollywood, which has the English spelling.

Indian names are rare here; among the few are Point Mugu, Malibu and Cahuenga.

IT HELPS TO KNOW WHERE YOU ARE

One of us phoned the Cañon Theatre for tickets and had a conversation about it with the fellow who answered.

Him: *Hello, Cannon Theatre.*

Me, a native, automatically: *Hello. It's "canyon."*

Him: *What?*

Me: *The name is pronounced "canyon."*

Him: *Cannon Theatre.*

Me: *Step outside and look at the sign. There's a tilde over the n.*

Him: *What?*

Me: *When did you get here from New York?*

Him: *Six months ago. What?*

Me: *And where are you now?*

Him: *Cannon Theatre.*

Me: *I give up. Adios.*

 # Traveling With Pets

If you are thinking about bringing your pet, here are some good reasons why Prince or Fluffy should stay home.

◆ **Planes** – Pets must travel in a crate and have health certification. Cargo holds are not heated, cooled or sound-proofed.

◆ **Hotels** – Many do not allow pets. They cannot stay alone in the room while you are out, because the maid must come in to clean.

◆ **Public Transportation & Attractions** – City buses, subways, tour buses and sites of interest do not allow pets, except for seeing-eye dogs.

◆ **Leash Laws** – Your pet must be on a leash whenever it is outdoors, including on beaches, where there is no running free, on pain of a stiff fine.

◆ **Losing a Pet** – Even well-trained pets can get stressed and nervous when traveling. Trying to find a lost pet in a strange city will sink any vacation.

▥ FILM GLOSSARY

Barn Doors – Black flaps attached to the front of a light on the set to control shadows and the light's spill.

Information Sources

Tourist Information

For general information about the Los Angeles area, contact the **Los Angeles Convention & Visitors Bureau** (LACVB), ☎ 800-228-2452; 24-hour hotline, ☎ 213-689-8822; www.lacvb.com.

For specific local information, see **Visitors Information listings in the** *A to Z* section of each chapter.

Hollywood on Television – *The Stanley Dyrector Show*, Channel 36, daily, 8:30am. Most TV shows about Hollywood are lightweight chitchat about stars, occasionally accurate. There is one local show done by a knowledgeable pro, writer Stan Dyrector, who has been in the business for years. He interviews real people – writers, directors, actors – who tell it the way it is, with sometimes hilarious anecdotes about what *really* happened. The time for the 30-minute show is always subject to change; see www.la-36.org for details.

News & Entertainment Publications

Though there are several other smaller newspapers, the 800-pound gorilla here is the *Los Angeles Times*. The daily *Calendar* section covers events relating to motion picture people.

LA Weekly, a giveaway found in some hotel lobbies and most liquor stores, plus markets and other shops, pub-

The Los Angeles Times' *Thursday and* Sunday Cal-endar *sections are heavy with movie and theater reviews.*

lishes approximately 200 pages every Wednesday. It features incisive investigative reporting on local and state politics and enormous listings and reviews of every movie and theatrical event around.

Entertainment Today is another free weekly that you can pick up on Fridays. Very good for film and theater reviews, nightclub and comedy club listings and everything interesting that is happening around town.

Most of the hotels have some sort of free local guide, which you may find in your room or at the check-in counter. Some of these guides list current schedules for film festivals and major theatrical events.

FILM GLOSSARY

Screen Actors Guild (SAG) – The actors' union, which negotiates basic contracts with the studios, independent producers and producers of commercials, and sees to the actors' residuals.

Downtown Los Angeles

I don't want to live in a city where the only cultural advantage is that you can make a right turn on a red light.
  — Woody Allen, *Annie Hall*

Overview

To start off a book about Hollywood with a chapter on Downtown Los Angeles may seem quirky, but "Hollywood" is a metaphorical term; the Hollywood phenomenon influenced the entire area, and Downtown is where it made its earliest marks.

Movies were shot in Downtown Los Angeles for a half-dozen years before Cecil B. De Mille made the eight-mile trek out to the sleepy farming village of Hollywood. But the city saw its first moving image on the screen way before that, in 1896 at the Orpheum Theatre on Broadway, when the life-sized figure of Anna Belle Sun dancing was projected onto a white sheet. It lasted about a minute. But Los Angeles was always about much more than the movie industry.

History

The 18th & 19th Centuries

The original *pobladores* (colonizers) were 11 couples with 22 children, mostly Indians, blacks and mestizos. It wasn't until 1781, a few weeks before the British surrendered to George Washington at Yorktown, that the governor of Spanish California declared Los Angeles important enough to be called a town. After he read the proclamation making LA official, his men fired a lone cannon and the governor left, leaving a lowly corporal in charge.

Downtown Los Angeles

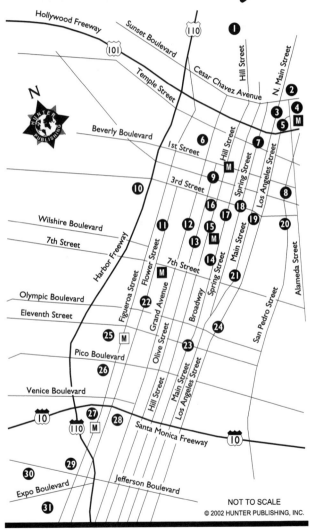

NOT TO SCALE
© 2002 HUNTER PUBLISHING, INC.

Key to Attractions
Downtown Los Angeles

Downtown Los Angeles

By 1784, the *pobladores* had replaced their original huts with adobe homes and laid the foundation for a church. Later, the Carillo, Olvera and Sepúlveda families built much fancier houses on the plaza near the church.

Today's plaza is not in the original location. It was rebuilt on higher ground after a flood.

The town grew slowly all through the Spanish and Mexican periods. It was the commercial center for a vast area of ranches, but since there was little contact with the outside world, commercial activity was limited. Though there was a wave of immigrants following the discovery of gold in 1848, almost all of those sensibly headed for northern California, where the gold was.

In spite of that, enough newcomers drifted into Los Angeles that soon the newly arrived whites outnumbered the long-settled Hispanics. Los Angeles in 1850 was barely a city; with a population of 1,610 it was more of a cowtown, with unpaved streets and little law – almost everyone toted a gun. Yet by the time the 19th century ended there had been a great change.

Between 1920 and 1924, 100,000 people a year poured into Los Angeles, mostly home-seekers.

The 20th Century

*Through the
1950s Broad-
way was the
prime shop-
ping street in
all of South-
ern Califor-
nia.*

From that time on, almost until the present day, Los Angeles' history has been shaped by the goal of selling all the
land surrounding it to everyone who could be enticed to
come here. The city's borders were extended to take in
that land, and the process was repeated as Los Angeles expanded in all directions. Downtown Los Angeles was the
center of it all. None of the other little towns around it really counted. That's the way it was when the motion picture industry arrived.

Thomas Edison was probably the first movie-maker to
reach Los Angeles, well before those who came later to escape the long arm of his company. Edison arrived in 1898,
mounted his giant early camera on a horse-drawn wagon
and shot the bustling life of Spring Street. The result was
a 60-second film, *South Spring Street, Los Angeles, California*, shown for a nickel on Edison Kinetoscope Peep
Shows.

🎬 FILM GLOSSARY

Focus puller – First assistant camera operator, whose job it is to control
focus, especially during movement, and
to maintain the camera.

*Until the
1960s, the
height limit
on buildings
in Los Angeles
was 12 stories;
City Hall was
the only excep-
tion, with 26
floors.*

Once the motion picture studios were built, the producers
liked to shoot as much as possible in the studio to save
money and time. But balancing that was a desire for reality, and sometimes the opportunity to use already-existing
structures rather than building new sets. Many of the ear-

liest pictures were shot on the streets of Downtown Los Angeles and the neighborhoods just to the west.

During the first half of the 20th century, LA's Downtown finally grew into a major city. Though it didn't have any skyscrapers, it was the financial and commercial center of the southern part of the state. After World War II, vast tracts of newly built single-family homes were thrown up in the San Fernando Valley and other outlying areas, and big shopping malls were built to service them. Gradually people stopped coming to downtown Los Angeles. To this day that hasn't changed.

Bringing It Up to Date

When visiting a place for the first time, travelers often automatically book a downtown hotel, feeling they are sure to be in the center of things. Los Angeles is different, there is no real center. There are places to see and walks to take downtown, but mostly it is a starting place for tours going elsewhere. In the daytime, the office buildings are full and the Hispanic stores that line Broadway are crowded with shoppers. But after 5 o'clock everyone goes somewhere else. Bewildered tourists ask about downtown Los Angeles at night, "Where is everyone?"

Los Angeles has a large theater-going population that takes the freeways to the Music Center, parks in the garage underneath the structure and afterward drives away again without ever setting foot on the downtown streets. The city-subsidized Music Center, consisting of a symphony/opera hall and two legitimate theaters, was cleverly built very near to where the Hollywood, Santa Ana, Harbor and Pasadena freeways all merge in a giant cloverleaf.

Visitors think of downtown Los Angeles as central because it is between Disneyland and Universal City.

Downtown Los Angeles

Getting Here

From LAX

By Car

From the airport, drive south a short distance to the Century Freeway (I-105) and go east. Proceed to Harbor Freeway (I-110) and head north. For most downtown hotels, exit from 9th to 4th streets east.

By Bus or Train

Take the free bus marked "Lot C" from in front of any terminal. Once at Lot C, walk a few steps to the Transit Station and get Metro Bus #40, 42, or 439. The fare is $1.35. Or, you can take the free Green Line shuttle bus, which also leaves from Lot C, to Aviation Station, where you catch the Metro Green Line train going east, then transfer to the Metro Blue Line train going north into Downtown Los Angeles. The fare is $1.60.

From Burbank Airport

Exit the airport, then go south to Victory Boulevard. Take Victory Boulevard east to the Golden State Freeway (I-5); go south to the Harbor Freeway (I-110), and continue south until you exit the freeway onto downtown streets headed east.

★ TIP

Metrolink has a double-decker commuter train that makes a 25-minute trip from Burbank Airport to Union Station, where you can connect with other Metrolink trains, subways and buses. It is about a five-minute walk from the air terminal to the Metrolink station, or you can take an airport shuttle. The fare to Union Station is $5. Check the Metrolink schedule at ☎ 800-COMMUTE or www.mta.net.

Downtown Los Angeles

From Ontario Airport

Take the San Bernardino Freeway (I-10) west, to the Hollywood Freeway (101) going north; exit at downtown streets and head south.

From Santa Monica & the Beaches

Take the Santa Monica Freeway (I-10) east to the Harbor Freeway (I-110) north. Exit on downtown streets.

Getting Around

By Bus & Trolley

DASH buses (the letters stand for Downtown Area Short Hop) follow six short routes on weekdays and three on weekends. Everyone who works downtown uses these buses for quick trips. Pick up a map of routes and a schedule at your hotel or from a DASH bus. Buses run Monday-Friday, 9am-5pm; Saturday, 10am-2pm. Fare is 25¢, with one free transfer to another route. All DASH buses are wheelchair-accessible. ☎ 808-2273 (from all LA area codes).

Angels Flight had an accident in 2001 and has stopped working indefinitely. The well-known funicular railway climbed the steep side of Bunker Hill from Hill Street at the bottom to the California Plaza by Olive Street near the top. It's a problem now to get from one to the other without Angels Flight. If you need a workout there are 153 steep stairs alongside the empty funicular tracks. If you would rather take it easy, the new **Bunker Hill Trolley**, a small bus with wooden seats and a bell at the front, picks up at Grand Central Market on Hill Street, goes up 2nd Street to Olive and drops passengers at an elevator or staircase that goes to California Plaza. The downhill trip is via 4th Street on a counterclockwise route. Hours are weekdays, 6:30am-6:30pm; weekends, 10am-5pm. Fare is 25¢.

HOW FAR IS IT?

From the center of Downtown LA (around Pershing Square):

Hollywood Boulevard . . . . 6 miles
Universal Studios . . . . 9 miles
Santa Monica Beaches . . . . 16 miles
Disneyland . . . . 26 miles
Los Angeles International Airport . . . . . 27 miles

FILM GLOSSARY

Gaffer – The senior electrician and lighting assistant, who rigs lights on the set under the direction of the director of photography.

 # Who Lived Here?

Los Angeles' wealthy set began moving out of the Downtown area in the late 1800s. Suburbs developed near the new University of Southern California, south of the city. The new district, called **West Adams**, was named for Adams Boulevard, west of Figueroa Street. The big, opulent homes, many of which still stand, fit in with the architectural styles of the day – Tudor, Elizabethan and Italianate.

When actors arrived in Hollywood, their first move was to check into the Alexandria Hotel at 4th and Main streets; the next move, when the real money flowed in, was to the Adams District. One home at **649 West Adams Boulevard** housed numerous stars; Roscoe "Fatty" Arbuckle was the first to live here, then Theda Bara, who became a star in 1917 with *Cleopatra*. She was followed by Raoul Walsh, then an actor but who later became a famed director, with his wife, Miriam Cooper, who portrayed the Southern belle in Griffith's *Birth of a Nation*. And finally the house was occupied by producer Joe Schenck, whose wife was Norma Talmadge. The house is still there, between Figueroa and Hoover.

IN CASE YOU'RE FEELING QUEASY

Los Angeles, built on a desert, saves water when it is plentiful by storing it in the ground underneath the city, and then draws on it when needed. But it has lately discovered there are unforeseen consequences. So much water is pumped in and out of the underground aquifers that stretch 25 miles south from beneath downtown Los Angeles, that much of the landscape rises and falls more than four inches each year. From fall until spring the water is pumped into the aquifers, causing the land to rise. In summer months the unseen reservoirs slowly collapse as they are drained.

On Location

Downtown Los Angeles has been the most filmed area ever since Thomas Edison set up his camera on Spring Street in 1898. Location shooting has only increased since. Different blocks double for big cities everywhere. Spring Street appears as Wall Street; the round, glass, futuristic Bonaventure Hotel shows up in countless sci-fi movies; the high-rise landscape evokes nameless urban areas; gritty warehouse streets echo to infinite gun battles. Over 7,000 film permits are issued every year for the downtown area; draw a two-mile-diameter circle around the area and 14,000 "shooting days" are spent each year within it.

Downtown Los Angeles

Los Angeles as a Film Set

In the decades that followed, downtown Los Angeles stood in for hundreds of other cities. Now, visitors to Los Angeles are apt to find themselves in the middle of a movie or television shoot, even downtown; sometimes it seems *especially* downtown. Not long ago Arnold Schwarzenegger's action pic *End of Days* closed down several intersections on a Monday morning, causing a horrendous rush-hour traffic jam. Production crews usually try to schedule long street shoots on weekends to avoid that problem.

A few summers ago the *Godzilla* crew spent 22 nights shooting in the streets downtown. If you recall the opening sequence of *Armageddon* and the meteors of molten rock plunging into the heart of Manhattan, that was really Fourth and Main streets. You can orient yourself by the Barclay Hotel, which was prominently displayed in the background. Another shoot that tied traffic in knots occurred when three blocks of Main Street were closed to re-create 1940s Los Angeles for *Devil in a Blue Dress*.

The AOL / Time Warner post-Grammy party held at Los Angeles Center Studios attracted 2,500 guests.

A new film studio downtown, the **Los Angeles Center Studios**, the first built in the area for at least 50 years, is just west of the Harbor Freeway (110) between 4th and 6th streets. In the few years it has been open, several movies, including *Charlie's Angels* and *Bounce* were shot here, and principal photography was done for *Planet of the Apes*, plus the TV shows *The X-Files, The Huntress*, and *The Titans*. Because it is so handy, many of the companies filming on the streets downtown use this studio to run dailies and for pick-up shots. See *Studio Tours*, page 543, for more information.

The organized walking tours cover some of the studios' favorite sites to film; some places downtown have shown up in so many movies that they will probably seem familiar to you; see pages 88 through 94 for walking tour information.

In The Heart of Downtown

The **Alexandria Hotel**, at Fourth and Main streets, was *the* place to stay in the early movie-making era when Downtown was more important than Hollywood. Charlie

Chaplin, Mary Pickford, Douglas Fairbanks and D.W. Griffith met here in 1919 to form their own movie-making organization, United Artists. The ballrooms are empty now – even the Palm Court with its stained Tiffany glass ceiling – and stars come into the lobby only to shoot pictures, anything from *Seven* to *American's Most Wanted* to music videos by the likes of Amy Grant and Fiona Apple.

Sarah Bernhardt and Enrico Caruso stayed in the once-elegant Alexandria Hotel.

The **Biltmore Hotel**, at Fifth and Olive streets, was at the heart of filmdom's social life all during the 1920s, and is still the most elegant hotel downtown, even amidst all the modern tower hotels surrounding it. It has been a favorite place for movie-makers to shoot since it was built. You might recognize scenes from dozens of movies as you stroll through its opulent lobbies (see page 69 for more about the Biltmore).

The **Bradbury Building**, at 304 South Broadway, has been especially attractive to makers of films noir. Consider *Chinatown*, *Wolf,* and *Murder in the First.* In the 1976 TV series *City of Angels*, Wayne Rogers played a 1930s Los Angeles gumshoe who had his office here. And Harrison Ford searched the building for 21st-century "replicants" in *Blade Runner.*

Farther downtown is a bar called **Torchy's**, at 218½ Fifth Street, where a big scene in *48 HRS.*, with Eddie Murphy, was shot. A few years ago a part of *Condor* was shot there.

The **Rosslyn Hotel**, 111 Fifth Street, opened during the last century as an elegant lodge; now it is sadly reduced in stature. But it had the title role in the movie *The Million Dollar Hotel*, starring Mel Gibson. The name referred to the "Million Dollar" sign, which still stands on the hotel.

In the futuristic film *Armageddon*, there is a sequence in a lavish strip club with 14-foot chandeliers, a crystal fountain and marble fish statuary. None of it was built on a set; it was the lush Louis XIV interior of the **Los Angeles Theater**, at 615 South Broadway. Charlie Chaplin put up more than $1 million to build the theater to premiere *City Lights*. The theater closed in 1994 when the street fell on hard times. But then it began a new life, showing up in films instead of merely screening them. Up to 170 production days a year are shot here, including features, music videos and commercials.

Downtown Los Angeles

The nine-story **Pacific Electric Building**, at 6th and Main streets, opened in 1905 as the downtown hub of the Red Cars, the largest inter-urban rail system in the world until it shut down in 1953. Now it is used almost entirely as a film location. The long hallways with marble wainscoting evoke countless past noir films; surely Philip Marlowe is still behind one of the frosted glass office doors. On the third floor of the building is the space used as the detectives' headquarters in *Seven* and, later, in *L.A. Confidential*. On the fifth floor is the apartment set from *Grace of My Heart*. There is the chemistry lab from *Paulie*, and *Fame L.A.* was shot in the loft, which was later taken over for several weeks for the shooting of *Face/Off*. Unfortunately, the building is closed to the public. There is one reason to visit it, though – **Cole's P.E. Buffet**, on the ground floor (see page 80).

▰ SCENES YOU MIGHT HAVE SEEN

Do you recall Ron Rifkin dangling by his ankles over Main Street from the P.E. Building in *L.A. Confidential*? Or New York cabs whizzing in and out of the building's garage for *Godzilla?*

If you had walked down **Hill Street** at night a few years ago, it's likely that you would have seen the Second Street Tunnel filled with hysterical extras fleeing alien invasions for *Independence Day*, or scenes from *Con Air* or *The X-Files* being filmed.

The **Subway Terminal Building**, 345 South Hill Street, is where we used to board the Red Cars for Hollywood. The trip started here through a long underground tunnel. The building's beautiful lobby is well preserved and is always included on architectural tours; you might recognize the tunnel from *Primal Fear*, *Absolute Power* or *Escape from L.A.*

The tunnel under the Subway Terminal Building has water dripping down mossy stalagmites in the dank darkness – perfect for MTV videos.

South of Downtown

The **Variety Arts Center**, at 940 South Figueroa Street, is dedicated to film and entertainers. It houses the Earl Carroll Lounge, the W.C. Fields Bar, the Masquers Theatre and the Roof Garden Ballroom, where scenes were shot for *Copacabana*. The Ed Wynn Bar & Lounge was used for TV's *Highway to Heaven*. You might have seen various parts of the center in *Cagney & Lacey*, *Falcon Crest* and *Murder, She Wrote*.

The ***Herald Examiner*** **Building**, at 11th Street and Broadway, has been closed for years now since the newspaper ceased publication. But it is still busy, its newsroom used as the setting in countless movies, including *Babylon 5*, *Baywatch Nights*, *Unsolved Mysteries* and *The Usual Suspects*.

The **LA Convention Center**, at Figueroa and Pico, has masqueraded as everything from a hospital to a futuristic lair and (not surprisingly, since it was the scene of the 2000 Democratic Convention) as a political stomping ground; the doors of *Chicago Hope* were actually the Pico Street entrance of South Hall. Hundreds of film crews are drawn to the building's many aspects, and two or three productions a month are filmed here. The high-tech look and striking towers were the villain's headquarters in Sylvester Stallone's *Demolition Man*. In *Jade* it is the lobby windows you see. The scene in *The Net* in which someone is thrown from a catwalk was filmed in the exhibit hall. For *Showgirls* a boat show was staged. The exterior is seen in *Heat*. The center has also been seen in *Escape from L.A.*, *Message in a Bottle*, *My Fellow Americans* and the *Power Rangers* movie.

South of the Freeways

Although much of Los Angeles' Downtown is contained between the Harbor and Santa Monica freeways (I-110 and I-10), there are sights to see beyond those boundaries. **Olympic Auditorium**, built in 1925 at 1801 South Grand Avenue at 18th Street, is just south of I-10; the auditorium attracted many celebrities on fight nights during the 1920s and '30s. The fight scenes for the films *Requiem for a Heavyweight* and *Rocky* were shot here, and many others before and since.

There has been a **Patriotic Hall** on Figueroa near 18th Street since the original was built in 1886 to honor the Grand Army of the Republic, a Civil War veterans group. The current 10-story building dates from 1926. During World War II, Hollywood's biggest stars, like Bob Hope, Bing Crosby and Dorothy Lamour, entertained the troops in the Hall's main auditorium. That same stage, with a huge US flag backdrop, was used for the opening scene of *Patton*, starring George C. Scott. Patriotic Hall's 10-story staircase was used in Alfred Hitchcock's *Vertigo*. The hall has been seen in more than 300 films, including *Heat*, *Iron Eagle*, *Native Son*, *Stand and Deliver* and *The Wedding Planner*. The final scene of *Flashdance* was filmed in the building's Nimitz Room.

The **University of Southern California** is next to Exposition Park, sprawling east to west between Figueroa and Vermont and north to south from Exposition to Jefferson. USC is where Dustin Hoffman earned his college degree in *The Graduate*. The school was also featured in *Forrest Gump*, *A League of Their Own* and *Young Frankenstein*.

North of Downtown

North of LA's Historic Core are the Civic Center, Olvera Street, Chinatown and Little Tokyo neighborhoods. Some of the buildings in these neighborhoods have been filmed countless times over the years. One building, the 12-story Beaux Arts-style **Spring Street Towers** at 650 South Spring, was used for scenes in *Fatal Vision*, *Prizzi's Honor* and *St. Elmo's Fire*, plus episodes of *Cagney & Lacey*, *Matlock*, *Hill Street Blues* and *Hardcastle & McCormick*. The massive **US District Court Building**, at 312 Spring Street, became the "Armed Forces Public Information Office" in *War of the Worlds*, and was a court building in *Oh, God! Book II*.

☞ **DID YOU KNOW?**

The **Clara Shortridge Foltz Criminal Justice Building** (the Criminal Courts Building), at 210 West Temple Street, was the site of the Heidi Fleiss and O.J. Simpson cases in the 1990s. It was named for the first woman admitted to the state's first law school; she was also the first woman admitted to the bar in California, the first woman to serve as a deputy district attorney in Los Angeles County, and a founder of our public defender system.

At 26 stories, **City Hall**, 200 North Spring Street, dominated Los Angeles' downtown skyline when it opened in 1927 and for years thereafter. Surely it is the most recognizable city hall in the world, having appeared in hundreds of movies and TV series. It was a stand-in for the Vatican in the TV miniseries *The Thorn Birds*. It served as the Daily Planet building in the 1950s series *Superman*, it was destroyed by the Martians in 1953's *War of the Worlds*, but showed up later in *Seems Like Old Times*, *Dragnet*, *48 HRS.*, *Ricochet* and *The Jimmy Hoffa Story*, to name a few.

Although it was built in 1939, visitors are still awestruck by the interior of **Union Station**, at 800 North Alameda just east of Olvera Street, with its soaring ceiling, black walnut beams and 3,000-pound chandeliers. Among the films shot here are *The Way We Were*, *To Live and Die in L.A.*, *Bugsy*, *L.A. Confidential* and *True Confessions*, based on one of Los Angeles' most famous unsolved crimes, the Black Dahlia murder case.

There was a 1950 movie about Union Station. It was called – Union Station.

HISTORIC NOTE

Union Station's most famous moment
has become an enduring Los Angeles
legend. In 1939 the city's flamboyant
district attorney, Buron Fitts, sent a
deputy to meet the arriving Mae West,
with instructions to give her a kiss,
saying "This is from Buron." Mae replied, "Is that a gun in your pocket, or
are you just glad to see me?"

Along the Los Angeles River

The cement bed of the Los Angeles River where it circles
around the northeast side of downtown has been used as a
location for film and television. One well-known scene was
the car race sequence with John Travolta in *Grease*, which
took place between the 6th Street and 4th Street viaducts
on the west side of the riverbed. The same location was
used in the comedy picture *The Gumball Rally*, and in episodes of *Moonlighting*, *Hunter* and *CHiPs*. While you are
there, take a look at the tunnel under the 6th Street Via-
duct. That is where the giant mutated ants swarmed in
Them! (1954), and it was used for various frights in *The
Annihilator*, *The Oldest Rookie* and *Moonlighting* (again).
In *Volcano* you will notice it is quick-thinking Angelenos
who guide the lava into the river channel and save the
city!

DID YOU KNOW?

The Los Angeles River is at present a
58-mile-long concrete-lined ditch. For
years, the group Friends of the River
has tried to do something about it
and, at last, parts of the city government have joined in to begin to restore
the riverbed and construct parks and
bike paths along its banks.

Best Places to Stay

Paul, if the honeymoon doesn't work out, let's not get divorced. Let's kill each other.

Let's have one of the maids do it. I hear the service here is wonderful.

– Jane Fonda and Robert Redford, *Barefoot in the Park*

Hotels

Most of the national chains are represented downtown. Keep in mind that hotel rates here, at least downtown, are lower in summer and higher in winter. At the big chain hotels they can vary daily. A room might be $140 for Wednesday night, $170 on Thursday and back to $140 Friday. It's also worthwhile to ask about senior rates, if that designation applies to you. A few hotels marked with stars have strong, long-running connections to the industry.

WILSHIRE GRAND
930 Wilshire Boulevard
Los Angeles, CA 90017
☎ 213-688-7777, fax 213-612-3989
www.wilshiregrand.com
Moderate-Expensive

This big, 900-room hotel attracts large numbers of Asian guests. The Wilshire Grand has two specialty restaurants: **Kyoto**, a Japanese tempura and sushi bar; and **Seoul Jung**, which features Korean barbeque, as well as **Cardini** for Italian food, and **City Grill** for American cuisine. For those who prefer to dine in-room, there is 24-hour service. Other amenities include a swimming pool (open 24 hours), a hydrotherapy pool, retail shops and a car rental desk.

The accommodations price scale can be found on page 39.

Downtown Los Angeles

★★ FIGUEROA HOTEL

939 South Figueroa Street
Los Angeles, CA 90015
☎ 213-627-8971, 800-421-9092, fax 213-689-0305
Moderate

LA's finest hotel in the 1870s was the Pico House, which still stands on the old Plaza, in need of restoration.

Built in the 1920s in the Spanish style, with hand-painted furniture, wrought iron beds and ceiling fans in most rooms. There are refrigerators in the rooms, a pool and hot tub, spa and exercise room, concierge and, what is unusual and a money-saver, free parking. The hotel also has two bars and a dining room. We hesitated at first to stick those stars by the name of this hotel, which has certainly never been an attraction for celebrities before. But Staples Center, the big new downtown arena for sports and concerts, is nearby and the Figueroa Hotel seems to be attracting some who want to party afterward. Following a recent concert, for example, Keanu Reeves and Depeche Mode showed up to keep the good times going.

HYATT REGENCY LOS ANGELES

711 South Hope Street
Los Angeles, CA 90017
☎ 213-683-1234, 800-233-1234, fax 213-629-3230
Moderate

The Hyatt is in the middle of things, and within walking distance to everywhere downtown, and there are first-class views from the upper floors of this tall building. The hotel has two restaurants – **The Grill** is the good one – and a karaoke lounge with, they tell us though we haven't counted, 3,000 Japanese and American CDs. There are no-smoking floors, a concierge and a separate concierge floor, room service, and an exercise room.

OMNI LOS ANGELES

251 South Olive Street
Los Angeles, CA 90012
☎ 213-617-3300, fax 213-617-3399
www.omnihotels.com
Moderate

The Omni Hotel overlooks California Plaza and its open-air concerts and entertainment in summer.

The sleek, Asian-accented Omni is near the top of Bunker Hill, next to California Plaza. Rooms offer panoramic views, and have telephones in the bathrooms, with a separate bath and shower in most; robes; and 24-hour room service. There is an outdoor swimming pool, and fitness facilities. The **Grand Café** serves California cuisine, and the **Angels Flight Lounge** has piano music every night. Close to the Music Center and MOCA (the Museum of Contemporary Art).

★ REGAL BILTMORE HOTEL
506 South Grand Avenue
Los Angeles, CA 90071
☎ 213-612-1575; 800-245-8673; fax 213-612-1628
www.millennium-hotels.com
Moderate-Expensive

When the Biltmore was built in 1923 it was the most elegant of Los Angeles' hotels. A recent multi-million-dollar renovation has made sure that it still is. The 11-story hotel occupies most of the block between Olive and Grand, from Fifth to Sixth streets. The main entrance is now on Grand, but the original, one-floor-lower Olive Street lobby exiting onto Pershing Square is opulently done, with handsome ceiling paintings.

Downtown Los Angeles

☞ **DID YOU KNOW?**

The **Academy of Motion Picture Arts & Sciences** was dreamed up in the Biltmore during a 1927 entertainment industry banquet. An award statue was sketched on a napkin and a name penciled in: Oscar.

Pershing Square is the last remaining public parcel of the original Spanish land grant on which Downtown Los Angeles is built.

The architectural style is Italian Renaissance. There are over 600 rooms, including 55 suites, with 24-hour room service. The Health Club ($7 per usage) offers all services, including a pool. The eight places to eat and drink range from casual (a big sports bar with complimentary snacks and moderately priced food, plus a deli and a bakery with coffee) to a *ristorante* with Italian and California cuisine; try **Sai Sai** for Japanese food or **Bernard's Bistro** for modern French and continental dinners (oddly, Bernard's hasn't been appreciated lately in the local press for its fine food and good service).

Forget the hotel's formal name – it has always been known simply as The Biltmore.

The hotel's very popular **Gallery Bar**, always crowded after downtown's offices empty out at 5pm, showcases photos from the 1920s and '30s depicting Academy Award ceremonies held at the Biltmore. Next to it is the **Cognac Room**, open from 4:30pm to 1:45am, with a piano tinkling from 7pm.

THE BILTMORE IN FILM

The number of feature films shot partially at the Biltmore is mind-boggling; we counted 128 just since 1974, and there must have been hundreds more before they started keeping track. We know part of *Vertigo* was set here way back when. Some pics used the hotel's interiors so pervasively that you easily recognize parts of the Biltmore when you look at *True Lies* and *Beverly Hills Cop*. Other films with scenes shot at the Biltmore are *Chinatown*, *A Star is Born*, *Rocky III*, *Pink Panther*, *Misery*, *Bugsy*, *The Bodyguard*, *The Nutty Professor*, *Independence Day*, *Escape From L.A.*, *Message in a Bottle*, *13 Days*, *What Women Want*, *Blow*, *Ocean's Eleven*, *Deeds*, *Spider-Man* and *Stuart Little 2*.

There have been 94 weekly episodic television shows shot at least partially in the hotel; some, like *Kojak*, *Cagney & Lacey*, *Murder, She Wrote* and *The West Wing*, have used the hotel as a location many times. A few of the others were, over the years since 1975, *McMillan and Wife*, *Columbo*, *The Bionic Woman*, *Charlie's Angels*, *Knots Landing*, *Dynasty*, *Hill Street Blues*, *Matlock*, *L.A. Law*, *Beverly Hills 90210*, *Chicago Hope*, *ER*, *NYPD Blue*, *JAG*, *Judging Amy*, *Ally McBeal* and *Providence*.

Scenes for half-a-dozen mini-series, including *Rich Man, Poor Man* and *Roots* were shot here. The Biltmore has also been the scene of dozens of movie-of-the-week specials and shows for cable and pay-per-view and, what we are all most likely to have seen, over 50 commercials.

📖 HISTORIC NOTE

Seven US Presidents have been Biltmore guests: Harry S. Truman, John F. Kennedy, Gerald R. Ford, Jimmy Carter, Ronald Reagan, George Bush and Bill Clinton. Other notable guests have included Princess Margaret and the Duke of Kent, Eleanor Roosevelt, Howard Hughes, Mary Pickford, John Wayne and Barbra Streisand.

★ THE WESTIN BONAVENTURE
404 South Figueroa Street
Los Angeles, CA 90071
☎ 213-624-1000, 800-228-3000
Moderate-Expensive

Instantly recognizable because of its appearance in so many films and television shows, the Westin Bonaventure's tower glows against Los Angeles' nighttime skyline with a dozen glass elevators sliding ceaselessly up and down the outside of its 35 stories – a spectacular urban sight. Of its 1,354 guest rooms, 135 are suites. There is a 9,000-square-foot spa, a half-acre garden deck with a 50x100-foot heated pool, a running track and a health, tennis and fitness center next door reached by a sky bridge. The Bonaventure has 19 different places to eat, including fine dining, fast dining, coffee bars, cocktail lounges, a chowder bar and a micro-brewery, plus 24-hour room service.

Four US Presidents have stayed at the Bonaventure, along with countless celebrities, including Elizabeth Taylor and Bob Hope.

For fantastic views of the city, try dining on the top floors of the Bonaventure. On the 35th floor is **L.A. Prime**, featuring steaks, Maine lobster and seafood; one floor down is the revolving **BonaVista Lounge**, which makes a full revolution every hour for a 360° view, ranging from the San Gabriel Mountains to Hollywood and the ocean.

Before the hotel even opened in 1976, the sci-fi thriller *Logan's Run* was shot in the six-story atrium, which has been the setting for many films since, including *Blue Thunder, Breathless, Final Analysis, Forget Paris, Heat, In the Line of Fire, Lethal Weapon II, Rain Man, Ruthless People, Strange Days, The Driver* and *True Lies*. On televi-

The Bonaventure Brewing Co. has live jazz Saturday nights.

sion you may have seen the hotel in *General Hospital, L.A. Law, Moonlighting, Remington Steele, Starsky and Hutch, The Insiders, The Return of Mike Hammer* and *Wonder Woman*.

★★ WYNDHAM CHECKERS

535 South Grand Avenue (between Fifth and Sixth)
☎ 213-624-0000, 800-WYNDHAM, fax 213-626-9906
Contemporary American
Expensive

The Wyndham Checkers, Los Angeles' only small, European-style hotel, is a very good hotel with a central location; it is across the street from The Biltmore. Former President Nixon and Soviet Prime Minister Gorbachev met in the private library in 1992 to discuss Soviet/US relations. Since then, Stefanie Powers has shot several PBS specials here, and Ray Charles is a regular guest.

When the Checkers opened in the 1920s, the rates ranged from $2.50 to $7 per night.

In 1999 Carol Burnett lived in the penthouse suite during her three-month run in Stephen Sondheim's *Putting It Together* at the Ahmanson Theatre. At the end of long days of rehearsal and performances she would signal to Joe the Bartender for a Skyy Vodka martini to be sent up to her suite. Cher spends the day of every Grammy Awards Show in the penthouse suite with a load of costumes and hairpieces to prepare for the evening. Jim Carrey lived in the penthouse suite during the filming of *Man on the Moon*.

In 2000, Gwyneth Paltrow "checked in" to a typical exclusive Paris hotel in a lobby scene for *View from the Top*, then shot a scene in a suite redesigned with French provincial furniture and the Paris skyline depicted on canvas outside the window.

The hotel was built in the 1920s as The Mayflower, which explains the two carved ships embedded in the sides of the entrance. One is the *Mayflower*; the other is the *Santa Maria*, the first ship to follow the Pacific shores and discover California harbors. The exterior is modern with Spanish design elements; the lower three floors are especially striking in modeled stone. The hotel reached the 12-story height limit in effect at the time of its construction.

There is a very fine dining room (see Checkers Restaurant, page 75) and a lobby bar; 24-hour room service; a rooftop spa with a lap pool; complimentary shoeshine; and complimentary limousine service to downtown.

Bed & Breakfast

INN AT 23RD
657 West 23rd Street
Los Angeles, CA 90007
☎ 213-741-2200, 800-347-7512
Moderate

No movie stars stay here, but it is one of the best bargains in lodging, at least downtown. Compared to the rest of the hotels in the area this is a very small place, with only 13 suites. It is not centrally located; it is off by the University of Southern California (in fact there is a USC tram stop just outside the door). People who have work to do at the University, such as Jane Goodall, stay here. Living rooms are good-sized, with sofas and easy chairs, and big dining tables. There are also kitchens with microwaves, and private entrances off the garden. The room rate includes a big breakfast with ham and French toast, pancakes and eggs Benedict, and local phone calls are free.

Best Places to Eat

During one of my trips through Afghanistan, we lost our corkscrew. Had to live on food and water for several days.

> – W.C. Fields, *My Little Chickadee*

Most Downtown hotels have at least one fine restaurant, and many visitors eat well without stirring out onto the streets. The reason there are so few really good free-standing restaurants here is that very few people, except for those in the handful of condos on Bunker Hill, actually live downtown. And those who drive downtown from elsewhere are going to the Music Center to see a play or Staples Center for a basketball game. The hotels depend on their captive audiences. An occasional celebrity may come in but, except for places open late enough for actors to drop in after shooting, don't count on it.

The dining price scale can be found on page 42.

Fine Dining

CBS SEAFOOD RESTAURANT
700 North Spring Street
☎ 213-617-2323
Cantonese
Inexpensive-Moderate

Even though this is a Chinese seafood restaurant with a menu that would challenge a good Hong Kong restaurant in its scope, many do not come here for the straight seafood, but for something different: dim sum. Dim sum are in Canton what tapas are in Spain – small dishes to pick and choose from. Here, when the dim sum carts roll by the tables, you will see shrimp dumplings, crabmeat wrapped in bean curd, barbequed pork buns, heaps of shrimp, soup, barbequed meats and sweets. Each goes for $1.70 to $9. Dim sum is served only 8am-3pm, though CBS is open until 10pm. Regular meals emphasize fish and seafood. This is not in Chinatown itself, but a few blocks east.

MORTON'S OF CHICAGO
735 South Figueroa Street
☎ 213-553-4566
www.mortons.com
Steakhouse
Expensive

There are over 60 Morton's scattered around the country. The restaurant has a club-like atmosphere with mahogany paneling and leather banquettes. Morton's features prime aged beef; fish and seafood are flown in daily. Open for lunch Monday-Friday, 11:30am-2:30pm; dinner Monday-Saturday, 5:30-11pm; Sunday until 10pm; bar opens at 5pm. Valet parking.

CAFE PINOT
700 West 5th Street
☎ 213-239-6500
French-California
Expensive

The food is basically French, but with an emphasis on the use of fresh California produce, without making a religion of it. The onions in the onion soup come from Bakersfield, for instance, but the porcini mushrooms in the salad made their way here from Europe. Entrées are very wide ranging. It is a good-looking place, basically a glass box sitting in the gardens of the Main Library, with the restaurant's patio verging on the greenery. Lunch is popular with the downtown business crowd; early dinners with pre-theater people (there is a free shuttle from Café Pinot to the Music Center).

Café Pinot is the only free-standing restaurant in downtown Los Angeles.

Café Pinot is open for lunch Monday-Friday, 11:30am-2:30pm; dinner daily, 5-9pm. There is a limited menu on weekdays in the afternoon between lunch and dinner. Valet parking is available on 5th Street at night; self-park at lunch around the corner on Flower Street (with validation, it's $3). If you are coming here on the Harbor Freeway, exit at 6th Street, go east to Olive, turn left, and left again on 5th Street.

★★ CHECKERS RESTAURANT
535 South Grand Avenue
☎ 213-891-0519
California cuisine
Expensive

This is one of the places people drive downtown for. It's in the Wyndham Checkers (page 72), across Grand Street from the Biltmore Hotel. The décor is blessedly peaceful and quiet. You can dine on the patio or inside in the handsome dining room; in either case the noise level is low and the food is very good. In fact, it was voted "Best Restaurant of 2001 in Downtown Los Angeles" by *LA Downtown News*, placed in the "Top 10 Restaurants in Los Angeles" by *Gourmet Magazine*, and praised as being "as good as it gets in Downtown Los Angeles" by *Zagat Guide 2000*. The hotel attracts celebrities, too, especially when they are shooting downtown or attending a performance at the Music Center. The food here is eclectic; you will recognize lots of Mediterranean flavors and Asian touches. We recommend the crab cakes with pancetta if they are on the menu. Breakfast served daily (hours vary); lunch Monday-Friday, 11:30am-1:30pm; dinner every night, 5:30pm-8:30pm.

CIUDAD

445 South Figueroa Street
Union Bank Plaza, Suite 100 (ground floor)
☎ 213-486-5171, fax 213-486-5172
www.ciudad-la.com
Latin American-Spanish
Moderate

If you ask for directions to Ciudad and are told it is at "5th and Fig," know that locally Fig means Figueroa Street.

You may have seen television's *Too Hot Tamales'* Mary Sue Milliken and Susan Feniger, the photogenic chefs whose show, in the '90s, made Mexican street food suddenly popular with the upscale crowd. They've also written a string of cookbooks, including *Mexican Cooking For Dummies*. Their place in Santa Monica, the Border Grill, became so popular with celebrities that they opened Ciudad downtown (in case you are Spanish-challenged, the name means "city"). This is a fun place; be ready to try something new, from menu items you would find in Havana, Rio, Lima, Buenos Aires, Lisbon and Barcelona.

The menu features authentic dishes Milliken and Feniger learned from cooks in Central and South America, such as Argentine empañadas, Puerto Rican tamales, and seared calamari Bilbao; they've also created new dishes with Latin ingredients. The colors on the walls and furniture must have been chosen because you can eat them all: avocado, pumpkin, lemon, and mocha; it is definitely a bright room. There is a full bar with American cocktails plus a wide selection of sipping rums (a three-rum sampler is $7). The wine list is heavy with wines from Spain, Chile and Argentina, as is fitting.

Weekday lunchtime is usually crowded (Ciudad is not open for lunch on weekends), with the patio full. Check out the big Cuban sandwiches made with house-baked buns stuffed with pork, ham and cheese. Early on Friday nights, when the office workers celebrating TGIF throng the lively bar munching *cuchifritos* (little snacks), it is usually packed and too noisy to carry on an intelligible conversation. Other weeknights you don't have to worry about reservations.

A free shuttle service runs from Ciudad to the Music Center or Staples Center – but you must make reservations.

This is definitely not a place haunted by celebrities, but the restaurant does cater meals for many of the film companies shooting downtown. Open for dinner every night; for lunch Monday-Friday from 11:30. Happy hour, Monday-Friday, starts at 3pm and goes to 7pm. Parking at lunch for up to two hours is free in the Union Bank Plaza Garage with Ciudad validation. Other times it's $3 with validation; valet parking is available from 5pm for $3.50.

☞ **DID YOU KNOW?**

The City of Los Angeles sprawls over 467 square miles and, with 3.6 million residents, is more populous than 25 states.

Downtown Los Angeles

MON KEE'S SEAFOOD
679 North Spring Street
☎ 213-628-6717, 877-550-5010
Chinese seafood
Moderate

Lobster, clams with oyster sauce, a sizzling platter of shrimp with garlic sauce, both freshwater and saltwater fish, and all the soups and appetizers to lead up to them are here. Mon Kee's has been in business a long time, putting out what may be the best Chinese seafood in town. A very popular place. Open Sunday-Thursday, 11:30am-9:45pm; Friday and Saturday until 10:15pm.

NICK & STEF'S STEAKHOUSE
Wells Fargo Center
330 South Hope Street
☎ 213-680-0330
Steakhouse
Expensive

Entrées are 10 steaks and chops, plus one chicken and one lobster item, for a total of 12. Along with it are 12 starters and salads on the menu, 12 vegetables, 12 sauces, and 12 kinds of potatoes. Someone wanted everything to balance evenly. Located on Bunker Hill, just a few blocks from almost everywhere downtown, this place has the feel of a traditional steakhouse with lots of wood, deep booths and large, angular chairs. The beef, which is the main concern here, is dry-aged on the premises. Nick & Stef's is open for lunch Monday-Friday, 11:30am-2:30pm; and for dinner

Monday-Thursday, 5:30-9:30pm; Friday until 10:30; Saturday, 5-10:30pm; and Sunday, 5-9pm. Valet parking is available, or park under the big Wells Fargo building. The restaurant is up one flight.

★★ PACIFIC DINING CAR

1310 West Sixth Street
☎ 213-483-6000
Steakhouse
Expensive-Very Expensive

Pacific Dining Car was named the number one steakhouse on the West Coast, and among the top five in the nation, by Wine Spectator *magazine.*

Any place with Dining Car in its name sounds as if should be serving casual food. But this restaurant, in the same family since it opened in 1921, has grown beyond the original faux dining car into a memento-filled, mahogany-paneled affair, with a large and lush interior.

You will find prominent politicians here as well as show-biz celebrities, a tradition that goes way back. The baseball steak, for instance, a round, fat top sirloin, used to be named for Buddy Ebsen, who preferred it. We have promised we won't name names, to keep up the restaurant's age-old policy of protecting celebrities' privacy; except for Nicolas Cage, as it is well known that his father used to bring him here when he was a child and he still has the habit. Since it is one of the few restaurants open 24 hours daily, celebrities drop in after seeing a play at the Music Center, or following a late-night shoot on downtown streets.

Incidentally, a free shuttle bus is provided for those who want an early dinner before going to the Music Center or Staples Center to see the Lakers.

The menu is large, as is the selection of steaks: cowboy steak, a ribeye on the bone; T-bone; Delmonico; filet mignon; New York and Dining Car Steak, which is a narrow section from a New York cut. To go with it, one order of fried onion rings will feed four, and the Dining Car Potatoes are what Easterners call O'Brien potatoes, or so the waiter told us. Other dishes, including some seafood, are served, but the restaurant is primarily known for steaks and chops. Coming here for breakfast is a long-standing tradition, as you might guess from the hours it is served: weekdays, 11pm-11am; weekends, 11pm-4pm.

TIP

Pacific Dining Car is one of those restaurants where you are wise not to order all at once. Portions are so large that after eating soup and an appetizer you may discover you don't want an entrée after all.

★★ PROMENADE RISTORANTE
710 West First Street
Promenade Plaza
☎ 213-437-4937
Italian
Expensive

Placido Domingo, the tenor and artistic director of the Los Angeles Opera, is a fairly regular presence here when he is in town, along with celebrities dining before attending a play at the Music Center. Besides entertainment industry types, you will find the place filled at lunch on weekdays with judges, lawyers and jurors from the nearby courthouse. You will find the restaurant across from the Music Center and near the Civic Center on Bunker Hill.

The décor will not win any prizes, but if you are a fan of Italian cooking you have come to the right place. Owner Orazio Afrento may greet you at the door and tell you today's specialties on the way to your table. Last time we were there he recommended some seafood that he had picked out himself at the fish market that morning. Contrary to the trend at many Los Angeles restaurants, the portions here are not overwhelmingly large. You might want an *antipasti misti*, a mixed antipasto plate, for the table. It is a generous dish and you should enjoy trying the different delicacies while you are investigating the menu. As we write this the restaurant serves wine and beer, but does not have a full bar. Open for lunch, Monday-Friday, 11:30am-2pm; for brunch on Sunday, 11am-2pm; for dinner, Monday-Saturday, 5:30pm-10pm, and Sunday, 5-10pm. Park underneath.

At lunch, Promenade also serves the original Italian thin sandwiches called panini. The panino with molten provolone cheese and prosciutto inside is a classic.

Downtown Los Angeles

Casual Dining

★★ COLE'S P.E. BUFFET
118 East Sixth Street
☎ 213-622-4090
French dipped sandwiches
Inexpensive

Cole's, which opened in 1908, is the oldest restaurant in Los Angeles, a few months older than Philippe (see page 81).

The restaurant's odd name refers to the Pacific Electric Railroad, the once-immense trolley system that linked all parts of the far-flung area together before the freeways. Cole's is located in what was the main terminal. When the trolley lines were dismantled in the 1950s, the café lost its supply of daily commuters, but the regulars kept coming back. It has always had a certain amount of fame because of the hundreds of movie and TV scenes shot here, including *The X-Files* and scenes in many episodes of the *NYPD Blue* television series. You might remember it from *L.A. Confidential* and the New Year's scene in *Forrest Gump*.

Cole's tables are built from the old LA Red Cars that ran on the trolley lines.

Check out the photos of celebrities on the walls. Cole's is a popular spot for actors who drop in to eat after a shoot, and the upper floors of the otherwise unused P.E. Building have been used as a location for many movies and TV episodes. Food is served daily, 9am-7pm; the bar stays open later.

ORIGINAL PANTRY
877 South Figueroa Street
☎ 213-972-9279
Old-fashioned American
Inexpensive

The Original Pantry is ancient by Los Angeles' standards; it opened in 1924 and has been extremely popular ever since. In fact, it has never been without a paying customer since its opening day. Everyone knows about the Pantry and, though it seats only 84, it serves several thousand huge portions every day. You walk into a long, plain room that no decorator has ever messed with and order old-timey stews, roasts or chops. They have been making the same baked salmon all these years; the menu also features corned beef and cabbage. The entrées come with canned vegetables and a choice of mashed or fried potatoes. The Original Pantry is open 24 hours daily. Incidentally, The Pantry is owned by the ex-mayor.

PANTRY BAKE & SANDWICH SHOPPE
875 South Figueroa Street
☎ 213-627-6879
Old-fashioned American, plus sandwiches
Inexpensive

No alcohol is served at either of the two Pantry restaurants, and no credit cards are accepted.

When a vacancy opened up next door to the Original Pantry a dozen years ago, the owners opened a second place to take the pressure off the crowds at breakfast and lunchtime. It is a little brighter, with curtains on the windows, but the menu is about the same, except for added sandwiches on weekdays. And there are daily specials at both, dishes you are never going to find on the menu in the high-toned, upscale joints, things like liver and onions, franks and beans and Swiss steak. The Sandwich Shoppe is open daily, 6am-3pm.

PHILIPPE THE ORIGINAL
1001 North Alameda Street
☎ 213-628-3781
www.philippes.com
Inexpensive

This is an old place, down by the railroad tracks and warehouses past Union Station. Philippe Mathieu, an emigré from Aix-en-Provence, opened it in 1908 as a deli that also sold sandwiches. It achieved fame in 1918 when he accidentally dropped a roll in a pan of roasting juices. The customer took it anyway and then came back the next day and asked that his sandwich be "dipped" again the same way. Philippe became known as the "Home of the French dipped sandwich."

Another old-time downtown café, Cole's on 6th Street, claims the French dip was invented there.

A long French roll is dipped in gravy and a thick layer of meat is piled on. You add the homemade house mustard that is on every table, but watch out, it is hot! Try the coarsely grated coleslaw with its creamy dressing. The meat, either lamb, pork or turkey (pass on the ham), is all nicely moist. The turkey is a late addition, tacked on as a heart-healthy choice. Wines are inexpensive, and most are pretty good. From October through June there is apple pie for dessert. Breakfast always includes homemade dough-

Downtown Los Angeles

Philippe's is a Los Angeles institution. It seems every-one has eaten here at least once, and a lot of people have made a lifelong habit of it.

nuts rolled in powdered sugar or cinnamon, crusty corned beef hash and eggs with a spicy salsa. And coffee is always 10¢ a cup!

Philippe has moved a couple of times, but nothing has really changed. The sawdust on the floor, the matter-of-fact waitresses behind the counter, some of whom have worked here for decades, and the long, shared tables are all part of the restaurant's long-standing appeal. Open every day, 6am-10pm.

Shop Till You Drop

I remember every detail – the Germans wore gray, you wore blue.

— Humphrey Bogart, *Casablanca*

Broadway

For a hundred years shopping meant Broadway, but that has not been the case since the 1960s. As the department stores closed and immigration, legal and illegal, from Mexico and points south greatly increased, Broadway recovered as a shopping mecca but with a decided difference. Now it is packed with stores – most of them small – all selling to the Latino trade. It most resembles a very busy shopping street in Mexico City. There are, however, a few specialized stores and areas where, though you may not see any celebrities, you might find something you can't get anywhere else.

★ TIP

Grand Central Market is a collection of at least 100 independent food stalls that extends from Broadway to Hill Street, just south of Third Street. It has been here for 75 years and is a great place to pick up casual meals to eat on the spot or take out.

Books, Maps & Music

CARAVAN BOOK STORE
550 South Grand Avenue
☎ 213-343-4772

Downtown was a thriving center for specialty bookstores from the 1920s to the '80s, but reduced foot-traffic in the neighborhood, combined with the arrival of the big chain stores, has eliminated the majority of independent shops. Caravan, one of the few survivors, first opened its doors more than 50 years ago, when this was booksellers' row. The store has a section on early movie history, with things like 1920s casting directories. If you are interested in learning more about the city, the store specializes in Western American History, which includes early Los Angeles and Southern California. You will also find books on travel, food, wine and antiques. Open Monday-Saturday, 11am-6pm.

THOMAS BROS. MAP STORE
521 West 6th Street
☎ 213-627-4018

Thomas Bros. sells maps for the traveler who really wants to know where he or she is at all times. Open Monday-Friday, 8:30am-6pm.

MUSIC MAN MURRAY
5055 Exposition Boulevard
☎ 323-734-9146

If you are interested in old records, or just in music, you will never find another place like Murray's. When you walk into this industrial-style building you are faced with around 200,000 records – even Murray is not sure how many are here – with another 200,000 or so in storage. Movie studios call here when they are looking for music they cannot find elsewhere, and Louis Armstrong, Duke Ellington and Mae West used to call for copies of their own records. Now, customers include Jason Alexander of *Seinfeld*, and Gene Wilder.

What is here? Classical, jazz, opera, Broadway shows, rock, pop, salsa, mariachi, marching bands, Yugoslavian music, Bohemian – with prices ranging from $3 to $2,000. You will find every Beatles album ever released, Bing Crosby, Herb Alpert and Paul Robeson; Frank Sinatra and Judy Garland almost fill a wall. Most of the inventory is on vinyl; a growing amount is on compact discs.

Fashion District

Shops with childrens' clothing are clustered on Pico, Julian and Wall streets.

Los Angeles is one of the greatest apparel resources in the country; manufacturers and wholesalers are concentrated in the Fashion District. Showrooms were traditionally open "to the trade only," but many wholesalers and manufacturers are now selling to the public; some are open to the public every day, some only on certain days. You can find samples and overstock at 20-50% below mall prices, though some shops, especially in Santee Alley, sell strictly retail. Within the 82-block Fashion District, 220 stores sell retail only, and 800 sell both wholesale and retail. Those that sell to the trade only will have signs stating their policy.

Every Saturday over 1,000 stores offer wholesale prices, 30% off retail, to the public.

The area of main interest to the general public stretches from 7th Street to Pico Boulevard, north to south, and from Main to San Pedro streets, west to east. Hours are Monday-Saturday, 10am-5pm for most stores. You'll need to take plenty of change for meters, or use paid parking lots. Lots closer to CaliforniaMart and Santee Alley are more expensive. A free trolley tour of the fashion district is offered on the last Saturday of the month. Call ☎ 213-488-1153. More information at www.fashiondistrict.org.

Marketplaces

CaliforniaMart, 9th and Main streets, is a 1,200-showroom fashion center and the district's showcase; the showrooms traditionally sell only to store buyers, who come from all over the country, especially to its lobby shops. Stylists come here weekly, many borrowing items for magazine photo shoots. CaliforniaMart is open Monday-Friday to the trade only, but opens to the public on the last Friday of each month for a sample sale and on select Saturdays for special sales in the exhibit hall. For dates and times, contact ☎ 213-630-3600 or check online at www.california-mart.com. **New Mart**, though prominent on the Fashion District's Web site, is almost entirely devoted to the wholesale trade.

FOR FASHION DESIGN BUFFS

From mid-February through April the costumes from many of the previous year's films are displayed at the **Fashion Institute of Design and Merchandising**, 919 South Grand Avenue, Los Angeles, ☎ 213-624-1200, in their annual Art of Motion Picture Costume Design Exhibit. Even though the costumes are selected months in advance, the choices usually line up with the Oscar nominations. The show also includes broader exhibits, such as "A Decade of Film Style." The collection can be viewed at the Fashion Institute's museum, Monday-Saturday, 10am-4pm. Admission free. Parking is available under the college building, entrance on 9th Street.

Santee Alley, Olympic Boulevard to 12th Street between Maple Avenue and Santee Street, is an outdoor market, a three-block bazaar. Some of everything is available, a lot of it at pretty good prices, but there is a big variety in quality. Nevertheless, it is fun, since most places allow bargaining. Most also prefer payment in cash, some will accept credit cards. Trendy club dresses are sold in Santee Alley for $7, T-shirts are three for $10. Costume designers with a small budget and a sitcom cast to dress each week flock here for bargains on up-to-the-minute fashions. Hollywood designers also shop the textile stores in the district for fabrics to make their own creations or to re-cover furniture. Costume jewelry is a big item here for music videos and album covers. Look for chain belts and rhinestone jewelry at discounted prices.

★ TIP

Watch clothing sizes: a large in Santee
Alley is sometimes closer to a mall's
small. And most of these marketplace
shops do not have dressing rooms.

HUNGRY FROM ALL THAT SHOPPING?

The following places are handy spots to grab a
bite near the Fashion District:

◆ **Coffee Bean & Tea Leaf**, 210 East Olympic
Boulevard, No. 120, ☎ 213-749-5746.

◆ **Sam's Famous Deli**, 121 East 9th Street,
☎ 213-622-2008.

◆ CalMart's **food court** is near the 9th Street
entrance, 110 East 9th Street.

◆ On the south side of CalMart is **Massimo Ris-
torante**, ☎ 213-689-4415, a full-service Italian restaurant serving lunch Monday-Friday
till 3pm (the bar is open till 8pm).

◆ **Angelique's Café**, 840 South Spring Street
at the fork between Spring and Main streets,
☎ 213-623-8698, is a French restaurant that
you might recognize if you saw *Rush Hour*.

◆ Also handy is **Cole's P.E. Buffet**, at 118 East
6th Street (see page 80).

Jewelry District

Most of the tall buildings on **Hill Street** and **Broadway**
between 5th and 8th streets are devoted solely to jewelry
making; you'll find hundreds of jewelry manufacturers,
wholesalers and retail shops, most above street level;
Look for custom-made fine jewelry, precious stones and
watches at discount prices. Most shops are open 10am-
6pm, Monday-Saturday.

Toy District

If you have a little person back home and want to find a gift, this may be the place for you. Instead of one store like Toys "R" Us you can visit dozens of small shops, each one with a specialty, and pick and choose not just among a few toy guns or dozens of stuffed animals, but hundreds of different kinds, all in one place. You will find plush animals at both **David's Toys**, 346 South 4th Street, ☎ 213-680-8928, and at nearby **Fancy Zoo**, 340 South San Pedro Street, ☎ 213-680-0034; and babies' toys and strollers at **A-Mart Toys**, 305 East 4th Street, ☎ 213-628-1389. There are many other stores. The Toy District is located primarily along San Pedro and Los Angeles streets between 3rd and 6th. Hours for most stores are Monday-Saturday, 9am-5pm. Parking is available at curbside meters or in paid parking lots.

Sunup to Sundown

Walks & Tours

There are quite a few downtown walks to choose from, guided and self-guided, none specifically associated with the movies except as they might incidentally pass through a place like the Regal Biltmore Hotel.

CARROLL AVENUE HOMES

A cluster of grand, still lived-in Victorian houses in the 1300 block of Carroll Avenue in Angelino Heights was the center for refined living in Old Los Angeles. Number 1345 is popularly known as the Haunted House; it was prominent in Michael Jackson's Thriller video. From Downtown, take Temple Street west to Edgeware Road, then turn right; Carroll is over the freeway and to the left.

Angels Walk

This non-profit group offers two 40- to 50-page booklets covering downtown walking tours that focus on architecture, history and culture; each of the walks takes about two hours, depending on the time spent lingering or lunching. The tour routes are designed with mass transit in mind so visitors can start and stop a walk at various points. Each booklet includes maps.

The first is ***Bunker Hill-Historic Core District***. This walk includes the unique, much-used-in-movies Bradbury Building; the Million Dollar Theater where premieres were first staged as spectacles; Grand Central Market; the Museum of Contemporary Art; the familiar-from-movies Westin Bonaventure Hotel and more. It also includes the Victor Clothing Co. building on South Broadway, where a 100-foot-tall mural depicts Anthony Quinn in his Oscar-winning role as *Zorba the Greek*. The second, ***Union Station/El Pueblo/Little Tokyo/Civic Center***, takes you to Olvera Street and the oldest part of Los Angeles, plus Chinatown, Little Tokyo, and the Music Center.

To have one or both of the booklets sent to you, call Angels Walk LA, ☎ 213-683-0080; or write to them at 304 South Broadway, Suite 494, Los Angeles 90013. The booklets are free; shipping is $4 for one title or $6 for both. The booklets are sometimes available at the Los Angeles Public Library, 630 West 5th Street, ☎ 213-228-7000 (check at the information desk inside the 5th Street entrance; library hours are Monday-Thursday, 10am-8pm; Friday and Saturday, 10am-6pm; Sunday 1-5pm).

Los Angeles Conservancy Walks

The Conservancy is currently attempting to preserve the historic Ambassador Hotel on Wilshire Boulevard.

The Los Angeles Conservancy is a non-profit organization dedicated to preserving and revitalizing Greater Los Angeles' architectural heritage. They have organized several docent-led walks of the downtown area that are very popular with both visitors and residents. Among the tours offered are **Pershing Square Landmarks**, with architectural styles from Victorian to art deco; **Broadway Theaters**, covering the largest concentration of pre-World

War II movie houses in America; **art deco** architecture walks; **Little Tokyo**; the glamorous **Biltmore Hotel**; **Angelino Heights**, one of Los Angeles' first suburbs; and **Union Station**, the last of the great railway stations built in America, a combination Spanish Colonial revival and art deco style. Self-guided tour literature is also available. Most tours cost $8 and begin at 10am; they last about 2½ hours, with a few exceptions. Days vary, so call or check their Web site for the complete schedule. No strollers or young children are permitted on any of the tours. Advance reservations are necessary; ☎ 213-623-CITY (2489), or reserve on the Web at www.laconservancy.org (click on "Tours" at the top of the page).

☞ DID YOU KNOW?

The 1931 **LA Theater** was decades ahead of its time, with a glass-fronted "crying room" for parents with noisy children, and a pre-televison form of sound and light transmission that simultaneously showed the picture on the auditorium screen and on mini-screens in the downstairs lobby.

Music Center Tour

During the summer, the Music Center offers free one-hour tours of the city's three primary theaters: the **Dorothy Chandler Pavilion**, the **Ahmanson Theatre** and the **Mark Taper Forum**. Highlights include artwork, costumes and photos of theatrical events. Tours are also available in French and Spanish. ☎ 213-972-7483.

The Bradbury Building

The Bradbury Building at 304 South Broadway has been Los Angeles' architectural gem for over 100 years, and none of the new buildings going up now are threatening its standing. It opened in 1894, predating motion pictures, and filmmakers have taken advantage of this unique structure from the start.

Lewis Leonard Bradbury, who came West from Maine in the 1850s, struck it rich in the Mazatlan (Mexico) gold mines. He married 20-years-younger Simona Martinez and ended up six children later in a 50-room Victorian mansion on Bunker Hill. (Much altered Bunker Hill – what is left of it – is between Hill and Figueroa, and Temple and 5th streets.)

▬ FILM FACTOID

The headquarters of Hal Roach's film company was later in Leonard Bradbury's Bunker Hill showplace, where he made two comedies, *Just Nuts* (1915), and *Haunted Spooks* (1920), both starring Harold Lloyd.

Wyman took his concept of the building's design from Looking Backward, a novel by Edward Bellamy that imagined the 21st-century world.

Bradbury wanted to construct a building for his office that would still be modern 100 years later. He improbably hired a $5-a-week draftsman to design it. George Herbert Wyman, like Frank Lloyd Wright with no academic architectural training, at first turned down the offer, but then received a message on an Ouija board: "Take the Bradbury assignment. It will make you famous." It did.

In the design of the five-story, utterly unorthodox masterpiece, the architect used Italian marble and Mexican floor tiles to beautiful effect, along with the largest plate-glass windows in Los Angeles. But the focal point is the stunning interior courtyard under a towering glass roof that bathes all the floors with soft, filtered sunlight.

The inside of the Bradbury Building's is probably the most often-filmed interior in Los Angeles.

Most ingenious were the delicate water-powered birdcage elevators. When excavation uncovered a spring underneath the building, instead of capping it, the water was used to supply tenants with steam heat and to power the elevators. Water pumped into a suspended cylinder made the elevator descend. When water was released, the cage ascended. These days it is operated with a hydraulic jack and electric pump. The Bradbury Building is open Monday-Friday, 9am-5pm, and Saturday, 9am-4pm. You can wander through and see it all, or join the Los Angeles Conservancy's two-hour Pershing Square Tour, which includes the Bradbury Building, every Saturday at 10am (see LA Conservancy tours, pages 88-89).

El Pueblo & Olvera Street

North of the Civic Center and just west of Union Station, between Alameda and North Main, is the site of El Pueblo de Los Angeles, where the city began. In 1781, 11 families from Mexico put up mud huts. The area gradually became the core of the new city. Look for the **Old Plaza Firehouse**, 134 Paseo de la Plaza, Los Angeles' first fire station, which dates from 1884. It has been restored as a museum, and is open Tuesday-Sunday, 10am-3pm. The nearby **Avila Adobe**, 10 Olvera Street, is the oldest home in Los Angeles, built in 1818 by Francisco Avila, who was mayor. Open daily, 9am-4pm. Free tours.

Just off the plaza is **Olvera Street**. Its shops and stalls offer a wild assortment of souvenirs. Originally named Wine Street because of the nearby vineyards, it was eventually abandoned; by the early 1900s it had become a trash-filled alley. In 1930, a group led by Christine Sterling, who became known as "the mother of *Calle Olvera*," created what could be called Hollywood's idea of an open-air Mexican market. It has been a success ever since, and is usually filled with tourists and locals who come here to eat at the many restaurants. The street has been featurd in many films, including *Death Wish II*, with Charles Bronson; *True Confessions*, with Robert De Niro; and TV episodes of *CHiPs* and *Lou Grant*, among others.

In 1932 the Mexican Revolutionary soldier, communist and painter David Alfaro Siqueiros was commissioned to paint an outdoor mural in Olvera Street with the theme "Tropical America." He accomplished that, but included within the painting an additional theme, the crucifixion of a Mexican peon by American imperialism. The mother of Calle Olvera quickly covered the painting over with whitewash. The mural by Siqueiros, one of the great painters of North America, is there still – neglected, boarded over – restorable, but with no money in sight to do the work.

Downtown Los Angeles

Olvera Street was named for Judge Agustín Olvera, a member of one of the area's founding families.

📖 **HISTORIC NOTE**

Look for the bricks in the pavement on Olvera Street. They mark the path of the *zanja madre*, the mother ditch that was the city's first water system when it was built in 1781.

Olvera Street merchants sell Mexican and Indian artifacts, leather goods, jewelry, clothing, art and lots of kitsch.

Get more information at the **Olvera Street Visitors Center**, located in the **Sepúlveda House**, 622 North Main Street, ☎ 213-628-1274; open Monday-Saturday, 10am-3pm; or visit the street's Web site at www.olvera-street.com. The building, dating from 1887, shows a combination of Mexican and Anglo styles; the period kitchen and bedroom are exhibited. There is an 18-minute film on the early history of Los Angeles.

Little Tokyo

Before 1942, Little Tokyo took in more than three square miles of boarding houses, mom-and-pop markets and Buddhist temples. After the end of World War II the residents returned from the internment camps but they gradually left downtown for the suburbs. These days Little Tokyo consists of only nine blocks, though Los Angeles as a whole still has the largest Japanese community outside of Japan.

Little Tokyo is located between 1st and 4th streets, Los Angeles Street (three blocks east of Broadway) and Alameda Street. In 1982 a killer helicopter in *Blue Thunder* bombed the Far East Café with special effects. Earlier, in 1975, the same café (which served Chinese food) was used as a location for a scene in *Farewell, My Lovely*, adapted from Raymond Chandler's novel, in which hero Philip Marlowe was having lunch when "a dark shadow fell over my chop suey."

The **Little Tokyo Walk** takes you along 1st Street between San Pedro Street and Central Avenue, where 13 buildings have been designated as national historic landmarks. Brass plaques embedded in the sidewalk tell the story of six decades of Japanese-American life from 1890s immigration through World War II internment camps.

The **Higashi Hongwangi Temple**, 8505 East 3rd Street, is an authentic Buddhist temple with a spectacular golden altar. The **Japanese Village Plaza**, a few blocks away on 1st street between San Pedro and Central, includes Japanese restaurants, food stores and gift shops.

Guided Tours are conducted Monday-Friday between 10am and 3pm, by the **Little Tokyo Business Association**. Tours last 1½ hours and visit the **Japanese American Cultural & Community Center**, the **James Irvine Japanese Garden**, **Buddhist Temple & Sanctuary**, the Japanese Village Plaza, and **Weller Court**. The fee is $1 for ages 14 years and up; 50¢ for younger children. Reservations are required; ☎ 213-628-8268 or fax 213-625-0943.

▪ FILM GLOSSARY

Key light – The primary source of a subject's illumination.

Downtown Los Angeles

Chinatown

LA's original Chinatown had almost 1,000 inhabitants, almost all of whom were laborers; the district was torn down in the 1930s to make way for the construction of Union Station. A few prosperous Chinese businessmen built **New Chinatown**, bordered by Alpine, North Spring and Yale streets and Bamboo Lane, in 1938. Today, many of the shops rely predominately on tourists. As many as 10,000 Chinese, mostly the elderly and the rawest newcomers, live in the area; authentic markets and restaurants are found on North Spring Street.

The 1974 movie China-town *had nothing to do with China-town and was not filmed here.*

There is an ornamental pagoda-style gateway on **Gin Ling Way** at 900 North Broadway; nearby is a statue of Dr. Sun Yat-sen, who liberated China from the Manchu dynasty in 1911. The **Chinatown** branch of the Los Angeles Public Library, at 536 West College Street, has a good collection of books in Chinese and English.

Guided walking tours are offered by the **Chinatown Tourist's Center** about once a month on a Sunday. The tour lasts 1½ hours and is followed by a show featuring acrobats, and a brunch. The fee for the tour only is $10 for adults; $5 for children under 11. For the tour, show and brunch the cost is $42 for adults; $28 for children under 11. For AAA members it is $33 for adults; $17 for children under 11; Phone for reservations, ☎ 323-721-0774, www.chinatowncenter.com.

Several new art galleries, some with good contemporary art rather than Chinese tourist kitsch, are located on **Chung King Road**, off Gin Ling Way between Hill and Yale streets. You will often find the biggest crowds in the evenings.

Winery Tour

San Antonio Winery, Los Angeles' oldest (and now its only) winery, is located at 737 Lamar Street, ☎ 323-223-1401, www.sanantoniowinery.com. Free tours are offered daily, every hour on the hour, 11am-4pm. The winery is not far from the Alameda/Union Street Station exit off the Hollywood Freeway (101); call for specific directions or check the map on the winery's Web site.

MTA Public Art

Art for Rail Transit. A self-guided tour highlights the public art of the downtown subway stations. ☎ 213-922-4ART (4278).

Farmers' Markets

In most states any place can call itself a farmers' market, but in California you must actually be a farmer, baker or beekeeper, and be certified, to sell directly to the public at specific times and places. (The famous Farmers' Market at Third and Fairfax started out as a real one in the 1930s but became a regular commercial enterprise.)

St. Agnes Church Farmers' Market, Adams Boulevard and Vermont Avenue, is open Wednesdays, June-August, 1:15-6pm; and September-May, 2-5:30pm.

735 South Figueroa Street, Thursdays and Fridays, 11am-4pm.

The newest market is **Mercado La Paloma**, 3655 Grand Avenue, Saturdays, 2-5pm. South of Jefferson Boulevard, entrance for parking is on Hope Street.

Museums

The **California African-American Museum**, Exposition Park, 600 State Drive (between Figueroa and 39th Street), ☎ 213-744-7432 or 892-1333, www.caam.ca.gov. At press time, the museum was undergoing a $3 million renovation and scheduled to reopen in early 2003.

California Science Center, 700 State Drive, Exposition Park (next to the LA Memorial Coliseum, between Figueroa and Vermont streets), ☎ 323-SCIENCE (724-3623), www.casciencectr.org. Hands-on and interactive exhibits on environment, aerospace, math, energy and health. Open daily, 10am-5pm. Free.

Japanese American National Museum, 369 East First Street (a former Buddhist Temple), Little Tokyo, ☎ 213-625-0414 or 800-461-5266, www.janm.org. Changing exhibits are dedicated to the Japanese-American experience. Open Tuesday-Sunday, 10am-5pm, Thursday until 8pm; closed Mondays and major holidays. Adults, $6; seniors, $5; students six-18, $3; children five and under, free.

Latino Museum of History, Art & Culture, 112 South Main Street, ☎ 213-626-7600. A look at the history of Latin American culture. Open Wednesday and Friday-Sunday, 10am-4pm.

Museum of Contemporary Art (MOCA), 250 South Grand Avenue at California Plaza; and **MOCA at the Geffen Contemporary Art Museum**, 152 North Central Avenue, ☎ 213-626-6222, www.moca.org. Both locations are dedicated to contemporary art. Open Tuesday-Sunday, 11am-5pm; Thursday, 11am-8pm; closed on major holidays. Admission for adults, $8; for seniors 65+ and students, $5; for children 12 and under, free (one admission fee covers both MOCA locations if you visit on the same day). Free to all on Thursdays, 5-8pm. Baby strollers and wheelchairs are available at no cost; the museums are handicapped-accessible.

Museum of Neon Art, 501 West Olympic Boulevard (entrance on Grand), ☎ 213-489-9918, www.neonmona.org. Historic neon signs, contemporary fine art. Open Wednesday-Saturday, 11am-5pm; Sunday, noon-5pm. Admission for adults is $5; for seniors and students, $3.50; for children under 12, free.

Natural History Museum of Los Angeles County, 900 Exposition Boulevard (between Figueroa and Vermont), ☎ 213-763-DINO (3466), www.nhm.org. Continuing exhibits of many aspects of natural history. The big hit is always the dinosaur fossils. Open Monday-Friday, 9:30am-5pm; Saturday and Sunday, 10am-5pm. Admission for adults is $8; for seniors and students 13-18, $5.50; for children five-12, $2; for children under five, free. Admission is free to all on the first Tuesday of every month.

Southwest Museum, 234 Museum Drive (take the Pasadena Freeway (110) north to Avenue 43, follow signs), ☎ 323-221-2164. Art and artifacts of indigenous cultures from Alaska to South America, including one of the best collections of Southwest Native American Indian artifacts in the country. The museum is open Tuesday-Sunday, 10am-5pm. Admission for adults is $5; for seniors and students, $3; for children seven-18, $2; for children six and under, free.

Outdoor Concerts

Grand Performances at California Plaza, on Olive between 4th and 5th streets, ☎ 213-624-2146. Noontime summer concerts at the Watercourt; free.

Pershing Square Concert Series, Olive and 5th streets, ☎ 213-847-4970. The music is eclectic: folk, swing, classical. Tuesday and Thursday, noon-2pm; Tuesday, 5:30-7:30pm; free.

Spectator Sports

Enjoy baseball at **Dodger Stadium**, 100 Elysian Park Avenue ☎ 323-224-1500.

Staples Center, at 1111 South Figueroa Street, is a new arena that is home to various sports and teams. Contact the stadium for ticket information, ☎ 877-305-1111, www.staplescenter.com.

LA Avengers (football) . . . . ☎ 877-4-AVENGERS
LA Clippers (basketball) . . . . ☎ 213-742-7500
LA Kings (hockey) . . . . ☎ 888-KINGS LA
LA Lakers (basketball) . . . . ☎ 310-419-DUNK

After Dark

The natives, they are restless tonight.
          – Charles Laughton, *Island of Lost Souls*

Clubs

Despite the things we have said about downtown being dead at night, that does not include club life, which is livelier than ever. But note that clubs have a habit of suddenly going dark, while new ones just as unexpectedly open; call ahead.

FIRECRACKER
Grand Star Lounge
943 North Broadway (at College Street)
☎ 626-454-7447

This club is in the heart of Chinatown. It began a few years ago with a poetry slam party for a few friends, and have evolved into a bit of everything; guests come from different neighborhoods and ethnic groups in a spirit of one big family. Downstairs is a jazz trio; upstairs, DJs spin mostly hip-hop. You may hear poetry or see a film; as we write this the work of Chaz Bojorquez, godfather of West Coast graffiti art, is on exhibit. First and third Fridays of every month, 10pm-2am, 21 and older, $8 to $10 cover.

GRAND AVENUE NIGHT CLUB
1024 South Grand Avenue (at Olympic Boulevard)
☎ 213-747-0999
www.grandavenightclub.com

A big place with a young crowd (minimum age 21), with live music, plus a DJ spinning disco, hip-hop, reggae, '80s. Dance all night to different flavors. Salsa lessons are given Saturday, 8-9pm. No jeans, tennis shoes or hats are permitted.

LITTLE J'S
1119 South Olive Street
☎ 213-748-3646

Salsa classes are held here on Thursdays from 8 to 9:30pm, then you can dance till 2am. Fridays and Saturdays are old school and a little hip-hop; Friday, 5pm-2am; Saturday, 9pm-4am. Dress code is professional attire. Complimentary soul food is served. This is a really popular place with dancers in their 30s and up; the music is not as popular with those in their 20s. Thursdays free; Fridays before 9pm, $5; after 9pm $10. Saturdays before 10pm, $10; after 10pm, $12.

THE MAYAN
1038 South Hill Street
☎ 213-748-4287
www.clubmayan.com

People of all age groups (over 21) start arriving at 9pm Friday and Saturday and party till 3am, to a wide variety of music on two floors. No food service. Dress code is shirt with collar. Valet parking is available for $5, or park in the lot for $2.

THE STOCK EXCHANGE
618 South Spring Street
☎ 213-489-1195

This bar actually was the stock exchange until the brokers moved out. Happy hour starts on Friday at 4pm, with complimentary appetizers and music all night long. Dress code is upscale casual – look cool. One possible drawback is that this is a lousy neighborhood, especially at night. Open Friday, 9pm-2am; Saturday, 9pm-3am.

ONLY IN LA

The Los Angeles cop who posed out of uniform for the July 2001 issue of *Playboy* said the nude photos didn't affect her credibility – the magazine buyers don't recognize her when she is in uniform.

Lounges & Happy Hours

ANGELS FLIGHT RESTAURANT & LOUNGE
Omni Hotel
251 South Olive Street
☎ 213-617-3300

At the top of Bunker Hill (see page 58). Cool piano. Open daily, 11am-2am.

BONA VISTA LOUNGE
Westin Bonaventure Hotel
404 South Figueroa Street
☎ 213-624-1000

Way up at the top. If you get tired of the fantastic view that goes along with the booze, take a glass elevator down to the hotel's Lobby Court Lounge and try your luck there. The Bona Vista Lounge is open from 4pm-1am daily.

CHECKERS LOUNGE
Checkers Hotel
535 South Grand Avenue
☎ 213-624-0000

Ask Joe the Bartender to make you Carol Burnett's favorite – a Skyy Vodka martini. A really cool, upscale place. Mind your manners. Open 10am-11pm.

Theaters

After New York City, Los Angeles is the prime theatrical town in the country, and with far more small houses all over town than New York. These are right downtown.

The Music Center, 135 North Grand Avenue (the Center is bounded by Grand Avenue and Hope Street, 1st and Temple streets), houses the city's three prime theaters.

◆ The **Ahmanson**, ☎ 213-628-2772, presents plays and musicals, mostly road shows from Broadway, and revivals.

◆ The **Dorothy Chandler Pavilion**, ☎ 213-972-7211, presents ballet performances, the LA Opera season from September to June, and the LA Master Chorale.

◆ The **Mark Taper Forum**, ☎ 213-972-7353, presents small plays, new and from off-Broadway.

Another venue, the **LA Theatre Center** at 514 South Spring Street, ☎ 213-627-6500, showcases independent theater group productions.

 # Downtown A to Z

Currency Exchange

American Express, 901 West 7th Street, ☎ 213-427-4800.

AMFOREX Foreign Currency Exchange, 350 South Figueroa Street, ☎ 213-617-2133.

Bank Notes Exchange, 406 West 6th Street, ☎ 213-627-5404.

Foreign Currency Express, Bonaventure Hotel, 404 South Figueroa Street, Suite 604, ☎ 213-624-3693.

Hospitals

California Hospital Medical Center, 1401 South Grand Avenue, ☎ 213-748-2411.

Hospital of the Good Samaritan, 616 South Witmer Street, ☎ 213-977-2121.

Orthopedic Hospital, 2400 South Flower Street, ☎ 213-742-6509.

Pacific Alliance Medical Center, 531 West College Street, ☎ 213-624-8411.

Medical Referrals

Medical Society referrals, multilingual, ☎ 213-483-6122, Monday-Friday 8:45 am-4:45pm.

Dental Society referrals, 24 hours, ☎ 213-481-2133.

Newspapers

Los Angeles Times, 202 West 1st Street, ☎ 213-237-5000, www.latimes.com; daily.

L.A. Downtown News, 1264 West 1st Street, ☎ 213-481-1448, weekly, on the stands Monday.

Parking

Metered parking can generally be found at the curb. Parking lots are located throughout the downtown area at varying rates, from 15 minutes to all day.

Pharmacies

Kelly's, 611 South Broadway, ☎ 213-629-2288.

Horton & Converse, 735 South Figueroa Street, ☎ 213-623-2838.

Rite Aid, 501 South Broadway, ☎ 213-628-8997.

Downtown Los Angeles

Roosevelt Pharmacy, 729 West 7th Street, ☎ 213-623-3283.

Police & Fire

Emergency (fire, ambulance, police). . . . . ☎ 911
Police, non-emergency, multilingual . . . ☎ 213-485-3294

Post Offices

Arcade, 508 South Spring Street.

ARCO Plaza, 505 South Flower Street.

Bunker Hill, 300 South Grand Avenue.

Macy's Plaza, MCI Center, 750 West 7th Street.

Federal Section, 300 North LA Textile, and 100 West Olympic Boulevard.

Market, 1122 East 7th Street.

California Plaza, 350 South Grand Avenue, Suite B1.

Public Transportation

MTA . . . . ☎ 800-COMMUTE, www.mta.net
METRO buses . . . . ☎ 213-626-4455
DASH buses . . . . ☎ 213-808-2273
Metrolink . . . . ☎ 800-371-LINK
Pick up schedules and maps for all of the above at CalMart in the Fashion District, 9th and Main Streets; at the MTA Building, 1016 South Main Street; and at Union Station, 800 North Alameda Street (1 Gateway Plaza).

Taxis

Bell Cab Co. . . . . ☎ 213-388-3177
Independent Cab Co. . . . . ☎ 213-385-8294
LA Checker Cab Co. . . . . ☎ 213-624-2227
LA Taxi Co. . . . . ☎ 213-627-7000

Time & Weather

Time .... ☎ 853-1212 (in all area codes)
Weather .... ☎ 213-554-1212

Visitor Information

The **Los Angeles Convention & Visitors Bureau**, at 685 South Figueroa Street, LA, CA 90017, ☎ 213-689-8822, has hundreds of brochures and maps, and a multilingual staff. They are open Monday-Friday, 8am-5pm; and Saturday, 8:30am-5pm. The LACVB is located between Wilshire Boulevard and 7th Street; DASH "A" Line stops at 7th and Fig; the nearest METRO Station is at 7th and Flower, one block away.

Six **Information Kiosks** on wheels roam downtown, staying for two hours at a time in places with heavy contingents of tourists, such as Pershing Square. The kiosks are staffed by "ambassadors" in purple polo shirts.

Downtown Center Business Improvement District, ☎ 213-624-2146.

LA Convention Center, ☎ 213-741-1151.

Travelers Aid Society, ☎ 323-468-2500.

☛ DID YOU KNOW?

When you phone the Business Improvement District office and are put on hold, the music you hear is – of course – *Downtown.*

Downtown Los Angeles

Hollywood

The stuff that dreams are made of.
 – Humphrey Bogart, *The Maltese Falcon*

Overview

Hollywood is, in one sense, an abstraction. When people say they are going to Hollywood, they usually mean they are going somewhere in Greater Los Angeles where they can see as much of the aura and glamour of the motion picture business as possible. Visitors find that it's spread out over a large area, from Studio City to Culver City, and from Westwood to Malibu.

But Hollywood is also an actual place. Look at an area map and you will see it is roughly the part of Los Angeles that stretches from Hyperion Avenue (a half-dozen blocks east of Vermont Avenue) on the east to Doheny Drive on the west, and from Melrose Avenue on the south to the top of the Hollywood Hills, which rise just a few blocks north of Hollywood Boulevard.

Hollywood is just a small part of the City of Angels, though the residents are trying to change that, as we write, by attempting to secede and form their own city, much as smaller West Hollywood successfully did a few years ago.

DISTANCES FROM HOLLYWOOD

Beaches	15 miles
Beverly Hills	5 miles
Burbank Airport	10 miles
Disneyland	40 miles
Downtown Los Angeles	8 miles
Los Angeles Int'l Airport	15 miles

History

At first what is now called Hollywood was mostly empty land in the boonies about eight miles west of Los Angeles, which, in the late 1800s, was a small town spreading out along the Los Angeles River. It was mostly sagebrush out here, with farms and some orange groves and a few dirt roads.

A 1900 law made it illegal to drive more than 2,000 sheep down Hollywood Boulevard.

Horace and Daeida Wilcox owned a ranch that was the center of the town when it was incorporated in 1903 with a population of 700. The name Hollywood came from the summer home of a friend of Mrs. Wilcox. The people who lived here were, by all accounts, staid and upright citizens. The joke in Los Angeles was that after nine o'clock at night you could shoot a cannonball down Prospect Avenue and not hit a living soul.

Then the first movie studios arrived, and with them hard-drinking cameramen, hell-raising stuntmen, and actors with questionable morals. Prospect Avenue was renamed **Hollywood Boulevard**. And there went the neighborhood.

But how all these people ended up making magic in a place called Hollywood is a more complicated story; it starts back east in 1889 when **George Eastman** and **Thomas Edison** solved the basic problem of how to make photographic images move by putting film on a one-inch, frame-lined, flexible celluloid strip. By 1892 "moving pictures" could be seen in penny arcades and kinetoscope parlors.

By the early 1900s dozens of upstart "producers" were cranking out short "features" one reel of film long. Edison contended that he owned the underlying patents involved in the production of these films, but while he argued it in court, millions of nickels were pouring into nickelodeon box offices instead of into his pocket. Edison finally gave up trying to shut everyone else out, and in 1909 went into business with his largest competitors. Together they formed the **Motion Pictures Patents Company**, which had a monopoly on production, distribution and exhibition.

The small producers who were shut out as a result of the merger were mostly nickelodeon owners who resented paying exorbitant prices for the Patents Company's films; however, every time one of them tried to shoot a bootleg movie in the wilds of Long Island the Patents Company's agents would swoop down with a writ and put them out of business.

By 1908 there were more than 10,000 nickelodeons throughout the country.

▚ HISTORIC NOTE

How The Nickelodeon Worked – Viewers dropped a penny in the slot and turned a crank: a light flashed on and they could see a one-minute-long production entitled *How Bridget Served the Salad Undressed.*

The Birth of Hollywood

Desperate to get out of the reach of the monopoly, a few producers packed up their cameras and actors and boarded trains headed west. Los Angeles was the end of the line.

Cecil B. De Mille produced the first feature film in Hollywood, *The Squaw Man*, in 1913 in a barn at the corner of Vine and Selma, one block south of the corner of Hollywood and Vine. The film cost a grand total of $15,000 to make and grossed $225,000, which made it one of the first nationwide hits. There is a plaque dedicated to *The Squaw Man* on the northeast corner of Vine and Selma, but the location is wrong; it should be on the southeast corner where the barn/studio was.

The little town was soon awash in motion picture people. As if that wasn't bad enough for the original upright Protestant inhabitants, its political independence didn't last long, either. Nearby Los Angeles was becoming a metropolis by annexing every bit of land it could get its hands on, one way or another.

Hollywood

📽 FILM TRIVIA

De Mille's original barn studio was later moved to the Paramount lot on Melrose and became part of the *Bonanza* set when that television series was shot in the 1960s.

Having outgrown the water available in the Los Angeles River, the city of Los Angeles secretly bought up the water rights to most of the Owens Valley, a beautiful place of ranches and farms high up on the eastern slope of the Sierra Nevada Mountains a few hundred miles north. Then it pumped all the water south, effectively destroying the farms and the valley but assuring Los Angeles' future monstrous growth.

📖 HISTORIC NOTE

The first real movie shot here was *The Count of Monte Cristo*. William Selig started the short in Chicago, at Lake Michigan's beach. Fleeing Thomas Edison's writ-serving agents, he brought his camera, but not the actors, and finished the picture at the beach 18 miles west of Los Angeles with local look-alikes. The year was 1907.

A few small towns, like Beverly Hills and Santa Monica, had enough water wells to make it on their own, but Hollywood was dry. Los Angeles refused to sell water to the burgeoning film capital unless it agreed to be swallowed up by the big city. Hollywood had no choice. It was annexed to Los Angeles in 1913. Since 1913 Hollywood has been the name of only one small part of Los Angeles. But it is the part that made all the rest famous all over the world.

Hollywood & Glamour: Synonymous

Hollywood is the sort of place you expect to find down a rabbit hole.

– Alexander Woolcott

By 1920 the population of Hollywood was 30,000 (now it is nearly 300,000). It really was the height of glamour up to World War II. There were nightclubs and restaurants, and the big movie premieres were held at the Egyptian and Chinese theaters. Eventually the big-name stars simply moved away, mostly to Beverly Hills, Malibu and West LA. They stopped coming to Hollywood except to work in one of the few studios that were left, mostly RKO, Paramount and the old Warner Bros. lot on Western. When the stars didn't dine, shop or play here any longer, only the rest of us were left. Hollywood has always been full of writers and other less-well-known film folk.

The reputation of the Brown Derby on Vine Street wasn't all publicity hype; hundreds of movie stars really did dine and drink there.

The area went downhill in the '60s; T-shirt shops and stores selling tchotchkes moved in, as well as panhandlers and assorted weirdos. A revival is taking place now, anchored by the new Kodak Theatre on Hollywood Boulevard next to the Chinese Theatre, part of the Hollywood & Highland complex (see page 145). Within a few years, the area, especially Hollywood Boulevard itself, may be transformed. We can hope.

Getting Here & Getting Around

From LAX

By Car

From the airport, drive north to the San Diego Freeway (I-405); go north to the Sunset Boulevard off-ramp, then go right (east) on Sunset to Hollywood (about eight miles).

Hollywood

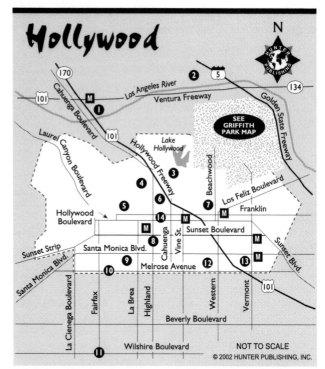

Hollywood

N

Los Angeles River

Ventura Freeway

Cahuenga Boulevard

Laurel Canyon Boulevard

Hollywood Freeway

Lake Hollywood

SEE GRIFFITH PARK MAP

Golden State Freeway

Beachwood

Los Feliz Boulevard

Franklin

Hollywood Boulevard

Sunset Boulevard

Sunset Strip

Santa Monica Blvd.

Cahuenga

Vine St.

Santa Monica Blvd.

Melrose Avenue

Sunset Blvd.

La Cienega Boulevard

Fairfax

La Brea

Highland

Western

Vermont

Beverly Boulevard

Wilshire Boulevard

NOT TO SCALE

© 2002 HUNTER PUBLISHING, INC.

1. Universal City & Studios
2. NBC Studios; Disney Studios
3. John Anson Ford Amphitheatre
4. Hollywood Bowl; Runyon Canyon Park
5. Magic Castle; Yamashiro
6. Hollywood Studios Museum
7. Château Elysée
8. Hollywood High School

9. Warner Hollywood Studios
10. Melrose Avenue Shopping District
11. Petersen Automotive Museum; Zimmer Children's Museum
12. Paramount Studios; Hollywood Memorial Cemetery
13. Los Angeles Community College & Theatre Academy
14. Hollywood Boulevard Walk of Fame; The Janes House/Visitors Center

Ⓜ Metro Red Line stops

- - - - - - Hollywood boundary

By Bus

Take the free bus marked "Lot C" from the front of any terminal, then transfer at Lot C to Metro Bus 42; take that bus to La Brea Avenue and Overhill, and transfer to bus 212 to Hollywood Boulevard. The fare is $1.60. For schedules, call the MTA at ☎ 800-COMMUTE (266-6883); for hearing-impaired TTY, ☎ 800-252-9040.

From Downtown Los Angeles

By Car

Take the Hollywood Freeway (101) west; get off at Sunset Boulevard or Hollywood Boulevard exit. Use the parking lots on side streets off Hollywood Boulevard, or look for street parking, which is metered on the boulevards.

By Public Transportation

Take Metro Red Line (subway) at the Pershing Square (at 5th Street betwen Olive and Hill) or the 7th and Flower stations; exit at Hollywood and Vine or Hollywood and Highland. The fare is $1.35.

Plenty of buses run on the east-west boulevards: Hollywood, Sunset, Santa Monica and Melrose; there are occasional Metro Buses (number 212) running north-south on La Brea and on Vine (numbers 210 and 426). Fare is $1.35, plus 25¢ for transfer.

Who Lives Here?

Don't these big, empty houses scare you?
Not me, I was in vaudeville.
> – Paulette Goddard & Bob Hope,
> *The Cat and the Canary*

The Hollywood Hills

Starting in about 1915, many of Hollywood's stars moved to the hills; among those who made the move were Charlie Chaplin, W.C. Fields, Jean Harlow and Groucho Marx. A surprising number of celebrities still live there. A few years ago the Hollywood Hills were home to Nicolas Cage, Kelsey Grammer and Madonna; more recent arrivals include Drew Barrymore, Leonardo DiCaprio and Ellen

DeGeneres. For a while these hills were iffy as a residential area. We still see a lot of celebrities moving out, usually going to the Westside, or back to New York.

You find older, established stars in mansions in Beverly Hills and farther west. The Hollywood Hills are for younger stars, and the houses are more unassuming, which is "in." Ben Affleck washed his old cars and motorcycles in the street outside his house until he moved to Beverly Hills.

The area starts at **Beverly Hills** on the west. It takes in everything from just above the **Sunset Strip** up to **Mulholland Drive**, which runs along the top ridge line of the mountains, east to **Riverside Drive**. It is made up of four main sections, each with subdivisions.

Whitley Heights

Developed in the early 1920s, Whitley Heights was Los Angeles' first celebrity neighborhood.

This neighborhood is in the hills above the Hollywood Boulevard Walk of Fame, north of Franklin Avenue from Cahuenga Boulevard to Highland Avenue. To get to Whitley Heights from Franklin Avenue, turn north on Whitley Avenue, two blocks west of Cahuenga. The neighborhood was split in two by the construction of the Hollywood Freeway; to reach the smaller part, take Cahuenga north and go under the freeway.

Patrick Bauchau, who stars in the TV series *The Pretender* and whose wife is the sister of French actress Brigitte Bardot, has lived for many years in a villa-like house built in 1921. Louise Brooks, Zsa Zsa Gabor and George Sanders previously lived in the house, one of the 196 Mediterranean-style homes in the Whitley Heights Historical Preservation Zone. None of these homes can be repainted, added to or altered in any way without the hard-to-get okay of the local architectural review board.

A builder named H.J. Whitley envisioned the hilltop overlooking Hollywood Boulevard as a small Mediterranean village, its white stucco homes with red tile roofs set among narrow winding streets lined with palm trees. The idea was an immediate success with film people. Jean Harlow lived here in the 1920s, among some of the best Spanish architecture in the city. At one time or another

Wallace Beery, Francis X. Bushman, Charlie Chaplin, Bette Davis, William Faulkner, Jean Harlow, Carmen Miranda, Harold Lloyd, Chester Morris, Tyrone Power, Rosalind Russell, Norma Shearer, Gloria Swanson and W.C. Fields all lived here. But the new crop of stars doesn't seem to be moving into Whitley Heights.

Beachwood Canyon

This beautiful neighborhood has always been popular with celebrities. Beachwood Drive is a winding road off Franklin Avenue five blocks east of Vine Street; you can follow it up to the Hollywood sign just under the crest of the mountain. The area includes the hills on both sides of Beachwood Drive with scores of crooked little streets.

Those who remember with fond nostalgia the original *Invasion of the Body Snatchers* (1956) should be aware that **Beachwood Village** is where the last 15 minutes of the film was shot. The townspeople of "Santa Mira" chased Kevin McCarthy and Dana Wynter through the village (then still called Hollywoodland) near the top of Beachwood Canyon Drive, then up the long stairs from Westshire Drive to Hollyridge Drive. The final scenes take place on the bridge that crosses the Hollywood Freeway near the John Anson Ford Amphitheatre.

Los Feliz

To get to Los Feliz Boulevard, drive east on Hollywood or Franklin to Western Avenue, then take Western to its end a few blocks north of Franklin at the foot of the hills. Everything along both sides of Los Feliz Boulevard, down to the Los Angeles River, is the Los Feliz district of Hollywood. The big building at Western and Franklin is the American Film Institute, a school for writers and directors.

Red Hot Chili Peppers' bassist Flea, who appeared in *Mascara*, *Psycho* (the 1998 remake), and other films, recently sold his 1924 Moorish-style house here to John Getty, grandson of the unimaginably rich, now deceased oilman, J. Paul Getty. Bob Dylan, Andy Warhol and actor John

Phillip Law previously lived here. In 1928 Walt Disney owned a small English Tudor-style home in the 2400 block of Lyric Avenue, where he worked on his animation projects in the garage.

Actress-comedian-writer Lily Tomlin, who has won Tony, Emmy, Grammy and Peabody awards, lived in a 1920 house in the Laughlin Park area of Los Feliz. Cecil B. De Mille and the singing actress Deanna Durbin each lived in it, and W.C. Fields leased the house for many years. Charlie Chaplin also lived in a Laughlin Park Mediterranean-style, gated home built before 1920. All of these houses are still considered very desirable and sell now in the $2- to $3-million range.

☞ **DID YOU KNOW?**

Leonardo DiCaprio (*Titanic*) donated $35,000 for a computer center at the new Los Feliz branch of the Los Angeles Public Library. The new library at 1874 Hillhurst Avenue is on the site of the DiCaprio family home, where Leonardo spent his teens just a few years ago.

From Highland to Doheny

Moving west, **Outpost Estates** takes in the area from Highland to La Brea (Outpost Drive goes up off Franklin Place), with mostly Spanish architecture. There is a six-bedroom, Spanish-style home built in 1927 for Dolores Del Rio, later lived in by Maria Montez and then by fashion designer Richard Tyler (whose designs have been worn by Julia Roberts, Janet Jackson and Sigourney Weaver). Alan Hale Sr. (star of over 300 films, including *The Adventures of Robin Hood*) and Alan Hale Jr. (*Gilligan's Island*) lived at 1940 Outpost Circle. Living on or just off Outpost now are Bob Barker, Rebecca De Mornay, Howard Hesseman, Billy Idol and Penny Marshall.

WOMEN WHO WORK IN HOLLYWOOD

Women who might be considering moving to Hollywood to work in the film industry should take a look at some recent statistics before burning any bridges. Here's the San Diego State University's analysis of behind-the-camera employment of 2,462 individuals working on 222 films in 2000:

◆ **Executive Producers** – 16% were women

◆ **Producers** – 24% were women

◆ **Writers** – 14% were women

◆ **Editors** – 19% were women

◆ **Cinematographers** – 2% were women

And the celluloid ceiling lives on.

The Gothic mansion at 7001 Franklin Avenue, located below Yamashiro Restaurant, was once Janet Gaynor's home. Now it is the **Magic Castle**, a non-profit private club for professional magicians. We were fortunate to be taken there as guests and found they have a hilarious bar, where seats may mysteriously change in height, and terrific shows. If you are a magic enthusiast you could call and try: ☎ 323-851-3313.

A bit farther west is **Nichols Canyon**, where the homes are all high up. You have to like driving on winding mountain roads to live here. The neighborhood has lots of Spanish-style houses built in the 1950s.

Then comes **Laurel Canyon Boulevard**, steep, twisting and only one narrow lane in each direction, yet it has always been a major road between Hollywood and the San Fernando Valley. If you have to drive it during rush hour give yourself an extra half-hour to get where you are going. Frank De Felitta, best-selling novelist and screenwriter (*Audrey Rose, The Entity*) lives off Laurel and Mulholland, among many in the film colony. This is where we met Robert Wise, the great director, at many of Frank's annual Super Bowl parties. **Mount Olympus**, an area of Laurel Canyon (Mount Olympus Drive goes off near the bottom of Laurel), is an upscale 1970s development with wide streets and great views.

From Laurel west to Doheny is the **Sunset Strip** area, which encompasses everything above Sunset Boulevard. Orson Welles lived at 8545 Franklin Avenue. Errol Flynn lived at 3100 Torreyson Place, a short street off Mulholland Drive west of Nichols Canyon. The house was the scene of legendary parties. The new, hip, Strip hotels, bars and restaurants have made the lower area, centered on Sunset Plaza, very desirable. Johnny Depp lives one block north of Sunset in Bela Lugosi's former home. Living on or just off Doheny Drive are Herbie Hancock, Ricardo Montalban and Judd Nelson.

Hitting the road recently out of the hills were Joel Grey, Nicolas Cage, Dan Aykroyd, Larry Drake (*L.A. Law*), Kelsey Grammer and singer-songwriter Lionel Ritchie, who moved with his wife to Beverly Hills.

Madonna put her Hollywood Hills house on the market after she moved to London and then decided to stay there and have a baby. Kathy Bates moved just a bit south of Hollywood to Hancock Park (more about that area later), selling to actor-writer Jon Cryer.

⚠ WARNING!

At Madonna's former place this sign was posted: "Madonna No Longer Lives Here. Dogs Attack at the Command Word *Madonna*."

Christian Slater sold his house to Tim Allen, and Ben Stiller and Leonardo DiCaprio have both moved here, as have René Auberjonois, Sandra Bullock and Cameron Diaz. Jenna Elfman (*Dharma and Greg*) bought Madonna's home in the hills, and Paul McCartney bought Courtney Love's place, which she had purchased from Ellen DeGeneres several years ago when DeGeneres moved to Ojai. Then DeGeneres sold the place in Ojai and bought once again in Hollywood Hills. Now she has put the new pied-à-terre on the market.

PEOPLE WE WISH WERE STILL WITH US

Pulitzer Prize-winning authors **Will** and **Ariel Durant** wrote most of their 11-volume *The Story of Civilization* in the Los Feliz home where they lived for 40 years. **Aldous Huxley**, brilliant English novelist and author of *Brave New World*, lived in the Hollywood Hills from 1937 until his death in 1963. **Christopher Isherwood**, also British, had his long-time home in Santa Monica canyon, and **Thomas Mann** moved here from Austria and bought a home in Pacific Palisades, which became a salon for famous European refugees during the 1930s and '40s.

Down From the Hills

Where the Non-Hip Live...

There is a stretch of **Rossmore Avenue** – the southern extension of Vine Street between Melrose and Beverly – that has been lined with desirable apartments since the 1920s. **Mae West** lived in the Ravenswood Apartments, 570 North Rossmore, across from the Wilshire Country Club, from the time she hit town in 1932 until her death in 1980. She first came here to do a small part in *Night After Night*, which was supposed to star George Raft. This is where Mae had her famous first scene in moving pictures. She walked into a nightclub in a long white satin gown, loaded with jewelry, and had the following exchange:

> Hatcheck Girl: *Goodness! What beautiful diamonds!*
> Mae: *Goodness had nothing to do with it, dearie.*

George Raft said later, "Steal the picture? She stole everything but the camera!"

Hancock Park

South of Melrose Avenue is, strictly speaking, outside of Hollywood proper, but many of the people who live here

Hollywood

think of themselves as Hollywoodians – except those who live in the area between **Beverly** and **Wilshire** boulevards and from **Rossmore** to **Highland** avenues. They are definitely in quiet, polite, upscale Hancock Park.

HANCOCK PARK'S TENNIS CLUB

May Sutton, who at the age of 18 was the first American to enter a singles match at Wimbledon, built the Los Angeles Tennis Club in Hancock Park near Melrose and Vine. May played there against Joan Bennett, Charlie Chaplin, Marlene Dietrich, Clark Gable and Jean Harlow, and gave lessons to actress Bebe Daniels (*The Maltese Falcon*, 1931 version, and *42nd Street*). May's husband, Thomas Clark Bundy, went into real estate. Bundy Drive (of O.J. Simpson fame) is named after him.

Richard Schiff, who plays White House communications director Toby Ziegler on *The West Wing*, bought a home here, as did French Stewart of *3rd Rock from the Sun*, and David Schwimmer of *Friends*; and when Kathy Bates sold her Hollywood Hills home it was to move to Hancock Park.

REMEMBERING THE 1940s

The late, great singer **Nat King Cole's** house came on the market recently. It is an English Tudor-style, built in 1924 on a large corner lot in Hancock Park. When Nat and his wife, Maria, bought the place in 1948, an attorney for the nearby all-white property owners said, "We don't want undesirable people coming here." The singer replied, "Neither do I, and if I see anybody undesirable coming into this neighborhood, I'll be the first to complain."

On Location

Hollywood Boulevard has been the site of many scenes on film. The intersection of **Hollywood** and **Vine** was the centerpiece of a 1936 picture called *Hollywood Boulevard*, and showed up again in a Gene Wilder-Richard Pryor comedy, *Another You*. Farther up the street, the 6600 block was prominent in *Alex in Wonderland*; and **Grauman's Chinese Theatre**, 6925 Hollywood Boulevard, the location of many film premieres, was where a famous scene in *The Day of the Locust* was filmed. It is also where Janet Gaynor went to see the footprints in cement when she first arrived in Hollywood as a naive wannabe actress in *A Star Is Born*. And it is the first place many visitors to Hollywood go even today.

The **Hollywood Bowl**, 2301 North Highland Avenue (see page 157), is also in *A Star Is Born*, as the place where Gaynor, the soon-to-be star, meets Frederic March, the aging star. The Bowl was also in *Hollywood Hotel*, *Three Smart Girls* and various TV episodes.

The movie *Chinatown* was all about Los Angeles getting water from the Owens Valley. **Lake Hollywood** was used several times in that picture, and it is the lake's waters that threaten to flood the city in *Earthquake*. Also in the Hollywood Hills is the house where Barbara Stanwyck talked Fred MacMurray into killing her husband in one of the best detective films (along with *The Maltese Falcon*) of all time, *Double Indemnity*. The house is still there at **6301 Quebec Drive**, at the intersection of El Contento Drive, in a maze of hard-to-find streets. Get the Chamber of Commerce's free map of Hollywood, and find Franklin and Vine: the house is about an inch above there.

A few of the more memorable places in Hollywood include a house at **565 Cahuenga Boulevard**, which was used as the Cunningham home in *Happy Days*. **Crossroads of the World**, at Sunset Boulevard and Las Palmas Avenue, was built in the 1930s as one of the first-ever shopping malls, with a Streamline Moderne design, and was used as the office of the *Tattler*, the tabloid newspaper in *L.A. Confidential*. And hilltop restaurant **Yamashiro**, 1999 North Sycamore Avenue (off Franklin, west of Highland),

Ronald Reagan was a member of the American Legion's Hollywood Post, 2035 North Highland Avenue.

Hollywood

has been seen in a number of features, most prominently in *Sayonara*.

Best Places to Stay

Will I see you tonight?
I never make plans that far ahead.
– Humphrey Bogart to Madeleine LeBeau, *Casablanca*

Hotels

The accommodations price scale can be found on page 39.

Stars don't stay in hotels in Hollywood any more. They used to, back in the early days when the famed Hollywood Hotel, a rambling white wooden building, stood on the northwest corner of Hollywood and Highland. It was in sad shape when it was finally torn down in 1957. There are a couple of still-famous hotels that are steeped in movie-making lore, though; both are on the Hollywood Boulevard Walk. See the Knickerbocker (page 151) and Hollywood Roosevelt (below).

BEST WESTERN HOLLYWOOD HILLS HOTEL
6141 Franklin Avenue
Hollywood, CA 90028
☎ 323-464-5181; fax 323-962-0536; reservations (CA) 800-287-1700 (in California); 800-528-1234 (elsewhere)
www.bestwestern.com/hollywoodhillshotel
Moderate

The Hollywood Hills Hotel is two blocks from the Walk of Fame.

Judith Altadine tells us her family has owned this hotel since 1948. Before that, British novelist Aldous Huxley stayed here (he wrote the screenplays for *Pride and Prejudice* and *Jane Eyre*), as did Aaron Spelling, who produced *The Love Boat* among many TV series. (We count among our minor sins a few episodes of *Starsky & Hutch* we wrote for Spelling.) These days the hotel's coffee shop is better known than the hotel (see page 124). The four-story hotel has no suites, but standard rooms ($109) and larger executive rooms. There is a pool and – a rarity in this area – free covered parking. Lots of Hollywood atmosphere here, starting with the murals.

★ HOLLYWOOD ROOSEVELT HOTEL
7000 Hollywood Boulevard
Hollywood, CA 90028
☎ 323-466-7000, 800-950-7667
www.hollywoodroosevelt.com
Moderate

The Hollywood Roosevelt has been *the* Hollywood hotel since it was built in 1927. And it is in a great location. This is where the first Academy Awards ceremony was held. The swimming pool is the one Marilyn Monroe favored when she was starting out. For more about the hotel's history, see *Walk of Fame*, page 142. Despite its age, frequent renovations have kept the place up. There is a cabaret and a restaurant, where we especially like the lavish Sunday brunch buffet.

For a few years the Hollywood Roosevelt was owned by a Japanese hotel chain, and Japanese tour groups still like it for their Hollywood vacations, but you are just as likely to hear other languages in the lobby as the hotel is well known in Europe.

RENAISSANCE HOLLYWOOD HOTEL
1755 Highland Avenue
Hollywood, CA 90028
☎ 323-323-1200
www.renaissancehollywood.com
Expensive

The 22-story Renaissance Hollywood Hotel is part of a big project called Hollywood & Highland that includes cinemas, restaurants, shops and the new Kodak Theatre, designed to house the Academy Awards. There are 640 accommodations, from oversized luxury rooms to VIP suites. There is a restaurant, a lobby lounge bar and a pool bar that serves lunch and cocktails. The pool terrace has cabanas and views of the Hollywood skyline. Look for a concierge, dry cleaning, and staff fluency in French, German, Italian, Japanese and Spanish. This massive development may, indeed, do much to revitalize Hollywood. The hotel is in a great location, around the corner from the Chinese Theatre and next to a Metro Rail subway stop.

Hollywood

Best Places to Eat

Feed me! Feed me!

> – Audrey Jr. (the carnivorous plant),
> *The Little Shop of Horrors*

The dining price scale can be found on page 42.

Hollywood has always been a mecca for hopeless optimists who dream of owning a restaurant. Oddly, the core area, on and around Hollywood Boulevard, has never supported many really serious places. Two restaurants have been here forever (as time is counted in Hollywood): **Musso & Frank's** and **Miceli's**; the rest – excepting, of course, **Les Deux Cafés** – are mainly for casual food and stuff you eat with your hands.

In the past decade, however, **Melrose Avenue** has become the center of one of the city's prime concentrations of good restaurants. You will find them mostly in the stretch of a dozen blocks west of La Brea Avenue. Those with a handful of tables out on the sidewalk serve primarily light fare, but quite a few of the city's serious eateries are also along here.

Fine Dining

★★ AGO
8478 Melrose Avenue
☎ 323-655-6333
Nuevo American-Italian
Expensive

The restaurant's name is properly pronounced AH-go.

A two-level dining room with a wood-burning pizza oven as its centerpiece. The moment you sit down, a chap will appear with a bottle of water in each hand. Would you like still or sparkling? Either bottle will add about $6 to your tab. We prefer tap.

While you nibble on complimentary flatbread from the pizza oven, drizzled with olive oil, you can look around and get your bearings. Any celebrities present are probably seated toward the back of the room, the preferred area. The place averages a high celebrity quotient, which perhaps accounts for the median price for a bottle of wine: in the low $100s. The owner's name is Agostino Sciandri, called Ago for short, thus the name of the restaurant; he'll probably be there. Open for lunch, Monday-Friday, noon-2:30pm; dinner, Monday-Friday, 6-11:30pm; Saturday, 6-11pm; Sunday, 6-10:30pm.

☞ **DID YOU KNOW?**

Ago is co-owned by Robert DeNiro, along with Miramax Pictures producers Harvey and Bob Weinstein and directors Tony and Ridley Scott, which may help lure the customers in.

★★ CAMPANILE

624 South La Brea Avenue
☎ 323-938-1447
www.campanilerestaurant.com
California/South of France
Very Expensive

We must confess, we are partial to Campanile; Nancy Silverton, the owner, is the daughter of a friend of ours, Doris Silverton, who died not too long ago. We had dinner at the restaurant after the memorial service there. So when we say this is a very good restaurant, you will have to believe we are putting personal feelings aside. It is hard to pick out any one item as superior. Entrées lean mostly to fish, steaks and lamb in the winter, though the menu changes constantly. Much as we like it, we do not eat here too often, primarily because appetizers are $9 to $15, and entrées $25 to $38.

The unusual building it occupies was built by Charlie Chaplin as his office in 1928. The main dining room is in the rear downstairs, but there are more rooms up a flight of stairs to the mezzanine, where the windows overlook the space below. We promised not to divulge any names, to protect people's privacy, but this is obviously a popular place with celebrities. Open for lunch, Monday-Friday, 11:30am-2:30pm; and brunch, Saturday and Sunday, 9:30am-1:30pm. Dinner is served Monday-Thursday, 6-10pm; Friday-Saturday, 5:30-11pm.

Campanile *means bell tower in Italian and is pronounced camp-an-EEL-ay.*

Hollywood

★★ HOLLYWOOD HILLS COFFEE SHOP

6145 Franklin Avenue
☎ 323-661-3319
American-multiethnic
Inexpensive

This is one of the places that at first glance (or second, or fourth) doesn't seem to be a hangout for celebrities. The first time someone mentioned seeing the likes of Brad Pitt and Michelle Phillips we thought they had been imbibing too many baked hot chocolates (a specialty here, a cross between a pudding and a soufflé with thousands of calories lovingly tucked inside). Then someone else told us Sandra Bullock and Nicolas Cage are among others who have been known to make this scene.

The attraction is probably the talent of Susan Fine Moore, whose background is in classic French cuisine, and who took the place over a few years ago. So the food is very good, even though a specialty of the house is not *poulet truffé* but rather cowboy chili (there are a lot of Mexican dishes on the big menu).

We didn't see anyone *that* well known when we were chowing down on *huevos rancheros* and *torta tortilla*, but there was background talk of studios and scripts while we were eyeing the *Swingers* poster on the wall (a scene from the movie was shot here, probably because this is where the writers sketched out the plot between bites). Monday-Thursday, 9am-11pm; Friday-Saturday until midnight.

★★ LES DEUX CAFES

1638 North Las Palmas Avenue
☎ 323-465-0509
French
Expensive-Very Expensive

People know about Les Deux Cafés strictly by word of mouth; the restaurant doesn't advertise. This place – with a garden behind stone walls off a parking lot – is deliberately hard to find. There is no sign out front and no entrance on Las Palmas, but it is two doors down from the very visible Miceli's. Owned by Michelle Lamy, the lady with the French accent who is also an actress, the restaurant is intimate, and protective of the celebrities who come here, such as Sharon Stone, and Madonna. Bill Murray is a part-owner, and his brother John tends bar. Sting threw a birthday party here. At lunch one day we saw k.d. lang and Prince, with other musical types.

Some nights there is a DJ, and on other nights you'll hear live jazz. Les Deux Cafés is open for lunch on weekdays, 11:30am-2:30pm; dinner is served every night, from 6-10:30pm on weekdays and until 11:30 on weekends. (that is when the kitchen closes but the café is open until 2am). There is a microphone, and occasionally you'll hear the owner or one of the celebrity guests get up and sing. Someone told us, "Les Deux is like the nighttime living room or a salon for the people in entertainment and music who live in the Hills, a place to meet and talk."

Look for the entrance to Les Deux Cafés in a corner of the parking lot.

★★ MICELI'S

1646 North Las Palmas Avenue
☎ 323-466-3438
American-Italian
Inexpensive

Next door to the newer, higher-priced Les Deux Cafés, Miceli's is like a weathered, experienced uncle towering over an eager youngster. Carmen Miceli has seen a lot of Hollywood go by since he opened his doors most of a lifetime ago. The restaurant still looks the way Italian restaurants did a half-century back, with reed-wrapped Chianti bottles hanging from the ceiling and all the tables covered with red-checked cloths. Some things haven't changed in 50 years. The bread isn't made with lard anymore, but the great rolls are still made with pizza dough. And Toni, the waitress, has been here since 1942. The menu still has lots of pasta with pomodoro sauce, lasagna, and cacciatore. Old-fashioned Italian-American comfort food. But, hey! That is just what we love.

Joe DiMaggio and Marilyn Monroe used to meet here; John Kennedy came in, and The Beatles; these days you might see Joe Pesci. Do you remember the *I Love Lucy* episode where Lucy got a job flipping pizzas? She spent three days in Miceli's learning how to do it, making pizza for startled customers. There are no photos on the walls of celebrities with a smiling owner; as Carmen always says, "They come here to be left alone. Leave 'em alone."

When Miceli's was the first pizzeria west of the Mississippi in 1949, pizza went for 35¢.

Hollywood

Scenes from the original *Terminator* were shot here, and some from *Vampire in Brooklyn*. The place was closed for 10 days in October last year while a picture was shot inside (we don't know which one; it had a working title). There is music on an intermittent basis – a jazz combo, sometimes a big band in the cellar; call ahead to find out what is scheduled. A good time to see celebs is at night after a show at the Pantages, or a premiere at the Egyptian. Posted hours are Sunday-Thursday, 11am-midnight; Friday and Saturday, 11am-12:30am. But actual hours are rather casual; they may not open for lunch until closer to noon, and if there are a bunch of congenial customers at the bar they'll stay open way past midnight. From Thursday through Saturday the cellar lounge is open until 2am.

★★ MUSSO & FRANK'S GRILL
6667 Hollywood Boulevard
☎ 323-467-7788
Old fashioned-American cooking
Moderate-Expensive

Musso's, as it is known, is the oldest restaurant in Hollywood and the one most closely associated with movie-making people throughout its history. Many of the studios moved away from Hollywood but the studio people still come back. There are two rooms; one has banquettes and open tables and a long bar; the other has a counter facing the grill and its flames, plus three rows of booths with high backs so you are never sure who is sitting behind you until you walk down the row and look. If you are alone, sit at the counter and watch the cooks searing the chops. You might see Lily Tomlin there having her usual: sautéed scallops, mashed potatoes, salad with thousand island dressing and a martini with olives to start it off properly.

At Musso's order "macaroni au gratin" to get macaroni and cheese, made with cheddar and parmesan.

For about 80 years, expert tipplers have gone to Musso's for the best martinis in town. But don't expect fancy food to go with them. What you will eat here now is just what you would have had in the 1920s – perhaps because they have had almost the same menu since 1922. William Saroyan always had the charcoal broiled rack of lamb with mushrooms and onions – it is still on the menu. In France they call this kind of food *cuisine bourgeois*; we know it as comfort food. And the menu is immense. Lois Dwan, former *Los Angeles Times* food writer, once wrote, "A man I know went to Musso's every day for three weeks, never ate the same thing twice, never had a poor meal and never got through the menu."

Make dinner reservations for 8pm or later; the restaurant is always crowded earlier with theater-goers to the Pantages Theatre down the street. Parking (partial validation available) in rear; enter on Whitley. (For more about Musso's, see *Walk of Fame*, page 147.)

★ TIP

Musso's waiters (all men) have worked here an average of 35 years. They know their business better than anyone, so be sure you treat them with respect.

★★ PATINA

5955 Melrose Avenue
☎ 323-467-1108
California-continental
Very Expensive

Joachim Splichal, *chef extraordinaire*, owns a gaggle of restaurants now, but this is where it all started 11 years ago. This place was a big hit with famous film folk back then, and still is. A recent remodeling has tripled the size of the formerly tiny kitchen, and there is a new dining patio. Patina is a prime star-watching venue. It's also a favorite of those who labor at Paramount Pictures up the street. Dinner, Monday-Friday, 6-10pm; Saturday, 5:30-10:30pm. Lunch is served only on Fridays, noon-2pm.

★★ PINOT HOLLYWOOD

1448 North Gower Street
☎ 323-461-8800.
Nouveau-continental, bistro fare
Expensive

This is one of Joachim Splichal's Patina spin-offs; during TV season it is always crowded after 11pm, when casts and crews come here after work (most shows are filmed

Hollywood

Patina is one of only two restaurant members of Relais & Châteaux in the Los Angeles area. The other is L'Orangerie (see page 206).

Tuesdays and Fridays). Whoever's currently shooting at Sunset-Gower Studios (the old Columbia lot) is usually in here at lunch. The martini bar always has a crowd; on the patio you can order salads and sandwiches. The pancetta-penne pasta is delicious and so is the gnocchi. Serves lunch Monday-Friday, 11:30am-2:30pm; after 2:30 a light lunch menu is served. Dinner hours are Monday-Saturday, 5:30 until 9:30 or 10pm, depending on the crowd. There is a late bar menu served until midnight.

★★ YAMASHIRO

1999 North Sycamore Avenue
☎ 323-466-5125
www.yamashirola.com
American/Asian
Expensive

Yamashiro is on a hilltop, just a few blocks behind Grauman's Chinese Theatre, and has views over the basin (for views from the restaurant, go online to www.earthcam.com; search for Yamashiro). We are not the only ones who come here because of the fabulous view. Manager Andy Ulloa told us that recent guests have included Ben Affleck, Johnny Depp, Faye Dunaway, Mel Gibson, Danny Glover, Anjelica Huston, Penny Marshall, Gwyneth Paltrow, Dolly Parton, Joe Pesci, Rene Russo, George Clooney and Tim Allen.

The Gothic mansion below Yama-shiro is the Magic Castle, a club for magicians.

Yamashiro is a sprawling, spread-out place. It could be full of stars and you wouldn't know it unless you happened to be sitting at the next table, which is why it is a favorite of many celebs. They don't have to sit in VIP rooms; they are simply not bothered here. The choice seats are on the lower tier by the windows, so sometime during the evening take a stroll along there and see who you might spot. But please keep going; don't make a big deal of it.

You might hear that Yamashiro was the home of silent film star Sessue Hayakawa (from *Family Souls*, 1916, and *Bridge on the River Kwai*). In fact, it was built in 1911 as a reproduction of a mountain palace near Kyoto, with imported antique walls and a 600-year-old pagoda. Later it became home to the exclusive "400 Club," a group of silent film stars and directors, including Bebe Daniels, Lillian

Gish and Ramon Novarro. At one time Richard Pryor and Pernell Roberts lived in apartments on the grounds.

Yamashiro has shown up in countless movies to indicate "Now we are in Japan." It was the officers' club in *Sayonara*, and was seen in TV series such as *I Spy*, *Route 66*, *Perry Mason* and *My Three Sons*. More recent shoots include *Gone in 60 Seconds*, *Blind Date*, *A Thousand Men and a Baby* and a Toni Braxton video. The restaurant is often used as a setting for premiere and wrap parties, recently *Lethal Weapon 4*, *Rush Hour* and *3rd Rock from the Sun*.

Appetizers include an extensive list of sushi and sashimi; entrées include lamb chops, tuna and chicken, all done with an Asian (not just Japanese) touch.

To get here (it is not actually on Sycamore and can be bewildering to find the first time), you can turn off Franklin onto a private road that twists uphill when you see the Magic Castle sign, but we find it easier to go a block farther west to the street marked Sycamore and follow that twisting road uphill. Dinner is served Sunday-Thursday, 5:30 to 10pm; Friday and Saturday, 5:30 to 11pm.When you make a reservation ask for a window table. We suggest you get here early to give yourself time to stroll through the exquisite gardens that cover the hillside, accented with pagodas and miniature trees and pools filled with koi.

Yamashiro means "mountain palace."

Hollywood

Casual Dining

★★ PINK'S
711 La Brea Avenue
☎ 323-931-4223 (for recorded directions)
☎ 323-931-7594 (to speak to a live person)
Hot dogs, hamburgers, burritos
Inexpensive

When you first see Pink's, you are not going to believe it is a place where you would ever find a celebrity. It looks like an ordinary hot dog stand. And it *is* a hot dog stand, but not ordinary. In 1939 the late Paul and Betty Pink bought a pushcart for $50 and set it up here. This was all vacant land then, so they had to rig up a *looonnnng* extension

At Pink's, ask for extra chili or extra cheese – they pile it high.

cord for their steamer and plug it in at a friendly hardware store a block away.

The current little building dates from 1946. By then, word had gotten around about how good the hot dogs were and celebrities were already dropping by. Michael Jackson first came here when he was a child. Richard and Gloria Pink, the son and daughter-in-law of the original owners, run the stand now, and celebrities are still dropping by.

Maybe the draw is the Hoffy 100% beef Kosher dog the Pinks have been serving since 1939. There is also a spicy Polish dog, a pastrami Reuben dog, a guacamole dog – 21 kinds in all, plus burgers (including a turkey dog and turkey burger).

Sandra Bullock comes here; so do Goldie Hawn, Jay Leno and John Malkovich. They say Bruce Willis proposed to Demi Moore here, and Orson Welles ate 18 of Pink's dogs at one sitting (still the record). Pink's sent hot dogs to Las Vegas for Diana Ross, to Tom Hanks for a wrap party, and to Rosie O'Donnell for her studio audience. Pink's was featured in Eddie Murphy's *Golden Boy*.

Not long ago, a television interviewer was talking to Gloria Pink on the air. Just as he skeptically asked if stars *really* ate here, Bill Cosby drove up, walked over to the counter and ordered 13 chili dogs to go.

We drove by here the other night about 7pm on our way to Yamashiro's and there was a crowd on the sidewalk. We went by again about 9:30 and there was *still* a crowd. There *always* seems to be a crowd. If you have a sudden yen for heartburn in the middle of the night, they are open till 2am; until 3am Friday and Saturday.

Shop Till You Drop

I can't wait forever for those shoes!
— The Wicked Witch of the West
(Margaret Hamilton), *The Wizard of Oz*

Melrose Avenue

One thing has been certain for a long time: whatever fashion is going to be hot and hip in the rest of the country six months or a year from now, is already happening on Melrose. This is the heart of young, trendy Los Angeles. The blocks of Melrose roughly from La Brea Avenue to just past Fairfax Avenue are the first destination of whole planeloads of young, fashion-hungry tourists. Many shops on the eastern strip, from La Brea to Fairfax, are less expensive than those in the western section. Just walk up one side and down the other; the shops are packed in, one jammed against the next. This is where you will find polite and knowledgeable clerks with lavender spiked hair and rings in their ears, noses, tongues, lips and belly buttons, one or all at the same time. In any case, though it may get strange, it is always lots of fun. Most shops on Melrose are open daily, usually 11am-8pm.

*If you miss the news from your home town, **Global Newsstand** at Melrose and Hayward has newspapers and magazines from many US cities and countries worldwide.*

Hollywood

THE SHOPPING MELROSE AVENUE TEST

Here is a test we have devised to see if you are ready to shop Melrose. Ask yourself if you will be 1) delighted, 2) tolerant, or 3) horrified by massive manifestations of black leather pants, visible tattoos, see-through belly shirts (crop-tops), body piercings, green hair, and thigh-high stiletto boots. If you answer 3) to any of the above perhaps you would like the Beverly Place Mall (Beverly and La Cienega) better.

Japanese sometimes seems like the lingua franca on Melrose Avenue.

> ⭐ **TIP**
>
> Bring plenty of quarters – the parking
> enforcers mean business!

Between La Brea and Fairfax

★★ RED BALLS ON FIRE
7365 Melrose Avenue
☎ 323-655-3409

How au courant can one be? Well, Patricia Field, costume
designer for Sarah Jessica Parker's character, Carrie, on
HBO's *Sex and the City*, said if she were shopping in Los
Angeles instead of New York, she would come to Red Balls
on Fire for new things. Various celebs drop in here, from
Nicolas Cage to Dennis Rodman; it is popular with bands,
such as Motley Crüe.

WASTELAND
7620 Melrose Avenue
☎ 323-461-4445

*RocketBaby
Sleeves are
sold only at
Wasteland;
they cost from
$18 to $40 a
pair.*

Wasteland sells mostly "rediscovered" clothing. Buyer Evan
Hughes says he is a sucker for bad '80s clothes. This is the
place to find a denim jacket with its sleeves hacked off and
Motley Crüe hand-painted on the back, or a reversible
Chinese silk jacket. Another Wasteland exclusive is Rocket-
Baby Sleeves, made to go with sleeveless summer wear.
Fiona Apple, songstress and MTV fashion plate, wore a
long-fringed, over-the-shoulder fuchsia set for a concert at
the Wiltern Theatre. Now actresses Claire Danes, Alyssa
Milano and Julianne Moore sport them. Micki Oberdorfer,
who came to Melrose and Wasteland from St. Louis, cre-
ated the fad and makes them herself.

West Melrose

West Melrose starts at about Fairfax and runs just a few
blocks. This stretch used to be solidly antique stores and
flower shops; now there are high-fashion boutiques, some
of which are spin-offs from New York or Europe.

> ⭐ **TIP**
>
> Expect high prices and small sizes. A recent fashion article in the *Los Angeles Times* said, "This is where those who are too rich and too thin come to stay too gorgeous."

Two-hour street parking is available on Melrose – if you are very lucky – and on most cross-streets. Patience is a virtue here.

★★ RUBY MAE
7975½ Melrose Avenue
☎ 323-651-4086

You might bump into the likes of Cher, Penelope Cruz, Jennifer Lopez or Lisa Marie Presley examining the sexy clothes reminiscent of 1940s screen sirens. Printed T-shirts at $58 give a hint of the price range.

FANTASIES COME TRUE
8012 Melrose Avenue
☎ 323-655-2636

This store has everything to remind you of Disney's movies, starting with 50¢ Disney-character baseball cards and topping off at $3,000 for *101 Dalmatians* figurines. Something for every tot in between.

MIU MIU
8025 Melrose Avenue
☎ 323-651-0072

Italian designer Miuccia Prada has plenty of fans among the Hollywood hip who can afford his trend-setting line. If a top (at perhaps $270) and skirt ($550) tempt you, there are bags, shoes and even lingerie to accessorize with. This is the only Miu Miu shop in the US to carry menswear.

Hollywood

Miu Miu has limited parking.

★★ FRED SEGAL MELROSE
8100 Melrose Avenue
☎ 323-651-1800

Fred Segal carries the collections of international designers, along with those of up-and-coming local ones. Don't get run over by stars arriving in limos, shopping for his funky high-fashion men's, women's and kids' clothes and accessories. Parking is free in the lot behind the store.

★ **TIP**

Fred Segal Melrose has the only quick-service café around, a good place to grab a bite while resting your by-now-tired feet.

★★ DECADES

8214 Melrose Avenue
☎ 323-655-0223

Resale sounds like buying tacky used clothing in some thrift shop, right? Not here. Trust us, Decades is high-end hip. Winona Ryder once hauled around 200 items into the shop so owner Cameron Silver could donate them to an auction for U2's Third World Relief Fund. She is size 2, they tell us, and those were for auction, but there is a lot more here for retail sale.

Specialty Shopping

A single-strap tank top is called a "bambi."

While the primary shopping area of Hollywood, known around the world, is Melrose Avenue, here and there you will find wee nooks and crannies with bits of interesting loot to carry away.

Hollywood Boulevard

OUTFITTERS WIG CO.

6626 Hollywood Boulevard
☎ 323-462-3088

There are five or six wiggeries along Hollywood Boulevard, mostly selling to the general populace (the most popular style at those is the Marilyn Monroe look); Outfitters Wig Co. is the one that does business primarily with the studios and independent productions. The walls are filled with signed photos of celebrities in drag.

HOLLYWOOD MAGIC STORE
6614 Hollywood Boulevard
☎ 323-464-5610

Magic tricks are for sale here, from simple to mind-boggling, for both the professional and the amateur.

HOLLYWOOD TOYS & COSTUMES
6600 Hollywood Boulevard
☎ 323-464-4444

You can choose from a staggering variety of toys, everything from a simple checkerboard to a full-size R2D2.

★ **HABLA ESPAÑOL?**

Espresso Mi Cultura, 5625 Hollywood Boulevard, ☎ 323-461-0808, has coffee, Chicano-Latino books, folk art and gift items.

Vine Street

★ IRISH IMPORT SHOP
738 North Vine Street
☎ 323-412-8922

This wee bit of Ireland tucked away in a nondescript strip mall just north of Melrose and south of Hollywood Boulevard is a destination for something special: claddagh rings. This is especially the case since they were featured on an episode of *Buffy the Vampire Slayer*. These traditional Celtic rings, used in weddings or as a token of friendship, feature a crowned heart held by two hands; here, they go for $349.

But *shure an begorra*, you will find enough goods from Eire to tempt a leprechaun, including gooseberry jam, *Riverdance* tap shoes and fishermen's sweaters.

Just before St. Patrick's Day, Irish expatriates head to the Irish Import Shop from all over Southern California.

Hollywood

La Brea Avenue

JERRY SOLOMON
960 La Brea Avenue
☎ 323-851-7241

We guarantee you have never heard of Jerry Solomon. He has been in business 42 years and has yet to advertise, and his off-the-street walk-in traffic is zero. But if you have a good painting that needs framing someone might tell you about him.

Art museums, galleries and interior designers know about Solomon; so do individual collectors like Jack Nicholson and Barbra Streisand, and artists such as David Hockney, who has been known to come into the studio and paint on the frames around his pieces. Jerry Solomon is open Monday-Friday, 8:30am-5:30pm.

★ *TIP*

Jerry Solomon says, "It's not about the frame; it's about the art. If you're not aware of the frame, then it's a good framing job." A point to remember.

Sunset Boulevard

SAMUEL FRENCH BOOKSHOP
7623 Sunset Boulevard (west of La Brea)
☎ 323-876-0570; fax 323-876-6822
www.samuelfrench.com

This stretch of Sunset Boulevard is too far east to be part of The Strip (that is in West Hollywood).

If being in Hollywood has inspired you to want to know more about its history; or if you're thinking, in a moment of madness, about becoming an actor yourself, here is a place to fill in some of the blanks. This shop, which has been here since 1947, is owned by Samuel French, Inc. of New York, which has published plays for over 170 years. The shop is open Monday-Friday, 10am-6pm; Saturday,

MIDNIGHT SPECIAL

```
03/01/04    14:18   H    20      10749
   1@  29.95  1585671886     $     29.95
             MARILYN ENCY
   1@  22.95  0312206461     $     22.95
             L.A. EXPOSED:STR
   1@  16.95  1843530589     $     16.95
             ROUGH GUIDE LOS
   1@  17.95  1588432866     $     17.95
             HOLLYWOOD & THE
SUBTOTAL                     $     87.80
SALES TAX @  8.250%          $      7.24
TOTAL                        $     95.04
TENDER CreditC               $     95.04
```

*****OUR RETURN POLICY*****
Returns MUST be made in 2 weeks with a
receipt. Exchange/store credit only.
***
ALL DISCOUNT ITEMS NON-RETURNABLE
***
Magazines/Journals are NON-RETURNABLE

10am-4pm. Parking is available on the street, and in a small lot in the rear.

> **★ TIP**
>
> For wannabe screen writers, Samuel French has books of collected screenplays, books on how to write screenplays and books about why, alas, you are blocked from writing a screenplay.

HOLLYWOOD SHEET MUSIC
7777 Sunset Boulevard
☎ 323-850-1075

This wonderful little store is included because no one under the age of 99 has ever seen a sheet music shop. They haven't existed in most towns for 70 years or more, but we have one in Hollywood because the movies and the music business need a place like this. Open Monday-Saturday, 10am-6pm; Sunday, noon-5pm.

Los Feliz District

★★ SKYLIGHT BOOKS
1818 North Vermont Avenue
☎ 323-660-1175
www.skylightbooks.com

A few blocks north of Sunset is the ultimate neighborhood bookstore that everyone knows. Buddy Ebsen was there one night not too long ago (yes, *that* Buddy Ebsen – the one who danced with Shirley Temple in *Captain January* and then spanned the decades to *Beverly Hillbillies* and *Barnaby Jones*). Now a nonagenarian, he was talking about a novel he had just written. A week later Margaret Cho, the stand-up and TV comedian, was there signing her new book. Skylight keeps from getting crushed by the megabookstores by sponsoring these events on a regular basis. Get Skylight's quarterly newsletter and you will see a half-dozen or more personal appearances by authors each month; in addition to signings, a half-dozen book groups meet here, everything from the Sisterhood Lesbian Book

Club to a brave group that does nothing but discuss James Joyce's *Ulysses*. Open seven days, 10am-10pm.

JOE BLASCOE MAKE-UP CENTER
1670 Hillhurst Avenue
☎ 323-467-4949

The Make-Up Center trains Academy Award-winning make-up artists, and offers courses in make-up and hair styling for film and television. You may not want to take classes in old age, monster, bald cap or injury simulation, where you learn to create liver spots, broken capillaries, broken noses and bullet holes. But the retail store selling professional cosmetics is open to the public on weekdays, 9am-4:30pm.

Sunup to Sundown

Hollywood Boulevard Walk of Fame

Most of the places you want to see in Los Angeles are spread out from downtown to the beach, so you need to drive or take public transportation. One of the few exceptions is Hollywood Boulevard, where it is better to walk.

The easy way to get to Hollywood Boulevard from downtown Los Angeles is via the **Metro Red Line Subway** that runs from Union Station or Seventh and Flower downtown to North Hollywood. There are two Hollywood Boulevard stops: one is at Argyle Avenue (the east end) and the other is at Highland (near the Chinese Theatre and its footprints). The ride takes about 20 minutes from downtown, or about five minutes from the Lankershim Boulevard station in the San Fernando Valley. Fare is $1.35 one-way.

⭐ **TIP**

If you drive, you'll need to park. Metered street parking is available at 25¢ per 30 minutes, with a one-hour limit. Hard-to-find free parking and lots are on side streets off Hollywood Boulevard.

There are 2,472 stars embedded in Hollywood Boulevard; only about 300 are still blank.

The section of the boulevard known as the Walk of Fame extends from La Brea Avenue, at the west end, to Argyle Avenue, a block east of Vine; this is 15 blocks along the north side of the boulevard and 12 blocks along the south side.

Seeing Stars

The name Walk of Fame was tagged on in 1958 when the Hollywood Chamber of Commerce, trying to put some pizzazz back into the fading street, began its project of embedding star-shaped brass plaques in the sidewalk along both sides of the boulevard and a half-block north and south on Vine.

At first the Chamber of Commerce decided who would get a star and installed 1,558 of them. The procedure now is for someone (usually a star's publicity person, a studio about to release a big picture, or a fan club) to petition the Chamber; a committee representing the entertainment industries screens potential honorees on the basis of longevity in the field of entertainment, awards they have received and charitable contributions they have made to the community (or so they say). The petitioner pays a $15,000 sponsorship fee to cover expenses and maintenance. See the *Calendar* section of the *Los Angeles Times* for announcements of when stars will be on hand to dedicate their plaques in the Walk of Fame. Because there are five categories (movies, recordings, radio, television and theater), some individuals have more than one star, although only Gene Autry has all five.

Gene Autry's star for theater was awarded for his personal appearances at rodeos an' such-like.

It seems there have been times when the Chamber of Commerce relaxed its own rules: there are stars honoring the Apollo Astronauts, and advice-to-the-worried columnist Ann Landers got one on Valentine's Day in 2001 because years ago she read her stuff on the radio. Who remembers?

Around 24 names are added every year to the Walk of Fame.

The stars in the sidewalks begin between Sycamore Avenue and El Cerrito Place, just east of La Brea Avenue. Our walk starts here. You may decide to walk up one side of the boulevard and down the other in order to see all the stars in the pavement, as well as the other sights along the way. If you'd like a list that tells where on the boulevard each plaque is, pick one up at the Visitors Information Center (see below), or contact the Hollywood Chamber of Commerce, 7018 Hollywood Boulevard, Hollywood, CA 90028, ☎ 323-469-8311, www.hollwoodcoc.org. There is no charge for any of the maps.

VISITORS INFORMATION CENTER
THE JANES HOUSE

The Janes House is the last of the Victorian mansions that lined Hollywood Boulevard in the early days of the 20th century.

6541 Hollywood Boulevard
☎ 213-689-8822

This is the place to get a map of Hollywood, a map to movie stars' homes, or a list of the stars on the Walk of Fame, and the answers to practically anything else you want to know about Hollywood. Information by phone is available in English, French, German, Japanese and Spanish; the center is open Monday-Saturday, 9am-5pm.

WALKING THE BOULEVARD

Red Line Tours offers an excellent 1¼-hour walking tour of Hollywood Boulevard, which goes inside the Egyptian and El Capitan theaters and thoroughly explores the history and architecture of Old Hollywood and the movies. Tours begin at 10 and 11am, 2 and 4pm daily. Cost is $20 for adults; $18 for seniors; $15 for children nine to 16; under nine, free. Call ☎ 323-402-1074.

☛ DID YOU KNOW?

The celebrity honoree must promise to show up for the installation ceremony, or no star.

Polishing the Stars

It wouldn't do to go see Marilyn Monroe's star and find wads of gum stuck to it, so the city applies a weekly power wash to the sidewalks and all 2,472 of the stars. The Hollywood Entertainment District pitches in on the cost of upkeep, some stores along the boulevard keep the ones outside their own doors shiny, and sometimes fans or fan clubs adopt a star.

John Peterson is probably the only person who knows from memory where every one of the named stars are.

As you walk along you might see John Peterson, who's usually out there shining the stars with his glass cleaner, bronze polish and soft cloth. John lost a leg in childhood and worked as a repairman in a television shop on Los Feliz most of his adult life until the place closed in 1996. Unable to get another job, he started polishing the stars on the boulevard, "because they needed it," depending for income on tips from appreciative shopkeepers. He became such a well-known fixture he was finally put on salary.

Stop and chat when you see him with his Hollywood Entertainment District T-shirt, down on the sidewalk polishing a star. John will be happy to tell you anything about the boulevard.

Walking The Boulevard

CARMEN MIRANDA SQUARE
Sycamore Street & Hollywood Boulevard

For those too young to remember, Carmen Miranda was a Brazilian singer who was big in movie musicals, back when there was such a thing as movie musicals; she is easily remembered by her extravagant hats that sprouted bananas and pineapples and such. Her first big picture, the one everyone remembers, was *Down Argentine Way*.

Hollywood

About 70 Brazilian diplomats gathered here when the sign naming the square was installed.

★ HOLLYWOOD ENTERTAINMENT MUSEUM

7021 Hollywood Boulevard
(Hollywood Galaxy, lower level)
☎ 323-465-7900

This museum celebrates Hollywood as a place, as well as the entertainment arts of film, television, radio and recording. There are interactive exhibits, some permanent and some new, and memorabilia; one feature is the entire collection from the Max Factor Museum, which closed several years ago. There is the Starship Enterprise set from *Star Trek* and one from the most famous bar in the nation, *Cheers*.

In July and August the museum is open daily, 10am-6pm; from September through June it is open daily except Wednesday, 11am-6pm; open all holidays except Christmas. Admission is $7.50 for adults; $4.50 for seniors (60+) and students; $4 for children five-12; under five, free (CityPass accepted, see page 147). Parking under the building is $2 with Museum validation (entrance on Sycamore Avenue).

★ HOLLYWOOD ROOSEVELT HOTEL

7000 Hollywood Boulevard
☎ 323-466-7000, 800-950-7667
www.hollywoodroosevelt.com

The architectural style of the Hollywood Roosevelt is Spanish Colonial.

This historic gem was built in 1926 across Hollywood Boulevard from Grauman's Chinese Theatre, and was an immediate hit with the film crowd. The décor includes lots of tile and wrought iron. A remarkably lifelike Charlie Chaplin seated on a bench is the first thing you will see as you come in. The room to your left as you enter is the **Cinegrill**, a popular cabaret (see page 177). Dozens of stars have performed here. George Liberace, Liberace's brother, led the band here for many years, and lived in the penthouse at the top of the hotel.

The tiled staircase directly across the lobby from the Cinegrill is, so legend tells us, where Bill "Bojangles" Robinson taught Shirley Temple the step dance they did in

The Little Colonel. Since Marilyn Monroe's death, her image, faint and ghostly, has appeared to various people in the tall mirror at the end of the short corridor just to the right, by the elevators. Of course, this being Hollywood, it is possible that some ordinary ghost is grabbing the spotlight and making people think she is Monroe. But it is true Marilyn spent many nights in the Cinegrill.

☞ DID YOU KNOW?

Marilyn Monroe's first modeling job was a picture of her in a bathing suit by the Hollywood Roosevelt pool.

Perhaps the most historic place in Hollywood is the **Blossom Room**, the big room off the balcony above the lobby. This is where the first Academy Awards were held in 1929. The event started with a dinner in those days. On that first momentous evening, the awards went to *Wings*, for best picture; Janet Gaynor for best actress (*Seventh Heaven, Street Angel, Sunrise*); and Emil Jannings for best actor (*Way of All Flesh, Last Command*). The room is still used for special events, though it hasn't housed the Academy Awards since 1931.

The balcony itself has been turned into a museum of the early days of motion picture history, especially the silent film era, with photos and artifacts. Give yourself time to browse.

There are many stories about the hotel's past. David Niven relates that when he arrived in Hollywood and was trying to crash the movies, broke and with no place to live, the reception clerk took pity on him and let him stay for practically nothing in a tiny room situated between a noisy elevator and the primitive, very loud air conditioning machinery. He was grateful to have any place at all until he started getting acting jobs.

Montgomery Clift lived here while he was shooting *From Here to Eternity*. He drove the other guests crazy by incessantly practicing the trumpet in the hall. A number of people have heard the sound of a ghostly trumpet in that hall in the years since his death.

Hollywood

Up on the top floor is the **Gable-Lombard Suite**, number 1200, where Clark Gable and Carole Lombard had a regular weekend tryst while he was divorcing his second wife. The hotel's owner lives in the Gable-Lombard suite now; it used to cost $1,200 a night.

☞ DID YOU KNOW?

Hollywood is full of ghosts. There are at least three in the Hollywood Roosevelt.

★ GRAUMAN'S CHINESE THEATRE
6925 Hollywood Boulevard
☎ 323-461-3331
www.manntheatres.com

Marilyn Monroe and Jane Russell put their handprints side by side in the Chinese Theatre Forecourt in 1953.

Sid Grauman, the consummate showman, built this most opulent of movie houses, and named it the Chinese Theatre. It is big, with 1,492 seats; the acoustics are perfect, and décor is lush, even for the 1920s. Over the years, many pictures premiered here. In the days of silent films, Grauman staged lavish shows, some with chorus lines of 40 or more girls, each designed specifically to go along with the film being shown. Since 1927, there have been nearly 200 handprints, footprints, signatures and, in the case of Jimmy Durante, a noseprint, pressed into wet cement in the Forecourt of the Stars. Whenever an imprint is about to take place, there will be a story in the *Calendar* section of the *Los Angeles Times* beforehand. It is probably the single most visited spot in Southern California; many tours leave from here. The Forecourt is open 24 hours a day with no charge. Call for movie ticket information.

EL CAPITAN THEATRE
6838 Hollywood Boulevard
☎ 323-467-7674

Built in 1926 for live theater, the El Capitan, with its East Indian-style interior, is probably the most beautiful movie house in Hollywood – perhaps in Los Angeles. Gertrude Lawrence opened it in *Charlot's Review*; in later years Buster Keaton, Clark Gable and Rita Hayworth were featured in live productions. It became a movie theater with the world premiere of *Citizen Kane* in 1941. Disney owns it now, and has refurbished it beautifully. It is a great place to see a movie.

★ KODAK THEATRE
In the Hollywood & Highland Complex
☎ 310-247-3020
www.oscars.org

This big, newly built structure is the first permanent home for the Academy Awards ceremonies. In the same complex you will also find the 22-story, 640-room Renaissance Hollywood Hotel (see page 121); a broadcast studio; and lots of retail stores. Oscar's new theater has 3,300 seats and is appropriately sumptuous. The building also contains a 35,000-square-foot ballroom, which will house the Governor's Ball, where everyone touches base after the Academy Awards and before the chosen ones go on to much more exclusive parties. Two plaster elephants rear up on pedestals above the Babylon Courtyard at the center of the complex, a reminder that D.W. Griffith's gigantic set for *Intolerance* once stood nearby on Sunset Boulevard.

★ HOLLYWOOD MOVIE POSTERS
6727-6731 Hollywood Boulevard
Between Las Palmas & Highland Avenues
☎ 323-463-1792

This is a fascinating place, with great original posters for sale, along with black-and-white and color stills, press kits, press books and monster magazines. If you have any questions, especially about the sci-fi and horror genres, Ron Borst really knows what he is about; he wrote the book – *Graven Images*. Open Monday-Saturday, 11:30am-5pm.

Hollywood

★ EGYPTIAN THEATRE
AMERICAN CINEMATHEQUE
6712 Hollywood Boulevard
☎ 323-466-FILM (3456)
www.egyptiantheatre.com

Legendary theater owner Sid Grauman had already built the Million Dollar Theater in downtown Los Angeles, but there was no grand movie palace in Hollywood until he opened the Egyptian in 1922, on the site of what had been a five-acre lemon ranch. Grauman, wanting something exotic, chose an Egyptian theme. The forecourt was 150 feet long, with towering statues of the Egyptian god Isis. Tall, muscled "warriors" garbed in ancient Egyptian costumes and carrying scimitars patrolled the battlements on the roof overlooking the street.

The grand opening was celebrated with the first movie premiere to be held in Hollywood, for *Robin Hood*, starring Douglas Fairbanks. Premieres in subsequent years included De Mille's *The Ten Commandments* (1923), and *The Thief of Bagdad* with Fairbanks (1924). The last big star-studded premiere was *Funny Girl* (1968). The following years were tough on the neighborhood, and on the theater, which closed in 1992.

The City of Los Angeles bought The Egyptian Theatre and sold it for $1 to the non-profit foundation American Cinematheque with the promise that the theater would be restored to its original grandeur. It has reopened as a movie-lover's dream house, showing everything from Hollywood classics to new films from every part of the world, with opportunities for the public to meet actors, writers and directors.

A good introduction to Hollywood and the Egyptian is *Forever Hollywood*, an hour-long film that celebrates a century of movie-making, related by two dozen stars and filmmakers; it screens Saturday and Sunday, at 2 and 3:30pm; there is an 11:45am screening during public tours on one Saturday and one Sunday each month. The dates of these additional screenings vary, so call ahead. Admission to the screening is $7 for adults; $5 for seniors and students. General admission to most films at Cinematheque is $8 for adults; $7 for seniors 65+ and students. Tours of the theater are $5 and can be combined with a screening of

Forever Hollywood, for $10 (CityPass accepted, see below). Parking validation (partial) for several lots.

★ TIP

If you plan to visit more than one or two attractions, you can save money and time by buying a **CityPass** ($49.75 for adults, $38 for children three to 11) at the first attraction you visit. It's good for nine days, and covers admission to Universal Studios, the Egyptian Theatre, the Hollywood Entertainment Museum, the Autry Museum, and several other attractions. It's a bargain: admission to Universal Studios alone is $43.

★ LAS PALMAS HOTEL
1750 North Las Palmas Avenue

Take a look to your left as you cross Las Palmas and you will see the spot where Julia Roberts hung out, plying the tricks of her trade, before she caught the eye of Richard Gere and moved to Beverly Hills in *Pretty Woman*.

★★ MUSSO & FRANK'S GRILL
6667 Hollywood Boulevard
☎ 323-467-7788

There is so much to tell about Musso's. It is by far the oldest café in Hollywood; it was founded by Joseph Musso and Frank Toulet in 1919 when there wasn't much else on the Boulevard. In 1926 the partners sold out to Joseph Carissimi and John Mosso (different spelling, different man). The place is run by those two families to this day.

Probably everyone who was anyone in the movie business has eaten here. Mary Pickford, Claudette Colbert, Bette Davis, Cesar Romero, Edward G. Robinson, H.B. Warner, Greta Garbo, Bing Crosby, Alan Hale. John Barrymore did some of his legendary drinking here. Mack Sennett came every day; people still ask for Charlie Chaplin's booth in the corner by the window, facing the boulevard (on the

Hollywood

days he couldn't make it he sent his chauffeur to pick up his lunch and bring it back to his studio on La Brea).

📖 HISTORIC NOTE

In 1919 there was an avocado grove across the street from Musso's all the way down to Sunset, eucalyptus trees in the back parking lot and a gentle stream running down what is now Franklin Avenue.

Even more than for actors, Musso's has always been a writer's place. Until a few years ago there was a bookstore next door where all the writers working at the studios and laboring over novels met. Nathaniel West lived in an apartment on Ivar and could be found here while he was writing his fiercely anti-Hollywood novel, *Day of the Locust*. Others who frequented Musso's include Bill Lippman (*Little Miss Marker*); Scott Fitzgerald when he was writing *Tender is the Night*; occasionally Thomas Wolfe; Elliott Paul; William Faulkner; Max Brand; Jo Pagano; John Fante, and Ernest Hemingway.

☞ DID YOU KNOW?

Matt Drudge, the Internet gossip, had his apartment just a few steps from here before he moved to luxury digs in Miami. He used Musso's like his own dining room and did his interviews in one of its booths.

★ LARRY EDMUNDS BOOK STORE
6644 Hollywood Boulevard
☎ 323-463-3273

This bookstore has been here as long as we can remember, and for all that time has been the place to come for stuff about Hollywood. You will find the largest collection of film- and theater-related books in Los Angeles, plus thousands of black-and-white photos and stills from famous and forgotten films. You'll find posters, too. Open Monday-Saturday, 10am-6pm.

★ FREDERICK'S OF HOLLYWOOD
6608 Hollywood Boulevard
☎ 323-466-8506

You can't miss it, as the building is painted a delicious slut-purple. Frederick's is practically world-famous for its lingerie guaranteed to revive any marriage, no matter how dull. But we are here to see the **Celebrity Lingerie Museum**, which features items such as Cher's bra, Mae West's peignoir, Madonna's pointy corset, and Tony Curtis' brassiere from *Some Like It Hot*. It's a hoot, and it's free. Open Monday-Friday, 10am-9pm; Saturday, 10am-7pm; Sunday, 11am-6pm.

THE PERFECT LITTLE GIFT
The "Marabou-trim Babydoll," designed by founder Frederick Mellinger in the mid '50s, is the bestseller. Adapted from a French lingerie style, it has a short, sheer nylon body, feather trim at hem and breast, with spaghetti straps. This style was worn by Cindy Margolis and other "Fembots" in *Austin Powers: International Man of Mystery*. Price, $38.

Hollywood

WARNER PACIFIC THEATRE
6423-6445 Hollywood Boulevard

Before the anti-trust laws stepped in, when Warner Bros. owned hundreds of movie houses nationwide, the Warner Pacific Theatre, at Hollywood Boulevard and Wilcox Avenue, was their flagship. But nobody cares about that now; the theater is famous because Carol Burnett was an usherette here in the 1940s. At the moment it is closed.

SECURITY TRUST & SAVINGS
6381-6385 Hollywood Boulevard

This bank has been on the northeast corner of Hollywood and Cahuenga since the 1920s. It is where Charlie Chaplin banked, as did the slightly paranoid W.C. Fields, who had accounts under several names. But most important, Philip Marlowe had his office upstairs. Author Raymond Chandler called it the Cahuenga Building in his books set in a *noir* Hollywood of the '30s. That's why this intersection is named Raymond Chandler Square. (You will find the plaque on the southeast corner.)

★ PANTAGES THEATRE
6233 Hollywood Boulevard at Argyle Avenue
☎ 213-365-5555 tickets

The Pantages was the location of the Academy Awards from 1949 to 1959.

The Pantages was built as as a movie palace in 1930, back when going to see a motion picture was still a special experience. This is where many of the big, kleig-lit premiers were held. The décor is art deco and the 18-foot-high lobby is a riot of architectural details, including a statue of a movie director standing behind his cameraman. It was converted into a legitimate theater in 1978 and is now one of the prime Los Angeles houses in which to see big musicals.

Ivar Avenue

1817 IVAR AVENUE
Go one block east of Cahuenga and turn left to find the house where Nathaniel West lived while he was writing the classic Hollywood novel, *The Day of the Locust*. He divided the rest of his time between hanging out at Musso & Frank's and writing screenplays (*Ticket to Paradise*, *It Could Happen to You*, *Five Came Back*, *I Stole a Million* and *Let's Make Music*).

1851 IVAR AVENUE
Cross Yucca Street and continue along Ivar; you might recognize the Alto Nido Apartments as the rundown building where Joe Gillis (William Holden) lived before he splashed into Norma Desmond's (Gloria Swanson) pool in *Sunset Boulevard*.

▄ FILM GLOSSARY

Script Supervisor – The person responsible for ensuring that the film matches the script – and itself – in terms of detail and continuity; e.g., that an actor who starts a scene wearing a red tie has the same tie on when shooting resumes, perhaps days later, and not a blue one.

1850 IVAR AVENUE

Across the street from the Alto Nido is the Spanish-style house where Marie Dressler lived. She was in Greta Garbo's first talkie, Eugene O'Neill's *Anna Christie*; George S. Kaufman and Edna Ferber's *Dinner at Eight*, where she had a classic comedy scene with Jean Harlow; and a series of *Tugboat Annie* films with Wallace Beery.

1714 IVAR AVENUE

As you head back toward Hollywood Boulevard you'll see the **Knickerbocker Hotel**; a lot of faded glory resides here. It was built in 1925, at the height of what some call Hollywood's Golden Age, to meet the housing needs of the swarms of actors and would-be actors arriving daily.

Until he died in 1926, Rudolph Valentino rode his horse down Ivar on moonlit nights from Falcon Lair, his house in the hills, to drink at the Knickerbocker's bar and dance his seductive tango with oh-so-willing women. Bette Davis, Doris Day, Errol Flynn, Judy Garland, Cary Grant, Dick Powell, Frank Sinatra, Gloria Swanson and Orson Welles stayed in the suites at one time or another – some for long periods. The lovely and forlorn actress Frances Farmer lived here in 1943 when she was dragged out in confusion to be housed in a mental institution. In the mid-1950s Marilyn Monroe used to sneak in through the kitchen on her way to meet Joe DiMaggio in a dark corner of the bar.

D.W. Griffith, who made the movie business possible and then (after *Intolerance* in 1916) was ignored by the industry, died in the lobby in 1948. A plaque on the Knickerbocker marks it as Griffith's one-time home. Two years later Elvis Presley stayed here while he made his first

Valentino Place, a street in Hollywood, was named for Rudolph Valentino, and there is a bust of him in DeLongpre Park, south of Sunset Blvd. off Cherokee Avenue.

Hollywood

film, *Love Me Tender.* But by 1970 the place had faded; it is now a home for seniors.

★ FRANCES HOWARD GOLDWYN BRANCH, HOLLYWOOD PUBLIC LIBRARY
1623 North Ivar Avenue
☎ 323-856-8260

Cross Hollywood Boulevard and go a half-block down Ivar to the Hollywood Public Library. Fittingly, it holds a large collection of books on movies and Hollywood. It's a good place to browse. The library is open Monday-Thursday, 10am-8pm; Friday and Saturday, 10 am-6pm; Sunday, 1-5pm.

★★ HOLLYWOOD FARMERS' MARKET
This block of Ivar (between Hollywood and Sunset, and along Selma from Vine Street to Cosmo) is closed to traffic on Sunday for an open-air farmers' market, where you will sometimes see celebrities. We noticed Janel Moloney among the great fresh fruit and vegetables, and Kirsten Dunst another time. Hey, actors have to eat, too! Open Sunday, 8:30am-1pm, come rain or shine. (Don't confuse this with The Farmers' Market, a permanent open-air mall at Beverly and Fairfax.)

Vine Street

Head back to Hollywood Boulevard and mosey a bit farther east; you are on the famed corner of Hollywood and Vine. What's to say, except to be in awe of the enduring power of hype over reality. There's nothing much of note here and, frankly, my dear, there never really was.

CAPITOL RECORDS BUILDING
1750 Vine Street

A light on the rooftop spire of the Capitol Records building flashes "H-O-L-L-Y-W-O-O-D" in Morse code.

Turn left onto Vine Street. Ahead is the Capitol Records Building; it has 13 stories and is shaped like a stack of records with a stylus in the groove on top. Nat "King" Cole, Frank Sinatra and The Beatles all recorded here. Gold albums are on display in the lobby; in the sidewalk out front are stars with the names of Capitol Records' artists, including John Lennon.

PALACE THEATRE
1735 Vine Street

This theater, on the west side of Vine Street, was built in 1930 as a legitimate theater. Ken Murray's *Blackouts*, starring comedian Ken Murray and Marie Wilson (remember *My Friend Irma*?), played here all through World War II, packing 'em in at every show. From the early 1950s on it was the origination site for many TV shows like the *Colgate Comedy Hour, This is Your Life* and the *Lawrence Welk Show*. Now it's a venue for TV shoots, special events and occasional rock concerts.

HOLLYWOOD PLAZA HOTEL
1637 Vine Street

Walk on down Vine to the south side of Hollywood Boulevard. On the west side of Vine is the hotel where Ronald Reagan lived when he first hit town. Doris Day and Jackie Gleason once lived here (not together, we assume).

In 1937 Clara Bow installed the It Café on the ground floor to the left of the entrance; the café was only briefly "it" in a town of many short-lived endeavors. By the time we personally paid any attention to the hotel, much later, the bar was the Carousel, or something like that. The bar and its seated customers revolved around the bartenders, who stood in the middle. You could never tell if you'd had too much to drink or were just experiencing *mal de mer.*

At one time the hotel was a popular hang-out for hookers. Now it has become a senior citizen home. We assume the hookers have moved on.

THE DOOLITTLE THEATRE
1615 Vine Street
☎ 323-462-6666

The theater was originally the CBS Radio Playhouse. *Lux Radio Theater, Your Hit Parade* and many other shows were broadcast from here in the 1930s and '40s. During the 1950s and '60s it became the Huntington Hartford, a jewel of a legitimate theater. There was a dining room on

The Doolittle Theatre is now a Latino-oriented performing arts center owned by the Ricardo Montalban Nosotros Foundation.

the mezzanine level, where we used to go and often see celebrities also having dinner while we were dining and then, moments before the curtain went up, we would stroll to our theater seats.

SITE OF CECIL B. DE MILLE'S BARN

There is a plaque on the northeast corner of Vine and Selma commemorating the site where Cecil B. De Mille made *The Squaw Man* in 1913, first feature film shot in Hollywood, in a barn he had rented. Trouble is, like a lot of things in Hollywood, you can't believe everything you see. The actual barn was not here but on the southeast corner.

THE HOLLYWOOD CHRISTMAS PARADE

This parade is held each year on the first Sunday after Thanksgiving. The Grand Marshal is always a star, and up to 100 celebrities are sprinkled among other marchers. The parade follows a rectangular route on Hollywood Boulevard, Vine Street, Sunset Boulevard and La Brea Avenue. There are bleachers for onlookers on Hollywood Boulevard in the block from Orange to Highland; tickets are required. You may choose to stand along the route; people begin arriving early in the day at favored spots.

Hollywood's Christmas Parade is the largest celebrity parade in the world.

TV cameras are set up in front of the bleachers, and interviews and performances are televised. For tickets call Sharp Seating, ☎ 626-795-4171; tickets cost $22, $29 or $35. You can also buy guaranteed parking at the same time. An easy way to enjoy the day without a parking hassle is to come by Metro; exit at Highland for the bleachers, at Vine Street for the other end of the parade route. Contact the Hollywood Chamber of Commerce, ☎ 323-469-8311, for more information, or check the parade Web site, www.hollywoodchristmas.com.

Elsewhere in Hollywood

HOLLYGROVE ORPHANAGE
1815 North El Centro Avenue

One block east of Vine Street between Melrose and Santa Monica is the place where Norma Jean Baker lived for two years. We remember her better as Marilyn Monroe. Hollygrove, Los Angeles' first privately run orphanage, opened in Chinatown in 1880 and was later moved to Hollywood and changed its name. Norma Jean's aunt put her here from 1935 to 1937, before she metamorphosed into MM.

WHAT GOES AROUND COMES AROUND

There are plans, or at least talk, about Monroe's estate building a Marilyn Monroe Theatre at the Hollygrove Orphanage.

Now the debt is being repaid. During the time she was a star, Marilyn was also one of the best known students at Lee Strasberg's Group Theatre in New York. A couple of years ago, more than 30 years after her death, some of her effects were auctioned off at Christie's, enough to raise $13 million. Now, Anna Strasberg, who has looked after Marilyn's estate since Lee Strasberg died in 1982, has made a donation to Hollygrove.

HOLLYWOOD ATHLETIC CLUB
6525 Sunset Boulevard
☎ 323-462-6262

This was a very popular place to work out, especially in the 1920s and even in the '30s. Douglas Fairbanks Sr. and Rudolph Valentino were members, as were Johnny Weismuller and Buster Crabbe and, later, Edgar Bergen. Charlie McCarthy was an honorary member. These days it is used heavily for premiere parties, wrap parties and the like. At night various promoters turn it into a popular nightclub.

Hollywood

HOLLYWOOD HIGH SCHOOL
1521 North Highland Avenue
☎ 323-461-3891

Hollywood High School's mascot is The Sheik; songleaders wear Arabic robes.

Just two blocks off Hollywood Boulevard at the corner of Sunset is perhaps the most famous high school in the country, simply because it is in Hollywood and so many kids who later became stars went here. Carol Burnett, James Garner, Jean Peters, Stefanie Powers, John Ritter, Jason Robards and Mickey Rooney are a few. Rick and David Nelson were students here when Ozzie and Harriet were shooting *Ozzie and Harriet* just a 10-minute walk away at Hollywood Center Studio on Las Palmas Avenue.

Not only soon-to-be actors went here. Warren Christopher attended, and delivered the *Hollywood Citizen-News* after school, as did one of the authors of this book (the author didn't grow up to become Secretary of State, though).

If your age is advanced enough you probably have heard about how Lana Turner was discovered while she was a student here. According to the story, she cut fifth period typing class and was sitting on a stool at the malt shop across Highland on the northeast corner of Sunset. Billy Wilkerson, publisher of the *Hollywood Reporter*, a movie-industry trade paper, spotted her and said something original like, "How would you like to be in the movies, kiddo?" She was probably wearing one of those popular sweaters, which makes the tale more credible; though any girl attending the school at the time would have had more sense than to go for a line like that. The malt shop was torn down long ago.

The phone at Hollywood High is answered in English, Spanish, Japanese and Armenian.

The art deco science and liberal arts buildings were built by the WPA in the 1930s. The school was once almost completely white; now, like most of Los Angeles, it is a mix of races and ethnic groups, everything from Armenian to, probably, Zairean. But, still reflecting the heritage of the celebrities who attended in the past, the school has an Academy of Performing Arts.

★ CHAPLIN STUDIO

(now Jim Henson Studio)
1416 North La Brea Avenue (between Sunset Boulevard
and De Longpre Avenue)
☎ 323-802-1500

Charlie Chaplin, perhaps the only real genius in the history of filmmaking, made most of his films on this small lot. He could control every detail here. The lot originally extended to Sunset Boulevard; the corner was sold off after Chaplin was shamefully banished from this country in the 1950s. Herb Alpert used the lot as a recording studio for many years. Tours are not available at this writing.

★★ THE HOLLYWOOD BOWL

2301 N. Highland Avenue, at Hollywood Bowl Road
Information and tickets, ☎ 323-850-2000
Restaurant, ☎ 323-850-1885
www.hollywoodbowl.org

The Bowl, in a narrow canyon cut into the Hollywood Hills off the Hollywood Freeway, offers concerts and much, much more; it's a place to see celebrities by the score, picnicking in style. Here you will find that much-photographed concert shell, with great acoustics, facing a curved hillside covered with over 17,000 seats. The season runs July-September. There is a restaurant, Sunset Grill (reservations needed), and take-out places to get food to eat in the open air. Down front are the boxes, where the stars dine al fresco, especially on occasions like the opening night of the Los Angeles Philharmonic season in July.

Hollywood

★ **TIP**

Show up at 9am in summer to hear rehearsals. Sit anywhere. No celebrities – except the world-famous singers and musicians – and free! ☎ 323-850-2000; speak to an operator to confirm rehearsal dates and times.

WHERE TO GET A PICNIC BASKET

◆ **La Brea Bakery**, 624 South La Brea Avenue, Hollywood, ☎ 323-939-6813. $16-$18. Order day before or before 10am for late afternoon pickup.

◆ **Ammo**, 1155 North Highland Avenue, Hollywood, ☎ 323-871-2666. A la carte (salad $8, chicken sandwich $10), pick up curbside.

◆ **Basix**, 8333 Santa Monica Boulevard, West Hollywood, ☎ 323-848-2460. $18-$35 in a gift basket. Order a day ahead.

◆ **Bistro Garden/BG To Go**, 12930 Ventura Boulevard, Studio City (San Fernando Valley), ☎ 828-FOOD-2-GO. Various baskets are available for $21 to $32.50 per person. Order at least an hour ahead.

JOHN ANSON FORD AMPHITHEATRE
2580 Cahuenga Boulevard
(cross over Hollywood Freeway)
☎ 323-461-3673

The Ford is a natural amphitheater on the east side of the Hollywood Freeway as it goes through Cahuenga Pass out of Hollywood. See page 183 for information about events held here.

LAKE HOLLYWOOD (HOLLYWOOD RESERVOIR)

Lake Holly-wood, in the Hollywood Hills, just 10 minutes' drive above the Boulevard, is the lake that flooded Hollywood in Earthquake!

Lake Hollywood is not a natural lake; it is a reservoir that, in the past, supplied drinking water to a portion of Hollywood; the water in the lake now is simply held in reserve for emergencies, since two immense tanks to hold potable water were recently constructed underground. This beautiful, tree-lined lake has long been a popular place for filming, as it is much closer to reach than Lake Arrowhead way up in the San Bernardino Mountains. Most of the exteriors of the old comedy series *Camp Runamuck* were shot here, and Lake Hollywood played a big role in the movie *Earthquake*.

There is a walking and jogging path all around the fenced-in lake, a 3.2-mile loop with only a short stretch along a road with traffic. Part of it crosses Mulholland Dam and gives a good view of the Hollywood sign in the Hollywood Hills above to the east. The westernmost stretch of a finger of Griffith Park (see pages 164-175) reaches the lake.

To get here, take the Hollywood Freeway (101) or Cahuenga Boulevard out of Hollywood to Barham Boulevard, then right (east) a short distance to Lake Hollywood Drive; turn right. Street parking. There are several access gates through the fence. Gates generally open 6:30am-7:30pm, but call to check current times; ☎ 323-463-0830.

PETERSEN AUTOMOTIVE MUSEUM
6060 Wilshire Boulevard (at Fairfax)
Los Angeles
☎ 323-930-CARS (2277)
www.petersen.org

Just south of Hollywood you can see famous vehicles on display that were owned by stars and used in movies, along with an array of milestone cars in US history. Open Tuesday-Sunday, 10am-6pm; closed Monday, except for major holidays. Admission is $7 for adults; $5 for seniors and students; $3 for children ages five-12.

ZIMMER CHILDREN'S MUSEUM
6505 Wilshire Boulevard, Suite 100
Los Angeles
☎ 323-761-8989
www.zimmermuseum.org

The Zimmer is a great place for kids ages three to 11. There is a Piper Cub airplane to "fly," a space capsule, and a dozen "businesses," where they can play cook in the diner, or sell books at Bubbie's Bookstore or put on white coats and scrubs and play "rescue" from the real ambulance. Every exhibit is fun, yet each offers subtle lessons. Open Tuesday-Thursday and Sunday, 12:30 to 5pm. Admission is $5 for adults; $3 for children ages three to 12; free for children age two and under and for grandparents accompanied by a grandchild. It is on the ground floor of the Jewish Community Center, just south of Hollywood.

Hollywood

In the Hollywood Hills

Listen to them, children of the night! What music they make!

– Bela Lugosi, *Dracula*

THE ACKERMANSION

Forest Ackerman Museum of Horror and Science-Fiction Film History
Hollywood Hills above Los Feliz
☎ 323-666-6326

More than 50,000 science-fiction books, over 100,000 film stills, uncounted movie posters, a model dinosaur from the classic 1933 film *King Kong* – that's just the beginning in the 18-room mansion stuffed to the *Creature From The Black Lagoon's* gills with movie memorabilia.

Forest Ackerman is the man who coined the word "sci-fi."

Forest J. Ackerman, now 85, has been a horror-science fiction flick fan since he was nine. He was Isaac Asimov's literary agent, and L. Ron Hubbard's and Ray Bradbury's. He has appeared in more than 56 cameo film roles, so when he starts telling stories about Lon Chaney Jr. and Boris Karloff, you know you are getting it right from the Wolf Man's mouth, so to speak. Newspaper clippings and movie lobby cards share the walls with space aliens and robots, witches and warlocks. Don't miss the first edition of *Dracula*, signed by Bela Lugosi, Vincent Price and the curator of Dracula's castle in Transylvania. Open most Saturdays, 11am-noon (call for directions); admission is free.

THE HOLLYWOOD SIGN
Beachwood Drive

The world-famous Hollywood sign was erected in 1923 to publicize a land development there. The original said Hollywoodland, though the last four letters later blew down in a storm; the developers eventually blew away, too. When the Hollywood sign was lit at midnight, December 31, 1999, each letter glowed with 250,000 watts of light.

The Hollywood Chamber of Commerce holds the copyright on the sign now, and controls how it can be used in advertising and publicity. They are strict; for instance, they vetoed covering the white letters with black spots to publicize the film *101 Dalmatians*. The Chamber has discovered that it can't control everything, though. On one occasion, college students modified the sign to say "Hollyweed," and "Olliewood" appeared during the Iran-Contra scandal starring Oliver North. To reach the sign, go two blocks north of Hollywood Boulevard to Franklin Avenue, then turn right and continue to Beachwood Drive. The sign has its own Web site, www.HollywoodSign.org.

In 1987, the Hollywood Sign was changed to read HOLY-WOOD in honor of Pope John Paul II's visit to Los Angeles.

☞ DID YOU KNOW?

The peak that is the home of the Hollywood sign is called Mt. Lee. Mack Sennett of *Keystone Kops* and bathing beauty movies fame once owned it, but never built a house there as he planned. That low, white building on top, just above it, was the first experimental television station in Los Angeles, one of the first in the country.

CHATEAU ELYSEE
5310 Franklin Avenue

If you continue past Beachwood on Franklin you will see a longtime Hollywood treasure that is now an official historic landmark. It was known as the Château Elysée, a celebrity hotel and hideaway when it was built by Eleanor Ince in 1927. She was the widow of Thomas Ince, the pioneer film producer who died under mysterious circumstances on William Randolph Hearst's yacht one dark and stormy night.

It was widely believed that Thomas Ince was killed by Hearst in a dispute over Hearst's significant other, movie star Marion Davies. In any case, Hearst afterward reportedly put up the money for the hotel.

Those who have stayed here at one time or another in the apartment-style accommodations include Humphrey Bogart, Errol Flynn, Clark Gable, Lillian Gish, Carole Lombard, Mary Pickford and Ginger Rogers.

Hollywood

Villa Carlotta, an apartment building on the corner of Tamarind Avenue, was originally the Château's staff quarters. The buildings were connected by a tunnel. The strip of stores and cafés that line the opposite side of Franklin is in the spot where the stables used to be.

The Château Elysée building now is the Celebrity Centre International, the headquarters for the Church of Scientology, which saved it from demolition in 1972 and undertook the lengthy and expensive restoration.

East Hollywood

For the purposes of this book, when we talk about East Hollywood we are talking about the area east of Gower Gulch.

> ☞ **DID YOU KNOW?**
>
> Gower Gulch was so named when many "oaters" were filmed in and around Gower Street. "Oaters" were Western movies, first called that by *Variety*, the Hollywood daily trade paper.

The big Disney Studios were later built in Burbank, where you will still find them.

In 1923, the 21-year-old Walt Disney rented a vacant lot at the corner of **Hollywood Boulevard** and **Vermont Avenue** and started his career, filming a combined live action-animated series of 13 short films about a four-year-old girl named *Alice*, who was played by Virginia Davis. That mouse named Mickey didn't arrive until five years later.

When Davis was commemorated for her pioneering work as an actress in 1998, at the age of 79, she mentioned that Disney was "long on creativity but low on cash," even to the point of borrowing her mother's car whenever he dated his future wife.

Go south of Sunset a few blocks on Vermont; there, between Santa Monica Boulevard and Melrose Avenue, is **Los Angeles City College**, which has one of the nation's most respected training programs in its Theatre Academy. Alumni include Alan Arkin, James Coburn, Al Freeman

Jr., Mark Hamill, Hugh O'Brian, director José Quintero, Donna Reed, Alexis Smith, Louise Sorel, Robert Vaughn, Cindy Williams and Paul Winfield.

After Mel Torme left Hollywood High he came here and sang with the Mel-Tones, a successful professional group he organized made up of students. Billy Barty, the less-than-three-feet-tall actor, attended during World War II when most men were away in the service so the football team had to take whoever it could get. Barty complained that, for the rest of his life, no one believed him when he told them he played college football.

LACC's Theatre Academy stages plays that are open to the public at its campus theater. The quality of acting and directing is consistently high while box office prices are absurdly low. ☎ 323-953-4000, extension 2990, for announcements of current productions (see page 184).

Recreation

Bowling

Hollywood is not much of a place for sports, organized or otherwise, except of course for the indoor kind. Long ago, in the '30s and '40s, when the American Legion Fight Arena was still open on Gower between Sunset and Hollywood, it was different – that is where you *really* saw stars every Friday night. There is one notable exception.

★★ HOLLYWOOD STAR LANES
7750 Sunset Boulevard
☎ 323-671-1100

It's a typical bowling alley, and we can't guarantee lots of celebrities work on their short steps here, but we happen to know Kirsten Dunst (*Get Over It!*) comes in with her girlfriends some Saturday nights. And what else are all the stars who live in Hollywood going to do with themselves? Open seven days, 24 hours – if you can't sleep at 4am, hey! Why not get some exercise?

Hollywood

Runyon Canyon Park

This park is west of Lake Hollywood on the other side of the Hollywood Freeway from the lake. Just a few minutes above Franklin Avenue, the park still has birds, rabbits, coyotes and other wildlife, as it did a century-and-a-half ago. To reach the park, take Franklin west from Highland, past La Brea Avenue to Fuller Avenue; go right on Fuller to the entrance gate. The park is open from dawn to dusk.

From 1862 to 1863 the US Army Camel Corps carried freight from Wilmington to Fort Tejon, by way of Los Angeles.

The wooded canyon has a history. Originally part of a land grant, it was given to "Greek George" Caralambo for his service as leader of the Army Camel Corps. **Carmen Runyan** (also spelled Runyon) bought it in 1919.

Soon after you walk through the gates, you will see the ruins of San Patrizio, the mansion built by actor/singer John McCormick (*Song of My Heart*). John Barrymore, Wallace Beery and Basil Rathbone were frequent guests.

Go left to join the road (you must walk, no cars are permitted) rising uphill along the west side of the canyon. Near the head of the canyon the trail meets a dirt road going back down the east side. Return down the steepish dirt road to Inspiration Point and the ruins of a pool house built by Frank Lloyd Wright for Huntington Hartford. Errol Flynn lived here in 1957-58. The site has nice views over Hollywood. Walk back to the dirt road and complete the loop to the beginning. Total distance is less than three miles, with a rise of more than 500 feet.

Griffith Park

A rock's a rock, a tree's a tree, shoot it in Griffith Park!
— Old studio saying

This is one of Los Angeles' treasures, an undeveloped park in the heart of the city, twice the size of New York's Central Park and San Francisco's Golden Gate Park combined. You can walk wooded trails, ride horseback, go to the Los Angeles Zoo, play golf, have a picnic or watch a movie being shot, all virtually in the lap of Hollywood.

The site was originally part of the land grant Rancho Los Feliz. The redundantly named **Colonel Griffith J. Griffith**, a gold speculator and curious character (he spent a year in prison for attempting to murder his wife), magnanimously gave 3,000 acres to the city for a park, along with $100,000 to build an observatory in it. His generosity may have been inspired by the belief that there was a curse on the land, which had taken its toll on several previous owners, so he couldn't sell it. The city, originally suspicious, finally accepted his offer and later added another 1,200 acres.

Griffith Park is five square miles in area, much of it mountainous.

It has certainly been a boon for movie-makers. Since the earliest days of silent movies, picture companies have trekked the few miles to Griffith Park to take advantage of its varying locales. The switchblade fight scene between James Dean and another teenager in *Rebel Without a Cause* was filmed near the Observatory, as was the scene in *Terminator* where Arnold Schwarzenegger steals clothes from a trio of bad guys.

We always thought Bronson Caves was the most-used area in the park, seen in countless old serials and movies, such as *King Kong*, as well as doubling for the Batcave in the 1960s series and the newer film versions of *Batman*, a villain's hideout in *The X-Files* and home base for the *Mighty Morphin Power Rangers*. But we learned that Cedar Grove, off Commonwealth Canyon Drive, is the most popular filmmaking locale. It is hard to believe, but the park is so popular that, in the year 2000, 2,148 film, TV and still productions used it as a locale.

With elevations from 384 to 1,625 feet, much of the park is mountains and canyons. There are plenty of deer and coyotes here, and not always in remote areas. There's an occasional rattlesnake in the scrub for hikers to avoid, and poison oak in some areas. You'll see lots of opossums, skunks, raccoons and red foxes, but no mountain lions. In

Hollywood

If you saw the controversial Dixie Chicks video, it is in Griffith Park where the body of the abusive husband is dumped.

Griffith Park

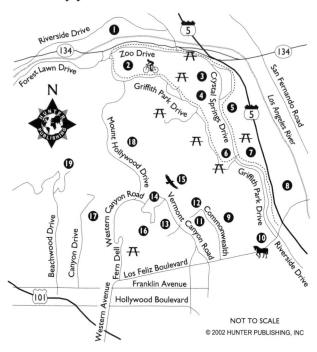

NOT TO SCALE

© 2002 HUNTER PUBLISHING, INC

1. Los Angeles Equestrian Center
2. Travel Town Transportation Museum
3. Los Angeles Zoo
4. Wilson/Harding Golf Course; golf clubhouse
5. Autry Museum of Western Heritage
6. Merry-go-round; tennis courts
7. Ranger station; Metro Bus #96
8. Los Feliz Municipal Golf Course
9. Park Nursery; Cedar Grove

10. Park Entrance; GP&S Railroad; tennis courts; pony rides; Metro buses #180, 181
11. Roosevelt Municipal Golf Course
12. Tennis courts
13. Greek Theatre
14. Tunnel
15. The Bird Sanctuary
16. Griffith Observatory
17. Bronson Caves
18. Mount Hollywood; Dante's View
19. Hollywood Sign

 Bicycle route

�ూ Picnic areas

the sky above you will see red-tailed hawks, turkey vultures and blue jays.

While three sides of the park are defined by major roads and freeways, the west side simply blends into the Hollywood Hills and Beachwood Canyon. One thin section goes all the way to Lake Hollywood (see page 158).

Getting to the Park

For those traveling by car, Griffith Park's southern boundary is Los Feliz Boulevard, with five streets leading in. On the east are Riverside Drive and the Golden State Freeway (I-5), with three off-ramps: Los Feliz, Zoo Drive and Griffith Park Drive. Forest Lawn Drive and the Ventura Freeway (134), are on the north.

Griffith Park borders the towns of Burbank, Glendale and Hollywood.

You can also reach Griffith Park by bus. From Downtown Los Angeles, METRO Bus 96 runs north on Olive; it takes 30 minutes to get to the Ranger Station, the merry-go-round, and picnic areas. From Hollywood, METRO buses 180 and 181 run east on Hollywood Boulevard to Riverside Drive and Los Feliz at the entrance to the park.

Park Regulations & Information

While the park is so large you could fit the entire city of Beverly Hills within its boundaries, the crime rate is extremely low. But there are penalties for minor transgressions. Bicycling on hiking trails will get you a $135 ticket. Dogs off leash, up to $81 (there are off-leash areas at Runyon Canyon and adjacent to the John Ferraro soccer fields); littering, $105; speeding over 25 mph anywhere in the park, $76. The most serious infraction is smoking in a fire district, which can cost you up to $675.

The park is open daily, 6am-10pm. Bridle trails, mountain roads and hiking paths close at sunset. Contact the **Park Ranger Station**, ☎ 323-913-4688, www.cityofla.org/RAP/grifmet/griffith.htm, for general information.

Hollywood

GRIFFITH PARK'S FESTIVAL OF LIGHTS

The mile-long Festival of Lights, on a one-way section of Crystal Springs Drive off Los Feliz, starts around November 25 and runs through December 26; lights are on daily from 5-10pm. It is a very popular attraction, and the closer it gets to Christmas, the slower the traffic moves; on weekends this can lead to long waits.

Autry Museum of Western Heritage

You might expect a simple tribute to the movies' favorite singing cowboy, but this is much more. There are memorabilia from movie cowboys Gene Autry, John Wayne and Roy Rogers along with artifacts from the lives of historical figures such as Annie Oakley, Buffalo Bill and Teddy Roosevelt. Permanent galleries and changing exhibitions explore both the mythological and the authentic Old West. There have been excellent exhibits on the role of black soldiers in the US Cavalry and the lives of Japanese women in the West. It is certainly worth a few hours. The museum is open Tuesday-Sunday, 10am-5pm; Thursday, 10am-8pm. Admission is $7.50 for adults; $5 for seniors 60+ and students 13-18; $3 for children ages two-12. 4700 Western Heritage Way, off Griffith Park Drive, which is off Los Feliz Boulevard; or use the Golden State Freeway (5). ☎ 323-667-2000, www.autry-museum.org.

★ TIP

The Autry Museum has hands-on exhibits where visitors can learn history through games and exploration.

Griffith Observatory

With its astronomy museum, telescopes and planetarium theater, this has been by far the most popular place in the park. Unfortunately, the Observatory closed for a three-year renovation in January 2002. The bust of James Dean, commemorating his role in *Rebel Without a Cause*, will be retained, and there will be a new Leonard Nimoy Event Horizon Theatre, partially funded by "Mr. Spock" of *Star Trek*. 2800 East Observatory Road, ☎ 323-664-1191, www.griffithobs.org.

Greek Theatre

An open-air, 4,700-seat natural amphitheater. Performances range from ballet to rock to musicals. Season runs May through October. 2700 North Vermont Avenue, ☎ 323-665-5857, www.greektheatrela.com.

Like the Hollywood Bowl, the Greek Theatre is an outdoor amphitheater with wonderful acoustics.

Bicycle Paths

Bikes are available for rent near the **Ranger Station**, 4730 Crystal Springs Drive, Friday-Sunday in summer, weekends only in winter; ☎ 323-662-6573. You can also rent from **Woody's Bicycle World**, 3157 Los Feliz Boulevard, ☎ 323-661-6665. Woody's is a few blocks from the park, handy to both Crystal Spings Road in the park and the Los Angeles River bike path.

An easy ride follows **Crystal Springs Drive** (begin at the park entrance at Los Feliz, if you get bikes at Woody's). It's eight miles for the entire round-trip, with light grades. You will pass the mini-railroad on your right, and later the Visitor's Center/Ranger Station. Where Griffith Park Drive splits off to the left, continue on Crystal Springs past the picnic grounds and between the golf courses. At the zoo go straight on Zoo Drive (a bike path also loops around the parking lot) and continue to Travel Town, with big locomotives and small live steam trains. Return to the starting point by the same route.

A moderate ride follows the same path as above to **Griffith Park Drive** (one mile from start). There is a short, steep upgrade, then you go left around the merry-go-round and past Cedar Tree Picnic Grounds. At the junction beyond the picnic area, bear left and continue by the golf course. Past the driving range the road goes uphill to

Hollywood

the Mineral Wells Picnic Area (2.7 miles); for about a half-mile there is an uphill grind, then the road goes downhill past Mt. Hollywood Drive to Travel Town (4.2 miles). Follow Zoo Drive and Crystal Springs Drive back to the starting point.

Bird Sanctuary

Located in a wooded canyon with a stream, this sanctuary is home to many species of indigenous birds. Open daily, 10am-5pm. The Bird Sanctuary is off Vermont Canyon Road.

Bronson Caves

Several TV series, including *The Lone Ranger*, *Gunsmoke*, *Bonanza*, and *Have Gun, Will Travel*, have been shot here, along with innumerable Westerns, Easterns, Southerns and everything else. You don't use the regular park entrances to get here. Drive up Canyon Drive (four blocks east of Beachwood Drive) to the park entrance (the Azalea Garden is to the left). There is a white gate to the right of the last parking lot; walk up about a quarter-mile on the trail. The caves are shown as "Rock Quarry" on some maps.

> ### ⚡ SAFETY TIP
>
> Griffith Park is exceptionally well patrolled and as safe as any park; it has a much lower crime rate than many. However, while it is perfectly all right to drive to the Greek Theatre after dark, exploring the park on foot at night is not advisable.

 ## Fern Dell

This is a popular place for mothers to bring children, and for couples with romance in mind. Ferns and tropical plants grow, a brook babbles, there's cool shade on a hot day, a place to picnic. It's by the **Western Avenue** entrance to the park.

Golf & Tennis

Wilson/Harding Golf Course, 18-hole, par 72. Clubhouse, locker room, rental clubs, hand and electric carts, pro shop, driving range; the restaurant serves breakfast, lunch and dinner. ☎ 323-663-2555.

Los Feliz Municipal Golf Course, Nine holes; par 27. Club rental, coffee shop. ☎ 323-663-7758.

Roosevelt Municipal Golf Course, Nine holes; par 33. ☎ 323-665-2011.

Griffith Park Drive tennis courts are free; after one set, make way for the next players. Located at Park Center, by the merry-go-round.

There is a snack stand by Griffith-Riverside Tennis Courts.

Griffith-Riverside, across Los Feliz Boulevard from Los Feliz-Riverside park entrance. Open during daylight hours; ☎ 323-913-4688 for hourly fees and reservations.

Griffith-Vermont courts are free before 5 and after 7pm; from 5 to 7pm the fee is $6 per hour. Make reservations the same day. Drive up Vermont Avenue into park, turn right onto Los Feliz and left on Commonwealth Drive. The courts are across from the Greek Theatre; parking is free. ☎ 323-664-3521.

Horseback Riding

The park has three pony tracks for children, from infants to pre-teens (riders must weigh less than 100 pounds). The tracks are open Tuesday-Sunday, 10am-4:30pm; cost is $1.50. Find them at Crystal Springs Drive, off Los Feliz near Riverside Drive; ☎ 323-664-3266.

Horses and guided trail rides are available at several locations; a few are listed below.

Los Angeles Equestrian Center, livery and rental stables, riding academy, indoor and outdoor show rings. Trail rides are available daily, 8am-4pm. Children must be at least six years old and four feet tall; adult maximum weight is 220 pounds. Rides are $20 per person for an hour, $30 for 1½ hours, $35 for two hours, $40 for the sunset ride; cash only. 480 Riverside Drive, Burbank, ☎ 818-840-8401.

Bar S Stables, open Monday-Friday, 8am-4pm; Saturday and Sunday, 8am-4:30pm. A one-hour ride is $15 for adults, $12 for children under 13; a two-hour ride is $25 for adults, $20 for children; additional hours are $13. 1850 Riverside Drive, Glendale, ☎ 818-242-8443.

Riders may walk, trot or canter horses; they must remain on marked trails, fire and patrol roads.

J.P. Stables, open daily, 7:30am-6pm; the cost is $15 for one hour, $10 for additional hours. 1914 Mariposa Street, Burbank, ☎ 818-843-9890.

Sunset Ranch Hollywood Stables, open daily, 9am-5pm; cost is $15 for one hour, $10 for additional hours. A popular event is their 10-mile trail ride into the park on Friday evenings. Reservations are not accepted; it's on a first-come, first-served basis. The ride sets off between 5:30 and 6pm; you need to get there by 4:30 or so to get a horse. The group stops at a honky-tonk Mexican restaurant on the other side of the park for dinner; cost is $40, plus dinner. Sunset Ranch also offers a lunch ride Monday-Thursday at 10am, for $40. 3400 North Beachwood Drive, Hollywood, ☎ 323-464-9612, www.sunsetranchhollywood.com.

Hiking

From easy lower slopes and chaparral-covered foothills to densely forested valleys – any place you walk you can be totally away from civilization within minutes. There are 53 miles of hiking trails, and with the exclusive Los Feliz area backing up to the park you are likely to pass well-known actors on the trails. Open fires and smoking are not allowed. For more information about trails in Griffith Park, ☎ 323-913-4688.

Bronson Caves are an easy half-mile round-trip – a walk rather than a real hike. Drive up Canyon Drive or Bronson Avenue (both go north off Franklin Avenue and then join). Continue about a mile into hilly Griffith Park. Use the lot by the picnic area or at the road's end. On the east side of Canyon Drive look for a white gate and a park sign marked "49"; take the fire road south to the caves where so many films have been shot.

Dante's View is a moderate hike, about four miles. Take Fern Dell Drive, just east of the end of Western Avenue, off Los Feliz. The main parking area is on the left about a half-mile into the park. Take the Mt. Hollywood Trail along Western Canyon for a half-mile, then upward and eastward to a view point. Cross the road leading to the closed Observatory, resume climbing on the trail. At a junction of trails bear right to Dante's View, 2.5 miles from the start. The area was cultivated over a period of years by a hiker who wanted to improve on nature.

Griffith Park has elevations up to 1,625 feet.

For the **Mt. Hollywood** trail, continue on from Dante's View by taking the Hogback Trail west a short distance to the continuation of the Mt. Hollywood Trail; go right and uphill to the highest point in the park. On your return keep on straight, crossing Hogback Trail, and you will come to Captain's Roost, a small picnic area with a water fountain. Continue on to the trail junction where you turned off to Dante's View on the way up, and go back down the original trail.

Sierra Club hikes take place year-round. The club meets in the upper parking lot by the merry-go-round on Tuesday, Wednesday and Thursday at 7pm; they occasionally meet on other days, or for weekend or moonlight walks. Drawback: sometimes big crowds show up, as many as 100, a bit much for a decent hike. Free. ☎ 323-387-4287.

Hollywood

Los Angeles Zoo

The most popular attraction after the chimpanzees, which have finally gotten out of cages and into a more natural setting, is the **Komodo dragon** area, since Phil Bronstein, editor of the *San Francisco Chronicle* and Sharon Stone's husband, stuck his bare foot into one's mouth. The zoo is open daily, 10am-5pm, except for Christmas Day. Admission is $8.25 for ages 12 and up; $3.25 for ages two-12; $5.25 for seniors (65+). Rentals are available for strollers ($7), wheelchairs ($6), and electric wheelchairs ($25). Parking is free. The fare for the **Safari Shuttle Tram**, which runs around the perimeter of the zoo (with stops), is $3.75 for ages 12 and up; $1.75 for children under 12; and

$1 for seniors. 5333 Zoo Drive; ☎ 323-644-6400, www.la-zoo.org.

Merry-Go-Round

A lovingly maintained 1926 wooden carousel with hand-carved horses goes 'round and 'round to the tunes of a brassy band organ. This is where the climactic scene of *Strangers on a Train* was filmed. Cost is $1 per ride, 11am-5pm; open daily in summer; Friday, Saturday and Sunday in winter. ☎ 323-665-3051. Crystal Springs Drive, in the northeast section of the park.

Miniature Train Rides

The **GP&S Railroad** (Griffith Park & Southern) is very near the park entrance off Los Feliz near Riverside Drive. Kids love this (as do some adults). Daily, 1pm to 5pm; adults, $2; children, $1.50; seniors, $1.25. Free parking. ☎ 323-664-6903.

Picnics

Picnicking is allowed practically everywhere in Griffith Park, but if you want a barbecue grill and tables try one of these designated spots.

Fast food stands are located in the park near the major attractions.

There are a few tables in the small area near the Bird Sanctuary off Vermont Canyon Road. At **Cedar Tree**, near the merry-go-round, there is a big, grassy area. **Crystal Springs**, near the Ranger Station, is the only place reservations are needed; it is a favorite area for large groups. **Fern Dell** is very accessible by car – Western Avenue crosses Los Feliz and becomes Fern Dell Drive; you can park along the street and walk over the stream to a picnic table. **Mineral Wells**, off Griffith Park Drive near Harding Golf Course and driving range, is near the zoo and gets crowded on weekends. **Old Zoo Road** picnic area is secluded and peaceful; it's off Griffith Park Drive, with tables around obsolete animal cages from the old zoo. **Park Center**, near the Merry-Go-Round, has picnic tables, playground equipment and free tennis courts. **Pecan Grove** is past the zoo toward Travel Town.

Ice cream trucks and other food vendors roam through the picnic areas, mostly on weekends.

☞ DID YOU KNOW?

During the 1970s, the Cedar Tree picnic area was the site of "Love- Ins," which were attended by thousands every Sunday.

Travel Town Transportation Museum

Travel Town is on the site of a regular campsite along the Anza Trail, founded in 1776.

This is a train museum with a large collection of steam locomotives, passenger cars, box cars, cabooses and retired streetcar trolleys. Inside the museum building is a very large, wonderfully detailed and working small-scale model train layout. Outside is a large-scale model train on a track for children and adults to ride on. The red barn, first seen as a set in Walt Disney's feature film *So Dear to My Heart*, was moved here from Disney's Holmby Hills home. Large-scale model railroading was his hobby – he had his own one-eighth-scale, steam-powered train in his backyard.

Open Monday-Friday, 10am-4pm; Saturday and Sunday, 10am-5pm. General admission is free; the model train ride is $1.75. 5200 West Zoo Drive (off Forest Lawn Drive), ☎ 323-662-5874, www.cityofla.org/RAP/grifmet/tt.

Hollywood

MARATHON, ANYONE?

The **Jimmy Stewart Marathon** is run every April to benefit St. John's Child and Family Development Center. It is named for the late Hollywood star who was its original host. Celebrities and leading runners participate; Robert Wagner co-hosted with Olympic champion Jackie Joyner-Kersee in 2001. The team relay marathon usually has 35,000 runners in 20 divisions; each participant runs 5.2 miles before passing the baton. In addition to that event, there is a Celebrity Race, with usually a bunch of movie and TV stars participating. There are a variety of performers on stages, with a petting zoo and face-painting for kids. For more info, ☎ 310-829-8968, www.st-johns.org.

 A(te> Da>k

What do you feel like doing tonight?
I don't know, Ange. What do you feel like doing?
    – Ernest Borgnine, Joe Mantell, *Marty*

Hollywood bustles all day long, but when it gets dark it is like an iron curtain clangs down. We drove up Hollywood Boulevard one night, headed for a Dramatists Guild event at the Stella Adler Theatre. There was a crowd on the sidewalk in front of the Pantages Theatre, east of Vine, because *The Lion King* was playing. Up at the other end, past Highland, there were masses of fans behind police barricades on the sidewalks in front of the Chinese Theatre and the El Capitan across the street, all screaming at the stretch limos arriving for some Grammy event. The whole length in between was like some dour post-apocalypse movie. Solid iron gates were pulled down in front of most of the shops, others had accordion grates pulled across the front windows. An occasional lonely pedestrian walked by, about one to a block. Yet the traffic crawled, maddeningly slow. A bummer.

TIP

If you are going for a stroll anywhere in Hollywood, you will usually be happier if you do it in the daytime.

Bars

★★ MICELI'S
1646 North Las Palmas Avenue
☎ 323-466-3430

Old-fashioned Italian restaurant, celebrities still drop in. Jazz pianists, big bands occasionally, but fun when they are here. Phone. (See Miceli's restaurant, page 125.)

Cabaret

THE CINEGRILL
Hollywood Roosevelt Hotel
7000 Hollywood Boulevard
☎ 323-466-7000

Hands-down best cabaret in Los Angeles. Call to see what's on. Cover $10-$25, two-drink minimum, over 21.

Comedy

ACME COMEDY THEATRE
135 North La Brea Avenue
☎ 323-525-0202

Proscenium theater space, no booze, all ages, valet parking. There's a different show every night, and ticket prices vary; call ahead.

Hollywood

THE GROUNDLINGS THEATRE

7307 Melrose Avenue
☎ 323-934-9700
www.groundlings.com

Famous improv group. No booze, but not recommended for those under 17. Thursday-Sunday, times of shows vary; ticket prices are uually between $11.50-$18.

THE IMPROVISATION

8162 Melrose Avenue
☎ 323-651-2583
www.improv.com

This is where "The Improv" show that was formerly on TV originated. It's the place to see well-known comics, many who started here and became stars, as well as unknown talent. Open every night. Full bar, two-drink minimum, over 18, $10-$15.

FILM GLOSSARY

Three-Camera Comedy – A situation comedy performed in front of a live audience on a sound stage, with three cameras filming simultaneously. Madelyn Davis, who with Bob Carroll Jr. wrote all the *I Love Lucy* shows, tells us the technique was developed by Desi Arnaz so they could do the show on film out here and not have to move back to New York to do it live there.

POETRY, ANYONE?

Greenway Court Theatre, 544 North Fairfax Avenue, ☎ 323-655-7679, has Da' Poetry Lounge, Tuesdays, 9pm to midnight. Free.

Clubs

Oddly, until the last few years Hollywood has never been a prime venue for nightclubs. Even in its heyday the only one of note was the Montmartre Café on the second floor at 6753-63 Hollywood Boulevard (just east of Highland, north side; the Stella Adler Theatre is in there now), where Joan Crawford was discovered, and where Rudolph Valentino and Clara Bow used to shake it at tea dances in the '20s.

People often complain it is impossible to get into the really popular clubs, unless you are 1) a celebrity, 2) a handsome, sexy and hiply dressed Gen-X guy, or 3) a gorgeous young thing who wears a size 2. That is true, but there is one other way: have the concierge at your hotel make you a dinner reservation there. Never fails. If you don't have access to a concierge, phone and do it yourself several days ahead. It has to be a dinner reservation; a club reservation by itself won't work.

These days there is quite a bit of club action in these parts, but things change overnight, so call to be sure the joint is still in business.

DEEP
1707 Vine Street
☎ 323-462-1144
Rock/Pop

At the moment this is the hottest place in town, even though it is located improbably at Hollywood and Vine. Deep was inspired, so they say, by the risqué nightclubs of Amsterdam. You come here expecting excess and hedonism, hoping for titillation and voyeurism. Good luck.

There is no sign on the door but those in the know, such as Russell Crowe, Heidi Fleiss, Hugh Hefner (who brings a half-dozen bunnies along), Helen Hunt, Nicole Kidman and more make this scene (as they say). When President Bush's two daughters were in town, this is where they were brought by friends (with Secret Service tagging along).

The main room is for dinner. Comely dancers in stylishly shredded lingerie groove in glass boxes above and behind the bar. The back room is the people dance room, a mirror-enclosed space with a glass cube above the ceiling where a *ménage à trois* of professional dancers move seductively. Admittance is by a strict guest list.

🎬 FILM GLOSSARY

Writers Guild of America (WGA) – The writers' union, which negotiates minimum payments for screenplays and teleplays with the studios, and has final say over screen credits. Also handles residuals for writers.

★★ THE DERBY
4500 Los Feliz Boulevard
☎ 323-663-8979
www.the-derby.com
Swing and rockabilly

Whoopi Goldberg held her birthday bash in the Derby.

There are those who claim that the whole national return to swing dancing started here, when this place was re-opened as The Derby in 1993. Before that it had been an offshoot Brown Derby, and was originally built in the 1920s by Cecil B. De Mille. Among early habitues of the '90s Derby were the writer and director of the low-budget 1996 movie, *Swingers,* who said this place was the genesis of the film. Now, TV shows host parties in the club and some who hone their skills here are regularly hired to appear in films, television shows and ads. You see all generations here, from Matt Dillon to Mitzi Gaynor.

CATALINA BAR & GRILL
1640 North Cahuenga Boulevard
☎ 323-466-2210
www.catalinajazzclub.com
Pure jazz

This is perhaps the city's premier jazz club. Major figures perform here and customers come to listen, not dance. Good sight lines, and service is discreet while performers are playing. Food is good, with an emphasis on pasta and seafood. Open Tuesday-Saturday, with shows at 8:30pm

and 10:30pm; and Sunday, 7pm and 9pm. Full bar. Cover
$10-$20. All ages.

★★ FARFALLA'S BAR F2

143 North La Brea Avenue
☎ 323-938-2504
Jazz, blues, cabaret, hip-hop – pick a night

At street level is a very good Italian restaurant. Upstairs
is Bar F2, a showcase for music, comedy and singers, depending on the night of the week. Saturday is usually
funky jazz, Wednesday is comedy, Friday is sometimes a
surf rock group, other times a blues singer. Thursday is
the biggest night, when the cabaret chanteuse Morganne
appears; that is when celebrities like Jim Carrey and Mira
Sorvino show up. On Tuesdays, the hip-hop club Heat
takes over both upstairs and downstairs, with live entertainment and DJs spinning underground rap. This place
has a history. It used to be the Swanee Inn, where the King
Cole Trio played in its early days (they started out across
the street at the smaller Pirates Den). All nights free, except Tuesday. Call for schedule.

*Farfalla
means "but-
terfly" in
Italian.*

HOLLYWOOD ATHLETIC CLUB

6525 Sunset Boulevard (entrance on Schrader)
☎ 323-462-6262 (recorded information)

When it is not being used at night as a film location or for
premier or wrap parties (it was the site of the official Madonna World Tour party in September 2001 when she did
Drowned World in Los Angeles), the Hollywood Athletic
Club is used by outside promoters as a popular venue as a
nightclub. Check the *Los Angeles Times Calendar* section
or *LA Weekly* to see what is happening, or phone.

KNITTING FACTORY

7021 Hollywood Boulevard
☎ 323-463-0204
www.knittingfactory.com/kfla
Jazz and Rock

Different nights, different live groups. A big place with a
Main Stage for well-known bands, the smaller AfterKnit
Lounge for lesser-knowns. Cover at both is $20 for men, $7

for women, all ages. Bar and restaurant open daily, 11am-2am. Very popular.

★★ SUNSET ROOM
1430 Cahuenga Boulevard
☎ 323-463-0004
Rock

Sunset Room is very difficult to get in to, unless you use your concierge – then it is easy. And it's a place that is worth your while to come see and participate in the action. Good food, beautiful people and celebrities are common. Friday and Saturday nights are the biggies – the street is clogged with late-model BMWs and SUVs impatiently waiting for the valet parkers to take over. Then there is the line hoping to get past the velvet ropes and the intimidating guy with the clipboard at the door. Inside with the hip clientele are often hip celebs, the likes of Val Kilmer, et al. Book dinner through the concierge at your hotel, or phone at least several days in advance for dinner reservations.

*California license plate **A1ANA2** belonged to Lawrence Welk. (Get it? "A-one and a-two.")*

★ TIP

In the Sunset Room, expect to mingle with the same 20s- and 30-types who watch *Sex and the City*.

Flamenco

CAVA RESTAURANT
8384 West Third Street
☎ 323-658-8898

This is not strictly in Hollywood, as it is south of Melrose and Beverly, between Fairfax and La Cienega. There are shows on Wednesdays, at 8:30 and 10pm.

EL CID SHOW RESTAURANT
4212 Sunset Boulevard
☎ 323-668-0318
www.elcid-ca.com

This is in East Hollywood, east of Vermont and Virgil. One-hour shows Wednesdays, 8pm; Thursdays and Sundays, 8 and 10pm; Fridays and Saturdays, 8pm, 10pm and midnight.

For Teenagers

ONE SEVEN
Hollywood & Highland
6801 Hollywood Blvd.
☎ 323-461-1517

This fairly new spot is in the Hollywood & Highland complex, and caters to 15- to 20-year-olds on weekends. It has a big dance floor and a stage, but so far has featured mostly DJs. The look is sleek and posh with the usual bright lights, video spheres and projection screens, a light show and a deafening sound system – just what everyone wants. Girls (who woefully outnumber boys so far) dress in standard-issue capri pants and navel-baring tops and stay on the lookout for the talent scouts (someone is spreading tales of starlet discoveries). Open Friday, Saturday and before school holidays, 8pm-1:30am. The $20 cover charge is a little steep.

Theaters

JOHN ANSON FORD AMPHITHEATRE
2580 Cahuenga Boulevard
☎ 323-461-3673

A natural amphitheater on the east side of the Hollywood Freeway as it goes through Cahuenga Pass out of Hollywood. There is also a smaller theater, Inside the Ford. They present chamber music, ballet, jazz, and plays.

Hollywood

LOS ANGELES CITY COLLEGE
THEATRE ACADEMY
855 North Vermont Avenue
Los Angeles, CA 90026
☎ 323-953-4000

LACC has been Los Angeles' premier training institution
for actors for 70 years. Performances are open to the public at low prices, with high theatrical quality. Phone or
write for the season's program.

SILENT MOVIE THEATRE
611 North Fairfax Boulevard (south of Melrose Avenue)
☎ 323-655-2520
www.silentmovietheatre.com

The Silent Movie Theatre is the only fully operational cinema in the US that is still showing silent movies. If you
can remember seeing John Gilbert in *The Big Parade* (*The
New York Times*' Best Picture, 1925), or the wonderful
Janet Gaynor in *Seventh Heaven* (Best Actress, first Academy Award, 1927), or Mary Pickford, Douglas Fairbanks,
Louise Brooks, Charlie Chaplin or W.C. Fields, you should
visit the theater out of nostalgia. Anyone younger than
that should go just to see what all the shouting was about,
and why many people were sorry when movies started
talking out loud and a fantastic art form was left behind.
Shows are Friday and Saturday at 8pm; Sunday at 1, 4
and 8pm.

 # Hollywood A to Z

Medical Services

Childrens' Hospital, 4650 Sunset Boulevard, ☎ 323-
876-4000.

Hollywood Presbyterian Hospital, 1310 North Vermont Avenue, ☎ 323-764-9900.

Kaiser Permanente Hospital, 4871 Sunset Boulevard,
☎ 323-455-7778.

Outreach Services

Gay & Lesbian Services Center, 1245 North Highland Avenue, ☎ 323-698-2121.

Police & Fire

Hollywood Police, 1310 Cahuenga Avenue, ☎ 323-233-8888; emergency, 911.

Post Offices

Hollywood Main Station, 1615 Wilcox Avenue (at Fountain), ☎ 323-464-2355.

Los Feliz Station, 1825 N. Vermont Avenue, ☎ 800-275-8777.

Santa Monica Boulevard Branch, 6457 Santa Monica Boulevard, ☎ 800-275-8777.

Visitor Information

Hollywood Entertainment District, 6425 Hollywood Boulevard, Suite 401, Hollywood 90028, ☎ 323-463-6767, www.hollywoodbid.org. Write for a map, information and coupons for restaurants and shops. See map, photos and information at their Web site.

Hollywood Chamber of Commerce, 7018 Hollywood Boulevard, Hollywood 90028, ☎ 323-469-8311, www.hollywoodcoc.com. Write, call or stop in for map and list of stars on the Walk of Fame.

Hollywood

West Hollywood

As long as they have sidewalks, you have a job.
     — Joan Blondell to Claire Dodd, *Footlight Parade*

Overview

Once upon a time there were Hollywood and West Los Angeles, both part of the City of Los Angeles, and there was Beverly Hills. Squeezed in between those heavyweights was a slice of leftover land the cities hadn't claimed so it belonged to LA County. Because it was long and thin the whole piece was called the County Strip, and the section of the boulevard running along the northern edge is called the Sunset Strip.

At its eastern end, the city of West Hollywood is only two blocks wide, from Fountain Boulevard to Romaine Avenue. Santa Monica Boulevard, the city's "main street," runs between them from La Brea Avenue (West Hollywood's eastern border), to the center of town at La Cienega Boulevard. At that point Santa Monica Boulevard turns south, and the road that was Santa Monica becomes Holloway Drive for a few blocks before merging with Sunset Boulevard.

Marilyn Monroe and Shelley Winters shared an apartment at 8573 Holloway Drive in 1951.

Both Sunset and Santa Monica boulevards continue west to Doheny Drive, where they cross into Beverly Hills. West Hollywood widens as you go west, stretching southward from Sunset Boulevard in the foothills of the Hollywood Hills to Beverly Boulevard, which borders the City of Los Angeles in the flatlands.

We must mention hipness, which is in the psyche of the beholder. Hollywood has it in limited quantities these days, only in a few clubs competing in the "who's hippest?" race and some shops on Melrose. Beverly Hills is too self conscious to be hip, Malibu is too private to be anything and Culver City never had it. But West Hollywood exudes hip from La Brea to Doheny without even trying. That is precisely why it's hip.

History

The 19th Century

As with everything around here, this land was originally home to the Gabrieleno Indians. Mexico gave it to Don Antonio José Rocha in 1828 as part of the Rancho La Brea land grant. By the late 1800s the land was subdivided and sold to newly arrived settlers. In 1898 Moses Sherman, who wanted his Pacific Railway Co. to reach out from downtown Los Angeles to Santa Monica and the ocean, built rail yards at what is now San Vicente Boulevard and Melrose Avenue. There's a great big glass building called The Blue Whale standing there now – you can't miss it.

The 20th Century

Historic Route 66 runs through the middle of West Hollywood as Santa Monica Boulevard.

The rail yard was called Sherman's Station, and railroad workers' homes and stores sprang up around it. Pretty soon it was known as the town of Sherman. By the 1920s it had really begun to build up, especially with the advent of the movie studios, and it was known by then as West Hollywood. It remained unincorporated, and with little government oversight and the advent of prohibition it became a haven for speakeasies and assorted forms of decadence. Glamour was added in the '30s when supper clubs along Sunset Boulevard were the resorts of Hollywood's elite.

Bringing It Up to Date

The famed Sunset Strip clubs like Trocadero and the Mocambo faded, but in the 1970s a different type of club,

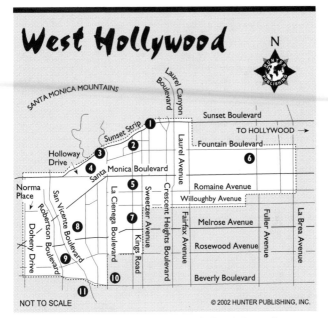

West Hollywood

N

1. Château Marmont, Mondrian, Standard and Argyle Hotels
2. William S. Hart Park
3. Tiffany Theatre
4. Sunset Plaza; Sunset Strip
5. Kings Road Park
6. Plummer Park
7. Schindler Studio & Residence
8. Pacific Design Center; Avenues of Art & Design
9. West Hollywood Park
10. Coronet Theatre
11. Cedars-Sinai Medical Center; Beverly Center Mall

- - - - - West Hollywood boundary

NOT TO SCALE   © 2002 HUNTER PUBLISHING, INC.

epitomized by Whisky A Go-Go and the Roxy, was created here. The interior design and decorating business found a home near Beverly and Robertson boulevards and soon the area became internationally known as a design center.

By the 1970s, West Hollywood had attracted large numbers of gays and lesbians, who historically have made their way to major urban areas to find safety in numbers; there was also a large senior citizen population. In the early 1980s the gays were fighting the homophobia of the Sheriff's Department, and the seniors felt vulnerable to the county's threat to end rent control. The two groups

West Hollywood

joined hands and overwhelmingly voted to incorporate as West Hollywood in 1984.

The new city signed a contract with the LA County Sheriff's Department to continue providing law enforcement services, but now that they answer to West Hollywood's City Council, deputies' attitudes toward gays have changed considerably. In fact, many gays are now Sheriff's Deputies. And senior residents feel considerably safer; new laws make it very difficult to arbitrarily evict a senior from an apartment.

PET LOVERS, TAKE NOTE

You are not your pet's "owner" in West Hollywood, although that doesn't mean your pet necessarily owns you, either. The City Council voted last year to amend the municipal code to remove all references to "pet owner." From now on those persons will officially be called "pet guardians." Mayor Jeffrey Prang said the resolution is aimed at reminding those with pets that animals have rights, too. The kindhearted city previously affirmed the rights of renters to have pets, and created a "no-kill" animal shelter.

Getting Here

From LAX

By Car

From the airport, take the San Diego Freeway (405) north to the Sunset Boulevard off-ramp; then go right (east) to Hollywood (about seven miles).

By Bus

Take the free shuttle to Lot C, then transfer to Metro Bus #220, which takes you to Santa Monica and San Vicente boulevards. Fare is $1.35. Phone ☎ 800-COMMUTE (266-6883).

By Shuttle

The waiting area is on the island in front of each terminal. Fare for one passenger is $22; for two passengers, $31. Try **Prime Time Shuttle**, ☎ 800-262-7433, www.primetime-shuttle.com; or **Super Shuttle**, ☎ 323-775-6600 or 310-782-6600, www.supershuttle.com.

By Taxi

The fare from the airport to West Hollywood is $24, plus a $2.50 airport fee.

> ### ★ TIP
>
> West Hollywood is within easy reach of both Los Angeles International and Burbank airports. LAX is served by international, national and commuter airlines and lies 15 miles southwest of town. Burbank is served by national and commuter lines and lies 10 miles to the north.

Getting Around

By Car

Driving around this area is easy, but parking is hard. West Hollywood was built up in the 1920s, and streets are narrow, especially those north of Santa Monica Boulevard that rise into the hills. There is not enough off-street parking space for current needs; most spaces are on-street and metered. Some neighborhoods, to ensure enough parking space for their own residents, have restricted parking zones at certain times. When parking on a residential

Telephone area codes for West Hollywood are easy to remember: 323 east of La Cienega Boulevard, 310 west of La Cienega.

West Hollywood

street, be sure to read the signs regarding times permitted.

By Bus & Shuttle

The legendary Sunset Strip is only 1.6 miles long, from Hollywood's Laurel Canyon Boulevard (Laurel Avenue in West Hollywood) to Doheny Drive.

West Hollywood's shopping areas of Santa Monica Boulevard, Sunset Boulevard and the design district are very walkable. And, to make things even easier, the CityLine shuttle bus loops around town on weekdays between 9am and 4pm, making frequent stops. There are four buses running continuously on two routes, starting at La Brea and Fountain on the east end of town, and cruising Santa Monica Boulevard and the side streets, ending at Beverly Center (the shopping mall) and Cedars-Sinai Medical Center; the fare is 50¢. Get a map of CityLine bus routes by contacting the West Hollywood Chamber of Commerce, ☎ 323-650-2688, www.wehochamber.org, or write or drop in at their office, 8278½ Santa Monica Boulevard, West Hollywood, CA 90046.

By Taxi

Fares are $1.90 to start the meter, then 30¢ for each tenth of a mile.

Beverly Hills Cab . . . . ☎ 310-273-6611
Checker Cab . . . . ☎ 800-696-4919
Independent Taxi Co. . . . . ☎ 800-521-8294
United Independent Taxi . . . . ☎ 800-411-0303

⚠ WARNING!

There are an estimated 2,000 "bandit cabs" on the west side of town. Some unscrupulous drivers buy an old taxi-cab, slap a fake city logo on the door and install a black-market meter set at any mileage rate they choose, and go into business. Be sure the cab you get into has an official seal; this assures it has passed strict inspections and gets regular safety checks, has doors that lock, air conditioning, proof of insurance and a meter that has been certified by the state. The driver must also understand English, which often comes in handy.

Who Lives Here?

Despite the fact that West Hollywood is full of people working at the studios, not many are celebrities. Loretta Young lived here, at 1308 North Flores Street near De-Longpre Avenue, early in her career (this section of Flores is four blocks east of La Cienega, north of Fountain Avenue; it doesn't go through to Sunset). Marilyn Monroe, early in her career, lived just two blocks east at 1301 Harper.

West Hollywood is one mile from Hollywood and one mile from Beverly Hills.

☞ DID YOU KNOW?

Lots of DINKs live here in West Hollywood: that's Dual Income, No Kids.

Liberace lived in the hills at 8433 Harold Way (a twisting street that runs between Kings and Queens roads a couple of blocks uphill from Sunset) during the 1960s and '70s. He wanted to make a museum out of the big mansion, but the neighbors understandably complained. Dorothy Parker lived at the stucco bungalow at 8983 Norma Place (east of Doheny between Sunset and Santa Monica) in the

West Hollywood

The boutiques and restaurants on the north side of Sunset Boulevard are in West Hollywood, but the houses in the hills directly above them are in Hollywood.

1960s while she was writing screenplays. The short little street was named after actress Norma Talmadge. For those either very young or exceedingly forgetful, Dorothy Parker wrote the screenplays for *A Star Is Born* (both the 1937 and 1954 versions) and for Hitchcock's *Saboteur*, and the still-haunting 1930s short story *Big Blond*.

Quite a few celebrities have homes just above Sunset Boulevard in the hills – but that is in Hollywood. There are few residing within West Hollywood.

> ☞ **DID YOU KNOW?**
>
> Sammy Glick, anti-hero of Budd Shulberg's classic Hollywood novel *What Makes Sammy Run?*, supposedly lived at 1416 Havenhurst Drive, near Sunset. Real-life stars who did live there include Carole Lombard, Dick Powell, and, more recently, Julia Roberts.

On Location

Quite a few films are shot here; West Hollywood even has its own Film Office where the studios go to get permission to clutter up the streets. A scene from *Annie Hall* was shot at 8301 Sunset Boulevard in an organic foods restaurant (then it was called the Source; now it is Cajun Bistro). Other films (and some of their West Hollywood locations) include *The Big Lebowski*, *Bowfinger*, *Circuit*, *Color of Night*, *Dr. Doolittle 2*, *L.A. Confidential* (the Formosa Café), *The Majestic*, *Night at the Roxbury* (Crunch Gym), *Timecode* (Book Soup), and *Living Dangerously*.

Best Places to Stay

The accommodations price scale can be found on page 39.

Several good, large hotels on Sunset Boulevard are favored by celebrities. Rock stars tend to flock together. A couple of places have legendary histories, and are still going strong. Below Sunset are several smaller, boutique hotels that have their own fans. In all, West Hollywood is a good place for hotels, with a nice range of choices.

Hotels

★★ THE ARGYLE
8358 Sunset Boulevard
West Hollywood, CA 90069
☎ 323-654-7100, 800-225-2637, fax 323-654-9287
www.argylehotel.com
Expensive-Deluxe

The Argyle is built on a hill; only 11 of its 15 stories can be seen from Sunset Boulevard.

This is real style, and has been since it opened in 1931 as The Sunset Tower, a luxury apartment building. At 15 stories it was always a spectacular sight with its elegant silver and gray façade. Now there are higher buildings, but none nearly as striking as this one.

The Argyle, with its art deco elegance, represents all that Hollywood aspired to in the 1930s. Friezes above the front door and along the setbacks express a tangle of typical art deco designs mixed in with flora and fauna, mythological creatures, zeppelins and Adam and Eve. If you get down the hill to the underground garage, the sculpted panels over the entrance depict the radiator grille of a 1920s car.

The first literary mention of The Argyle was in Raymond Chandler's Farewell, My Lovely.

Those were the days when, at one time or another, Billie Burke, Clark Gable, Zsa Zsa Gabor, Paulette Goddard, Jean Harlow, Howard Hughes, Marilyn Monroe, Zazu Pitts, the mobster Bugsy Siegel (who was evicted for taking bets), Frank Sinatra, John Wayne and James Dean had apartments here.

If the building looks familiar that might be because you have seen it onscreen; the hotel has appeared in *Indecent Proposal*; *Murder, My Sweet*; *Wayne's World Part II*; *Pretty Woman* and *Strange Days*. One of the apartments was John Travolta's in *Get Shorty*; and a terrible story for a picture was pitched to Tim Robbins poolside in *The Player*.

The suites have art deco furnishings and floor-to-ceiling windows; some have steam showers, Jacuzzi tubs and terraces. Everything comes with plush robes and oversized marble baths; amenities include 24-hour room service and a 24-hour concierge. There is a health center, heated pool and the **fenix restaurant**. Both the hotel and the restaurant are still magnets for celebrities. You will know why when you see them.

★★ CHATEAU MARMONT

8221 Sunset Boulevard
West Hollywood, CA 90046
☎ 323-656-1010, 800-242-8328, fax 323-655-5311
Expensive-Deluxe

Talk about the spirit of Hollywood; Château Marmont *is* Hollywood. One curious touch here is that you will find a script on the dressing table in your room; there's a different one in every room. A writer who was staying there a few years ago noted that the script in his room was *Reality Bites*, starring Ethan Hawke; the next time he came in he shared the elevator with his next-door neighbor, who happened to be Ethan Hawke.

George Plimpton reported that he encountered Boris Karloff roaming the halls late at night when he stayed at Château Marmont.

The seven-story hotel on the hillside just above Sunset was built as an apartment house in 1929, modeled after the royal Château Amboise on the Loire River. But the timing was bad. When the Depression almost immediately depressed everything, it was sold and turned into a hotel. That is why all of the hotels' 50 rooms and suites, except the smaller, basic rooms, have full-size kitchens and dining rooms. Celebrities have enjoyed staying here from its very early days. And while the Garden of Allah (right across the street), Schwab's Drugstore (catty-corner) and Mocambo and the Trocadero (up Sunset a few blocks) are all gone, Château Marmont is going along better than ever.

Its past guests are a roster of Hollywood's stars – Orson Welles, Marilyn Monroe, Harry Belafonte, Robert Mitchum. A young, unknown Warren Beatty took the cheapest room and was locked out for not paying. Judy Garland spent an afternoon playing the piano in the lobby. Paul Newman and Joanne Woodward first met here. Greta Garbo, thinking no one recognized her, signed the register as Harriet Brown. Robert de Niro lived in the penthouse for two years, Boris Karloff lived here for five years, and Keanu Reeves doesn't even own a house in Los Angeles, he just stays at the Marmont. Billy Wilder conceived *Sunset Boulevard* here and *Butch Cassidy and the Sundance Kid* was written here.

The stories go on. James Dean climbed in the window of Bungalow 2 when Natalie Wood was waiting there for the first reading of *Rebel Without A Cause*. After Hedy Lamarr, nee Hedwug Keisler, was given her new name by Louis B. Mayer she checked into Château Marmont but signed the register Hedy Lamar – she didn't yet know how to spell it. In the loud 1980s, Jim Morrison of the Doors, high as a kite, jumped off the roof of a poolside cabana to see if he could really fly. He couldn't. Members of Led Zeppelin raced their Harley-Davidsons through the halls, the Eagles immortalized the hotel in *Hotel California*, Alice Cooper joined a pick-up football game – naked. And John Belushi died of a drug overdose in Bungalow 3.

A warning about rampant celebrities, though. Although the model-infested bar, which is actually next door, was for years a hangout mainly for music industry people (a lot of civilians come there now), the hotel itself is very private. The restaurant is small, and many guests eat in their rooms, taking advantage of those kitchens and the hotel's 24-hour room service. While casting directors often hold casting sessions here, with bit players hanging around the lobby awaiting their turn, the elevator goes directly from the garage to the upper floors, so many of those who stay here don't even go through the lobby.

After millions of dollars of refurbishing, the Marmont has changed enough to be considered up to date, but not enough to lose the romance it has always had. Each room and suite is unique. There is a pool, used only by guests and their guests; above the pool are bungalows on a hillside that is a tangle of fragrant eucalyptus, honeysuckle, midnight jasmine and rose bushes. Some rooms open onto a private colonnaded courtyard where guests may have breakfast and lunch; some look out on the gardens; others have wonderful panoramic views of the Strip and all of West L.A. Hotel amenities include 24-hour shoeshine service, and rental car delivery to the airport.

West Hollywood

HYATT WEST HOLLYWOOD
8401 Sunset Boulevard
West Hollywood, CA 90069
☎ 323-656-1234, 800-233-1234, fax 323-650-7024
www.hyatt.com
Moderate-Expensive

The Hyatt West Hollywood attracts a young clientele and tends to fill up during spring break and summer. Book early.

Rock 'n roll fans love this place because of its history. While the Sunset Strip was the center for luxurious nightclubs in the 1930s and '40s, those were replaced by the 1960s with clubs drawing a younger crowd. That is when Gene Autry opened Hotel Continental, which soon attracted the rock bands that were in town playing the clubs; Hyatt Hotels took it over a few years later. Guests included Led Zeppelin, The Doors, the Rolling Stones and Alice Cooper. Mostly, they were not quiet, retiring types, and the hotel was soon nicknamed The Riot House instead of Hyatt House. In the 1980s the hotel was a favorite of bands such as Guns N' Roses and Poison. The hotel appeared in the rock parody *Spinal Tap*, and still gets many of the bands playing the Strip as guests.

There is a rooftop pool, a fitness center, concierge service, currency exchange and postage stamps. Their restaurant, **Tramonto on the Strip**, serves continental food, and the Tramonto bar is a handy place for cocktails. South rooms overlooking Sunset Boulevard have a view over West Hollywood and beyond; rooms on the north side look up at the Hollywood Hills. Overnight self-parking is $15.

★★ LE MONTROSE SUITE HOTEL
900 Hammond Street
West Hollywood, CA 90069
☎ 310-855-1115, 800-637-7200, fax 310-657-9192
Expensive-Deluxe

See West Hollywood without polluting the atmosphere: borrow complimentary bicycles at Le Montrose.

Though there are 132 suites, this gem of a place in a quiet residential area two blocks downhill from Sunset and just east of Doheny seems smaller. The hotel, protecting privacy, is loath to name names, but we know it gets its share of celebrities; it is popular with those in the music business, and someone saw Ann-Margret there recently.

Each suite has a sunken living room with a fireplace; most suites have a kitchenette and all have a refrigerator. You can dine in your suite, or on the rooftop terrace where we attended a party and can attest to the great city views, or in the small **Library Restaurant**, open only to hotel guests and their friends. And there are suites designed for the handicapped.

Just a few of the extras that make Le Montrose appealing: 24-hour room service, roof-top heated salt-water pool and spa, lighted tennis court, private trainer and tennis pro, health club with sauna, in-suite massage therapy, on-site car rental, 24-hour concierge, multilingual staff, and currency exchange.

★★ MONDRIAN

8440 Sunset Boulevard
West Hollywood, CA 90069
☎ 323-650-8999, 800-525-8029, fax 323-650-5215
www.ianschragerhotels.com
Expensive-Deluxe

The two 40-foot high mahogany doors outside the Mondrian's front entrance are there strictly to impress you.

The Mondrian was built in 1958 as an apartment building on Sunset; it is part-way up into the foothills, so the south-facing rooms had a view. Now it is a hotel, but it still has the view. It was named after the early 20th-century Dutch painter and the exterior was originally painted like one of his artworks. The hotel was bought several years ago and refurbished by its new owners. Now it is stark white and people wonder why it is named the Mondrian.

The rooms (everything, including the lobby, is white-on-white) are good-sized and have kitchens, a legacy from the days when these were apartments. There is an extensive room service menu, with a large international selection for breakfast. Breakfast, lunch and dinner are also served in **Asia de Cuba Restaurant** (see page 202). **Seabar**, the lobby sushi bar, has a 42-foot-long alabaster table lit from below and is mostly a late night spot, as is the popular **Sky Bar**, which is not up on the roof, as you expect from the name, but off the lobby. The hotel, restaurant and bar are all places you might see celebrities; some, Kevin Costner and Robert Downey Jr., for instance, have stayed here. There is a gymnasium, personal trainers, steam room; massages and aerobics classes are available, as is a 24-

West Hollywood

hour concierge, handy for tickets and reservations for anywhere. The Mondrian delivers fruit and cookie platters to each room every afternoon.

★★ THE STANDARD
8300 Sunset Boulevard
West Hollywood, CA 90069
☎ 323-650-9090, fax 323-650-2820
www.standardhotel.com
Inexpensive-Moderate

You'll need plenty of quarters for the coin-operated telescopes on The Standard's pool deck so you can check out the views of Beverly Hills and West LA.

Where the Château Marmont definitely has more geriatric Hollywood in mind, The Standard (note that the name of the hotel is always shown upside-down, beginning with their sign) is positively made for Gen-X- and Gen-Y-ers. It is hard to believe this hotel was built in 1962 as the Thunderbird Motel and then became a retirement home. Now the coffee shop is open 24 hours and the maids don't vacuum the halls until noon – they might wake some of the guests if they made noise earlier than that. That is why check-in time isn't until 4pm.

As soon as we walked in we knew this place was anything but standard. The lobby has a conversation pit (much used for cocktails), with shag carpet that goes up the wall to cover the ceiling; a disc jockey's booth built into the registration desk; and a big vitrine behind the desk where you will usually see a performance artist (perhaps a nude woman asleep).

The Standard's coffee shop is usually crowded between 2 and 3am, after the other places on the Strip have closed.

The lobby also has video art projected onto a wall, a screening room, a barber/tattoo shop where Matt Dillon, Jennifer Lopez, Paula Abdul, Gloria Estefan, Rose McGowan and Roberto Benigni have dropped in to sample the $19 cuts ($14 for a buzz) and peruse the tiny, eccentric gift shop (we found bi-coastal clocks labeled "Here" and "There").

Ever since it opened, The Standard has been a place to be seen for those in one of Hollywood's three big industries – television, music and film.

The food in the coffee shop, which has no name, has been described as American coffee shop casual, but it is more than that. Where else can you get spicy crab noodles with grapefruit and avocado or a steak with red wine mushroom sauce at 4am? Not many places, even in Los Angeles.

And the sophisticated little wine list is surely un-coffee shop-like. The décor is sort of '60s-chic and there is a full bar, at which the 40 oz. Colt 45 is served in a brown paper bag. This is one of their little jokes – like the air conditioning settings in the rooms, labeled Blow, Hard, Harder and Stop. There's no art on the walls in the rooms, but the décor makes up for that – you'll see Andy Warhol-print curtains and silver beanbag chairs. Some rooms have inflatable sofas (maids carry air pumps on their carts), surfboard tables and ultrasuede floor pillows. The minibars are stocked with Gummi Bears, licorice, Vaseline and condoms wrapped like gold coins.

Andre Balazs, who also owns the Château Marmont a block east, created The Standard with the young, hipper-than-thou in mind. The interiors were done by film set designer Shawn Hausman (*The People vs. Larry Flynt)*, which is possibly why it all has the feeling it would have been perfectly at home in an *Austin Powers* film. Leonardo DiCaprio, Cameron Diaz and the Smashing Pumpkins' D'arcy Wretzky and James Iha are investors; DiCaprio is sometimes glimpsed out by the pool, sipping a drink and taking in the view.

There are five room categories at The Standard: Budget Sunset, Sunset, Medium, Large and X-Large.

The corner rooms with a southeast exposure are best; they face the pool and also have their own view of the city. Your fellow guests are likely to be actors who tend to spend more on their wardrobes than on their hotel rooms. But it is definitely a fun place.

★★ WYNDHAM BEL AGE HOTEL
1020 North San Vicente Boulevard (just off Sunset)
West Hollywood, CA 90069
☎ 310-854-1111, fax 310-854-0926
www.wyndham.com
Expensive-Deluxe

This hotel is located on the south side of the Strip at its highest point, with great views from private balconies out over the basin (ask for room on the south side of the building). This is a class act: all suites, many with the bedrooms up a half-level so you can see the views from bed, a world-class art collection on every wall. The hotel has two restaurants; **Diaghilev** is one of the most elegant in town (see page 203); the less formal **Club Brasserie** is lined

West Hollywood

with big windows for the view (it is also a top jazz club at night; see page 228).

For workouts, the Bel Age has a rooftop pool and fitness center.

The Bel Age is a popular place for celebrities who don't have a home in Los Angeles; we know of a star who is staying here for a week as we write this. The hotel is packed when the Los Angeles Film Critics Awards are held here each year, and it always fills up at Emmy and Oscar award times. Quite a few films and TV shows are shot here. The hotel doesn't give out names, but we know that the Bel Age was home to the character Dylan McKay on *Beverly Hills, 90210*, and countless scenes were shot here as guests watched. *Ally McBeal* filmed a few segments here. And the movie *Showtime*, released in 2002 with Robert Di Niro and Eddie Murphy, lit up the West Hollywood skyline for three nights when they shot on the rooftop.

▬ FILM GLOSSARY

Rifle Mike – a microphone that is aimed at an actor's mouth from a distance (also called a shotgun mike).

Best Places to Eat

The dining price scale can be found on page 42.

There are probably more good places to eat in West Hollywood than in downtown Los Angeles, Beverly Hills or Hollywood itself, though it is much smaller in size. Parking is the problem, which is why every place, even nondescript, casual Barney's Beanery, has valet parking.

Fine Dining

★★ ASIA DE CUBA AT MONDRIAN
Mondrian Hotel
8440 Sunset Boulevard
☎ 323-848-6000
Nouveau Asian-Latino
Very Expensive

The food is modeled on the cuisine that supposed developed in Cuba after many Chinese settled there in the early

1900s. It is not Chinese and not Cuban, but a very nouveau and tasty combination of both. The portions here are huge! The items listed as "shooters" on the menu, probably so-called because they are served in small glasses, are really appetizers. The "appetizers" are meals. The "entrées" are feasts. Recently the two of us ordered one appetizer and one entrée and staggered home under a load of leftover goodies. Whether your party is two, three or four, we suggest you start with a couple of shooters to go along with drinks, then order one appetizer for the table before going any further.

Asia de Cuba serves breakfast, lunch and dinner; eating out on the terrace by the hotel's pool is most popular in any kind of decent weather because of the view (the Mondrian is up on the hilly part of Sunset with nothing in the way to block the sight of West Hollywood and beyond). We also like the dining room, with its white on white décor and romantic candlelight at night. Because it is a narrow room there are only four tables by the windows; if you want one, reserve it early. Celebrities are here daily at breakfast, lunch or dinner. Reservations strongly suggested. The hotel is set close up to busy Sunset Boulevard; watch for the sudden, narrow, short driveway. And watch for the $15 valet parking fee. If you are staying anywhere in West Hollywood it would behoove you to taxi here.

★★ DIAGHILEV

Wyndham Bel Age Hotel
1020 North San Vicente Boulevard (just off Sunset)
☎ 310-854-1111
Franco-Russian
Very Expensive

To get the name out of the way, Sergei Diaghilev was the famous ballet impresario who brought Russian ballet to Paris, London and New York in the early 20th century. And celebrities dine here for the same reason ordinary mortals do: it is opulent and romantic. Start with ice-cold Russian vodka and caviar while you enjoy the balalaika or harp music. The mirrored room has gold-framed paintings from Diaghilev's era, and long-stemmed roses grace the tables.

West Hollywood

The California Restaurant Writers Association voted Diaghilev its supreme achievement, the 5-Star Award.

Don't miss the piroshki served with the borscht. The menu is wide ranging: sturgeon, duck and venison, each served with a caviar and lemon emulsion, truffles or port wine sauce. Dimitri, the manager, is the most gracious host you will ever encounter. Diaghilev offers a great dining experience with the possibility of seeing a star stuff herself on chicken Kiev (only here it is called *Poulet Kiev Façon Diaghilev*). Dinner only, Tuesday-Saturday, 6:30-10:30pm.

★★ DAN TANA'S
9071 Santa Monica Boulevard
☎ 310-275-9444
Italian
Moderate-Expensive

Show-biz types have been having dinner at this little yellow bungalow just south of the Sunset Strip ever since 1964. We have been going there ourselves most of that time. It is a really comfortable place with red leather booths and checkered tablecloths; Dan Tana wouldn't dare change it, this is exactly what his customers want. We go in, see the same waiters, the same bartender, year after year. Dan Tana was named "Restaurateur of the Year" by the California Restaurant Writers Association.

The 1980s TV show Vega$ named its lead character, Dan Tanna, after the restaurateur, with Robert Urich playing the lead role.

We keep going back because Mate Mustac, the chef, turns out what the French call *vielle cuisine*, food that is well cooked but with no pretentions. The mozzarella marinara has been on the menu as an appetizer forever, although we usually go for an antipasto platter for both of us to munch on while we are deciding on what is to come. Linguine with clams; lasagna; chicken Florentine; and New York steak are all are long-time favorites with the regulars who fill the booths.

There are two rooms, neither very large, with the bar in the middle. We have concluded that the smaller side room is a better place to find celebrities, like George Clooney and Alec Baldwin, separately and recently (we happened to notice them there; Dan Tana doesn't give out names). Only dinner is served, but the kitchen is open Monday-Saturday, 5pm to 1am; and Sunday, 5pm to 12:30am – one of the few places that is open and even lively after a show or a game. Reservations are supposed to be a must, but we have dropped in on the spur of the moment many times and have always been seated, though sometimes after a wait at the bar. It is just east of Doheny, next door to the Troubadour. Valet parking.

Don't worry about the overhanging Chianti bottles in Dan Tana's – they are carefully dusted three times a week.

★★ THE IVY
113 North Robertson Boulevard
☎ 310-274-8303
Contemporary American
Very Expensive

"Star-studded" is what this place is sometimes called, especially the front patio on Robertson on a nice day. Definitely the home of power meals. If you saw *Get Shorty* you remember that lunch scene: that was here. On the menu you'll find meat loaf, crab cakes, even a hamburger – but at prices that take it out of the "hamburger joint" class. Lunch and dinner daily, 11:30am-10:15pm (last orders taken), Sunday brunch starts at 10:30am.

★★ LE DOME
8720 Sunset Boulevard
☎ 310-659-6919
California-continental
Expensive

Everyone who is anyone in Hollywood has eaten or is eating at Le Dôme. It is like a rite of passage – coming here validates one's rise to stardom. It's popular with the more established celebrities, but all the generations – everyone from Liz Taylor to Britney Spears, from rockers to opera stars – are seen here sooner or later.

Le Dôme was started 25 years ago by 50 people who put money in a pot; investors included some movie stars, but also people like Walter O'Malley, owner of the Dodgers, and a butcher at the farmers' market. The result was an elegant place with soft, flattering lighting. You are as likely to see celebs at lunch as at dinner. Like a lot of places, the continental cooking has taken on light California touches. Open for lunch and dinner, Monday-Friday, noon to 10:30pm (sometimes a bit later, especially on Friday); Saturday, dinner only, 5:30pm until 11 or midnight.

West Hollywood

★★ L'ORANGERIE

903 North La Cienega Boulevard
☎ 310-652-9770
www.orangerie.com
French
Very Expensive

L'Orangerie is one of only two restaurant members of Relais & Châteaux in Los Angeles.

Celebrities dine here, of course, but so does much of the Westside's power elite and what passes for society. This was probably the last place in town that required ties for men (a policy that has since been relaxed). The formal dining room with candlelight, potted orange trees and a towering lily arrangement suggests the fantasy of an 18th-century orangerie; the garden room, with a roof that opens when the weather is warm, has its own charm.

The food is very French, as we can attest (we have eaten here a few times). Even if you order something very ordinary, such as a filet of fish or a steak, it will have a treatment or a sauce that gives it a different taste than you had expected. There is an eight-course prix fixe menu for $95, and a four-course vegetarian one for $58. The wine list starts at $25 and goes to $4,000, but you are bringing your platinum credit card, right? *Très chic, très cher.*

☞ DID YOU KNOW?

The only restaurant in Los Angeles that is more expensive than L'Orangerie is **Ginza Sushi-Ko** in Beverly Hills, a sushi place that is the most expensive restaurant in the US, at around $300 a person.

There are more than 120 eateries in West Hollywood, from sidewalk tables to glamorous dining.

The list of celebrities who dine here seems endless: Warren Beatty and Annette Bening, Marlon Brando, Sean Connery, Mel Gibson, Dustin Hoffman, Gregory Peck, Sidney Poitier, Arnold Schwarzenegger, Kevin Spacey, Barbra Streisand, Elizabeth Taylor, Billy Wilder, Denzel Washington and many more. L'Orangerie is open Tuesday-Sunday, 6 to 11pm; call for reservations after 9am weekdays, after 3pm Saturday and Sunday. The restaurant is between Melrose and Santa Monica, on the west side of the street. Valet parking.

★★ LUCQUES

8474 Melrose Avenue
☎ 323-655-6277
Mediterranean
Expensive

Silent star Harold Lloyd once owned this building on Melrose just east of La Cienega; it was built as a carriage house, and the original bricks and half-timbers have been kept. The chef lets the food itself be the star, rather than making a showy presentation, which is all to the good. You can dine on the patio, but inside seems nicer, with leather sofas in front of the fireplace. This place has been a very hot ticket, so reservations are highly recommended. Tuesday-Saturday, noon-2:30pm and 6-11pm; bar menu served until midnight. Sundays, 5:30-10pm, with a prix fixe dinner for $30.

The name of the restaurant (pronounced "Luke") is a type of French olive.

★★ MORTON'S

8764 Melrose Avenue
☎ 310-276-5205
New American
Expensive

Even though two stars by the restaurant's name means a place where you might see celebrities, we are tempted to put three stars in front of Morton's. It has been for some years *the* power restaurant for the industry. The biggest stars come here after the Oscar ceremony. One year the restaurant threw a party on what would have been Marilyn Monroe's 75th birthday to raise funds for Hollygrove Orphanage in Hollywood, where she lived for a time.

The dining room is large and tables are spaced well apart; this is good for those holding private conversations, but it makes celeb-spotting more difficult. Monday night is the big night for star-watching. Many ordinary people are discouraged from even trying for reservations then; we noticed a guidebook that said about Mondays, "tourists are discouraged with vehemence." We have not found this to be so. We phoned one weekend for a reservation Monday at 8:30pm and got it. And cheerfully, with no vehemence in sight.

The food, incidentally – which is not what most people come here for – is standard fare with nouvelle touches,

West Hollywood

and strong on steak. And yes, you do see beaucoup stars. Lunch, Monday-Friday, noon-2:30pm; dinner, Monday-Saturday, 6-9:30pm. Valet parking.

★★ PALM
9001 Santa Monica Boulevard
☎ 310-550-8811
Steak, lobster
Expensive

Don't worry about what to wear to dinner at Palm; you will see everything from jackets and ties to T-shirts.

Palm started in New York 75 years ago. There is a story that the original restaurant was founded by two emigrants from Parma, Italy, who planned to call it after their hometown but their accents got in the way and it has been Palm ever since. This one has been here 25 years. We remember that when it opened, show-biz folk flocked in right away; they still do. Probably more picture deals are made here than at Paramount, so many that there is a handy notepad on every table.

We were here for dinner recently. It still has the same booths with upright, not-too-comfortable wooden backs; narrow aisles; stamped tin ceiling; and a noise level so high it is hard to hear what the other person in your booth is saying (which might explain some of the pictures we have been seeing).

The waiters (male and female), are a good combination of New York efficiency and Los Angeles friendliness. The first thing the waiter does is set down a basket that contains four or five kinds of bread. The sourdough is tart and tastes as if it is flown in fresh from San Francisco. We know that the cheesecake, at the other end of the meal, is flown in from the Bronx.

The main thing to remember here is that portions are big. We mean *huge*. Filet mignon, pork chops, double lamb chops; the specials might be 24-oz. steaks and four-pound lobsters. One of us had a salmon filet that must have weighed two pounds, the other had a double order of the shrimp served as an appetizer, which was just right as an entrée. There are also a few pasta dishes. We have never ordered one of them, but we are sure you would be up to your elbows in pasta.

There is a bar, but it isn't a neighborhood place where people hang out. A lot of industry people come here, writers and directors as well as actors. The night we were here we noticed Blythe Danner at a nearby table. She seemed to be having a good time. As we left with our doggie bags we stopped to talk for a moment with manager Louis Deomaestro, whom everyone calls Gigi, who has been here from the beginning. We inquired if there was anyone else here we might know. He eyed us doubtfully and asked if we had ever heard of a Gen-X band called Limp Bizkit. Of course we had! Then we should know Fred Durst, the lead singer. Of course we did! How old did he think we were? He didn't answer. Open Monday-Friday, 11:30am-10:30pm; Saturday, 5-10:30pm; Sunday, 5 to 9:30pm. Valet parking.

Casual Dining

★★ TAIL O' THE PUP
329 North San Vicente Boulevard
(near Beverly Boulevard)
☎ 310-652-4517
Hot dogs
Inexpensive

The thing that distinguishes this hot dog stand from every other hot dog stand is its shape – it looks like a giant hot dog bun with mustard and an extra long wiener sticking out both ends. LA used to be full of this kind of eye-catching, vernacular architecture, but it is almost all gone now. Stars drop by here occasionally. Eddie Blake, the owner, has photos on the wall of Pamela Anderson, Ryan O'Neal, Barbra Streisand and Denzel Washington when they happened by. Magic Johnson comes in fairly often. Jay Leno's a regular (but not very loyal, he goes to Pink's for hot dogs, too), and Neil Diamond recently sent Eddie tickets to his concert. Woody Allen used a passing shot of it in *Annie Hall* (of course, that was to illustrate Hollywood's general tackiness). Tail o' the Pup is open daily, 6am-5pm.

The "Boston Celtic dog" with baked beans is the Tail's most popular item.

West Hollywood

IN THE VERNACULAR

Tail o' the Pup is one of the few remaining examples of what has been called vernacular architecture – buildings shaped like the things they sell. Starting in the 1920s and lasting through the '40s, you could find these buildings all over LA – ice cream stands shaped like giant cones, "Dutch" bakeries topped with working windmills, enormous coffee pots. There were a few examples of similar structures elsewhere in the country, but LA was where it really proliferated. The idea behind it was logical: to draw the attention of someone speeding by in a car as no ordinary sign ever could.

For architecture purists, the Tail is almost one of a kind these days. There is a much-photographed donut stand in Inglewood with a gigantic donut up in the air on top of it, but that is not the same thing – the stand itself is just a stand, not shaped like a donut. And the famed original Brown Derby restaurant had a hat on the roof, the slogan was "Eat in the Hat," but that missed the mark, too. It would have been vernacular architecture only if they had sold *hats*.

Tail o' the Pup has been seen in over a hundred films and TV shows.

Where did all the rest of the vernacular buildings go? Most of them were cheaply made and when the land they sat on became too valuable, they were simply torn down. That almost happened to Tail o' the Pup, but Eddie Blake saved it and moved it to its present location. Some people ridicule it as tacky, others love it for the same reason. In any case, it certainly represents Hollywood's golden age.

★ BARNEY'S BEANERY
8447 Santa Monica Boulevard
☎ 323-654-2287
American
Inexpensive

We have been coming here for years, when we just feel like a beer and a sandwich or bowl of chili, at lunch or on the way home after a show. It is always open and always crowded with a young show biz crowd, lots of actors and dancers. It started as a wooden shack with a bar and is now three or four (it is hard to tell) connected shacks with many booths, a few pool tables and a high noise level. It has the biggest menu you will ever see: scores of hamburgers, dozens of sandwiches, tens of omelets, countless variations on basic chili, and over 200 brands of beer from all over the world. This is not the place to come and settle for a plain burger and a bottle of Bud. Live!

Barney's Beanery on Santa Monica Boulevard was Ronald Reagan's hangout in his early Hollywood days.

Barney's is just east of La Cienega, at the bend where Santa Monica Boulevard curves to the left and the street going on straight ahead becomes Holloway Drive. Open for breakfast, lunch and dinner daily, until 1:30am. Parking is available on the street and in the lot next door.

Shop Till You Drop

Take off the red shoes.
— Moira Shearer, *The Red Shoes*

If you are looking for things you can get in any department store or chain store, duplicates of which are found in every city, don't bother shopping in West Hollywood. You won't find it here. The same goes for furnishings, décor and design. This is the place where you will find new things before anyone else in the country has imagined them. That is why so many celebrities shop here.

★ **TIP**

You can find a particular shop in West Hollywood through the Web site www.shopsmb.com.

West Hollywood

There are concentrations of stores in three primary areas; where you shop depends on what you are looking for.

Santa Monica Boulevard

Free parking is available behind the storefronts.

The boulevard is a great place just to stroll and look at the window displays. Most of the action is between Crescent Heights and Robertson; shopping is all along here amid lots of sidewalk dining. Look for men's clothing, especially very sharp casual wear.

TRASH WITH CLASS
8271 Santa Monica Boulevard
☎ 323-654-8789

In this shop, west of Crescent Heights Boulevard, the focus is on used theatrical gowns, feather boas, wigs, and knickknacks. It is an eccentric place, but the signed photos of celebrities on the wall attest to something.

DREAM DRESSER
8444 Santa Monica Boulevard
☎ 323-848-3480

Drop in for the kind of erotic apparel you definitely won't find in most small towns. The store is just before the bend in Santa Monica Boulevard.

Stars such as Julia Roberts drop by The Paper Bag Princess to check the racks.

THE PAPER BAG PRINCESS
8700 Santa Monica Boulevard
☎ 310-358-1985

You'll find the shop about halfway between La Cienega and San Vicente; it stocks hard-to-find vintage couture.

Sunset Boulevard

Sunset Boulevard in the Sunset Plaza area, between La Cienega and San Vicente, is rife with boutiques full of high-end women's clothes.

CLUB MONACO
8569 Sunset Boulevard
☎ 310-659-3821

This store, just west of La Cienega, is known for trendy casual wear.

★★TRACEY ROSS
8595 Sunset Boulevard
☎ 310-854-1996

Just a few doors from Club Monaco and next door to a bustling coffee shop. Tracey Ross, a Farrah Fawcett look-alike, has an intimate little hangout with blue walls and chandeliers, that she seems to run as much like a place for her friends to drop by as a shop. But quite a few of her friends happen to be celebrities and the goods are very high-end and chic. Look for bias-cut slip dresses, hip-hugging trousers and little cashmere sweaters. A few items – T-shirts, a scarf or two – are under $100, but most things sell for $200 to $500.

HERVE LEGER
8619 Sunset Boulevard
☎ 310-360-6740

This is the place to shop if you are in the market for a gown to attend the Oscars; it is a few doors down from Tracey Ross.

⚠ WARNING!

If you are what most of the country considers a "normal" size – 10, 12 or 14 – you might have problems finding much you can squeeze into at many of the boutiques along Sunset. Tracey Ross, for instance, carries a few items in sizes 10 and 12 (huge by Hollywood standards), but the most popular sizes are definitely 4, 6 and 8.

West Hollywood

TOP SUNSET BOULEVARD BOUTIQUES

◆ **Calypso**, 8635 Sunset Boulevard, ☎ 310-652-4454.

◆ **Nicole Miller**, 8663 Sunset Boulevard, ☎ 310-657-6121.

◆ **Anna Sui**, 8669 Sunset Boulevard, ☎ 310-360-6224.

◆ **Kenzo**, 8711 Sunset Boulevard, ☎ 310-360-0433.

HUSTLER HOLLYWOOD
8920 Sunset Boulevard
☎ 310-860-9009

Hustler Hollywood is billed as "the world's premier erotic department store."

This large place, near San Vicente a few blocks west of Sunset Plaza, is owned by Larry Flynt, publisher of *Hustler Magazine*. A big assortment of hip, alternative clothing, with a full line of luxurious lingerie. But you will also find sensual candles, soaps and creams, adult novelties and a coffee and juice bar, plus a huge newsstand-bookstore.

☞ **DID YOU KNOW?**

Sunset Boulevard is one of Los Angeles's oldest and longest thoroughfares. Originally a footpath used by the Indians to get from the LA River to the coast, it was later used as a wagon road by the earliest settlers in the pueblo. Today, the boulevard follows the route of the old trail along the lower edge of the foothills for 22 miles from Downtown Los Angeles to the sea.

Robertson Boulevard

★★ KITSON'S
115 South Robertson Boulevard
☎ 310-859-2652

Kitson's carries a wide range of clothing (including baby clothes), gift items, jewelry, and cosmetics. Although it is not particularly a haven for denim, Cher once spotted an embellished denim jacket hanging on a rack. "How much?" she asked the salesgirl. The girl was embarrassed to say it was her own jacket, so she pulled a figure out of the rarified air and told Cher it was $850. Cher ordered two more.

Art & Design District

AVENUES OF ART & DESIGN
That is how the city is promoting this pedestrian-friendly area centering around Melrose Avenue and Beverly and Robertson boulevards, in the section of town west of La Cienega. You will find over 100 interior design and furniture showrooms, and stores selling fine fabrics, imported tile, antiques and specialty items alongside high fashion boutiques. These few blocks are frequented by studio set designers looking for ideas.

There are 30 art galleries in the Art & Design section of West Hollywood.

PACIFIC DESIGN CENTER
8687 Melrose Avenue
☎ 310-657-0800

The Design Center, on the north side of Melrose Avenue near San Vicente Boulevard, anchors the district, with 130 showrooms in one building. All of the shops are open to public to come in and look, but some sell only to the trade, and even those shops occasionally have public sales. The Museum of Contemporary Art has a satellite MOCA Gallery in the Pacific Design Center; ☎ 310-289-5223.

West Hollywood

Specialty Stores & Services

Antiques

ANTIQUARIUS
8840 Beverly Boulevard
☎ 310-274-2363

A collection of antiques and estate jewelry stores under one roof; just west of Robertson.

THE COLLECTION
315 South Robertson
☎ 323-876-2245

This building houses a huge showroom filled with antiques and collectibles. North of Beverly Boulevard.

Bakeries

BASIX
8333 Santa Monica Boulevard
☎ 323-848-2460

Basix is a café that serves breakfast, lunch and dinner, but the bakery is the big attraction for us, especially the big muffin made from sour cream pound cake dough and topped with cinnamon streusel ($1.60). Open daily, 7am-11pm.

EXOTIC CAKES
1068 South Fairfax Avenue
☎ 323-938-2286

Roger Rodriguez says that of the 60 to 80 cakes he bakes each week, about 40% are naughty. Whitney Houston, before she was married, ordered a cake in the shape of boobs and had the decorative writing on it say "I'm here, where are you?" and added her phone number. Now there is an idea. Whoopi Goldberg, Madonna and Sylvester Stallone are also customers. You will have to guess at their messages. Anyway, if you are in the market for a cake...

★★ SWEET LADY JANE

8360 Melrose Avenue
☎ 323-653-7145

This bakery, a few blocks east of La Cienega, is where the celebrities come to get their brownies.

Beauty & Health

BORRELLI SALON

8623 Santa Monica Boulevard
☎ 310-652-9597

If you need your hair colored or cut while you are here, visit Borrelli, just west of La Cienega.

FACE PLACE

8701 Santa Monica Boulevard
☎ 310-855-1150

This salon is a few doors down from Borrelli; come in and pamper your skin.

JESSICA'S NAIL CLINIC

8627 Sunset Boulevard
☎ 310-659-9292

For more pampering, luxurious manicures and pedicures are the specialty at Jessica's, in the Sunset Plaza area.

OLE HENRICKSEN FACE & BODY SALON

8601 Sunset Boulevard
☎ 310-854-7700

Skin care in a spa atmosphere, offering facials, massages, and more. By appointment only.

★★ CRUNCH FITNESS

8000 Sunset Boulevard
☎ 323-654-4550

This gym at the east end of the strip is where *A Night at the Roxbury* was filmed, and it's a place where you are apt to see stars sweating as well as preening. Besides the usual bench press and walkers, popular classes include

West Hollywood

The movie Perfect was filmed at another West Hollywood gym, The Sports Connection, at 8612 Santa Monica Boulevard.

the **Goddess Workout** (belly dancing with scarves), **Circus Sports** (tumbling and acrobatics), and **DJ Ride** (aerobics accompanied by a disc jockey). Get a day pass ($23) to try it out. We were told that Margaret Cho, Fabio, Ellen DeGeneres, Taye Diggs, Jerry and Charlie O'Connell, and Ian Ziering worked out during a recent two-day stretch.

⚡ WARNING!

At Crunch Fitness both the men's and the women's shower stalls are frosted glass; the silhouettes of those inside are visible from the lobby. If your silhouette is not all that perfect, you can always shower at your hotel.

Books

AUDUBON HOUSE
Plummer Park
7377 Santa Monica Boulevard
☎ 323-876-0202

You'll find everything for the birder here, with over 2,000 books on birds for sale, plus audios, videos and gift items, including clocks that sing each hour in a different bird song.

Beverly Center Mall, at Beverly and La Cienega, is where Scenes From a Mall *was shot.*

☛ DID YOU KNOW?

Plummer Park in West Hollywood is the center of LA's Russian community, which has been emigrating from the Soviet Union, then Russia, over the last 50 years.

A DIFFERENT LIGHT
8853 Santa Monica Boulevard
☎ 310-854-6601

Books for and about the lesbian-gay community; frequent author signings and events.

HERITAGE BOOK SHOP
8540 Melrose Avenue
☎ 310-659-3674

This shop, just off La Cienega, is a primary source for first edition, rare and unusual books.

ELLIOT M. KATT BOOKS ON THE PERFORMING ARTS
8568 Melrose Avenue
☎ 310-652-5178

Elliot M. Katt specializes in hard-to-find books on the performing arts, and has a large film book collection; a few doors from Heritage.

BODHI TREE BOOKSTORE
8585 Melrose Avenue
☎ 310-659-4428
www.bodhitree.com

In the same stretch of Melrose as Heritage and Elliot M. Katt, this shop specializes in Eastern and Western religions, astrology and occult books.

★★ BOOK SOUP
8818 Sunset Boulevard
☎ 310-659-3110
www.booksoup.com

Book Soup is strong in subjects of interest to its show-biz clientele: art, photography, film and literary fiction. They also have general fiction and non-fiction titles. You might see Nicolas Cage or Marlee Matlin browsing; celebrities do readings and book signings here. Open 365 days, 9am-midnight.

West Hollywood

Home Items

LEMON TREE BUNGALOW
8727 Sunset Boulevard
☎ 310-657-0211

Shop for candles and home fragrances in, of course, a cute lemon-colored bungalow.

HOMEBODY
8500 Melrose Avenue
☎ 310-659-2917, 800-838-5507

You'll find a good selection of candles, incense and aromatherapy items.

Farmers' Market

PLUMMER PARK
Fountain Avenue at Vista Street
North Parking Lot
☎ 323-848-6502

In addition to great fruit and veggies, the market has flowers, bonsai plants, honey and handmade craft items. Mondays, 9am-2pm.

Shoes

★★ ANDRE NO. 1 SHOE DESIGN
7914 Sunset Boulevard (next to the Director's Guild)
☎ 323-876-5565

A must for those who want the best shoe made just for them. Andre Rostomyan makes platform boots for members of the band KISS and leather shoes for Prince. He will measure your feet and make whatever you desire, whether it's elegant shoes for evening, or casual little numbers; he also makes shoes for professional dancers. Choose satin, cotton, velvet, imitation suede or leather; Andre can shape them all, as he has for Drew Barrymore, Neil Diamond, Amy Irving, Keanu Reeves and Alicia Silverstone, among many others.

KENNETH COLE
8752 Sunset Boulevard
☎ 310-289-5085

This designer is well known for funky footwear.

Sunup to Sundown

Historic Architecture

R.M. SCHINDLER STUDIO & RESIDENCE
835 North Kings Road
☎ 323-651-1510
www.makcenter.com

This building, once architect Rudolph Schindler's residence and studio, is one of the most significant works of architecture in West Hollywood. Exhibitions, lectures, performances and workshops are held seasonally. The exhibition space is open to the public Wednesday-Sunday, 11am-6pm, with docent-led tours on Saturday and Sunday; admission is $5. The center's bookstore is open daily, from 11am-6pm.

★ **TIP**

The City of West Hollywood distributes a special events calendar every six months. Call ☎ 800-368-6020.

Recreation

Plummer Park, 7377 Santa Monica Boulevard, is the largest of the city parks. It has tennis and basketball courts and picnic tables. Two parking lots.

West Hollywood Park, 647 North San Vicente Boulevard, has tennis, basketball, softball, children's play equipment, lots of green areas, and a few picnic tables. Free parking.

West Hollywood

Kings Road Park, 1000 Kings Rd., is very small, with a few picnic tables, children's play area, and pond. Street parking.

William S. Hart Park, 8341 DeLongpre Avenue, has grassy areas, benches and a fountain. The home of early film star William S. Hart is here, but not open to the public. Street parking.

SUMMER SOUNDS

Outdoor concerts are held on Sundays in June, July and August in various West Hollywood parks. Performances range from Broadway tunes to Eastern European klezmer to country – a great excuse for a picnic. Call ☎ 323-848-6530 or visit www.visitwesthollywood.com.

 A(te> Da>k

Here's looking at you, kid.
– Humphrey Bogart, Casablanca

Sunset Strip

Fat Tuesday is celebrated in West Hollywood with costumes, music, eats and typical Mardi Gras entertainment.

This is the part of West Hollywood that has always been famous. The TV series was called *77 Sunset Strip*, not West Hollywood. This is where the glamour was to be found at night, from the late 1920s through the '30s. The Mocambo nightclub was on Sunset then, near Sunset Plaza. That is where the stars went, and the paparazzi followed (only they weren't called that in those days) to take flash pictures with Speed Graphics of beautiful people and wild doings.

Marie Windsor was working as a cigarette girl at **Mocambo** where producer Arthur Hornblow Jr. saw her and recommended her for a part in a picture. Hollywood's elite, from Betty Grable and Lana Turner to Clark Gable and Humphrey Bogart, came to hear acts like Lena Horne and Vic Damone.

It was at the Mocambo that Charlie Chaplin, who was with Marion Davies, paid the doorman for his uniform and directed traffic in the middle of the street. And some star (was it Franchot Tone?) hit another star and knocked him down. There was a fair amount of that, perhaps because there was a lot of booze consumed in those days. Or at least the papers played it up. It closed in 1958 and was demolished (we always need more parking lots).

SUNSET STRIP GRIDLOCK

The Strip is such a potent attraction that young drivers from the Valley and other parts of Los Angeles have made a tribal habit of cruising, especially on summer weekend nights. It sometimes becomes so difficult for patrons to reach the restaurants and clubs that a cruising ban is clamped down: Sheriff's Deputies are stationed and drivers caught passing more than twice through the checkpoints are cited; fines go up to $500.

In 1934 Billy Wilkerson, publisher of the trade paper *Hollywood Reporter*, opened **Café Trocadero**, a French-themed late-night club on Sunset Boulevard. The stars flocked there: Fred Astaire, Bing Crosby, Sonja Henie, Jean Harlow, William Powell, Tyrone Power and Robert Taylor. It all seemed more glamorous when they rubbed elbows with gangsters Mickey Cohen, Tony Cornero, Johnny Roselli and Bugsy Siegel. In the cigar smoke-filled backroom every Saturday night the moguls who ran the studios, Sam Goldwyn, Carl Laemmle Jr., Joseph Shenck, Irving Thalberg and Darryl Zanuck, had a high-stakes poker game.

West Hollywood

★ TIP

The old Troc is long gone but a new **Sunset Trocadero Lounge** has risen a few blocks away. It is smaller and less glamorous, but with a lively bar scene and a patio out on the Boulevard to see and be seen. Open 6pm to 2am, dinner served to 1:30am; valet parking ($4.50). 8280 Sunset Boulevard, ☎ 323-656-7161.

West Hollywood's normal population of 37,000 swells to 250,000 on summer weekend nights.

Ciros, another famous nightclub also owned by Billy Wilkerson, was a few blocks east, toward La Cienega. That is where Lili St. Cyr, a well-known stripper, was busted in 1951 for taking a bubble bath on stage in a giant champagne glass that was short on bubbles.

Because it was the County Strip, not the city, law enforcement was provided by the Sheriff's Department and somehow the Sheriff didn't notice there was a gambling casino a few feet up the hill, looking down on the Boulevard.

Bars

BAR MARMONT
8171 Sunset Boulevard
☎ 323-650-0575

The walls are horsehide, the hanging lights came from a Dutch turn-of-the-century factory, the floor is from a building in Paris and the bricks from a 1920s Fairfax district market. It all adds up to... something. But the guys like it because a lot of models, and girls who look like they should be models, hang out here. And if you happen to be around the third Sunday of the month, Constance, the exotic hostess, throws a "Bad & Beautiful" bash.

The downside is some of the drinks the bar pushes. Like a Butterfly's Kiss (vanilla vodka and Frangelico with a cinnamon stick); or a Marmont Cosmo (raspberry vodka, triple sec and lime). Other than that, while the Sky Bar and Standard Lounge sometimes seem to want to X-ray a fella's credentials to be sure he is authentically hip, any of the rest of us who are not-sure-we're-really-that-cool can just sidle in here. No cover, 21 and older.

★★ SKY BAR
Mondrian Hotel
8440 Sunset Boulevard
☎ 323-848-6025

Despite its name, this bar is on the lobby level of the Mondrian Hotel, so the view is good, but not spectacular. Given the stylish, white-on-white hotel where it is located, the décor is incongruously rustic, but it is still a magnet for hip Hollywood types, including celebrities. A hard place to get into on good nights; reservations are strongly advised.

Be aware: The Mondrian Hotel has a $15 valet parking charge.

Cabarets

Cabaret started in Paris' Montmartre district in the late 1800s, but didn't get anywhere in this country until Prohibition, when it came about spontaneously as chanteuses began singing in basements and back rooms while patrons quenched their illegal thirst. After Prohibition, speakeasies became supper clubs, where alcohol was now sold legally. The definition of a cabaret is a venue that sells booze; otherwise is it a theater. In a cabaret, the entertainment is usually either musical comedy or torchy, ironic, sophisticated material.

GARDENIA
7066 Santa Monica Boulevard
☎ 323-467-7444

This is one of the two prime cabarets (the other is Cinegrill in Hollywood, see page 177) in the Los Angeles area. Quite a few new performers try out their material here. Andrea Marcovicci, probably the top cabaret diva in the country, got her start at Gardenia and still plays in this small, peach-tinted room when she is in LA. Gardenia is open Monday-Saturday; dinner (International-Italian) is served from 7 to 10pm, and shows are at 9pm; $10 cover, two drink minimum, over 21.

West Hollywood

WATCH OUT FOR...

The latest fad, concocted in Taiwan and known as "boba teas," has washed up on Westside shores. The sweet drinks, sipped through wide, brightly colored straws, are blended like martinis in metal cocktail shakers. The secret ingredient is gummy balls of tapioca. Sells for $3 to $4. We are not making this up, honest!

★ TIP

When you hear someone refer to "the Westside" (or you read it in these pages), the term refers to the area west of Downtown LA, which takes in, roughly, the area past Western Avenue, including Hollywood, West Hollywood, Beverly Hills, and all the the neighborhoods out to the coast.

Comedy

THE COMEDY STORE
8433 Sunset Boulevard
☎ 323-656-6225
www.thecomedystore.com

Robin Williams, Richard Pryor, Jim Carrey and Andy Kaufman are some of the best-known alumni of this place. Stand-up comedy, sketch comedy and themed shows. The club has three stages, with shows nightly; call to see what is playing where. Full bar, two drink minimum. $5-$20.

Clubs

BARFLY
8730 Sunset Boulevard
☎ 310-360-9490
Rock, Pop

There is a Barfly in Paris; this is a spinoff with a restaurant for dinner and a spacious bar. The velvet rope is often up, so call ahead to make reservations, either for dinner or for what comes after. Tuesday and Wednesday are Moulin Rouge nights, with dinner dancing, in keeping with the French twist. Thursday is dinner dancing with a DJ, Friday likewise with a mix of music. The whole lineup may change while you are reading this, but it looks as if it will continue to be an easygoing, popular place. Tuesday-Saturday, 7:30pm to 2am; no cover, dress is upscale casual. Phone for new information and reservations.

★★ BELLY
7929 Santa Monica Boulevard
☎ 323-692-1068
Hip-hop, R&B, Jazz and Funk

This is a relaxed, casual tapas lounge with a DJ and tiny dance floor that may be the best place for singles in town. Everything is reasonably priced, and tapas portions are large. The place doesn't seem to be trying to attract celebrities, but they come in regardless. Whitney Houston and Bobby Brown have been seen here; Farrah Fawcett was here for San Francisco Giant Barry Bonds' birthday bash. Belly is open nightly, 6pm to 2am; food is served until 1am. 21 and older; no cover. Casual dress; not everyone is in that black-on-black club tradition, but the women still tend to dress up more than the guys. Just west of Fairfax; valet parking.

West Hollywood

CLUB BRASSERIE
Wyndham Bel Age Hotel
1020 North San Vicente Boulevard
☎ 310-358-7776 evening; 310-854-1111 days;
310-358-7712 for recorded jazz information

Jazz afficionados like this place, especially on Friday and Saturday nights from October to May, when it becomes home to the **Thelonious Monk Institute of Jazz**; scheduled performers are frequently joined on stage by major jazz artists. You can come in and hear jazz all summer. Happy hour from 5-8pm; dinner, 8-12pm; music, 9pm-1am. Dress code: casual-hip; no plain T-shirts, but "semi-formal" T-shirts are fine. Cover $10, valet parking $2.

HOUSE OF BLUES
8430 Sunset Boulevard
☎ 313-848-5100
Rock, Jazz, Blues, Rap and Reggae

Outside it looks like an ancient Southern Delta gin mill sheathed with corrugated tin. Inside it is big, with 1,000-person capacity, and faux-Mississippi décor, but the sight lines and the sound system are good. Cuisine is "new Southern." The cover is $10-$40, depending on who is headlining. Full bar, over 21. There is a Sunday brunch with gospel singing.

★★ KEY CLUB
9039 Sunset Boulevard
☎ 310-274-5800 (information); 310-274-5800 (tickets)
Old-school Punk, Rap, Rock, R&B to Tango

Keanu Reeves, Wesley Snipes, comedian Pauly Shore, and basketball stars Dennis Rodman and Shaquille O'Neal have been known to show up here. Some nights you will see **Camerata Tango**, a showy dance and aerial performance; other times you'll join rock-industry types and talent agents sizing up the bands on stage. One night each month they hold "The Carnival, a Choreographer's Night." Some of the best young dancers and working choreographers try out their new material in a two-hour show in front of an inside crowd connected to the world of professional dance and music. It is always standing-room-only. Try for reservations.

Key Club has three bars, plus a "tequila library," and serves California cuisine until 1am. The club is generally open Tuesdays-Saturdays, 7pm-2am, but that changes according to what is on the program. There's usually dancing after shows Wednesday-Sunday. The age limit varies, along with the cover charge (from $10 to $22.50), again depending on the program. There is always a line here; have your concierge make reservations.

THE STANDARD
8300 Sunset Boulevard
☎ 323-822-3111
A mixed bag

The bar in the Standard Hotel (see page 200) starts in the lobby conversation pit, where there is a DJ at the nearby registration desk (doesn't every hotel registration desk have a DJ?), continues into the Joshua Tree mural lounge, and wanders out poolside where you can watch the twinkling lights of the city. There are lots of young actors and wannabes in the 25- to 30-something crowd. To gain admission to the lounge (especially on weekends) you first have to get by Anya Varda, the petite presence with clipboard and the velvet rope. Of course, it is easy if you are staying here.

The lounge has its own entrance to the left of the lobby's main doors. It is a smallish room, with a few swings (de rigueur these days) and a low egg-carton ceiling. The bar is very dark. 21 and older; you had better have reservations.

★ TIP

Looking for something different after dark? **Du-Par's Restaurant & Bakery** (a well-known chain in Southern California) has a location in the lobby of the Ramada West Hollywood, 8585 Santa Monica Boulevard. You can come in for hotcakes and fresh baked stuff, 6am-1am weekdays; to 3am Friday and Saturday.

West Hollywood

TROUBADOUR
9081 Santa Monica Boulevard
☎ 310-276-6168
Folk, Rock, Comedy

Clubs come and go, but Troubadour is forever, since more than 40 years qualifies as forever in Hollywood. The acts that have played here make quite a list: Lenny Bruce, the Byrds, Judy Collins, Bill Cosby, the Committee, Bo Diddley, Arlo Guthrie, Richie Havens, Elton John, Gordon Lightfoot, Steve Martin, Roger Miller, Joni Mitchell, Mort Sahl, Kris Kristofferson and Nina Simone. Some played here at early, crucial points in their careers, and have come back repeatedly since they have been anointed as stars; Linda Ronstadt and Emmylou Harris returned as a duo recently. There are three bars; the cover may be anywhere from $0 to $20, depending on the act. All ages are welcome, but sometimes there is a small (like $3) entrance fee for those under 21.

★★ VIPER ROOM
8852 Sunset Boulevard
☎ 310-358-1880
Rock

Johnny Depp created this Hollywood haven on the Strip. You might see Ben Stiller and Charlize Theron, Cameron Diaz, George Clooney, Cher, or Sex Pistol Johnny Rotten at the bar. Nicolas Cage and Sean Penn were in on the same night. But it will probably always be known best as the place where River Phoenix collapsed on the sidewalk outside. Everything from heavy metal to a very wet T-shirt contest on Mondays. Monday-Saturday, cover $7-$15, full bar, over 21.

★★ WHISKY A GO-GO
8901 Sunset Boulevard
☎ 310-652-4202
Rock, all styles

Children as young as 13 may come to the Whisky with their parents, as long as they don't drink.

This practically historic place has been here over 35 years. This is where bands like The Doors, KISS, Chicago, and Guns N' Roses started. More recently, Rage Against the Machine, Korn and Limp Bizkit made a name for themselves here. It is still a crucial spot for touring bands and local aspirants, and draws fans such as Nicolas Cage and Rosanna Arquette. Open nightly, with two bars; cover $10 weekdays, $12-$15 weekends; all ages.

⭐ *TIP*

Escape to tranquility at **Elixir Tonics and Teas**, a haven of quiet in a Japanese-style teahouse in the midst of West Hollywood's buzz. 8612 Melrose Avenue (at San Vicente), ☎ 310-657-9300. Open daily, 9am-9pm; Sunday, 11am-7pm.

Theaters

Most live theaters in town are 99-seat or smaller, and there are literally hundreds, with new productions all the time. See the *Los Angeles Times Calendar* section, or *LA Weekly* (free) theater listings. There are a few larger houses in West Hollywood.

TIFFANY THEATRE
8532 Sunset Boulevard
☎ 310-289-2999

A mid-size house with good views from all seats, the Tiffany presents new plays, with a leaning toward self-absorbed one-person shows.

CORONET THEATRE
366 North La Cienega Boulevard
☎ 310-657-7377

This venue often presents interesting plays (of course, that depends on what interests you) in a comfortable 284-seat theater. Valet parking is $5 if you don't find a space on La Cienega. Do not park on the side streets, as that is permit parking for residents only, and you will be ticketed.

West Hollywood

West Hollywood A to Z

Counseling

Statscript Pharmacy, 8490 Santa Monica Boulevard, Suite J, ☎ 310-657-4333. Consulting and pharmacy for living with HIV/AIDS.

Women Helping Women Counseling Talkline, ☎ 323-655-3807. Help with depression, crisis, domestic problems.

Currency Exchange

Hyatt West Hollywood Hotel, 8401 Sunset Boulevard, ☎ 323-656-1234, exchanges foreign to US as courtesy for guests, but bank rates are better.

Thomas Cook Exchange Service, 806 Hilldale Avenue, ☎ 310-659-6093, provides currency exchange, travelers checks and other financial services.

Libraries

West Hollywood Library, 715 North San Vicente Boulevard, ☎ 310-652-5340, (between Santa Monica and Melrose, across from the Blue Whale). Open Monday-Wednesday, 10am-8pm; Friday and Saturday, 10am-5pm.

Durant Branch, 1403 North Gardner Street, (one block south of Sunset Boulevard), ☎ 323-876-2741, is open Monday and Tuesday, 12:30-8pm; Wednesday and Thursday, 12:30-5:30pm; Friday and Saturday, 10-5:30pm. Parking is at the corner of DeLongpre. Call for information about upcoming special programs such as magic shows for children.

The Durants never used the Will & Ariel Durant Branch of the library, as they lived in the Los Feliz area.

The June L. Mazer Lesbian Archives has 2,300 fiction and non-fiction books, over 500 periodicals, a large video/audio tape collection, photos, recordings, sculpture, drawings, lithographs. Open every Tuesday and the first Sunday of each month, noon-3pm, and by appointment. 626 North Robertson Boulevard, ☎ 310-659-2478, www.lesbian.org/mazer/.

Locksmiths

In case you get locked out of your rental car:
A-Al's Lock & Key Service. . . . . ☎ 310-672-7988
Academy Locksmith . . . . ☎ 310-815-8300

Medical Services

Cedars-Sinai Medical Center, 8700 Beverly Boulevard, ☎ 310-855-5000, 310-423-3277, www.csmc.edu.

Los Angeles Free Clinic, 8405 Beverly Boulevard, ☎ 323-653-1990.

Newspapers

West Hollywood Independent, ☎ 323-932-6397. Comes out Wednesdays, with local news and tips on entertainment; free.

Police & Fire

Emergency. . . . . ☎ 911
Sheriff & Fire Departments. . . . . ☎ 800-855-8850

West Hollywood

Post Offices

Cole Branch, 1125 North Fairfax Avenue, ☎ 323-654-8236, 800-275-8777.

West Branch, 820 North San Vicente Boulevard, ☎ 310-652-5435, 800-275-8777.

Postal Center, 8205 Santa Monica Boulevard, Suite 1, ☎ 323-654-4090. Copies, fax, FedEx, packaging and sending.

Visitor Information

West Hollywood City Information Hotline, ☎ 323-848-6361.

West Hollywood City Information Hotline, Russian translation, ☎ 323-848-6532.

West Hollywood Convention & Visitors Bureau, Pacific Design Center, 8687 Melrose Avenue, Suite M38, West Hollywood, CA 90069, ☎ 310-289-2525, 800-368-6020, fax 310-289-2529, www.visitwesthollywood.com.

> ★ TIP
>
> Ask the Visitors Bureau to send you the very informative booklet, Only In West Hollywood. Inside is a Travel Club card good for up to 50% off on various hotels, restaurants, clubs, pubs, shops and museums.

Beverly Hills

All right, Mr. De Mille, I'm ready for my close-up.
— Gloria Swanson, *Sunset Boulevard*

Overview

Hollywood, the San Fernando Valley and Culver City are where the studios are; Downtown Los Angeles is just a place for location shooting; and Malibu is where the stars have second or third homes. Beverly Hills is where more stars live, more expensive shopping is concentrated, and more wealth is stashed and sometimes flaunted, than almost anywhere else on the planet.

History

Like everywhere else in Southern California, Beverly Hills was a land grant, *El Rancho Rodeo de las Aguas*, "The Ranch of the Gathering of the Water." Streams cascaded down *Cañada de las Aguas Frias* and *Cañada de los Encinos* and ran southeast to where a *cienega*, a swamp, formed in the rainy season. The streams are gone, and the swamp, but the mountain area is still close enough to its original state so you can picture what Coldwater and Benedict canyons must have looked like less than 100 years ago.

☞ **DID YOU KNOW?**

The reason most people visit Beverly Hills is "The Golden Triangle," the area bounded by Cañon Drive, Wilshire Boulevard and Little Santa Monica, one of the most expensive shopping districts in the world.

Beverly Hills

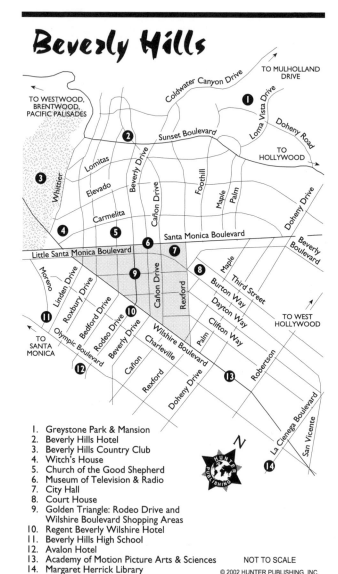

TO MULHOLLAND DRIVE

Coldwater Canyon Drive

TO WESTWOOD, BRENTWOOD, PACIFIC PALISADES

Loma Vista Drive

Doheny Road

Sunset Boulevard

TO HOLLYWOOD

Lomitas

Beverly Drive

Foothill

Maple

Palm

Doheny Drive

Whittier

Elevado

Cañon Drive

Carmelita

Santa Monica Boulevard

Beverly Boulevard

Little Santa Monica Boulevard

Moreno

Linden Drive

Roxbury Drive

Bedford Drive

Cañon Drive

Rexford

Maple

Third Street

Burton Way

Dayton Way

Clifton Way

TO WEST HOLLYWOOD

TO SANTA MONICA

Olympic Boulevard

Rodeo Drive

Beverly Drive

Wilshire Boulevard

Charleville

Palm

Robertson

Cañon

Rexford

Doheny Drive

La Cienega Boulevard

San Vicente

1. Greystone Park & Mansion
2. Beverly Hills Hotel
3. Beverly Hills Country Club
4. Witch's House
5. Church of the Good Shepherd
6. Museum of Television & Radio
7. City Hall
8. Court House
9. Golden Triangle: Rodeo Drive and Wilshire Boulevard Shopping Areas
10. Regent Beverly Wilshire Hotel
11. Beverly Hills High School
12. Avalon Hotel
13. Academy of Motion Picture Arts & Sciences
14. Margaret Herrick Library

N

HUNTER PUBLISHING

NOT TO SCALE

© 2002 HUNTER PUBLISHING, INC.

The land passed through the hands of several gringos from the East, and by the late 1800s was farmed as "one vast field of lima beans." By 1906 it was subdivided, and wide streets with easy sweeping curves were lined with palm, acacia, eucalyptus and pepper trees. The name Beverly Hills came from Beverly Farms, Massachusetts. But buyers were few, Benedict and Franklin Canyons had to be added to bring the population up to the 500 needed to incorporate as a city.

It all changed in 1919 when Douglas Fairbanks and Mary Pickford bought land and built their home, Pickfair. The migration of motion picture people into Beverly Hills began then and has never ended. The city that started with just 500 population has 32,000 now, which is about capacity.

Getting Here

From LAX

By Car

From the airport, go north on Sepulveda Boulevard to the San Diego Freeway (405). Take that to Santa Monica Boulevard, then go right (east). You are in Westwood as you get off the freeway; soon you will go through Century City. You'll pass the Los Angeles Country Club on your left, and in another few blocks you'll be in Beverly Hills.

By Bus

Take the free shuttle to Lot C; at the nearby Transit Center, go to public bus stop 9 and take Metro Bus #561 to Wilshire Boulevard and Veteran Avenue. Transfer to Metro Bus #20 going east. It will take you to the heart of Beverly Hills on Wilshire Boulevard. Fare is $1.85, plus 25¢ for transfer. Bus #561 runs 5:49am-12:20am, #20 runs 24 hours.

★ PARKING TIP

Because of a lack of parking space for residents, some Beverly Hills streets are out of bounds for visitor parking, and fines are steep. Watch out for South Bedford Drive, 400 block; South Elm Drive, 100 block; South Reeves Drive between Cañon Drive and Crescent Drive, the 100 and 200 blocks; and Charleville Boulevard and Gregory Way between Reeves and Elm, including the 300 block of South Cañon.

By Shuttle

Fees vary by company, but generally $20-$24 for one person, $9 for each additional person, plus tip; no airport fee. Try **Prime Time Shuttle**, ☎ 800-733-8267, www.prime-timeshuttle.com; **Super Shuttle**, ☎ 310-782-6600 or 323-775-6600, www.supershuttle.com; or **X-Press**, ☎ 800-427-7483.

By Taxi

The fare is about $27, depending on time of day and traffic, plus a $2.50 airport fee and tip.

 # Getting Around

By Car

For Beverly Hills traffic information, tune your radio to AM 1500. Street parking is usually hard to find, but there are a number of public parking facilities with one, two or three hours free parking.

If you are in the market to tool around Beverly Hills in something a bit more exotic than the usual compact rental, you can hire a Mercedes from Budget Rent-A-Car of Beverly Hills, ☎ 310-274-9178 or 800-729-7350. They also have some new Ferraris you might like; the F355 and F355-F1s have a 24-hour rate of $1,500, and the 550 Maranellos go for $2,500 per day (that does not include the additional charge of $1 per mile). Rental of a Mercedes SUV for an afternoon from Budget Rent-A-Car will cost you $140.

☛ **PARKING TIP**

There are public parking structures between Santa Monica and Little Santa Monica boulevards on every block from Beverly to Linden; they are metered, at 25¢ for 15 minutes, with a three-hour limit.

By Bus

For schedules and route information, contact **MTA** (Metropolitan Transit Authority), ☎ 213-626-4455; and **Santa Monica's Big Blue Bus**, ☎ 310-451-5444

By Taxi

Taxis are available at all Beverly Hills hotels. Try **A Taxi Co.**, ☎ 310-829-4222; **Beverly Hills Taxi Co.**, ☎ 310-273-6611; or **Independent Taxi**, ☎ 310-521-TAXI.

By Limousine

There are 16 chauffeured limousine companies serving Beverly Hills, among them: **Dav El Limousines**, ☎ 310-550-0070; **Mercedes Limousine Service**, ☎ 310-271-8559; and **Rocket Express Limousine**, ☎ 310-559-5162.

> **■ FILM GLOSSARY**
>
> **Grip** – Crew member responsible for the moving and operation of camera support equipment: tripod, dolly, etc.

▊▊ Who Lives Here?

The obvious answer to that question is "lots of stars." In the beginning there were two favored residential areas: one was between Santa Monica Boulevard and Sunset Boulevard, and the other was in the foothills above the Beverly Hills Hotel, north of Sunset. Douglas Fairbanks and Mary Pickford built Pickfair there on Summit Drive, which was Hollywood's Shangri-la for decades. Now Pia Zadora has it. Harold Lloyd built Greenacres, an oversize mansion on 20-some acres, on Greenacres Drive off Benedict Canyon. Ron Berkle, a supermarket mogul, owns it now. Bill Clinton stayed there often when he was president, and big money-raising parties are held in its opulent rooms and on its terraces and lawns.

L.A. Alive is the name of the biennial bash held at Greenacres, which raises $1 million in an evening for the Performing Arts Center.

The area between Santa Monica Boulevard and Sunset is lovely and reeks of old movie money. The streets all slowly curve as they rise on a gentle slope toward Sunset, each lined with trees on both sides, either shade trees with wide branches that meet overhead or tall, majestic royal palms.

Jean Harlow lived in that area in a Spanish bungalow at 512 North Palm Drive, though she also lived at times in other parts of town. Lana Turner lived at 730 North Bedford Drive when her boyfriend was stabbed by her daughter. George Burns and Gracie Allen lived at 720 Maple Drive when Bob wrote for George. Occasionally they worked in the den instead of at the studio, but arboriculturally-deficient Bob doesn't know if the trees on Maple Drive are maples, or the ones on Elm are elms. Carl Reiner lives in the area now, as does Kirk Douglas.

Beverly Hills

📖 **HISTORIC NOTE**

Warren Beatty's film *Bugsy* was based on the life of Bugsy Siegel, the bad-tempered mobster who brought glamour to Las Vegas when he built the Flamingo casino. The house at 810 Linden Drive at Lomitas, a few blocks from Santa Monica Boulevard, was the home of Siegel's girlfriend; this is where he was rubbed out by even more disgruntled mobsters.

Lucille Ball and Desi Arnaz lived just above Sunset and just west of the Beverly Hills Hotel at 1000 North Roxbury Drive. Also on Roxbury were Jack Benny and Jimmy Stewart. In the hills back of and above the hotel were Marion Davies at 1700 Lexington Road (where William Randolph Hearst died), Glenn Ford at 911 Oxford Way, and Frank Sinatra at 915 Foothill Road, though his main residence the 20 years before his death was in Palm Springs. Cary Grant lived in the hills a bit to the west at 9966 Beverly Grove Drive. George Hamilton, Stephanie Powers and Jack Palance live in the area now.

No one who is anyone lives south of Santa Monica Boulevard. All the celebrities live north of that boundary, and most are north of Sunset. Many film people live even farther south, past Wilshire, actors like Frank Sutton, who was the Sergeant on *Gomer Pyle*, and his wife Toby, where we went to great parties when they lived at 205 Rodeo Drive in the non-chic south of Wilshire flats. It is just that no one whose name goes above the title lives down in those sylvan slums between Wilshire and Olympic.

World-famous Beverly Hills is a small town, encompassing only 5.7 square miles (14.7 square kilometers).

BROTHERLY LOVE IN THE
CITY OF STARS

Coldwater Canyon Drive starts at Sunset Boulevard on the east side of the Beverly Hills Hotel and runs up over the mountains and down into the San Fernando Valley. We ran out of gas one time on Coldwater, fortunately on the long straight stretch where there is a sidewalk and houses side by side. Bob walked up to the door of the nearest one, intending to ask to use the phone. He rang the bell; a curtain twitched but no one came to the door. It was the third house before a frightened voice behind the unopened door said she would call the Auto Club. In case you are ever pregnant and looking for shelter on Christmas Eve, our advice is don't come to Beverly Hills.

Will Rogers was the first honorary mayor of Beverly Hills in 1925.

Bert Lahr built a home in Coldwater Canyon in 1941 and lived in it, then sold it to Betty Grable and Harry James. For the last 10 or 12 years Don Johnson has owned it, first with his wife Melanie Griffith until they divorced. Michael Caine has a house right on Coldwater (there are many little short, dead-end streets that run off it), and Carrie Fisher and Charlton Heston are there.

On the ridge along the top of the Santa Monica Mountains runs Mulholland Drive, with views down over Beverly Hills and all of Los Angeles, or across the San Fernando Valley on the other side, or even, to a few fortunate homes, both ways. This is outside the city limits of Beverly Hills and is part of Sherman Oaks, but the Beverly Hills Post Office brings the mail, so these are BH addresses. Marlon Brando lives up here, and Jack Nicholson a few doors away. Sharon Stone sold her house just off Mulholland when she moved to San Francisco to marry that editor of the *Chronicle* who got the weird idea, at the LA Zoo, of sticking his foot in a Komodo dragon lizard's mouth.

☞ DID YOU KNOW?

While Beverly Hills may not actually be "the best-policed six square miles on earth" (the Principality of Monaco probably deserves that title) the wealthy residents of this little village certainly do get unusually good police protection. While the undermanned Los Angeles Police department has a response time of 20-some minutes, Beverly Hills' is less than two minutes.

Actors Matthew Perry (*Friends*) and James Woods have recently sold their Beverly Hills houses. Rosemary Clooney still lives here after 40 or so years. Recent arrivals are pop singer Christina Aguilera; comedian Louie Anderson of *Family Feud*; Eddie Murphy (who knows the area well after making *Beverly Hills Cop*, and who bought a couple of acres to build on); rock star Ozzy Osbourne; Debbie Reynolds, who has moved back from Las Vegas; Sylvester Stallone; Denzel Washington, who left Toluca Lake near Universal and NBC in the Valley to move here; Samuel L. Jackson and his actress wife, LaTanya Richardson, who recently left Encino in the Valley and bought Roseanne's house in the gated and guarded Amestoy Estates; and Diane Keaton, who sold her Beverly Hills home to Madonna. She, in turn, sold her Hollywood Hills home and moved to London, if you are still with us.

Tour buses are allowed to drive Beverly Hills' streets on "Movie Stars Homes" tours, but the buses must weigh less than three tons.

Now that you have seen it, if you are toying with the idea of moving to Beverly Hills, there's a Mediterranean-style house for sale that was built by Lionel Barrymore in 1926, and later became the residence of Marilyn Monroe. As we write this, it's on the market for $2 million. Talk to Barbara Tenenbaum or Lea Porter of Fred Sands Real Estate. And the five-bedroom house where Herman Mankiewicz and Orson Welles wrote much of *Citizen Kane* (the rest was written at a guest ranch where we have stayed near Victorville) is on the market for $2.4 million.

On Location

The house at 614 North Walden Drive (off Wilshire west of its intersection with Santa Monica Boulevard, turn north) was featured in *Beverly Hills Cop II* when Eddie Murphy moved into it. The house where Richard Dreyfuss and Bette Midler lived in *Down and Out in Beverly Hills* is at 802 North Bedford Drive. Bedford is three blocks east of the intersection of Wilshire and Santa Monica. Pictures have been shot at the Beverly Hills Hotel since the early 1900s, and at the Regent Beverly Wilshire (see page 250), where everyone remembers *Pretty Woman*.

Anywhere But Here was filmed all over Beverly Hills, including BH High School. Other films shot here include *Almost Famous*, *15 Minutes*, *Crocodile Dundee in Los Angeles*, *Swordfish* and *Legally Blonde*.

A HALLOWEEN TREAT

The **Witch's House**, the name it is known by in Beverly Hills (516 North Walden Drive, at Carmelita Avenue), has Black Forest architecture with steeply pitched roofs and angled panes on its windows. It was built in Culver City many years ago as a film set. Since it was moved to Beverly Hills it has attracted thousands, especially at Halloween, when the owner runs up a large bill for candy.

Best Places to Stay

No wire hangers!
    – Faye Dunaway as Joan Crawford, *Mommie Dearest.*

The accommodations price scale can be found on page 39.

You will find few motels or flophouses in this tidy little community. Most places are top-notch, and each of the following is definitely a haunt of celebrities.

Hotels

★★ AVALON HOTEL
9400 West Olympic Boulevard
Beverly Hills, CA 90212
☎ 310-277-5221, 800-535-4715, fax 310-277-4928
www.avalon-hotel.com
Moderate-Expensive

This was once a smallish (88 rooms) Beverly Hills hide-away hotel called the Beverly Carlton; Marilyn Monroe lived here for a while. Now it has been completely redone, renamed and restyled back to '50s art deco – and is becoming a Beverly Hills hideaway once more, catering heavily to the movie and fashion crowd. The layout is unusual in that there are three different buildings on three lots; it includes a residential neighborhood, in addition to the hotel, that stretches from Beverly Boulevard to Cañon Drive, so there are the Olympic, Beverly and Cañon buildings.

Avalon's best rooms are those in the Olympic building with balconies overlooking the amoeba-shaped pool.

There is concierge service, in-room massages and aroma-therapy facials, and 24-hour room service from **Blue on Blue** restaurant and bar in the lobby. In addition to the buildings are two residential villas on Cañon, available by the month for those planning a longer stay. Each has a large dining room, two bedrooms, a kitchen and office. A posh home away from home, with all the amenities of the hotel, for $9,000.

★★ BEVERLY HILLS HOTEL & BUNGALOWS
9641 Sunset Boulevard
Beverly Hills, CA 90210
☎ 310-276-2251, 800-283-8885, fax 310-887-2887
www.beverlyhillshotel.com
Deluxe

Limousine service within Beverly Hills is compli-mentary for guests of the Beverly Hills Hotel.

Stars have been drinking here, dining here and staying here ever since there were stars in Hollywood. Harold Lloyd starred in *Tailor-Made Man*, shot at the hotel in 1923, long before *Designing Woman, Move Over Darling* and *California Suite* were filmed here. The hotel was owned, during the 1940s, by Loretta Young, Irene Dunne and Harry Warner. The Polo Lounge was christened that because Will Rogers, Darryl Zanuck and their friends used

Beverly Hills Hotel's bungalow 5 has a private swimming pool, built for businessman Walter Annenberg, who stayed here often.

to drop in after their weekly polo matches. Charlie Chaplin stayed here when he returned from exile to accept a special Oscar.

Howard Hughes came here in 1942 and stayed in bungalow 3 off and on for 40 years. Clark Gable had trysts with Carole Lombard in bungalow 4, in between their weekends at the Hollywood Roosevelt. When Marilyn Monroe and Yves Montand were filming *Let's Make Love*, Monroe and her husband, Arthur Miller, stayed in bungalow 21, while Montand and his wife, Simone Signoret, were in bungalow 20. And Liz Taylor liked the hotel's bungalows so much she honeymooned with six of her husbands in them.

Raquel Welch was discovered by the Beverly Hills Hotel pool, one of the reasons so many aspiring actresses lounge about there now.

What promotes all this loyalty is that the Beverly Hills is a very comfortable hotel. We stayed in a corner room in the wing a few years ago, went down to the pool for dip among the agents and starlets in the afternoon, had a drink at the **Polo Lounge**; it is all very gemütlich. The rooms are large, each has a walk-in closet and an extra touch, a TV in the bathroom. About a third have balconies, fireplaces, terraces or patios.

The 21 bungalows are all different. Each has a living room, dining room and wood-burning fireplace. Some have pianos, Jacuzzis or treadmills for those who want to make music, get wet or work out.

There are tennis courts, lighted at night, and a pool where Katharine Hepburn dove in fully clothed one day after a hot set of tennis. This is where pool manager Svend Petersen taught Faye Dunaway to swim for her role in *Mommie Dearest*. You also see it in *American Gigolo* and the opening of the 1957 film *Designing Woman*. The **Cabana Club Café** is open to the public from 9am-5pm for poolside dining, and a tradition of serving pool guests sorbet at 4pm is still observed.

Service is assured at the Beverly Hills Hotel by the high staff ratio: three per guest.

Oh yes, one other thing we like: there are fresh macaroon cookies on the pillow at night. The hotel is easy to find: it is at the spot where Cañon, Rodeo and Camden all reach Sunset Boulevard.

★ TIP

Beverly Hills' hotel occupancy tax is 14%, plus an additional 1.2% surcharge, which some hotels call by a different name. But a surcharge by any name is still a tax.

★★ FOUR SEASONS HOTEL
300 South Doheny Drive
Los Angeles, CA 90048
☎ 310-273-2222, fax 310-385-4927
www.fourseasons.com
Deluxe

We have been here several times for lunch meetings; although we have never stayed overnight, we are very aware that this is one of those special, large, fine hotels that a city is lucky to have in its midst. On palm-lined Doheny Drive, with lush landscaping outside, and what must be half a marble quarry in the lobby. All rooms and suites have balconies overlooking Beverly Hills and western LA. Amenities include 24-hour room service, overnight shoeshine, packing and unpacking service, an in-house seamstress and one-hour pressing and valet service.

The hotel has an outdoor swimming pool on the fourth floor terrace with panoramic views, and an extensive spa. Complimentary limousine service to nearby Rodeo Drive, and 24-hour concierge. The **Gardens Restaurant** is fairly formal: oil paintings on one side, windows overlooking the gardens on the other, Limoges china on the table linens. The food is California-Pacific, a broad designation that covers a multitude of pleasures. Tea is served in the afternoon, Monday-Saturday, and a lavish Sunday buffet brunch served 10am-2pm, for $49. The café is decidedly more casual, with a more informal menu.

Windows Lounge & Bar is a popular place for movie industry people at night. There is a late-night supper for the after-theater crowd, and a pianist, with even more entertainment Friday and Saturday.

The Four Seasons Hotel offers translation and interpreting services.

LUXE HOTEL RODEO DRIVE
360 North Rodeo Drive
Beverly Hills, CA 90210
☎ 310-273-0300, 800-HOTEL-411
www.luxehotels.com
Moderate-Expensive

Luxe Hotel offers pickup and return from LAX in luxe Towncars.

A stylish boutique hotel (86 rooms) in the middle of Rodeo Drive, that shopaholic's heaven. Breakfast, lunch and dinner are served in the small, skylighted **Café Rodeo** with its even smaller bar. Full, 24-hour room service for meals en suite, if preferred. Robes and slippers, concierge and valet service.

★★ PENINSULA BEVERLY HILLS
9882 South Santa Monica Boulevard
Beverly Hills, CA 90212
☎ 310-551-2888, 800-462-7899
www.peninsula.com
Deluxe

The oval marble and glass Creative Artists Agency next door to the Peninsula hotel was designed by famed architect I.M. Pei.

Just off Wilshire on Little Santa Monica is the top-of-the-line Peninsula. Well known as the site of power breakfasts (it is next door to Creative Artists Agency), it seems to attract celebrities all day and into the night. There are luxuriously furnished rooms, and some villas and suites have private garden entrances. The hotel has a well-known spa, and a pool with cabanas (even the cabanas have telephones, fax and TV). **The Belvedere** restaurant is quiet, intimate and elegant, with California cuisine. There is a Sunday brunch. The Peninsula offers courtesy chauffeured Rolls Royce service to the neighborhood and Century City.

★★ MERV GRIFFIN'S BEVERLY HILTON
9876 Wilshire Boulevard
Beverly Hills, CA 90210
☎ 310-274-7777, 800-922-5432
www.merv.com
Deluxe

We have never heard anyone actually call this hotel Merv Griffin's Beverly Hilton (although, when you phone the hotel and are put on hold, you can while away the time listening to what sounds like ol' Merv singing). It is the

Beverly Hilton and it has been here at the crossroad of Wilshire and Santa Monica boulevards for almost 50 years. There are so many movie industry meetings and parties and dinners taking place here that, if you stand in the wide corridor to the right of the lobby, by the doors to the International Ballroom, almost any evening between 6 and 8pm you are likely to see some celebrities. The main restaurant is Trader Vic's, with "Polynesian" food and umbrellas hovering over rum drinks. The Beverly Hilton is host every year to the Golden Globe Awards and the Academy Award nominees luncheon.

★★ RAFFLES L'ERMITAGE BEVERLY HILLS

9291 Burton Way
Beverly Hills, CA 90210
☎ 310-278-3344, 800-800-2113, fax 310-278-8247
Preferred Hotels & Resorts, 800-323-7500
www.lermitagehotel.com
Deluxe

Raffles L'Ermitage is situated between the centers of Beverly Hills and West Hollywood, a few minutes from each.

This is one of the best hotels in the entire area. A renovation that cost more than the national debt of some small countries has transformed it into a modern hotel with light blond wood paneling. It has always been a quiet haven for celebrities, located just a few blocks from Beverly Hills Golden Triangle.

The choice in accommodations is fairly simple: standard guest rooms are good-sized as hotel rooms go; deluxe rooms are slightly larger; and grand luxe rooms have a separate sitting area, which makes them suites. Other than these, there are only two really big suites. Each room has a large, low bed, with a telephone on each side (there are five phones in every guest room), a desk, a vanity area separate from the bathroom, a 40-inch-screen television, and CD/DVD player. Ask for a room above the third floor (there are eight stories), as traffic on Burton Way can be noisy.

We especially like the extra touches: personalized business cards and letterheads are on the desk in the room when you arrive. And it is the only hotel we know with 24-hour check-in. If you want to arrive at 8pm, no problem – on the last day of your stay you have until 8pm to check out. Another great idea that no other hotel provides: your

L'Ermitage has a fitness center on the 8th floor, with weight training, massage and steam rooms.

L'Ermitage's 3,000 sq. ft. Presidential Suite, with four balconies and a grand piano, costs $3,800 a night.

room has a cell phone to take with you whenever you go out, so you never miss a call.

The **Living Room**, off the lobby, serves afternoon tea, cocktails and snacks by the fireplace. The **Library Bar** has its own fireplace, a cozy place for a cocktail before dinner or a drink after. The **Executive Center**, on the second floor, is a place for champagne before or drinks after dinner, and cigars in a club-like atmosphere. This is possible because California's no-smoking law was enacted to protect the employees from second-hand smoke. There is presumably no service within the room.

The **Restaurant**, with its dome-shaped ceiling, big chandelier and oversized windows serves breakfast, lunch or dinner; there is also an outside patio with its sycamore trees and fountain. Any of the menus are available 24 hours a day in your room, in the Restaurant, in the Library Bar, the Living Room or wherever you would prefer. Dining by the rooftop pool in the evening, with its 360° view of the city and the mountains, is a nice treat.

★★ REGENT BEVERLY WILSHIRE

9500 Wilshire Boulevard

The population of Beverly Hills was fewer than 1,000 when the Regent Beverly Wilshire was built.

Beverly Hills, CA 90210
☎ 310-275-5200, 310-274-2851
www.fourseasons.com
Deluxe

The hotel was built in 1928 at the intersection of Rodeo Drive and Wilshire Boulevard, on the site of one end of the Beverly Auto Speedway, where residents of Los Angeles came out by steam railroad to see Model T auto races on Sunday afternoons. Beverly Hills High School was built at the other end of the racetrack when the Golden Triangle hadn't been dreamt of. It was a far cry from *Pretty Woman*.

The Beverly Wilshire's two penthouse suites are the most expensive in Los Angeles: $5,000 and $7,500 per night.

The hotel has been a hangout for stars from its early days. Fred Astaire and Cary Grant caroused here. Elvis Presley lived in a suite for a while, Warren Beatty had a rooftop suite for 15 years. Steve McQueen took his motorcycle with him into his suite, and the Beatles trashed their suite while celebrating Ringo's birthday. When Barbara Walters pinched the towels the hotel suggested politely that she had made a mistake, undoubtedly because she and they shared the same initials. Elizabeth Taylor, Richard

Harris, Carol Channing, Robert Mitchum and Drew Barrymore have all stayed here, among many others.

Much of *Pretty Woman* was shot in the Presidential Suite in the Wilshire Wing; *Wag the Dog* used the same suite. *Clueless* and *Father's Day* filmed the exteriors of the hotel. *Color of Night* shot around the pool and driveway, *Indecent Proposal* filmed in suite 975 of the Beverly Wing, and *American Gigolo* used several locations in the hotel. We also see the hotel in *Escape From the Planet of the Apes* (1971) and *Beverly Hills Cop*.

The Beverly Wilshire is actually two hotels. The Wilshire wing, built in 1928, which fronts on Wilshire Boulevard, has a classic, traditional feel. Witness the Italian Renaissance façade of white Carrara marble and Tuscany stone. But when you walk through the opulent lobby and across a cobblestone drive lined with gaslight lanterns from a Scottish castle, you enter the much newer Beverly wing. There the décor is contemporary chic, a mixture of silks and wools and pink and gray marble.

Two weeks before the Academy Awards show, Oscars for technological achievement are awarded in the Beverly Wilshire's ballroom.

DID YOU BRING YOUR PET ALONG?

You will be happy to know that the Beverly Wilshire treats pets like royalty. A veterinarian, pet-sitter, groomer are on call, along with "meow mix" and water in bowls served on linen. If that is not enough, you may have squeeze toys delivered on a silver tray.

Nine categories of rooms vary in size, location and view, but most have good-size bathrooms of Italian tile and marble, with separate shower and deep soaking tub.

The art deco-style **Dining Room**, with Murano glass chandeliers suspended from *trompe l'oeil* ceilings, towering bay windows and oil murals, is an elegant place to try the California-continental dishes. Breakfast, lunch and dinner are served here, with a pianist nightly and a jazz duo Saturday nights. The **Lobby Lounge**, with a casual cuisine, is really a neighborhood bistro, it just happens to be in a very sophisticated neighborhood. We like the way it overlooks Rodeo Drive through 15-foot-tall windows. There is a nice three-course dinner until late at night for

The Beverly Wilshire has 120 suites – more than any other hotel in Los Angeles.

Jackets are recommended in the evening in the Beverly Wilshire's Dining Room, but ties are not essential.

$25. Friday and Saturday nights an all-you-can-eat dessert buffet for $10.

Then there is **The Bar**, also off the lobby in the Wilshire wing, where we have probably rubbed elbows with more celebrities over the years than anywhere else in the hotel.

NOT TO FORGET THE KIDS...

The Beverly Wilshire has a special program for overnight guests ages two-12. Start with strollers and cribs available, go on to a stuffed toy animal, a teddy bear T-shirt, coloring book with crayons, teddy bear tearless shampoo, bath soap and bubble bath, and milk and cookies served on a silver tray. The main danger of this "Comforts of Home" program is that your children will want to go on being treated this way when they *are* home.

Best Places to Eat

Almost all of the hotels in Beverly Hills are expensive, most of the shops very expensive, so you are expecting something different from the restaurants?

Fine Dining

The dining price scale can be found on page 42.

CHADWICK
267 South Beverly Drive
☎ 310-205-9424
California
Very Expensive

Chadwick, featuring fresh, locally grown vegetables, is owned by chef Ben Ford, son of Harrison Ford. Dinner only, Monday-Saturday, 6-10pm; Sunday, 6-9pm.

DELMONICO'S SEAFOOD GRILLE
9320 West Pico Boulevard
☎ 310-550-7737
Seafood/Steaks
Moderate-Expensive

An old-style New York restaurant, complete with booths, transported to Beverly Hills (actually, it's between Beverly Hills and West Hollywood in a never-land called West LA). No nouveau California menu here, still plenty of rich sauces; mostly seafood, with enough steaks to keep the others happy. Reservations recommended. Open Monday-Friday, 11:30am-10pm; Saturday from 5pm; Sunday from 4pm. Valet parking.

★★ JAAN
Raffles L'Ermitage Beverly Hills
9291 Burton Way
☎ 310-385-5307
Asian-French-American
Very Expensive

If you are bored with the thought of another Italian restaurant or are weary of steak houses, you will find that Jaan is definitely different. Their cuisine expresses a fusion of Indochinese, French and American cooking, and the flavors are delicate and subtle. The menu changes often, usually listing one soup, a half-dozen each of salads and entrées, and several desserts. Each meal starts with a complimentary appetizer. Ours, on a recent visit, was of sweet onion, melted feta cheese, and raw ahi tuna. There was a salad of Maine lobster, Belgian endive, watercress and sprouts with a misting of green apple vinaigrette; it was so good that Phyllis ordered a second portion and skipped the entrée. The wild black bass with Manila clams and risotto was delicious, but the bass was served rare, as is much of the fish here. There are meat dishes available, such as roasted lamb loin, as well as vegetarian items.

"Jaan" is Cambodian for dish or bowl.

The room is impressive; there is a small floor area with only about eight tables, but the ceiling is at least two stories high. The table settings are modern and attractive, with comfortable chairs. Huge windows overlook a fountain, and there's a patio that is popular in warm weather.

Beverly Hills

L'Ermitage attracts show-biz people, which means those in the production or business end, as well as celebrities. Rockers tend to stay at this high-end, decorous hotel, perhaps as a respite from the put-on stage antics. The other night one of us said, "Isn't that what's-her-name?" And the other replied, "No, I think it's, you know, what's-her-name." The trouble is, we are of the wrong generation to remember rock stars' names, and of course the maître d' won't divulge anyone's identity in this expensive hideaway. Open daily for breakfast, lunch and dinner; call for hours. Reservations recommended.

★★ IL CIELO

9018 Burton Way
☎ 310-276-9990
Italian
Expensive

So many weddings are celebrated at Il Cielo it is best to call ahead for reservations to make sure the restaurant will be open to the public.

This is a place for couples. Romance is as big on the menu here as the risotto. Even the lobster-stuffed ravioli is heart-shaped. Though that sounds hokey, it *is* a romantic place; it looks like a Tuscan cottage with a wrought-iron gate, a patio and garden, and two dining rooms, complete with fireplaces. Lesley Ann Warren and advertising executive Ron Taft had their first date, and then were married, here. Shirley Jones and Marty Ingels, after separating, came here when they reunited.

Though owner Pasquale Vericella was born in Sorrento much of the food is Northern Italian, fairly light and contemporary. There is a six-course tasting menu for two. Il Cielo is open Monday-Saturday, with lunch from 11:30am-3pm, and dinner from 5:30-10pm. It is located between Doheny Drive and Robertson Boulevard. Incidentally, *cielo* (the sky) is pronounced "chee-EL-o."

★★ NIC'S

453 North Cañon Drive
☎ 310-550-5707
American-continental
Expensive

The dinner menu (Nic's is only open for dinner) does not overwhelm with its size, but what is here offers a nice range of appetizers and salads, and then entrées. The

Beverly Hills

chef's continental training shows up with the way each dish is finished off: the crusted swordfish with basil and capers, the prime rib of pork with maple soy glaze. If you are dining a bit on the late side you will be right on hand for the popular Nic's Martini Lounge club for an after-dinner drink. (See Martini Lounge, page 276.)

It is just up the street from the Cañon Theatre; parking is available in a nearby lot or with valet service. Dinner on weekdays is served 6-10pm, on weekends to 11pm.

WHAT'S IN A NAME?

The beach restaurant Gladstone's 4 Fish lists its address as Malibu, but it is actually in Pacific Palisades. A number of places have Bel-Air in their names even though they are nowhere near Bel-Air. As the Beverly Hills border runs downs Doheny Drive and the Four Seasons Hotel is on the east or Los Angeles side of the street, the hotel lists its address as "Los Angeles at Beverly Hills." We applaud truth in advertising.

★★ THE POLO LOUNGE
Beverly Hills Hotel & Bungalows
9641 Sunset Boulevard
☎ 310-276-2251
Oak-grilled food with an Asian flair
Very Expensive

Celebrities have been coming here ever since the hotel was opened, not long after Hollywood was opened. The hotel has changed owners several times, with a long gap when it was closed for extensive renovations a few years ago, during which time quite a few people who formerly took power meetings here got used to wining and dining elsewhere. But a number are coming back. You'll usually see more celebrities at breakfast and lunch, combining a meal with a meeting, than at dinner.

Humphrey Bogart used to hang out here, as did Frank Sinatra, Sammy Davis and the others of that pack. Marlene Dietrich was supposed to have broken the code that ladies couldn't wear pants into the Polo Lounge in the 1940s. If so, it didn't take. The maître d' handed Phyllis a skirt to put on over her slacks when we were there to meet our agent in the '70s. That ritual has been done away with, although jackets are still "suggested" after 7pm.

The Polo Lounge is a favored lunch spot for the ladies of Beverly Hills, as well as with movie people making deals. Sunday brunch has mariachi music accompaniment. The Polo Lounge is a favorite of ours for dinner. We like sitting out in the patio, under a tree, with piano music in the background. Open daily, 7am-1:45am.

> ★ **TIP**
>
> Although dinner is served at the Polo Lounge only until 11pm, a limited menu is available after that, with pizza, omelets, pasta and sandwiches. And, though they don't advertise it, the kitchen staff will make anything you care to order until the bar closes at 1:30am.

★★ SPAGO BEVERLY HILLS
176 North Cañon Drive
☎ 310-385-0880
California-French-Austrian
Very Expensive

Spago's owner-chef Wolfgang Puck first became known as chef at the now-closed restaurant Ma Maison, which had an unlisted phone number.

When Wolfgang Puck closed his Spago Restaurant just above Sunset Boulevard in West Hollywood, where items like nouvelle pizza made him the most famous chef in the country, it was to open Spago Beverly Hills. Whereas the original place was open and casual, this one is intimate and much more obviously about power and money. After all, this is Beverly Hills.

The main room has much glass art, with panels, patio doors and skylights, ceramic art and a couple dozen paintings, including Hockneys, Miró lithos and Picasso sketches. The outdoor patio, which many prefer, is built around a few hundred-year-old olive trees (these are not native trees; they were planted, according to one story, by missionaries in Sylmar in the San Fernando Valley, and saved from being bulldozed), and a fountain.

It is hopeless to name the celebrities who come here, as the list would be too long. Someone mentioned seeing Maria Shriver, Arnold Schwarzenegger and producer Al Ruddy dining here. But one pair of diners intrigues us most of all: Jim Carrey and Henry Kissinger. Together.

The menu changes daily; dishes are derived from Puck's classic French training, with California cuisine's insistence on fresh, never-overcooked vegetables. They include lots of pastas and seafood as well; if you are a steak-and-potatoes person, go to Palm or Pacific Dining Car. Dinner is served every day from 5:30pm to 9:30 or 10:30, depending on the reservations. Lunch Monday-Friday, 11:30am-2:15pm; Saturday, noon-2:15pm. Valet parking.

Wolfgang Puck also owns Chinois on Main in Santa Monica, and Granita in Malibu.

★ TIP

Get the *Beverly Hills Visitors' Guide*, containing a wealth of information, from the Beverly Hills Visitors Bureau, 239 South Beverly Drive, Beverly Hills, CA 90212, ☎ 310-248-1015, or 800-345-2210.

Casual Dining

★★ BARNEY GREENGRASS
9570 Wilshire Boulevard
☎ 310-777-5877
Moderate-Expensive

This is a branch of the New York deli, from whence the smoked sturgeon and salmon is flown in. It's on the top floor of Barney's New York, and is definitely fancier than the original, with a caviar-vodka bar and a terrace, from which to view the hills of Beverly while munching imported (also from New York) bagels. Open 8:30am-6pm daily; Saturday to 7pm.

At Barney Greengrass you get New York-style seltzer for 2¢ a glass, with free refills.

MULBERRY STREET PIZZA
347 North Cañon Drive
☎ 310-247-8998
Pizza
Inexpensive

Actors James Caan and Cathy Moriarty, homesick for the kind of pizza they used to get in New York, opened Mulberry Street. The décor features lots of signed movie posters on the walls. Mulberry Street serves all the basic types of pizza but with a thin New York-style crust. They also offer a few meaty Italian sandwiches, though we have never got the knack of eating a sandwich with three big meatballs without losing at least one to gravity. Open daily, 11am-10pm.

★★ NATE 'N AL'S
414 North Beverly Drive
☎ 310-274-0101
Deli
Inexpensive

Nate 'n Al's is a half-block south of Little Santa Monica Boulevard.

As long as we can remember this has been the Beverly Hills place for celebrity schmoozing, especially for comics and comedy writers. Groucho Marx used to come in here, and Milton Berle. You might see Rodney Dangerfield or Carl Reiner. Definitely Larry King. Very big as a power breakfast spot for film people.

On top of that, the food is good deli fare, with everything from noodle pudding to cold beet borscht. And they make over 70 kinds of sandwiches. Open daily, 7am-9pm.

Afternoon Tea

When high tea is mentioned, one always thinks of Britain and Jane Austen (well, *we* do), but tea's popularity as a beverage really began in China, 4,000 years or so ago. According to legend, the process of brewing tea was discovered by accident when a leafy branch fell into a pot of hot water, which the farmer's daughter, a virgin (this is possibly the movie version of the story), tasted and cried out, "Eureka!," or the Chinese translation thereof. Tea got to Europe by way of Portuguese merchants in the 16th century and spread to America with the colonists. Now it has spread to Beverly Hills.

FOUR SEASONS HOTEL
300 South Doheny Drive (at Burton Way)
☎ 310-273-2222

The Four Seasons serves a formal tea, with meticulous service and all the goodies that go along with the choicest blends. Tea is served in the impressive Gardens Restaurant, Monday-Saturday, 3-4:30pm. The price is $24; with champagne it is $27.

RAFFLES L'ERMITAGE
9291 Burton Way
☎ 310-385-5344

Tea at L'Ermitage starts with champagne and continues with a three-course service that includes delicious finger sandwiches, scones with Devonshire cream and homemade jams, and finally sweets, each course accompanied by the appropriate teas. The presentation has Asian touches, courtesy of Raffles' origins in Singapore. The price is $30.

REGENT BEVERLY WILSHIRE
Lobby Lounge
9500 Wilshire Boulevard
☎ 310-275-5200

Tea selections range from Earl Grey to China Rose or Jasmine Blossoms at the Regent Beverly Wilshire.

The Beverly Wilshire serves a traditional tea with finger sandwiches, toasted teacakes and scones with Devonshire cream and fruit preserves, then follows up with French pastries and chocolate-dipped strawberries. Tea is served in the Lobby Lounge, with sofas and plush chairs and a piano playing in the background. From 3-5pm, $21; $25 with sparkling wine or sherry.

Shop Till You Drop

I always say a kiss on the hand might feel very good, but a diamond tiara lasts forever.
— Marilyn Monroe, *Gentlemen Prefer Blondes*

We recognize that some people come to Los Angeles not to see the stars of Hollywood but to spend their entire time shopping in Beverly Hills. But that too fits right in with the purposes of this book; Beverly Hills is the place you are most likely to serendipitously do one while expensively accomplishing the other.

Beverly Hills has several distinct shopping areas. The best way to do each of them is to walk, window-shop, go in and browse. Fortunately, each area is compact and easy to cover at a leisurely saunter. Following the districts, we will point out a few specialty places where celebrities shop that you might otherwise miss.

★ TIP

If you ask someone "Where's RO-dee-oh Drive?" they will look at you as if you are speaking another language. Pronounce it the Spanish way, Ro-DAY-oh, to make yourself understood.

The Golden Triangle

There are only 16 blocks within the Golden Triangle; it can be walked in stages, between stops in cafés.

Most of the upscale shops are concentrated here, between Wilshire Boulevard and Little Santa Monica, which cross at a point; the base of the triangle is Cañon Drive. Only six short streets bisect the area at a northwest-southeast angle, and only three that run parallel to Little Santa Monica cross those. It is possible to walk the whole area, and interesting upscale stores are on every street, along with a scattering of cafés, some with sidewalk tables, for occasional relaxation.

★★ Rodeo Drive

Within the triangle is a street that, though only three blocks long, is famous around the world because of the stores found here. If you are interested in shopping it is worth spending an hour or so walking up one side and down the other. Here are some of the places to look for, listed in order by their address, starting from Wilshire. All phone numbers have a 310 area code.

Beverly Hills

> ☞ *DID YOU KNOW?*
>
> **2 Rodeo**, which begins at Rodeo Drive and Wilshire Boulevard, is the first new street in Beverly Hills since its incorporation in 1914.

◆ **Tiffany & Co.**, 210 Rodeo, ☎ 273-8880.

◆ **Cartier**, 220 Rodeo, ☎ 275-5155.

◆ **Christian Dior**, 230 Rodeo, ☎ 859-4700, women's clothing.

◆ **Valentino**, 240-250 Rodeo, ☎ 247-9691, women's apparel.

◆ **Van Cleef & Arpels**, 300 Rodeo, ☎ 276-1161, jewelry.

◆ **Battaglia Shop**, 306 Rodeo, ☎ 276-7184, men's clothing and accessories.

◆ **Cartier**, 370 Rodeo, ☎ 275-4272; this branch is larger and carries the company's high-end jewelry.

◆ **Chanel**, 400 Rodeo Drive, ☎ 278-4700, fragrance, women's ready-to-wear.

◆ **Lladró**, 408 Rodeo, ☎ 385-0683, porcelain figurines from Spain.

◆ **Hermès of Paris**, 434 Rodeo, ☎ 278-6440, leather goods, men's and women's apparel.

◆ **Giorgio Armani**, 436 Rodeo, ☎ 271-5555, men's and women's apparel.

◆ **Polo Ralph Lauren**, 444 Rodeo, ☎ 281-1500, apparel for men, women.

◆ **Tommy Hilfiger**, 468 Rodeo, ☎ 888-0132, men's and women's apparel.

◆ **Alfred Dunhill of London**, 465 Rodeo, ☎ 274-5351, cigars and gifts.

◆ **Lacoste**, 447 Rodeo, ☎ 385-0655, clothing for men, women and children.

Not all the shops in the Golden Triangle sell clothing; there are 24 bakeries, coffee houses and specialty gourmet shops here.

Dior and Armani gowns are seen every year at the Academy Awards ceremony.

Amphora Arts and Antiques, 308 Rodeo Drive, has Oscars – or entire estates – for sale.

♦ **Gucci**, 347 Rodeo, ☎ 278-3451, men's and women's apparel.

♦ **Lalique**, 317 Rodeo, ☎ 271-7892, fine crystal.

♦ **Louis Vuitton**, 295 Rodeo, ☎ 859-0457, luggage, shoes for men and women.

☛ **DID YOU KNOW?**

The common perception that salesclerks in Beverly Hills stores are rude and snooty is called "*Pretty Woman* Syndrome," referring to Julia Roberts' experience in the movie of that name. The Beverly Hills Chamber of Commerce holds customer service workshops for shop owners and clerks to make sure that does not happen.

Wilshire Boulevard

There are restaurants inside each of the three big department stores on Wilshire Boulevard.

If larger stores are more to your taste, hie thee to the south side of Wilshire Boulevard where the department stores are lined up. Don't let their lack of expensive intimacy put you off, it doesn't deter the celebs who shop here. Start in the block west of the Regent Beverly Wilshire Hotel.

★★ BARNEYS NEW YORK
9570 Wilshire Boulevard
☎ 310-276-4400, 310-277-5742
www.barneys.com

Barneys is known for hot, up-to-the-minute designers, plus a full range of well-known labels. And you'll enjoy the New York deli, Barney Greengrass, on the top floor. (See Barneys maternity line on page 267.) The store is open Monday-Saturday, 10am-7pm; Thursday to 8pm.

★★ SAKS FIFTH AVENUE

East Building, 9600 Wilshire Boulevard
☎ 310-275-4211
West Building, 9634 Wilshire Boulevard
☎ 310-275-4211

Saks nurtures new designers, and continues to offer classics like Pamela Dennis' collections (see Neiman Marcus). Saks brought its East Coast reputation for service to Beverly Hills. They have two buildings on Wilshire. The east building, at the corner of Peck, has women's clothes; the west building, at the corner of Bedford, is primarily men's, with a floor for ladies' petite sizes and one for womens' large sizes. Open Monday-Wednesday and Friday, 10am-6pm; Thursday, 10am-8:30pm; Saturday, 10am-7pm; and Sunday, noon-6pm.

★★ NEIMAN MARCUS

9700 Wilshire Boulevard
☎ 310-550-5900, 310-975-4335
www.neimanmarcus.com

At Neiman's you'll find top-end as well as popular designer labels, a shoe department with a wide selection, and men's and children's apparel as well as women's. Look for Pamela Dennis' gowns here (she has dressed stars like Ellen DeGeneres, Anne Heche, Helen Hunt, Meg Ryan and Kate Winslet for the various award shows in her $3,000-$4,000 creations). The store also carries the Pamela Dennis Collection at the $1,000 level.

★ WHO GOES THERE?

Celebrities like bargains as much as the rest of us. Check out Neiman Marcus' 70% Off! sale held in July. Last year one of the bargain hunters was Nancy Reagan, with two discreet Secret Service agents in tow.

★ **TIP**

The gentleman decked out in a red-and-black frock coat, top hat, black tie and white gloves, greeting shoppers under the clock at the corner of Rodeo Drive, Via Rodeo Drive and Wilshire Boulevard, is Gregg Donovan. He greets people in their own language (Gregg can say hello in 30 languages) as they enter the piazza of 2 Rodeo. For tourists asking where the stars are, he has pointed out such fellow shoppers as Warren Beatty, Dennis Hopper, Anthony Hopkins, and Sharon Stone.

Specialty Stores & Services

Latin American Masters gallery, 264 North Beverly Drive, specializes in art from Latin America.

There are some stores that, though not on Rodeo Drive, are in the area and should not be missed if you are serious about shopping where celebs shop.

Books

RIZZOLI BOOKSTORE
9501 Wilshire Boulevard
☎ 310-278-2247

The store hosts poetry and prose readings, book signings and musical performances. Open daily, 10am-6pm; Thursday and Saturday to 7pm; Sunday, 11am-6pm. Rizzoli is across the street from the Beverly Wilshire.

STORYOPOLIS
116 North Robertson Boulevard
☎ 310-358-2500

This shop specializes in children's books; they also have a great collection of greeting cards inspired by classic children's stories. Open Monday-Saturday, 10am-6pm.

Bridal

★★ RENEE STRAUSS
8692 Wilshire Boulevard
☎ 310-657-1700

Raquel Welch, Victoria Principal and Roseanne all
shopped here for their wedding finery. Gowns from Renée
Strauss have appeared on *ER*, *Beverly Hills 90210* and
Melrose Place.

If you are shopping for the perfect wedding dress, you may
also wish to look into **Bridal Images**, 9740 Wilshire Boulevard, ☎ 310-274-4090; and **Brides International**, 275
La Cienega Boulevard, ☎ 310-652-8447.

Clothing

★★ LILY ET CIE
9044 Burton Way
☎ 310-274-5757

Rita Watnick has had an obsession with clothes for most of
her life, which has resulted in her amassing one of the
largest collections of high-quality clothing in the country.
The vast, open main space of the building is filled with
racks of Diors and Valentinos, with Galanos gowns and
Oleg Cassini designs. Demi Moore wore a navy jersey
Norell at the Emmys and Renee Zellweger a Jean Desses
at the Oscars – both came from here. Every year at the
awards shows stars are wearing dresses from Lily et Cie.

It is possible to find a dress or sweater for $100 or less, but
most prices are higher, into the thousands. Open Monday-
Friday, 10am-6pm; Saturday, 11am-4pm. Park on street,
or try for a space behind the store (turn into the alley off
Weatherly, go to the end).

★★ LISA KLINE
136 South Robertson
☎ 310-246-0907

Call this a youthful boutique. Shop here for T-shirts, pajamas, halter tops, wrap skirts and the like. Julia Roberts,
Courteney Cox, Jennifer Aniston and Drew Barrymore

have. Open Monday-Saturday, 11am-7pm; Sunday, noon-5pm. This is just outside Beverly Hills in a little intrusive bit of Los Angeles, between Beverly Boulevard and Third Street. Parking lot is across the street, as is Lisa Kline's Men's Store at 123 Robertson.

★★ CARROLL & COMPANY
425 North Cañon Drive
☎ 310-273-9060

This has been a favorite of many gentlemen in show biz for many years. Cary Grant had a suit tailor-made for him here. After the third fitting, when the tailors were proud they had finished and done perfect work, he said, "Well, fellows, I think we're starting to get there." Most men, the tailors are happy to tell you, are easier to please. Of course, most men don't look like Cary Grant. Now they sell their goods off-the-rack, and they are friendly folk. Open Monday-Saturday, 9am-6pm.

Maternity Wear

When Lucille Ball was expecting during *I Love Lucy* you couldn't even say the word "pregnant" on TV. But ever since Demi Moore's 1991 nude magazine cover, stars have made it fashionable to be fashionably enceinte. There are a few places in Beverly Hills they can go to achieve that status.

★★ A PEA IN THE POD
352 North Beverly Drive
☎ 310-273-3522
www.apeainthepod.com

This company is nationally known for maternity versions of styles from upscale lines, including ABS, Nicole Miller, Bisou Bisou and Robin Piccone. Here you can find the black leather pants like Marlee Matlin bought, the snake-skin pants that Melina Kanakaredes (*Providence*) wore to a premiere, or a stretch-mesh Vivienne Tam dress. Open Monday-Saturday, 10am-6pm; Sunday, noon-5pm.

★★ BARNEYS NEW YORK
9570 Wilshire Boulevard
☎ 310-276-4400
www.barneys.com

Barneys carries the Procreation line, plus designer labels L'Atessa and Mamma Luna, with capri pants, slit slim skirts, stretch cashmere sweaters and raw silk drawstring pants. The maternity department is on the third floor.

Gourmet Foods

BEVERLY HILLS CAVIARTERIA
158 South Beverly Drive
☎ 310-285-9773
www.caviarteria.com

Well stocked in these difficult times for roe lovers, with the Caspian Sea polluted and pirated, so every variety is not always available. But there is probably more here in this small shop than anywhere else. Open Monday-Saturday, 10am-5:30pm.

THE CHEESE STORE OF BEVERLY HILLS
419 North Beverly Drive
☎ 310-278-2855

For cheese-lovers, this is like reaching paradise. You have never seen such cheeses. They are also strong in the olives department, with imported varieties that are hard to find in the US, and offer a good selection of caviar and wine. Open Monday-Saturday, 10am-6pm.

★★ EDELWEISS CHOCOLATES
444 North Cañon Drive
☎ 310-275-0341, 888-615-8800

Maple creams from Edelweiss were Frank Sinatra's favorites, though there are more than 60 other types for celebrities and the rest of us to choose from. By the pound, $24. Open Monday-Friday, 10am-6pm; Saturday to 5:30pm.

Farmers' Market

This market is on North Cañon Drive, in the 200 block between Clifton and Dayton ways. There are over 45 vendors offering breads, fresh seasonal produce, juices, flowers and prepared foods. A good place to shop for celebrities. For *The Young and the Restless* fans, Lauralee Bell is a regular. Sundays, 9am-1pm.

☛ **DID YOU KNOW?**

While only 32,000 people live in Beverly Hills, over 200,000 work here.

Jewelry

So you are in Beverly Hills on vacation and you met a well-dressed, friendly man who seemed sincere and liked you so much he let you in on a fabulous deal. Now you have no money and need cash to get home, so...

★★ SOUTH BEVERLY WILSHIRE JEWELRY & LOAN
157 South Beverly Drive, a block south of Wilshire
☎ 310-888-1818

The Hands On nail salon, 243 South Beverly Drive, ☎ 310-860-1037, is owned by Michael Wolper, son of producer David Wolper.

There is one defining word missing in the name. This is, after all, a pawn shop. But why would the filthy-rich people of Beverly Hills need a pawn shop? As Susan Emerling said, writing about the subject in the *LA Times*, "Being wealthy doesn't come cheap." This is a town where conspicuous displays of wealth are considered compulsory. If you don't have a new Mercedes and a mansion in the hills, who would do business with you? So if you are famous and have an Oscar but suddenly need cash – discreetly – you come to see Yossi Dina. Yossi, of course, won't reveal who brought in the original Tiffany lamp, Ming jade vase or fully restored classic Harley-Davidson. Most of his loans are made on jewelry (such as engagement rings); George Hamilton comes here to buy for his collection of antique watches. Monday-Saturday, 10am-5:30pm.

★★ MELANIE BERG & CO.
9363 Wilshire Boulevard
☎ 310-278-4248

Pearls should be restrung once a year, especially if there is play between the pearls, or if the thread looks yellowish or frayed. A standard preppy choker costs about $100 to restring. Magdalena (her professional name), following in the footsteps of her mother, Melanie, has restrung pearls for Jacqueline Bisset, Judith Krantz, Ed McMahon, Helen Reddy, Don Rickles and many other celebrities. Magdalena restrung the pearls that Joe DiMaggio gave to Marilyn Monroe on their honeymoon (but years later, when Susan Strasberg had them). Look for a rather plain building on Wilshire; the shop is on the second floor, suite 202. Call for an appointment.

Shoes

★★ TOD'S
333 Rodeo Drive
☎ 310-285-0591

Tod's (sometimes listed as JP Tod's) D-bag, a boxy leather tote, was carried by Princess Diana, who had a tan version. Hilary Clinton has one. The evening shoes and bags always get a lot of red carpet time at the awards shows. This large new store has cut down on opportunities for celebrity-watching with the creation of VIP room for stars who wish to shop in private. Unless you are a VIP, too, of course. Monday-Saturday, 10am-6pm; Sunday, noon-5pm.

Reweaving & Shoe Repair

★★ TOSHI'S INVISIBLE REWEAVING
427 North Cañon Drive
☎ 310-274-3468

There's a cigarette hole in your blazer? Moths munched on a favorite cashmere sweater? Toshi Ichihara put the word 'invisible' in the name of the shop because her repairs really are. Generations of stars, from Jack Benny to Kevin Costner, have thought so, too. Call for an appointment.

★★ ARTURO'S SHOE FIXX
9643 Little Santa Monica
☎ 310-278-9585

Do you need shoes or a bag dyed, altered or completely re-built? Kim Basinger needed shoes dyed to match the dress she wore to accept her Oscar; likewise Kim Cattrall for the Golden Globes, and Laura Bush just before the presidential inauguration. Arturo's hole-in-the-wall shop is where they come to get it done (though perhaps the first lady wasn't in here herself pleading with him to get her order back right away). Stand-up comedian Rosee Brumfeld was in to get her thigh-high suede boots tightened. Open Monday-Saturday, 8am-6pm. Between Camden and Bedford drives, on the north side.

Sporting Goods

BOBBY JONES GOLF
310 North Beverly Drive
☎ 310-860-9566

This shop is well known for sports apparel as well as golfing stuff. Open Monday-Saturday, 10am-6pm.

Wines & Spirits

Find your favorite beverages at **Beverly Hills Liquor Castle**, 212 South Beverly Drive, ☎ 310-273-6000; **Cañon Liquor & Café/"**, 350 North Cañon Drive, ☎ 310-246-9463; **Vendome**, 9153 Olympic Boulevard, ☎ 310-276-9463; and **The Wine Merchant**, 9467 Little Santa Monica Boulevard, ☎ 310-278-7322.

Sunup to Sundown

Film History

ACADEMY OF MOTION PICTURE ARTS AND SCIENCES

8949 Wilshire Boulevard
☎ 310-247-3000

This building houses a theater and the offices of the Academy. The galleries in the lobby and upstairs have exhibits that change every few months and are open to the public Monday-Friday, 10am-5pm; Saturday and Sunday, noon-6pm. It is great seeing films here as they should be seen – not in a living room-size box in a multiplex, but in a big, really comfortable theater with a huge screen and wonderful sound – the way all cinemas used to be. Most screenings are for Academy members only, but special showings are occasionally open to the public. Announcements are made in the *Calendar* section of the *LA Times*.

Phone the Academy for information on screenings open to the public.

MARGARET HERRICK LIBRARY, ACADEMY OF MOTION PICTURE ARTS AND SCIENCES

333 South La Cienega Boulevard
☎ 310-247-3020

Beverly Hills always has done things in style. The city long ago built its striking water purification plant in a Spanish-Romanesque style. When it was abandoned the Academy took it over and used the old storage tanks as film vaults. The building is now a unique library housing one of the most complete collections of film-related material ever assembled. It includes books, pamphlets, periodicals, still photos, scripts, press clippings, personal and business correspondence, production memoranda, sketches, sheet music, music scores and scrapbooks.

The Academy film archive is one of the largest repositories of motion pictures in the US.

It is all for research, nothing can be checked out, but if you want to look up arcane details on a favorite actor or film, this is the place. Open Monday, Tuesday, Thursday and Friday, 10am-5:30pm. Parking is next door, under tennis courts; first two hours free, then 50¢ per hour.

IT'S A GREAT LIFE

The real **Beverly Hills High School** is not the one that was shown in *Beverly Hills 90210* (those scenes were shot at much less affluent Torrance High, some miles to the south). Some parents cheat, lie and scrounge to get their kids enrolled in Beverly Hills High, such as falsely using the address of a relative or friend who lives in the district. Academic standards are high (just think what Monica Lewinsky learned when she attended), but according to friends whose kids have gone here, it can be tough on a less-than-rich student.

For years the school had its own producing oil wells on the grounds, which brought in extra bucks that were invested in lavish facilities. For instance, the gymnasium floor recedes and reveals a swimming pool that we see every holiday season when *It's a Wonderful Life* plays on TV again. Lots of stars went to school here: Richard Chamberlain, Richard Dreyfuss, Carrie Fisher and Rob Riener for instance.

It is at 244 South Lasky Drive, in the little triangle of streets east of Little Santa Monica between Wilshire and Moreno. Or if you are on Olympic going west toward Century City, you see it to your right at Spalding.

★ CINEMA ARTS GALLERY
179 South Beverly Drive
☎ 310-246-9333

Showings like a Clark Gable exhibition, with pictures of Gable from all stages of his life, are frequent. Call to see what is on.

GREYSTONE PARK & MANSION
905 Loma Vista Drive
☎ 310-550-4654

Many movies have been filmed at this gorgeously impressive mansion, including *All of Me*, *The Beautician and the Beast*, *The Bodyguard*, *Death Becomes Her*, *The Fabulous Baker Boys*, *Guilty by Suspicion*, *Indecent Proposal*, *The Marrying Man*, *Nixon* and *The Witches of Eastwick*.

A nicely *noir* story goes with Greystone. Edward Doheny, the very rich oil man who was involved in the Teapot Dome scandal, built the 55-room mansion in 1927 for his son and daughter-in-law, a couple who apparently needed a lot of room. But shortly after they moved in the son was shot to death in his bedroom by his male secretary. Rumors flew about a lover's quarrel, but since the secretary also killed himself we will never know.

The 23 acres of grounds are beautiful, with views of Beverly Hills and beyond. From Sunset Boulevard between Doheny and the Beverly Hills Hotel, turn north on Mountain Road to the first block, Loma Vista Drive, then right to Doheny Road. At the closed double wrought-iron gates there is a gate house where you can get a brochure that tells the whole story. Or drive up to the parking lot (parking is free) and get a brochure from a Park Ranger.

The mansion is closed to the public, though the city rents it out for opulent weddings and immense parties. The park is open daily; in summer, 10am-6pm; in winter, to 5pm.

MUSEUM OF TELEVISION & RADIO
465 North Beverly Drive
☎ 310-786-1000

The museum hosts screenings and presents radio broadcasts, and has collections of films and television episodes. Open Wednesday-Sunday, noon-5pm; Thursday, noon-9pm.

There is no admission charge at the Museum of Television and Radio, but donations are requested.

Tours

Walking Tours

THE AMBASSADEARS
These professionally trained, multilingual guides are the
Beverly Hills Visitors Bureau's official docents (they are
really much better than that embarrassing name). They
are available to give walking tours to leisure travelers,
business travelers and journalists interested in learning
more about Beverly Hills. The tour is $80, with a four-
hour maximum time limit. Phone ☎ 310-248-1015.

☞ DID YOU KNOW?

The **Church of the Good Shepherd**, 505 North Bedford Drive (north
of Wilshire and Santa Monica boulevards), is where Elizabeth Taylor and
Nicky Hilton, her first husband, were
married in 1950. The funerals of Jimmy Durante, Alfred Hitchcock and
Gary Cooper were held here. The exterior has been seen in many movies.

CIVIC CENTER PUBLIC ART WALKING TOUR
Art-loving Beverly Hills has large-scale works by Charles
Moore, Claes Oldenburg, Auguste Rodin and others, and
is acquiring more. For a close-up look join a docent-led
tour, usually held on the first Saturday of each month;
tours are available from May-September, 1-2pm. Meet at
the door of City Hall, 450 North Crescent Drive, on the
west side of the building. Free. Phone beforehand in case
of schedule changes, ☎ 310-288-2201.

☞ DID YOU KNOW?

The **Writers & Artists Building**, 9507 Santa Monica Boulevard at Beverly Drive, is where creative types have had offices since the early 1920s. Charlie Chaplin, Eddie Cantor, Ray Bradbury, Jack Nicholson and Billy Wilder have labored here. The building is still a hive of activity for the talented.

Trolley Tours

Beverly Hills Trolley Tours cover Beverly Hills at a nice pace and in comfort as a docent, steeped in local history, gives the lowdown on everything. There are two separate tours; both run May-December, Saturday only. The Art and Architecture Tour departs at 11am; it is 50 minutes long. The Sights and Scenes Tour departs on the hour from noon-4pm; it is 40 minutes long. All tours depart from the corner of Rodeo Drive and Dayton Way; the cost for adults is $5; for children 12 and under, $1. Phone ☎ 310-285-2438. There is no tour if it rains.

Seats are not reserved on Trolley Tours. Arrive a bit early for a good spot.

Recreation

Tennis

La Cienega Tennis Center, 325 South La Cienega Boulevard, ☎ 310-550-4765. Call for hours and fees.

Roxbury Park, 471 Roxbury Drive, Tennis Club House, ☎ 310-550-4979. Call for hours and fees.

La Cienega Tennis Center is next door to the Academy of Motion Picture Arts & Sciences Library.

After Dark

Of all the gin joints in all the towns in all the world, she walks into mine.

— Humphrey Bogart, *Casablanca*

Beverly Hills' club scene is not nearly as frenetic as Hollywood's or West Hollywood's, but there are a few clubs worth mentioning.

Clubs

★★ BACKSTAGE CAFE
9433 Brighton Way
☎ 310-777-0252
www.backstagecafe.com

Top musicians, such as Herbie Hancock, Sting, and Dr. Dre, show up here sometimes to jam on their off nights; they are occasionally joined by Tom Hanks. Tuesday is a good night for music. The food is a mélange of California cuisine with French, Italian and Middle Eastern touches. Sunday is barbeque night, with a picnic-style menu starting at 7pm. Open 11am-2am. No cover.

★★ THE MARTINI LOUNGE
453 North Cañon Drive
☎ 310-550-5707

The Martini Lounge has a pianist Thursday nights, and Friday-Saturday a band playing R&B, jazz and blues. You mostly see the young, hip celebrities in here, where they blend in with the generally young, hip crowd. There is also a dining room, with good food (see Nic's, page 254).

Theaters

CAÑON THEATRE
205 North Cañon Drive
☎ 310-859-8001

The Cañon is a mid-size house, with around 400 seats; they have an erratic schedule presenting new plays and smaller imports from Broadway; shows usually run for about a month.

WILSHIRE THEATRE
8440 Wilshire Boulevard
☎ 213-468-1700

A large house, with around 1,200 seats, this theater is used only occasionally for national touring companies of large musicals when the Nederlander organization's other big house, the Pantages, has a long-running booking.

Beverly Hills A to Z

Counseling

Alcohol & Drug Abuse Helpline	☎ 800-ALCOHOL
Alcoholics Anonymous	☎ 310-644-1139
Be Sober Hotline	☎ 800-237-6237
Los Angeles Free Clinic	☎ 213-653-8662
Nineline (counseling for teens)	☎ 800-999-9999

All phone numbers in Beverly Hills have a 310 area code.

Currency Exchange

Associated Foreign Exchange, 443 North Beverly Drive, ☎ 310-274-7610.

Bermuda Financial Inc., 9025 Wilshire Boulevard, 310-385-0725.

Thomas Cook Currency Service, 421 North Rodeo Drive, ☎ 310-274-9177.

Hospitals

Cedars-Sinai Medical Center, 8700 Beverly Drive, LA, ☎ 310-855-5000, 310-423-3277, www.csmc.edu.

Century City Hospital, 2080 Century Park East, Century City, ☎ 310-558-6211.

UCLA Medical Center, 10833 Le Conte Avenue, Westwood, ☎ 310-825-9111.

Library

Beverly Hills Library, 444 North Roxford Drive, ☎ 310-288-2220.

Locksmiths

Academy Locksmith . . . . ☎ 310-450-9444
A-Al's Lock & Key Service . . . . ☎ 310-672-7988
Metro Locksmith . . . . ☎ 310-441-2755
Oakley Lock & Key . . . . ☎ 310-474-4704

Police & Fire

Emergency . . . . ☎ 911
Police Department . . . . ☎ 310-550-4951
Fire Department . . . . ☎ 310-281-2701

Post Office

Beverly Hills: 325 North Maple Drive, 90210, ☎ 310-247-3470.

☞ DID YOU KNOW?

The Beverly Hills Post Office is listed on the National Register of Historic Places.

Time & Weather

Time . . . . ☎ 853-1212
Weather . . . . ☎ 213-554-1212

Translation Services

Beverly Hills International School, PO Box 6188, Beverly Hills, CA 90210, ☎ 310-557-1711.

Beverly Hills Lingual Institute, 9601 Wilshire Boulevard, Suite GL-4, Beverly Hills, CA 90210, ☎ 310-858-0717.

Visitor Information

Beverly Hills Conference & Visitors Bureau, 239 South Beverly Drive, Beverly Hills, 90212, ☎ 310-248-1015, 800-345-2210, www.bhvb.org.

Beverly Hills Chamber of Commerce, 239 South Beverly Drive, Beverly Hills, 90212, ☎ 310-248-1000, 8:30am-5pm. www.beverlyhillscc.org.

The Glamour Communities

I never knew it could be like this.
> – Deborah Kerr to Burt Lancaster,
> *From Here to Eternity*

The Santa Monica Mountains run to the coast, and **Sunset Boulevard**, which begins in downtown Los Angeles, curves its way west along the foothills all the way to the beach. A lineup of star-studded communities stays close to the boulevard on both sides. Above Sunset these communities occupy the canyons back up into the hills; only in Brentwood, where Wilshire Boulevard intersects with San Vicente, does the glamour reach the flatlands. Hills are classy, flatlands are déclassé.

From Beverly Hills, going west, are **Bel-Air**, **Brentwood** (with Mandeville Canyon and the Cliff May Estates), and finally **Pacific Palisades**.

Bel-Air

Toto, I have a feeling we're not in Kansas anymore!"
> – Dorothy (Judy Garland), *The Wizard of Oz*

Bel-Air is poshest of the posh. Areas like Brentwood and Pacific Palisades, which most of us would consider idyllic, are positively bourgeois in comparison. Bel-Air is where you can be a hip star, with a screen image as a common-as-dirt man or woman of the people, and at the same time live like a preciously cocooned member of royalty, surrounded only by more of the same.

There is no commercial life in Bel-Air – no markets, no bars, no boutiques – just great homes and the wonderful Hotel Bel-Air.

The Glamour Communities

N

1. Hotel Bel-Air
2. UCLA Campus
3. J. Paul Getty Museum
4. Sepulveda Pass Walking Trail
5. Will Rogers State Historic Park
6. Temescal Canyon; Children's Nature Institute
7. Palisades Park
8. Santa Monica Canyon

NOT TO SCALE

© 2002 HUNTER PUBLISHING, INC.

History

Bel-Air's Beginnings

Bel-Air is the creation of one man, **Alphonso Bell**, who made a lot of money in Southern California as an oilman and land developer. At some point he acquired the Buenos Aires Ranch in the foothills of the Santa Monica range, and then in 1922 added 600 contiguous acres in the canyons, foothills and mountain slopes west of Beverly Hills and north of what is now Westwood.

He replaced the native chaparral with trees and lush, exotic vegetation to line his new winding roads and to blanket a raw country club. Bel-Air Stables opened so the residents could board their horses and enjoy miles of equestrian trails winding through the canyons.

Bel-Air soon became the most exclusive address in Los Angeles. The area attracted stars and producers who bought large plots of land, often measured in acres rather than feet, though there are smaller lots as one drives up the steeper slopes toward Mulholland Drive along the top ridge of the mountain range.

▀ FILM GLOSSARY

Looping – The re-recording of actors' dialogue, used mostly when the original recording is poor due to conditions on location (noise, airplanes, etc.). In a special studio the film is projected and the actors match their words to the lip movement on the screen.

Bringing It Up to Date

In 1946 a hotel man named Joseph Drown bought 18 acres off Stone Canyon Road in the heart of Bel-Air. He converted the mission-style building that was originally built as Bell's land sales office into the main building of the new **Hotel Bel-Air**. He closed the stables and built the oval-shaped pool at the site of the original riding ring, transformed the grounds into lush gardens and added romantic Swan Lake.

In addition to the celebrities already living in this beautiful area – close to the studios and the city, yet quiet and peaceful – the new hotel attracted privacy-seeking stars like Grace Kelly, Jackie Gleason, Cary Grant, Elizabeth Taylor and Marilyn Monroe, (though her favorite over the years was always the Beverly Hills Hotel).

The Glamour Communities

Because most of the estates have extensive grounds, and because the still-chaparral-covered canyons are deep and the hillsides are steep, there is plenty of wildlife remaining. Squirrels, raccoons and dozens of species of birds (hummingbirds are attracted by the exotic imported vegetation) are common. Deer are less often seen than in earlier days.

Getting Here

From LAX

By Car

Take Sepulveda Boulevard from the airport exit to the San Diego Freeway (405) going north; get off at Sunset Boulevard going east (to the right). Stay on Sunset (the UCLA campus will be on your right) for about five minutes to Stone Canyon Road on your left.

By Bus

You cannot really get here by bus. If you take the free airport shuttle to Lot C, go to Dock 9 and get Metro Bus #561. That will take you to Hilgard Avenue and Charing Cross Road near UCLA, a block from Sunset Boulevard and about a mile walk to the Bel-Air Hotel. If you wonder how the cleaning people and non live-in help get to the homes they work in, someone drives from the house to the bus stop to pick them up.

By Taxi

Late morning and midday fare is about $30 (plus $2.50 airport fee); later in the afternoon and evening it's more, due to traffic.

The Glamour Communities

TO HYPHENATE OR NOT
TO HYPHENATE?

Alphonso Bell put a hyphen in the area's name when he called it Bel-Air Estates in 1922. The Hotel Bel-Air and the residents' Bel-Air Association are both hyphenated, but Thomas Bros. Maps, LA's gazetteers, has it as Bel Air Estates (hyphenless), and the Bel Air City Planning Department is also missing the hyphen.

Commercial businesses like the Bel Air Postal Center are, you will notice, hyphen deprived, but that doesn't really count since they are located at Beverly Glen Circle, on the edge of but not actually in Bel-Air.

Getting Around

Two of Los Angeles' primary east-west roads border Bel-Air – Sunset Boulevard is to the south, and Mulholland Drive (along the top of the Santa Monica Mountain Range) is to the north; on the eastern edge of the community is Beverly Glen Boulevard, a road that climbs up a canyon from Sunset to Mulholland; and to the west is Sepulveda Boulevard, which parallels the San Diego Freeway (405). Between those, Stone Canyon, Stradella and Roscomare roads run south to north, connected by a system of winding streets.

None of the streets in Bel-Air Estates have sidewalks.

But life is seldom that simple: only the west side of Beverly Glen in the first eight blocks above Sunset is within the original Bel-Air. Farther up the road near the top, a commercial development with stores on an offshoot called Beverly Glen is a 1970s development. Over on the other side of Bel-Air, on Mulholland at Roscomare Road, there is a gate that says, "Bel-Air, North Gate," but when you enter here, you are in a more recent development.

Jan Berry and Dean O. Torrence (more familiarly known as Jan & Dean) wrote their famous hit song *Dead Man's Curve* after Mel Blanc was almost killed in an auto accident on the portion of Sunset Boulevard that borders Bel-

Air. The whole up and down, twisting section of Sunset from west of the Beverly Hills Hotel to the San Diego Freeway is accident-prone, but the stretch that divides Bel-Air from UCLA is the most dangerous. The specific part of the road that the song warns about is on the curve just west of a small cross street, Groverton Place, especially dangerous when going east (downhill) toward the UCLA athletic field, which is behind a row of trees.

▬▬ **Who Lives Here?**

Large tour buses are not allowed on the roads in Bel-Air.

Henry Fonda, whose extraordinary career included the films *The Grapes of Wrath*, *The Lady Eve*, *Mister Roberts* and *On Golden Pond*, lived in a Spanish Colonial-style home on Chalon Road for many years until his death. Son Peter Fonda, seen on the screen in films from *Easy Rider* to *Ulee's Gold*, lives not far away in upper Bel-Air. Our favorite Hungarian, Zsa Zsa Gabor, lived on Bel-Air Road, and Quincy Jones, film composer nonpareil, lives on Bel-Air Place. Elizabeth Taylor lived on a one-acre estate on Nimes Road back when she was married to Richard Burton.

Holmby Park at Beverly Glen and Comstock Avenue is a good place to see stars jogging.

Robert and Rosemary Stack have lived here for many years. Johnny and Joanna Carson moved in when they were first married; now divorced, Joanna is still here. And this is where ex-President and Nancy Reagan live. Farrah Fawcett recently sold the three-acre gated place she purchased with Lee Majors when they were married; Tony Curtis got a smaller place in Las Vegas but kept his house in Bel-Air; and Nicolas Cage moved into the Bel-Air home he bought after he sold his Hollywood Hills house.

Not all residents are movie stars. Novelist Judith Krantz has a golf course view from her house on the 17th hole of the Bel-Air Country Club. A small drawback is the sliced balls that sometimes plunk into her pool. Boxer Oscar De La Hoya, who is also making a career as a singer, recently sold his Bel-Air estate that had a 300-foot driveway and, of course, its own gym.

And then there is Wilt Chamberlain's place, high on a Bel-Air mountaintop above it all. The living room is five stories high; you can swim into the living room from the moat swimming pool; there is a playroom with a wall-to-wall waterbed floor; the mirrored ceiling above the jumbo-size bed in the main bedroom retracts to reveal open sky; and the sunken Cleopatra-inspired bathtub at the foot of the bed can be filled at a touch of the pillow-side control panel. Wilt called it "a little kinky, with kinky details."

After the Hall of Famer died the bachelor pad went on sale for $7.4 million. Apparently there are not too many people who want a place like that; after a while the price dropped to $5.2 million. If it sounds like your kind of place, it is still available as we write this for $4.3 million. You had better snap it up quick!

On Location

Shooting is allowed here, but is almost always done on private property. There are occasional scenes of an exterior of one of the mansions, or someone may allow their interior to be used. The streets are all so narrow that there is really not room to park the necessary trucks on the public roads.

Best Place to Stay

There is only one place to stay in Bel-Air, but fortunately it is, for many, the best hotel in the city... maybe the country.

Room rates at Hotel Bel-Air are subject to a 14% city tax.

★★ HOTEL BEL-AIR

701 Stone Canyon Road
Los Angeles, CA 90077
☎ 310-472-1211, 800-648-4097
www.hotelbelair.com
Member Leading Hotels of the World
Deluxe

Hotel Bel-Air has won the "Number One Hotel in the World" award from Institutional Investor *four times.*

We stayed here a few years back. After checking in during the middle of the afternoon at a tiny desk that seemed more appropriate for a country inn, we then realized that is what the Bel-Air is, a country inn in the city. We were escorted down a curving path to a pink-stuccoed bungalow with a red-tiled roof that turned out to be our suite. Inside was a large, bright sitting room, then a few steps down to a good-size bedroom with a fireplace piled with wood ready to light. Beyond French doors was a bubbling hot tub in a small, high-walled patio. We fell in love with it all, right then.

A gardening staff of 11 changes flowers and plants with the seasons on the grounds of Hotel Bel-Air.

We went for a walk, first on cobbled paths around Swan Lake where two stately white swans, Eros and Aphrodite, were gliding over the dark water below the ancient sycamore trees, some of whose twisted limbs were growing almost horizontally. Ferns framed other walkways that led to the stream that flows beautifully in the rainy season, but dries up in summer along with almost all Southwest streams.

Hotel Bel-Air guests can get on a treadmill at 3am if the mood strikes: the Fitness Center is open 24 hours.

It was all really remarkable. The fern-like leaves of the largest silk floss tree in North America (or so a little sign informed us), a 12-foot-tall bird of paradise, a 200-year-old California live oak, even a grove of coastal redwood trees. Down in the southwest corner we found a big herb garden with basil, rosemary, oregano, sage, tarragon, cilantro and mint ready for use in the hotel's kitchen. And, on the way back to our digs, we passed by the dining room terrace where the thick branches of a 60-year-old East Indian lonchocarpus tree blanketed everything in a cloud of pale purple flowers. All this in the bottom of a canyon with slopes rising steeply on each side. As we arrived back, complimentary tea service was just being set up with tea and cakes in our bungalow. It was yummy.

Of the 92 rooms, 40 are suites, and all are different. Some have private patios with fountains; some have fireplaces. A number of celebrities who don't have homes in LA make a habit of staying here when they are in town. Around Oscar time this place is wall-to-wall stars.

Best Place to Eat

There is only one place to dine inside Bel-Air, the Restaurant at the hotel. Breakfast and lunch are casual, and dinner certainly doesn't call for a tuxedo, or even a tie as long as the rest of you is presentable, but we would never show up looking like slobs. Not at Hotel Bel-Air.

★★ THE RESTAURANT
Hotel Bel-Air
701 Stone Canyon Road
☎ 310-472-1211
French-Californian cuisine
Expensive

We celebrated Phyllis' birthday here in 2001. It is an attractive dining room with good food, impeccable service, and tables far enough apart so you can talk without your neighbors hearing every word. When the weather is right, floor to ceiling windows open out onto the Terrace, where you can dine year-round because of the heated terra-cotta tile floor and overhead heating system.

"Table One" is a private dining room in the Hotel Bel-Air kitchen, with a large picture window so guests can see the chef prepare their meal.

In addition to the three daily meals, afternoon tea and Sunday brunch are served. Celebrities who live in this area often eat here, and some stars who live out of town always stay at the Bel-Air when they are here to make a picture. Nancy Reagan used to have lunch on the Terrace every Tuesday; we suppose she still does. Breakfast is served Monday-Saturday, 7-10:30am and Sunday to 9:30; Sunday brunch, 11am-2pm. Lunch, Monday-Saturday, noon-2:30pm; dinner daily, 6:30-10:30pm.

Shopping

THE BOUTIQUE
Hotel Bel-Air
701 Stone Canyon Road
☎ 310-440-5858

Guests who want to take a pleasant reminder of the hotel home may get a robe here, or a creamy swan-shaped soap. There are usually soft sweaters, delicate gold necklaces and scented candles within hand-blown glass, but the selection is constantly changing. Much of the inventory is from abroad and sold here exclusively. The Boutique is open Monday-Saturday, 9am-9pm; Sunday, 9am-8pm.

 # After Dark

★★ THE BAR
Hotel Bel-Air
701 Stone Canyon Road
☎ 310-472-1211

This is one of the nicest bars in town. There is a wood-burning fireplace, walnut paneling, private niches and cozy tables. A pianist makes music at the baby grand piano every night. This has always been a favorite meeting place for Bel-Air residents and hotel guests.

■ FILM GLOSSARY

Cookie – An abstract pattern, usually cut from wood, suspended in front of a light, causing the pattern to be thrown onto the scene.

There is a story we heard when we were having lunch in The Bar one time, about George C. Scott, who had been banned for getting in his cups and slugging Richard Zanuck. He showed up a few days later, sheepishly stood in the doorway and called to the bartender to send over a Scotch.

We used to come here a lot when we were writing daytime soaps. For some reason soap production executives always stayed here when they came to town, so The Bar is where we would meet around lunchtime. If it was a late afternoon meeting it was usually in their suite. At first we thought it was a Proctor & Gamble quirk, but it turned out that no matter which soap we were writing the execs always stayed here.

Brentwood

Is there ever such a thing as enough?
– Pearl Bailey, *All the Fine Young Cannibals*

Going west on Sunset Boulevard from Bel-Air, you pass Westwood and the San Diego Freeway (405). Everything on the other side is tranquil, upscale Brentwood. It was not intensely developed until rather late in the scheme of things and yet, especially along Sunset, many of the lots are oversize and the houses, consequently, large. There are two village-like shopping centers, a small one just off Sunset west of the freeway, and a much larger one along San Vicente Boulevard from Bundy Drive down to Wilshire Boulevard, a stretch of about six blocks with a contiguous neighborhood of apartments and condos. It is an exceedingly pleasant place to live – quiet and safe and relatively remote from the fast-track transportation routes. We cannot remember ever seeing a tour bus prowling the streets of Brentwood. So it follows, as the night the day, that lots of show-biz folk who have made it have ended up here in one of Hollywood's Promised Lands.

Gary Cooper became the first Honorary Mayor of Brentwood Village in 1949.

History

Brentwood was part of Rancho San Vicente y Santa Monica, 31,000 acres of mountain, mesa and ocean shoreline, granted in 1839 to Don Francisco Sepúlveda, a retired soldier of the King of Spain. The land stretched from Sepulveda Pass to the sea, and what is now Santa Monica Boulevard to the top of the Santa Monica Mountains.

Brentwood Village is the only commercial shopping area on Sunset Boulevard between the Palisades and West Hollywood.

At first it was one vast cattle ranch. In 1872 Sepúlveda's heirs, who wanted to divide their inheritance and who thought the land would never be worth more than it was at that time, sold it for $2 an acre. Later the western part became the city of Santa Monica. In 1887 the new owners donated 300 acres to the federal government to establish the National Home for Disabled Volunteer Soldiers, which became the present Veterans Administration at Wilshire and Sepulveda boulevards.

The San Vicente shopping area began as a cow path along the side of the Veterans Home property. The homes and stores for the families of these veterans, built along there, became the first settlement of Brentwood.

Brentwood Village, at Sunset Boulevard and Barrington Avenue, has maintained its quaint character since the 1920s. Originally there was a hitching post for horses and a goat farm down the street; its continued friendly and still "quaint" character is an asset for the upscale businesses here now.

Mandeville Canyon Road is a long cul-de-sac and does not reach Mulholland Drive.

Mandeville Canyon is the western border of Brentwood. There must have been a cabin there in the early days, perhaps for the *vaqueros* who would search for stray cattle, because historic accounts from the 1880s call it Casa Viejo (old house) Canyon. In the 1920s there was a polo field at the mouth of the canyon, and a large botanical garden, with plantings from all over the world, in the first stretch; many of the plantings are still here. The headquarters for the botanic garden park later became the home of Richard Widmark.

Getting Here

Sepulveda Boulevard follows an Indian trail through the mountain pass to the San Fernando Valley.

From LAX

By Car

Take Sepulveda Boulevard north to the San Diego Freeway (405), and go north. For San Vicente and Wilshire boulevards, get off at Wilshire. Go west, through Veterans Home; the first street on the right is San Vicente Boulevard. For Sunset and Barrington (Brentwood Village) get off at Sunset Boulevard, go west a few blocks to Barrington.

By Bus

Take the free shuttle bus marked "Lot C" from the terminal; when you reach Lot C, walk to the nearby Transit Center and take Santa Monica Bus #3 to Wilshire and Federal in Brentwood.

From Downtown Los Angeles

By Car

There is no fast way to get to Brentwood from downtown. Take Wilshire Boulevard all the way out and it will carry you along a good swath of the west side of the city, through the heart of Beverly Hills and Westwood's high-rise condo canyon. After driving under the San Diego Freeway you see the Veterans Center on both sides of Wilshire. The next street is San Vicente Drive to your right. This is Brentwood's larger village.

Or, take the Hollywood Freeway (101) to Sunset Boulevard and drive west through Hollywood, the Sunset Strip and the scenic part of Beverly Hills. Either way, it is no use being in too much of a hurry.

By Bus

From 5th Street (at Main, Broadway or Grand) take Metro Bus 720 to Wilshire and Barrington in Brentwood.

Getting Around

Brentwood's southern boundary is Wilshire Boulevard, and Sunset Boulevard makes the northern boundary; most of Brentwood's classiest homes go up into the hills on the north side of Sunset. Sepulveda Boulevard is the east boundary; the west boundary consists of 26th Street and Mandeville Canyon.

👓 Who Lives Here?

Brentwood has been popular with celebrities since the 1930s; at least for those looking for a tucked-away, less obvious and glitzy place than Beverly Hills. Billie Burke, Linda Darnell, Audrey Hepburn, Frederic March, Steve McQueen and Pat O'Brien lived here. Shirley Temple lived at 209 North Rockingham Avenue before 1951, Cole Porter at 416 North Rockingham Avenue and Joan Crawford at 426 North Bristol Avenue.

Kate Mulgrew of the Star Trek Voyager *TV series was named honorary mayor of Brentwood a few years ago.*

Incidentally, Phyllis knew Christina Crawford in New York. The first time Christina took Phyllis home to meet her mother, Joan Crawford's first words were to scream, "Don't walk on my white carpet! Take your shoes off!" When Christina later wrote her book, *Mommie Dearest,* we were not too surprised.

SCHOOL DAYS

In the 1930s, Grace Moore bought the property at 12001 Sunset Boulevard, and distinguished Los Angeles architect Paul Williams designed her house. Tyrone Power bought it in 1939. In 1947, part of the property, but not the house, became Marymount Jr. School. The children of Jimmy Durante, Lucille Ball and Desi Arnaz, Randolph Hearst, Barron Hilton and Peter and Pat Lawford were students here.

When it became Brentwood School in 1993 the students buried a time capsule, which included an AIDS awareness ribbon, Internet Yellow Pages, newspaper coverage of the O.J. Simpson trial, a Windows '95 ad, music from the Grateful Dead and Coolio, and a Starbucks cup.

The original Tyrone Power family house is still next to the school, behind a tall hedge.

Others who own or have owned homes in Brentwood include Bea Arthur, Phyllis Diller, Sally Field, Harrison Ford, Tom Hanks, Dustin Hoffman, Angela Lansbury, Hal Linden, Dylan McDermott of *The Practice*, Rob Reiner, Ving Rhames of *Mission: Impossible*, Patrick Stewart, Sally Struthers and Betty White. Gary Cooper lived behind what is now St. Martin of Tours Catholic Church, 11967 Sunset Boulevard. The church purchased its property in 1954. Current residents also include Ted Danson and Mary Steenburgen; actress Shiva Afshar, who purchased a home recently from Melanie Griffith and Antonio Banderas; Michelle Pfeiffer and writer-producer David Kelley. Mandeville Canyon, the westernmost part of Brentwood, was home to Lorne Greene of *Bonanza*, composer Meredith Wilson, Robert Taylor, Don Defore, and Esther Williams, as well as Dick Powell. Michael Douglas and Gregory Peck live there now.

The Cliff May Estates, next to Mandeville on the canyon floor, has no sidewalks. It was developed as a horsey area; there are narrow, tree-lined roads, and split rail fences fronting all the properties. Like Mandeville, this out-of-the-way area is heavily favored by show-biz people. Robert Wagner lives here, and Steven Spielberg is building a horse ring, though only after a noisy fight with the neighbors reduced its size from gargantuan to merely very big.

Composer Arnold Schoenberg lived on Rockingham Avenue across the street from Shirley Temple in the 1930s and '40s. Richard Nixon lived at 901 North Bundy Drive after losing the 1960 presidential election; this is where he wrote *Six Crises*. At the other end of the political spectrum, Tom Hayden lives in Brentwood now. Marilyn Monroe died at 12305 Fifth Helena Drive, off Carmelina Street.

O.J. Simpson lived at 360 North Rockingham Avenue when he was arrested for allegedly killing Nicole Brown Simpson and Ronald Goldman at what is now 875 South Bundy Drive (the new owner had the address changed). And Dr. Bernard Lewinsky lives just a few blocks away. You may better know him as Monica's father.

The Glamour Communities

On Location

Archer School has continued Eastern Star's annual Maypole tradition, to the great appreciation of the neighborhood.

The attractive Spanish Colonial Revival building at 11725 Sunset Boulevard, just across from Brentwood Village, was built in the 1930s as the Eastern Star retirement home. It has been used many times as a location for movies and television, perhaps the most notable was *Chinatown*.

Whenever a film was shot here the home's supervisor always insisted that the residents be given first chance if any elderly extras were required. The property is now Archer School for Girls; we do not know if the principal insists that the casting director hire her schoolgirls.

Best Places to Stay

The accommodations price scale can be found on page 39.

Brentwood is much more an upscale residential community than a tourist destination. There are only a few places to stay.

Hotels

HOLIDAY INN
170 North Church Lane
Los Angeles, CA 90049
☎ 310-476-6411, 800-HOLIDAY
www.holiday-inn.com/brentwood-bel
Inexpensive/Moderate

This 17-story round hotel, like a non-leaning Tower of Pisa, is at the handy intersection where Sunset Boulevard crosses the San Diego Freeway (405). Most of the rooms have a balcony with a view, either of the freeway or the mountains. There is a swimming pool, Jacuzzi and fitness center. The dining room for breakfast, lunch and dinner is on the top floor with views all around. Room service is available, as is complimentary shuttle service to Westwood, UCLA, Brentwood and the Getty Museum. Valet and self-parking.

LUXE SUMMIT HOTEL BEL-AIR
11461 Sunset Boulevard
Los Angeles, CA 90049
☎ 310-476-6571, 800-HOTEL-411, fax 310-471-6310
www.luxehotels.com
Moderate

The name says Bel-Air, but that is putting on airs a bit. Bel-Air ends on the other side of the freeway, this is actually the edge of Brentwood, the corner of Sunset Boulevard where Sepulveda and the San Diego Freeway start into the Sepulveda Pass. It is easy to find because the Getty Museum tops the hill just above.

This is still a very nice place with a pool, tennis, exercise facility and beauty treatments and massages, concierge, a café for breakfast, lunch and dinner and hors d'oeuvres and light dinner in the piano lounge. There is shuttle service to the Getty Center and UCLA (this is a very popular place for visiting scholars to stay, just few minutes from the campus), and airport towncar service for pick-up and return from LAX.

If you are driving from the airport, get on the San Diego Freeway (405) and get off at Sunset Boulevard. The hotel is on the northwest corner.

Motel

BRENTWOOD MOTOR HOTEL
12200 Sunset Boulevard
Los Angeles, CA 90049
☎ 310-476-9981, fax 310-471-0768
Inexpensive

The only motel on all of Sunset Boulevard from West Hollywood to the beach, the Brentwood is a good choice for anyone who prefers a small, simple place to a grand, luxurious hotel. It has been sitting here for over 50 years, only 20 mostly single-level bungalows nestled in greenery, providing a little splash of old-time character and intimacy in the midst of elegant Brentwood.

There is a refrigerator in each room, continental breakfast, voice mail, fax and Internet access available. Additional persons $5 per person, weekly rates available.

Best Places to Eat

I'll have what she's having.
– Estelle Reiner, *When Harry Met Sally*

The dining price scale can be found on page 42.

Brentwood's two business areas are relatively small, and the number of restaurants is accordingly few. But with only a few very good places in an area where many celebrities live, the star-gazing possibilities are high.

PEPPONE RESTAURANT
11628 Barrington Court
☎ 310-476-7379
Italian
Expensive

Sometimes we yearn for the old-fashioned Southern Italian food of our childhood: huge portions of pasta covered with heavy sauces in an atmosphere of red leather booths and dim lights. That is when we go to Miceli's in Hollywood, Matteo's in Westwood, or here. An extensive menu includes about 18 pasta dishes, meat dishes from sausage to filet, many fish and seafood items, and a dozen chicken preparations. If you would still prefer something else, just ask. This place has one of those congenial kitchens that is usually happy to oblige.

The restaurant is located in that little neighborhood village off Sunset Boulevard a few blocks west of Sepulveda and the San Diego Freeway. Open for dinner only, 5:30-11pm; Sunday from 4:30; last orders around 10:30. Full bar.

★★ TOSCANA

11633 San Vicente Boulevard
☎ 310-820-2448
Italian
Moderate-Expensive

Usually crowded, this restaurant is a favorite of show-biz types who live on the Westside, but not necessarily stars; you hear a lot of producer talk. Some people come here just for the pizza, but there are also other menu items, such as *medaglioni de manzo boscaiola* (filet mignon with porcini mushroom sauce), seafood, and, of course, pasta. Wine and beer only.

Open Monday-Saturday, 11:30am-3pm and 5:30-11pm; Sundays, 5-10:30pm. Although they try to take walk-ins, you may have a long wait if you don't have a reservation; you can book several days in advance. For lunch a reservation is recommended if you want to eat between 12:30 and 1:30pm. Valet parking available; street parking is very difficult around here.

★★ VINCENTI RISTORANTE

11930 San Vicente Boulevard
☎ 310-207-0127
Italian
Expensive-Very Expensive

This attractive, contemporary Italian restaurant has blond woods and modern Italian light fixtures, and a wood-burning grill and oven scent the air with enticing flavors. The pasta is made in-house, Mediterranean fish and seafood are flown from Italy. The risotto with shrimp, zucchini, zucchini blossoms and cheese is fine; meat enthusiasts tell us the steak and pork are excellent.

Maureen Vincenti is mum about naming her guests, always careful to protect the privacy of the celebrities who dine here. After all, you would not want to wade through a battery of paparazzi to get to the front door; think how embarrassing it would be when none of them took your picture. Open Tuesday-Saturday 6-9:30pm, Sunday 6-9pm; lunch Friday only noon-2pm. Valet parking.

★★ ZAX RESTAURANT
11604 San Vicente Boulevard
☎ 310-571-3800
California cuisine
Moderate-Expensive

This small place with plain brick walls has become very popular, for good reason. The young chef does not try to do everything in the world; weekdays she puts out a one-page menu, with some added specials on weekends, and does them all very well.

Zax features California cuisine, using fresh local ingredients available at the farmers' markets and from the produce grown for the restaurant in the Veterans Hospital garden right across the street. Salads might include jumbo asparagus or baby arugula, enhanced with fig balsamic vinaigrette or sheep's milk cheese.

The chicken glazed with lavender honey is a winner, and the New York steak is smeared with Roquefort-shallot butter to good effect. The risotto at Zax (you can tell risotto is a favorite of ours because we keep mentioning it) is made with white asparagus, morel mushrooms, and fava beans. There are also imaginative fish dishes.

A lot of tables are squeezed into this space, so it is a bit noisy when the room is full. Lunch Tuesday-Friday, 11:30am-2pm; dinner Tuesday-Thursday, 5:30-10pm; Friday-Saturday, until 10:30pm; Sunday, 5-9pm. Valet parking.

 Shop Till You Drop

San Vicente Boulevard north of Wilshire is Brentwood's primary shopping area: it has some restaurants, some boutiques, a few bookstores. There is a median with grass and trees that runs all the way to the ocean from Bundy Drive. If you are on Sunset Boulevard, go a few blocks west of the freeway and you will see Brentwood Village, the smaller shopping area, to your left. Keep in mind that Brentwood is a small community, so you will not be overwhelmed by shopping opportunities; Hollywood, West Hollywood and Beverly Hills are the places for that.

The trees in the San Vicente Boulevard divider are coral trees.

Books

DUTTON'S BRENTWOOD BOOKSTORE
11975 San Vicente Boulevard
☎ 310-476-6263
www.duttonsbrentwood.com

A fine bookstore, with lots of contemporary fiction and
non-fiction and a good selection of travel books, too, plus
CDs and a café. We have been to several author readings
and book signings. Open Monday-Friday, 9am-9pm; Saturday, 9am-6pm; Sunday, 11am-5pm.

Bakeries

THE CHEESECAKE FACTORY
11647 San Vicente Boulevard
☎ 310-826-7111
www.thecheesecakefactory.com

This is definitely not a mom-and-pop bakery; actually, it is
one branch of a big company. Still, it is the most popular
place in Brentwood, always crowded. Is that because it
has the best cheesecake? That is too important a question,
too personal a taste for us to advise anyone. You will have
to try it for yourself. In any case, they have more varieties
here than anywhere else. Open Monday-Thursday,
11:30am-11pm; Friday and Saturday, 11:30am-12:30am;
Sunday, 10am-11pm. Between Barrington and Darlington
avenues. There are branches of The Cheesecake Factory
in Beverly Hills, 364 North Beverly Drive, ☎ 310-278-
7270; Marina del Rey, 4142 Via Marina, ☎ 310-306-3344;
and Woodland Hills, 6324 Canoga Avenue, ☎ 818-883-
9900.

The Glamour Communities

Natural Foods

★★ WHOLE FOODS MARKET
11737 San Vicente Boulevard
☎ 3120-826-4433
www.wholefoods.com

This is a big chain that bought up a very small local chain called Mrs. Gooch's. But it kept the organic produce, non-hormone-injected meats and antibiotic-free chicken and things that people like Jamie Lee Curtis and Diane Keaton look for when they are shopping, which is why you see them in here. Stop in, if you want to munch on an apple that tastes like an apple should. Open daily, 8am-10pm.

Other branches are in Beverly Hills, 239 North Crescent Drive, ☎ 310-274-3360; Sherman Oaks, 4520 North Sepulveda Boulevard, ☎ 818-382-3700, and 12905 Riverside Drive, ☎ 818-762-5548; West Hollywood, 7871 Santa Monica Boulevard, ☎ 323-848-4200; West Los Angeles, 11666 National Boulevard, ☎ 310-996-8840; and Woodland Hills, 21347 Ventura Boulevard, ☎ 818-610-0000.

 Sunup to Sundown

Getty Museum

J. PAUL GETTY MUSEUM
Getty Center
1200 Getty Center Drive
☎ 310-440-7330
www.getty.edu/museum

The Getty Museum is on the top of a hill on the west side of the San Diego Freeway, just north of Sunset Boulevard.

Brentwood's big attraction (almost the only attraction), is the Getty Museum. Built just a few years ago, the museum has revealed a surprising, and embarrassing, feeling of inferiority on the part of Los Angeles. Just a few months ago we again read in the *LA Times*, "The J. Paul Getty Museum... disproves any notion that Los Angeles lacks culture." Many of us, however, doubt that one museum is all that stands between Los Angeles and the barbarians.

For a month before the grand opening there was a story every day in the *Times* about the monumental event to come. The wonderful art we would see... the fabulous architecture... the gardens... the architect... the marble... the architect... The paper was gushing every morning like a schoolgirl.

Since its completion, the Getty has been referred to often as a contemporary Acropolis. To paraphrase a well-known remark, we know the Acropolis, and believe us, this is no Acropolis. Every time we passed while it was being built we tried to guess whether, from the Freeway's viewpoint, it looked more like a Silicon Valley smokeless factory or ineptly designed condominium buildings.

You can judge for yourself, whether you make the journey up to where it looms on the hill or merely pass by down below on the San Diego Freeway. We admit that up there, within the circle of buildings, it is impressive – some think world-class. But about a million cars passing by every day on the freeway see only the back of the buildings.

The Glamour Communities

J. PAUL GETTY

J. Paul Getty was an obscenely wealthy oilman who lived in England in a castle filled with artwork. He had another place in Malibu that he turned into an museum filled with Greek art. When he died he left the largest art legacy in history to the Getty Foundation, which finances art education and restoration. The foundation built the Getty Museum, and now funds studies in art research and related fields.

The buildings are more or less low-rise, built largely of travertine that came from the same quarries used to build the Colosseum in Rome. Outside there are fountains, reflecting pools and gardens that change with the seasons.

The museum's collection includes European paintings, drawings, sculpture, illuminated manuscripts and photographs. There is a café and, on a clear day, good views from downtown Los Angeles to the ocean. The Getty Museum is open Tuesday-Thursday and Sunday, 10am-6pm; Friday and Saturday, 10am-9pm closed Monday. Admission is

Visitors take a driverless tram up the hill to the Getty Museum's central courtyard.

free, but parking is $5, and advance parking reservations are required; phone on weekdays before 4pm.

To get here by car, take the San Diego Freeway (405) going north (toward the San Fernando Valley); pass Wilshire and Sunset boulevards and continue to Getty Drive. Follow the road to parking structure. If you are using public transportation, from the beaches take Santa Monica's Big Blue Bus #1 on Santa Monica Boulevard, and ask for a transfer to bus #14 on Bundy Avenue. From Downtown Los Angeles get Santa Monica Big Blue Bus #10 at 6th Street and Grand Avenue going east on Grand, and transfer at Bundy and Pico to Santa Monica bus #14. All those buses run every 10-15 minutes during peak weekday hours; every 20-30 minutes during off-hours and on weekends. The fare is $1.25. Get schedule information at ☎ 310-451-5444, Monday-Friday, 8am-5pm, or online at www.bigbluebus.com. There is no direct bus service from Hollywood to the Getty.

📖 HISTORIC NOTE

The Chevron station at the corner of Sunset and Barrington was built in 1938 in Spanish Colonial style. Its most distinctive feature is the 40-foot tower that houses a 20-by-20-foot room; this was rented in the 1950s and '60s by writers who liked its solitude and large windows. James Poe wrote *Lilies of the Field* here, as well as *They Shoot Horses, Don't They?*, and the screen adaptation of *Around the World in 80 Days*, for which he shared an Oscar.

Sepulveda Pass Walking Trail

The bottom of Sepulveda Pass is almost filled in with the San Diego Freeway (405), where the traffic flows in two directions 24 hours a day. But the pass above that level is surprisingly wild. The walking trail starts just north of the Getty Center Drive exit and zigzags its way over 500 feet up the chaparral-covered east side of the pass to the top. The distance is 2½ miles round-trip; it is fairly easy, with some climbing.

At the top is the East Sepulveda Fire Road. There is a golf course up here, too, but it is primarily a big, undeveloped, wild canyon. Up here, quail are common, and deer are seen occasionally. Walk south, to your right, for good views of the Getty Museum across the pass. Walk the other way for a view of the San Gabriel Mountains. Morning or late afternoon might be best, since there is no shade.

To get here by car, take the San Diego Freeway or Sepulveda Boulevard to the Getty Center Drive exit. Just north of the exit, on Sepulveda, is a parking area where the trail starts. For information phone the Santa Monica Mountains Conservancy, ☎ 310-589-3200.

Pacific Palisades

Pacific Palisades is a beautiful little community along the ocean; not as long as Malibu but wider, it stretches atop the palisades a few hundred feet above the sand and extends up into the foothills of the Santa Monica Mountains between Santa Monica and Malibu. As you drive along Pacific Coast Highway between these communities, it is Pacific Palisades that you see on top of the cliff that looms over the road.

The name comes from the coastal cliffs. A palisade is a wall of logs standing upright, usually built to defend a fort. From a sailboat at sea, as we have seen it often, this cliff merely looks like a crumbling embankment, but from the shore, looking up the coast, the eroded gullies in its face make the intervening parts stand out like a line of logs that form a barricade. Well, sort of...

The original vegetation on the rolling terraces at the top of the cliffs and going a little way up the mountain slopes was coastal sage, at higher elevations was the chaparral. It is still that way in the untouched areas; whatever has been developed is mostly exotics from elsewhere: trees, shrubs, flowers and grasses from all over the world that look beautiful now, but nothing like the original look.

History

The Gabrieleno Indians lived on the Palisades mesa starting sometime after AD 500. This was near their northern boundary, while Malibu was the Chumash's southern boundary. The tribes were similar, but the Gabrielenos arrived in this area much later. They were a highly evolved people who had shared with the Chumash boats made of wooden planks and had a monetary system based on shell beads. Religious and solstice shrines were located on the mountain tops and, 1,500 years before Hollywood, there was a ceremony that used jimson weed, a hallucinogenic plant.

In 1838 the governor in Monterey awarded a land grant to Francisco Marquez and Ysidro Reyes. It was named *Boca de Santa Monica*, or Mouth of Santa Monica, referring to the fertile flatland in Santa Monica Canyon where it was possible to farm. But most of the grant was the hilly and mountainous land above the canyon to the north.

Official cordbearers measured out the land. Two riders, carrying poles tied together with a line 100 *varas* long (a *vara* was 33.3 inches, a unit based on the length of a man's arm), would start at Topanga Point on horseback; the two took turns riding the length of the cord. With the first man's pole anchored, the second rode on until the cord stretched taut, then jammed his pole in the sand. They continued until they measured 7,500 *varas* along the beach, ending past Santa Monica Canyon where Montana Avenue now reaches the bluff. The eastern boundary was the ridge line of the Santa Monica Mountains.

Rancho Boca de Santa Monica was rich with game, including bear. The Marquez family hunted in the mountains above Pacific Palisades until the 1930s.

The land was used as a cattle ranch. In the 1870s families from Los Angeles began camping out in Santa Monica Canyon on excursions. Some tents and cabins were built, even a hotel, and dances were held at night. In the 1880s the land was divided and awarded to the heirs of the original families. Much of it was sold off.

The Movies

Santa Ynez Canyon was first used as a location for silent pictures in 1909. Thomas Ince started making pictures there in 1911, when he leased 18,000 acres that stretched for 7.5 miles inland from the ocean, which gave him picturesque terrain from seashore to mountains. Ince hired an entire Wild West Show, complete with a Sioux Indian tribe, and began shooting Westerns.

THE BATTLE OF PACIFIC PALISADES

One of the last battles between the independent filmmakers and Thomas Edison's Trust, which held patents on the cameras and film, was held here. The Patent Trust men, intent on destroying Thomas Ince's studio, were coming up the coast road toward Inceville when Ince opened fire with some cannons he had been using in a Civil War picture. The Patent Trust's henchmen turned and ran. The future of movie-making in Hollywood was saved.

Ince kept a herd of cattle on the mesa for cowboys to round up in his Westerns. A brigantine was anchored offshore for pirates to attack. He built a Swiss village, a Puritan settlement, even a Japanese hamlet, whatever was needed to make motion pictures. Inceville was maintained as a Western location even after Ince built the studio that became MGM in Culver City, until it burned down a few years later.

It was at Inceville Studios in Pacific Palisades that William S. Hart first made movies and became a star.

The old Inceville Studio reached on down to the beach at the mouth of Santa Ynez Canyon. To find the site, drive out Sunset Boulevard and pass the parklike grounds of the Self-Realization Fellowship, near the northern end.

The 1920s & 1930s

There were no real settlements in Pacific Palisades until 1922, when a group of Methodists established a "Chautauqua of the West," emulating a popular cultural center

The Glamour Communities

Mack Sennett shot many of the two-reel, silent Keystone Kops comedies in Pacific Palisades.

in New York State. After years of economic problems, outsiders were allowed to buy lots. The area soon became popular with artists, writers, theater people, architects... and wealthy entrepreneurs. The community expanded to its present size, but never incorporated as a city. It is one more part of far-flung Los Angeles.

Will Rogers started building his ranch in Pacific Palisades in 1923. He ended up with six miles of private roads, five miles of bridle paths, a nine-hole golf course and a polo field where other movie stars would join him in matches (see page 318).

Pacific Palisades was half-built by the 1930s when the Depression hit. Homes rented for as little as $15 a month, with the first month free. Raymond Chandler, poet laureate of Los Angeles, lived for a time on Hartzell Street.

Many celebrities have lived in Pacific Palisades over the years, almost always tranquilly, providing few salacious headlines. An exception occurred in 1935 when movie star Thelma Todd, who owned Thelma Todd's Sidewalk Café, was discovered dead, covered in blood and asphyxiated, in producer Roland West's nearby garage. In the following years there were many speculations, with lurid theories involving different Hollywood personalities, but it was never discovered what actually happened.

You will pass Thelma Todd's café as you drive up Pacific Coast Highway along the Castellammare bluff between Santa Ynez Canyon and Topanga Canyon. Driving north it is on your right just past the pedestrian overpass. It is the building at the south end of the block, which looks the same now as it did then.

The Emigrés

Hitler's ascension to power in Germany in 1933, and his 1938 conquest of Austria, with Austria playing the too-willing victim, led to an unexpected bonus for this area: as scores of actors, directors, writers and composers fled Europe, Pacific Palisades became for a time one of the great intellectual centers of the US.

Writer and director Berthold Viertel and his wife, Salka, an actress, arrived in 1929, with Berthold under contract to Fox Studios. Salka took early morning walks along the beach with a neighbor, Greta Garbo, and later at MGM she wrote the screenplays for several of Garbo's pictures, including *Queen Christina* and *Anna Karenina*. The Viertels' house at 165 Mabery Road in Santa Monica Canyon became a haven for many who emigrated out of necessity.

Sunday gatherings at the Viertel house included guests like Dmitri Tiomkin, Max Reinhardt, Arnold Schönberg, Thomas and Heinrich Mann, Lion and Marta Feuchtwanger, Charlie Chaplin, and Oscar Levant. Katia and Thomas Mann (author of *The Magic Mountain* and winner of the Nobel Prize for literature) lived on San Remo Drive; Austrian composer Arnold Schönberg on nearby Rockingham Drive.

The Feuchtwangers bought a house on the more remote Paseo Miramar, where Chaplin and playwright Bertolt Brecht were frequent guests and where Charles Laughton, whose house was on Corona del Mar, gave Shakespearean readings in their garden. Brecht lived over the border in Santa Monica, where he wrote *Mother Courage* and *The Good Person of Szechwan*. Laughton and Brecht worked on the English translation of Brecht's *Galileo* in Laughton's garden.

The postwar period of the 1950s was a shameful one for the US when it came to Hollywood and the arts. Not only were hundreds of American-born writers, directors and actors blacklisted, but many emigrés were caught up in the Cold War paranoia. Ironically, the charge usually leveled against these artists who had been persecuted by Hitler was "premature anti-fascism." Bertolt Brecht was summoned by the House Un-American Activities Committee, and returned to Berlin. Lion Feuchtwanger was called to testify in the McCarthy hearings. Salka Viertel was blacklisted. Thomas Mann, protesting these injustices, also returned to Europe.

The Glamour Communities

Getting Here

From LAX

By Car

From the airport take Sepulveda Boulevard and head north, staying in the left lane. At the second traffic light the road curves left onto Lincoln Boulevard. Stay with Lincoln to Pico Boulevard in Santa Monica, then turn left on Pico; continue to Ocean Avenue and go right to the next light at Pacific Coast Highway; turn left and go down the hill. Drive along the beach to Santa Monica Canyon and take Chautauqua up the hill. You are now in Pacific Palisades. At the top, at Sunset Boulevard, the village is a half-mile to the left.

By Bus

Take the free shuttle to Lot C and take Santa Monica Bus #3 (request a transfer); transfer at 4th and Broadway to bus #9, which goes up Sunset Boulevard to, and through, the village. Fare 50¢, seniors 25¢. ☎ 310-451-5444.

By Shuttle

Prime Time Shuttle, ☎ 800-733-8267, www.primetimeshuttle.com, $26 first person, $9 each additional.

By Taxi

Taxis are not found at the island in front of the terminal, but on the street, usually to your right. Fare will be around $40, plus a $2.50 airport fee; time involved around 45 minutes.

By Limousine

Try **Ace Limousine**, ☎ 310-452-7083, which charges $75 plus tax, tip and $5 airport fee; or **Gemstar Limousine**, ☎ 800-922-5466, with rates of $85 plus tax, tip and $5 airport fee.

☛ DID YOU KNOW?

The fee limo companies actually pay the airport is $1.50 per pickup (there is no charge for passenger drop-offs). Unlike taxis that have official meters, limousines can charge whatever they want. We have no idea why some of the approximately 900 limos that service LAX charge this additional fee.

The Glamour Communities

Getting Around

By Car

Talk of getting around Pacific Palisades and you are talking about Sunset Boulevard. The community starts just west of Mandeville Canyon, where Sunset Boulevard climbs up onto the mesa. Driving west on Sunset, you pass the Will Rogers State Historic Park and Ranch. At this point, Sunset turns north and runs parallel to the coast above Palisades Park. The boulevard passes through the village and continues curving its way north, then west, to finally reach the Pacific Coast Highway.

Most streets in Pacific Palisades branch off Sunset Boulevard.

THE PALISADES TOPOGRAPHY

Six major canyons crease their way down through Pacific Palisades from the Santa Monica Mountains to the sea. Some of the canyons have lush vegetation, underground springs and meandering streams; some abound with wildlife.

The altitude of Pacific Palisades ranges from sea level to 2,126 feet at Temescal Peak.

Who Lives Here?

Residents refer to Pacific Palisades as "The Palisades."

Cuba Gooding Jr. (*Pearl Harbor*) bought a house here in 2000; Jeffrey Tambor (*How the Grinch Stole Christmas*) and Kasia Ostlun (of *Never Again* with Tambor) bought a place in 2001. Nanette Fabray, who launched her career by winning a talent contest at the Million Dollar Theatre downtown, and graduated from Hollywood High, lived here for years, and still keeps an office.

Arnold Schwarzenegger and Maria Shriver, who have four children, recently bought yet another house in Pacific Palisades. They bought their first place here 15 years ago; eight years ago when neighbor John Forsythe was ready to sell they added his place and its tennis court. Two years later their neighbor on the other side, Daniel Travanti (*Hill Street Blues*) sold them his place. The most recent purchase was the property of one of the owners of the Pittsburgh Pirates who moved back to Pittsburgh; the Schwarzeneggers' compound at this point adds up to 5.5 acres.

When Ronald and Nancy Reagan were first married they lived in a ranch-style home on North Amalfi Drive. A few years later they built a new home on San Onofre Drive.

> ### 📽 FILM GLOSSARY
>
> **Housekeeping Deal** – A deal, usually between a studio and producer, in which the producer gets an office on the lot and a secretary in exchange for the studio getting first look at any projects he creates.

We have noticed a few professional athletes around; Kobe Bryant of the LA Lakers has been here for some time, and recently LA Dodger Shawn Green moved here.

PACIFIC PALISADES' HONORARY MAYORS

Anthony Hopkins was elected Honorary Mayor of Pacific Palisades for 2000-2002. He said his qualification for the job is that he loves the town. He has spent every year of his mayoralty riding in the 4th of July Parade. The first Honorary Mayor was Esther Williams in 1949; others have included Jerry Lewis, Vivian Vance, Walter Matthau, Dom DeLuise, Chevy Chase, and Martin Short.

The Glamour Communities

Best Place to Stay

Pacific Palisades has no hotels, not even any motels, but it has one wonderful inn. Well, it *almost* has one inn, which is at the bottom of one-block-wide Santa Monica Canyon. Pacific Palisades starts on top of the bluff on the north side of the canyon, and Santa Monica ends on top of the bluff on the south side of the canyon. Even though the Santa Monica Post Office delivers mail to this narrow slice of land in between, Pacific Palisades nevertheless claims the inn as its own.

CHANNEL ROAD INN BED & BREAKFAST
219 W. Channel Road
Santa Monica, CA 90402
☎ 310-459-1920, fax 310-454-9920
www.channelroadinn.com
Moderate-Expensive

The accommodations price scale can be found on page 39.

We loved this place the first time we saw it. Warm, inviting, comfortable, and relaxing are the words that came to mind as we walked into the living room and then saw the upstairs bedrooms. Just a block off the beach, three stories of wood painted a robin's-egg blue with white trim and a shake roof, it was built in 1910. The living room on the ground floor, with its big, tiled fireplace, evokes the 1920s. except for the computer that guests may use to check their e-mail. The comfortable library is stocked with books and video tapes (all the rooms have VCRs).

There are 14 rooms in all, each one different; two are on the ground floor, one of which is handicapped-accessible. The rooms upstairs look out either on the flowering hillside or down Channel Road and out over the ocean. Many rooms have balconies with chairs and a table. The beds are all big; some fourposters, a few king-size. Room 3 in front has a a fourposter bed, a fireplace and a huge bathroom with whirlpool bath and a daybed for a child or extra guest. Room 5, the "romance suite," has a whirlpool bath with windows on three sides, just steps from the large bed.

A full breakfast is served in the breakfast room or out on the patio; tea and cookies are available from 3-5pm, and wine and cheese from 5-7pm. There are bicycles to borrow for pedaling along the oceanside path, good restaurants in Pacific Palisades and nearby Santa Monica, and free parking. To get here, drive from Santa Monica up Pacific Coast Highway to Channel Road.

Best Places to Eat

The dining price scale can be found on page 42.

Pacific Palisades is not known as a great restaurant town, but there are a few places that attract celebrities, simply because they live here or nearby. Aren't there times you go to the neighborhood place rather than getting dressed up and schlepping downtown?

Fine Dining

★★ DANTE PALISADES RESTAURANT
1032 Swarthmore Avenue
☎ 310-459-7561
Italian
Inexpensive/Moderate

Dante's is unusual in that there are really two restaurants here. One is inexpensive, a casual place for families and kids. The other, to the left as you enter from the street, is more formal, much more for adults and serious dining. We, and many Palisades residents, like this idea. The food is Italian with a slight twist – Angelo is actually Basque – but his heart and marinara sauce are definitely in the right place. At least Goldie Hawn and Michelle Pfeiffer seem to like it here.

Casual Dining

GLADSTONE'S 4 FISH
17300 Pacific Coast Highway
☎ 310-573-0212
Seafood
Moderate

It is big, always crowded, and you usually have to wait outside until they call your name on the loudspeaker. They serve several thousand meals each day. No one ever puts it on a list of best gourmet restaurants, but it is on the beach where Sunset Boulevard ends at Pacific Coast Highway, with a view. Big portions, big drinks. The parking lot is on the beach side of the highway, by the restaurant.

★★ TERRI'S CAFE
1028 Swarthmore Avenue
☎ 310-454-6467
Seafood, eclectic
Moderate

Families, kids and dogs seem to prefer Terri's. We have found it noisy inside, on occasion, but tables outside are very nice. People even bring along their dogs, especially on weekends, when breakfast is served all day. You might see Anthony Hopkins (he *is* the mayor, after all) and Goldie Hawn; Tommy Lee Jones and Tom Hanks eat here occasionally.

★★ MORT'S PALISADES DELICATESSEN
1035 Swarthmore Avenue
☎ 310-454-5511
Delicatessen
Moderate

Right across the street from the other two restaurants on Swarthmor is Mort's, a typical deli with a salad bar, too.

You can sit down inside, though the television always seems to be too loud; maybe that is why the tables out on the sidewalk are more popular. Our Palisades informants tell us of seeing Anthony Hopkins, Martin Short, Billy Crystal, Tom Cruise and Matthew Perry here.

VILLAGE NEWS

The little Village Green is a volunteer effort. Some put in the bench, others keep the grass mowed. There is a movement to erect a statue of Walter Matthau, who lived in the Palisades for many years and whom everyone knew, but it will probably come to naught. Some people feel if you start putting up a statue of one celebrity, where will it end?

 # Shopping & Services

No one drives to The Palisades from other parts of LA to shop, simply because there are no well-known boutiques of trendy shops of any kind here. Although celebrities have always lived here, the total population of only 27,000 is probably not enough to support a lot of high-end shops. But there are a couple of places worth mentioning.

Market

★★ GELSON'S MARKET
15424 Sunset Boulevard
☎ 310-459-4483

Some claim this is the market where you are more likely to spot a star among the succotash than in any other, including the Gelson's in Malibu. Someone told us of seeing Charlton Heston and Meredith Baxter at different times. Another friend mentioned seeing Peter Graves there.

Books

VILLAGE BOOKS
1049 Swarthmore Avenue
☎ 310-454-4063

The small town of Pacific Palisades is lucky to have such a complete bookstore; only a place that is so heavily weighted with writers and university professors could support one. Owner Katy O'Laughlin has interesting authors, many local, doing readings and book signings here at least once every week.

Dry Cleaning

★★ EMERSON LAMAY CLEANERS
1045 Swarthmore Avenue
☎ 310-454-4015

Helen Campbell is a person who takes a lot of care with what she does. Clothes she has cleaned look so good that Billy Crystal, Michelle Pfeiffer, Diana Ross and Lakers basketball star Kobe Bryant are among those who bring (or more usually send) their clothes. Of course, the prices are commensurate: cleaning a dress or a suit is $12.95 and up, a dry-cleaned shirt $4.95, a shirt washed and hand-finished here is $2.95.

Sunup to Sundown

My ancestors didn't come over on the Mayflower, but they met the boat.

— Will Rogers

WILL ROGERS STATE HISTORIC PARK & RANCH
1501 Will Rogers State Park Road
Pacific Palisades, CA 90272
☎ 310-454-8212, fax 310-459-2031

Will Rogers was a cowboy, a vaudeville performer, a comedian, an actor and one of the most famous personalities in America in the 1920s and '30s. He was part Cherokee, and

Smoking is not allowed on trails in Will Rogers State Historic Park.

The Glamour Communities

Dogs must be kept on-leash in Will Rogers Park, and are allowed only on trails and developed areas.

was born in Indian Territory. Rogers bought this large property above Sunset Boulevard and built the ranch house in the late '20s. The house has been preserved exactly as it was when he and his family lived here (Rogers died in 1935). There are guided tours every hour on the half-hour from 10:30am-4:30pm; Will Rogers' films – both silents and "talkies" – are screened at the Visitor Center.

The park makes a nice place for an outing. There is a picnic area, and barbecue pits are available on a first-come basis. There are several walks and hikes (see below). Parking is $3, near the polo field or the ranch house. Will Rogers Road is off Sunset Boulevard on the east side of Pacific Palisades; from Brentwood, top the hill past Mandeville Canyon Road. From Santa Monica take the Coast Highway north to Chautauqua and turn right; go right again on Sunset. Less than a mile from Chautauqua turn left on Will Rogers State Park Road. Parking is at the end.

See a polo match (free) every weekend at Will Rogers State Park, ☎ 310-454-8212.

Will Rogers played polo often on his private grounds with others like Clark Gable and Walt Disney; after a match, the players would repair to the Beverly Hills Hotel for libations – this is the derivation of The Polo Lounge's name. This is now the last outdoor polo field in LA County (there were, remarkably, 30-some in the 1930s), and matches are played here every weekend during the summer season. Celebrity guests are often seen at the charity matches; call ☎ 310-573-5000, or see www.willrogerspolo.org for information.

The Rustic Canyon hike is the beginning of the 55-mile Backbone Trail that runs the length of the Santa Monica Mountains, from Will Rogers State Park to Point Magu.

HIKING TRAILS

The **Inspiration Point Trail** is two miles round-trip, about a 300-foot rise, rated easy. The trail starts near the tennis courts, just west of the ranch house. Take the widest trail, a bridle path. It is eucalyptus-lined and ascends a ridge; turn off at a junction to Inspiration Point. The clear-day views are remarkable; you can see from Aaron Spelling's 123-room mansion all the way to downtown Los Angeles on one side, and to Catalina Island on the other.

Rustic Canyon Trail, five miles round-trip, about three hours, 900-foot elevation gain, moderate. Start out on main trail west of ranch house. Pass Inspiration Point turnoff (trail is well marked) look for Backbone Trailhead. The first two miles are uphill, then, after crossing a bridge, descends into Rustic Canyon with lush, overgrown vegetation and old abandoned buildings. Be careful of poison oak in the canyon. The trail criss-crosses the stream, then leads back to the park.

Take plenty of bottled water with you when hiking the trails here.

Temescal Canyon, west of Will Rogers State Park; three miles round-trip, 800 feet elevation gain, about 1½ hours. Drive west on Sunset Boulevard past Will Rogers Park, through the village of Pacific Palisades; turn right on Temescal Canyon Road. From Santa Monica, drive north on the Coast Highway, and turn right on Temescal. Park at entrance to Presbyterian Conference Grounds at the end of the road. The trail starts by the booth at the far end of the parking lot; it goes to the left and climbs the west ridge of the canyon to Skull Rock at the top. About a half-mile past that, the trail on the left goes down to the canyon floor where you will see a waterfall, and takes you back to the starting point.

The Glamour Communities

⚡ WARNING!

Hike or bike only on designated trails. Wandering off the trail increases your chances of coming into contact with poison oak, rattlesnakes and ticks.

The word temescal, as in Temescal Canyon, is an Indian word for sweat house.

CHILDREN'S NATURE INSTITUTE
Temescal Gateway Park
1560 Sunset Boulevard
Pacific Palisades
☎ 310-998-1151
www.childrensnatureinstitute.org

Adults and children explore nature at a leisurely pace on an activity-filled nature walk with a friendly, knowledge-able guide. Kids search for animal homes and hideaways. Walks are held at county parks, beaches, canyons and marshes. Most are "stroller-friendly." Free, but a donation of $7 per family is requested. Reservations are highly recommended. Call or check the Web site for upcoming dates and places. The institute holds an annual festival in late May or early June that is filled with hands-on outdoor activities; admission is charged for this event.

❓ *The Glamour Communities A to Z*

Cameras & Photography Supplies

Brentwood Camera Shop, 225 26th Street, ☎ 310-394-0256.

Car Rental

Westwood Rent-A-Car, 2100 Westwood Boulevard, ☎ 310-474-2333.

Hospitals

Brentwood Ambulatory Surgical Medical Center, 11645 Wilshire Boulevard, ☎ 310-442-9262.

UCLA Medical Center, 10833 LeConte Avenue, Westwood, ☎ 310-825-9111.

Library

Donald Bruce Kauffman Library, 11820 San Vicente Boulevard, Brentwood . . . . ☎ 310-575-8273.

Locksmiths

Bel Air Locksmith (West LA) . . . . ☎ 310-207-1414
Bel Air Locksmith (BH). . . . . ☎ 310-273-8238
Brentwood Locksmith . . . . ☎ 310-207-1414
Brent Air Lock & Key . . . . ☎ 310-447-5625
Locksmith of Pacific Palisades. . . . . . ☎ 310-823-9221

Newspapers

Pacific Palisades Post, 839 Via De La Paz, ☎ 310-454-1321, comes out every Thursday. We always look for Barry Blitzer's column, which is often about local doings.

Pharmacies

Brent-Air Pharmacy, 134 South Barrington Avenue, ☎ 310-476-2211.

Brentwood Plaza Pharmacy, 11980 San Vicente Boulevard, ☎ 310-820-1496.

Knoll's Pharmacy, 16630 Marquez Avenue, Pacific Palisades, ☎ 310-454-6000 or 454-0604.

McKiernan Prescription Center, 900 Via de la Paz, Pacific Palisades, ☎ 310-454-0377.

Police & Fire

Emergency. . . . . ☎ 911
Bel-Air Police . . . . ☎ 310-575-8402
Brentwood/Pacific Palisades Police. . ☎ 310-451-5273
Lifeguard, Will Rogers Beach . . . . ☎ 310-394-3261
Poison Control . . . . ☎ 800-876-4766

Post Offices

Brentwood, Barrington Station, 200 South Barrington Avenue, 90049, ☎ 800-275-8777.

Pacific Palisades, 15209 W. Sunset Boulevard, 90272, ☎ 310-454-3475.

Public Transportation

Brentwood is served by both Los Angeles' Metro Buses and by Santa Monica's buses. For route and schedule information contact **MTA**, ☎ 800-COMMUTE (266-6883) and **Big Blue Bus**, ☎ 310-451-5444.

Taxi & Limousine Services

Westwood Cab. . . . . ☎ 310-234-0709

Westwood Yellow Cab . . . . ☎ 310-207-3394

Brentwood Cab. ☎ 310-478-6669

Brentwood Taxi . . . . ☎ 310-234-0709

Brentwood Express Lim. Service . . . . ☎ 310-820-2253

Independent Taxi . . . . ☎ 310-659-8294

Pacific Palisades Yellow Cab. . . . . ☎ 310-828-7777

United Checker Cab . . . . ☎ 310-393-9699

Veterinary Services

Brentwood Pet Clinic, 11718 Olympic Boulevard, ☎ 310-473-0957

Pacific Palisades Veterinary Center, 853 Via De La Paz, ☎ 310-573-7707.

Visitor Information

Pacific Palisades Chamber of Commerce, 15330 Antioch, Pacific Palisades, CA 90272, ☎ 310-459-7963.

Below the Foothills

I remember you. You used to be big.
I am big. It's the pictures that got small.
        – William Holden and Gloria Swanson,
                     Sunset Boulevard

To the south of Wilshire Boulevard is a broad plain that stretches to the ocean. Here are found a handful of communities with strong connections to the movies – one was a studio backlot until 40 years ago. They are **Century City**, which borders on Beverly Hills on the south side of Santa Monica and Wilshire boulevards; **Westwood**, also bordering Beverly Hills to the west; and **Culver City**, another cradle of the movies located a bit to the south toward the airport.

Century City

Century City is truly a child of the movie industry – it was built on 20th Century Fox Studio's back lot. Where once Tom Mix chased the bad guys across the chaparral, now only 30-story office towers and massive hotels grow.

History

20th Century Fox started when Beverly Hills was not much more than a minor stop on the rail line from downtown Los Angeles to the beach at Santa Monica. Most of the land past Beverly Hills was bean fields, so it did not cost much for the new studio to take in a big chunk of land to use as a back lot. But the fortunes of big studios wax

Below The Foothills

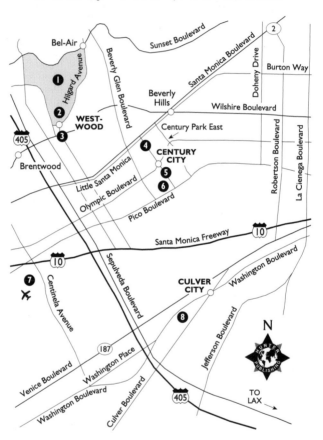

1. UCLA Campus
2. Geffen Playhouse
3. Armand Hammer Museum
4. Century City Shopping Center
5. Avenue of the Stars
6. 20th Century Fox Studios
7. Santa Monica Airport
8. Sony Studios

NOT TO SCALE   © 2002 HUNTER PUBLISHING, INC.

Hotel Bel-Air.
(Photo by Brian Leatart, courtesy of Victoria King Public Relations)

Beverly Hills Hotel, Crescent Wing.
(Courtesy of CarryOn Communication, Inc.)

The entrance to Paramount Pictures in Hollywood.
(© Paramount Pictures)

Above: *The lobby of the Beverly Hills Hotel.*
Below: *The hotel's famous Polo Lounge.*
(Both photos courtesy of CarryOn Communication, Inc.)

Above: *The Moreton Bay fig tree at the Fairmont Miramar Hotel in Santa Monica was planted in 1890.* (Photo courtesy of the hotel)

Below: *The intimate Spago restaurant in Beverly Hills.* (Photo courtesy of Spago)

Asia de Cuba restaurant at the Mondrian Hotel in West Hollywood.
(Photo courtesy of Michelle Bolton & Associates)

Above: *Lioness at the Los Angeles Zoo.*
(Photo by Tad Motoyama, provided by the zoo)

Below: *The Autry Museum of Western Heritage, in Hollywood's Griffith Park.*
(Photo courtesy of the museum)

Tippi Hedren and friend at Tippi's Shambala Preserve.
(Photo © Bill Dow, courtesy of Shambala Preserve)

Universal Studios offers a behind-the-scenes look at movie-making.
(Photo © Universal Studios Inc.)

and wane, and in 1961, 20th Century sold off all its land not being used for sound stages to Alcoa, which built a city.

It is not a city in the sense of having a mayor; like Hollywood, it is a part of Greater Los Angeles. Century City is a carefully planned mixed-use development, which includes office towers, a few large hotels, a mall with department stores and boutiques, cinemas and restaurants, thousands of apartments and condos, and a hospital – all on the edge of Beverly Hills. In fact, the office towers on the eastern edge of Century City look down on Beverly Hills High School.

Century City is built on only 178 acres of land; every inch was planned in advance.

Getting Here

From LAX

By Car

Head north on Sepulveda Boulevard to the San Diego Freeway (I-405); then go north on 405 to the Olympic Boulevard off-ramp. Go right (east) to Avenue of the Stars, which crosses over Olympic, and take the on-ramp to the right, which puts you in the middle of Century City.

By Bus

Take free shuttle bus to Lot C, then walk to the Transit Center and Culver City Bus #6, which will say "Sepulveda Boulevard." Transfer at Sepulveda and Santa Monica boulevards to Metro Bus #4 on Santa Monica Boulevard, going east to Avenue of the Stars.

From Downtown Los Angeles

By Car

Drive out Wilshire to Santa Monica Boulevard, or take the Hollywood Freeway (101) to the Santa Monica Boulevard

Below the Foothills

Bus schedules differ from weekdays to weekends; make sure you are looking at the correct day's schedule.

off-ramp and go west on Santa Monica. Where Wilshire and Santa Monica cross, continue straight ahead on Santa Monica to Avenue of the Stars (the next stop light) and turn left.

By Bus

Get Metro Bus #27 or #28 on Spring Street, going south, anywhere between 1st and 7th streets. Either bus takes you to the Century City Shopping Center at Little Santa Monica and Avenue of the Stars; fare is $1.35. Phone ☎ 800-COMMUTE (266-6883).

 ## Getting Around

Finding your way here is not difficult because Century City is so compact. It takes in the area from Century Park East to Century Park West – two blocks with Avenue of the Stars between them. From north to south it goes from Little Santa Monica Boulevard to Pico Boulevard. In the downtown area those two streets would be miles apart but they converge as they come west so they are close together here.

Former President Ronald Reagan's Western White House when he was in office – and his own office thereafter – was on the 34th floor of Fox Plaza in Century City.

20th Century Fox is in the southwest corner of Century City, at Avenue of the Stars and Pico Boulevard, with the entrance on Pico. Century City Shopping Center is in the northwest corner at Avenue of the Stars and Little Santa Monica Boulevard. Office towers take up the northeast quarter, north of Olympic Boulevard, and condominiums the southeast quarter, south of Olympic.

 ## Who Lives Here?

There are no mansions in Century City, no single-family homes of any kind, just condominiums. Billy Wilder lived in one for years, Dennis Franz (*NYPD Blue*) moved here from Bel-Air. Another who left a big Bel-Air home for a condo here is Judge Joseph A. Wapner, of television's *The People's Court* and *Animal Court*.

FILM GLOSSARY

Dailies, a.k.a. **Rushes** – Footage shot, edited and projected the day after shooting for the director and production executives.

On Location

20th Century Fox has probably made use of locations in Century City more than most other studios; it is right here, just outside the back door, after all. In the years when the new city was being developed, the studio was making *Escape From the Planet of the Apes*. Only the four buildings at the corner of Little Santa Monica and Avenue of the Stars were in existence then, plus the bridge over the Avenue of the Stars from the Shopping Center. The film made extensive use of these structures, especially the bridge.

Die Hard, with Bruce Willis, shot all of its exteriors here and used the tall glass and granite structure of Fox Plaza, 2121 Avenue of the Stars, which will be familiar to anyone who has seen the film.

Best Places to Stay

There are only a few high-end places to stay in Century City, but they are very good.

Hotels

★★ THE CENTURY PLAZA
2025 Avenue of the Stars
Century City
Los Angeles, CA 90067
☎ 310-277-2000, fax 310-551-3355
Expensive

This is a high-profile hotel well used to catering to celebrities; seeing presidents and stars traipse through the lobby

The accommodations price scale can be found on page 39.

is not unusual, as there are banquets and charity dinners here every week, sometimes every night.

The marble lobby is floor-to-ceiling glass walls. The Plaza also has a new restaurant, **Breeze**, that has been called one of the two best in Los Angeles and one of the 20 best in the nation (see page 329). Other amenities include the largest spa in LA, and there are spectacular views from the 15 penthouse suites. This is the kind of hotel that makes you say "Wow!"

★★ PARK HYATT LOS ANGELES
2151 Avenue of the Stars
Los Angeles, CA 90067
☎ 310-277-1234, 800-778-7477, fax 310-785-9240
www.parkhyatt.com
Expensive

The Park Hyatt is a fine hotel, with more suites than rooms; the executive suites have large sundecks, and all the rooms and suites have private balconies. The **Park Grill** restaurant is a meeting place for folks in the industry, especially at breakfast. The staff is multilingual, the gift shop carries international newspapers, and there is a florist shop. Room service is available 24 hours, as is valet service, and the hotel offers a complimentary health club with indoor pool, sauna and steam room, and complimentary limousine service to Beverly Hills and the Rodeo Drive shopping area.

THE ST. REGIS
2055 Avenue of the Stars
Los Angeles, CA 90067
☎ 310-277-6111, 877-787-3452, fax 310-277-3711
www.stregis.com
Deluxe

Call this a quiet, elegant haven for luxury travelers. Just off the lobby, in the stylish **St. Regis Bar**, is a huge mural of flamenco dancers; it's reminiscent of the Maxfield Parrish mural over the King Cole Bar at the St. Regis in New York. The **Encore** restaurant (see page 330) has floor-to-ceiling windows looking out over the gardens. Spacious guest rooms feature electronic controls in the bedside telephone console for most of the equipment in the room: the entertainment system with surround sound; the lighting and air conditioning. The marble bathrooms have their own telephones and plush robes for guest use.

AS PRESIDENTS GO...

The entire top floor of the St. Regis was Ronald Reagan's presidential digs when he was in LA; he and Nancy stayed here 82 times. After a recent renovation, the suite's first guest was Bill Clinton. We were taken up there for a look; it is a great place for views, with glass everywhere and balconies on all four sides.

Amenities include spa and fitness rooms, outdoor pool and whirlpool. Services include fresh fruit daily, complimentary in-suite pressing and shoeshine, 24-hour butler service (an extra $150 per day), 24-hour concierge, limousine service, complimentary transportation within five miles. The staff is multilingual.

Best Places to Eat

There are dozens of places to eat in Century City; most are casual coffee or sandwich shops. You will find the best dining rooms in the hotels.

Fine Dining

★★ BREEZE

The Century Plaza
2025 Avenue of the Stars
☎ 310-551-3334
California cuisine
Expensive

Breeze offers a California grill menu that changes daily. We cannot tell you what we recommend, but the selection will be heavily influenced by what is fresh – there is lots of seafood, so you can count on stone crab and softshell crab in season, as well as seasonal fruits and vegetables. The

The dining price scale can be found on page 42.

Below the Foothills

herbs that are a big part of the cooking are grown right here at the hotel.

The food is fairly uncomplicated, not adorned with heavy sauces, and the presentation is straightforward. Breeze is more than a hotel dining room; it has its own entrance on Avenue of the Stars. There is a traditional bar facing the entrance, and a seafood bar on the opposite side facing the dining room. There you find carpaccios and tartares, and oysters and mussels on the half-shell. The tables on one side look out through a glass wall to a fountain; on the other side, the view is of an enormous coral tree and lush landscaping. Open daily for breakfast, lunch and dinner. Valet parking at all times.

ENCORE
The St. Regis
2055 Avenue of the Stars
☎ 310-277-6111
Provençal
Expensive

The menu shows an emphasis on seafood, plus a few steaks and one free range chicken dish. All are prepared simply, with very fresh ingredients. The arc-shaped restaurant has floor-to-ceiling windows looking out on gardens, and a patio area among the foliage and fountains for relaxed dining.

★★ PARK GRILL RESTAURANT
The Park Hyatt
2151 Avenue of the Stars
☎ 310-277-1234
www.parkhyatt.com
California cuisine with Asian influences
Expensive

The menu is not very adventurous, but even ordinary dishes are superbly cooked and presented here. Items such as seared sea bass, grilled filet, angel hair pasta with prawns, and herb crusted chicken breast are usually on the menu, exactly what most people like best. The Park Grill attracts a lot of people in the business talking film projects, especially at breakfast.

Shop Till You Drop

Century City Shopping Center is the place to go. Fortunately, this fairly compact open mall is worth a visit.

★★ CENTURY CITY SHOPPING CENTER
10250 Little Santa Monica Boulevard
☎ 310-277-3898

The mall is at Little Santa Monica and Century Park West, with entrances to underground parking on Little Santa Monica, Century Park West and Constellation Boulevard. Bloomingdale's is an anchor here, and it's a favorite of many celebrities who are originally from New York. While many of the shops are branches of chains, such as BCBG and Max Mara, enough of them are high-end that it is not uncommon to see stars. The mall also has a 14-screen cinema.

★★ BRENTANO'S
Next door to the Cinema
☎ 310-785-0204

Many celebrities browse the aisles here, and practically every star who writes a book, and most seem to sooner or later, comes here to do readings and book signings. It is a general interest bookstore, with a strong performance arts section and lots of expensive gift books. We have always found it a great place to spend time while we were waiting to go to a movie next door.

Westwood

A college widow stood for something in those days. In fact, she stood for plenty.
    – Groucho Marx, *Horse Feathers*

Westwood Village is a unique blend of historic buildings (historic in LA usually means they go all the way back to the 1920s), with a mix of small businesses and theaters. Beyond the Village is the larger Westwood community extending east and south to Beverly Hills and Century City, and bordered on the west by the LA National Cemetery and on the north by the UCLA campus.

 # History

Like almost all of the land stretching west of downtown Los Angeles to the ocean, Westwood's history begins with a land grant, this one to Don Maximo Alanis, a soldier in the Spanish Army and an early settler. He was awarded 4,400 acres extending from what is today Sepulveda Boulevard east to Beverly Hills, and from the foothills south to Pico Boulevard. Señor Alanis named his spread Rancho San José de Buenos Ayres and remained there from the 1820s through the 1840s.

The land went through the hands of several families until the 1920s, when a developer convinced the state to move UCLA out here. By the time the new campus opened in 1929 the first part of the Village was built and residential lots were being sold to the south. It all grew in concert from then on.

The original buildings in the Village were Mediterranean-Revival style; many were designed by LA's famed architect Paul Williams, including the Italian Renaissance-style building now occupied by Tanino restaurant (see page 339). At first there were a few shops and restaurants and an outdoor skating rink, all aimed at creating a social and academic atmosphere that would appeal to the university population.

PAUL R. WILLIAMS

Paul Williams was one of Los Angeles' most famous and distinguished architects; he was also the first African-American member of the American Institute of Architects. He designed dozens of homes for celebrities – Lucille Ball, Tyrone Power, Bill Robinson and Frank Sinatra, among others. His public buildings include Franz Hall at UCLA, the LA County Courthouse and the UN Building in Paris.

In the past 30 years, 600,000 Iranians have moved to Southern California. Westwood-Beverly Hills has become the center of Iranian life, as you will notice if you drive the stretch of Westwood Boulevard from Santa Monica to Wilshire boulevards, where there are many Iranian restaurants.

The second most prevalent language in Westwood is Farsi.

Getting Here

From LAX

I-405 is called the San Diego Freeway even though San Diego is 100 miles south and even if you are driving north.

By Car

Take Sepulveda Boulevard and go north to the San Diego Freeway; keep going north to the Wilshire Boulevard off-ramp, then go east on Wilshire. Turn left after a few blocks onto Westwood Boulevard.

By Bus

Take the free shuttle bus to Lot C, then Metro Bus #561 to Westwood Boulevard and Lindbrook Avenue; $1.85.

By Taxi

The fare is approximately $25, plus $2.50 airport fee and tip. Try **Westwood Cab**, ☎ 310-234-0709; **Westwood Yellow Cab**, ☎ 310-207-3394; or **Yellow Cab Co.**, ☎ 310-301-9211.

From Downtown Los Angeles

By Bus

Take the Rapid Metro #720 (the red bus) from 5th Street and Grand Avenue going west to Wilshire and Westwood boulevards; $1.35.

Below the Foothills

Getting Around

Westwood Village is compact. It's bounded by Wilshire Boulevard on the south and by Le Conte Avenue and the UCLA campus on the north; on the east is Hilgard Avenue and on the west is Gayley Avenue; in all it's only four by five blocks. The affluent residential area outside the Village proper extends alongside the UCLA campus, up to Sunset Boulevard and down to Wilshire.

The larger Westwood community encompasses the area from Beverly Glen Boulevard on the east to Sepulveda Boulevard on the west, about 15 blocks; and from Sunset Boulevard down to Santa Monica Boulevard. Many people living south of Santa Monica, down to Olympic and even Pico, think of their neighborhood as part of Westwood rather than the amorphous West Los Angeles.

Parking is metered on the streets and usually difficult to find, but there are several parking structures and lots. The parking structure on Broxton Avenue just south of Weyburn has one hour free parking daily from 8am-6pm; the second hour is also free with validation from a local merchant.

> ### ▬ FILM GLOSSARY
>
> **Clapperboard** or **Slate** – Two pieces of wood that are slapped together at the beginning of a shot to precisely synchronize picture and sound.

 # Who Lives Here?

In a switch from the usual star's-mansion-with-lawn, celebrities in Westwood live primarily in the tall buildings that line Wilshire's **Golden Mile**, the stretch from Beverly Hills to Westwood Boulevard. It is home for those who favor a New York style of high-rise living, such as Tom Selleck, Charlie Sheen, Jessica Simpson and Tori Spelling (perhaps only those whose names begin with S are allowed in?). Many of these places include services and amenities such as a concierge, valet, fitness center, swimming pool and sundeck.

On Location

My mother wanted me to go to college. I wanted to go to UCLA but I couldn't find a place to park."
— Goldie Hawn, *Butterflies Are Free*

Westwood is well-used by the studios. Here are a few of the movies shot here, according to Steven Sann, local film buff: *American Gigolo* (the Bruin Theatre on Weyburn Avenue); *Gotcha!*; *Heaven Can Wait* (the remake with Warren Beatty, with scenes filmed on the 15th floor of the Oppenheim Tower); *I Am Sam* (many scenes were shot at the Starbucks next to the Fox Westwood Village Theatre, Weyburn and Broxton); *The Nutty Professor; and Welcome to L.A.*

You never see the UCLA campus identified as such on film, as the university won't permit it. But it has been used many times to double for other campuses in, for example, *Gross Anatomy*; *Love, American Style*; and many episodes of the TV series *Buffy, the Vampire Slayer.*

Best Places to Stay

Hotels

DOUBLETREE HOTEL
10740 Wilshire Boulevard
Los Angeles, CA 90024
☎ 310-475-8711, 800-472-8556, fax 310-475-5220
www.losangeleswestwood.doubletree.com
Moderate-Expensive

The Doubletree is on Wilshire Boulevard, in handy walking distance to everything in the Village. It is a big, tall hotel with good views from the upper rooms. There is a café that serves breakfast, lunch and dinner, plus 24-hour room service, concierge to make it easier to get tickets and

The accommodations price scale can be found on page 39.

Below the Foothills

reservations around town, a swimming pool, exercise room, and a shuttle to the Getty Museum and UCLA.

HILGARD HOUSE HOTEL
927 Hilgard Avenue
Westwood, CA 90024
☎ 310-208-3945, 800-826-3934, fax 310-208-1972
Moderate

This is a small, European-style hotel, with just 55 comfortably sized rooms. No restaurant, no bar, no pool, no gift shops, but a free continental breakfast is served, free covered parking, there are Jacuzzi tubs in some rooms and the residential suites have kitchens. It is perfect – a small, very nice, quiet place without the bustle of a big hotel.

Hilgard Avenue runs along the east side of the UCLA campus; the hotel is between Weyburn and Le Conte (Hilgard House is directly across the street from the W Hotel).

W LOS ANGELES
930 Hilgard Avenue
Los Angeles, CA 90024
☎ 310-208-8765, 877-WHOTELS, fax 310-824-0355
www.whotels.com
Expensive-Deluxe

On the eastern edge of the Village, W is an all-suite hotel, with two pools, an extensive spa and gym, concierge, newsstand, and **Mojo**, an upscale restaurant (see page 337).

A lotta bucks were recently put into redoing what we thought was already a good hotel; it shows up in the design touches, like the use of fiber-optics at the entrance, giving guests the illusion they are walking on water. So it is no surprise to learn that the design was done by Dayna Lee, a set designer with many feature film credits, including *Dances With Wolves*.

The spa and gym are lavish, with a dozen types of massages and facials (try a poolside cabana massage) and private training sessions in the gym; plus steam rooms and a fully-equipped fitness facility. And to give anyone the chance to experience the life of a Hollywood mogul there is an "Extreme Weekend" package that includes the use of a luxury convertible.

Best Places to Eat

Fine Dining

★★ MATTEO'S
2323 Westwood Boulevard
☎ 310-474-1109
Italian
Moderate

The dining price scale can be found on page 42.

Matteo's is not technically in Westwood because it is south of Olympic Boulevard (almost to Pico), but everyone thinks of it as part of Westwood.

We have been coming here for many years, we hate to think how many, usually on a birthday. But it has not changed an iota in all that time. Dark wood paneling, red booths, food like your mother made (if your mother was Italian). Sinatra and the Rat Pack used to hang out here eons ago, and the older generation of celebrities still does on occasion. Sunday is the best day for star-peeking. Matteo's is open for dinner only, Tuesday-Sunday, 5 to 11pm. Valet parking. Watch which door you enter; Matteo's Taste of Hoboken next door is their down-scale, family joint.

MOJO
W Los Angeles
930 Hilgard Avenue
☎ 310-443-7820
Nuevo Latino
Expensive

Located in the W Hotel, Mojo has been stylishly designed by Dayna Lee. You won't find exotic dishes with unpronounceable names. Instead, the menu consists of mostly steaks, pork chops, lamb chops and fish, but all are cooked with spices and touches that give them a new taste. Mojo is open daily for breakfast, 6:30-11:30am; and lunch, 11:30am-2:30pm; dinner is served Sunday-Thursday, 5:30-10pm; Friday and Saturday to 11pm. Valet parking.

Mojo, named for a Latino spice, is pronounced moe-hoe.

Below the Foothills

★★ PALOMINO

10877 Wilshire Boulevard
☎ 310-208-1960
Mediterranean
Moderate-Expensive

Palomino has big floor-to-ceiling windows, and it is a high ceiling; you can look out on the street for the entire length of the dining room. In other words, this is not a cozy, intimate kind of place. It is an attractive room, though, and the big bar in a separate room with high marble tables has its own menu.

The regular dinner menu has a dozen permanent items. A large handful of specials is added each day. The menu leans very much toward fish, though there were a few gestures at meat and pasta. We wish we could say nicer things about the food, as it is supposed to be inspired by "the simple and rustic dishes of Europe," but we found everything overcooked, and the service was slow. But, we have to add, others may have a better experience; the place was quite busy even though we were there on a rainy Monday night.

You may have trouble finding Palomino. The address is on Wilshire Boulevard, but we drove around a bit looking for it before we found the valet parking on Lindbrook Drive (a block north of Wilshire in the Village). We then walked back to the restaurant's entrance a block east of Westwood on the corner of Glendon Avenue and Wilshire. They are open for lunch, Monday-Friday, 11:30am-4pm; dinner, Sunday-Thursday, 4-10pm; Friday and Saturday, to 11pm. Reservations are advisable, especially on weekends.

★★ TENGU SUSHI LOUNGE

1085 Lindbrook Drive
Westwood Village
☎ 310-209-0071
Japanese
Moderate-Expensive

We are not, as a rule, great devotees of Japanese food, but we have become fans of this place. It is like a tapas bar. We go in and, while enjoying a perfect classic martini or a bottle of Kirin beer, we munch on a little of this and a sample of that and a platter of those, and sometimes are filled before we even get to one of the main courses.

Tengu is an attractive place, popular with movie people. We like the small, romantically dim room (though the conversation at the next table is less likely to be about *amor* than about problems on the set). There is also a big, bright, sunken room with small tables and a long, busy sushi bar. And the separate cocktail lounge seems to be a neighborhood gathering place.

We recommend starting with a drink and a bowl of edamame to nibble while perusing the menu (they are as addictive as peanuts, but better). We usually order a small bowl of miso, a soup made with tofu, seaweed and scallions, which may not sound good but is actually delicious. They offer many types of sashimi and sushi, and raw seafood dishes such as tuna carpaccio or tuna tartare.

Edamame are fresh soybeans boiled in salted water. Bite off the tip of the pod, then squeeze the beans out with your teeth.

If you still have appetite enough for a main course there is filet mignon, five-spiced duck, twice-cooked chicken or grilled sea bass, each perfect in its own way. Although we are not usually dessert people we do eat the chocolate tartufo here, which may be the best ice cream we have ever had, including the gelati in Rome.

One anomaly: don't expect Japanese waiters. The last time we were here one of our servers said, as he put a plate down, "*Es caliente.*" But all the waiters have been knowledgeable, enthusiastic about the food and ready to guide us through the menu. Tengu is in the Village, a block north of Wilshire and two blocks east of Westwood Boulevard. Valet parking.

Below the Foothills

TANINO RISTORANTE AND BAR
1043 Westwood Boulevard
Between Kinross and Weyburn Avenues
☎ 310-208-0444
www.tanino.com
Italian
Moderate

This is Italian food with a Sicilian emphasis; you see it right away on the menu, with the salad of marinated anchovies and pasta with sea urchin. Among the entrées is a lamb and polenta dish, and this is one of the few places in town to find *coniglio al forno*, roasted rabbit. The décor is striking; it's in one of the dozen buildings in Westwood that date back to the beginnings of the village. Famed architect Paul Williams designed the Italianate building after the Pitti Palace in Florence; the restaurant is in a two-level space with the original ceiling frescos and carvings, elaborate wall murals and artisan plaster work intact. The bar is popular locally. Lunch, Monday-Friday, 11:30am-3pm; dinner, Monday-Saturday, 5:30-11:30pm; Sunday until 10pm. Reservations recommended.

Casual Dining

JERRY'S FAMOUS DELI
Westwood Village
10925 Weyburn Avenue
☎ 310-208-3354
Deli
Inexpensive

If you are in a mind for deli food, this one is handy to walk to from anywhere in the Village. Open Sunday-Thursday 7am-2am, Friday-Saturday 24 hours. Parking in daytime in lot in back, valet parking in evenings, may even find a space on the street late at night.

 # Shopping

Westwood Village started out as a small, pretty little place next to the UCLA campus, with lots of local stores featuring youthful, casual items. It became so popular that chains like Gap and Ann Taylor moved in; rents eventually became so high that the small entrepreneurs moved out. Then the crime rate rose, frightening many people away from the area. Right now it is in a down period, with many empty stores. However, if you need a camera or photographic supplies, you'll find a large selection at **Bel Air Camera**, 10925 Kinross Avenue (at Gayley), ☎ 310-208-5150.

Sunup to Sundown

ARMAND HAMMER MUSEUM
10899 Wilshire Boulevard
Los Angeles, CA 90024
☎ 310-443-7000, tours 310-443-7041
www.hammer.ucla.edu

Eclectic collections and exhibits from old masters to the newest unsung artist. The museum plans to close in the fall of 2004 for refurbishing, reopening in 2005. Admission is $4.50 for adults; $3 for seniors 65+; free for ages 17 and under; free for everyone on Thursdays. Hours are 11am-7pm, Tuesday-Saturday (open until 9pm on Thursday); 11am-5pm on Sunday. Closed Monday. Parking is $2.75 for three hours with museum validation.

FARMERS' MARKET
Weyburn Avenue, between Westwood Boulevard and Tiverton Avenue

The market is held every Thursday, year-round, from 2-7pm. Two blocks on Weyburn and one on Glendon are blocked off. There are usually around 70 organic food vendors, plus craftspeople, flower vendors, cooking demos, and live music, usually jazz.

After Dark

Games

THE WESTWOOD ARCADE
10965 Weyburn Avenue
☎ 310-443-4316

Since video games for home computers have become more sophisticated and adult-oriented, local arcades have become playgrounds, not only for kids but for Westwood's ubiquitous stockbrokers. This is one of the most active arcades, where you might see anyone. Jason Alexander, of *Seinfeld*, hangs out here. Hours are 10:30am-1am; in winter they close at 12:30am during the week.

Movies

Watch the LA Times *or* LA Weekly *movie ads for notices of premieres.*

Westwood, which used to be a village with a couple of really nice movie theaters for the college students and locals to see a picture once a week, has turned into the movie capital of the world. More premieres are held here than anywhere. There are seven cinemas in a few blocks.

All of the following telephone numbers have a 310 area code; those numbers indicated with an asterisk (*) are for ordering tickets in advance.

AVCO General Cinema, 10840 Wilshire Boulevard, ☎ 475-0711.

Mann Bruin, 948 Broxton Avenue, ☎ 239-MANN*.

Most premieres are held at the Bruin and the Village (known to locals by its old name, Fox).

Mann Festival, 10887 Lindbrook Drive, ☎ 208-4575*.

Mann Four Plex, 1050 Gayley Avenue, ☎ 208-7664*.

Mann National, 10925 Lindbrook Drive, ☎ 208-4366*.

Mann Plaza, 1067 Glendon Avenue, ☎ 208-3097*.

Mann Regent, 1045 Broxton Avenue, ☎ 208-3259*.

Mann Village, 961 Broxton Avenue, ☎ 208-5576*.

Theater

GEFFEN PLAYHOUSE
10886 Le Conte Avenue
Westwood Village
☎ 310-208-5454, fax 310-209-8383
www.geffenplayhouse.com

The playhouse offers a season of five plays each year, in both classic and contemporary theater. Their programming is eclectic, offering musicals as well as traditional productions, including both West Coast and world premieres.

Culver City

I don't know nothin' 'bout birthin' no babies, Miss Scarlett.

— Prissy (Butterfly McQueen), *Gone With the Wind*

When it comes to where the movies were actually made, from about 1918 on, Culver City was at least as important as Hollywood. This is where MGM had their studio, joined later by Selznick and Hal Roach, who was incredibly meaningful to the world of comedy.

The "burning of Atlanta" for Gone With the Wind *was achieved on the back lot of the Selznick International studio in Culver City.*

Culver City's star has dimmed a bit since those days. MGM moved to Santa Monica and, while the physical studio remains, its fabulous back lots have disappeared under acres of cookie-cutter condos. Hal Roach's studio was razed, which was (or should have been) a criminal act; a nondescript industrial park has risen where Laurel and Hardy's water tank had been. Now, there is one ancient hotel, known mainly for its association with one picture; and one restaurant that has reason to be known outside the boundaries of Culver City itself. But for 40 years it was really something.

History

The 19th Century

In 1820 the settlers from Sonora, Mexico, were living in a Los Angeles that was steadily increasing in population. There was little cash coming in from Mexico, and few foreign ships called to leave any currency behind, so the residents developed a barter system. Two young men, Agustín Machado and Felipe Talamantes, saw that cattle provided hides, tallow and meat for bartering, and petitioned for exclusive grazing rights to an area called La Balloña Valley, 15 miles southwest of the town.

They were granted rights to an area that one person could circle on horseback between sunup and sundown in one day. Agustín camped overnight at the foot of the Del Rey hills by the seashore (just south of Marina del Rey) and set off at sunrise. By the day's end he was able to claim 14,000 acres of land.

The name "Balloña" is probably a mispronunciation of the Spanish town of Bayona, ancestral home of one of the founders of the Rancho.

Besides grazing cattle and sheep on the green hills, Rancho La Balloña produced corn, pumpkins, beans, wheat, and grapes that turned out a prized white wine. La Balloña Creek, which drained all the land west of downtown LA from the Santa Monica Mountains south, flowed clear and full of fish, with fruit trees along the banks. When you are driving in the area now and pass over a concrete ditch about 10 feet wide and 10 feet deep you are gazing at the pitiful remains of La Balloña Creek. You can credit the Army Corps of Engineers and its mania for burying everything in cement; witness the Los Angeles River.

The rancho prospered, declined and prospered again. Fortunately the general trend was up, and Agustín, who ran the operation, became wealthy; but after the Americanos arrived in the 1850s his partners sold off (or lost to debt) pieces of their shares of the land. By 1867 there were 32 owners.

A SHORT & EASY HISTORY LESSON

La Balloña School was built in 1865. Miss Craft, from Boston, was paid $50 a month to instruct 160 children, though average attendance was 19.

While Northern Californians sympathized with the North in the Civil War, Southern Californians had a 100-year history of holding Indians as slaves, and they tended to support the South. During the war the army established a base at Camp Latham on La Balloña Creek, near the present Jefferson Boulevard, to keep Southern sympathy in check.

When Agustín Machado died in 1865 the Rancho was divided into 25 long, narrow strips so that each inheritor would have some fertile land near Balloña Creek, some higher land for dry farming, hillside land for pasture and some "worthless" coastal swamps. Gradually, during the real estate booms of the 1870s, '80s and '90s the land was divided and re-divided until hardly any was owned by descendants of the original owners. Except for that owned by Macedonio Aguilar, who not only kept his portion but bought up some of the others. It was his land on which Culver City was built.

Bringing It Up to Date

In 1910 a 30-year-old Nebraskan, Harry Culver, went to work for real estate man I.N. Van Nuys, whose name you will see prominently in the San Fernando Valley. After Harry learned the ropes he staked out the barley fields around Washington Boulevard and announced his plans for a city. Like Van Nuys, he modestly named it after himself.

Harry Culver was, above all, a salesman. He installed an 80,000-watt revolving searchlight that could be seen for 30 miles on the roof of his real estate office. He staged a polo game featuring Fords rather than horses. He promoted a marathon that started in Los Angeles and ended, predictably, at his sales office in Culver City. There were parades with brass bands, and the prize of a building lot to the parents of Culver City's Most Beautiful Baby. Anything to put Culver City on the map.

Culver City's official seal is inscribed with the words, "The Heart of Screenland."

In 1915, Culver saw an odd sight on La Balloña Creek: actors costumed as Indians with painted faces rowing down a mighty "river." It was Thomas Ince shooting a Western. Culver convinced Ince to move his Inceville studio from north of Santa Monica to Culver City. There just happened to be, right on Washington Boulevard, an 11-acre portion remaining from Macedonio Aguilar's La Balloña ranch. This site became the first of the three major motion picture studios that provided Culver City's economy with a base.

Thomas Ince built Ince Studios at 10202 Washington Boulevard; the landmark colonnaded structure is backed by a two-story administration building that stretches along Washington Boulevard to this day. The first picture shot there, *Civilization*, helped elect Woodrow Wilson to the presidency in 1916 on a "he kept us out of war" platform. Two years later Ince's company became Triangle Studios with D.W. Griffith and Mack Sennett as partners; a 16-acre expansion made Culver City home to the largest motion picture studio in the world.

Below the Foothills

The stages had glass walls, as they depended on natural light; actors in those early pictures included Western star William S. Hart, Billie Burke from Broadway, "Iron Eyes" Lew Cody, and Leo Carrillo, who was himself descended from a Mexican Land Grant family. Douglas Fairbanks, a minor star on the Broadway stage, was brought out by Triangle to appear in one of its first releases, *The Lamb*.

LIFE IMITATES ART

In the early days of Culver City studios a film crew set up to shoot a scene of a make-believe robbery at the Culver City Commercial and Savings Bank. When the crew broke for lunch a man walked into the bank and put a revolver in the cashier's back. While employees and customers applauded, thinking it was a rehearsal for the afternoon shooting, the cashier was locked in the vault and the real robber walked out with the real money, never to be seen again.

In 1918 Samuel Goldwyn bought Triangle Studios. He is the one who established the screen trademarks Leo the Lion and "Ars Gratia Artis" (Art for Art's Sake). Later there was a merger; the Metro Company moved from Hollywood, Louis B. Mayer Studios left East Los Angeles for Culver City, and Metro-Goldwyn-Mayer was created. Goldwyn soon pulled out, but his name and trademark lion remained behind.

The first sound film shot at MGM was White Shadows of the South Seas, 1929. The first sound heard was the roar of Leo the Lion.

Goldwyn had started shooting *Ben Hur* in Italy before the merger; the new company found that the Colosseum's walls were too high to shoot in natural light except during a short time at noon. The picture was finished back home at an enormous cost which included rebuilding the Colosseum at Venice Boulevard and La Cienega – with lower walls. The stands were filled with Culver City residents who were enticed to double as Romans for $5 a day and a box lunch. Efforts paid off; *Ben Hur*, the first MGM movie, was the screen's biggest grosser for many decades.

FILM GLOSSARY

Line Producer – Though a dozen "producers" may be listed in the credits, the line producer is the one who supervises the actual production.

Thomas Ince moved east a few blocks and built a new studio at 9336 Washington Boulevard. The first building was the colonial mansion that still stands facing the boulevard. Ince built the lot up and produced a full schedule of films for several years until he died mysteriously on William Randolph Hearst's yacht in 1924. The Pathé Company, a French studio, owned the lot in 1929 when talkies came in. The company was called RKO-Pathé in 1933 when *King Kong* was shot.

It was the King Kong sets that were destroyed in the burning of Atlanta for Gone With the Wind *in 1939.*

The third of the big Culver City studios was built by Hal Roach in 1919 farther east on Washington. *The Little Rascals*, *Our Gang*, *Laurel and Hardy* and other comedies spilled out of the studio onto the surrounding streets; Hal Roach produced 50 comedies a year plus features.

The 1930s and '40s were MGM's golden days, with a succession of memorable stars and pictures. In 1941 more than half of all American-made films were produced in Culver City, and MGM captured eight Oscars. Ten years later the studio was in trouble and L.B. Mayer was forced to resign.

The onset of television delivered the *coup de grâce* to the studio system. MGM pretty well committed hari-kari when it sold its entire library of all the films it had ever produced to Ted Turner for use on television. Then it auctioned off most of its fabulous props and costumes, and finally disposed of 153 of its 183 acres, all five of the back lots. Only the original Lot #1 was left; Samuel Goldwyn would have recognized it easily.

We always disliked working at the studio, where you were supposed to go regularly to an office and spend a reasonable number of hours five days a week. We much preferred working at home. But we were trapped for a couple of years in the '70s at MGM. Whenever we would get stuck on a script and take a walk, hoping for inspiration to

Below the Foothills

strike, it was sort of sad to see how little activity there usually was on the lot. There were a few TV series, hardly ever any features. It was a transition period between the golden days of films and the present golden days of money.

Raintree, a condo and apartment development, occupies what was MGM Lot #3. You can still see part of the lake where the HMS Bounty *and the riverboat from* Show-boat *floated.*

The old MGM lot is owned by Sony Corp. now, and divided between Tristar and Columbia Pictures. MGM has some offices in Santa Monica.

At the studio that Ince built, RKO-Pathe became Selznick International Studios. This was the period in the 1930s when *Gone With the Wind*, *A Star is Born* and *Intermezzo* were made. After television and changing times decimated the movie business the lot was owned by various entities, at one time by Desi Arnaz and Lucille Ball's company, Desilu.

During World War II the Hal Roach Studios became "Fort Roach." Most of the Army and Air Forces training films were made there. Ronald Reagan spent the war here working with some of the writers he later helped to blacklist.

For many years there had been abortive campaigns to establish a real museum dedicated to the history of motion pictures. The Roach lot, a small, historic studio that had fallen on hard times, would have been perfect and a wonderful destination for tourists. Instead, Culver City, "the heart of screenland," allowed it to be torn down in 1963 and a barely functioning industrial tract put in its place. (Los Angeles also paid no attention when the same fate befell Eagle-Lion Studio on Santa Monica Boulevard.)

▄ FILM TRIVIA

Look for a marker on a strip of grass at Washington and National, the former site of Hal Roach Studios. It was placed there by the "Sons of the Desert," a Laurel and Hardy appreciation group, to commemorate the "Laugh Factory to the World."

Getting Here

From LAX

By Car

Exit airport to Sepulveda Boulevard, turn left and stay on it to Washington Boulevard, then turn right – you are in Culver City.

By Bus

Take the free airport shuttle to Lot C. Board the Culver City Bus #6, which follows Sepulveda Boulevard; transfer at Washington Boulevard to Bus Line #1 going east for downtown Culver City. Line 1 continues to Washington and Fairfax. Fare 75¢, children 50¢, seniors 35¢. ☎ 310-253-6500, recorded 310-253-6510.

By Shuttle

Fare to Culver City is about $16 for one person, $25 for two. Shuttle operators include **Prime Time Shuttle**, ☎ 800-733-8267, www.primetimeshuttle.com; **Super Shuttle**, ☎ 310-782-6600 or 323-775-6600, www.supershuttle.com; and **X-Press**, ☎ 800-427-7483.

By Taxi

Pick up a taxi by the island in front of terminal. Fare is $15-$18 plus a $2.50 airport fee.

From Downtown Los Angeles

By Car

Take any downtown street south to Washington Boulevard, turn right.

Below the Foothills

By Bus

Get Bus 33 or 333 going south on Spring Street and out Venice Boulevard to Culver City. Fare $1.35. ☎ 800-COM-MUTE (266-6883) for information.

 # Getting Around

The Top employer in Culver City is Sony Pictures: over 2,000 residents work there.

Washington Boulevard is Culver City's main street. It runs the length of the city, from where the Santa Monica Freeway (10) crosses it in the east all the way out the shoe-string strip to Lincoln Boulevard in Marina del Rey.

Culver Boulevard also crosses Washington, though at the opposite angle. From that point for the dozen blocks west to Overland Avenue is the heart of the city's business district. It also contains Sony's studio; Culver Studio is to the east. Look at an area map for the six streets that extend south of Culver Boulevard across from Sony (starting at Overland). They form an oval because the race track used to be there.

Culver City originally covered 1.2 square miles; through annexation it now covers almost five square miles.

The strangest part of Culver City is a long, thin strip that extends from the core of the city out to the west, reaching almost to Lincoln Boulevard in Marina del Rey. This umbilical cord, only 300 feet wide in places, was annexed in 1926 because there was a chunk of land at the end where some mover and shaker wanted to build a midget auto racing track. Hughes Aircraft later built helicopters there. Culver City wanted to allow a big mall on the site but Los Angeles blocked it: Culver City would get all the tax money and LA would get all the traffic grief. Now there is a Costco, which generates its own waves of traffic just one block from the corner of Washington and Lincoln, LA's busiest intersection.

🕶 Who Lived Here?

The enchanting Hobbit Houses, as they are called locally, were built by Lawrence Joseph between 1946 and 1970. The architecture will remind you of buildings from *Snow White*; crooked trees shade slanting roofs, their domes covered with mossy wooden shingles; walls are made of aged bricks and bulging mortar. A path wanders through rich vegetation to a thick, handcarved door. Former residents include Gwen Verdon, Nick Nolte, and Paula Prentiss and Richard Benjamin (as a couple).

The architecture was called Fantasy Revival Style (it was also known as Storybook Style), and was popular briefly during the 1920s and 30s. Arrol Gellner and Douglas Keister have a new book out, *Storybook Style*, which pictures the Hobbit Houses.

The houses are still here, on a one-block stretch of Dunn Drive between Venice and Washington boulevards. The site is near a hospital and movie theater on Washington, so there are open-air parking lots and a parking structure on this block. But if you look behind the trees and ferns and cool pools with fish you will find Culver City's hidden treasure. The houses are occupied, so just look; don't bother anyone.

On Location

Culver City's streets have shown up in literally thousands of films, especially if we are counting all the early silent two-reelers. Think of the Laurel and Hardy comedies: most of the off-the-lot shooting in all of them was done right here. *Putting Pants on Philip*, Laurel and Hardy's first two-reeler for Hal Roach Studio, was shot on the street with the Culver Hotel in the background. Another Laurel and Hardy film was *County Hospital*, which used the old City Hall. Their early *Hog Wild* was shot on the 4100 block on Madison Avenue.

Culver City's historian, Julie Lugo Cerra, told us that her father was one of the extras hired for the mob scenes when the original *Ben Hur* was shot at Venice and La Cienega boulevards. He and hundreds of other residents were also extras in *Last of the Mohicans*.

A few other films and TV series that used Culver City streets are *King Kong*, and the television series *Police Story* and *CHiPS*. The interior of the police station in *The Mad Bomber* was the actual Culver City police station; the exterior of that building was used in *Coming Home*.

Below the Foothills

★ **TIP**

Pick up a copy of the *Culver City News*, a weekly that comes out Thursdays, to see the column by Julie Lugo Cerra, the city's official historian.

Several episodes of Rod Serling's *Twilight Zone* were shot in part at Carlson Memorial Park, at Braddock and Le Bourget, a block south of Sony Studio in the old racetrack area. The old City Hall was the location for much of the *Hunter* series; the new City Hall was used by the more recent *Party of Five*.

The TV series *The Wonder Years* frequently used many of Culver City's residential streets; the Veteran's Memorial Auditorium at Overland Avenue and Culver Boulevard became the Court House for *Knots Landing*. For *Under the Rainbow* several blocks of Washington and Culver boulevards were closed off for the day. The remake of *Planet of the Apes*, shooting in 2001, filmed on some Culver City streets. And you may very well recognize the one-block stretch of Main Street between Washington and Venice boulevards, because it has been used so many times as "small town 1950s."

 Best Place to Stay

★ CULVER HOTEL
9400 Culver Boulevard
Culver City, CA 90232
☎ 310-838-7963, 888-328-5837, fax 310-815-9618
www.culverhotel.com
Moderate

The accommodations price scale can be found on page 39.

When *The Wizard of Oz* was filmed at MGM, 124 little people were recruited from all over the country to play the Munchkins. Most were put up at the Culver City Hotel, just a few blocks from the studio. What happened next was the stuff of legend, with endless drunken parties and drunken brawls.

The stories were good enough to inspire *Under the Rainbow* (1981), which used the hotel to shoot that comedic take on the making of *The Wizard of Oz*. Other movies shot here included early Laurel and Hardy silents and *Our Gang* two-reelers. More recently were *The Last Action Hero*, with Arnold Schwarzenegger, and parts of the TV series *Party of Five*.

In 1924, Harry Culver built this oddly shaped hotel that sits in the middle of the intersection of Washington and Culver boulevards. Ronald Reagan and Joan Crawford were residents, and at one time it was owned by John Wayne. Clark Gable kept a suite here for a while, Red Skelton and Greta Garbo were among the guests over the years.

For many years the six-story Culver Hotel was the tallest building in Culver City.

New owners spent a lot of money renovating the hotel a few years ago, and the high-ceilinged lobby reflects this. But the décor is erratic and some of the rooms are rather frumpy. Room service can be fast, or it can be slow, but overall we liked the place; it has a homey feeling. Note: you can save money by booking your room on the internet.

Best Place to Eat

VERSAILLES RESTAURANT
10319 Venice Boulevard
☎ 310-558-3168
Cuban
Inexpensive

This is the most interesting and probably the best place in Culver City. People all over the Westside are aware of it, the line outside the door every night attests to that. The line also tells you they don't take reservations. There used to be a French restaurant here and when the new owners moved in they didn't bother to change the sign, but it was also serendipitous: a famous restaurant in Cuba and a knock-off in Miami have the same name.

Most people rave about the garlic chicken, but the black beans are very good, too. Add spicy pork dishes, fried plantains, fast service and cold beer. What more could anyone ask? Open daily, 11am-11pm. Parking in lot at front.

The dining price scale can be found on page 42.

Below the Foothills

Shopping

Culver City is definitely not known as a place to go for shopping. Fox Hills, the mall on the southwest end of town, is pretty old and dowdy now, and there's not much of note downtown. But there are a few places that are special and worth checking out.

SORRENTO ITALIAN MARKET
5518 Sepulveda Boulevard
☎ 310-391-7654

The Vera family, which owns Sorrento, has a ranch in the Central Valley where they grow the fruit, wine and olives sold here.

Perhaps you are looking for some unique food or cooking implement as a gift for someone, or say you are simply hungry for something special. Sorrento has been here for 40 years with food from South America, Asia, Europe and the Middle East as well as Italy. It is the kind of place where you want to spend time browsing among the cans and bottles and deli cases, or order something hot and homemade to take along to eat. Open Monday-Saturday 7am-7pm, Sunday 7am-4pm. Parking lot in rear.

★★ ALLIED MODEL TRAINS
4411 Sepulveda Boulevard
☎ 310-313-9353

Here you will find one of the world's largest model train stores in a scaled-down replica of Union Station downtown. The displays are fantastic, with trains rolling along a track near the ceiling and others gliding through model villages and intricate landscapes in front of the large windows.

Don't turn your nose up at the small HO trains: one hand-crafted locomotive can cost from $500 to $2,000.

The store has provided layouts and equipment for many pictures, including *Star Trek*, *The Rat Pack*, and *Stuart Little*, and you would be surprised at how many celebrities have their own trains at home. Allen Drucker, the owner, declines to name individuals, to protect their sense of privacy when they drop in here, but he assured us they do, almost every week.

The store has everything from tiny half-inch Z gauge trains to the big nine-inch LGB gauge. But Allen told us that the standard HO gauge is the most popular. There is a separate room full of the most amazingly complete and detailed model villages. What we like especially about this store is that there are separate departments for each type of train model, each staffed by an expert salesperson. Open Monday-Thursday and Saturday, 10am-6pm; Friday 10am-7pm.

A STAR-STRUCK CHIEF OF POLICE

California state law empowers local law enforcement authorities to issue concealed weapon permits. Except for a few rural counties up in the Sierra Mountains in the north of the state, few of these permits are handed out, especially in the big cities. A glaring exception is Culver City, where Police Chief Ted Cooke likes to help celebrities pack heat. In 1999, Culver City licensed over 400 gun toters; in contrast, the cities of Santa Monica, Torrance and celebrity-packed Beverly Hills combined issued a total of three. Over the years the chief has handed out concealed-weapon permits to scores, including Sammy Davis Jr., Johnny Carson, Sylvester Stallone, James Caan, Gary Coleman and Jim Belushi. Mostly in response to Chief Cooke's profligate scattering of permits to stars, none of whom lived in his jurisdiction, state law now mandates that permits can be issued only to persons who live in the same municipality.

Sunup to Sundown

If you are from colder climes and miss ice skating already, **Culver Ice Arena** is here. It is open Monday-Friday and Sunday, 1:30-5pm; Saturday, 11:30am-2pm and 2:30-5pm; plus Thursday-Sunday nights, 8-10:30pm. General admission (13 years and up), $6.25; kids, $5.25; skate rental, $2.50. 4545 Sepulveda Boulevard, ☎ 310-398-5719; for recorded information, ☎ 310-398-5718.

Below the Foothills

After Dark

JAZZ BAKERY
3233 Helms Avenue
☎ 310-271-9039

One of the best places to hear jazz. No tables, no dinner service, not even drink service, just respectful listening. Mostly top groups play here; shows are at 8 and 9:30pm. Cover charge $15 to $25, no minimum, all ages. Café Cantata in the lobby serves coffee, beer and wine, and munchies. Half-price tickets are sometimes available for students (with student ID) 30 minutes before showtime.

 # Below the Foothills A to Z

Automotive Services

Goodman's Towing, Culver City . . . . . . ☎ 310-839-2281

Hospitals

Century City Hospital, 2070 Century Park East, ☎ 310-553-6211.

Century City Hospital Out-Patient, 2080 Century Park East, ☎ 310-551-1463.

Brotman Medical Center, 3828 Delmas Terrace, Culver City, ☎ 310-836-7000. A large, full-service hospital with roots in the community since 1927.

UCLA Medical Center, 10833 Le Conte Avenue, Westwod, ☎ 310-825-8611; emergency room, ☎ 310-825-2111.

Locksmith

Metro Locksmith (Century City, Culver City, Westwood), ☎ 310-441-2755.

Miller's Lock Shop (Westwood), ☎ 310-393-8025.

Oakley Lock & Key (Culver City, Westwood), ☎ 310-474-4704.

Newsstands

News Spot, 10953 Kenross Avenue, Westwood ☎ 310-208-4408; daily, 8am-midnight

Westwood Village Newsstand, 1101 Westwood Boulevard, ☎ 310-208-5315; daily, 7am-midnight.

Pharmacies

Century City Pharmacy, 2080 Century Park East, ☎ 310-553-3434. Open Monday-Friday, 9am-6pm.

Culver City Medical Pharmacy, 4340 Overland Ave., Culver City, ☎ 310-559-6555. Open Monday-Friday, 9am-6pm.

Westwood Center Pharmacy, 10921 Wilshire Boulevard, ☎ 310-208-6666. Open Monday-Friday, 9am-7:30pm.

Police & Fire

Emergency................................. ☎ 911
Century City Police (West LA) .... ☎ 310-575-8400
Culver City Fire Dept............... ☎ 310-253-5900
Culver City Police .... ☎ 310-837-1221
Westwood Police .... ☎ 310-575-8404

Post Offices

Westwood, Village Station, 11000 Wilshire Boulevard, (not in the Village), Los Angeles, CA 90024, ☎ 310-235-7443.

Culver City, Main Branch, 11111 Jefferson Boulevard, Culver City, CA 90230, ☎ 310-391-2704; Gateway Station, 9942 Culver Boulevard, Culver City, CA 90232, ☎ 310-204-0843.

Public Transportation

Culver City Municipal Bus. . . . . ☎ 310-253-6500
Metro Bus . . . . ☎ 800-COMMUTE (266-6883)

Taxis

Beverly Hills Cab Co. . ☎ 310-273-6611 or 800-273-6611
Independent Taxi Co. . . . . ☎ 310-800-9498
Yellow Cab Co. . . . . ☎ 800-200-0011

Veterinary Services

★ **Culver City Animal Hospital**, 5830 Washington Boulevard, ☎ 310-836-4551. For more than 40 years this facility has specialized in small animal care. Because it is located just a few blocks from MGM, the staff here have cared for the pets of many stars over the years, including Yul Brynner's black German shepherd, Elvis and Priscilla Presley's two Great Danes (Snoopy and Brutus), Rod Stewart's collies, John Candy's menagerie of cats and dogs, and Sammy Davis Jr.'s Great Dane.

Visitor Information

Westwood Village Community Alliance, 1081 Westwood Boulevard, Suite 218, Los Angeles, CA 90024; ☎ 310-208-1984, www.westwood-village.org, www.yournorthvillage.org/westwood. Open Monday-Friday, 8:30am-5pm.

Century City Chamber of Commerce, 2029 Century Park East, Concourse Level, Century City, CA 90067, ☎ 310-553-2222, www.centurycitycc.com.

Culver City Chamber of Commerce, 10767 Washington Boulevard, Culver City, CA 90232, www.culvercitychamber.com, ☎ 310-287-3850.

Culver City Public Information, ☎ 310-253-5914.

The Beach Communities

God opens the sea with a blast of His nostrils!
– Old Man, on the parting of the Red Sea,
The Ten Commandments

They say everything in the US that was loose rolled westward and ended up in California, and that's certainly true here: the hippest, the wealthiest, the flakiest, the loosest, all eventually find their way to the beach. We hate to comment; we live here.

Marina del Rey

The westside beaches start with **Marina del Rey** on the south and move north through **Venice**, **Santa Monica**, **Topanga** and **Malibu**. Each is a very different kind of community, from tiny, rural Topanga to big, commercial Santa Monica; from eccentric, who-knows-what-might-happen-next-and-who-cares Venice to wealthy, very private Malibu.

Marina del Rey is Spanish for "Marina of the King."

History

Marina del Rey did not exist before 1965; now, with 6,000 boat slips, it is the largest marina in the country. Many who like to stay near the airport choose this area just a few miles from LAX, and quite a few TV series have been filmed here.

This area was a marsh for thousands of years, popular with the shore Indians for its abundance of seafood and birds. Jump ahead to 1905. It was still a marsh, still a haunt of fishermen, but that is when Abbot Kinney built Venice by giving his Grand Canal an entrance to the sea

Marina del Rey is not truly a city; it is administered by the LA County Department of Beaches and Harbors.

The Beach Communities

1. Los Angeles Int'l Airport
2. Fiji Way; Fisherman's Village; Burton Chace Park
3. Venice Pier; Boardwalk
4. Museum of Flying; SM Airport
5. Santa Monica Pier; Muscle Beach
6. Third Street Promenade; Main Street; Historical Museum
7. Gold Coast
8. Douglas Park
9. Palisades Park; Temescal Canyon Park
10. Theatricum Botanicum
11. Malibu Pier; Surfriders Beach
12. Pepperdine University

5 MILES

© 2002 HUNTER PUBLISHING, INC.

The local pelican population was almost wiped out a few decades ago by DDT, but it has now come back.

here, so tidal waters could flush the canals out twice each day.

These wetlands areas are incredibly important. The tidal mixture of freshwater and saltwater in a safe, marshy environment is what many species of fish and other creatures require to propagate and grow to a size where they can venture into the deeper ocean waters. Every time another wetland is destroyed we are all poorer for it.

Unfortunately, not enough attention is paid to this fact. In the 1950s people saw this area as a big useless swamp, so

Los Angeles County "put it to better use." It took a lot of digging to destroy it all, but in 1965 Marina del Rey was dedicated.

When the county built the marina they didn't just put in slips and let a few sailmakers, boat supply and fishing tackle places open up. Instead, they leased all the land between and around the basins to private corporations, which run the slips and put up apartment buildings. Of course, that cuts off some of the wind and most of the view, which seems odd for a small boat harbor. But, hey! Who is going to hand over more money to the county, some guys with dinky 17-foot sailboats or giant real estate corporations?

Of the 21 separate marinas that make up the total of Marina del Rey, 20 are private. The California Yacht Club, on Admiralty Way near the Marina del Rey Library, has private parking lots so its many celebrity members can discreetly come and go. And the trend lately is to take out the smaller boat slips available to the public and replace them with fewer larger slips. There is more money in it. But it is a beautiful place, and messing around on the water, or just sitting and looking at someone else doing it, is still one of our favorite things to do.

★ **TIP**

Actor Ted Danson is very involved in a non-profit organization called **Heal the Bay**. To learn the present quality of the bay's water, and the areas where it is inadvisable to go swimming or surfing, check their Web site: www.healthebay.org.

Getting Here

From LAX

By Car

The corner of Lincoln and Washington boulevards is the busiest intersection in Greater Los Angeles.

Take Sepulveda Boulevard north to Lincoln Boulevard (Highway 1), where you turn left; go through Westchester and over the Balloña Creek bridge to Fiji Way. The distance is 4.3 miles. Marina del Rey stretches from Fiji to Washington Boulevard, less than a mile. The marina and the beach are to your left, west of Lincoln Boulevard.

By Bus

Take the free airport shuttle to Lot C, then the Big Blue Bus #3; fare 50¢; seniors and disabled, 25¢.

By Shuttle

Approximate fare to the area is $13 for one person, $8-$10 for each additional passenger. Shuttle operators include **Prime Time Shuttle**, ☎ 800-733-8267, www.primetimeshuttle.com; and **Super Shuttle**, ☎ 310-782-6600 or 323-775-6600, www.supershuttle.com.

By Taxi

Call **My Taxi**, ☎ 800-4 MY-TAXI (469-8294); or **Celebrity Executive Car Service**, ☎ 310-398-8779. Approximate fare is $14, plus $2.50 airport fee.

From Downtown Los Angeles

By Car

Take the Santa Monica Freeway (10) west, to the San Diego Freeway (405); go south to the Marina Freeway (90) exit. Continue on 90 to Lincoln Boulevard.

By Bus

Santa Monica's Big Blue Bus #10 starts at Union Station and can be picked up at 3rd, 4th, or 5th streets on Flower, and 6th and 7th streets on Grand. It goes to 4th Street and Santa Monica Boulevard in Santa Monica. You can transfer to #3, which goes down Lincoln Boulevard to Fiji Way in Marina del Rey. Fare is $1.25; call ☎ 310-451-5444 for schedule.

> ☞ *DID YOU KNOW?*
>
> The Marina Freeway was originally named the Richard Milhouse Nixon Freeway. It was supposed to slash through the middle of Marina del Rey to Pacific Avenue in Venice. An uproar from the residents stopped that, which is why is it now so short, and after Watergate the name was changed.

Getting Around

Marina del Rey is a rectangle with the beach running down its west (ocean) side; the main channel into the marina is at the south end of town along Fiji Way. The marina is between the beach and Lincoln Boulevard, the big thoroughfare; there are shopping centers and a few blocks of apartments and condos to the east of Lincoln. The streets that encircle the marina, Admiralty Way and Via Marina, are connected to the piers by streets named after South

Pacific islands. Between these are the boat basins designated by letter: Basins A through H. At the north end of the town is Washington Boulevard, which forms the boundary with Venice and runs out to the Venice Pier. Half the town is taken up by the water of the marina.

On Location

This is a popular place to film; there is lots of color and activity with boats rocking at their slips and moving around on the water. Scenes from the remake of Disney's *The Parent Trap* were shot here, and there has been a flurry of movies filming here in the last year or so; among them are *National Security* with Martin Lawrence; *Enough*, with Jennifer Lopez; Disney's *Big Trouble*, with Tim Allen, which was partially shot at the corner of Fiji and Admiralty Way; and *Simone*, starring Al Pacino, shot in part at Burton Chace Park on Mindanao Way and at various boat slips.

The most popular place to film in Marina del Rey is at the pier and boat slips of the Ritz-Carlton Hotel.

Television shows with episodes filmed in Marina del Rey include *Dallas* and *Knots Landing*. Later came *Baywatch*, which was shot at various times at Burton Chace Park, on the bike path and on different boat slips. Fisherman's Village, with its Cape Cod-style buildings, looks great on film and can fill in for fishing villages. The *Mission: Impossible* TV series filmed here several times, as did *The Mod Squad, The F.B.I.* and *Trapper John, MD.*

Best Places to Stay

This is a nice area, especially if you plan to spend some time enjoying the marina and the beaches, or if you just like to stay in a place with a view. It is not too far from Hollywood and Beverly Hills if you have a car; however, it can be a less-than-handy location if you are going to depend on public transportation.

The accommodations price scale can be found on page 39.

There are only a handful of hotels in Marina del Rey. Four are either right next to boat slips or the beach; two (Marina Beach Marriott and Marina International) are across the street but have views of the marina; and one (the Courtyard by Marriott) is a couple of blocks away, with no view. We've also included some hotels near Los Angeles International Airport, in case you are arriving late in the evening or have an early flight out.

If seeing celebrities is your number-one priority, this is not an area where you will find yourself stumbling over them, unless someone is filming right under your nose. But you are close to Venice, where a lot more movie-making goes on.

COURTYARD BY MARRIOTT

13480 Maxella Avenue
Marina del Rey, CA 90292
☎ 310-822-8555, 800-321-2211
www.courtyard.com/laxcm
Moderate

This hotel does not overlook the water; it is in a large shopping complex with several restaurants and two movie multiplexes within a few minutes' walking distance. The Courtyard is a medium-size hotel with 276 rooms, including handicapped-accessible and smoking rooms; amenities include an outdoor swimming pool and a Jacuzzi, fitness room and bike rental (the bike path is very near). A breakfast buffet is offered, and the **Courtyard Café**, which has prices in the Moderate-Expensive range, is popular with local people, especially on holidays. There is free self-parking, and complimentary coffee in the lobby.

Aunt Kizzy's Back Porch restaurant, with Southern down-home style cooking, is a two-minute walk from the Marriott Courtyard.

MARINA BEACH MARRIOTT

4100 Admiralty Way
Marina del Rey, CA 90292
☎ 310-301-3000, 800-228-9290, fax 310-448-4870
www.marriott.com/marriott/laxmb
Moderate-Expensive

This Marriott is a big hotel, located a few steps from the marina, a few turns of the wheel from the bike path, a couple of blocks from Venice Pier. It has an impressive lobby, with acres of marble and massive pillars; there is an outdoor swimming pool, concierge and valet service, **Stone's Restaurant** for breakfast, lunch and dinner, and a lobby bar.

The Marina Beach Marriott is right across the street from Mother's Beach.

TIP

Fisherman's Village, once a thriving shopping place in Marina del Rey, has lately lost its luster, and many of its shops have closed. Only a few shops and eating places are open now. There are rumors it will be revived, but who knows when?

MARINA DEL REY HOTEL
13534 Bali Way
Marina del Rey, CA 90292
☎ 310-301-8167, 800-882-4000
www.marinadelreyhotel.com
Moderate

The Marina del Rey is one of only two hotels here that are right on the water (the upscale Ritz-Carlton is the other). The best rooms have a full view of the water and a balcony or patio; others are sans balcony; some have only a partial view. There is an outdoor pool and a putting green, a small dining room and a small cocktail lounge, and complimentary limousine service to and from LAX.

MARINA INTERNATIONAL HOTEL & BUNGALOWS
4200 Admiralty Way
Marina del Rey, CA 90292
☎ 310-301-2000, fax 310-301-6687
Inexpensive-Moderate

This is a medium-size hotel, across the street from the marina. Most rooms have private patios and balconies, and there are 25 bungalows. Amenities include dining room and lounge, swimming pool and Jacuzzi, complimentary parking and complimentary shuttle service to and from the airport.

But when we were there in 2001, we found things pretty run-down. There was no bellman on duty; the room was a nice size, but the bath had a loose shower head and the shower stall did not drain; room air conditioning could not be controlled; and the dining room was closed at lunch. Needs work.

☞ DID YOU KNOW?

The TV series *Baywatch* got its inspiration from the **County Lifeguard Baywatch Patrol**, which is based in Marina del Rey. When not on patrol, the real Baywatch boats can be seen docked near Fisherman's Village.

★★ THE RITZ-CARLTON

4375 Admiralty Way
Marina del Rey, CA 90292
☎ 310-823-1700, 800-241-3333, fax 310-305-0019
www.ritzcarlton.com
Expensive-Deluxe

As you might expect from the name, this is the top place to stay in Marina del Rey. The hotel stands on the bank of one of the basins; all of the rooms have balconies with views of the marina, with its hundreds of boats tied up directly below. The hotel has several dining rooms and lounges, including the **Lobby Lounge**, where tea is served in the afternoon. The concierge staff is multilingual and there is 24-hour room service and valet service. It is that kind of hotel.

It is a place where celebrities hole up, and more films, TV episodes and commercials are shot here than anywhere else in Marina del Rey. Some filmed in the last few years were *Melrose Place*, *Party of Five*, *The Game*, *The Parent Trap*, *Old Friends*, *Dance With Me*, *Chicago Hope*, *Seventh Heaven*, *Providence, Time of Your Life*, *JAG* and *Curb Your Enthusiasm*.

BALANCING YOUR PRIORITIES

Is staying at a very good hotel more important to you than waking up to see a movie being shot on your doorstep? Marina del Rey has good hotels, but less location shooting. Venice is deficient when it comes to hotels, but is used as a location for more films than any of the other towns along the coast.

Near LAX

The big hotels (and they are all large here) start practically at the entrance to the airport and stretch back down the north side of Century Boulevard for a dozen blocks. The biggest advantage to staying near the airport is that you will be in your room and unpacked shortly after landing. Each hotel has its own shuttle bus to pick you up at the terminal. Ask, when making your reservation, if you need to call from inside the terminal for transportation. Some hotels, such as the Westin, have vans running continuously; for others you need to call for pickup. Don't worry about the noise from planes, as all the hotels have double-glazed windows for soundproofing. The disadvantage is that public transportation is not that good; if you don't have a rental car you may spend long periods of time waiting, only to find that no bus goes where you want to go.

Just Outside the Terminals

COURTYARD BY MARRIOTT LAX
6161 West Century Boulevard
Los Angeles, CA 90045
☎ 310-649-1400, 800-321-2211, fax 310-649-0964
Inexpensive-Moderate

Smaller than most of the other airport hotels, the Courtyard by Marriott has more than 180 rooms, each with a separate sitting area. There is an outdoor spa, a café and lounge, complimentary parking and 24-hour free shuttle to and from LAX. The hotel is only two blocks from the airport. Head north on Sepulveda Boulevard, turn right on 98th Street, then right again on Vicksburg; the hotel is on the left.

FOUR POINTS SHERATON
9750 Airport Boulevard
Los Angeles, CA 90045
☎ 310-645-4600, 800-LAX-HOTEL, fax 310-649-7047
www.fourpointslax.com
Inexpensive

Only a quarter-mile from the airport with complimentary shuttle service every half-hour. The staff is multilingual, and there is 24-hour room service, an outdoor, Olympic-size pool, and a 24-hour fitness center. The **Palm Grill** serves breakfast from 6am, a lunch buffet, and dinner 5-10:30pm. **T.H. Brewster's Lounge** has California wines, Pacific Coast microbrews and Belgian ales. There are beer tastings and beer dinners for those who cannot get enough beer. To reach Airport Boulevard, go east on Century Boulevard out of LAX and continue for a few blocks; turn left on Airport Boulevard to the hotel.

★ TIP

When a brochure from a hotel near LAX says "less than 15 minutes from the Los Angeles Convention Center," they must be counting as the crow flies. However, you will not be flying with the crow, but traveling via the freeways, so give yourself between a half-hour and 45 minutes, depending on the time of day.

HILTON LOS ANGELES AIRPORT
5711 West Century Boulevard
Los Angeles, CA 90045
☎ 310-410-4000, 800-HILTONS, fax 310-410-6250
www.losangelesairport.hilton.com
Inexpensive-Moderate

The largest hotel by the airport, the Hilton has more than 1,200 rooms. Some of the nicest, we think, are lanai rooms that open onto a garden terrace or poolside deck. There is an outdoor swimming pool and several whirlpool spas, and the largest fitness center in the city, open 24 hours, with

Every large hotel in the city seems to now have a multimedia sports bar. The Hilton's is Landings.

aerobics classes and racquetball courts. **The Café** is a good choice for families, with breakfast, lunch and dinner buffets and a Sunday buffet brunch. The more romantic **Andiamo** serves northern Italian cuisine, while **The Bistro** has deli fare. There is also 24-hour room service.

LOS ANGELES AIRPORT MARRIOTT
5855 West Century Boulevard
Los Angeles, CA 90045
☎ 310-641-5700, 800-228-9290, fax 310-337-5358
www.marriott.com
Moderate

The Airport Marriott is a huge hotel with over 1,000 rooms, including three concierge floors. There is an outdoor swimming pool, whirlpool and sauna and a health club, as well as several places to eat, including **Allie's American Grille** for family dining, **JW's Steakhouse** for more casual fare, and **Champions**, a sports bar with light food and pizza. There is also complimentary coffee in the lobby, and room service from 6am-2am. The hotel provides complimentary transportation to LAX every 10 minutes, 24 hours a day, and there's a Hertz car rental desk in the lobby.

RENAISSANCE LOS ANGELES HOTEL – AIRPORT
9620 Airport Boulevard
Los Angeles, CA 90045
☎ 310-337-2800, 800-HOTELS 1, fax 310-216-6681
Moderate

A large hotel, with over 500 rooms, it's a half-mile from the airport. There is a fitness center, outdoor swimming pool, sauna and Jacuzzi; for those who prefer to exercise in private, a stationary bicycle can be delivered to the guest's room. The **Library Steakhouse** is an intimate room with an art collection, marble fireplace and candlelit tables; The **Conservatory** is a more casual brasserie; the **Lobby Lounge** has piano entertainment in the evenings. The hotel provides a complimentary shuttle to airport.

SHERATON GATEWAY HOTEL
6101 West Century Boulevard
Los Angeles, CA 90045
☎ 310-642-1111, 800-325-3535, fax 310-410-1267
Moderate

A big hotel, with over 700 rooms and suites, very near the airport. The Club Level serves a continental breakfast and evening hors d'oeuvres in the **Club Lounge**. Amenities include an outdoor swimming pool and spa; the **Brasserie** for breakfast and lunch (6am-5pm); and **Landry's** for dinner (5-11pm), which also features the **Daimon Sushi Bar**; and 24-hour room service.

THE WESTIN LOS ANGELES AIRPORT
5400 West Century Boulevard
Los Angeles, CA 90045
☎ 310-216-5858, 800-WESTIN, fax 310-670-1948
www.westin.com
Moderate-Expensive

The Westin, located four blocks from the airport, has over 700 rooms and suites. Their amenities include an outdoor pool, whirlpool and sundeck, fitness center and sauna, concierge, airline and rental car desks, gift shop, and a big, colonnaded lobby with groupings of deep, comfortable chairs and couches in case you intend to spend much time sitting around the lobby. Same-day laundry service is available, but there is also an unusual amenity for a hotel: a self-service laundry for guests' use. The hotel has valet and self-parking and frequent, 24-hour transportation to the airport. The Westin's **Charisma Café** is open 6am-11pm, and there is 24-hour room service. Wednesday night is Jazz Night in the **Lobby Lounge**, from 5 to 9pm. It's a major gathering spot for local Angelenos. Better still, there's no cover, no minimum, and validated parking.

North of the Airport

FURAMA HOTEL
8601 Lincoln Boulevard
Los Angeles, CA 90045
☎ 310-670-8111, 800-225-8126, fax 310-337-1883
www.furama-hotels.com
Inexpensive

The Furama is not in the cluster of hotels near the airport entrance; it's about halfway to Marina del Rey and the beach towns. That still puts it only five minutes away from the airport. It is a deceptive-looking building; you would never guess there are 773 rooms and suites, including poolside rooms with patios. There is nightly entertainment and dancing, complimentary scheduled shuttle service to Marina del Rey, Venice and Santa Monica, and complimentary airport transportation 24 hours a day. To get here from LAX, go north on Sepulveda Boulevard, and turn left on Lincoln Boulevard at the corner of the airport; the hotel is about a mile ahead, on your left.

Best Places to Eat

It used to be a pretty apt observation that the quality of the food declined as the quality of the view increased; restaurants right on the marina didn't have to worry because customers were going to come in anyway. These days, dining seems to have improved in many places here.

In Marina del Rey

ALEJO'S
4002 Lincoln Boulevard
☎ 310-822-0095
Italian
Inexpensive

The dining price scale can be found on page 42.

No celebrities come in here that we know of, but we include it because it is our favorite neighborhood place and a great bargain. Alejo's is on the southeast corner of Lincoln and Washington, in a six-store strip mall. There are only a dozen tables crowded together and it is always full at night, often with a line outside. Alejo's is also open for lunch on weekdays.

Sit down and enjoy chunks of bread dipped in garlic oil while you scan the menu. The bread here is baked daily, and we stop by at least once a week to buy a loaf or two to take home. The family is Italian from Argentina, but the food is basically home-cooked southern Italian. It's good and there's plenty of it.

Prices are incredibly low, even lower than usual because you bring your own bottle of wine; you might want to stop at a liquor store en route. Parking in the mini-mall is limited to 20 minutes; park on Del Rey Avenue, the little street right behind the restaurant, parallel to Lincoln Boulevard. Open Monday-Friday, 11am-10pm; Saturday-Sunday, 4-10pm.

★★ AUNT KIZZY'S BACK PORCH
4325 Glencoe Avenue
☎ 310-578-1005, fax 310-306-1715
Southern American
Inexpensive

Not many inexpensive restaurants attract celebrities in large numbers; Aunt Kizzy's is the exception. This down-home place is a favorite of the elite. Willie Nelson comes here, and so do Stevie Wonder and Eddie Murphy, Rosanne Barr, Johnny Cochrane and Jesse Jackson. The menu features items like pork chops cooked slowly in a rich brown gravy, with collard greens and black-eyed peas.

Aunt Kizzy was the name of Leslie Uggams' character in Roots.

Items such as Aunt Johnnie's fried chicken, Miss Flossie's chicken and dumplings, Uncle Wad's ribs or Sister Zethel's meat loaf are all named for relatives. No attitude here, just really comfortable food.

It is an attractive, homey place. No alcohol is served, but you can bring your own bottle of wine. Lemonade, iced tea or wine are all served in mason jars, just as they were in owner Adolf Dulan's childhood in Oklahoma. Cornbread arrives as soon as you sit down. The next thing that happens is the cornbread is all gone and you ask for more.

Adolf, the tall, distinguished gentleman who owns the place, told us about the name. In the south there are a lot of shotgun cabins with a porch in front and in back. If you sit on the front porch you dress up a bit for the neighbors. But the back porch is the real comfortable, casual place to lounge.

Park free for Aunt Kizzy's in front or by the rear entrance.

When looking for Aunt Kizzy's, the street address does not mean much of anything because it is in the middle of a big, low-rise shopping area. There are four shopping areas within a few blocks, but you want the one with the Von's market (see page 39). Coming south from Washington Boulevard on Lincoln the first traffic light is Maxella Avenue. Turn left on Maxella and right on Glencoe. Von's is in the middle of the block, Aunt Kizzy's is next to it in the corner of the little strip mall.

There are no appetizers or soups, just entrées that come with vegetables; the most expensive entrée is $12.95. All desserts, like peach cobbler, are $2.95. It is really hard to spend much money here. Lunch is served Monday-Saturday, 11am-4pm; Sunday brunch buffet, 11am-3pm; dinner Sunday-Thursday, 4 to 10pm; Friday and Saturday, 4 to 11pm.

CAFE DEL REY
4451 Admiralty Way
☎ 310-823-6395
www.cafedelrey.com
California-French-Asian
Expensive

Café Del Rey has a sensible rule for stress-free dining: no use of cell phones in dining room.

The French-trained Japanese chef puts out a wide range of tastes. Courses start with Cuban black bean soup and go on to smoked salmon sushi roll and Hawaiian ahi tuna tartare. There is everything from pasta to Peking duck to osso buco Milanese on this fusion menu. The restaurant is on the water, overlooking the boats and the marina. Open for lunch, 11:30am-2:30pm; (they serve a light menu from 2:30-5:30); dinner is served on weekdays, 5:30 until 9:30; a bit later on Saturday nights; they close earlier on Sunday nights. An à la carte brunch is served on Sunday beginning at 10:30. Parking is available in a lot.

RÖCK
13455 Maxella Avenue
☎ 310-822-8979
California Casual
Inexpensive-Moderate

In case you wonder about the unusual name, this is a spin-off from a restaurant in Santa Monica named Röcken-wagner. It is a casual place with a simple menu, but it is well regarded. Try the spicy tortilla soup or the chilled Spanish gazpacho soup to start; main courses include pasta, fish and steaks. Röck is open for lunch, Monday-Friday, 11:30am-2:30pm; for dinner nightly, 5:30-10pm; Friday and Saturday until 10:30. It is located off Lincoln Boulevard on the corner of Del Rey, on your left.

TONY P'S DOCKSIDE GRILL
4445 Admiralty Way
☎ 310-823-4534
American
Moderate

This unassuming, casual place right on the water was the location for scenes from the movie *Martial Law*, and before that *Clueless*, and several of the *Blind Date* shows. *V.I.P.* shot its dock scenes here. You can see why it is popular with directors as soon as you walk in – its location at the head of the main channel is perfect. Seat a couple of actors at one of the outside deck tables and the shot will pick up all the activity in the marina going on in the background.

Food ranges from sandwiches to steaks, and be warned: the dinners all start with a few loaves of homemade bread hot from the oven, and then the portions are huge. There is an extended four-hour happy hour, Monday-Friday, from 3 to 7pm, with appetizers and cheap drinks.

The long, narrow dining room has big windows that overlook the marina. The outside deck is really nice when the weather is good. And, if you are a sports fan, the adjoining Tavern has 20 TV sets going, all at the same time. (For nightlife at Tony P's, see page 389.)

Near LAX

Most dining around the airport is found in the hotels. But there are a few interesting stand-alone places.

ENCOUNTER RESTAURANT & BAR
209 World Way, LAX
☎ 310-215-5151
California
Moderate

This is the airport's theme restaurant, located in the middle of the U of terminals. It's up in the air on stilts, and looks like a flying saucer. Surprisingly, most guests are not waiting for planes but are locals or staying at nearby hotels. You can get sandwiches or a full menu at lunchtime. Dinner entrées emphasize seafood, but there is also poultry, pasta and meat. Big windows offer a view of planes arriving in an endless stream.

A few years ago Walt Disney Imagineering, the folks who do Disney World and such, redesigned the interior as a 1960s vision of the future, starting with the space-age elevator. Walls are curved; amoeba-shaped lighting structures are embedded in the ceiling; and lava lights help the ambiance, along with bar guns that emit laser lights and futuristic sound effects when bartenders pour a drink.

There is a sign at Terminal Two indicating where to turn left for the restaurant. Use the multi-level parking structure in the daytime; valet parking is available at night. Open daily, 11am-9pm.

★ TIP

If you have a long wait for a plane and would like to enjoy a leisurely meal or drink with a view of the airport, take the free shuttle that makes the rounds of all the terminals; get off at Terminal 6 and cross the street to Encounter Restaurant & Bar.

PROUD BIRD
11022 Aviation Boulevard
☎ 310-670-3093
American
Moderate

This well-known place serves lunch and dinner, but is best known for its big Sunday brunch, which encompasses three rooms with omelets and waffles to order, ham and roast beef carved for you, along with a dozen-and-a-half other hot entrées, a large spread of seafood, salads and desserts. Brunch is served 9am-3pm, for $18.95; kids $10.95. Lunch and dinner are served Monday-Thursday, 11am-10pm; Friday and Saturday, 11am-11pm; Sunday to 10pm. Take Century Boulevard east from LAX, almost to the San Diego Freeway, then turn right on Aviation Boulevard and head south a few short blocks to the corner of 111th Street. Self-parking is available on a lot.

★ BUGGY WHIP
7420 La Tijera Boulevard
Westchester
☎ 310-645-7131
Moderate-Expensive

We love this kind of place – dark wood paneling, red leather booths, a piano tinkling in the background, and a fine, really cold martini to start with. The warm and relaxing ambiance here provided a backdrop for a scene in the film *Blow*, starring Johnny Depp.

The Buggy Whip is just a block off the San Diego Freeway (I-405) on the way to LAX, so a lot of people stop off here en route. It is not just handy, though; the food is very good, especially if you are tired of nouveau-this-and-that and are hungering for steak, fish, seafood, or maybe ribs. If you are a lobster fan, they feature a 2½-lb. lobster tail at $49.95; the fresh 1¼-lb. Maine lobster, whole and sweeter, is $19.95. Steaks are big, up to 22 ounces. Many people come here just for the stone crab claws.

Be warned about ordering, as the portions are very large. We stopped in the other night, sat at the corner booth in the lounge (preferable to the dining room), and chatted with owner Paul Darricarrere, who knows lots of people in the movie business, while we looked at the menu. We couldn't make up our minds so we ordered appetizers – the calamari strips sautéed in scampi batter and smoked Scottish salmon. We never got any further; that became our meal.

Shop Till You Drop

No one comes to Marina del Rey for shopping, though it is grossly oversupplied with shopping malls for such a small area. There are three within a few blocks. Waterside Shopping Center is bordered by Fiji and Mindanao, Lincoln Boulevard and Admiralty Way; two quasi-malls with similar names are off Lincoln Boulevard on Maxella Avenue, right across from each other. They are known locally as "the one with the Von's (market)," and "the one with the Gelson's (market)."

Sunup to Sundown

Beaches

There are two beaches in Marina del Rey, a big one on the Pacific Ocean and a small one in the marina.

Venice City Beach

Metered street parking near the beach is $1 an hour. If you plan to stay some time, bring plenty of quarters.

The Marina del Rey section of this beach begins at Washington Boulevard and runs south to Via Marina and the jetty, where the main channel of the marina enters the ocean. It is wide, clean and seldom-used; on weekdays you can often go blocks without seeing a single person on the sand or in the water.

The reason for this is a simple lack of access. The only parking is at hard-to-find metered street spots and in one public lot at the end of Washington by the Venice Pier. It is difficult to reach the sand any other way; the bike path turns away from the beach at Washington and, although the coast is lined with houses, apartments and condos for its entire 26-block length in Marina del Rey, there is no sidewalk.

The Beach Communities

TIP

Cross-streets are easy to find along Pacific Avenue: beginning a block south of Washington, the streets are named alphabetically and nautically: Anchorage, Buccaneer, Catamaran and so forth to Westwind and Yawl.

Great numbers of the hoi polloi crowd the boardwalk in Venice, tramping along noisily in front of the houses and apartments at the edge of the sand. The bike path, 20 feet farther out, further clutters up the sight lines of those who live there. The people south of Washington Boulevard didn't want everyone who comes out to get a breath of the ocean walking and talking in front of *their* places of abode. Every time it is proposed that either the bike path or the boardwalk be continued down the beach to the channel, the residents have blocked it, and they are successful largely because they have a potent ally.

A BIRD'S-EYE VIEW OF THE BEACH

The most politically powerful residents of Marina del Rey's beach are not the Yuppies, Buppies and Dinks who live here year-round. Rather, it is a group of several hundred seasonal residents who fly up from Central and South America each year starting in mid-April, and stay only until August. They are the endangered **California least terns**.

The small, glossy-black, gray and white birds, called "least" because they are the smallest of the tern species worldwide, each year head for the beach north of the Marina del Rey harbor inlet. They have one goal: finding a mate. After a lively aerial courting ritual, the birds couple up and the female lays up to three eggs in a simple nest in the sand.

Once the eggs are laid, the California Fish and Game Service puts up a "chick fence" around the nesting area, not only to keep humans out but to prevent the hatchlings from wandering away from the protected area.

The folks who live along here are protective of and grateful to the terns, and often join the volunteers who help guard the tiny birds from crows who try to steal the eggs. Whenever there is a proposal to extend the walkway down this beach, locals always point out that would increase human activity here and further endanger this already endangered species.

The terns have been coming back to this same spot, probably for thousands of years, because of its proximity to Balloña Lagoon Marine Preserve channel (just south of the marina's main channel), where they snatch anchovies, sardines and other small creatures from the shallow waters to feed their chicks. Unfortunately, LA's government is in the process of allowing a huge commercial development to be built that will destroy most of those ancient wetlands.

If you are in this area between mid-April and August and would like to volunteer to help guard the least terns for a period of time, phone Doug Korthof at ☎ 562-430-2495. You'll find more information about the project at www.lawetlands.org/leastern.

☞ DID YOU KNOW?

Another enemy of the least tern is the **peregrine falcon**. We have seen a pair of falcons on top of the tallest building in Marina del Rey, at Admiralty and Mindanao ways, only a few minutes' flight from the least terns' beach. Ironically, the falcon was endangered itself and was reintroduced into the LA area in a successful effort to increase its numbers. It was removed from the endangered list only a few years ago.

Mother's Beach

Also called Marina Beach, it is at the inland end of Basin D, with access from Admiralty Way and Via Marina. The sand curves around the basin, with no boat slips and no moving boats permitted at the end so there is an expanse of calm, safe water. It is a place mothers like to bring children, hence the name. There is parking and public restrooms, and a place to get snacks. Sounds perfect, right? Not so fast...

Unfortunately, this swimming area is inside a 6,000-boat marina, so tidal action is limited, and the water is full of gas, engine oil, paint and other pollutants. Even though Heal the Bay's latest test gave it a good dry-weather score, other tests over many years have repeatedly shown problems.

It is an easy place to get to, and has no rough surf to frighten small children. But you might want to make sure no one swallows any water. Young children and the elderly are most susceptible to waterborne bacteria and viruses, and it can take only one exposure to get sick. Symptoms can show up a day or two after exposure, usually in the form of respiratory or gastrointestinal infections.

⚠ WARNING!

Many people like to collect mussels from the rocks in the beach communities. At certain times of the year, toxins found in mussels along this coast can cause paralytic shellfish poisoning, which affects the central nervous system. There is no antidote, and cooking the shellfish will not destroy the toxin. Sport harvesting of mussels is quarantined from May 1 to October 31 along the entire coast of California. Clams are quarantined at some times in some areas. Call the Biotoxin Information Hotline, ☎ 800-553-4133, to hear a recorded update.

Bike Trails

Bike riding is popular in Marina del Rey because every-thing is flat, there are interesting views everywhere and, except for one long stretch of Washington Boulevard and a short stretch of Fiji Way, riders are not sharing space with cars. Bike rentals cost from $4 to $7.50 an hour, $10-$20 per day; skates are about $5 an hour, $12 per day. Here are a few places that provide rentals:

Bike & Skate Rentals, 4175 Admiralty Way (across from Marina Beach Marriott Hotel), ☎ 310-306-3332.

Marina del Rey Hotel Gift Shop (bike rentals), 13534 Bali Way, ☎ 310-301-8167 or 800-882-4000.

Venice Pier Bike Shop (bike rentals), 27 Washington Boulevard, ☎ 310-301-4011.

South of Fisherman's Village

There is a water stop by some palms, 2.1 miles from the starting place. Another one is farther along at 4.1 miles from the start.

This ride takes you from Marina del Rey south to Man-hattan Beach; it is 7.3 miles one-way.

Start at Fisherman's Village, or anywhere along the bike path in the marina. Follow Fiji Way south for .2 mile to its end, then proceed another .1 mile to the fence along Bal-loña Creek. Pass through the fence – to the left is the Balloña Creek Bikeway, and the Balloña Wetlands are across the creek; turn right along the levee beside the creek. Pass the UCLA crew boathouse. Ride along the levee to a small bridge; cross and continue west down the other side to where the path swings south down the strand. The trail goes by Del Rey Lagoon and Del Rey La-goon Park, then on down to the beach. From here on it is all beach and ocean. Continue south .7 mile, pass a play-ground area with sculpture; .5 mile farther on you will be passing under the busy LAX flight path.

☞ DID YOU KNOW?

About 50 of the 6,000 boats in the marina are live-aboards. Most are power- or sailboats, but you will see an occasional well-appointed houseboat. Strict regulations make sure they are seaworthy, and have a working engine capable of propelling them, although most never leave the dock.

Another .2 mile farther on, you'll see bluffs to your left; this is a historic spot where the sport of hang-gliding was largely developed. Stopped for safety reasons, according to local government, they are now being used again for this sport.

The beach here is El Segundo. South of the power station it is El Porto Beach. You will see "Volleyball City" around the foot of Rosecrans Avenue. You are now 6.1 miles from the starting point; the Manhattan Beach Pier is straight ahead.

North of Fisherman's Village

From Marina del Rey to Venice Pier it is 2.7 miles one way. Beginning at Fisherman's Village, the route goes north alongside Fiji Way, then crosses Fiji into the boat storage and repair area. As you cross Mindanao Way, a short side path leads to Burton Chace Park. Cross Bali Way next (these are dead-end streets, not heavily trafficked). You'll pass boat yards and parking lots while skirting the basins off the main channel. Go by the fine little Marina del Rey County Library at Bali and Admiralty. Cross busy Admiralty Way into Admiralty Park, a long, narrow green strip alongside the street, where there is a fitness trail.

The light-house in Fisherman's Village is not used for navigation.

☞ **DID YOU KNOW?**

Marina del Rey Public Library, 4533 Admiralty Way, ☎ 310-821-3415, has the one of the largest and best collections of boating- and sea-related books in Southern California.

The water level of the flood control basin, which some call "The Duck Pond," varies each time you see it because it is tidal. It is the last remnant of the original Balloña Wetlands in this area.

When you reach the fenced-in Oxford Flood Control Basin, the bike path leaves the park to follow its eastern edge. On the other side of the basin is Washington Boulevard. Cross the boulevard, turn left and head toward the ocean along Washington. After several long blocks you'll pass over the Venice Grand Canal, and there, at the foot of Washington, is the Venice Pier. Turn right here to follow the bike path up the beach. Windward Avenue and the heart of the Venice boardwalk are a bit more than 0.5 mile farther north, if you wish to push on.

Boat Charters

Taking a boat down the main channel and out through the breakwater into the Pacific is a great way to spend a day, or even just a few hours of an afternoon. Simply renting a kayak, electric boat or canoe to tour the marina and the various basins at leisure can be a lot of fun. When we kept our sailboat docked at the marina, we would go over in the late afternoon with some appetizers and a bottle of wine and just poke around, looking at all the boats – from little 14-footers up to 100 feet of palatial yacht.

MARINA BOAT RENTALS
13719 Fiji Way
Fisherman's Village
☎ 310-574-2822
www.boats4rent.com

Tom York has a wide variety of watercraft for rent: powerboats, sailboats, kayaks, electric boats and one canoe. These are not big yachts; the powerboats range up to 19 feet, the sailboats to 30 feet. (You must demonstrate the ability to handle sailboats 22 feet and above.) The boats are docked in the main channel right in front of Fisherman's Village. From Memorial Day to Labor Day, hours are 9am-8pm daily; reserving ahead is advised in season. The rest of the year he's open 10am-6pm.

BOATING TIPS

If you take a sailboat or powerboat out, here are a few suggestions from the Coast Guard.

◆ File a **float plan**. Tell someone on shore where you are going and when you plan to leave and return.

◆ Wear a **life jacket**. See there is one on board for each person.

◆ Check your boat and equipment. make sure **fire extinguishers**, **running lights**, and **radio** (if you have one) are working before you cast off.

◆ Bring a **compass** and **signaling device** such as a whistle, horn or mirror.

◆ **Avoid alcohol**. If anything happens you want your wits about you. Do not drink outside the breakwater; wait until you return.

◆ Monitor **weather conditions**. Check the forecast, keep an eye out for changes.

For more safety tips, go to the US Coast Guard's Web site at www.uscgboating.org.

N BEWARE!

Renting a sailboat here is great sport. You should know, though, that the entrance/exit from the main channel at the south end of the breakwater is usually silted up, unless the government has recently been cajoled into paying to have it cleared out once again. Ask at the dock before you sail away.

Harbor Tours

JUST FUN STUFF TOURS
Fisherman's Village
13755 Fiji Way
☎ 310-577-6660
www.justfunstuff.net

This company offers a 40-minute boat ride around the harbor. In summer, tours leave the dock every hour from noon to 5pm, daily; in winter, tours are Saturday and Sunday, 12 to 4pm only. Adults, $10; seniors (65+), $8; kids two to 12, $6; infants, $2. Get tickets 15 minutes ahead of time. There is also a sunset champagne cruise in summer, which is even more fun if you like the bubbly; Friday and Saturday, 7 to 8:30pm, $25; reservations required.

Picnics

Chace Park, at the end of Mindanao Way, off Admiralty Way between Basins G and H, is a pleasant place to enjoy a picnic. Get a table with a view and you'll see boats of every type in their slips and going by in the main channel.

Where to get Picnic Food

CHACE PARK FOOD CONCESSION
☎ 213-739-9913

The standard park fare includes hamburgers, hot dogs, turkey-burgers, veggie-burgers, ice cream sodas... you get the idea. The stand is open seven days in summer; weekends only in winter.

MR. PICKLES DELI
13354 Washington Boulevard
☎ 310-822-7777

There are tables at Mr. Pickles as well as take-out.

This deli and kosher market is about three blocks east of Lincoln, in a little corner strip mall; it is officially in Culver City – this is Culver City's shoestring strip that is two miles long and only 200 feet wide, with this part embedded deep into Marina del Rey.

The moment we step inside we always have the feeling that this is the cleanest place we have ever been. Everything glistens – the walls, the floors, the refrigerator cases. And the food is wonderfully fresh. Soups, knishes, lots of good, freshly made salads, corned beef, pastrami, brisket sandwiches, and of course pickles, lox, whitefish and herring, along with cookies and pastries.

Yosef Beit-Halahmi, the owner who looks a lot like Zero Mostel with a beard, is French by way of Tunisia, which explains the tasty Tunisian salads that are sometimes on hand. No beer or wine. Mr. Pickles is open Tuesday-Thursday and Sunday, 11am-9pm; Monday, 11am-6pm; Friday, 8:30am-4pm; closed Saturday. Parking is in front in the little mall.

After Dark

The first time we stayed in Marina del Rey we came out to spend a weekend at the Marina del Rey Hotel, which is at the end of Bali Way, right on the main channel. We looked down from our balcony and saw lights glowing from the windows of half the boats docked in the slips below us and thought, "There are people living in all those boats. What a romantic life that must be!"

Much later we discovered that most small boats tied at a dock where they can plug into shore electricity leave a light burning for heat, not light. It is to fight the mold that develops from constant moisture in the air.

In fact, it turns out, the vast majority of boats docked at the marina never go anywhere. Either people don't have time to take them out, or they just use them for occasional entertaining.

The Marina is not a hot destination after dark. Most of those who are out and about are seated in restaurants, eating and drinking. There are a few exceptions.

Concerts

FISHERMAN'S VILLAGE
Lighthouse Plaza
13755 Fiji Way
☎ 310-823-5411 (recorded information)

Free concerts featuring local bands with a wide variety of styles and content: pop rock, rock, jazz, smooth jazz, Latin, Latin reggae, R&B and funk are held year-round, Saturday and Sunday, 2 to 5pm.

Music & Dancing

BRENNAN'S
4089 Lincoln Boulevard
☎ 310-821-6622

Brennan's is a nicely raucous joint. They have live music Wednesday-Saturday, but their big claim to fame are the turtle races every Thursday at 9pm. The patrons shout and cheer and have a great time, but we have never heard the turtles say they are enjoying it. No cover.

BURTON CHACE PARK
13650 Mindanao Way
☎ 310-305-9545

From July to August, free twilight summer concerts (7-9pm) alternate between **Summer Symphonies** (Thursdays) and **Pop Saturdays**. Past performers have included Monica Mancini, The Buddy Rich Big Band and James Darren. There is plenty of parking at $2 for the evening. Lot 4, at Mindanao and Admiralty Way, is close at hand. If that fills up, Lot 5 is one block away at Bali and Admiralty. Plan to come early and have a picnic in the park; the Chace Park Food Concession, ☎ 213-739-9913, offers a special menu for the concerts. Order ahead and your picnic will be waiting for you. Bring your own wine or beer.

TONY P'S DOCKSIDE GRILL
4445 Admiralty Way
☎ 310-823-4534

Live swing bands play here Saturday nights, and there is dancing in a big, boozy, noisy room separated from the dining room. Friday nights there's a DJ, but it is still a place to go dancing. The music starts at 9pm; there's no cover charge if you have dinner; or $7 at door.

Venice

We were in England a dozen years ago, turned on the telly in the hotel room – and watched a documentary about roller-skating in Venice. A few years ago, in Italy, we met a couple who asked where we were from. Once we had cleared up the confusion about *which* Venice, the husband immediately exclaimed, "Oh, yes! Roller skates!"

We hastened to assure them there was more to our little Eden-by-the-sea than in-line skating. After all, Venice is where skateboards were developed, too.

☞ DID YOU KNOW?

Venice drew many silent film stars. Fatty Arbuckle, Clara Bow, Charlie Chaplin, Tom Mix and Rudolph Valentino all had beach houses here.

Venice was the city's fun destination during both the first and last decades of the last century. For 15 years after the city was created people flocked here by the thousands every week: Venice was the most spectacular thing Los Angeles had ever seen. After a long period of decline and decay it is only in the last 20 years that the area has become known world-wide as a "must-see" destination for travelers.

History

Venice owes everything to a man named **Abbot Kinney**. He was wealthy, an heir to a cigarette fortune, but he wanted to do something more in life, something bigger. He wanted to bring culture to Los Angeles.

Venice was first known as the "Playland of the Pacific."

Around the turn of the century Kinney was in business with two real estate developers; their corporation owned nearly all the land between what is now Pico Boulevard in Santa Monica and Marina del Rey, including four miles of seashore. While the northern part, which became Ocean Park, could be sold as prime beachfront lots, the southern half was mostly marsh.

When Kinney and his partners disagreed on how to develop the land, they decided to divide it between them. They flipped a coin, and Kinney won the toss, but surprisingly he took the marshland.

But Kinney had a plan. He had been to Italy and he dreamed of creating another city just like Venice, with canals where gondolas would drift under arched bridges; where artists, musicians and intellectuals would create a cultural renaissance just 20 miles from downtown Los Angeles. And, of course, to everyone who was inspired to live in this new paradise, he would sell a lot to build on.

There are now three miles of canals in Venice.

Kinney dug eight miles of canals; there was a Grand Canal that ran from what is now Marina del Rey to the traffic circle at Windward Avenue, with other canals branching off. What is now the traffic circle was the Grand Lagoon.

Windward Avenue, the heart of his creation, was lined with Italian Renaissance buildings with arched colonnades. At the foot of Windward a long pier thrust out into the ocean. There was the famous Ship Café at the pier, and a huge indoor "saltwater plunge," a swimming pool, next to it on the beach.

On July 4, 1905, over 40,000 visitors came to opening day, and that night marveled as 17,000 electric lights all sparkled on at once. A private railroad car stood by for two days and nights while Sarah Bernhardt sang on the pier. There were lecturers and musicians. But the people of Los Angeles mostly came for the rides. Originally there were only a few, as Kinney wanted to improve and uplift people, but he gave in. He built a roller coaster, chute-the-chutes and a miniature train. Venice became the biggest attraction on the coast, and people bought lots to build simple weekend or summer beach houses.

LIVING IN VENICE

We live in Venice, near the beach. Our sandy lot is 30 feet wide, and the houses are close together. The original handwritten deed dated 1905, when the lot was first sold, tells us that we cannot "sell alcohol or keep cattle or pigs" on the property, and that we must build a structure costing at least $500. As we are law-abiding citizens, we don't have even one cow or pig, and we managed to spend more than $500 when we built our house. What gives the area much of its charm is that many streets are only eight feet wide and are strictly "walking streets," with no auto traffic.

The Sporting Life

The automobile was new and auto racing became a national craze just after the turn of the century when Abbot Kinney brought daredevil Barney Oldfield, the king of the racing drivers, to Venice for a series of races. The street that parallels Ocean Front Walk one block inland is still named Speedway for that reason.

In 1913 Kinney built the Venice Baseball Park at what is now the intersection of Abbot Kinney and Venice boulevards. He brought a minor league team from Vernon, a small town southeast of downtown Los Angeles. The opening game was against the Chicago White Sox, who won 7 to 4. The ballpark lasted only a few years. Apparently the problem was that while Los Angeles was dry, Vernon was wet and the games were played at 10:30 Sunday mornings when the Venice Tigers still had hangovers.

The ballpark was razed in 1916 when the Crawford and Faunders Flying Field was built on the same southwest corner. The stunt pilots staged exhibition flights featuring

The Beach Communities

Early maps show that the walk alongside the beach was originally named Broad Walk.

plane-to-plane wing-walking, and later flew in *Wings* (1927) and *The Dawn Patrol* (1930). Today you will see some one-story apartments and a small commercial building on that corner.

The End of an Era

Nothing is ever perfect; Adam and Eve were probably slapping at mosquitoes. In Kinney's case, winter storms damaged the pier, which had to be rebuilt several times; the canals had problems with drainage; and narrow streets and bridges made access difficult for the increasing number of cars. But despite obstacles, for 15 years Venice was the brightest, liveliest and most popular destination for Angelenos out to have fun.

Kinney died in 1920. The pier burned down one month later. With Prohibition, speakeasies moved into Venice (there are still basements that were speakeasies, and a tunnel under the Town House on Windward was used to smuggle booze in from the beach).

The remaining Venice Canals, difficult for some to find, are from Washington to Venice boulevards, just east of Pacific Avenue.

Venice's original high moral standards had been slipping for some time; now they went into free-fall. The city treasurer stole $20,000 from the city, which teetered on the edge of bankruptcy. In 1925 a majority voted to let Los Angeles take over. Then oil was discovered and oil derricks sprouted everywhere, with no thought to the environment.

☞ DID YOU KNOW?

Venice once had gondolas imported from Italy, along with singing gondoliers to pole the boats along in the shallow water.

The city of Los Angeles was determined to fill in the canals, regarding them a nuisance and an impediment to auto traffic. In 1929 the canals in northern Venice were filled in; there are several stories about why it stopped there. Our favorite is that the contractor took the rest of the money and ran off to Brazil, thus saving the canals that are left.

During the Depression, Venice was pretty much forgotten, except for the rebuilt pier, which had a few rides, a lot of carny games and a ballroom, where bands like the Dorsey Brothers and Lawrence Welk played. In the late '50s the beatniks brought Venice into public view again, and in the '60s the hippies were attracted by the cheap rent and tolerant atmosphere. Today the atmosphere is still tolerant but the rents are way up.

Bringing It Up to Date

During the 1960s and '70s three groups formed the majority of Venice's population. The first was senior citizens living on social security, many of whom were Jewish, whose focal point was Bay Cities Synagogue at 505 Ocean Front Walk. Anthropologist Barbara Myerhoff made a well-regarded film, *Number Our Days*, about the Bay Cities congregation. Hippies living on air, and artists living for art, were the others. All of them co-existed very well. In the '80s and '90s, as Venice became gentrified, all three groups were largely forced out by skyrocketing prices.

Reyner Banham, author of Los Angeles – The Architecture of Four Ecologies, *in 1971 called it "romantically blighted Venice."*

✗ WARNING!

Because Venice's older buildings have inadequate parking, many residents park on the streets, leaving little space for visitors. On weekends, the few parking lots often fill up before noon.

In the early 1970s Venice was the only place on California's 1,000-mile-long, expensive coastline where poor people could live at the beach. That changed as those living inland realized that there was, miraculously, one place left in Los Angeles with both a great climate and low housing prices. Some were also attracted by the live-and-let-live atmosphere. As those with more money moved in, the ones with less were forced out. So there went the artists and a lot of the atmosphere.

We moved to Venice in the mid '70s when the smog in the San Fernando Valley got to be too much for us. At the time, Venice showed up in the newspapers only for violence and drug dealings, so much so that for years friends asked us, "Aren't you afraid to live there?" Actually the violence was (and still is) confined to an area called Oakwood, which is north of Venice Boulevard and east of Electric Avenue, several blocks from the beach, and has never affected the rest of the area. Even Oakwood is safer now. The biggest worry there now is that Oakwood's population will also be forced out by gentrification.

The better-off liberals who moved to Venice were called "affluhips."

Venice is now known all over the world primarily for Ocean Front Walk, a.k.a. **The Boardwalk**. Its revival began in the '70s with hippies selling pipes and pot-smoking paraphernalia, home-crafted jewelry and leather goods. Musicians played and put out hats to collect tips, comedians told stories, and tarot card readers set up card tables.

A new development has been the very welcome French influx. There is a growing expatriate community of artists, writers and those working in film – there is quite a French contingent in animation, especially at Disney. They tell us that those from the south of France are particularly drawn to Venice, which is as much like the Mediterranean as you can find in Los Angeles.

The Venice "boardwalk" is a misnomer that disappoints some visitors – it is actually a paved walkway.

What that has added to our life here are places like Normandie Bakery & Coffee on the first block of Washington, the bakery Le Pain du Jour near Pico and Lincoln, and Lilly's French Café and Slave, a clothing store, both on Abbot Kinney Boulevard. And, for all the French families, there is Ecole Clair Fontaine, a preschool. Alas, for all the Americans who would love to have their small children grow up speaking French, there is a waiting list a kilomètre long.

Getting Here

From LAX

By Car

Take Sepulveda Boulevard north to Lincoln Boulevard (Highway 1), and curve left. Stay with Lincoln through Marina del Rey to Washington Boulevard. If you keep going straight, everything from there to Rose Avenue is Venice; if you turn left on Washington and go to the last traffic light you'll come to Pacific Avenue, which parallels the ocean. Street parking, a parking lot and the Venice Pier are a block farther on at the end of Washington.

By Bus

Take the free shuttle to Lot C, then get on the Santa Monica Big Blue Bus #3 to Lincoln and Venice boulevards. Ask for a transfer to Metro Bus #33, which goes west on Venice Boulevard to Main Street.

By Shuttle

Shuttle service is available from **Prime Time Shuttle**, ☎ 800-733-8267, www.primetimeshuttle.com; and **Super Shuttle**, ☎ 310-782-6600 or 323-775-6600, www.supershuttle.com. Approximate fare is $15, plus $9 for a second passenger.

By Taxi

Taxi fare to this area runs $17-$20, depending on traffic, plus $2.50 airport fee. Try **My Taxi**, ☎ 800-4 MY-TAXI (469-8294); or **Venice Checker Yellow Cab**, ☎ 310-306-7440.

From Downtown Los Angeles

By Car

From Downtown Los Angeles, especially during rush hour, the easiest route is to head straight out Venice Boulevard to its end.

Take any of the main westbound streets (except Sunset Boulevard) to Ocean Avenue in Santa Monica, and turn left; as you go south, the street name changes to Neilson, then Pacific Avenue. Continue to Venice Boulevard, where you turn right to the beach parking lot. You can also take the Santa Monica Freeway (10) west from downtown, exit at the Fourth Street off-ramp, and turn left onto Broadway to get to Ocean Avenue.

There is a public parking lot at Venice Boulevard and Pacific Avenue, and another one a block farther west at the end of Venice Boulevard on the beach. The parking lots on the beach (one is at the end of Rose Avenue, Venice's northern border with Santa Monica, and the other is at the end of Washington Boulevard, the southern border with Marina del Rey), are usually less crowded. Prices vary from $3 per day in the early morning to as much as $14 on a packed holiday afternoon.

There are a few private lots: Angel's gas station at Pacific Avenue and Venice Way has one, and there is a small lot across the street. Their prices are usually lower than the public lots. There is a lot at Speedway and Market Street, one block north of Windward Avenue, and two more farther north at Speedway and Thornton.

A bit farther away are two DASH lots (Downtown Area Shuttle Hops – does everything have to be an acronym?) with free bus service to the beach. The lots are at 4551 Glencoe Avenue, Marina del Rey (Glencoe is off Washington Boulevard two blocks east of Lincoln Boulevard); and at 4220 Admiralty Way at Palawan. These are open daily, from Memorial Day to Labor Day, 11am to 7pm. Parking is $2 all day.

⚡ WARNING!

If you're parking on the street, observe the hours posted on the red "No Parking for street cleaning" signs. In most areas here, cleanings occur on Monday or Tuesday.

By Bus

Metro Bus #33 runs south on Spring Street (#333 is added during rush hours); catch it at 4th, 6th or 7th streets. It goes west out Venice Boulevard all the way to the beach. If you are downtown west of Pershing square, take #60 running south on Flower Street; at 7th Street it turns and connects with #33. Transfer (75¢) and continue as before.

Getting Around

The only reasons anyone comes to Venice are the beach and the boardwalk. The beach is great for its entire length (we are not saying the same for the water quality). Most of the Boardwalk/Ocean Front Walk action is centered at Windward Avenue, a few blocks south to Venice Boulevard and a dozen blocks north. If you arrive at the pier at the end of Washington Boulevard and want to see the crowds and the street performers, walk north a half-mile (a very nice walk along the beachfront). If you are parked at the north end by Rose Avenue you will have to walk south quite a ways.

Who Lives Here?

Venice is no longer a community of celebrities the way it was in the days of silent pictures. But a few are still attracted, such as Lauren Ambrose, who plays the daughter on HBO's *Six Feet Under*. Orson Bean, comic, Broadway actor, game show panelist and a permanent character on *Dr. Quinn, Medicine Woman* of a few years ago, started with one cottage on one of the canals. After he married ac-

Dogs are not allowed off the leash on Venice beach.

tress Alley Mills of *The Wonder Years* and *Dr. Quinn*, they gradually added three more cottages next door to them, so they now have a compound.

Anjelica Huston lives here with her husband, sculptor Robert Graham, who also has his studio in Venice. Graham did the torsos in front of the 1984 Los Angeles Olympic Games, the Duke Ellington sculpture in New York's Central Park and the Charlie Parker memorial in Kansas City. He recently sculpted the massive main doors for the new Cathedral of Our Lady of the Angels in downtown Los Angeles.

Dudley Moore (*10, Arthur*) lived for many years in his beachfront home and sometimes played piano in 22 Market Street, the Venice restaurant he owned with Liza Minnelli and producer Tony Bill (Bill still has his offices across the street from the restaurant, which is now the Globe; see page 404).

 # On Location

Venice practically crawls with film crews. You see the town on the screen over and over, whenever the star comes out of an ancient hotel onto Ocean Front Walk. If it's a film noir the scene will be set at dawn and a few carefully placed newspapers will blow forlornly along the misty, deserted walkway. In the comedies the hero emerges to find bikini-clad blondes roller-skating nonchalantly by in the bright sunlight.

When you see the big white equipment trucks and smaller white dressing-room trailers you will know some company is shooting. If it is a big shoot that is going to take a while there will also be a white commissary tent.

Venice is one of the most-used filming locations in Los Angeles.

Because a lot of space is needed to park everything for a big shoot, look at the large parking lots at the ends of Rose, Venice and Washington. The two parking lots back from the beach are most used: the one between North and South Venice from Pacific Avenue back to the next street, Dell, and the one from Dell back to Venice Way/Ocean Avenue (the street name changes here).

Even if you don't see equipment trucks, there are other clues to the presence of a production crew; you might see a hand-painted cardboard sign on a lamp post, with just a word and an arrow, like "WIND," or "CHARLIE." That is shorthand for the name of the picture being shot. Follow the arrows, which will lead to where the crew is parked.

Some pictures have used Venice extensively for exteriors, like *Bounce, The Doors* and *L.A. Story. White Men Can't Jump* was shot here at the basketball courts on the beach, as well as *Baywatch*, which has used all the beaches along the coast at one time or another.

The most famous picture ever shot here was Orson Welles' *Touch of Evil* (1958). The sinister alleys, the shadowy, threatening arcades, stagnant canals and brooding buildings all lent a prophetically ominous atmosphere. The three-story stucco building on the northwest corner of Windward and Pacific, built 90 years ago as a hotel and apartments, was prominently featured.

Other notable film spots include **Hinano**, 15 Washington Boulevard. It's a bar, the kind with sawdust on the floor, and is named after a Tahitian beer. The original owner made his way to Tahiti on a 32-foot sailboat in 1962, fell in love with the local beer and persuaded the brewery to let him bring back some brew and use the name. Scenes from *The China Syndrome* and *Falling Down* were shot here, and Jim Morrison carved his name on the wall somewhere. The place is also famous for having the best hamburgers in town. We don't know about best, since we haven't tasted all the rest, but they are pretty good.

Venice High School, 13000 Venice Boulevard, is not really in Venice but just over the border in Mar Vista, about two miles from the beach. The school's original location was in Venice, in Abbot Kinney's original bathhouse on the Grand Lagoon in 1910. Physical education classes consisted of rowing boats up and down the canals. The school was moved in 1914 when the bathhouse burned down.

The building's classic '50s exterior has been used in many films, but Venice High is famous for two things, only one of which is a film. It was the high school seen in *Grease*; John Travolta, Olivia Newton-John and Stockard Channing spent a lot of time there in 1977, and Olivia Newton-John showed up for a *Grease*-themed Homecoming a few years ago. The white statue of a slim young woman in front of the main building on Venice Boulevard was sculpted by

The Beach Communities

The building on the corner of Windward that was used in Touch of Evil *is now the Venice Beach Hostel.*

Hinano is on the corner of Speedway, a few doors stagger from the beach.

Harry Winebrenner in 1923, who styled it partly after Botticelli's Birth of Venus painting. The ninth-grade student who modeled for the figure was Myrna Williams, later known as movie star Myrna Loy.

Best Places to Stay

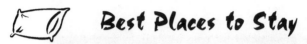

Hotels

You don't have many choices if you want to make Venice your headquarters during your stay. There are two hotels, but there also a B&B, one of the few in all of Los Angeles.

The accommodations price scale can be found on page 39.

THE INN AT VENICE BEACH
327 Washington Boulevard
Venice, CA 90291
☎ 310-821-2557, 800-828-0688
www.innatvenicebeach.com
Inexpensive-Moderate

A neat, small hotel three blocks from the pier and beach and almost next door to the Grand Canal. Rooms are a decent size, parking is free and there is complimentary continental breakfast. A modest, nice place.

MARINA PACIFIC (BEST WESTERN)
1697 Pacific Avenue
Venice, CA 90291
☎ 310-452-1111, 800-421-8151
www.mphotel.com
Moderate

This place, between Pacific Avenue and Speedway, has been here a long time. Not fancy, but a recent renovation has made it very nice. We went into an ocean-view room the other day, opened the drapes, and there were all the trucks and dressing-room trailers for a picture that was being shot under our noses. The clerk told us another pic was to start shooting on their rooftop sundeck, which has great views, in a few days.

Some rooms have kitchenettes, and there are suites available. All have a small refrigerator; breakfast is included and parking is $5 per day. The free shuttle to Santa Monica or Marina del Rey is handy. Higher summer rates start May 25. Reservations about a month in advance are needed in summer. For anyone wanting to see all the Venice action, the location just off Windward overlooking the beach can't be improved.

Bed & Breakfast

THE VENICE BEACH HOUSE
15 Thirtieth Avenue
Venice, CA 90291
☎ 310-823-1966, fax 310-823-1842
Inexpensive-Moderate

A big comfortable house built when Abbot Kinney was building his canals, the Venice Beach House has become a really nice nine-room inn for people who aren't all that crazy about staying in 400-room hotels where nobody knows your name. In the rooms are four-poster beds, rocking chairs and throw rugs. Breakfast features freshly squeezed juice and homemade breads with apple butter, and coffee in a sunny alcove or in your own room. In the evening guests share refreshments in front of a cozy winter fire or on the veranda at sunset.

The Inn is only a few steps from the beach, and there are bicycles to borrow for a long ride down the bike path. A few of the rooms share a bathroom, some are suites. Reserve as soon as possible; after all, this is one of Los Angeles' few B&Bs.

Venice Beach House is only a block from Washington Boulevard's shops and restaurants.

Best Places to Eat

Please, sir, I want some more. – Oliver Twist

There are four restaurants just steps from the beach between Pacific Avenue and Ocean Front Walk: two on North Venice Boulevard, one on Market Street (a short block north of Windward Avenue) and the fourth on Dudley Avenue (a short block south of Rose Avenue at the north end of Venice next to Santa Monica). We highly recommend all for excellent food and good star-watching.

Fine Dining

★★ 5 DUDLEY

5 Dudley Avenue
☎ 310-399-6678
California-continental
Expensive

The dining price scale can be found on page 42.

This tiny, but very good place is just two doors off the boardwalk, next to a funky art gallery. It is about 15 feet wide and perhaps 20 feet deep, there are only 10 tables inside and four out on the sidewalk for a total of 36 guests tops, so when celebrities are here, as they often are, they definitely are not hidden off in a dark corner. Reservations are strongly advised. There is no bar; only beer and wine are served. It is currently open for dinner Tuesday-Sunday, 6-10pm, and in the summer for lunch, Tuesday-Friday, 11:30am-2:30pm, but call ahead to confirm times.

JOE'S

1023 Abbot Kinney Boulevard
☎ 310-399-5811
French-California cuisine
Moderate-Expensive

The fare put out here has been described as the most sophisticated kind of comfort food. What better could be said? Here is a starter: "pistachio-crusted goat cheese, bartlett pears, red oak leaf lettuce, pomegranate vinaigrette." And an entrée: "tagine of monkfish with almond couscous, saffron broth, cherry tomato and preserved lemon salad." (Never having heard of "tagine," we had to ask to find out it is a clay crock used in Morocco to cook food and carry it in the desert.) There are four-course prix fixe menus at $38 and $48 as well as an à la carte menu.

No matter how new and trendy the restaurant, many still play 60-year-old Billie Holiday records for a romantic background sound.

The restaurant is in an old house dating from the days when Abbot Kinney himself was around. Open for lunch Tuesday-Friday, 11:30am-2:30pm; and for brunch (not a buffet) Saturday and Sunday, 11am-2:30pm. Dinner is served Tuesday-Thursday and Sunday, 6-10pm; Friday and Saturday until 11pm. Reservations are necessary for dinner Friday and Saturday. Abbot Kinney Boulevard angles off Washington Boulevard a dozen blocks from the beach and runs north to Main.

★★ THE CANAL CLUB

2025 Pacific Avenue
☎ 310-823-3878
Asian-Californian-Mexican
Moderate-Expensive

It is like several different places all in one: a sushi bar in the center front, a dining room with a high, exposed-brick wall to one side, a bar with tables and couches on the other side. And a palapa, a South Pacific bamboo and palm hut, hanging from the ceiling over all. Take your pick.

There is miso soup, sushi, a Chinese duck salad and shiitake sauce on the salmon for the Asian; and tortilla soup, guacamole and chipotle marinated albacore to take care of the Mexican influence. But mostly it is solid steak, chops and chicken. When we drop in it is usually at happy hour for the cut-rate beer and little bar dishes. The address is Pacific Avenue, but it is on the corner of North Venice Boulevard and the entrance is on Venice. Open only for dinner, from 5pm to 10pm, Sunday-Tuesday; to 11pm other nights; the bar is open later. Valet parking.

Canal Club is called that because it is a half-block from the end of the Grand Canal.

★★ JAMES' BEACH

60 North Venice Boulevard
☎ 310-823-5396, fax 310-823-5397
New California/American
Moderate-Expensive

This is our neighborhood restaurant (in North Venice, this is almost everyone's neighborhood restaurant). And that is in addition to the Hollywood crowd. The place is pared down to the essentials: stark white walls with a few choice pieces of art by local artists (and remember, Venice is an enclave of art and artists), a long, impressive bar all along one side. Beside it is a patio with heaters for winter and cool beach breezes in summer (the place is only a couple hundred feet from the sand). A pleasing look to it all, down to the famous "potato-chip" chairs, designed by Charles Eames, whose studio was in Venice. At lunch and on weekends there are usually more people on the patio than inside.

James Evans, the owner, wanted to make this "a young Musso & Frank's," and has succeeded nicely. The chef here does classic American food very well. Chicken pot pie, meat loaf, roast beef, Caesar salad. Look for the daily specials.

Dinner nightly; lunch Wednesday-Friday; brunch Saturday and Sunday. There is a late-night menu Thursday-Saturday, 10:30pm to 1am (it is really nice to find something more than a hamburger late at night in this part of town). Valet parking.

★★ GLOBE

72 Market Street
☎ 310-392-8720
American, Italian influenced
Expensive

This location was previously occupied by a restaurant called 72 Market Street, which was owned by Dudley Moore, Liza Minnelli, and producer Tony Bill. The real estate is still owned by Tony Bill but the restaurant is run by Joseph Manzare and Mary Klingbeil (they also own the Globe in San Francisco). The striking interior has been used as a location (for the film *Bounce*, and several commercials). Celebrities are beginning to try it on for size, led by Anjelica Huston, who lives nearby.

Dishes are basically seafood, pasta and meat, with one rotisserie grilled chicken dish. When it comes to appetizers, we heartily recommend the house-smoked salmon on grilled bread with dill crème fraîche. One serving at $9.95 is just right for two people.

The sign on the corner of Pacific and Market reading "72 Market Street" now points to Globe.

Lunch is served Wednesday-Friday, noon-3pm; dinner Tuesday-Saturday, 6pm-midnight; and Sunday, 6-10pm. The bar is open and snacks are available on weekdays, 3-6pm. Market Street is one block north of Windward (toward Santa Monica), between Pacific Avenue and Speedway (toward the beach). Valet parking, $4.

Casual Dining

SIDEWALK CAFE
1401 Ocean Front Walk
☎ 310-399-5547
Sandwiches, salads
Inexpensive

This is where Ron Kovic used to hang out, the kid who joined the Marine Corps and went off to Vietnam, and ended up a paraplegic in a wheelchair for life. Oliver Stone told his story in *Born on the Fourth of July*.

Inside the café there is a loud bar and music at night. Outside is the big attraction: an expansive view of the Boardwalk and the beach as you sit and enjoy a glass of wine or beer and eat a salad. Across the walkway in this section are the tarot card readers, but the best show is really the passing parade of tourists ogling other tourists and thinking how funny they look.

Shopping

Venice is not the place to come for shopping. There is none, except for Ocean Front Walk, where you will find dozens of small stores and stands all selling the same T-shirts and dark glasses. However, if you want to have your skin tattooed or pierced, you can do it here. **Tattoo Asylum**, 64 Windward Avenue, ☎ 310-450-1073, is open Sunday-Thursday, 10am-8pm; Friday and Saturday, 10am-10pm. **Muscle Beach Hair & Nail Salon**, 1811 Ocean Front Walk, ☎ 310-827-9923, does hair wraps and piercing; it's open daily, 10am-7pm. You can also have your fortune told in tarot cards from one of the many "readers" along the block west of Market Street on Ocean Front Walk.

Sunup to Sundown

Farmers' Market

There is a year-round market on Friday mornings, 7-11am, about four blocks inland from the beach on Venice Boulevard at Venice Way.

Recreation

Motorized scooters are banned from the bike path in Venice.

Bicycling and **skating** along the flat bike path allows you to travel along the beach from Venice to Santa Monica without getting on any streets. Technically, skaters are not supposed to use it, but there is no path just for skating. Try one of these shops for rentals: **Rental on the Beach**, 3001 Ocean Front Walk (next to Venice Pier), ☎ 310-396-1959; or **Venice Pier Bike Shop**, 21 Washington Boulevard, ☎ 310-301-4011.

★ TIP

The cement bike path on the beach extends from north of the Santa Monica Pier to the Venice Pier at the foot of Washington Boulevard, a distance of almost three miles.

Get a copy of paddle tennis rules at the Parks & Recreation office on the other side of the weight pen.

Paddle tennis courts are at 20th Avenue at Ocean Front Walk. There are 11 regulation courts where National tournaments are held annually. Open play, no fee or reservations. First-come basis. Racket rentals, 8am-sundown, $5.

Muscle Beach is at 19th Avenue at Ocean Front Walk, ☎ 310-399-2775. The original, legendary Muscle Beach was in Santa Monica. When it went poufft in the 1970s many of the muscle people moved here. Now this is the legendary one. A day pass to use the equipment is $5; monthly memberships are available. The stage behind the weight pen is the location of occasional powerlifting and physique contests; pick up a schedule at the office. The weight pen is open from 8am-sundown.

Basketball courts are at 18th Avenue at Ocean Front Walk. The book *Hoops Nation* (Chris Ballard, Henry Holt & Co.) called this the "most famous outdoor basketball court in the world." And that is not counting the fact that this is the court where *White Men Can't Jump* was shot. There are four courts, but the number one court is where pro players from the Lakers, Clippers and Sparks occasionally show up and join in. That is the court right by Ocean Front Walk, nearest the little building where the office is.

Skateboarding area. Venice is the birthplace of skateboarding; *Dogtown*, a documentary film on the history of skateboarding in Venice and South Santa Monica, follows the development of the sport. However, after the Boardwalk renovation in 2000-01, the skateboarders were left with only this circle, which has a few low curved walls and other areas for grinding. Here you'll see some phenomenal skateboarding and can show off your own skills. The skateboarders still hope to get a larger area of their own built, but because the Coastal Commission has a rule that structures on the beach cannot exceed four feet high, that rules out seven-foot-high Plexiglas dasher boards. Venice Skateboard Association, ☎ 310-392-2179.

The **Skate Park** is just a few feet away from the skateboarding area. There are skaters practicing their heel spins and backward glides here every day, but on weekends roller-skaters descend from all over for skate dancing. Everything from disco to pop to hip-hop spins from DJ Blue's boom box.

There are plans to build a roller hockey rink near the Skate Park.

Gold's Gym, 368 Hampton Drive (Main Street and Abbot Kinney Boulevard), Venice, ☎ 310-392-3005. This is a new building; the old one (now closed) where Arnold Schwarzenegger and many other mythic bodies trained was on Pacific Avenue. Men and women who are serious about sculpting their bodies still come here. You may also see people like fashion model and fitness guru Gabrielle Reece, who is tops in professional beach volleyball. A one-day pass is $20; one week, $50. Hours are Monday-Friday, 4am-midnight; Saturday and Sunday, 5am-11pm. Parking lots are nearby.

IF YOU ARE GOING IN THE WATER...

You should know that in some years lifeguards make more than 2,500 rescues along what they call "Venice North," the stretch of beach from Avenue 23, just south of Venice Boulevard, to the border with Santa Monica – and most of the rescues take place in the seven-block stretch between Avenue 23 and Windward Avenue.

There are rock jetties at either end of that stretch. Water gets trapped in between, and tunnel-like rip currents tear through. People can be standing waist-deep in the surf, or even only knee-deep, when a rip develops, and get swept out to sea moments later. A few years ago one lifeguard made 322 rescues in just 10 weeks of summer. That is why nine lifeguards watch over that one stretch, and two more patrol in a boat beyond the surfline. Enjoy the sun and sand, but when you go into the water, be careful.

Walking Tour

The space between North and South Venice boulevards was originally used by the Pacific Electric rail line, which delivered thousands of beach-goers from downtown Los Angeles each day. Our first walk takes you along crowded and bustling Ocean Front Walk (a.k.a. the Boardwalk).

☞ DID YOU KNOW?

You could get from downtown Los Angeles to Venice quicker in 1920 than you can today, by taking a Red Line rail car, which made the trip in less than 30 minutes.

Along Ocean Front Walk

The Beach Communities

There are many interesting places along Ocean Front Walk. Start where Ocean Front meets North Venice Boulevard, by the public parking lot. Note that other guidebooks sometimes mention that 517 Ocean Front Walk was once owned by comedian Eddie Cantor. Actually, that building was torn down in the 1980s and replaced by the present brick bungalow that now houses shops.

Jody Maroni's Sausage Kingdom, 2011 Ocean Front Walk, ☎ 310-453-2044, is a take-out place with a few tables and, very possibly, the best sausages in Los Angeles. It is known city-wide and has franchises in a dozen other places, but this is the original. Try a sample of the Polish sausage (beer and smoky flavor), and the Tequila chicken sausage (spicy with jalapeños) before you choose.

Tom Mix's House, 1915 Ocean Front Walk. Tom Mix made his first movie for Selig in 1910 in Oklahoma, where he was a sheriff (he was also a Texas Ranger for a few years), but he didn't become a Western star until the '20s, well after William S. Hart and Hoot Gibson. He was a big star, who became really wealthy even in those days when there were no 20-million-dollar paychecks for actors. This stucco, Spanish-style place was his beach house. You can tell by the now-battered architectural detail that it was once a fine place. It is sad to see what it has come down to, although it's hard to see much behind the racks of sunglasses for sale.

Snack food and outside tables are available at 517 Ocean Front Walk.

The **Town House**, 52 Windward Avenue, ☎ 310-392-4040, is a dark, cavernous saloon, though it's only half its original size. It has been here since 1915. During Prohibition it was called Manotti's Buffet. The name was a euphemism, as the buffet conisisted of a chunk of cheese and a bowl of hard-boiled eggs on the bar upstairs where soda and near beer were dispensed; downstairs in the basement was a speakeasy. A tunnel ran from there to the beach. In those days international waters began only three miles offshore (now the rule is 12 miles); boats full of Canadian liquor would wait just beyond the three-mile limit until after dark, then run in under the pier and unload cases of illegal booze that would be carried up the tunnel to Manotti's.

The tunnel that once connected the Town House to the beach is now closed.

Notice Buster Keaton's face on a workman in the Post Office mural.

Venice Post Office. Turn up Windward Avenue to Main Street and go inside the Post Office on the southwest corner. The mural by Edward Biberton, a WPA Depression project, shows Abbot Kinney and the entire history of Venice.

The **Traffic Circle**, at Windward and Main, is where Kinney's Grand Lagoon was located.

The **Arcades**, buildings on the north side of Windward from Pacific to Speedway with colonnades and arches over the sidewalks, are all that remain of Kinney's original vision.

☞ DID YOU KNOW?

The Byzantine- and Renaissance-style buildings, with shaded walkways and ornate columns, originally lined both sides of Windward from the Grand Lagoon to Ocean Front Walk and for several blocks up Ocean Front Walk.

The **Venice Beach Hotel** at 25 Windward Avenue was the St. Charles Hotel when this side of the street was solid hotels, one after another, during Venice's early glory years. The mural on the side of the hotel was painted by Terry Schoonhoven when it was still the St. Charles. The view is as it was if you turned around in 1979; sadly, it has faded. Across Speedway was the St. Mark's Hotel, where Orson Welles did most of his shooting for *Touch of Evil* (1958). During the beat and hippie years from the 1950s to the 1970s it was said you could get high on the pot fumes wafting out of the hotel by just passing by on the sidewalk.

A **mural** called Venice Reconstituted is on the west side of the Venice Beach Hotel; you can see it from Speedway. It was done in 1989 by Rip Cronk, and shows the surf, the bay up through Malibu and a representation of Venice's buildings and people. The turbaned in-line skater with the electric guitar is Harry Perry, the best-known Boardwalk habitue (if you meet him, he'll sell you cassettes of his own music). The sidewalk pianist is Berry "The Lion" Gordon. The artist himself is in there somewhere, too.

A LOT FOR A LOT

Surprisingly, neither Beverly Hills nor Bel-Air, with their mansions and movie star homes, have the most expensive real estate in Los Angeles. Venice now has the second-highest per-square-foot land value in Los Angeles County, even though 25 years ago lots here were, excuse us, dirt cheap. The only place more expensive is within the 90402 zip code in Santa Monica.

A few hundred feet up Speedway is **Market Street**, where a **mural** on the parking lot wall depicts a phantasmagoric Venice: Hollywood's blondes wearing sunglasses, Aztecs, and a modern-day scene all morphed together.

Small World of Books, 1407 Ocean Front Walk, ☎ 310-399-2360 is well known by the many writers who live in this area. The store covers fiction and non-fiction, childrens' literature and poetry, and quite a few books about different aspects of Los Angeles and Venice. Check the schedule of the Mystery Annex at the back for book readings and signings.

TV show tickets are often handed out at the corner of 17th Street and Ocean Front Walk, which will save you going somewhere to get them.

The **Waldorf Hotel**, 1219 Ocean Front Walk, a white glazed brick building on the corner, was built in 1914. Stars like Clara Bow and Charlie Chaplin were frequent guests. You see the same elegant brass marquee with white globes, though with more than 85 years of tarnish and dust.

The building off Ocean Front Walk at **17 Park Avenue** was Olivia de Havilland's home in the 1930s.

The first block on **Thornton Avenue** is filled with several interesting and historic houses. At **16 Thornton Avenue**, on the corner of Speedway, is a five-story, hexagonal building where dancer Isadora Duncan lived in the 1920s. The flaking stucco has faded badly. Surely the topmost apartment, with its windows facing the sea and its rooftop patio, must have been hers. Jane Fonda had the upstairs apartment at **18 Thornton Avenue** in the late '60s. When she and Tom Hayden married they lived a few blocks north of here in Ocean Park, and still later moved to a bigger house in Santa Monica, north of Montana Avenue. That was before she married Ted Turner, who owned the state of Montana.

You'll see a good example of a Craftsman-style house at **39 Thornton Avenue**, where silent film star Fatty Arbuckle lived in the '20s. Arbuckle was a big star, both physically (he weighed more than 250 pounds) and professionally (as a leading comedian), when he was falsely accused of causing the death of Virginia Rappe, a young wannabe-actress, during a three-day drunken party in the St. Francis Hotel in San Francisco. The case made headlines and, by the time Arbuckle went through three trials of hung juries and final acquittal, his career and life were effectively ruined. The sturdy porch pillars on the house are granite, rather than the usual wood ones typical of the Craftsman style. The beautiful mullioned windows appear to be original. The second-floor room in front with a wide, wall-to-wall window was a later addition. As you walk back down Thornton toward the ocean take a look at **30 Thornton**. The fascinating architecture of the gray-and-blue-trimmed clapboard building takes advantage of the view and breezes with decks and well-positioned windows at every level and a widow's walk at the top.

All the addresses cited here are private homes. Please do not disturb the owners.

Continuing along Ocean Front Walk to **Rose Avenue**, you'll find the **Ocean View Hotel** at #5. The big building on the corner, white with blue trim, was a deluxe beach hotel in 1926. On May 16 of that year, flamboyant evangelist Aimee Semple McPherson, who led services in her Four Square Church in Echo Park in a long, white satin gown, left her suite, walked across the beach and into the ocean for a swim – and disappeared from sight. Thousands gathered on the beach to pray she would be found. It was a headline story in newspapers nationwide. Finally, although there was no body, she was pronounced dead and an emotional memorial service was held at the beach.

A month later, however, Aimee McPherson miraculously walked out of the Arizona desert, claiming to have escaped from kidnappers. Her return to Los Angeles, where she was greeted by 100,000 rejoicing followers, was a hysterical mob scene. Unfortunately, it was later discovered that she had spent the missing month with her lover. Aimee's fortunes went downhill after that. The building is now a home for senior citizens.

The Canal Walk

For a charming – and quieter – walk through Venice, explore the streets around the remaining canals.

North Venice Boulevard at **Canal Street**. The Grand Canal, which currently ends here, originally extended along Canal Street, through the space now occupied by a large apartment complex at Mildred Avenue, and on to the Grand Lagoon. The rest of the canals were filled in; only the three miles from here south to Marina del Rey are left.

Take the sidewalk at canal level to South Venice Boulevard, cross the street and descend to **The Grand Canal**. The walk ahead of you is one of the most beautiful in all of Los Angeles. Fortunately for the peace and quiet of the people who live along the canal, few seem to know about it so it is never crowded. In fact, you will usually see only a handful of people between here and Washington Boulevard. Simply stroll along the narrow pathway, enjoying the houses and gardens, and take a few pictures of the ducks and paddleboats against the background of the picturesque arched bridges.

The Grand Canal goes straight from Venice Boulevard to Washington Boulevard. Four other three-block-long canals branch off it to the east, where Eastern Canal connects them all. If you take the right-hand pathway it is a half-mile walk to **Washington Boulevard**. The left path is longer because you will walk along each side canal, cross a bridge, go back down the other side and continue on to the next. Either way is a great walk.

There is no canal-side walkway from Washington Boulevard to the marina, where the Grand Canal starts.

Baja Cantina, 311 Washington Boulevard, the brown wooden building behind the parking lot to your left, is next door to where your canal walk ends. It's a handy place to sit for a bit and have a bottle of Mexican beer or a margarita (they serve huge ones) before starting back. They also have Mexican food, an outdoor patio and several dining rooms inside. It's hugely popular, especially on weekends when you'll end up on a long waiting list for a table.

From here you can either go back the same way, or perhaps explore the side of the canal you didn't visit, or walk down Washington to the right and return to the starting point on Ocean Front Walk.

C&O Trattoria, 31 Washington Boulevard, is another fine place to stop. Sit out at a sidewalk table or in the patio; if you order a glass of the house Chianti, they will bring you a whole bottle, on the honor system (it is only $2.95 a glass). They will also bring a plate of the most addictive just-baked little rolls, which are on the house. If you are still hungry after that, look at the menu, but be warned, the portions are huge!

The Venice Pier

Venice Pier, at the end of Washington, was just rebuilt again a few years ago. All the piers along this coast keep getting knocked out in storms. If you walk out to the end, you will encounter quite a few local fishermen. Because of the levels of pollution in Santa Monica Bay we wouldn't eat anything caught here, but apparently some people do.

There is a public parking lot on the beach at the foot of Washington Boulevard.

There is a good view of the coastline from the end of the pier. Looking north, the tall buildings are downtown Santa Monica. Farther on, where the coast curves west out to the point, is Malibu. To the south, the breakwater a mile down protects the entrance to the Marina del Rey channel; past that you see the planes taking off from LAX (unless there is a Santa Ana wind, in which case they come in over the ocean). Manhattan Beach is next, then Redondo Beach, where there is a breakwater and a small yacht harbor. After that the coast curves out to the west to Palos Verdes Peninsula, which is a point, not a peninsula.

You can see Catalina Island in the Channel past Palos Verdes.

From the foot of the pier walk back up Ocean Front Walk to where you started. The curving bike path parallels the walkway. The few old single-family residences along the way are all from around World War I or earlier, and some of the new apartment and condominium buildings are striking. Or unusual, anyway.

After Dark

THE TOWN HOUSE
52 Windward Avenue
☎ 310-392-4040

We have never seen the Town House without people inside, either to get cool on a hot sunny day or warm when the beach is foggy. In either case, George the bartender, a wonderful storyteller, will keep you entertained with tales of the "old days" while you consume a big 24-ounce bottle (the only size they have) of one of the dozens of brands of beer on hand. Most Saturday nights there is live music and dancing downstairs in the old speakeasy.

★★ THE CANAL CLUB
2025 Pacific Avenue
☎ 310-823-3878

The bar is open to midnight on weeknights, until 1am on weekends. Valet parking.

SIDEWALK CAFE
1401 Ocean Front Walk
☎ 310-399-5547

Inside the café is a loud bar where locals congregate. Open Sunday-Friday until 11pm, Saturday to midnight.

Santa Monica

It's better to be looked over than overlooked.
– Mae West, *Belle of the Nineties*

Santa Monica is one of the nicest towns in the Los Angeles region. Movie-makers have been taking advantage of its three miles of wide, clean beaches and its piers ever since movies have been made out here. It is a small town, in both size and population, and the people have long been proud of the fact that they are independent of and better run than the gargantuan next-door City of Los Angeles.

There are some good hotels, several well-known places to eat, three different shopping areas that attract people from all over Los Angeles, and incomparable beaches. What more could one ask?

History

Father Juan Crespi, whom we mentioned early in this book, was one of the first European arrivals on the scene; he was part of Gaspar de Portolá's expedition from Mexico, and is credited with naming this area. He saw a free-flowing natural spring and called the place Santa Monica (she was the saint who wept for her wayward son, who became Saint Augustine). Crespi was obviously a sensitive fellow. The spring still flows on the campus of University High School in West LA (not in Santa Monica).

In its first nine months, Santa Monica's population grew from almost zero to 1,000.

Fast forward almost 60 years to 1828, when Mexico freed itself from Spain. The region around what was to become Santa Monica was divided into three land grants: *Rancho San Vicente y Santa Monica*, *Rancho Boca de Santa Monica* and *Rancho La Balloña*.

WHAT'S IN A NAME?

It is possible to tell what area the land grants covered by the names they were given. Rancho San Vicente y Santa Monica was in the area of San Vicente Boulevard, north of the town; Rancho Balloña incorporated Balloña Creek, a small river that ran into the sea at what is now Marina del Rey; and "Boca," which means "mouth," referred to Santa Monica Canyon at the beach.

The city wasn't laid out until almost 50 years later, when John Percival Jones bought a big piece of the San Vicente y Santa Monica land grant and planned the streets and lots. His plan included room for ample parks, including Palisades Park, which runs along the bluff overlooking the ocean for a mile-and-a-half.

Jones kept a prime piece of property for himself; he built a mansion that he called Miramar at Wilshire Boulevard and Ocean Avenue. In 1890 he planted a Moreton Bay fig tree, which still stands. In 1924 the mansion became the Miramar Hotel, and the hotel – now called the Fairmont Miramar – was Greta Garbo's first residence when she arrived here.

A mile-long wharf was built in 1893; Santa Monica was Los Angeles' major port of call for the next 10 years, until Los Angeles annexed San Pedro, to the south. The present pier, the oldest pleasure pier on the West Coast, was built in 1909.

Bringing It Up to Date

Santa Monica is still used extensively for location shooting, as it has been from the time of the first movies shot in Hollywood. There is a new trend: motion picture studios are moving from their historic locations to Santa Monica, as when MGM left Culver City after its original studio was sold to Sony.

La Monica Ballroom, which was once at the Pier, could hold 10,000 dancers.

These days Santa Monica is a small but cosmopolitan city that lies between its own spectacular beach and the eighth-largest city in the world. The style of dress tends to combine urban sophistication and laid-back seaside casualness, with a dash of an ongoing Hollywood/Beverly Hills hipness. Comfortable, casual clothes work well here year-round. There is no formal dress code anywhere; jackets and ties are optional even at the city's most elegant (and expensive) restaurants.

Climate

In the beach area, a jacket, sweater or perhaps just a sweatshirt can come in handy. You may start out in a hot sun with the temperature around 72°F (22°C), but if a fog bank suddenly moves in from the ocean, the temperature can plunge to the mid-50s. Even though it is only 22 miles from downtown Los Angeles, Santa Monica's climate is vastly different because of the ocean breezes. Los Angeles is inland and has a desert-like environment.

*In Santa
Monica the
sun shines
more than
300 days a
year.*

MONTHLY TEMPERATURES & RAINFALL		
	HIGH/LOW	RAINFALL
JANUARY	64° / 50°F	5"
FEBRUARY	64° / 50°F	5"
MARCH	63° / 51°F	5"
APRIL	64° / 53°F	3"
MAY	65° / 56°F	1"
JUNE	68° / 59°F	0"
JULY	71° / 61°F	0"
AUGUST	72° / 63°F	0"
SEPTEMBER	72° / 62°F	1"
OCTOBER	70° / 59°F	1"
NOVEMBER	68° / 54°F	3"
DECEMBER	65° / 50°F	4"
AVERAGE	67° / 56°F	2.3"

Getting Here

From LAX

By Car

*Route 66
runs through
Santa
Monica as
Santa
Monica
Boulevard.*

Take Sepulveda Boulevard north; turn left on Lincoln Boulevard at the north edge of the airport. Follow Lincoln through Marina del Rey and Venice to Santa Monica. Turn left at Rose Avenue to get to Main Street; left at Pico Boulevard for beach hotels; or left at Wilshire Boulevard for downtown Santa Monica and the Fairmont Miramar.

By Bus

Take the free airport bus to Lot C, then get on Big Blue Bus #3, which stops at 4th Street in downtown Santa Monica; fare is 75¢.

By Shuttle

Catch the shuttle bus, really a van, on the traffic island outside the terminal. Approximate fare to Santa Monica is $17 for the first passenger, $11 for each additional person. Companies include **Prime Time Shuttle**, ☎ 800-733-8267, www.primetimeshuttle.com; or **Super Shuttle**, ☎ 310-782-6600, www.supershuttle.com.

By Taxi

Fares run between $25 and $30, plus a $2.50 airport fee. Call **Star One Yellow Cab**, ☎ 310-260-9941, or **United Independent Taxi**, ☎ 310-821-1000 or 800-822-TAXI.

By Air

Santa Monica Municipal Airport, 3223 Donald Douglas Loop South, ☎ 310-390-7606.

Santa Monica is only 8 miles (13 km) from LAX and 13 miles (20 km) from downtown LA.

From Downtown Los Angeles

By Car

Take the Harbor Freeway (110) south to Santa Monica Freeway (10) and go west to the end.

By Bus

MTA's Metro Rapid Bus #720 comes straight out Wilshire Boulevard from the downtown area, makes fewer stops than other buses, and an electronic device onboard changes all the stop lights to green, so it is faster; the fare is $1.35.

Santa Monica Big Blue Bus #10 comes out Santa Monica Freeway to Bundy, then down Santa Monica Boulevard; it's $1.25. Phone ☎ 800-COMMUTE (266-6883) for information on either.

Getting Around

By Car

Santa Monica is laid out in a grid of streets running north-south and east-west; those parallel to the beach are numbered, and run from 1st to 26th in the north part of town, to 34th south of I-10. Some of the north-south streets are named, so what would be 1st Street is Ocean Avenue; 8th Street is Lincoln; and 13th Street is called Euclid. East of 26th the streets are named after colleges: Princeton, Harvard, Yale, and so on. A few blocks farther east is Bundy, marking the edge of town.

When you reach Pico from the south on Ocean Avenue, the street that continues straight ahead is Neilson Way; Ocean Avenue veers off to the right and provides beach access.

DISTANCES FROM SANTA MONICA TO...

Venice . . . . 2 miles, center to center
Marina del Rey . . . . 3 miles
Malibu . . . . 4 miles
Beverly Hills . . . . 7 miles
West Hollywood. . . . . 8 miles
Hollywood . . . . 9 miles
Downtown Los Angeles . . . . 17 miles
Universal Studios . . . . 10 miles

All the major hotels and most restaurants and shops are close to the ocean in a 12-block stretch from Montana Avenue to just south of Pico Boulevard. North of Pico, most of the avenues running east-west are named for states (such as Montana). South of Pico you will see names that are common in California, such as Bay, Grant, Pine and Pacific streets, and names with a nautical sound, such as Pier and Navy.

It helps to know that building numbers start with the 100 block at Adelaide Drive on the north side of town and increase as you go south; Rose Avenue is the 3500 block. The north-south running Third Street Promenade, in the center of downtown between Wilshire and Broadway, is numbered from 1200 to 1400. Building numbers on east-west streets start with the 100 block at Ocean and increase as you go east.

By Bus

The Tide Shuttle is an electric bus that runs in a continuous loop every 15 minutes, starting at the Promenade and Broadway; it travels south on Ocean to Marine, then north again on Main and Fourth streets back to the Promenade. Shuttles run Sunday-Thursday, noon-10pm; Friday and Saturday, noon-midnight. The fare is 25¢; seniors and handicapped, 10¢.

Most Santa Monica and Los Angeles attractions can be reached by the Santa Monica Big Blue Bus or Los Angeles Metropolitan Transportation Authority (MTA). (Senior citizens travel on Santa Monica's Big Blue Bus at reduced fare by showing a Medicare Card.) For route information: Big Blue Bus, ☎ 310-451-5444; MTA Metro Bus, ☎ 213-626-4455, or 800-266-6883.

Santa Monica's Big Blue Bus has been named North America's Best Transit System three times.

Who Lives Here? 👓

The north end of Santa Monica is the preferred area for many celebrities. Popular neighborhoods are near San Vicente Boulevard, La Mesa Drive and Adelaide Drive, all just at the edge of town. The tall condo at the north end of the Palisades, at 101 Ocean Avenue, is also a favorite (it's a few feet over the line dividing Santa Monica from Pacific Palisades, but everyone regards it as part of Santa Monica). Anne Bancroft, Mel Brooks, Jeff Bridges, Larry Hagman, Dylan McDermott and Sylvester Stallone all live in this area.

☞ **DID YOU KNOW?**

Shirley Temple was born at 924 24th Street, just south of Montana Avenue (sorry, the house is not open to the public).

Other residents of Santa Monica are Jamie Lee Curtis, rocker Eric Clapton and Heather Graham, who lives in Ocean Park (the southern part of Santa Monica by the beach).

Santa Monica's first mayor was a descendant of one of the old Land Grant families, and the father of Leo Carrillo – an actor most famous as Pancho, sidekick to The Cisco Kid.

☞ **DID YOU KNOW?**

The 25-foot plastic statue of a ballerina with a clown's head that's perched above the front door of a building at Main Street and Rose Avenue is Jonathan Borofsky's Ballerina Clown; it was much acclaimed by our local art critics when it first went up. There has not been much said about it lately though; perhaps that is because the ballerina's leg, which used to kick, has not moved for several years. Arthritis?

On Location

From the earliest days of movie-making, Santa Monica has been an active site for every studio. How could it be otherwise? It is such an easy drive straight out the boulevard from downtown or Hollywood, and you arrive in a town with gorgeous beaches, a handy pier and a very special character.

The beach community was first invaded by the fledgling movie industry in 1908 when Kalem, Essanay and Vitagraph all had studios here. The brick building at 1438 Second Street was at one time Santa Monica's City Hall, and much later was the home of Vitagraph. By 1915 the studios had all moved to Hollywood, but Santa Monica continues as a popular place for location shooting to this day.

Second Street is where the original Gold's Gym was located, near what is now the Santa Monica Place mall. Gold's is where Arnold Schwarzenegger starred in his first pic, *Pumping Iron*. Later, Santa Monica Place itself was used in Schwarzenegger's *Terminator 2*.

Walk out the Colorado Street doors of Santa Monica Mall Place, go straight ahead down Main Street one block and you have arrived at the **Santa Monica Civic Auditorium**, where *The Astronaut's Wife* was shot a few years ago. The Civic was the site of the Academy Awards from 1961 to 1968.

If you walk out the Broadway doors of Santa Monica Place you will be facing the **Third Street Promenade**, where *PeeWee's Big Adventure*, among others, was shot. Scenic Ocean Avenue is a favorite backdrop for Hollywood films and TV shows such as *The Practice*, *Ally McBeal* and *Jack & Jill*; and movies, including *Jerry McGuire*, *Get Shorty*, *Pulp Fiction* and *Speed*. St. Monica's Church, 715 California Avenue, is where Barry Fitzgerald and Bing Crosby were priests in *Going My Way*.

The metal piece of "art" spanning Wilshire Boulevard as you enter Santa Monica is called "The Big Wave."

⭐ **TIP**

Most of Santa Monica's major hotels, attractions, shopping streets and better restaurants are conveniently located within a 14-block radius that includes the beach and the pier.

The Pier was the location for slapstick silent comedies from the moment the first hand-cranked camera arrived.

Charlie Chaplin, Ben Turpin and Laurel and Hardy all used the Pier and, in later days *They Shoot Horses, Don't They?* and *The Glenn Miller Story* were made here when the Pier still had a ballroom. It is also where Paul Newman made the carousel go round in *The Sting*; it stood in for Coney Island in *Funny Girl*; and Natalie Wood's mom was the fortune teller here in *Inside Daisy Clover*.

The Santa Monica Pier is at the end of Colorado Boulevard.

In fact, so many films have been shot at the Pier, we will just list a few. Feature films include *Ruthless People*; *The Next Best Thing*; *The Babysitter's Club*; *Deuce Bigalow, Male Gigolo*; *The Kid*; *Joe Dirt*; *Tom Cats*; *Forrest Gump*; *The Net* and *Mr. Bean*. Television series that have used the Pier include *Three's Company*; *Beverly Hills, 90210*; *Melrose Place*; *The Huntress*; *Snoops*; *Seinfeld*; *V.I.P.*; *Level 9*; *SPF-30*; *The X-Files*; *Seven Days* and *Follow the Stars Home* (Hallmark Movie). Among the performers who have shot music videos here are Selena, Jessica Simpson, Rod Stewart and Chris Isaac.

Santa Monica's Beach has stood in for beaches all over the world for almost a century, not always successfully. There is a story about a picture with an East Coast setting, where the screenplay called for a scene on a beach with the sun rising over the Atlantic. The producer, not wanting to spend the money to send a crew across the country, had a brilliant idea. "We'll shoot a sunset on the beach in Santa Monica and reverse the negative." So they did, and a few days later sat in a screening room at the studio and watched the result. A great-looking beach, the sun rising on schedule over the ocean – and the seagulls all flying backward.

Best Places to Stay

Hotels

The best hotels tend to be either on the bluff overlooking the ocean or on the beach at sea level. In Santa Monica, because of the beach and resort atmosphere, winter rates tend to be lower than summer rates. If you fly into LAX, look for a bank of telephones with direct lines to local hotels. Most have free buses they will send to pick you up.

The accommodations price scale can be found on page 39.

⭐ **TIP**

In Santa Monica, you have the right to inspect your room before you accept it. Report problems to City of Santa Monica, City Attorney Office for Consumer Affairs, 1685 Main Street, Santa Monica, CA 90401, ☎ 310-854-8336.

THE FAIRMONT MIRAMAR HOTEL
101 Wilshire Boulevard
Santa Monica, CA 90401
☎ 310-576-7777, fax 310-458-7912
www.fairmont.com
Expensive

When people in the LA area think of Santa Monica, they tend to think of the Miramar, now called the Fairmont Miramar Hotel. The original building was the home of John Jones, founder of Santa Monica, who built his mansion on this site on the bluffs overlooking the ocean. His family planted the Moreton Bay fig tree in the front yard in 1890; the tree still stands in front of the hotel. Greta Garbo moved into the hotel when she first came to Hollywood, and stayed four years. Betty Grable was singing with the band playing in the lounge when she was discovered.

Miramar is Spanish for "view of the sea."

The garden bungalows have hardwood floors, French windows, and marble bathrooms with oversize tubs; some have private balconies and terraces, some have ocean views. Jean Harlow stayed in one of the bungalows, as did, much later, Marilyn Monroe. Jean Simmons stayed seven months. Others who preferred the bungalows included Eleanor Roosevelt, Charles Lindbergh and Supreme Court Justice Earl Warren; President Clinton stayed several times in a tower suite.

Jane Fonda filmed several of her exercise videos in the Miramar bungalows.

The rooms are supplied with plush robes, and beds are made up with goose-down duvets and triple sheeting. The on-site restaurant, the **Grille**, is popular with the locals for dinner, afternoon tea and Sunday brunch. There is room service, concierge service, a health and fitness center and beauty complex and, because this is Santa Monica, bike and in-line skate rentals.

THE MIRAMAR FIG TREE

More than 100 years ago a sailor from Australia, whose name is now forgotten, got off his ship and went into a local watering hole carrying a sapling of a Moreton Bay fig tree. Unable to pay for his drinks, he gave the tree to the bartender in lieu of money. The bartender gave it to Georgina Jones, wife of the founder of Santa Monica, who planted it in their front yard. Their home eventually became a hotel, but successive owners have been careful not to disturb the Moreton Bay Fig.

The tree is now over 80 feet high and has a 120-foot network of branches. It is still a focal point for outdoor meetings and local festivities. The figs, incidentally, are ornamental, not edible, and fall off each year.

The hotel's appeal to celebrities continues down through the decades. In the 1930s, Gloria Swanson, Humphrey - Bogart, Noah Beery Jr., Claudette Colbert and Cary Grant were fans of the Miramar's nightclub. In the '40s it was a favorite of Randolph Scott and Jimmy Stewart. Stewart Granger was a visitor for more than 20 years; he liked to get his hair cut in the hotel barbershop. Dick Van Dyke was a regular for lunch. In the '50s Lana Turner was married at the Miramar, and Susan Hayward, Louis Jourdan and Anthony Quinn were frequent guests. In more recent years, Olivia Newton-John spent her honeymoon here, and Faye Dunaway, Judge Reinhold and Debra Winger have been long-term guests. John Travolta is an occasional visitor; and Michael Keaton brings his son for Sunday breakfast.

The Miramar has long been a favorite locale for movie shoots; movies include *That Touch of Mink* (with Cary Grant and Doris Day in the pool); *Oh, God!*; *The Joy of Sex*; and *The Check is in the Mail*. Many TV shows have been filmed here as well, including *Moonlighting*, *Dallas*, *Dynasty*, *Hart to Hart*, *Remington Steele*, and *Knots Landing*.

Alan Alda often stayed here while filming *M*A*S*H*, Anthony Quinn while making *A Walk in the Clouds*, and Mel Gibson while shooting *Tequila Sunrise*.

FOR PHYSICALLY CHALLENGED GUESTS

The Fairmont Miramar Hotel has special equipment available on request, including smoke detectors with strobe lights, superprint and supercom phone devices, sonic alert phone signalers and tub seats with handrails.

THE GEORGIAN HOTEL
1415 Ocean Avenue
Santa Monica, CA 90401
☎ 310-395-9945, 800-538-8147, fax 310-656-0904
www.georgianhotel.com
Expensive

This moderate sized hotel (56 rooms and 28 one-bedroom suites) is another that is in a great location: it's across the street from Palisades Park and the ocean, and two minutes' walk from the Santa Monica Pier and the Promenade. Eight stories tall and architecturally striking, the art deco style building was opened in 1933 as a seaside apartment hotel. Breakfast only is served in the **Speakeasy** restaurant, which was once a hangout for Fatty Arbuckle, Carole Lombard, Clark Gable and gangster Bugsy Siegel, whose dubious life was celebrated in Warren Beatty's *Bugsy*. A member of the Historic Hotels of America, it is an inviting hotel with a multilingual staff, concierge service and a complimentary reception Wednesday afternoon. Room service is catered in from nearby Ocean Avenue Seafood. There are non-smoking and handicapped-accessible rooms available.

The Beach Communities

★★ HOTEL CASA DEL MAR

1910 Ocean Front Walk
Santa Monica, CA 90405
☎ 310-581-5533, 800-898-6999, fax 310-581-5503
www.hotelcasadelmar.com
Deluxe

Casa Del Mar is one of only two hotels on the beach in Santa Monica. The others are on the bluff above.

Casa Del Mar has a history. It opened during the Roaring Twenties as the most opulent of the exclusive beach clubs that were built along the Santa Monica coast. Its elite, well-heeled membership included many Hollywood celebrities. There were Sunday afternoon concerts in the Grand Ballroom, barbecues on the sand, Saturday night dinner dances, elaborate floor shows, championship aquatic events in the Olympic size, heated indoor pool. Plus elegant hotel rooms and a private beach for members only.

Prohibition was in full force then, in 1926, but illegal booze (the good stuff, not bathtub gin) flowed at Casa Del Mar, along with the illegal slot machines and late-night skinny-dipping in "The Plunge" (the pre-World War II name for a big commercial swimming pool). The local newspaper, the now-defunct *Evening Outlook*, didn't mention any of it. Its big advertisers were all members of the club. Casa Del Mar got through the Depression but never recovered from World War II, when the Navy used it to house personnel. It reopened in 1999.

Present-day celebrities have returned to replace the old ones. Shaquille O'Neal, Oprah Winfrey, Sharon Stone, Martin Scorcese, Whoopi Goldberg, Kevin Bacon, Steven Spielberg and the Indiana Pacers when they were in the finals with the Lakers. There have been quite a few others since it reopened. We mention these only because they have already been mentioned in the local papers.

The hotel now re-creates the traditional look and feel of the '20s. We were impressed by the dramatic entry rotunda with a royal blue ceiling of stars, and the double staircase to the main lobby with its fruitwood paneling, plush rugs and stone fireplaces. The rooms have gauzy white floor-to-ceiling draperies, wood Venetian blinds and whirlpool tubs.

For dining, there is **Oceanfront**, with California cuisine; the **Veranda**, off the lobby, for light dining; and the **Palm Terrace** by the pool. Complete room service is available

24 hours, with a late-night menu until 6am. A 24-hour concierge provides service, service, service.

★★ HOTEL OCEANA
849 Ocean Avenue
Santa Monica, CA 90403
☎ 310-393-0486, 800-777-0758, fax 310-458-1182
www.hoteloceana.com
Deluxe

If you prefer a smaller, boutique-style hotel, the 63-suite Oceana may be for you. Some of the suites look out on a tropical palm-studded courtyard with pool, the others have a view of the Pacific. There is an outdoor garden area where you can enjoy a complimentary continental breakfast and newspaper, or you may have the meal served in your room. (The hotel is very big on service.) Every suite has a kitchen, and lunch or dinner can be served in your suite. There is a lounge, which we have found to be very nice for sipping a cocktail while gazing at the ocean, and a health club open 24 hours with Cybex equipment, treadmills, StairMasters, and facial and massage services.

Hotel Oceana's room service comes from the nearby Wolfgang Puck Café.

A nice walk of about a half-mile brings you to the upscale Montana Avenue shopping area; it is about the same distance to the more moderate Promenade. Across the street is long, thin Palisades Park (you look out across the thinnest part); below that are 189 steps to the beach.

This is a good, small, quiet, private hotel, which is why it has long been a favorite of many celebrities. The hotel strongly wishes to keep it that way, so we promised not to mention any names. If you check in and find yourself sitting next to someone whose autograph you would really like to have, please restrain yourself. Don't embarrass us.

LE MERIGOT
1740 Ocean Avenue
Santa Monica, CA 90401
☎ 310-395-9700, fax 310-395-9200
www.LeMerigotHotel.com
Expensive

On Ocean Avenue overlooking the beach (a block downhill) and the ocean, Le Merigot might be on the Côte d'Azur. Rooms have Frette linens, down comforters, feather pillows, oversize towels and plush robes. There is an outdoor pool, 24-hour in-room dining, valet service, and concierge. **Cézanne's** menu is California cuisine with a French flair, and has a popular Sunday brunch.

★★ HOTEL SHANGRI-LA

1301 Ocean Avenue
Santa Monica, CA 90401
☎ 310-394-2791, 800-345-STAY, fax 310-451-3351
www.shangrila-hotel.com
Moderate-Expensive

Five blocks south of the Oceana is another small hotel (only 55 rooms in a seven-story building). The striking art deco building is on a corner across the street from Palisades Park with a great view of the ocean, and it is only a block-and-a-half from the Promenade. It has been here since 1939, and from the beginning was a sort of hideaway for celebrities. It was the kind of wonderful seaside place where, in the old days, Hollywood couples would go for what used to be called a "dirty weekend." Couples still go, it simply isn't called that anymore.

Scenes for pictures and TV episodes are shot here every once in a while; we remember seeing the hotel in *Bodies of Evidence*. Even with that, people tend to forget about the place, the hotel hardly advertises and it is known for what it *doesn't* offer: pool, bar, restaurant, room service, or valet parking, which keeps some people away. But that very lack of publicity and paparazzi is what attracts others. Diane Keaton is a fan of the hotel, and Bruce Webber shoots here often (*Let's Get Lost* was filmed here).

There is an unusually wide range of prices, from studios with living/bedroom combinations, single or double, for $160 a day; to two-bedroom, two-bath with sundeck overlooking the sea for up to four people, for $450-$540.

★★ SHUTTERS ON THE BEACH

One Pico Boulevard
Santa Monica, CA 90405
☎ 310-458-0030, 800-334-9000, fax 310-458-4589
www.shuttersonthebeach.com
Deluxe

This is an attractive hotel. Seen from the beach – it sits right at the edge of the sand – it looks to us somewhat like a larger version of Marion Davies' beach house. And that is exactly the atmosphere Shutters intends to convey, invoking the casual, inviting architecture of historic beach resorts and cottages reminiscent of the Southern California coast of the 1920s.

Sliding shuttered doors and shuttered windows in the rooms and public rooms help give it its distinctive exterior look. Inside, throughout the hotel, is original art, lithos and *objets d'art* by artists like David Hockney, Jasper Johns and Roy Lichtenstein. The 186 rooms and 12 suites aim at, and achieve, comfortable luxury. The marble bathrooms contain large whirlpool tubs near windows that open to an outside view from the bath.

The main restaurant is **One Pico**, with windows that wrap around three sides for views of the coastline. **Pedals Café**, next to the bicycle path, serves both indoors and outdoors for breakfast, lunch and dinner. The **Lobby Lounge** is our favorite place for a cocktail at sunset. Afternoon tea is also served there; and the chef will make up an elegant picnic basket, which would be great to take along if you were lucky enough to be invited to a box at the Hollywood Bowl.

This is one of those places that is very protective of its celebrity guests, so we promised not to mention any names. But it has been popular with stars and sports figures who like to stay at the beach from the time it opened in 1993. It is losing some of its cachet, and some celebrity guests, now that the even grander beachfront Casa del Mar has opened across the street. The owners probably don't worry, though. They also own Casa del Mar.

A Santa Monica city room tax of 12% is added to your final bill.

★ TIP

A complete listing of more than 30 hotel accommodations is in the free *Visitors Guide* at the Visitors Center, 1400 Ocean Avenue, in Palisades Park.

Best Places to Eat

Man: *How do you like your coffee?*
Woman: *Alone.*
– Jeff Chandler, Joan Crawford, *Female on the Beach*

The dining price scale can be found on page 42.

For a long time anyone who drove to Santa Monica for lunch or dinner from somewhere else usually wanted an ocean view along with the meal, so the oceanfront restaurants tended to be popular; occasionally they were even among the best. But lately people have been coming to Santa Monica for the food itself. Several of the new gourmet places are on Ocean Boulevard, but in some, the dining room is inside where you can't see the water. This is pretty good territory for celebrity-spotting while dining.

There are more than 450 restaurants and cafés in Santa Monica.

There are several expensive, gourmet restaurants that fit the bill, but don't make the mistake of always going by fancy looks and high prices. One of the most popular eating places in Santa Monica with stars is the least expensive and least prepossessing of the restaurants we list here.

Fine Dining

★★ ABIQUIU
1413 5th Street
☎ 310-395-8611
Contemporary Southwestern
Expensive

If you saw the very funny movie *Get Shorty* a few years ago, there was a scene where John Travolta, during lunch in a modern Hollywood restaurant, threw a bad guy down the open staircase. That was shot in Abiquiu here in Santa

Monica. They were able to shoot a lunch scene because the restaurant is open only for dinner. The décor includes lots of blond wood and stark black-and-white photos evoking the Southwestern United States, which is the area that influences the menu. Lime, green chilis and tequila are used as accents to transform what might otherwise be ordinary dishes. Abiquiu is open Monday-Thursday and Sunday, 6-9pm; Friday, until 10pm; Saturday, until 11pm.

★★ CHINOIS ON MAIN
2709 Main Street
☎ 310-392-9025
Franco-Asian
Very Expensive

This fusion of French and Asian cooking has been extremely popular, especially here at Chinois. The "Asian" part is mostly Chinese and Japanese, with such dishes as tempura Ahi tuna, grilled Mongolian lamb chops and Shanghai lobster. There is one room, not large but with a lot of visuals to keep the eyes occupied while eating: green tabletops, a hammered copper range hood, neon signs. The counter is a popular place to eat, and to watch the cooks preparing the food. The noise level can get very high when it is crowded, enough so that we have friends who went once and loved the food but have never gone back because of the sound level. Chinois is open for lunch, Wednesday-Friday, 11:30am-2pm; for dinner nightly, 6-10:30pm; on Sunday, 5:30-10pm. Reservations are strongly advised.

★ TIP

As far as the high noise level inside restaurants like Chinois on Main is concerned, a highly scientific survey (it took us a half-hour) predicts that those people over 60 years of age hate noisy restaurants, where they have to shout to be heard across a small table, while those under 40 seek such places out. No results are in yet on those between 40 and 60.

The Beach Communities

THE GRILLE
The Fairmont Miramar Hotel
101 Wilshire Boulevard
☎ 310-319-3111
American cuisine
Moderate-Expensive

This is definitely not a place serving whatever-is-the-trend-of-the-moment food. The menu is traditional and solid, the setting is casually elegant. Look for Napoleon of filet mignon with roasted figs (definitely not from the Moreton Bay fig tree out front); bone-in pork with Calvados honey glaze; and grilled Ahi tuna. Breakfasts are the big, old-fashioned kind, and for lunch you might try a lobster club sandwich. A popular item is the Cobb salad, which you do not see on many menus these days. It makes a great lunch all by itself.

You have a choice of dining in the attractive dining room, with rich wood and an exhibition kitchen, or on an outdoor patio and terrace overlooking the gardens – perfect for sunny days and warm evenings. For those who might want a late lunch or early dinner, there is an afternoon menu served 3-6pm with a combination of lunch and dinner items, and on summer Sundays the classic buffet brunch served in the garden is a big community event. Open Sunday-Thursday, 6:30am-10pm; Friday and Saturday to 11pm. Sunday brunch is served from May to September, 11:30am-3:30pm.

★★ THE IVY AT THE SHORE
1541 Ocean Avenue
☎ 310-393-3113
American
Very Expensive

A spin-off from the original Ivy on Robertson in West Hollywood, this one has different décor but the same food and prices. Large portions of crab cakes, fried chicken, meat loaf, fish 'n chips and such are nicely cooked, but at these prices why shouldn't they be? The payoff is the celebrities who eat here; perhaps not as many as on Robertson, but it'll do. Lunch, 11:30am-4:45pm; dinner, 5-11pm; the kitchen closes earlier on Sunday. Brunch starts at 11am Saturday and Sunday.

★★ JIRAFFE

502 Santa Monica Boulevard
☎ 310-917-6671
www.jirafferestaurant.com
California-French
Expensive

Chef/owner Raphael Lunetta calls his menu "sophisti-cated comfort food with strong French influences." Roast-ed beet salad with caramelized walnuts, cherries and goat cheese cream is a signature item. Lobster is, for a change, *not* advertised as "flown in fresh from Maine;" they serve fresh spiny lobsters from the Santa Barbara Channel Is-lands. There are also four- or eight-course tasting menus, and the Saturday night specials include a really tasty osso buco. JiRaffe is open for lunch, Tuesday-Friday, noon-2pm; dinner, Monday-Thursday, 6-10pm; Friday-Satur-day until 11pm; Sunday until 9pm only. Look for valet parking around the corner on 5th Street during lunch and dinner hours.

★★ MELISSE

1104 Wilshire Boulevard
☎ 310-395-0881
American-French
Expensive

The main dining room, decorated in yellow and green, with green and gold brocade fabric and Empire-style chairs, has an elegant flair. The menu is based on tradi-tional French cuisine, and the wine list is impressive. Lunch, Wednesday-Friday, noon-2pm; dinner, Monday-Friday, 6-10pm; Saturday, 5:30-10:30pm; Sunday, 5:30-9pm. Valet parking.

★★ SCHATZI ON MAIN

3110 Main Street
☎ 310-399-4800
Austrian
Moderate-Expensive

Just across Marine Street from M. Hanks Gallery (see page 442), this Austrian restaurant was built by Arnold Schwarzenegger a half-dozen years ago. He sold the res-taurant a few years back, but still comes in for his favorite food, and still owns the building. Monday-Friday, 11:30am-midnight; Saturday-Sunday, 9am-midnight.

★★ VALENTINO
3115 Pico Boulevard
☎ 310-829-4313
www.welovewine.com
Italian
Very Expensive

This restaurant is on an unprepossessing stretch of Pico with no other grand restaurants anywhere near, but the Jags and Rolls Royces keep rolling into the parking lot. The restaurant has been here for over 25 years; we have eaten here several times, usually on a birthday or anniversary. Piero Selvaggio, the owner, who is originally from Sicily, expanded it a few years ago but, in our opinion, the new rooms lost the charm of the old.

Valentino has received Wine Spectator's *Grand Award every year since 1981.*

The celebrities keep coming because the restaurant's food keeps winning national praise for "outstanding" this and "best" that. The wine cellar is considered one of the best in the country, with over 100,000 bottles. Though the cellar was substantially damaged in the 1994 earthquake, it is now better than ever, with over 2,000 choices, partially due to the help of loyal patrons and wine lovers from around the world who sent a bottle or two each to help rebuild it.

Valentino is open for dinner, Monday-Saturday, 5:30pm-10pm; lunch is served Friday, 11:30am-2:30pm. Reservations are strongly recommended. Take Pico to just east of Santa Monica Freeway (10), between the freeway and Centinela Avenue. Valet parking.

Casual Dining

★★ CAFE MONTANA
1534 Montana Avenue
☎ 310-829-3990
California cuisine
Inexpensive-Moderate

A toney café whose walls are brightened with posters of Oscar-nominated movies. Someone who went in for break-

fast recently reported that, at a table under a poster of Anthony Hopkins in *Titus*, was – surprise! – Anthony
Hopkins. Apparently that's not an unusual sight here.
Café Montana is open daily for breakfast and lunch, 8am-
3pm; for dinner, Monday-Thursday, 5:30pm-9:30pm; Friday-Saturday, 5:30pm-10pm; Sunday, 5:30pm-9pm. Brunch
is served on weekends, 11:45-3pm.

★★ CHEZ JAY

1657 Ocean Avenue
☎ 310-395-1741
American
Moderate

Mellow is the word for this dark joint with sawdust on the
floor where you can toss the shells after you crunch the
free peanuts at the bar. Celebrities have been coming in
here since the place opened over 40 years ago. Part of the
appeal is that they can be anonymous for a while; it does-
n't hurt that owner Jay Fiondella is an engaging personality. Clint Eastwood used to come in often, before he moved
to Carmel; he still drops in when he is in town shooting.
Dennis Hopper, who lives nearby in Venice, is often spotted here; Sean Penn, Julia Roberts and others are here occasionally, sometimes late at night after the kitchen is
supposedly closed.

*Chez Jay
owner Jay
Fiondella
says his res-
taurant is
"so dark you
don't know
what you're
eating or who
you're with."*

The fare is mostly steaks, shellfish and seafood; the banana mashed potatoes (no kidding) are a longtime favorite. There are only 12 tables in this small place with
nautical décor, so you might want to call ahead. There are
also 12 bar stools, but you cannot reserve those. Lunch is
served Monday-Friday, noon-2pm; dinner daily, 6-
10:30pm; the bar is open in the afternoon and until 2am.
Breakfast is served Saturday and Sunday from 9am.

SURF DOGS

2522 Main Street
Inside Surf Liquor Store
☎ 310-392-2819
Inexpensive

This is a hot dog joint for purists. Buns are toasted,
weiners are meaty and in natural casings so there is that
traditional (but not often found) snap when you bite into

them. Polish sausages have real flavor, with lots of garlic, and pastrami is lean but still has flavor.

Choose from a selection that includes hot dogs, Polish sausages, pastrami and chili, then make a combination. A dog with mustard, sauerkraut and onions is a Hang Ten Dog; a Polish with the same combo is a Main Street. Sauerkraut and pastrami is a Reuben. They run $2.69-$5.59; no credit cards. We tried the chili, but thought it was sort of bland.

YE OLDE KINGS HEAD PUB
116 Santa Monica Boulevard
☎ 310-451-1402
Inexpensive

It seems as if everyone visiting from Britain comes in here at least once, along with all the Brits who live here (and there are many), and a lot of the rest of us who live in or near Santa Monica. It is not just for the fish and chips or the steak and kidney pies, though they are good, but to enjoy the warm and friendly atmosphere that goes with them. For more about the pub, see pages 455, 456 and 457.

Afternoon Tea

THE FAIRMONT MIRAMAR HOTEL
101 Wilshire Boulevard
☎ 310-319-3113

The tradition of afternoon tea in Santa Monica started at the Miramar in 1889 with Georgina Jones, who was both English and the wife of John Jones, founder of the city. She served tea on the terrace of the Jones mansion, where the hotel is now, and the tradition has been carried on. These days it is served in the Koi Pond Lounge and Garden Terrace from 3-5pm daily. It includes, depending on how hungry you are, champagne and fresh strawberries, tea sandwiches, freshly baked scones with Devonshire cream, strawberry jam, assorted pastries and banana nut bread and, of course, many tea selections. The cost is from $14.50-$24.50.

Shop Till You Drop

*If this is the way things are going to be around here, I'm
going back to the Bonjour Tristesse Brassiere Company.*
　　　　　– Judy Holliday, *Bells Are Ringing*

Santa Monica is prime shopping territory. There are three
distinct shopping neighborhoods, and many more interesting shops are scattered around town. It wasn't always
this way. Santa Monica used to have one venerable, old-
fashioned but well-loved department store – Henshey's –
the kind of store where, right to the end, your money and
the handwritten order slip were sent via a vacuum tube to
the cashier on another floor. Everyone hated to see it go,
but it was inevitable after the big, modern mall, Santa
Monica Place, arrived.

> ★ **TIP**
>
> For a free map of Santa Monica's cen-
> tral shopping district and a list of all
> merchants, with addresses and phone
> numbers, write to the **Bayside Dis-
> trict Corporation**, 1351 Third
> Street Promenade, Suite 301, Santa
> Monica CA 90401; ☎ 310-393-8355,
> www.downtownsm.com.

On a celebrity-rating scale, **Montana Avenue** is where
you are most likely to find someone famous looking at the
same expensive knickknacks as you. There are no hard
statistics on this, but our gut feeling is that **Main Street**,
while it does have Chinois on Main, Wolfgang Puck's restaurant, and a few celebrity-prone shops, sees fewer. The
Third Street Promenade is not a great place to go on a
celebrity-hunt, it is too crowded; if someone is recognized,
he/she is likely to find themselves in the middle of a mob.

Main Street

Edgemar, which houses a collection of shops and eateries at 2401 Main Street, was designed by famed architect Frank O. Gehry.

In about 12 blocks, from Pico Boulevard to Navy Street, this street offers a varied range of options for walking, browsing, shopping, eating and probably a few others things, depending on your personal predilections. If you have time and just want to saunter along seeing the sights and enjoying the smog-free air (one of Santa Monica's big attractions), the densest selection of shops is from Hollister Street (the 2400 block) to Marine Street (the 3000 block). Here is a small, selective sampling of the more than 160 merchants on Main.

★ TIP

For a good map of this district, contact the **Main Street Merchants Association**, ☎ 310-899-9555.

ZJ BOARDING HOUSE
2619 Main Street
☎ 310-392-5646, fax 310-392-9907
www.zjboardinghouse.com

Surely the biggest selection of boards and board fashions along the coast. We mean surfboards, snowboards and skateboards, plus everything to go with any of those: beach fashions, footwear and accessories for everyone from tots to the tottering. The staff is good about answering questions and providing help. Surfboard and snowboard rentals and surfing instruction are also available. Open Monday-Saturday, 10am-8pm; Sunday, 10am-6pm.

TIP

Street parking is hard to find on or near Main Street, but there are metered parking lots behind the buildings on the west side of the street the length of all the blocks from Kinney to Hollister.

IMPOLITIC
2665 Main Street
New Orleans Building
☎ 310-396-2720
www.impolitic.com

At Impolitic, look for original drawings of political cartoons by artists like Pulitzer Prize-winner Paul Conrad (*Los Angeles Times*). It's fun to go in and browse, even if you have no intention of buying, just to scan the art on the walls. This is really high-quality artwork. Open Wednesday-Saturday, 10am-5pm (hours vary).

★ SANTA MONICA TRADING CO.
2705 Main Street
☎ 310-392-4806

A long, narrow store specializing in movie posters and books; everything is on shelves against the walls up to the ceiling, on stacks on the floor; there are more books and posters heaped on tables down the middle, and on into the back room. Whatever you want to know is probably in an old book in there somewhere. It can be great fun to spend a while browsing among it all. Open Wednesday-Friday, noon-5pm; Saturday, 11am-5pm.

NEWS STAND ETC.
2726 Main Street
☎ 310-396-7722

This is where you'll find hometown and international newspapers and magazines. Open daily, 6am-11pm.

ANNIE ROSE
2806 Main Street
☎ 310-396-3377

Visit Annie Rose for hip women's beach attire as well as Hawaiian shirts for men. Open daily but with a laid-back schedule, so you might want to phone ahead.

★★ M. HANKS GALLERY
3008 Main Street
☎ 310-392-8820

You'll see good things on the walls in this gallery specializing in work by African-American artists; quite a few pieces sold here now hang in celebrities' homes. Owner Eric Hanks (M. is his daughter) has asked us not to name names of some of those who drop in here, but this is a well-known gallery in celeb circles. Thursday-Saturday, noon-5pm, and by appointment.

Montana Avenue

To appreciate what Montana Avenue is now you had to have known it in earlier times. Languid was the word for the collection of mom-and-pop shops – a barber shop, a coin-operated laundry, a hardware store, service station – that were strung out between 7th and 17th streets. It was a friendly place to shop and had most of what the neighborhood needed, and the neighborhood was insulated from the rest of the city: to the south, between Montana and Wilshire, are apartments and townhouses; on the other side as far as San Vicente are tree-lined streets with vintage single-family homes.

Like harbingers of things to come, a few boutiques appeared in the 1970s; by the mid-'80s out went the dry cleaners, gas stations and hardware stores, all replaced by spas, galleries, artsy home décor shops, trendy antique stores and coffee houses, coffee houses and more coffee houses. Since the area north of Wilshire Boulevard is upscale Santa Monica, and north of Montana is upper-upscale Santa Monica, it is all sort of upscale-chic. It is pretty much a replay of what happened to New York's Upper West Side: if you are a visitor it may be a delight, but if you live there and you want to buy a hammer and some nails, it can be a pain.

⚠ WARNING!

Parking is a problem along Montana. Have coins for the meters, and know that parking on some side streets is restricted; read the signs before parking.

Many celebrities shop along Montana. Kate Capshaw and Rita Wilson are seen often; so are Lauralee Bell from *The Young and the Restless*, and Madonna when she is in town. Arnold Schwarzenegger and his wife Maria Shriver and their children live in Pacific Palisades, just to the north, but are often here shopping. The attraction is that there are no big chain stores as yet, just unique shops, each imbued with the individual vision of its owner, which is what makes it worthwhile, and fun, to come to Montana.

You will soon see that the avenue is definitely aimed at women shoppers; while there are over 30 places showing women's clothes and five devoted to babies and children, you will find only two for men. More numbers: there are 17 antiques and furniture stores and seven coffee bars along the 10-block strip. You'll find more about Montana Avenue at www.montanaave.com.

★ JASON VASS GALLERY
1210-A Montana Avenue
☎ 310-395-2048, fax 310-395-4541

Vass is a well-known, respected dealer in international vintage Belle Epoch, art nouveau, art deco, propaganda and movie posters, circa 1880-1950. Open Tuesday-Sunday, noon-7pm.

WOVEN LEGENDS
1302 Montana Avenue
☎ 310-451-9008

This is truly an unusual carpet store. You will find neither handwoven antique carpets made with natural dyes, nor new, machine-made carpets made with cheap chemical dyes. Instead, remarkably, these are new carpets made with natural dyes, woven in remote Turkish villages by people who have re-created the long-forgotten artistry.

George Jevremovic, the owner, went to Turkey in 1978 and spent years nourishing the idea of revitalizing the carpet industry. The villagers had to learn how to make natural dyes, using such things as milkweed for yellow, madder root for red, indigo for blue and walnut for black. And they learned how to weave on hand looms, in the ancient way, using wool from "fat-tailed" sheep. In the book *Oriental Rugs Today, a Guide to the Best in New Carpets From the East* (Berkeley Hills Books, 2000), author Emmett Eiland says "Jevremovic was the first," and calls it a renaissance. Open Monday-Saturday, 10am-6pm; Sunday, 11am-6pm.

★★ ROOM WITH A VIEW
1600 Montana Avenue
☎ 310-998-5858

In this shop you'll find a wide range of fine housewares, from silverware to linens with an elegant country feeling; robes and towels; glassware; silver trays. Lauralee Bell of *The Young and the Restless*, who shops here, likes the "girly stuff. It's a chick store." There's parking in back. Open Monday-Saturday, 10am-6pm; Sunday, noon-5pm.

Third Street Promenade

The Third Street Promenade is a pedestrian-only bazaar.

In recent years the Promenade has become a popular destination for people from all over Los Angeles. Add to that the visitors from the rest of the country and abroad, mostly Europeans, and you'll know why it is so often crowded.

This busy part of Santa Monica is between Wilshire and Broadway, from Ocean Avenue to Fifth Street. The heart of the area is the three-block walking street (no cars, hence the name Promenade) along Third Street from Wilshire to Broadway. Browsers, diners, shoppers, moviegoers and people watchers stroll along enjoying the shops, boutiques, vending carts, eateries, bookstores, street performers and movie theaters, all in a lively, friendly atmosphere.

TATTOO ANYONE?

Henna tattoo artists were once prevalent on Santa Monica's Third Street Promenade. The brown-tinted designs wear off in about two weeks, which makes them perfect for someone who wants a temporary body adornment. But then someone used permanent hair dye instead of henna, and the patron sued the city. As of this writing, the city has banned henna tattoo artists from the Promenade, even though actress Michelle Phillips, one of the original members of The Mamas and The Papas, joined in a demonstration supporting the artists. If you still want a temporary tattoo, try the Venice Boardwalk, where they are endemic.

Mimes, jugglers, harpists and dueling saxophones are common on the Promenade.

To get here from out of town, take the Santa Monica Freeway to the Fourth Street exit; turn right. There are parking structures along both sides of the Third Street Promenade, accessible either from Second or Fourth. Spaces are metered, but the first two hours are free.

Elsewhere in Santa Monica

There are other hot spots away from the heavily publicized streets where you might find just what you need.

Pico Boulevard

This is a small district located 30-some blocks east of the beach along Pico, around the Centinela off-ramp of the Santa Monica freeway; the boulevard is known mostly for **Valentino**, probably the best-known Italian restaurant in Los Angeles (see page 436).

COLLEGE OF THE STARS

Santa Monica College, 1900 Pico Boulevard, was named by *Rolling Stone* among the "Ten of the Best" community colleges in the nation. The college's **Academy of Entertainment & Technology** trains students in digital animation and new media. The school's award-winning radio station, KCRW (89.9 FM), is the flagship station for National Public Radio. Alumni include actors James Dean, Dustin Hoffman, Arnold Schwarzenegger, Gloria Stuart (*Titanic)* and singer Rickie Lee Jones. Oh, yes, and Monica Lewinsky and madam-to-the-stars Heidi Fleiss.

CAPRICE FINE FRENCH PASTRIES

3213 Pico Boulevard
☎ 310-453-1932
www.capricefrenchpastries.com

Caprice is known for gourmet cakes, cookies and pastries, and particularly for their exquisite wedding cakes. Monday-Saturday, 7:30am-5:30pm.

McCABE'S GUITAR SHOP

3101 Pico Boulevard
☎ 310-828-4497
www.mccabesguitar.com

Pull the guitar-neck door handle and you will step into one of the most famous acoustic instrument stores in the nation. Nothing has a dangling wire that plugs into a stack here, it's strictly a matter of strummin' and finger-pickin' a mellow spruce-and-rosewood box. Probably every folk great and many jazz performers have been in, either for an instrument or to play (see *After Dark*, page 481).

The store, which carries guitars, banjos, mandolins and much more, was founded in 1958 by furniture maker and folk music fan Gerald McCabe as a quiet, friendly, unpretentious place, one of the reasons it still thrives. If you play, you might want to get yourself a free pick; if not, have a cup of coffee and simply browse among the hundreds of instruments and hard-to-find CDs and books lining the walls.

We have found there is even more to admire than the exquisitely made boxes: beautifully crafted instruments like Greek bouzoukis, Russian balalaikas and Tibetan singing bowls. For mariachi fans there are *guitarrons, sextos...* it goes on. Whether you are a musician or just a fan, you don't want to miss McCabe's. Open Monday-Thursday, 10am-10pm; Friday-Saturday, 10am-6pm; Sunday, 1pm-5pm.

Specialty Shopping & Services

Celebrity Gear

★ BRITS OVER HOLLYWOOD
3004 Lincoln Boulevard
☎ 310-392-7740
www.britsoverhollywood.com

You will find used clothing, some from celebrities, in Mo Potok's shop. Even though it is a tiny place, there are nooks and crannies to explore so allow time to browse. Mo was once an interior designer in London, which is why the place looks as if it belongs on Portobello Road.

Although this part of Lincoln Boulevard is certainly not a fashionable shopping area, Mo says she has a lot of celebrity friends who dispose of last season's alligator handbag or some such here. She points to a pair of sequined Gaultier bike shorts that used to hang in Madonna's closet.

Mo likes to find old designer gear and bring it back to life; in addition to her retail business, she supplies the costume departments on films and series like *The Nanny*. It is best to simply ask Mo what she has in the shop that came from celebrities.

The shop used to be open regular hours; we put one ★ by the name because, since it is now open by appointment only, you are not apt to run into any celebrities while you are there. On the other hand, Mo says it is the only shop where you will get the personal attention of the owner who will advise you about style, and not be waited on by "some little $8-an-hour twit of a salesgirl."

★★ STAR WARES
☎ 818-707-8500
www.starwares.com

This is a celebrity thrift store on-line. There was once a store by this name on Main Street, but a few years ago it closed and went completely electronic. If you'd like a jacket that belonged to Cher, or the glasses worn by secret agent Austin Powers, then this is the place for you.

In addition to movie collectibles purchased from studios and at auctions (there are dealers who specialize in only that), Star Wares' owner Marcia Tysseling also sells used clothing, but hers happen to be the discarded threads of well-knowns like Linda Blair, Shirley MacLaine, Rue Mc-Clanahan, Barbra Streisand and Elizabeth Taylor. Some of the clothing comes from the studio wardrobe people, but most of it is from the celebrities themselves, who give it to her on a consignment basis and donate the profits to charities.

In case you wonder how you can be sure those really were Rita Moreno's ski boots, Tysseling will not purchase anything unless there is proof through paperwork that the item is authentic and was obtained lawfully. On top of that, she spends hours fast-forwarding through movie videos to make sure the costumes and props were actually in the films they claim.

A tip about the prices: contrary to what you might expect, an item of clothing worn at home by a star often sells for less than something that was worn on screen. Tysseling cites a pair of pants that may have cost Cher $1,200, which sold here for $150 because they were used. Yet a shirt that a studio wardrobe department paid $20 for at the Gap may sell for $3,000 because Bruce Willis wore it in a movie. Celebrities sometimes shop Star Wares to fill in their own movie collections. For instance, Charlie Sheen bought a set of dog tags from *Platoon*, and Christian Slater collects items from *Batman* and *Star Trek* movies.

YOU'LL FIND IT AT STAR WARES

◆ Linda Blair's autographed Ann Taylor blouse – $20

◆ Cher's spaghetti-strap tank top – $55

◆ Burt Reynolds' tuxedo jacket – $150

◆ John Wayne's luggage tag – $475

◆ Ribbed tank top worn by Al Pacino in *Frankie and Johnny* – $2,000

◆ Suede boots worn by Harrison Ford in *Indiana Jones* – $5,500

◆ Army dress uniform worn by Tom Hanks in *Forrest Gump* – $20,000

Books

Angelenos buy and read more books than people in any other place in the country, and Santa Monica is a big part of that. For instance, if there is a book on any aspect of the arts you have been wanting, you have probably come to the right place. Here is a sampling of bookstores that host regular readings and other performance events.

HENNESSEY & INGALLS BOOKSTORE
1254 Third Street Promenade
☎ 310-458-9074

This is one of the most complete art and architecture bookstores in the area. Open daily, 10am-8pm.

ARCANA BOOKS ON THE ARTS
1229 Third Street Promenade
☎ 310-458-1499

At Arcana, you will find books on 20th-century art, architecture, design and photography, many of which are rare and out of print. Open Monday-Saturday, 10am-6pm; Sunday, noon-6pm.

MUSEUM OF CONTEMPORARY ART
(MOCA) STORE
2447 Main Street (at Edgemar)
☎ 310-396-9833

You will find books relating to contemporary art at this spin-off of the Museum of Contemporary Art in downtown Los Angeles. Open Sunday-Wednesday, 11am-6pm; Thursday-Saturday, 11am-9pm.

NOVEL CAFE
212 Pier Avenue
☎ 310-396-8566

The Novel Café is a bookstore and coffeehouse where you will find contemporary art on display. Open daily, 7am-1am.

HI DE HO COMICS
525 Santa Monica Boulevard
☎ 310-394-2820

You will find over 500,000 comic books, from *Batman* #1 to a variety of underground comics. Film studio researchers are among their customers. It is worth phoning before they open to hear the message on the answering machine. Open daily, 11am-7pm; Wednesday, 11am-9pm.

MIDNIGHT SPECIAL BOOKSTORE
1350 Third Street Promenade
☎ 310-393-2923

This is the place for poetry and prose readings, book signings and discussions with authors, current affairs panels, music performances, monthly art shows, classes, reading groups. Busy, busy! Open Sunday-Thursday, 10:30am-11pm; Friday-Saturday, 10:30am-11:30pm.

ACTS CHRISTIAN BOOKS
710 Broadway
☎ 310-319-1304
Open Monday-Saturday, 11am-4pm

THUNDERBOLT SPIRITUAL BOOKS
512 Santa Monica Boulevard
☎ 310-899-9279
Open daily, 10am-10pm

BARRY R. LEVIN SCIENCE FICTION & FANTASY LITERATURE
720 Santa Monica Boulevard
☎ 310-458-6111
Open Monday-Thursday, 10am-6pm; Friday, 10am-2pm;
Sunday, noon-5pm

CALIFORNIA MAP & TRAVEL
3312 Pico Boulevard
☎ 310-396-6277

Here you will find what may be the most extensive collection of travel books in the city, plus maps, including US Coast Guard topographical, and some wonderful globes, all sizes. Open Monday-Friday, 9am-6pm; Saturday, 9am-5pm; Sunday, 12pm-5pm.

Beauty, Health & Fitness

Santa Monica is a great spa town, with quite a few small, serene places to get pampered or pummeled, or both. If you are looking for something a bit more strenuous, there are a few gyms and health and sports clubs for real workouts. Most of them keep long and late hours.

AQUA DAY SPA
1422 Second Street
☎ 310-899-6222

This spa offers Vichy showers, Ayurvedic treatments, yoga, meditation and anti-aging programs, and a spectacular atrium. Open Monday-Thursday, 10am-10pm; Friday-Saturday, 9am-10pm; Sunday, 10am-8pm.

The Beach Communities

BURKE-WILLIAMS DAY SPA
& MASSAGE CENTER
1460 Fourth Street (at Broadway)
☎ 310-587-3366

At Burke-Williams you can opt for European style massage, hydrotherapy, hair, skin and nail care, body wraps, aromatherapy massages, facials and scalp treatments. Open daily, 8am-10pm.

CLUB SANTE
Fairmont Miramar Hotel
101 Wilshire Boulevard
☎ 310-576-7777

This salon offers massage and basic cosmetics services such as waxing, nails and facials to walk-in day clients as well as hotel guests. Open daily, 9am-10:30pm.

THE LEONARD DRAKE SKINCARE CENTER
2654 Main Street
☎ 310-452-6961

Facials, massages, body treatments, waxing and other services are offered here. Open Monday-Friday, 10am-8pm; Saturday and Sunday, 10am-5pm.

SPA LE MERIGOT
Le Merigot Hotel
1740 Ocean Avenue
☎ 310-395-9700, 800-926-9524

A full range of spa services is offered in this luxury day spa in the oceanfront hotel. The facility is open to the pool area and has an outdoor gym. Open Monday-Friday, 6am-10pm; Saturday and Sunday, 7am-9pm.

BODIES IN MOTION
2730 Santa Monica Boulevard
☎ 310-264-0777

This sports club offers boxing and kickboxing classes; visitors can take a class (the day rate is $20). Open Monday-Thursday, 5am-11pm; Friday, 5am-9pm; Saturday-Sunday, 7am-7pm.

FREE WORKOUTS

Surprisingly, the most popular place to get fit for free in Santa Monica is not Muscle Beach, but the Santa Monica Steps, a set of stairs that goes down the side of Santa Monica Canyon. Actually, there are two steep staircases – one concrete, one wood – both near 4th Street and Adelaide Drive, the city's northern boundary.

Look for the wide, grassy median that splits 4th street. Most people go there early in the morning, or after work. To do a set, start at the top, go down 189 steps to the intersection of Entrada Drive and Ocean Avenue at the bottom, then up again. The wooden staircase is east of the more popular concrete one, and has 168 steps.

However, some of the residents in this upscale area are not particularly happy that the stairs are so popular with locals and visitors tightening their glutes and firming their thighs. It can get pretty crowded, especially on Friday and weekend evenings when people stand around cooling off in the sea breeze while enjoying the wonderful view. Parking is an obvious problem.

EASTON GYM
1233 Third Street Promenade
☎ 310-395-4441

Top of the line fitness equipment, classes in boxing, kickboxing, aerobics are offered here. Day memberships are available, or phone ahead for a free workout (save the $13). The gym is on the building's second floor overlooking the Promenade. Open Monday-Friday, 5am-midnight; Saturday-Sunday, 7am-midnight.

QUEST
1455 19th Street
☎ 310-453-4536

Quest has individual sessions in body sculpting, cross-training and kick boxing. Private trainers are available in their 15,000-square-foot, top-of-the-line fitness facility, or just drop in to use facilities ($12). On Thursday nights there's a free-form "vibe" dance party. Open Monday-Thursday, 6am-9pm; Friday, 6am-6pm; Saturday and Sunday, 8am-3pm.

☞ DID YOU KNOW?

Though everyone calls them the Santa Monica Steps, they are mostly in Los Angeles. The city line runs down the middle of Adelaide Drive and even through the middle of some of the houses. Only the top 22 of the concrete steps are in Santa Monica, the rest are in Los Angeles. Of the shorter, lesser-known wooden steps, the top 14 feet are in Santa Monica, the bottom 214 feet in Los Angeles.

 # The British Are Here

The British began arriving in Hollywood in the 1920s, and by the '30s it became a flood that included expatriate actors like Brian Aherne, Ronald Coleman, Leslie Howard and David Niven; and writers like Christopher Isherwood, who lived in Santa Monica Canyon; Aldous Huxley; and Evelyn Waugh, whose novel, *The Loved One*, satirized his fellow expat Brits. Others, like Deborah Kerr, came in the early 1940s. And business people, students, tourists and film people still come. The majority seem to have chosen Santa Monica as the place to live, perhaps because it reminded them of home. After all, Santa Monica has more fog than anywhere else in Los Angeles County.

As a result there is a liberal sampling of English – and Irish – life found here in Santa Monica. We can understand the proliferation of pubs and tea rooms; they are a touch of home away from home for Brits living here as well as for visiting Brits. And those places have become very popular with the rest of us; some of the champion pub dart teams even have all American-born players. But we have never understood who is buying British goods in the shops; surely Brits wouldn't come all the way here to buy a pot of Devon preserves, or socks with a clan plaid design? Oh, well.

Sports the British Way

Head for the lawn-bowls area of Douglas Park, near Wilshire and Chelsea. You will see very serious lawn bowlers wearing proper white linen slacks, white shirts and white shoes. After you watch for a while you will appreciate how difficult this sport truly is, and how good they are at it. The park is open daily, 6am-11pm; tournaments are usually on weekends.

 TIP

To enjoy proper British lawn-bowling, visit Douglas Park on Wilshire Boulevard.

British Shoppes

THE CONTINENTAL SHOP
1619 Wilshire Boulevard
☎ 310-453-8655

Homesick expatriates know this place well. They carry a lot of goods from the continent in general, but their specialty is all things British, including food, films, cassettes, CDs, you name it. Open Monday-Saturday, 9:30-6; Sunday, noon-4pm.

YE OLDE KINGS HEAD SHOPPE
132 Santa Monica Boulevard
☎ 310-394-8765

On the corner of 2nd Street, next door to the Ye Olde Kings Head Pub, it is not a large place but it has a wide variety of everything – from tea to teapots, marmalade to candy, ties to china – made in Britain. How about showing up with your own darts when you challenge the locals in the pub next door? Open Monday-Saturday, 10am-6pm; Sunday, noon-5pm.

TUDOR HOUSE
1403 2nd Street
☎ 310-451-4107

Across the street from Ye Olde Kings Head Shoppe, this is an atmospheric place filled with nostalgia for the British who live here. Smallish, but an amazing variety of things to browse amongst. Open Monday-Saturday, 10am-6pm; Sunday, 11am-6pm.

Afternoon Tea

TUDOR HOUSE TEA SHOP AND BAKERY
1403 2nd Street
☎ 310-451-4107

Enjoy a proper tea for $10.75, and a larger menu with things such as meat pies like mum used to make back in Blighty. Open daily, 11am-5:30.

YE OLDE KINGS HEAD PUB
116 Santa Monica Boulevard
☎ 310-451-1402

They serve a very nice tea here, with sandwiches and freshly baked scones with fresh clotted cream. They also have a vegetarian tea (perhaps in reaction to mad cow disease?), and a children's version. All are served on bone china with good silver. Price is $12.95; reservations are necessary. Tea is served Monday-Friday, 3pm-5pm and Saturday, 2pm-4pm.

Pubs

The pubs listed here are the real thing, not the ersatz places for tourists that you find in some cities. They are especially busy during World Cup, or big football (soccer) matches back home; this is where local British and Irish go to escape the incomprehensible American indifference to the world's most popular sport.

YE OLDE KINGS HEAD PUB
116 Santa Monica Boulevard
☎ 310-451-1402

This is the patriarch of Santa Monica pubs. Everyone from back home stops in here at some time or another. There is the pub, a restaurant (see page 438), a tea room, and then the gift shop, all side by side, taking up most of a block. It all started with just the pub, which has been popular since it opened, not just with the British but with the rest of us. Darts are big here, and there are British beers and hard cider on tap, a favorite in Blighty. Most of the accents you hear are *not* American. Friendly atmosphere, feels like we are back in London. Pub is open 11am-1:30am.

We drop in at the restaurant once in a while at noon for authentic-tasting fish and chips (though they don't serve them in a greasy sheet from a tabloid). There is Yorkshire pudding, fish, bubble 'n squeak, the whole lot. The restaurant is open daily, 11am-10pm; till 11pm Saturday and Sunday.

O'BRIEN'S PUB
2941 Main Street
☎ 310-396-4725

O'Brien's is an Irish pub, which explains all the Guinness posters on the walls. Other than that, there's not much in the way of décor, just a bare wood floor and wood-backed booths in the long, narrow room. But there are dart boards and a warm atmosphere. The imported beers and ales on tap are served cold, "since we're in America." There is live music nightly, and a cover charge of $5 after 9pm. Call for hours.

THE COCK 'N' BULL PUB
2947 Lincoln Boulevard
☎ 310-399-9696

This is a bare sort of place with a bar and a few high round tables to perch at, but it attracts more customers than any other because of the big satellite dishes on the roof. When the important football (soccer) matches are aired live from back home this place gets so crowded that sometimes you can't get in – whether it is the middle of the night or at

6am! A half-dozen British beers and hard ciders on tap, and a limited menu. Small parking lot. Open 6am-2am.

THE DAILY PINT
2310 Pico Boulevard
☎ 310-450-7631

As we walked into this small neighborhood pub we saw the Red Sox playing the Yankees on one telly and Manchester United playing a Yugoslav soccer team on another. Sarah, the bartender, was British; so was the bloke down the bar who bought us a drink a few minutes after we sat down, and John, on our other side, who was enjoying a day off from his job as bartender at McCabe's – a sort of busman's holiday. It's an immediately friendly place.

Parking on the side streets in this Pico neighborhood is for residents only.

There is a better-than-usual selection of UK brews on tap, and two dozen single-malt scotches listed on a blackboard. No food, and no live music, but you can play the juke box all you want. A second room has pool tables and skittles. They're open 2pm-2am; parking is in a lot behind the pub.

O'BRIENS
2226 Wilshire Boulevard
☎ 310-829-5303

O'Briens is 100% Irish, from the staff to the food. It even received the Guinness "Perfect Pint" award for adherence to Irish serving traditions. There's lots of typical pub grub available; entertainment consists of a juke box and a pool table. O'Brien's is open 11am-2am, but the cook goes home at 11pm.

SONNY McLEAN'S
2615 Wilshire Boulevard
☎ 310-449-1811

This used to be The Red Setter, and was a British pub. The number of Irish pubs is growing (that's not necessarily bad or good, just an observation). Sonny's has three distinct areas, one each for dining, darts and a bar, with the bar in the middle. Back home these would have been separate rooms, closed off from each other, but here in Santa Monica the walls have disappeared and all is open. That might or might not mean something.

There are 23 beers and ales on tap, but half are those weak American national brews, so they shouldn't count. In the dining room are the same high-backed wooden booths seen in so many old country pubs, but more comfortable. The menu has succumbed to Southern California tastes, and offers things like stuffed jalapeños and teriyaki chicken, but the traditional favorites, like fish and chips and Guinness beef pie, are also here and are very good. And portions are large.

Darts are taken seriously here; there are always several tournaments in progress. There is often live music with an Irish band (but no dancing); at present it's every other weekend, but call ahead.

TEMPLE BAR
1026 Wilshire Boulevard
☎ 310-393-6611

The Temple Bar is named for an ancient district in Dublin on the bank of the River Liffey. There is a heavy emphasis on live music in the club room, which opens anywhere from 7:30pm-9pm with a cover of $3-$10, depending on who is booked. There may be four or five groups in one night; phone ahead to see who will be playing. They're open Monday-Friday, 7pm-2am; Saturday-Sunday, 6pm-2am. Valet parking is available.

THE WEST END
1301 5th Street
☎ 310-394-4647

No food is served here, but they have more beer varieties than you could ever drink, everything from Budweiser to Guinness and Harp, and many brown ales, most on tap. There's a dance floor, and live music. Open only at night, 6pm-2am.

Sunup to Sundown

What is there to do in Santa Monica? Anything you want. Things to make one healthy, or artistic, intellectual, or just pleasantly amused... it is all here.

Recreation

Santa Monica Pier

The Santa Monica Pier is the oldest surviving pleasure pier on the West Coast.

There has been a pier of one kind or another here for most of the last century. The present one was at one time much longer; the rest was knocked off bit by bit in storms. But it has been rebuilt and has, among other attractions, a roller coaster (not terrifying enough by some standards, but good for those who don't *want* to be terrified) and a really big Pacific Wheel, the world's first solar-powered Ferris wheel.

The problem with the Pier (the citizens of Santa Monica have been arguing about this for years) is that, while there are a few carnival-midway-type amusements and quick-serve eateries, the Pier Restoration Corp., which runs things for the city, doesn't want too much of a carnival atmosphere for fear the Pier will attract a "bad element." But what it needs is a lot more carny games run by carny people to create more noise and excitement.

There are two restaurants with great views (unfortunately, the first, the quirky Boathouse, which had been well-run by a local family for about 50 years, was inexplicably kicked out by the Restoration Corp. and is being replaced with a fast-food chain restaurant called Bubba's). The other, out at the end, is Mariasol, with Mexican food and a patio overlooking the fishermen and out over the ocean.

The 1909 building housing the Pier's carousel is known as The Hippodrome and is a National Historic Landmark.

One thing everyone wants to see is the carousel; it has been featured in so many movies including, prominently, in *The Sting*. There has been a carousel here since 1916, and the price is still just 25¢ for kids, 50¢ for adults. The carousel is open Tuesday-Friday, 11am-5pm; Saturday-Sunday, 11am-7pm.

The rides and amusements are open year-round. From Labor Day through April, hours are Monday-Thursday, 11am-6pm; Friday and Saturday, 11am-midnight; Sunday, 11am-9pm. From May to Labor Day the Pier is open Monday-Thursday, 11am-10pm; Friday and Saturday, 11am-midnight; Sunday, 11am-9pm. See page 479 for more on the Pier after dark.

The Beach Communities

DISTANCE FROM THE PIER

Palisades Park . . . . next door
Santa Monica Place Shopping Center . . . . 1 block
Main Street . . . . 3 blocks
Third Street Promenade . . . . 3 blocks
Wilshire Boulevard . . . . 4 blocks

The Beach

Santa Monica's beach is one of the big reasons many people come here. It is 3.5 miles long and quite broad, with plenty of room for tanning, wading and swimming. The remains of an old offshore breakwater north of the Pier almost disappears from sight at high tide, but it is enough to keep the surf gentle in this area, good for small children and bathers who don't like waves.

Cirque du Soleil, the Quebec-based acrobatic circus, regularly comes to perform on the sand next to the Santa Monica Pier.

Movies have been shot on this beach since there have been movies; more recently it has been a popular location for television series as well – *Baywatch* is one of many that comes to mind.

You will find parking lots on the beach side of Pacific Coast Highway (which runs along the beach at the base of the Palisades) from Montana to Arizona avenues, and a large one next to the Pier on the north side, at Colorado. There are some small lots just south of the Pier between Colorado and Pico, and two large lots farther south, between Ocean Avenue and Ocean Park Boulevard, accessible from Ocean Avenue. If you are on foot, take one of four pedestrian bridges spaced along Palisades Park north of the Pier that arch over Pacific Coast Highway down to the sand, or walk down the entrance ramp to the Pier, at the end of Colorado Avenue. (There are four public restrooms on the beach, and 14 along the entire length of the bike trail; telephones are numerous.)

Santa Monica has five public sculptures along its beach.

> ### ✗ WARNING!
>
> For safety reasons the police recommend you do not walk on the beach after dark.

Surfing

The average temperature in Santa Monica is 67°F (19.5°C) throughout the year.

North of the Pier, where the surf is usually higher, is good for body surfing; you may want to rent a boogie board – a short foam board – to lie on as you kick with your feet to catch a ride on an incoming wave (for rentals on the beach, see below).

If you are interested in more serious surfing but aren't ready to hang ten, you can rent soft-top boards (easier for novices) at ZJ Boarding House, which also rents hard boards (see page 440).

South Bay Bike Trail

The bike trail starts well north of the Pier around Montana Avenue and continues south uninterrupted for about four miles to Marina del Rey. (After a one-street detour around the marina it continues for another 15 miles south.) It is a fun and easy, non-worrisome ride with no auto traffic to contend with.

Bike & Skate Rentals

BLAZING SADDLES
Santa Monica Pier (next to Police Station)

There are clearly marked bicycle and skating paths throughout Santa Monica.

☎ 310-393-9778
www.blazingsaddles.com

Road bikes, mountain bikes and hybrid bikes (the best vehicles for tooling around town) are all here, and all come with lock and helmet. Hourly rate, $7-$11 (two-hour minimum); day rate, $28-$48. Trailers for kids are also available; open daily, 9am-6pm.

> ★ **TIP**
>
> If you're renting a bike, remember to request a bike lock, in case you want to pause somewhere along the way. Parents with small children can rent bike trailers so they can tow the kids along for the ride.

SEA MIST
1619 Ocean Front Walk (at the Pier)
☎ 310-395-7076

Road bikes, hybrids and mountain bikes, locks and helmets included. Rentals: one hour, $5-$6; all day, $14-$20; open daily, 9am-6:30pm.

PERRY'S CAFE & RENTALS
Four locations
☎ 310-372-3138

Perry's has two locations north of the Pier and two south. They rent (and sell) skates, bikes, boogie boards and volleyballs, and Perry's operates volleyball courts at all locations. Ask for a copy of their handy bike trail map with restrooms and pay phones marked. If you would like to skate but are a novice, they offer lessons. Perry's has small clusters of tables and umbrellas on the sand, and serves sandwiches, salads, pizza, snacks. Bike and skate rentals: one hour, $6; all day, $15. Open daily, 9am-sunset.

Perry's loans all-terrain wheelchairs at no charge to those who need them, making the beach fully accessible; there is a two-hour time limit, and they require someone to push.

> ☛ **DID YOU KNOW?**
>
> Santa Monica regards itself as the high-tech, dot-com, digital entertainment heart of southern California. It is home to more than 200 top post-production houses and is the regional and world headquarters for a handful of entertainment conglomerates.

Ocean Front Walk

The walk starts on the south side of the Pier and goes to about Bay Street. Walk out onto the Pier and look for the stairs going down just before the carousel.

The sound signals timed to the traffic lights on Ocean Avenue are for the benefit of blind pedestrians.

Right at the start is the **Ocean Discovery Center**, 1600 Ocean Front Walk, Santa Monica 90401, ☎ 310-393-6149, fax 310-393-4839, www.odc.ucla.edu/. With three primary display tanks, a shark and ray tank, touch tanks, a computer and microscope laboratory and a bookstore, it offers an eye-opening insight into the world of the fish and invertebrates that live under and around the piers and in the bay. You will get to know what lives in the sand and on the reefs as well as in the local waters. The Ocean Discovery Center is a non-profit facility run by the University of California at Los Angeles. Summer hours (July 1 to Labor Day) are Tuesday-Friday, 3pm-6pm; Saturday, 11am-6pm; Sunday, 11am-5pm; winter hours are Saturday and Sunday, 11am-5pm; admission is $3.

Next on the ocean side of the walk is a stone-walled **sandbox** for kids. You will recognize it by the big dragon's head and Viking ship play structures. Santa Monica's reputation as a mecca for beach volleyball is obvious with the row of public courts that run along the sand here. There are more beach volleyball courts farther down, but the ones here have bleachers for spectators to enjoy the action.

The large-scale chess-board set into the sidewalk is for matches played with people as living pieces.

The **International Chess Park** is usually crowded with local players, some of whom play from noon to sunset every day, which shows a lot of dedication. Even non-players will enjoy watching, for a while at least. Some homeless people in the area often make their way here and challenge a winner to a game, and the outcome is sometimes surprising. As one of the regular players told us, you shouldn't judge someone's intelligence by the way they look.

A bit farther south is **Muscle Beach**, which was once world-famous and is trying to regain that distinction. At first it was simply an impromptu gathering place for circus and vaudeville performers looking for a good spot to practice their more strenuous routines. Soon they were joined by Hollywood stuntmen and then by a new breed of athletes, both men and women, who practiced what they called "physical culture." From the 1930s through the '50s this place attracted every gymnast, wrestler and weight-lifter of note in the country, and around the world, to show their stuff. It was really the birthplace of the fitness movement.

Jack LaLanne, Vic Tanny, Joe Gold (who founded Gold's Gym and World Gym), all the Mr. and Miss Universes (there was no "Ms." then) posed, somersaulted, formed pyramids, threw pretty girls into the air – and pretty girls lifted big men over their heads. Celebrities had their photos taken looking buff: Kirk Douglas, Clark Gable, Tyrone Power, Mae West and Arnold Schwarzenegger before he was Arnold Schwarzenegger.

Jayne Mansfield and Jane Russell both met their muscular husbands here. Cecil B. De Mille hired Steve Reeves to star in *Hercules* after seeing him do things like balancing three people on his shoulders, and coming off the high rings with a double somersault.

The site was shut down by Santa Monica in 1959 because it was "attracting a bad element." Then, as Venice began attracting national attention, its Muscle Beach overshadowed this one. But there is new equipment here now, and a refurbished facility, and Santa Monica's Muscle Beach is coming back.

As you walk along, look for the public art installation **Singing Beach Chairs**, by Douglas Hollis. In a strong wind the aluminum tubes that rise behind the backrests of these oversized lifeguard chairs become 14-foot-tall pan pipes, creating unique music.

Kite-flying and volley-ball are favorite things to do on Santa Monica's beach. There are many free public volley-ball courts.

BEACH INFORMATION

Surf conditions . . . . ☎ 900-849-WAVE
LA County Lifeguards . . . . . . ☎ 310-394-3265
LA Harbor Patrol . . . . ☎ 310-458-8694

Farmers' Markets

There are four farmers' markets in Santa Monica every week. Each is run by a non-profit city organization, and all profits go to the farmers themselves. Each farmer certifies that he grows his own food, and everything must be grown in California.

Look for Asian pears in Santa Monica's farmers' markets during Chinese New Year.

Even if you are eating in restaurants every day during your time here, it is fun to walk through the colorful markets. Try some really fresh fruit that doesn't taste anything like what you buy at a supermarket. Commercial produce brokers would never buy a ripe peach because it couldn't last through shipping and storage, but local farmers can wait until the produce is tree-ripened before picking and bringing it to a local market. You will discover exotic varieties of fruit and vegetables rarely seen in commercial markets.

THE WEDNESDAY MARKET
Arizona Avenue & 2nd Street

This is the oldest farmers' market in Santa Monica and one of the largest in the state. Over 60% of the city's residents say they shop here often, which we don't wholly believe, though it may not be too much of an exaggeration. More farmers show up here than at the other markets, and we have found it is a treasure trove of exotic and experimental varieties, as well as the usual.

For instance, agretti showed up in this market on a recent Wednesday. A Northern Italian vegetable that looks sort of like chives, it has never been available in this country. But, we learned, the owner of a local café, tired of not having any to use in her cooking, got some seeds from Italy and gave them to several organic farmers in this area. Open 9am-2pm.

SATURDAY DOWNTOWN MARKET
Arizona Avenue & 3rd Street

This market specializes in organic food; over 60% of the produce sold here is organic. Open 8:30am-1pm.

★ *TIP*

Farmers' markets give you a chance to try fruit you may have never seen before. Here is where farmers can experiment with old-fashioned or new varieties that aren't grown commercially.

SATURDAY PICO FARMERS' MARKET
Pico Boulevard & Cloverfield Avenue

This market, the twin of the Saturday Downtown Market, is on the east side of Santa Monica (drive about 23 blocks out Pico Boulevard from the beach), with a good offering of organic produce. Open 8am-1pm.

THE SUNDAY MARKET
Main Street & Ocean Park

This market is the newest, and it is different. Besides the many produce booths, the local Main Street businesses participate with non-agricultural booths serving breakfast and lunch, coffee and tea. There is always live music, arts and crafts, and activities for children, such as facepainting, ceramics and pony rides. Open 9:30am-1pm; bring the whole family.

For more information on all four markets, contact Santa Monica Farmers' Market, 200 Santa Monica Pier, Santa Monica, CA 90401, ☎ 310-458-8712, fax 310-393-1279, www.farmersmarket.santa-monica.org.

Art Galleries

Santa Monica can boast more than a dozen public art exhibition spaces and more than four dozen private exhibition galleries. To get a full list – more than you ever imagined would exist in a town like Santa Monica – phone ☎ 310-458-8350, or try www.art.santa-monica.org. Listed here are a few of the bigger arts complexes, each with a number of galleries and other facilities in one place.

BERGAMOT STATION ARTS COMPLEX
2525 Michigan Avenue
(off Cloverfield, just north of Santa Monica Freeway)
☎ 310-459-7892

Back in 1875 this was a stop for the Red Line trolley that ran from Los Angeles to the Santa Monica Pier (the name comes from a flower of the mint family that once flourished in the area). Now it is home to over 20 galleries, plus the Gallery Café, custom framing by Art Concepts, Artworks Bookstore, and Colleagues' Gallery, a non-profit, very upscale thrift store where celebrities often shop (see below). Gallery hours are generally Tuesday-Friday, 10am to 6pm; Saturday, 11am to 6pm.

CALIFORNIA HERITAGE MUSEUM
2612 Main Street
☎ 310-392-8537
Free parking

The museum's Queen Anne-style Victorian building was built in 1894 for Roy Jones, son of Santa Monica's founder Robert Jones. It was first at 1000 Ocean Boulevard, a block from the senior Jones' Miramar home at Ocean and Wilshire. It was moved here in 1977 to become the California Heritage Museum. Rotating exhibits have subjects like Depression glass, quilts, Mexican pottery, Hawaiian surfboards and California history and decorative arts. Admission for adults, $3; for students and seniors, $2; children under 12, free. Open Wednesday-Sunday, 11am-4pm (arrive by 3pm).

★★ COLLEAGUES' GALLERY
Bergamot Station
2525 Michigan Avenue, Bldg. A4
☎ 310-828-1619

This is a non-profit shop raising funds for the Children's Institute International, which explains the odd hours it keeps. Some charity-minded celebrities shop here. The store takes in donations of antiques, household articles and clothes, mostly from the wealthy Westside, all great stuff. The clothing is mostly women's. Somebody picked up Nancy Reagan's old Adolfos here, and Jimmy Stewart's cashmere cardigan and some other things with his monogram on them, but that doesn't usually happen. Most of the time the celebrities exact a promise the Colleagues *won't* reveal who owned the items. Open Monday, noon-2pm; and Thursday, 10am-2pm.

18th STREET ARTS COMPLEX
1641 18th Street
☎ 310-453-3711

This facility is home to the Visual Art Gallery; Side Street Projects exhibition space, a studio for artists in residence and workshops; Highways Performance Space; the Cornerstone Theater Company and Electronic Café International. Gallery hours are 10:30am-5pm; openings are usually held on Fridays, 6:30-8:30pm.

Just For Kids

PUPPET AND MAGIC CENTER
1255 2nd Street
Santa Monica
☎ 310-656-0483
www.puppetmagic.com

Shows are given every Wednesday and on holidays at 1pm; Saturday and Sunday at 1 and 3pm. Tickets are $6.50.

Murals

Santa Monica is well-supplied with murals. Although some are hidden inside high schools and bank buildings, there are a few large murals on exterior walls that are easy to see. They are exuberant, sometimes clever, but all of it public art you will enjoy.

OCEAN PARK PIER
Ocean Park Boulevard and Main Street
(southeast corner)

Designed by Jane Golden, painted by Golden and Barbara Stoll, 1976, this is one of the best. The mural pictures a crowded boardwalk and beach at the well-loved pier with its ballroom, roller coaster and midway. The pier was torn down in 1974.

YOUR TRAVEL AGENT
a.k.a. *Waiting for the Train*
1842 14th Street
(between Pico Boulevard and Michigan Avenue)

This mural, painted by Jane Golden and Peggy Edwards in 1976, depicts expectant travelers waiting at the depot for an approaching train in an earlier era.

JOHN MUIR WOODS
John Muir School
Ocean Park and Lincoln Boulevard
(northwest corner)

The subject of this mural, done by Jane Golden in 1978, is a forest of redwood trees in Muir Woods National Monument in Northern California.

HISTORY OF THE PICO NEIGHBORHOOD
Santa Monica Freeway (I-10), Stewart Street underpass
Stewart Street at Virginia

Ann Elizabeth Thiermann painted this mural in 1983; it is a rather impressionistic depiction of the community's struggle to stay unified.

The Three Dinosaurs on the Third Street Promenade are officially Santa Monica Public Art.

PUBLIC ART

Chain Reaction, at Santa Monica Civic Center, 1855 Main Street, (just north of Pico) is a depiction of a 26-foot-tall atomic bomb cloud made of heavy chain by Pulitzer prize-winning political cartoonist Paul Conrad (*Los Angeles Times*).

WHALE OF A MURAL
Ocean Park Boulevard at Fourth Street underpass

The subject matter of Daniel Alonzo's 1983 mural is dolphins, whales and other underwater creatures. Not as alive as some of the others.

UNBRIDLED
Ocean Park Boulevard at Fourth Street underpass
(next to the whale mural)

David S. Gordon's 1985 mural, depicting horses frolicking
on the beach, means more when you know they are meant
to have escaped from the carousel on the Pier.

PARA LOS NIÑOS ("For the Children")
1601 Olympic Boulevard (at 16th Street)

As befits an exterior wall of the Police Activities League
Center, Daniel Galvez's 1993 rendering depicts adults and
kids together doing nice things.

TIP

For an online calendar of events in
Santa Monica, visit www.santamoni-
ca.com.

Museums

MUSEUM OF FLYING
2772 Donald Douglas Loop North
☎ 310-392-8822

This museum has permanent exhibits of antique and historic aircraft, and hands-on displays. There is even a flight
simulator. Open Wednesday-Sunday, 10am-5pm. Admission: adults, $7; seniors and college students, $5 (with ID);
children ages three to 16, $3.

★ SANTA MONICA HISTORICAL SOCIETY MUSEUM
1539 Euclid Street
☎ 310-395-2290

The museum has obtained photos and memorabilia relating to the history of Santa Monica and the Westside, including a collection of Stan Laurel's letters (he lived in
Santa Monica), photos of stars engaged in civic activities,
movie posters, etc. Open Tuesday and Thursday, 10:30am-

4pm; second and fourth Sunday, 1-4pm; suggested admission, $3.

Poetry Readings

ANASTASIA'S ASYLUM
1028 Wilshire Boulevard
☎ 310-394-7113

Anastasia's hosts poetry readings, performances, live music. Open Monday-Thursday, 6am-1am; Friday and Saturday, 6am-2am; Sunday, 8am-1am; phone for performance times.

LEGAL GRIND COFFEEHOUSE
2640 Lincoln Boulevard
☎ 310-452-8160

This is a neighborhood coffee shop with poetry readings, art exhibits and live music, along with free legal consultations, by appointment. Open at various times; phone ahead for a current schedule.

Palisades Park

Palisades Park is a long, thin strip squeezed between Ocean Avenue and the rim of the sandstone bluffs overhanging (and sometimes falling down on) the Pacific Coast Highway and the beach. It is a great place to walk or jog, lined with towering palm and eucalyptus trees and carpeted with lush grass.

An easy, level walk begins at Colorado Avenue, by the entrance to the Pier, and ends 1.6 miles north at Adelaide Drive (Santa Monica Canyon, just beyond Adelaide, is in Los Angeles). The southern part of the park, from California to Colorado Avenue, is much more crowded than the northern half.

The first and only building you'll see is the **Senior Center**. Outside are shuffleboard courts, reserved for seniors. Inside, upstairs, is a **camera obscura**, a delightful instrument that Bob's parents first took him to see when he was a child. From the camera obscura, look across the street to 1323 Ocean Avenue, the Gussie Moran House. The Queen Anne-style Victorian house is the kind that once lined Ocean Avenue. (If you are not a tennis buff, Moran was a world-famous star player.)

The screen is a round table tilted at an angle. By turning a ship's-wheel, light from a lens-mirror combination in a rooftop turret is beamed onto the tabletop. The lens, which rotates 360°, catches the scene outside: cars driving by in the street, a woman in a blue dress walking on the park path, an elderly man asleep on a bench under a palm tree, a sailboat on the ocean, all eerily silent.

THE CAMERA OBSCURA

In case you have never come across a camera obscura, the encyclopedia definition is "a light-tight box with a convex lens at one end and a screen for the image at the other." This particular light-tight box is an entire light-tight room which you enter, and the convex lens is in a turret in the center of the roof.

☞ DID YOU KNOW?

Santa Monica Civic Auditorium, 1855 Main Street, has played host to the Academy of Television Arts & Science's Emmy Awards, the Soul Train Women in Soul Awards and a number of other high-profile events. Call for a quarterly calendar of happenings at the Civic; ☎ 310-458-8555.

Just north of the Senior Center is the **Visitors Center**, a kiosk by the Ocean Avenue sidewalk. Pick up a map of Santa Monica, bus routes or driving directions and information in four languages.

A few steps away is the end of Santa Monica Boulevard, which is also the end of historic **Route 66**, the first national highway to cross the country from Chicago to Los

Angeles in the 1930s. A plaque calls it "This Main Street of America," and dedicates it the Will Rogers Highway.

The cement **statue of Santa Monica**, which faces down Wilshire Boulevard, was sculpted by Eugene Morahan as the city's namesake. Across the street at 100 Wilshire Boulevard, the 22-story General Telephone Building and the adjacent 16-story Champagne Tower Apartments are jointly known as **Lawrence Welk Plaza**. The band leader, who owned the buildings and had an apartment in the Tower, got his big break a mile down the coast at the Aragon Ballroom on the now-gone Ocean Park Pier.

Scenic Drive

The old name for the stretch of sand along Pacific Coast Highway north of the Pier is the **Gold Coast**, also once known as Rolls Royce Row. As the movie industry prospered in the 1920s, magnificent beach houses were built here for Cary Grant, Darryl F. Zanuck and Brian Aherne, among others. Louis B. Mayer, head of MGM, built a house at 625 Pacific Coast Highway. Peter Lawford lived there later, and hosted Jack and Robert Kennedy along with various starlets, including Marilyn Monroe.

William Randolph Hearst built the most lavish spread of all at 415 Pacific Coast Highway. There were several sprawling, two-story white wooden buildings containing, in all, 118 rooms and 55 baths. It was steps from the surf, but with its own protected pool spanned by a marble bridge. Of course, it was all for Marion Davies, Hearst's long-time mistress and screen star for Cosmopolitan Pictures (which, helpfully, Hearst owned).

Marion was very popular with most people, though not all, and practically every star of that era (the 1920s through the early '40s) was happy to be invited to Marion's fabulous parties. For the costume parties, some of the celebrities would come in great get-ups, which they borrowed from the studio wardrobe department.

The Sand & Sea Club is there now. The main buildings of Davies' complex were torn down; the remaining ones were merely the servant's quarters and the cabanas in Marion's time.

The Gold Coast is easy to get to; take California Avenue to Ocean Avenue and go down the pretentiously named California Incline from the top of the Palisades to the Pacific Coast Highway below. Or, take the Santa Monica Freeway to the PCH; drive north from there.

Picnic Areas

At **Palisades Park**, there are no tables, but many like to picnic here anyway, as there are almost always cool breezes and a wonderful view of the ocean from the top of the bluff. The northern part of the park, past California Avenue, is always less crowded and parking is easier.

Douglas Park, at Wilshire Boulevard at Chelsea Avenue (between 24th and 25th streets) is a very nice park, where the Brits come to lawn bowl; no picnic tables.

Los Amigos Park is up on the hill above Main Street, between Hollister and Strand, 3rd and 4th streets. No picnic tables here either, but there are a half-dozen benches with maybe one or two elderly men dozing in the sun and a young amorous couple or two. Lush grass, great views and gentle breezes.

Picnic Supplies

AMALFI
2400 Main Street
☎ 310-392-7466

This Italian deli has good sandwiches, a full range of goodies to go, and a nice little patio if you can't wait to start eating.

BAY CITIES DELI
1517 Lincoln Boulevard
☎ 319-395-8279

This is the largest deli in town, focusing on Italian foods, with a big cheese selection (both domestic and imported), fresh Italian bread every day, all sorts of packaged food and more wines than most liquor stores. Best of all, there are usually three or four clerks making thick sandwiches on large split rolls, to order. Parking lot.

★★ IZZY'S DELI
1433 Wilshire Boulevard
☎ 310-394-1131

Izzy's is a real Jewish delicatessen, where the pastrami or corned beef is piled high on rye bread and the kosher dills are really kosher. We sat with Karl Malden here at a back table some time ago to talk about a play we had written. The regular customers are used to seeing celebrities who live nearby (mostly north of Montana) and respect their privacy. Only one woman came over and interrupted to ask for an autograph, which Malden cheerfully supplied.

JUDY'S DELI
1415 Montana Avenue
☎ 310-260-8877

This place specializes in deli-quality soups, salads and sandwiches. If you want a bottle of wine to go with your picnic, Fireside Cellars is next door.

SHOOP'S DELICATESSEN
2400 Main Street
☎ 310-452-1019

Shoop's is next door to Amalfi; they share the same address, but aren't really in competition because Amalfi is Italian and Shoop's is German. About a third of the shop is dedicated to German imports, from mustard to magazines. Several dense varieties of rye bread (one center slice of *bauern* is enough for two sandwiches). Wide variety of cold cuts.

📷 FILM GLOSSARY

Above-the-line costs – Money paid to "talent" in film production: writers, producers, directors, stars.

After Dark

Art Movie Houses

Santa Monica is home to more than 20 movie screens on the Third Street Promenade showing virtually everything in current release. But if you are looking for theaters showing hard-to-see films, here are two.

LAEMMLE'S MONICA FOURPLEX
1332 2nd Street
☎ 310-394-9741

They specialize in foreign films and independents, and occasionally have a retrospective of someone interesting. See *Los Angeles Times Calendar* for current screenings.

NU WILSHIRE THEATER
1413 Wilshire Boulevard
☎ 310-394-8099

Features foreign and independent fare.

THE AERO THEATRE

When this theater was built by Douglas Aircraft Co. for its labor force during World War II, it stayed open all night so swing-shift workers would have someplace to go after midnight. The theater is still a favorite in the Montana neighborhood; it is one of the last single-screen theaters still around – and they even put real butter on their popcorn. Threatened with declining attendance, the theater was saved on the point of closing by Robert Redford's Sundance Film Center, which plans to put a bistro beside it to generate income, and to renovate the theater to show first-run independent films. 1328 Montana Avenue, ☎ 310-395-4990.

Friday Night Skates

This trend started in Paris, where 25,000 Friday Night Fever skaters speed through the streets. San Francisco picked it up; they get about 350 Midnight Rollers. Here in Santa Monica up to 80 skaters have been known to join in every week so far, weather permitting. If you can skate, and are looking for something wild to do on a Friday eve, this may be for you.

Skaters meet at the entrance to the Santa Monica Pier, at the northwest corner of Ocean and Colorado by the cannon, at 8pm. The skate begins promptly at 8:30. It is a 10-mile, 2½-hour trek through parts of Santa Monica, Venice and Pacific Palisades, with some hills (speed on the downslope is up to 30 mph).

A boom box strapped to the leader's back urges the group along with the sounds of disco, hip-hop and dance music. Rest stops are made so everyone can catch up and catch their breaths. The evening usually ends with the pack speeding down Montana Avenue to Ocean Avenue to the sounds of Richard Wagner's *Ride of the Valkyries* blaring from the boom box.

Provide your own skates – in-liners, quads or five-wheeled – and safety gear. For more information, ☎ 310-57-SKATE (577-5283), www.fridaynightskate.org.

Music & Dance

SANTA MONICA SYMPHONY ORCHESTRA
Santa Monica Civic Auditorium
1685 Main Street (Main and Pico)
☎ 310-996-3260

The Symphony presents four free classical concerts each year, including a family concert with an early starting time.

SANTA MONICA PIER
Colorado Avenue
☎ 310-458-8900
www.santamonicapier.com

The Twilight Dance Series features bands and performers of all kinds – jazz, swing, rock, folk – outside on the pier on summer nights, and it always draws big crowds. Past performers include Bo Diddley, Queen Ida, Jack Mack and the Heart Attack, Tito Puente, Pancho Sanchez and The Young Dubliners. Thursday nights, free, from the last Thursday in June through the first Thursday in August; 7:30-9:30pm. Free Sunday afternoon concerts are held from 2-4pm, February to May, and focus on pop, jazz and R&B.

▪ FILM GLOSSARY

Breakdown – A list of characters in a movie; or a concise description of each scene in a movie.

RUSTY'S SURF RANCH
256 Santa Monica Pier
☎ 310-393-7437, music line 310-393-7386

Just past the carousel, Rusty's is by far the swingin'est place on the Pier, and perhaps in Santa Monica. Thursday-Saturday there are usually three or four groups each night, starting at about 8:30pm; 4pm on Saturday. Lots of choices are offered, from friendly jazz, country western, rockin' blues, rock, roots rock, pop rock to R&B and reggae. Thursday is usually the night for "Women Who Cook," a showcase of top Los Angeles's female musicians and bands. Cover varies from nothing to $20, depending on the attractions. Karaoke is popular on Sunday from 4pm, and Monday from 8:30pm. Tuesday there's no music, but happy hour goes on all night.

Lunch and dinner are served every day at Rusty's Surf Ranch.

HEY, DUDE...

Rusty's Surf Ranch has probably the best collection in the world of vintage longboards from the surfin' '60s. There are 25 boards on the walls that depict the history of the sport.

VODA
1449 2nd Street
☎ 319-394-9774

Voda is an elegant space behind a large, anonymous brown door next to Hotel Carmel. Inside is a cozy, candle-lit lounge with some well chosen art and a few banquettes, and Santa Monica's only dedicated vodka bar, with heavy emphasis on martinis. Choose from more than 60 brands of vodka; any goes well with smoked salmon or one of the selection of caviars on the menu. Prices go up to $12 a glass for some of the trendy imports.

Clubs

14 BELOW
1348 14th Street
☎ 319-451-5040
www.14below.com
Eclectic

Live music is offered seven nights a week, alternating between rock, reggae, ska and funk. This is a big, sprawling place with two full bars (12 draft beers), pool tables, three different rooms. Happy hour Monday-Friday, 5pm-7pm. Parking adjacent.

GAS LIGHT
2030 Wilshire Boulevard
☎ 310-829-2782
Blues

This is a smallish place with a décor that tends to red tinsel and Christmas lights, but it's a good place to hear the blues, especially on Friday and Saturday nights, when

J.J. "Bad Boy" Jones is on. The club is packed then with young people who come to hear Jones, who must be 75 and learned everything that is in his songs in Deep South juke joints way before his audience was born.

HARVELLE'S BLUES CLUB
1432 4th Street
☎ 310-395-1676
Blues

In a town where clubs come and go so fast no one bothers to write the phone number in ink, Harvelle's has been here since 1931. Top local groups perform funk and rock, but the specialty is blues, jazz and R&B. Dancing or just listening. Opens at 8am. Park close by in the big public parking structure.

McCABE'S
3101 Pico Boulevard
☎ 310-828-4403
Eclectic

Wander through all the guitars and a myriad other instruments with strings on your way into this one-of-a-kind shrine to live music. Music starts nightly at 8pm; Sunday 7pm. Cover is $10-$20 for all ages. Coffee, tea and sweets only, no alcohol.

★★ MAGICOPOLIS
1418 4th Street
☎ 310-451-2241
www.magicopolis.com

There are two theaters here: the smaller Hocus-Pocus Room, which presents close-up magic and sleight of hand, and the Abracadabra Theater for larger illusions and stage events. Penn and Teller performed here (see their handprints and signatures in cement), Stephen King had a birthday party, and David Bowie comes to shows (see their signatures on the Wall of Fame). Call for show times and information.

Magic classes for kids are held on Tuesdays at Magicopolis.

UN-URBAN COFFEE HOUSE
3301 Pico Boulevard
☎ 310-315-0056

Try this place for stand-up comics on Thursday nights, a Song-Writers Soirée with an open mike on Fridays, and a new live band every hour on the hour on Saturdays.

Topanga Canyon

We took some pictures of the native girls, but they weren't developed. But we're going back again in a couple of weeks.

– Chico Marx, *Animal Crackers*

First were the Indians. Those who lived in the area of Topanga, to the south along the coast and well inland east of the Los Angeles River, and in the San Fernando Valley, were all called Gabrielenos by the Spanish who came along toward the end of the 18th century. But there was no large Gabrieleno tribe. They shared a Shoshonean language and a way of life in common, but each village was autonomous.

 # History

Remains of a Gabrieleno village were found at the mouth of Topanga Canyon, near the beach, and others were discovered farther up in the canyon – one at the site of the present post office and shopping area. The oldest excavated was occupied 8,000 years ago. During the Spanish and Mexican eras, Rancho Boca de Santa Monica, granted to Francisco Marquez and Ysidro Reyes, included the lower part of Topanga; Rancho San Vicente y Santa Monica, granted to the Sepúlveda family, took in the upper part; between them was unclaimed public land.

In the 1870s Jesus Santa Maria was the first to homestead in the canyon. He found that the famous bandit Tiburcio Vasquez had a hideout that became known as "Robber's Hut" on the creek bank near present-day Topanga Center. Instead of killing Santa Maria, the bandit said "You stay in your end of the canyon and I'll stay in mine." Later Vasquez, fleeing a posse, rode through Santa Maria's ranch, grabbed a fresh horse and threw some gold on the ground in payment – and escaped the posse.

Early settlers were born in Mexico, or in Los Angeles of Mexican parents. Later 19th-century settlers were Americans from back East. Early in the 20th-century inns and camps were established and Topanga became a popular vacation place. The road from the ocean to the valley was completed during World War I, and Topanga no longer seemed as remote as before.

Bringing It Up to Date

Topanga was still isolated enough in the 1960s, when the "hippies" were evolving, to become "Haight-Ashbury South." (Venice Beach really owned that appellation, but because the population of Topanga was so limited, a relatively small number of hippies had a big impact, especially on an uptight Chamber of Commerce.) Robert Bobrow wrote in the *LA Times*, "Like Mountain folk from the Ozarks to the Alps, the people of Topanga have only one thing in common – their individualism. Topanga is a thoroughly heterogeneous community, combining urban snob appeal and rural slob appeal in just the right proportions... "

Topanga is a Native American word for "the place where the mountains meet the sea."

Development

There was sufficient water from Topanga Creek and various wells to support the early settlements here. By the 1950s, with population climbing, though still under 3,000, a majority of residents voted to hook up with the city-wide Metropolitan Water District. With the water problem permanently solved, a seemingly endless queue of land developers showed up, each with bulldozers ready to reshape the hills into a series of tidy terraces just the right size for thousands of houses, all alike. In the process the developers planned to fill in the canyons and get rid of all those "unnecessary" live oaks that were in the way. One of the

*The small
Pine Circle
Shopping
Center has
bakeries, bou-
tiques, cafés
and galleries.*

early developments was planned for a population of 60,000 to 70,000.

Yet today as you drive up Topanga Canyon Boulevard you will see only a handful of homes, except for a few tracts way up at the top. You might wonder where all the houses are. They are out of sight, up narrow roads that disappear into ravines around the back of slopes and onto solitary knolls. Most of those who live in Topanga are here to live with those oak trees and everything else that grows here naturally just as it is. And probably to get away from crowds of other people.

A majority of Topanga residents organized to block or se-verely mitigate that first development and every one since – and there have been many more attempts to pack a large population into Topanga. One stage performance in the 1970s to raise money to help defeat yet another proposed development included locals Dean Stockwell, Russell Tamblyn, Billy Gray (Bud Anderson in *Father Knows Best)*, Lou Gossett and Tisha Sterling in the cast.

WATCHABLE WILDLIFE

*All phone
numbers in
Topanga
begin with
the prefix
455.*

When driving through Topanga Canyon look in the sky for turkey vultures (*Cathartes aura)*, of-ten seen soaring high overhead; red-tailed hawks (*Buteo jamaicensis)*, which nest on cliffs and dive into meadows for rodents; and red-shouldered hawks (*Buteo lineatus)*, which are endangered elsewhere, but are common in Topanga, and which feed on lizards and snakes.

A Haven for Artists & Musicians

At least since the 1950s Topanga has been home to artists. In this small town of diverse people with a live-and-let-live atmosphere, only a short distance from Hollywood and the money available there to support the arts, it is a natural fit. Bob De Witt was an early artist who made a living from real estate, but refused to rent or sell to people he consid-ered too bourgeois. Sculptors, weavers, print makers, cer-amicists make their homes here, including glass artist

Steven Correia, whose work is found in the Metropolitan Museum of Art, the Smithsonian Institute and the White House.

It seems that musicians have always been here. So many classical musicians have lived here, many of whom are members of the LA Philharmonic, that there is a Topanga Symphony and a Topanga Philharmonic. The Symphony performs three concerts a year, in spring, summer and fall, at the Topanga Community House, 1440 N. Topanga Canyon Blvd. Phone Jack Smith at ☎ 818-999-5775 for dates. The Philharmonic performs once a year, in April, at Theatricum Botanicum (see page 488).

Folk singer Woody Guthrie, who composed the American classic, *This Land is Your Land*, came to live in Topanga in 1952. The rock band Canned Heat, which played at Woodstock, was formed here; Neil Young bought a house here, as did Mick Fleetwood of Fleetwood Mac. The acts that played at the now defunct Corral included Joni Mitchell and the Eagles; Taj Majal was a regular, and the Rolling Stones appeared occasionally.

▣ FILM GLOSSARY

Trade Press – Newspapers and magazines devoted to the entertainment industry, such as the *Daily Variety* and *Hollywood Reporter*. The term does not refer to magazines filled with stories of stars' antics, which are written for fans – "the trades" are strictly about business. Note: Do not take as gospel every item announcing picture deals made or jobs won. Filling the trades with these stories describes a good deal of what press agents do.

Getting Here

By Car

There are two ways to get here, up the coast or over the mountains from the Valley; both are scenic. Coming in one way and out the other makes a lovely drive.

The Coast Route

To park at Topanga State Beach, use lot along Pacific Coast Highway, $5 to $8.

Drive out to Santa Monica (the Santa Monica Freeway, Route 10); or take the slower but more scenic route on Sunset Boulevard. Continue up the Pacific Coast Highway to Topanga Canyon Boulevard (State Highway 27).

The Valley Route

Drive out on the Hollywood Freeway (101), to the Ventura Freeway (still 101); go west to Woodland Hills, then go left (south) on Topanga Canyon Boulevard.

Who Lives Here?

Oddly, we don't know of any hugely famous celebrities residing here; they tend to cling to the coast farther up the Pacific Coast Highway in Malibu rather than venture into these narrow canyons. Among the few are Ben Stiller, Dean Stockwell and, on an incongruous note, the Shah of Iran's brother.

The Jacqueline Hansen Tough Topanga 10K run, held each Memorial Day weekend, is one of the more challenging runs in Southern California.

Dozens of writers have lived in Topanga over the years. Among them are Hugh Lofting, who wrote the *Dr. Doolittle Stories*; novelist Carolyn See; writer-archaeologist Marija Gimbutas, whose books *The Language of the Goddess* and *The Civilization of the Goddess* have become greatly popular and controversial. The community of writers in Greater LA is so small that we happen to have met Laurel Lee, author of children's books and *Walking Through the Fire*, the story of her recovery from cancer;

and Deena Metzger, poet and playwright, both longtime Topanga residents.

Best Places to Stay

Topanga is a very rural, private community. There are no places where visitors can stay overnight. The nearest place is the Channel Road Inn in Pacific Palisades (see page 313); slightly farther are numerous hotels in Santa Monica.

Best Place to Eat

There is just one place – but it is very well known – across the road from the little Topanga Village.

The dining price scale can be found on page 42.

★★ INN OF THE SEVENTH RAY

128 Old Topanga Canyon Road
☎ 310-455-1311
Healthy/New Age
Moderate

A romantic place with outdoor tables under the oak trees overlooking Topanga Creek. The ambiance is casual and leisurely; actor Dennis Weaver swears by the peaceful and beautiful outdoor atmosphere in the summertime and cozy interior dining by the fireplace in winter. Food is organic, mostly vegetarian, but with a few meaty items like free-range chicken. The bread is homemade and we can testify that the lasagna is very good. Friends who live in Topanga love the Sunday brunch, though we haven't tried it. They serve lunch Monday-Saturday; and dinner nightly. A New Age bookstore is attached, popular for browsing before or after a meal.

The Beach Communities

Sunup to Sundown

Picnic & Theater

THEATRICUM BOTANICUM
1419 Topanga Boulevard
Topanga Canyon, CA 90290
☎ 310-455-2322, box office 310-455-3723
www.theatricum.com

This rustic outdoor theater is nestled in the hills of Topanga. When actor Will Geer was blacklisted in the early 1950s for refusing to testify before the House Un-American Activities Committee, he and his actress wife Herta moved to Topanga Canyon and began to produce folk plays and concerts. There were performances by Woody Guthrie, folk singer Pete Seeger, the legendary singer Odetta and Rex Ingram, "De Lawd" in the play *The Green Pastures*.

Later, when the political climate changed and Geer could work in films and TV again, he rebuilt the theater in a natural bowl in a canyon, with magnificent California live oaks overhanging the open stage, and named it Theatricum Botanicum (Theater of Plants). Entrance is through the gates used in the original 1929 film *Ben Hur*. Arlo Guthrie and Burl Ives were among the early performers.

Topanga Creek, like most waterways in the Southwest US, is dry in the summer.

Will Geer, who played Grampa Walton on television, died in 1978 (on Shakespeare's birthday). A bust of Geer by Topanga artist Megan Rice in the Shakespeare Garden was dedicated by John Houseman. Every year during the drama season from June to October, when we attend a performance, we picnic beforehand in the Shakespeare Garden near Will's bust. Plan to have a picnic in the garden before seeing a stage production in the open-air natural amphitheater at Theatricum Botanicum; pick up food en route from a Santa Monica deli (see pages 475-476).

Malibu

He who hesitates is poor. – Zero Mostel, *The Producers*

Malibu is Hollywood plus. Everyone in the world knows about Hollywood; it is where dreams are made. Everyone has heard of Malibu; it is where the dream-makers go to rest luxuriously from their labors. It is the land of milk and honey, the place beyond imagination.

History

According to Chumash legend, the people were brought to what is now Malibu by the goddess Lemeuw. Supposedly, the tribe grew too large for Catalina and the other islands off the coast, so the goddess created a rainbow bridge for the Chumash to cross over onto the mainland. But a sudden storm knocked many of the people off the bridge. To save them, Lemeuw changed them into dolphins, which is why the dolphins are in the bay to this day, and the people are on the land.

The place at the foot of Malibu Canyon was called *Humaliwo*, "where the mountains meet the sea and the surf sounds loudly," which is what our word Malibu comes from. The Chumash lived along the coast from Malibu to San Luis Obispo, way to the north, and in some interior valleys.

> ### 📖 HISTORIC NOTE
>
> The local Indian tribes were named by the Spanish after the nearest missions, such as the Gabrielenos after the San Gabriel Mission and the Fernandeños after the San Fernando Mission.

The Chumash dressed either in skins or in nothing, depending on the weather. Their grass houses were well-constructed, spacious and dome-shaped; the beds were on frames; and they boiled or roasted all their food. Their planked canoes were unique, made with no tools but shells and flints. Whalebone wedges were used to split wooden planks and to pry abalone off rocks. Fish hooks were made of abalone shell. Their baskets were watertight and highly prized. They were an intelligent and peaceful people.

Juan Cabrillo anchored off Malibu Lagoon in 1542 and, without asking anyone's permission, claimed this land for the King of Spain. He named the town and lagoon in the ship's log, *Pueblo de las Canoas*, Town of the Canoes, because of the many well-crafted canoes that rowed out to meet his ship. Three days later he sailed away and the Chumash were blessed, as no other Europeans dropped by for more than 200 years.

In the 1770s King Charles III of Spain was feeling threatened by the English ships exploring the California coast and the Russians pushing down from the north. He sent Juan Bautista de Anza to lead an expedition north from Mexico with 250 people to settle in California. They made camp under the oak trees by Malibu Creek in February 1776.

José Bartolome Tapia, then in his teens, was a member of the de Anza expedition. When the group went on to Northern California, he joined the army and, in 1800, applied for a land grant to the area he had seen called Malibu. Tapia called the land Rancho Malibu; he and his wife and family lived on Vaquero Flats and raised cattle.

In 1844 Leon Victor Prudhomme, 22 years old, arrived in Los Angeles from France. He went to work for Tibúrcio Tapia, son of now-deceased José. When Tapia died three years later, his only daughter, 16-year-old Maria, married Prudhomme. The following year her grandmother, José's widow, sold Rancho Malibu to the young couple.

The deed was signed January 24, 1848, the day gold was discovered in California. For some years times were good, and cattle driven north from Rancho Malibu sold for incredible prices to the miners. But the boom was followed by a bust: in 1857 there was a depression.

Prudhomme sold the entire ranch to Don Mateo Keller, an Irishman, in 1857 for $1,400, about 10¢ an acre, and Keller continued to raise cattle. When he died in 1892, his son, busy elsewhere, sold the beautiful coastal property to

Frederick Hastings Rindge for $10 an acre. There was no one to put in a claim for the Chumash, they were all dead, all signs of them except for scattered rock paintings eradicated.

🎬 FILM GLOSSARY

Foley Artist – The one who re-records sound effects, such as footsteps or door slams, on a Foley Stage, to be added to the final sound track during the sound mix.

The Early 20th Century

When you ride Amtrak south from San Luis Obispo the railroad tracks hug the coastline most of the way until they reach Oxnard, 20 miles north of Malibu. There they turn abruptly inland to continue to Union Station in downtown Los Angeles. The reason for that is the Rindge family's determination to protect the sanctity of Rancho Malibu a century ago. When F.H. Rindge died in 1905, his widow, May, began a 20-year struggle to keep Malibu pristine.

The Southern Pacific Railroad had a line running from Los Angeles west to its Long Wharf, where ships loaded cargo in Santa Monica. It was only natural that its tracks coming south would link up by running along the coast through Malibu. But a little-known law prevented a second railroad from duplicating an already existing rail line. So May built the piddling 15-mile-long Hueneme, Malibu and Port Los Angeles Railroad, which, though it consisted of only a few flat cars and a small gasoline engine, stopped the mighty Southern Pacific in its tracks, as it were.

By that time her fight to prevent a coast highway from being built through Malibu had also begun. Suddenly there were more automobiles around, and people wanted a shortcut up the coast to get to Ventura and Santa Barbara. But May Rindge didn't want hordes coming through her property. Trespassing had already escalated to cattle rustling, vandalism and fires; the big ranch house had been burned down. May put locked gates across the existing private dirt road, and had armed guards patrol on horseback. The newspapers called her "Queen of the Malibu." She brought four cases to the California Supreme Court and two to the US Supreme Court, but in the end she lost; a county road was opened in the early '20s, and Pacific Coast Highway in 1929. Today, the sandstone cliffs that loom over most of the length of the highway as it goes through Malibu are unstable and often crash down after a rain, blocking the road in the same places May Rindge's fences and armed guards blocked it 80 years ago.

Bringing It Up to Date

When Malibu was developed in the 1920s the lots sold to stars became the "Malibu Movie Colony."

Malibu's modern development began in 1928. The first tract of land along the beach just above Malibu Lagoon was offered exclusively to movie stars, to set the tone for what this priceless place was to become. Anna Q. Nilsson built first. Ronald Colman, Jackie Coogan and Dolores del Rio followed, soon joined by Warner Baxter, Constance Bennett, Clara Bow, Gary Cooper, John Gilbert, Mervyn Leroy, Harold Lloyd, Barbara Stanwyck, Gloria Swanson and Jack Warner.

At the beginning no one lived here permanently; they built small beach houses for an average cost of $2,600. That stretch of beach became known as the Malibu Movie Colony, with gates and 24-hour security guards. Access to the Colony is a turn off from Pacific Coast Highway on Webb Way, which dead-ends a half-block later on Malibu Road. The Colony gates are to the left.

People who live in Malibu, no matter their degree of celebrity, eventually become fanatical about the place. Malibu has a lot of obvious advantages. It is very near a huge metropolitan area yet offers a great deal of privacy; it has some lovely beaches, and a Mediterranean climate the rest of the country would kill for. But it also has a propensity for disasters.

Every few years, usually around the Christmas season during a Santa Ana wind, a fire sweeps over those chaparral-covered, largely impenetrable mountains to the east and burns down a few dozen to a few hundred expensive homes. The following year, at the first rain, mud slides down the now-bare mountain slopes and takes out more homes. Many of the beach houses, most of them up on pilings in the sand, have their foundations washed out by fierce periodic storms coming in off the Pacific.

We have friends who live up in the hills off Big Rock Road. A big fire about six years ago destroyed their house, leaving only the concrete slab it was built on. We asked what they were going to do. "Oh," they replied, "we're going to build the same house at the same place. We love it!"

Malibu real estate agents say outsiders come in after a fire, thinking they will be able to pick up bargains. But there are no bargains because no one is selling. That's loyalty.

Getting Here

From LAX

By Car

Get onto Sepulveda Boulevard at the airport, and go left at Lincoln Boulevard, at the northern edge of the airport; then go through Westchester and Marina del Rey. At Washington Boulevard turn left onto Pacific Avenue; this is the last traffic light before the ocean. Go right on Pacific through Venice and into Santa Monica (Pacific Avenue's name changes in Santa Monica to Neilson Way, then to Ocean Avenue, but it is always the same street).

In Santa Monica, pass Pico Boulevard and turn left at the next light, going downhill onto Pacific Coast Highway; then continue north to Malibu.

If traffic is moving along it should take about 45 minutes. If it is the rush hour (approximately 4-7pm), or if there is an accident on PCH, or road work, or a rock slide, take a good book along.

By Bus

It is not realistic to stay in Malibu without a car.

Take the free shuttle bus to Lot C, and transfer to Santa Monica Big Blue Bus #3, get off at 4th Street and Colorado Boulevard, transfer to MTA Bus #434 going west on Colorado. Time to Malibu Civic Center is about 75 minutes at midday, longer at rush hours.

By Shuttle

The fare averages $25 for the first person, $10 for each additional person. Pick up the shuttle at the island in front of each of the terminals. **Prime Time Shuttle**, ☎ 800-733-8267, www.primetimeshuttle.com.

By Taxi

The fare is about $35 plus a $2.50 airport fee from LAX to Malibu. **Malibu Taxi**, ☎ 310-456-0500, charges $35 from Malibu to LAX, and $45 from LAX to Malibu, "because of the airport fee."

☞ DID YOU KNOW?

The City of Malibu covers about 20 square miles, and the land outside city limits, which also calls itself Malibu, takes in another 40 to 60 square miles.

 # Who Lives Here?

Everyone knows Malibu is where the stars live. Ten years ago, as we would drive up Pacific Coast Highway (Highway 1, or PCH) through one of those stretches where we were just 100 feet from the ocean but unable to see it because of a wall of homes between the road and the water, we always knew which was Steve Martin's house because his was the only roof that sprouted a satellite dish. Now rooftop dishes are as ubiquitous as surfers.

Unlike the earliest days, celebrities now live not just in the Colony but all over Malibu. It will be helpful to have a mental picture of how Malibu is laid out. As you drive up Pacific Coast Highway from Santa Monica, Malibu starts just past Topanga Canyon. First there is a long stretch of houses packed close together on the left, on a small bluff overlooking the beach (or just rocks in some places where there is no beach). Occasionally there is a break, where a stream comes down the mountains or for some reason houses couldn't be built there, so you have a view of the ocean. There is nothing on the right but the raw cliff, with houses in the hills above, most with magnificent views of the coastline and ocean.

Steve Martin and Burt Reynolds live on the beach side along here; Bruce Willis and Shirley MacLaine farther on. Olivia Newton-John has quite a large place in the hills in the Big Rock area. Jeff Bridges, George Wendt of *Cheers*, and Kris Kristofferson have homes in the hills past Big Rock. Sean Penn lives up above Carbon Beach.

After the coast, which has been tending westward, turns more to the north at Duke's Restaurant, the highway broadens and there are businesses on your right until you come to the Malibu Pier. After that is Cross Creek Road, a small business section, with the Colony and Malibu Road to your left.

Also to your right, but south of Malibu Creek, is the Serra Retreat high up on the hill where the Rindge family built their mansion. Charles Bronson lives near here and keeps horses on the hill.

In the Colony and along the beach live celebrities like Dyan Cannon, Bruce Dern, Adam Sandler, Whoopi Goldberg, Cher, Suzanne Somers (who has 90 feet of beachfront where the average lot has about 40 feet), Courteney Cox (*Friends*) and her husband, David Arquette (*The Grey Zone*). Add Tom Hanks, Mel Gibson, Dick Clark, Kelsey Grammer and Jaclyn Smith. Walter Matthau had his home on the beach, and Ed Begley Jr. and comic-actor Howie Mandel both recently sold their homes in the Colony. Jack Warden spends weekends at his Colony home, mainly for the tennis.

Former Malibu Mayor Tom Hasse said: "Malibu is only about a mile wide. We're like a big, long string bean of a city."

The Beach Communities

Pepperdine University, though only 100 yards from the beach, opted to stay outside the City of Malibu when it was formed.

The civic center is just past Cross Creek Road; Pepperdine University sprawls over the top of the hill ahead. This is also where Malibu Canyon Road heads north toward the San Fernando Valley. Continue on PCH to where the highway rolls down to the next cove and you see the end of Malibu Road, which joins Pacific Coast Highway here. You can exit from it to PCH, if you have chosen to drive along Malibu Road, which hugs the beach, but you cannot enter it here.

ABOUT PEPPERDINE UNIVERSITY

When the annual *Princeton Review* ranking of colleges nationwide came out last year it listed Malibu's Pepperdine this way:

◆ 5th for students who pray the most

◆ 11th for happiest students

◆ 15th for students who (almost) never study

Everyone assumes that the Smothers Theatre at Pepperdine University was named for the Smothers Brothers, but 'twas Frances D. Smothers, a benefactor.

North of Pepperdine, Malibu goes back more than a mile into the mountains, with wide upland pastures that have broad views over the ocean. The highway is farther inland from the edge of the bluff so there are larger estates on the ocean side. Director James Cameron (*Titanic*), for instance, last year bought 500 acres of pastureland with two small houses on the inland side. And if you think you might like to rent a place when you are here, the bluff-top home of Richard Gere and Carey Lowell, of *Law & Order*, is available as we write this. It has two guest houses, a pool and tennis court and 90 feet of private beach with a cottage on the sand. It rents for $75,000 a month in July and August.

Continue on PCH; when you come to Kanan-Dume Road splitting off into the mountains (a great mountain drive if you want to end up in tamed and manicured Westlake Village) you know you have reached Point Dume. The highway is well away from the beach here, leaving a great deal of space for homes on rural lanes. One tends to think that stars must have huge, palatial homes, but that is not always so. Rod Steiger lives here in a very nice, one-story house surrounded by a lot of foliage. It is ordinary looking rather than an outstanding eye-catcher, but really comfortable.

Johnny Carson lives in Point Dume, as do Pierce Brosnan, Dick Van Dyke, Martin Sheen, Lou Gossett Jr., Craig T. Nelson and Henry Gibson. Barbra Streisand and husband James Brolin have a three-acre place on the bluff on the ocean side of the highway in Point Dume. Here, too, rather than something visually overwhelming and out of scale, you'll find a few old-fashioned, low-slung farmhouses surrounded by gardens with an emphasis on native, drought-resistant plants.

Streisand bought her first place in Malibu almost 30 years ago, on the inland side of PCH in Ramirez Canyon. There was first a modest residence on the property called "The Barn." Over the years she added more land, built a recording studio, a bigger house and several guest cottages. She brought in 1,000 trees to join the native sycamores and relocated Ramirez Creek. By the time she moved out it was a stunning estate, which she donated to the Santa Monica Mountains Conservancy. You can take a two-hour guided tour of the property at 5750 Ramirez Canyon Road; the cost is $30. ☎ 310-589-2850.

Although the sign as you enter Malibu proclaims "27 miles of beaches," it is actually only 19.9 miles as the crow flies.

The highway continues north, going downhill to Zuma Beach, a long, long gated strand, much used by surfers and swimmers from the San Fernando Valley (those from metropolitan Los Angeles and the West Los Angeles area tend to go to Santa Monica and Venice beaches). The beach and area just past Zuma is Trancas.

If you continue, you will come to Broad Beach Road, which is especially thick with celebrities; it branches off PCH to run along the beach. Goldie Hawn, Tom Hanks, Sylvester Stallone and Steven Spielberg live on Broad Beach. Robert Redford sold his large place last year, along with the next door lot he bought from Neil Simon to protect his view, only to buy a smaller place in the same area.

Fires are not allowed on any Los Angeles County beaches, which includes Malibu.

The Beach Communities

On Location

Film shoots in Malibu are mostly on the beaches, with an occasional scene done at Malibu Creek State Park and in Malibu Canyon. Paradise Cove and Malibu Lagoon State Beach are where Hollywood's mythic version of the Los Angeles beach scene began – Annette Funicello romped on the sand in Paradise Cove in *Pajama Party*. (Paradise Cove is north of Geoffrey's Restaurant; there is a traffic light on PCH and a road going down to the beach.) The 1960s beach-flick craze went on with *Beach Blanket Bingo*, *Beach Party* and *Muscle Beach Party*. Then there was the beach-blanket revival movement with *Back to the Beach*.

Later Robert Redford and Barbra Streisand filmed scenes for *The Way We Were* at Paradise Cove, and Redford was here again in *Indecent Proposal*. Other films using Malibu locations include *Apollo 13*, *The Net*, *Deep Rising* and *Lethal Weapon 4*.

While other television series have filmed individual episodes at Paradise Cove, *Rockford Files* became a permanent tenant. Jim Rockford's trailer was part of the action on the sand here for 125 episodes in the 1970s and six movies in the 1990s, surviving storms, wildfires, mud slides and earthquakes.

City of Angels has some scenes filmed at Nicholas Canyon Beach; *Bounce* and *Pearl Harbor* used the beach below Point Dume; and a number of *Baywatch* episodes were filmed at Surfrider Beach, near the Malibu Pier.

Just inland, on the other side of the Pacific Coast Highway, is where a number of big films shot key scenes: *How the West Was Won*, *The Swiss Family Robinson*, *Planet of* *the Apes, M*A*S*H,* and *Butch Cassidy and the Sundance Kid.*

✏️ Best Places to Stay

The Beach Communities

Malibu tends to astonish and disappoint those who have never before seen it, and yet its very name remains, in the imagination of people all over the world, a kind of shorthand for the easy life. I had not before 1971 and will probably not again live in a place with a Chevrolet named after it.

– Joan Didion, *Quiet Days in Malibu*

There is only one real hotel in Malibu, a small one, plus an inn and a few motels. How can that be? Every hotel chain in the country would love to plant a 20-story Hilton, Sheraton or Marriott on one of these fabulous beaches in this place that exudes world-wide publicity on a daily basis. Well, there is a story behind that.

Just as two generations of the Rindge family fought to maintain their own little paradise by keeping outsiders outside where they belonged, the first celebrities who were allowed to buy land here valued Malibu for the privacy it afforded them, the opportunity to be themselves without thousands of curious eyes watching their every move. That privacy depended partly on its remoteness, and the fact that the Rindge family had kept it primitive. For instance, each house had to have its own septic tank. Voila! The lowly, not-mentioned-in-polite-company septic tank turned out to be Malibu's salvation.

The accommodations price scale can be found on page 39.

A big development like a hotel can't make it with a simple septic tank buried in the ground; it would immediately be overwhelmed. So the first time a large development wanted to build on the beach, Los Angeles County obligingly proposed to extend its sewer lines to Malibu. (Los Angeles' governments, both city and county, have never met a land development scheme they didn't like.) But there was a catch: there is a law that a majority of the homeowners who will have to pay for the new sewer line must vote in favor.

Overnight camping is allowed at Leo Carrillo State Park, just north of Malibu.

Malibu's residents voted down the proposal for a sewer line, and for the past 80 years have continued to vote it down every time the idea is reintroduced. It is the reason Malibu became an independent city in 1991: it was the only way the residents could stop the Los Angeles County Board of Supervisors, who were once again bent on forcing a sewer line and inevitable over-development on Malibu. Cityhood won easily. Malibu still has no sewers – and no big hotels.

MALIBU BEACH INN
22878 Pacific Coast Highway
Malibu, CA 90265
☎ 310-456-6444, 800-4-MALIBU, Canada 800-255-1007, fax 310-456-1499
www.malibubeachinn.com
Expensive

They call it "A small hotel on the beach." The long, low, three-story building is in Spanish-Moorish style with lots of tile and a soft beige color with a tile roof. The lobby floor is covered with big Mexican tiles. There are some good pieces of silver and turquoise available in the hotel's Native American Jewelry Gallery.

We like the rooms. Every one has a private balcony, and cane furniture that makes it feel like a cottage on the beach, rather than a hotel room. Some of the rooms have a two-person Jacuzzi on the balcony. The hotel is just south of the Malibu Pier, so that is in the foreground when the sun goes down over Point Dume. It can be a romantic spot.

Continental breakfast is complimentary, either in the lobby or out on the terrace overlooking the ocean. We thought that was a very nice way to start the day, and the thick terrycloth robes they provided were a nice way to end it.

MALIBU COUNTRY INN
6506 Westward Beach Road
Malibu, CA 90265
☎ 310-457-9622, 800-FUN-N-SURF, fax 310-457-1349
www.malibucountryinn.com
Moderate-Expensive

This place, well off the highway on a quiet bluff over the ocean, is a romantic country hideaway. The inn has nine standard garden-view rooms, two rooms with Jacuzzi tub, and five one-room suites with fireplace and Jacuzzi. All rooms have a refrigerator and coffee maker. There is a swimming pool, a rose garden and complimentary continental breakfast. A poolside restaurant, the **Hideaway Café**, serves breakfast and lunch daily, 8:30am-2:30pm.

To get here, take Pacific Coast Highway past Kanan-Dume Road to Heather Cliff Road, which is the next traffic light. PCH goes steeply downhill here. At the bottom of the hill take Westward Beach Road to the left, just before the entrance to Zuma Beach parking lot.

TONI BERGET
☎ 310-457-7119, 818-790-7788

Toni is not a real estate agent, but she owns a few houses that are available for short-term rental. There are two places in Point Dume with fabulous views over Zuma Beach and the ocean, and a two-bedroom place in the Malibu Colony with an ocean view. Rentals are approximately $200 a night for a one-bedroom, higher for a two-bedroom, with rates by the week or month.

Best Places to Eat

Fine Dining

I never drink... wine. – Bela Lugosi, *Dracula*

★★ GEOFFREY'S
27400 Pacific Coast Highway
☎ 310-457-1519
California
Expensive

The dining price scale can be found on page 42.

At Geoffrey's you'll enjoy great views of the coast and ocean, especially at sunset, along with excellent food; it's a natural habitat of celebrities. The menu is heavy with fish, but also offers filets for meat eaters. Open Monday-Friday, noon-9:30pm; Saturday and Sunday, 11am-9:30pm. If you take the Pacific Coast Highway from Santa Monica, Geoffrey's is up the next hill past Pepperdine. Go past the restaurant and make a U-turn.

★★ GRANITA

Malibu Colony Plaza
23725 Malibu Road
☎ 310-456-0488
California-Provençal
Expensive

Granita is an Italian shaved ice dessert.

Granita is a very popular restaurant for those who live in Malibu. The menu is strong on fish and seafood, but there are also chops, steak and even short ribs, and, since Wolfgang Puck owns the place, there is a wood-burning oven putting out several kinds of his signature exotic pizzas. It is a large place with an open kitchen, a lounge and bar upstairs, and front and side patios used in season. The restaurant is open for lunch, Saturday-Sunday, 11am-2:30pm; and for dinner, weeknights, 6-11pm; Saturday-Sunday, 5:30-11:30pm. Reservations are a must. Go out Pacific Coast Highway, past the Malibu Pier to Webb Way; the restaurant is in the shopping center.

★★ BEAURIVAGE

26025 Pacific Coast Highway
☎ 310-456-5733
Mediterranean
Expensive

Daniel Forge, a delightful man with a charming French accent, opened this place at the mouth of Corral Canyon 20 years ago when Mediterranean dining was unknown in Los Angeles. But after the first few years of confusion – food critics insisted on calling his menu continental or French – this has been a consistently valued restaurant by those who live in Malibu.

Beaurivage has the most extensive wine list in Malibu.

On one of our visits, Heather Locklear was having her birthday party in the wine cellar, which many, like Pamela Anderson of *Baywatch*, prefer for dining. There is also a patio and an upstairs terrace with a good view of the ocean, as well as the main dining room. Malibu is thick with celebrities and there are only a few really good restaurants, which is why people like Johnny Carson, Barbra Streisand and Jim Brolin, Robert Redford and dozens more drop in here for dinner. Beaurivage is open nightly for dinner, and on Sundays for brunch. There is a pianist on weeknights. Reservations advised, especially on weekends.

★★ SADDLE PEAK LODGE

419 Cold Canyon Road
☎ 310-456-7325, 818-222-3888
Game
Expensive

A romantic lodge in the country that draws couples, including celebrity couples, as it has for many years. It began as a cabin more than 100 years ago, was a general store, then in the 1920s was a roadhouse that drew the starlets and stars who were shooting at the nearby ranches owned by Paramount, Warner Bros. and 20th Century Fox. Charlie Chaplin and Mary Pickford, Errol Flynn and Clark Gable, Ernest Borgnine, Milton Berle and more found this "in" place. There are lots of stories; we are not sure if we believe that Richard Burton, and at another time the Hollywood Rat Pack, fed the coyotes with buffalo bones thrown from the back terraces at night.

Inside the atmosphere is rustic, with heavy, hand-hewn wood beams, rock walls, and mounted animal heads. They have always offered the kind of meals a hunting lodge should serve: rack of venison, roasted elk tenderloin, wild boar, pheasant, Sonoma duck and always a halibut or salmon dish. The lodge is open Tuesday-Sunday nights for dinner. From the Westside, take the Pacific Coast Highway to Malibu Canyon Road, go 4½ miles to Piuma Road (there is a traffic light), right ¾ mile to Cold Canyon Road, and turn left. From the Valley, take the Ventura Freeway (101) past Calabasas to Las Virgenes Road, turn left and go five miles to Piuma Road, then another left for ¾ mile.

★★ TRA DI NOI

3835 South Cross Creek Road
☎ 310-456-0169
Italian
Expensive

This is Dennis Weaver's favorite place when he is in Malibu. The restaurant not only has good pasta, but does good things with fish, too. Cross Creek is the little shopping area on the right when you come up PCH from the Santa

Monica direction. Start watching after you pass the Malibu Pier. Open daily, noon-10pm.

Casual Dining

CANYON GROCERY & GRILL
2598 Sierra Creek Road
☎ 818-991-0818
Hot dogs, burritos, fish & chips
Inexpensive

Take scenic Kanan-Dume Road from Malibu; from Point Dume the road punches through three tunnels to get through the straight-up mountains and then plunges down into the Agoura Valley. At the bottom of the hill, where Sierra Creek Road branches off, sits the only structure on the entire length of the Kanan-Dume Road. Owner Alladin Premji calls it "the Brown Derby of the mountains," because everybody who lives around here comes in at one time or another since it is all there is. Nick Nolte lives around here, and Mel Gibson just bought some property, though Alladin tells us there are more rockers than movie stars, people like Tommy Lee of Motley Crüe.

Whenever we go to Westlake we try to arrange it so we come back through the canyon around noon, and stop to order a huge, oozing burrito, or a messy chili dog, and eat it outside under the sycamores. Open daily, 10am-8pm.

> ★ **TIP**
>
> The 10K Dolphin Run is held every fall in Malibu to benefit local charities. If you would like to participate, or just watch, phone ☎ 310-450-8540.

Shopping

One would naturally think that with Malibu's wealthy, fashion-conscious population it must be a shopping mecca with expensive boutiques around every corner. That isn't really the case. In fact, the best places to shop here are in the food markets, where you are more likely to see stars among the succotash than in any other markets in the country.

★★ RALPH'S MARKET
23841 Malibu Road
☎ 310-456-2917

When you drive up Pacific Coast Highway past Malibu Pier and Surfriders Beach and past Cross Creek shopping area on the right, the next street is Webb Way. The big market in the long shopping area on your left, on the other side of Webb Way, is Ralph's. It is one of a chain, they have dozens of sizeable markets like this all over Los Angeles. But because there are so many stars living in a small area (Malibu's population is only 12,000), and Ralph's is the only complete market, you are likely to find the most celebrities shopping here.

Services

Health & Fitness

Malibu Gym, 28955 Pacific Coast Highway, is a very well-equipped place to work out, with 12,500 feet of space and equipment: two steam rooms (male and female), cardiovascular room, an aerobics floor, and classes in yoga, tai chi and body sculpting. At the corner of Kanan-Dume Road and PCH. ☎ 310-457-2450.

Malibu Health, Fitness Center and Spa, 22917 Pacific Coast Highway, Suite 220, has a gym and health services. They offer more than a dozen types of massage, facial treatments, mud baths, seaweed baths; yoga, stretch and other classes, and fitness instructors, Olympic free weights and boxing training. Near the pier on the inland side of PCH. ☎ 310-456-7721.

Sunup to Sundown

The **Farmers' Market** is open every Sunday from May-October, 11am-3pm, at the Malibu Civic Center. Turn right at the traffic light at Webb Way (½ mile north of Malibu Pier); there's plenty of easy parking. Both organic and non-organic fresh fruit and vegetables are offered. Malibu-grown is preferred, so you will find local avocados and fresh-cut flowers. There is a food court for stuff to eat now; it may be Greek or grilled ears of corn, it changes. (Malibu's proceeds from the farmers' market go to plant gardens in elementary schools, and teach kids organic gardening.)

Malibu's Dan Blocker Beach is named after the co-star of the television series Bonanza.

This is where you will see stars with their hair down – or sometimes with it up. As a friend of ours said, "At the farmers' market you see stars only if you pay attention." He was at the market the previous Sunday and saw Suzanne Somers, only there she was just another neighbor wearing jeans and tennies, with her hair up under a baseball cap. Kelsey Grammer was easier to recognize the last time we were there. Dick Van Dyke, Shirley MacLaine and Mel Gibson are in attendance fairly often. ☎ 310-457-4537.

At **Adventures on Horseback**, 2666 Triunfo Canyon Road, Agoura Hills, ☎ 818-889-6918, a dozen different rides are offered at various skill levels, morning and night, through canyons and foothills. Several trips visit the Paramount Ranch, where *Dr. Quinn, Medicine Woman* was filmed, and one ride is along the Malibu Creek Trail, which was the film site for the series *M*A*S*H*. There are romantic sunset rides for couples, and some for children as well. To get here, take Kanan-Dume Road off Pacific Coast Highway; Triunfo is just west of Sierra Creek Road and Rustic Canyon Grocery & Grill. If you are in the San Fernando Valley you can catch Kanan-Dume off the Ventura Freeway (Highway 101).

Surfriders Beach, Zuma Beach and Leo Carrillo Beach are the most popular beaches in Malibu.

The best-known surfing beach in the country is here at **Surfriders Beach**, just north of the Malibu Pier. This is where Duke Kahanamoku brought his long board from Hawaii in 1926 and introduced surfing to the world. Though much of the year the waves are not exceptionally large, certainly nothing like the ones on Oahu, because of the slope of the bottom there are very long waves to ride. You will find surfers from around the world who are drawn here. We have *never* driven past on PCH that there weren't surfers in the water, patiently waiting, and wait-

The Beach Communities

ing, and waiting for that perfect wave. Park on Pacific Coast Highway.

☞ DID YOU KNOW?

Though surfing was first introduced in Huntington Beach 30 miles to the south, it was in Malibu in 1926 that the daring new sport became popular.

If you are here any time from February to early April, Point Dume is one of the best places along the Pacific Coast to see the **whales** migrating back north after their long trek from Alaska's Bering Sea to the warm mating and breeding lagoons of Baja California. Whales often pass less than 100 yards from shore; because deep water is close to shore here they sometimes come within 20 feet offshore to rub the barnacles attached to their skin off on the sand. Most of the whales are Pacific Gray and blue, but you can also see sperm, killer, finback and humpback whales. Like sighting celebrities, it is a matter of luck if any are passing by at the time you are here, but dolphins, sea lions and pelicans are often also here in abundance.

Half-day and full-day cruises to the Channel Islands can be taken from Oxnard Marina, 20 miles north of Malibu.

Take Pacific Coast Highway to Westward Beach Road, past the little Point Dume shopping area at the top of the hill and on down to the bottom of the hill just before Zuma Beach. Follow the road to Westward Beach, where parking is $5. Sit on the beach (near Lifeguard Station #1 is best) or climb the trail to the headlands for a view farther out. Bring binoculars. More info: Point Dume Lifeguard Station, ☎ 310-457-9891.

Malibu Kayak Rentals, 22935 Pacific Coast Highway, rents both one- and two-person kayaks, scuba gear and fishing tackle. Open daily, 10am-6pm. Near Malibu Pier on the inland side of the highway. ☎ 310-456-6302.

After Dark

MALIBU STAGE COMPANY
29243 Pacific Coast Highway
☎ 310-289-2999

The theater is housed in an odd building, a converted '70s-style Lutheran church. The company presents good, usually well-known plays on weekends.

? The Beach Communities A to Z

Automotive Service

Topanga Central Auto Service, 106 South Topanga Canyon Boulevard, ☎ 310-455-1568.

Cameras

Venice Camera Exchange, 2417 Lincoln Boulevard, Venice (near South Venice Boulevard), ☎ 310-821-5611.

Dog Park

Westminster Dog Park, Westminster and Main streets, Venice (three blocks north of the Windward Traffic Circle), is a block-and-a-half long, half-block wide, fenced park where dogs can run off the leash. It is one of the few on the Westside, and is extremely popular with dog owners.

E-mail, Fax & Internet Services

Global Gossip, 80 Windward Avenue, Venice, ☎ 310-450-5019, fax 310-450-5935, www.globalgossip.com. A place to keep in touch with the folks back home.

Hospitals

Freeman Marina Hospital, ☎ 310-823-8911, in Marina del Rey, has 24-hour emergency facilities. Other area medical centers include **Santa Monica UCLA Hospital**, ☎ 310-319-4000; **St. John's Hospital**, Santa Monica, ☎ 310-829-5511; and **Topanga Medical Clinic**, 395 South Topanga Canyon Boulevard, ☎ 310-455-2019.

Lifeguards

Emergency numbers for local beaches: **Marina del Rey**, **Topanga Beach**, and **Santa Monica**, ☎ 310-394-3261; Malibu (including Corral Beach, Nicholas Canyon, Point Dume and Zuma Beach), ☎ 310-475-2525; **Leo Carrillo Beach**, ☎ 310-488-0887.

Locksmith

Malibu Locksmith, 22775 Pacific Coast Hwy., ☎ 310-456-7045.

Newspapers

The Argonaut, Marina del Rey . . . . ☎ 310-822-1629
The Messenger, Topanga Canyon . . . . . . ☎ 310-455-1303

Newsstand

Malibu Newsstand, 23717½ Malibu Road, ☎ 310-456-1519, has domestic and foreign publications; it's on the side of the Bank of America building; open daily, 8 am-8pm.

Parks & Recreation Facilities

Malibu Parks & Recreation, ☎ 310-317-1364

Santa Monica Mountains Conservancy, ☎ 310-456-5046

Malibu Beach RV Park, 25801 Pacific Coast Highway, ☎ 310-456-6052. Some daily, weekly rental spaces. Reserve ahead.

Police & Fire

Emergency................................ ☎ 911
Crime Reporting .... ☎ 800-78-CRIME
Poison Control .... ☎ 800-876-4766
Suicide Prevention .... ☎ 310-391-1253, 877-727-4747
LA County Sheriff's Department .... ☎ 310-823-7762
Malibu Sheriff's Station .... ☎ 310-456-6652
Santa Monica Police .... ☎ 310-458-8491
Topanga Canyon Police .... ☎ 818-756-8543
Venice Police...................... ☎ 310-451-5273

Public Transportation

Culver City Bus Line, ☎ 310-253-6500; recorded information, ☎ 310-253-6510.

MTA (Los Angeles) .... ☎ 213-626-4455
Santa Monica Bus Co. .... ☎ 310-451-5444

Time & Weather

Time	☎ 310-853-1212
Surfing Conditions	☎ 310-578-0478
Weather	☎ 213-554-1212

Veterinary Services

Malibu Animal Hospital, 23431 Pacific Coast Highway, ☎ 310-456-6441.

Visitor Information

LA County/Marina del Rey Beaches & Harbors Visitors Center, 4701 Admiralty Way (corner of Mindanao Way), ☎310-305-9545. Open daily, 9am-5pm.

Venice Boardwalk Association, 8 Horizon Avenue, Venice, CA 90291; ☎ 310-392-4687 ext. 6; fax 310-399-4512; www.westland.net/Venice.

Santa Monica Convention & Visitors Bureau, 1400 Ocean Avenue, Santa Monica, CA 90401, ☎ 310-393-7593, www.santamonica.com.

Topanga Chamber of Commerce, PO Box 185, Topanga, CA 90290 (does not take phone calls). Additional information available from the **Topanga Historical Society**, ☎ 310-455-1969, or on the Web at www.topangaonline.com.

Malibu Chamber of Commerce, 23805 West Stuart Ranch Road, Malibu 90265, ☎ 310-456-9025.

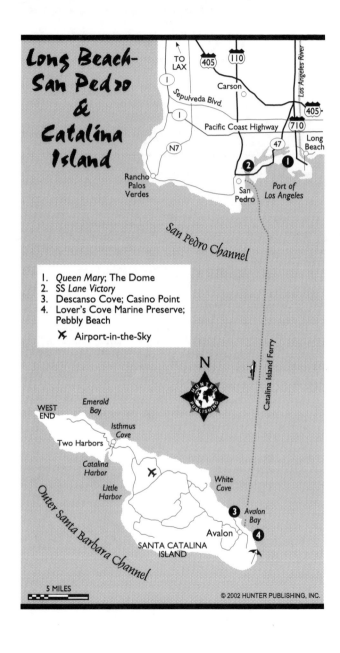

Long Beach-San Pedro & Catalina Island

TO LAX

405 110

Carson

Sepulveda Blvd.

405

Pacific Coast Highway 710

N7

Long Beach

❷ ❶

Rancho Palos Verdes

San Pedro

Port of Los Angeles

San Pedro Channel

1. *Queen Mary*; The Dome
2. SS *Lane Victory*
3. Descanso Cove; Casino Point
4. Lover's Cove Marine Preserve; Pebbly Beach

✗ Airport-in-the-Sky

N

HUNTER PUBLISHING

Catalina Island Ferry

Emerald Bay

WEST END

Isthmus Cove

Two Harbors

Catalina Harbor

Little Harbor

✗

White Cove

Outer Santa Barbara Channel

❸ Avalon Bay

Avalon ❹

SANTA CATALINA ISLAND

5 MILES

© 2002 HUNTER PUBLISHING, INC.

Day-Trips

There are a multitude of worthwhile places to go in Southern California outside the LA/Hollywood area. We have chosen a few sidetrips that are easy to get to and return from in one day, or where you can stay over if you would like. Each area has a fascinating history connected with the movies.

May August moon bring gentle sleep. Sayonara.
— Marlon Brando as Taki,
The Teahouse of the August Moon

Catalina Island

When you look out to the Pacific Ocean from the Hollywood Hills, that island you see off the coast to the south is Catalina. Mainlanders have been visiting the island for more than a century. And the ones who settle down to live there hardly ever want to return.

History

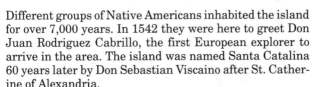

Different groups of Native Americans inhabited the island for over 7,000 years. In 1542 they were here to greet Don Juan Rodriguez Cabrillo, the first European explorer to arrive in the area. The island was named Santa Catalina 60 years later by Don Sebastian Viscaino after St. Catherine of Alexandria.

The 18th & 19th Centuries

In the 1790s, Americans, Russians and Aleut Indians hunted sea otter here in defiance of Spain. The island was a haven for Yankee smugglers during the Mexican era in the early 1800s. When the Americans took over California, squatters arrived with sheep and cattle.

Catalina was the Chicago Cubs' spring training camp while Wrigley owned both the team and the island.

Vacationers first showed up in the 1880s. William Wrigley Jr. bought the island in 1919 and made it an international fishing destination, as well as a center for tourism. But by the 1970s, as the popularity of the island increased, it became apparent that something must be done to preserve the island's charm. The Wrigley family deeded 88% of the land to a non-profit conservancy they formed in order to preserve and protect the island's native plants and animals.

Bringing It Up to Date

The Catalina Island fox is a much smaller version of the mainland gray fox, and is found only here.

Today, almost all permanent residents live in the town of **Avalon**, with a few at **Two Harbors**. The rest of the island is much as it was when the first European explorers arrived. The ground squirrels, quail and Catalina Island Fox are indigenous; the wild pigs, goats and deer are not.

The non-native plants and animals have been very destructive of the unique native species. Goats were brought over by Spanish missionaries in the 1800s, and over the next two centuries their grazing wreaked havoc on the island's topography. A decade ago there were more than 5,000; now, all but two females have been captured and removed. The last 300 tusked and shaggy feral pigs are targeted for removal. Of the 2,000 mule deer – descendants of the original 19 brought over in 1930 – about 850 are left.

FLYING FISH

The season to see flying fish is from April to September.

Catalina's flying fish are the world's largest; they can be up to 18 inches long, with bluish bodies and iridescent wings. Escaping underwater predators, the fish swims its fastest – up to 20 miles an hour – then as he breaks the surface wriggles his big tail fin for a final burst of speed. Most of the airborne fish a visitor sees are fleeing an approaching boat. On a calm day a flying fish can glide 75 yards through the air.

Catalina is a pleasant, small resort area with a mild climate and none of the pressures of the big city. For instance, there is not enough room for many cars in the small town of Avalon, so the number is capped; residents get on a 10-year waiting list for a permit to import a car. In the meantime, most people, including tourists, get around in motorized golf carts.

Catalina Islanders refer to Los Angeles, across the water, as "overtown."

Sports and recreation are mostly on and under the water: boating, diving, fishing. There is a postage-stamp-size beach and pleasant walks. Bus tours of the island can take up much of a visitor's time.

There is a story about Avalon that pretty much puts this small resort town in perspective. There has been a Mexican-American population here dating back about 100 years; in the late 1980s the City Council decided there were too many illegal aliens living amongst the descendants of some of the early settlers, and they called for the Immigration Service and the Coast Guard to do something. Those two agencies conducted a 3am raid with scores of uniformed men that, sure enough, netted around 200 Spanish-speaking people. Some had been born in the US but could not produce papers, so they were all hauled away. And pleased City Council members thought the problem was solved.

Except that every hotel and restaurant owner in Avalon showed up at the next Council meeting shouting that they did not have anyone to make beds, serve meals or do any of the work that needed doing. They threatened to recall every member of the City Council if they did not get their workers back, illegal or not. (No one appears to have suggested that paying better wages would bring legal workers.) In any case, within a week all the original workers were back, and no one has mentioned citizenship since.

Getting Here

By Sea

Catalina Express provides year-round service from the Port of LA to Catalina, with 30 daily departures; the trip takes about an hour. Take the Harbor Freeway (110) south from Los Angeles to its end at San Pedro, then take the Terminal Island-Long Beach exit to Harbor Boulevard. Follow signs to the Catalina Terminal entrance across

Harbor Boulevard. Catalina Express, Berth 95, San Pedro, ☎ 319-519-1212, 800-481-3470 or 800-618-5533, www.catalinaexpress.com. Round-trip fare for adults is about $45; call for reservations.

By Air

The Airport-in-the-Sky is so called because it is perched atop the island's highest point.

Bravo Aviation offers chartered helicopter flights from LAX to Catalina's Airport-in-the-Sky. Round-trip, all-inclusive day packages are available; the minimum rate is $360. To book a flight, contact Bravo Aviation, ☎ 800-77-FLYING, www.bravoair.com.

Island Express Helicopter Service goes from San Pedro to Avalon; the trip takes 15 minutes. Day package available. Island Express, San Pedro Boat Terminals, ☎ 800-2-AVALON (800-228-2566).

> ★ **TIP**
>
> The town of Avalon covers one square mile; its tight grid of narrow streets contains 300 businesses, including hotels and restaurants. It is an eminently walkable resort town.

 ## Getting Around

By Bus

The area code for Catalina Island is 310, and the prefix for all island phone numbers is 510.

Catalina Safari Bus, ☎ 310-510-2800. Scheduled bus service between Avalon and Two Harbors, stops at beaches, trails, campgrounds and the airport.

By Taxi & Golf Cart

Catalina Island Taxi Services, ☎ 310-510-0025. Taxis for hire, six-passenger vans for charter to the interior.

Cartopia Golf Cart Rentals, ☎ 310-510-2493. Week day specials.

Catalina Auto & Bike Rental, corner of Metropole and Crescent, ☎ 310-510-0111.

Island Rentals, at Holly Hill House, 125 Pebbly Beach Road, ☎ 310-510-1456. Gas-powered golf carts for rent.

Catalina Island is eight miles wide at its widest, and 21 miles long, with 48 miles of coastline.

By Bicycle

Brown's Bikes, 107 Pebbly Beach Road (across from basketball courts), ☎ 310-510-0986. Rent mountain bikes, tandems, children's bikes, also strollers and wheelchairs. Hourly and daily rates.

Catalina Auto & Bike Rental, Crescent Avenue on the beach, ☎ 310-510-0111, has mountain bikes ($10/hour, $25/day) and beach bikes ($5-$10). Open 9am-5pm.

On Location

Unlike everywhere else in the Los Angeles area, where records were lost and no one bothered to keep track anyway, you can look up every movie, documentary, travel film, TV show and commercial that has ever been shot on Catalina Island. The number is creeping up on 300 and counting. The first was *Feeding the Seals* in 1910 (we doubt that it had a terribly complicated plot). A film about whaling was shot in 1911, and *Man's Genesis*, by D.W. Griffith, in 1912. Four short silents were filmed here in 1913, and there were 13 in 1914. And so it went.

Universal Pictures made the first silent American version of *Treasure Island* here in 1918, and Paramount shot *Terror Island*, with Harry Houdini, in 1920. The silent version of *The Ten Commandments* was filmed here in 1923, and Buster Keaton shot parts of *The Navigator* in 1924. *King of Kings* and *Ben Hur* were partially filmed here in 1925. The first take on Somerset Maugham's tale *Sadie Thompson* was done here in 1928, and the version with Joan Crawford, called *Rain*, in 1932. The great silent film *Seventh Heaven*, with Janet Gaynor, was shot here in 1928, and the unforgettable *Treasure Island* with Wallace Beery in 1933.

Several soap operas have been filmed on Catalina, including Days of Our Lives in 2001.

Catalina, looking so much like a South Pacific island and so close to Hollywood, was just right in 1935 for *Mutiny on*

Two Harbors, in the north end of Catalina Island, is a favorite place for filming.

the Bounty, with Clark Gable and Charles Laughton, and for *Captains Courageous* in 1937. Hope and Crosby were here for part of *Road to Singapore*, 1940; in 1949 the island's first TV show was filmed, which opened the floodgates; it was followed by *The Lawrence Welk Show, Queen for a Day, The Wackiest Ship in the Army, McHale's Navy, Cannon, Mannix* and *Barnaby Jones*. Feature films that have used Catalina as a location include *Jaws* and *Jaws II, Waterworld, Amistad*, and *Pearl Harbor* in 2000.

Sunup to Sundown

On & Under the Water

AVALON BOATSTAND/JOE'S RENT-A-BOAT
On the Pleasure Pier
☎ 310-510-0455
www.catalina.com/rent-a-boat.html

Catalina Island is 10° warmer than the mainland in winter, and 10° cooler in summer.

Visitors can rent boats for sightseeing, fishing, snorkeling and scuba diving; choose a motorboat, kayak, pedal boat or paddle board. Fishing tackle is also available to rent. Open daily, April-October.

CATALINA ADVENTURE TOURS
☎ 310-510-2888, 310-510-0409
www.catalinaadventuretours.com

Glass-bottom boat and Yellow Submarines cruise over the Undersea Garden, a state marine preserve where sea life cannot be picked, caught or molested.

CATALINA DIVERS SUPPLY
☎ 310-510-0330, 800-353-0330
www.catalina.com/cds, www.diveinfo.com/cds

Guided snorkeling tours, introductory scuba diving, scuba cat boat diving, scuba cat snorkeling; Green Pleasure Pier Dive Shop, complete scuba and snorkel rentals, air fills. Open daily.

CATALINA JETSKI & WAVERUNNER RENTALS
☎ 310-510-1922, 877-AQUAFUN

Personal watercraft are available for rent here. Look for the booth 100 yards from the boat terminal, opposite the baseball and volleyball courts, or at Joe's Rent-A-Boat at Green Pier.

A PIER IS A PIER IS A PIER...

Some call it the Pleasure Pier, some say it is the Green Pier, and others insist on Green Pleasure Pier. To make it easier to find, the pier and all the buildings on it are painted green. The place where the ferries from the mainland dock is not the pier, though; it's called the Mole.

CATALINA SCUBA LUV
126 Catalina Avenue
☎ 310-510-2350 (information); 800-262-DIVE (reservations, dive packages)
www.scubaluv.com

Introductory dives, instructors, rentals, airfills. Dive the kelp forests.

CATALINA SNORKELING ADVENTURES
Lover's Cove
☎ 877-SNORKEL (766-7535)
www.catalinasnorkeling.com

Snorkeling is done in the marine preserve, where the fish are protected. Rentals and tours. Open daily, April-October.

DESCANSO BEACH OCEAN SPORTS & CATALINA ISLAND KAYAK EXPEDITIONS
☎ 310-510-1226
www.kayakcatalinaisland.com

Kayak and snorkel rentals by hour or day; rentals include instructions. At Descanso Beach, close to secluded coves. Guided Natural History kayak trips, kids classes.

Descanso Beach and Cove are just north of Avalon Bay, around Casino Point.

Day-Trips

DISCOVERY TOURS
☎ 310-510-TOUR
www.scico.com

Several different trips are offered by the Santa Catalina Island Company. The 45-minute **Undersea Tour** takes you out in a semi-submersible; their **Glass-bottom Boat Tour** explores Lover's Cove Marine Preserve kelp forest, and lasts 30 minutes. Take the **Sea Rocks Cruise**, 50 minutes, to see sea lions on the small islands off Catalina; 50 minutes, May-September. On the evening **Flying Fish Trip**, also 50 minutes, you'll see that fish really do fly; May-September. The 4½-hour **Sundown Isthmus Cruise** cruises the coastline to Two Harbors; you may see flying fish on this trip, too; May-September. Call for reservations and fee information.

A TOAST FOR THE MAYOR

Avalon is a small enough town that it had only one drunk, who was regarded as the official town drunk for around 40 years. One year at election time, during the 1980s, a lot of the bartenders and cocktail waitresses who knew him only too well got together and nominated him for mayor. He won, and for two years Avalon could boast it had what was undoubtedly the drunkest mayor of any place in the state.

HIGH TIDE TRADERS
415 Crescent, Avalon
☎ 310-510-1612

Fishing charters aboard a 35-foot sports fisher for local waters and offshore fishing; bait and tackle included.

ISLAND WATER CHARTERS
☎ 310-510-1707

Fishing out of Two Harbors.

SECOND WIND CHARTERS
☎ 310-510-1802
www.secondwindcharters.com

Sail on a 50-foot skippered sailing yacht, which accommodates two to six guests on trips from two to eight hours. Overnight packages are also available. Call for reservations.

Cruise boats and fishing charters operate year-round on Catalina Island.

ISLAND WATER CHARTERS
☎ 310-510-1707

This small, friendly company provides a full range of year-round water activities: fishing on a 21-foot Skipjack ($75/ hour for two, with everything provided, including soda and beer), local and around-the-island cruises, snorkeling, wakeboarding, and diving. The boat is at Green Pleasure Pier, but call for reservations.

On Land

Day-Trips

Casino

Not a gambling casino, this is where the Big Bands played in the 1930s and '40s. The **Catalina Island Museum**, ☎ 310-510-2414, with its photos of the history of the island, is in the Casino building, which is large enough to hold Catalina's entire year-round population. It's at Casino Point, and open daily, 10am-4pm, year-round. Museum admission is $2 for adults.

A half-dozen times a times a year, in summer, big bands play at the Casino for weekend dancing.

The Inn at Mt. Ada

This classic home built by William Wrigley in 1921 is on top of the hill overlooking Avalon Bay on the south side. Listed in the National Register of Historic Places, it is now an inn. We have stayed here and it is by far the best place for an overnight in Avalon, with wonderful views of the harbor. 398 Wrigley Road, Avalon, ☎ 310-510-2030. Those having breakfast or lunch at the inn may enjoy a tour of the splendid old house; others are discouraged in order to

Mt. Ada, the hill overlooking Avalon Bay, is named for Ada Wrigley, wife of the chewing gum magnate.

protect the privacy of overnight guests. Phone for meal reservations.

Zane Grey Hotel

The home of Western author Zane Grey has the original living room, fireplace and piano. On the hill on the north side of town, it is now a hotel with swimming pool and ocean views. 199 Chimes Tower Road, Avalon, ☎ 310-510-0966, 800-3-PUEBLO. Manager Michael Shehabi welcomes day-trippers and will give you a tour. There is no restaurant, however.

Shopping

Stroll **Crescent Avenue**, Avalon's main street, where you will find most of the island's shops and restaurants.

Tours

DISCOVERY TOURS
☎ 310-510-TOUR
www.scico.com

The Santa Catalina Island Company (SCICO) offers various bus and tram tours around the island, ranging from approximately one to four hours and costing between $12 and $45, depending on the tour selected. Call or check their Web site for details and reservations.

Fourteen buffalo were brought over in 1924 to use in a film called The Vanishing American. *Their 350 descendants are still here.*

CATALINA ADVENTURE TOURS
☎ 310-510-2888
www.catalinaadventuretours.com

This company offers bus tours of the island. Call for details and reservations.

CATALINA STABLES
600 Avalon Canyon Road
☎ 310-510-0478

Guided horseback rides are available through the mountains above Avalon. Open year-round.

JEEP ECO-TOURS
Catalina Island Conservancy
125 Claressa Avenue
☎ 310-510-2595, ext. 0

This company provides open Jeep tours of the island. Call for schedule and fee information.

Catalina Island has little fresh water; in times of drought it gets water by barge from the mainland.

Golf & Tennis

CATALINA ISLAND GOLF COURSE
Avalon
☎ 310-510-0530
www.scico.com

The nine-hole resort course is open for public play. Rental clubs and golf carts are available.

CATALINA RACQUET CLUB
Catalina Country Club
Avalon
☎ 310-510-0530

Two professional courts are available for public play. Open 7am until dark; court fee is $15 per hour. Call 24 hours in advance for reservations.

Long Beach-San Pedro

The Queen Mary

The *Queen Mary* was the most famous ship in the world from 1936 to 1967; she was a favorite of hundreds of celebrities and stars. When she was taken out of service she ended up at a special wharf in Long Beach, south of Los Angeles, where she is permanently docked as a sight-seeing attraction and a remarkable hotel.

Day-Trips

History

The Queen
Mary *was the
fastest pas-
senger ship,
going from
Southampton
to New York
in less than
four days, a
world record
she held for
14 years.*

She was called the Queen of the Atlantic, the largest and most luxurious ship ever built up to that time. She carried kings and potentates and movie stars galore, among them Fred Astaire, Richard Burton, Charlie Chaplin, H.M. Queen Elizabeth, Douglas Fairbanks, Greta Garbo, Rex Harrison, Laurel and Hardy, Harpo Marx, David Niven, Aristotle Onassis, Gloria Swanson, Elizabeth Taylor, Mae West and Loretta Young.

Hundreds of films and TV shows have been shot on the *Queen Mary*, starting with a Petula Clark Special in 1969. Most of *The Poseidon Adventure* was shot here, and parts of *Farewell, My Lovely*; *From Here to Eternity*; *Harlem Nights*; *Titanic*; *Pearl Harbor*; and *Vanilla Sky*. She was used in many television series, including *Cannon*; *Charlie's Angels*; *Quincy, M.E.*; *CHiPs*; *Murder, She Wrote*; *MacGyver*; *Alfred Hitchcock Presents*; *Melrose Place;* and *Diagnosis Murder.*

Visiting the Queen

Getting Here

The *Queen Mary* is at the south end of the Long Beach Freeway (710). From the West Side (Beverly Hills, Westwood and Santa Monica), take the San Diego Freeway (405) south to 710, turn right, and follow the "Queen Mary" signs. From Hollywood, take the Hollywood Freeway (101) east to Downtown LA, turn right onto the Harbor Freeway (110) and head south to 405, then turn left until you reach 710, and turn right for the ship. It is 25 miles from downtown LA; figure a half-hour to 45 minutes from there, depending on traffic, and about 45 minutes from Hollywood or the West Side.

▛ FILM GLOSSARY

Dolly – A wheeled platform on which to mount the camera to allow smooth camera movement. This is called a Dolly Shot; when the wheeled platform is mounted on a track it's called a Tracking Shot.

Touring the Ship

A tour will take you everywhere on board: through the immense engine room; around the broad teak decks; into the opulent first-class cabins and suites, the shops that glitter with art deco style, and the restaurants looking out onto the harbor. The tours are self-guided, and go behind-the-scenes. For dining there is the **Chelsea** seafood restaurant and **Sir Winston's** atop the fantail with continental cuisine and ocean views. Champagne Sunday brunch is served in the **Grand Salon** and live entertainment and dancing occur daily in the **Observation Bar**.

Staying On Board

For those looking for a wonderful place to stay in the Long Beach area, the ship has 365 original staterooms with rich wood paneling, art deco fixtures, original artwork and, of course, portholes. Rates are moderate. Actors working on film shoots in the nearby geodesic dome (see page 526) often stayed here.

In 1943 the Queen Mary carried 15,740 troops, with a crew of 943, for the greatest number ever on a vessel: 16,683.

Hours, Fees & Contact Information

The ship is open daily, 10am-6pm. General admission, which includes a self-guided tour, is $19 for adults; $15 for children ages three to 11; $17 for seniors and military personnel. A "First Class Passage" ticket adds a guided tour that visits more of the ship; adults pay $23; children, $19; seniors and military, $21.

Day-Trips

For information about visiting or staying aboard the *Queen Mary*, call ☎ 800-437-2934 from outside California; 562-435-3511 or 562-432-6964 in state; or visit the ship's Web site, www.queenmary.com. You can also write to *Queen Mary*, 1126 Queen's Highway, Long Beach, CA 90802.

THE DOME

On the pier beside the *Queen Mary* is the world's largest free-standing geodesic dome. The structure looms over the land; it is tall enough to enclose a 12-story building and roomy enough to hold a football field, plus fans. It was built in the '60s to house the world's largest airplane, Howard Hughes' *Spruce Goose*.

The Spruce Goose *can now be seen in McMinnville, Oregon, where it was shipped by barge.*

Howard Hughes, who produced and directed motion pictures, was also a pilot and aircraft designer. When World War II began he proposed to build the largest plane ever, with a 320-foot wingspan, to carry troops. Metal was scarce so it was made of wood, hence the name *Spruce Goose*. His contract with the government stipulated he would not be paid unless the plane flew. He finally got it into the air and flew it across Long Beach Harbor, a few feet above the water. It flew just that once; after that it was put into storage and never used again.

When the *Queen Mary* came to Long Beach, The Dome was built beside it to house the *Spruce Goose* as an added attraction. But a few years ago the city sold the plane and it went to a museum in Oregon. The vast, empty space became the world's largest sound stage. Most of *Batman Forever* and *Batman and Robin* were shot here, along with *Virtuosity*, *Stargate*, *Jack Frost* and *A.I.: Artificial Intelligence*.

Films are no longer shot in The Dome. The space is so huge (135,000 square feet) that, although Carnival Cruise Line is renovating part of it to use as a terminal for its ships, the rest will probably end up as an area with seating for a very large audience. The Dome is not open to the public.

SS Lane Victory

For those who love ships, especially ships that have been in the movies, the SS *Lane Victory* is not to be missed. She is in San Pedro, docked at Berth 94, next to the big cruise ship berths. Whenever an old cargo ship is needed for a movie, the studios head here, since she is the only one left in the area. The ship has been used in countless movies, TV episodes and commercials, including *Death Wish*; *Moving Target*; *Naked Gun 2½*; *Cloud Nine*; *Amelia Earhart*; *Outbreak*; *The Relic*; *Titanic*; *JAG*; *Murder, She Wrote*; *Unsolved Mysteries*; *Quantum Leap*; *Ninja Kids*; and the final episode of *MacGyver*.

One of the few Victory ships still in existence, the *Lane Victory* was built in 1945 and served in World War II, the Korean "police action," and the Vietnam War. Weighing in at 10,750 tons and still painted battleship gray, she is open daily for tours of the wheel house, engine room, guns tubs, all of it. An entire between-decks cargo hold has been turned into one of the best merchant ship/naval museums we have seen. To get here, go south on the Harbor Freeway (110), take the exit for Highway 47/Vincent Thomas Bridge; exit before the bridge at the Harbor Boulevard off-ramp, and go straight ahead across Harbor Boulevard.

The ship is open for viewing daily, 9am-4pm; admission is $3 for adults, $1 for children six-15 (those five and under get in free). During July, August and September, the *Lane Victory* goes on a day-long cruise toward Catalina Island. It is an exciting channel crossing, especially for children, as the ship is "attacked" by Nazi war planes while the crew defends the ship with the 20-millimeter guns in the gun tubs. The cruise fare is $100 for adults, $60 for ages 15 and under; it includes breakfast and lunch aboard. Call ☎ 310-519-9545 for more information.

Santa Barbara

Woman to man: "Is he as cute as you are?"
Man: "Nobody is."

– Martha Vickers and Humphrey Bogart
(Philip Marlowe), *The Big Sleep*

Santa Barbara, a pretty, genteel and wealthy little city, is an easy 90-mile drive northwest of Hollywood, along the coast. Like the rest of California, the Indians were here first, then the Spanish, the Mexicans and finally the gringos, who ended up owning everything, including tranquil havens along the coast like Santa Barbara.

Getting Here

From Downtown LA, take the Hollywood Freeway (101) through Hollywood to the Ventura Freeway (still 101), which runs along the south side of the San Fernando Valley through Oxnard, a poor, agricultural town, and Ventura, a not-so-poor middle-class town. Very few people get off the freeway to see any more of either of these places. From Ventura, Highway One goes along the coast.

Half the strawberries in the country are grown in Oxnard.

From the airport or the beach communities, you can take the Pacific Coast Highway. Drive west to Santa Monica, or out Sunset Boulevard if you have lots of time, and up through Malibu. The coast highway joins 101 at the north end of Oxnard. You might go out one way and return the other.

> ⭐ **TIP**
>
> Look for **Santa Barbara Hosts** on State Street, Thursday-Sunday, 10am-7pm, for tourist information and directions. They are the ones wearing safari hats and blue polo shirts. Very helpful.

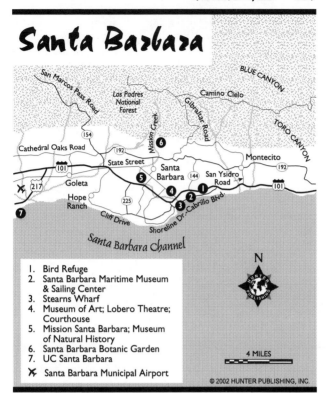

Santa Barbara

1. Bird Refuge
2. Santa Barbara Maritime Museum & Sailing Center
3. Stearns Wharf
4. Museum of Art; Lobero Theatre; Courthouse
5. Mission Santa Barbara; Museum of Natural History
6. Santa Barbara Botanic Garden
7. UC Santa Barbara
✈ Santa Barbara Municipal Airport

4 MILES

© 2002 HUNTER PUBLISHING, INC.

Day-Trips

Who Lives Here?

Santa Barbara folk are very protective of the privacy of the celebrities who have homes here. All we have been able to glean is that among current residents are Dennis Franz, Rob Lowe and Oprah, who has a big place (which she may never have visited since she built it, according to the story we heard).

Residents of Santa Barbara sometimes refer to themselves as Santa Barbarians.

On Location

One of the earliest West Coast studios was Flying A, which was located in Santa Barbara and shot over 1,200 silent

When The X-Files *stopped shooting in Vancouver, Canada, it shot an episode in Santa Barbara in 2001.*

movies here between 1912 to 1919. Of course, the films were only one and two reels long. In addition, because it is an easy drive up the coast from Hollywood, Santa Barbara has been a favorite out-of-town location almost from the beginning. Starting in 1910, even before Flying A Studio, *Winners of the West* was the first film made here. *The Perils of Pauline* was in 1914 and *The Ten Commandments* in 1923. W.C. Fields' *The Bank Dick* was done in 1940, the original *Batman* television series pilot in 1964, and parts of *The Graduate* and *Thoroughly Modern Millie* in 1967. Since then there have been *Lipstick*; *Rich Man, Poor Man*; *The Postman Always Rings Twice*; *The Two Jakes*; *Of Mice and Men*; *Nixon; G.I. Jane*; and almost 70 other films. And, of course, Santa Barbara was seen in every episode of the soap opera, *Santa Barbara*.

Best Places to Eat

If you are here on a day-trip you'll want to have lunch in Santa Barbara. Fortunately, this small, attractive coastal city with lots of wealthy residents is one of the best towns you will find anywhere for excellent food.

The dining price scale can be found on page 42.

Just north of Santa Barbara, where the highway turns inland, is where wine country begins. This vintners' locale is little known outside of California, but some very nice vintages are produced here, and the influence of the wineries on the local restaurants is obvious.

Fine Dining

San Ysidro Ranch may be the only place in the world that could please both Groucho Marx and Richard Nixon.

THE STONEHOUSE RESTAURANT and THE PLOW & ANGEL BISTRO

San Ysidro Ranch
900 San Ysidro Lane
Santa Barbara, CA 93108
☎ 805-969-5046
www.sanysidroranch.com
American Regional Cuisine/Comfort Food
Moderate-Very Expensive

The Stonehouse Restaurant is one of the prime places to eat on the West Coast, so you might want to take advantage of a drive up the coast to have lunch or dinner here before returning to Hollywood. The menu is based on fresh herbs, fruits, vegetables and edible flowers grown in their own organic garden. The kitchen receives so much acclaim because it accomplishes the most difficult feat of all – cooking simple dishes perfectly.

The Plow & Angel Bistro is a more casual place for dinner only. There is an excellent bar menu, for nibbles with your drinks, as well as a "small plates" menu and a "big plates" menu, and a three-course fixed meal that changes every night and is popular with Santa Barbarans.

San Ysidro Ranch is one of only two Southern California members of Relais & Châteaux, a prestigious world-wide hotel organization.

A PERSONAL NOTE

We stayed at San Ysidro Ranch some years ago, and when we arrived at our cottage we found our name hand-carved on a wooden plaque by the door, and matchbooks in the room printed with our name. Dinner was wonderful, there was a fireplace in the cottage, and the next morning we walked up to the swimming pool. We were sunning ourselves on lounges by the pool when a phone rang nearby. Since we were closest to it, one of us answered, and a moment later turned to the other half-dozen sunbathers and asked, "Is the countess here?" The countess got up and came over to take the phone. San Ysidro Ranch is that kind of place.

Day-Trips

San Ysidro Ranch has been popular with both Hollywood people and politicians since Ronald Colman created the present facility. Originally it was a way-station for Franciscan monks in the late 1700s. The 1825 adobe ranch house is still in use. Its 500 acres in the foothills of the Santa Ynez Mountains have been a retreat for celebrities like Fred Astaire, Lucille Ball, Jack Benny, Bing Crosby, Jean Harlow, Olivia de Havilland, Audrey Hepburn, Deborah Kerr, Groucho Marx, Somerset Maugham, Bertrand Russell and Gloria Swanson.

John Huston and James Agee finished the script for *African Queen* in one of the cottages, Vivien Leigh and Laurence Olivier were married at the Ranch, John F. and

The creators of the soap Santa Barbara, Jerry and Bridget Dobson, got their inspiration locally. They lived in Santa Barbara's wealthiest suburb, Montecito.

Jackie Kennedy honeymooned here. Political notables Joseph Kennedy (who was also a movie producer), Robert and Ethel Kennedy, Hubert Humphrey, Adlai Stevenson and Richard Nixon all stayed here. To get here from Highway 101, watch for San Ysidro Road on the right while you are still in the southern outskirts of Santa Barbara. Go uphill about five minutes, past Montecito Village to San Ysidro Lane; turn right, follow the lane to the ranch.

HARBOR RESTAURANT
210 Stearns Wharf
☎ 805-963-3311
Seafood and steaks
Moderate

The view here has been popular with visitors for a long, long time. There are tanks full of tropical fish, and windows all around with views of the mountains on one side and the harbor on the other. The window seats on the sunset side, where diners can see all the way out to the Santa Cruz Islands, are very desirable. The Harbor is open Monday-Friday, 11:30am-10:30pm; Saturday and Sunday, 8am-11pm. It is the first restaurant you will come to when you drive onto the pier, and there is valet parking.

BOUCHON SANTA BARBARA
9 West Victoria Street (at State Street)
☎ 805-730-1160
www.bouchon.net
California wine country cuisine
Expensive

bouchon means "wine cork" in French.

Despite what we said about lunch in Santa Barbara, bouchon (yes, with a small "b") is open only for dinner – but who knows, you may very well become entranced with Santa Barbara and linger. Owner Mitchell Sjerven describes his cuisine as wine country regional; he creates menus that interact well with wine. The cooking features products of the Central Coast: fresh produce, seafood, game and poultry; bouchon's wine list contains hundreds of Central California Coast and Santa Barbara County wines. There is a covered garden patio, and the main room showcases the open kitchen.

bouchon is open daily, from 5:30 to 9pm on weekdays and until 9:30pm Friday and Saturday. Street parking, and a city parking lot only three doors down.

★★ PALACE GRILL

8 East Cota Street (corner of State Street)
☎ 805-963-5000
www.palacegrill.com
Regional American: New Orleans-style cuisine
Moderate

This is considered one of Santa Barbara's finer eating joints, despite the moderate prices. This casual place, with no tablecloths on the wooden tables but art on the walls, is a favorite of the likes of Geena Davis, Michael Douglas, Michael Keaton and Kevin Costner, among others, when they drive up to Santa Barbara for the weekend, as lots of Hollywood folk do. And, of course, Dennis Franz, who lives in the area.

The food is not just cajun; owner Errol Williams makes sure it reflects all the ethnicities of New Orleans, so creole and Italian dishes are on the menu, too. Try the barbequed shrimp, or the redfish, available only when they can get it fresh. The menu reads as if you are in New Orleans, with house-smoked andouille sausage, Creole crawfish crab cakes and, for steak lovers, filet mignon stuffed with Louisiana crawfish tails and Creole spices.

The Palace Grill is open for lunch daily, 11:30am-3pm; and for dinner, Sunday-Thursday, 5:30-10pm, and Friday and Saturday until 11pm. Reservations are recommended. If you are on the Freeway (101), take the Garden Street exit; turn right and go 2½ blocks to Cota Street, then turn left and go another 2½ blocks to State. Parking is available on the street, and there are two city lots within a half-block.

Day-Trips

Palace Grill has a magician to entertain on Friday evenings and live music on weekends.

Casual Dining

★ MONTECITO CAFE

Montecito Inn
1295 Coast Village Road
Santa Barbara, CA 93108
☎ 805-969-7854, 800-843-2017, fax 805-969-0623
www.montecitoinn.com
Standard American with Italian accents
Inexpensive

Montecito Inn has a complete library of all of Charlie Chaplin's films.

Charlie Chaplin built the graceful, Mediterranean-style building in 1927 primarily as a romantic escape for the film colony. Among the first guests were Warner Baxter, Wallace Beery, Lon Chaney Sr., Marion Davies, Janet Gaynor, Carole Lombard, Conrad Nagel, Gilbert Roland and Norma Shearer. Lyricist Lorenz Hart was staying here with composer Richard Rodgers in 1936 when they wrote *There's a Small Hotel*. The "wishing well" in the lyrics is gone; there is now a fountain in its place. The café serves lunch and dinner.

 # Sunup to Sundown

On Land

MISSION SANTA BARBARA

2201 Laguna Street
☎ 895-682-4713

Santa Barbara's Old Spanish Days celebration is held in August.

The biggest attraction in Santa Barbara is the Mission. It sits up on a hilltop overlooking all of the city and the ocean, and is known as the Queen of the Missions. It has been knocked down a couple of times by earthquakes, but nicely restored. There is a self-guided tour and the usual gift shop. Open daily, 9am-5pm; admission is $3; children under 16 free.

THE RED TILE WALKING TOUR
1 Santa Barbara Street
☎ 805-965-3021

The Red Tile Walking Tour in downtown Santa Barbara is named that because of the red tiles on the roofs of all the old buildings to be seen on this 12-block, self-guided tour of the best of downtown. Pick up a map at the Visitors Information Center at the corner of Cabrillo Boulevard, down by the beach. The route includes the Historical Museum, the Museum of Art and Lobero Theatre, and ends at the Courthouse.

In the Santa Barbara News-Press *see* Barney Brantingham's *column of wise words about what is really happening locally.*

SANTA BARBARA BOTANIC GARDEN
1212 Mission Canyon Road
☎ 805-682-4726

The Botanic Garden takes in a large 65 acres of Santa Barbara Canyon, with Mission Creek running through it. There are more than 1,000 species of rare and indigenous plants, with big sections devoted to the native plants of the area. It is a wonderful sight for lovers of nature, both wild and tamed. The gardens are open Monday-Friday, 9am-4pm; on weekends to 5pm. Admission is $3 for adults; $2 for seniors 60 and over and teens 13 to 17; and $1 for children ages five to 12.

Day-Trips

THE LOBERO THEATRE
33 East Cañon Perdido Street
☎ 805-963-0761

A truly grand theater, the Lobero was built on the site of the 1870s Lobero Opera House and is now home to the Santa Barbara Grand Opera and the Lobero Stage Company. The elaborate Spanish-style architecture and interior is worth seeing.

There are tours available from time to time of the Lobero Theater. Phone ahead.

STEARNS WHARF
Foot of State Street

The wharf has been here since 1872 and is still a very popular place for residents and visitors alike. Stroll out to soak up the sea air and atmosphere. Harbor cruises depart from here, and there are shops and several seafood restaurants, the most famous of which is the Harbor Res-

Park on the wharf, or look for public parking lots on Cabrillo Boulevard.

taurant (see page 532). The Dolphin Fountain at the land end celebrates Santa Barbara's sister city, Puerto Vallarta, on the west coast of Mexico, where there is a much-photographed replica.

PEDAL & PADDLE OF SANTA BARBARA
848 Cathedral Vista Lane
Santa Barbara, CA 92110
☎ 805-687-2912
www.nvstar.com/pedpad

These bicycle tours are educational trips tailored to your interests by Judy Keim, focusing on wetlands, art, birds, or history. A three-hour minimum tour is $45 (see below for the paddle part).

SANTA BARBARA TROLLEY COMPANY
120 State Street
☎ 805-965-0353

The Santa Barbara Trolley Company's tour includes a 15-minute stop at Mission Santa Barbara.

Taking off from Stearns Wharf, Santa Barbara Trolley Company offers a 90-minute narrated tour of the city. The 32-passenger bus runs five times a day, every hour-and-a-half, and you can get off at any of the 14 stops, explore that part of town and then get back on the next bus. Fare is $14 for adults; $8 for children 12 and younger. Trolleys run daily, 365 days a year, at 10 and 11:30am, 1, 2:30 and 4pm.

On & Under the Water

SUNSET KIDD
125 Harbor Way
☎ 805-962-8222
www.sunsetkidd.com

Sunset Kidd *has a full bar on board.*

Take a two-hour coastal cruise or a romantic sunset cruise on a 41-foot ketch. These are for people who really like the experience of being on a sailboat, to hear the breeze in the rigging and feel the water lapping along the hull. No narration, just a tranquil boat ride. The cost is $30 for either of the cruises. From February 15 to May 15 there is a 2½-hour whale-watching cruise, also $30. As soon as the boat gets near the whales the engine is turned off and you drift silently along with them. A trained naturalist is on board to talk to you individually, with no loudspeaker narrations. These people are classy. Board the *Sunset Kidd* at Cabrillo Landing, by the Breakwater Restaurant.

PEDAL & PADDLE OF SANTA BARBARA
848 Cathedral Vista Lane
Santa Barbara, CA 92110
☎ 805-687-2912
www.nvstar.com/pedpad

Judy Keim does not rent kayaks, she takes you on a kayak tour along the coast, and will customize it for your interests and skill level. Along the way you will learn all about the coastline and the history around here, the birds you see, aquatic animals; it is an educational way to get out on the water and have fun. The cost is $45 for two-hour minimum.

★ TIP

Before going to sea you might want to check the weather hotline: ☎ 805-962-0782.

SANTA BARBARA MARITIME MUSEUM
113 Harbor Way
Waterfront Center
☎ 805-962-8404

A neat place for those with a nautical turn and families of all sorts. They have historic boats, all sorts of nautical gear such as a good collection of diving helmets. Lots of interactive stuff: you can catch marlin and sailfish, for instance. Films run all day in the theater, and kids can learn things like knot-tying. To get here, drive north on Cabrillo Boulevard a half-mile past State Street to Waterfront Center. Winter hours are Thursday-Monday, 11am-5pm; closed Tuesday and Wednesday. Phone for summer hours.

Day-Trips

SANTA BARBARA SAILING CENTER
133 Harbor Way
Santa Barbara, CA 93109
☎ 805-962-2826, 800-350-9090
www.sbsail.com

Go for an afternoon sail or a champagne cruise, or on a 53-foot sailing vessel exploring the Channel Islands. For those who know how to sail, boats are available for rent by the hour or day; they also rent kayaks.

🎬 **FILM GLOSSARY**

Montage – An editing process that results in a sequence of several brief scenes in quick succession, usually creating a time-lapse effect.

Shambala Preserve

*A*ctress Tippi Hedren, who starred in Alfred Hitchcock's *The Birds* and *Marnie*, is a long-time wild-animal protector. In 1983 she created a 72-acre game park, located in the hill country about 40 minutes north of Hollywood, as a haven for abandoned, abused and unwanted exotic animals. The resident animals include cheetahs, leopards, lions, cougars, tigers and an African elephant.

Shambala, in Sanskrit, means "A meeting place of peace and harmony for all beings, animal and human."

The Santa Clara River wanders through the Shambala Preserve; the tall cottonwood trees are native, and 800 more trees have been planted to create a forest canopy. There are flowering plants and shrubs everywhere, a waterfall, ponds and a small lake, home to a white egret and a grey heron. Tippi Hedren's conservationist **Roar Foundation** does not breed, buy, sell or trade animals; it is dedicated solely to saving wild creatures. Most of the animals that end up here come from California's Fish & Wildlife Department, the Department of Agriculture and other legal authorities who have rescued animals from deplorable conditions. Some have come from individuals who bought the animals as cute little pets and didn't know what to do

Shambala Preserve

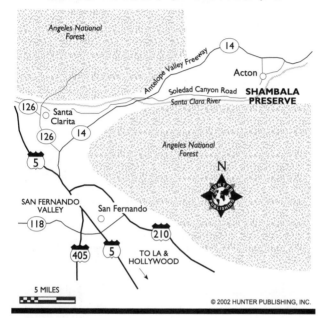

with them when they grew up to be wild beasts. The preserve's population includes 50 African lions, Royal Bengal and Siberian tigers, black and snow leopards, a bobcat, and a lynx.

Visiting the Preserve

Shambala is open one weekend a month to day visitors in groups of 30 or fewer, who are escorted on a special "safari" through the park. The animals are not in cages, they are free behind fences, with trees to climb, a body of water to play in and plenty of room. Tours take about three hours, including lunch (guests can buy snacks here or bring a picnic lunch). The cost is a $35 minimum donation; reservations in advance are a must, and no one under 18 is allowed. Ms. Hedren often joins the guests for a chat before the safari starts out.

Rugged Soledad Canyon, the location of Shambala Preserve, was once the hideout of the legendary Latin-American bandit Tiburcio Vasquez.

The Preserve is also open occasionally for overnight guests. There is one designer tent, and no more than two guests at a time are allowed, so no one has to worry about overcrowding. Visitors arrive in the afternoon for a private safari (which a staff photographer documents), then enjoy cocktails and a catered dinner on the tent's veranda. Tippi joins her guests for after-dinner coffee and drinks and then escorts them on a midnight walk to view the nocturnal animals. After that it's time to turn in on a big feather bed, while the sounds of the big cats and the elephant echo in the darkness. Shower in the morning in a bamboo enclosure with a window (through which a tiger may be watching you!). The price for this unusual adventure is $2,500 per couple, all-inclusive. The cost is steep, but most of it is tax-deductible as a donation to Hedren's nonprofit foundation, which raises money to sustain the animals.

We suggest bringing a camera for either visit (but be advised that any photos you take must be for personal use only). While you are here, you might want to pick up a copy of the adventure-action film *Roar*, shot both in Kenya and here on the preserve, starring Tippi Hedren and her daughter, Melanie Griffith. Contact Shambala Preserve at 6867 Soledad Canyon Road, Acton, CA 93510, ☎ 661-268-0380, www.shambala.org. Directions will be provided when you make your reservations.

❓ Day-Trips A to Z

Police & Fire

Emergencies . . . . ☎ 911
Harbor Patrol, emergency. . . . ☎ 911 or VHF channel 16
Avalon Harbor Patrol. . . . . ☎ 310-510-0535,
                  or VHF Channels 12, 16 (24 hours)
LA County Sheriff, Avalon. . . . . ☎ 310-510-0174
Santa Barbara County Sheriff . . . . . . ☎ 805-681-4100

Santa Barbara Police . . . . ☎ 805-897-2300
US Coast Guard . . . . ☎ 562-980-4445,
　　　　805-966-3093 (patrol boat) or VHF Channel 16
California Highway Patrol . . . . ☎ 805-967-1234

Medical Services

St. Francis Medical Center, 601 East Micheltorena, Santa Barbara, ☎ 805-962-7661; for emergency department call 805-568-5712.

Avalon Hospital, 100 Salls Canyon Road, Catalina Island, ☎ 310-510-0700.

Newspapers

Santa Barbara News Press, ☎ 805-564-5200, www.sbcoast.com; published daily.

The Catalina Islander newspaper, ☎ 310-510-0500; published every Friday.

Taxis

Catalina Island Taxi Services . . . . ☎ 310-510-0025
Island Rentals, Catalina. . . . . ☎ 310-510-1456
City Cab Co., Santa Barbara. . . . . ☎ 805-968-6868
Yellow Cab Co., Santa Barbara . . . . ☎ 805-965-5111

Visitor Information

Catalina Island Chamber of Commerce & Visitors Bureau, PO Box 217, Avalon, CA 90704, ☎ 310-510-1520, www.catalina.com.

Santa Barbara Visitors Bureau, 1601 Anacapa Street, Santa Barbara, CA 93101, ☎ 800-676-1266, www.santabarbaraca.com. When you are in town, stop in at the Visitors Center, at the corner of Cabrillo Boulevard and Garden Street (three blocks east of State Street); the local phone number is ☎ 805-965-3021.

Oudoor Santa Barbara Visitors Center, Maritime Building, 113 Harbor Way, 4th floor, ☎ 805-962-8404 or 805-884-1475, for information about outdoor activities in the City of Santa Barbara, Channel Islands National Park and Sanctuary, and US Forest Service. To find the Maritime Building, from the south take Exit 101 at Hot Springs Road/Cabrillo Boulevard, turn left (west) on Cabrillo to Harbor Way.

The Movies & More...

Studio Tours

I don't want realism. I want magic!
– Vivien Leigh, *A Streetcar Named Desire*

For anyone at all interested in how pictures are made, a good studio tour is invaluable. Fortunately, several excellent ones are on tap. The surprising thing is how easy it is to take these tours, only because most people coming to Hollywood do not take advantage of this opportunity. But it is best to call as far ahead as you can to get the date and time you want.

All the studios tend to be busier, with more chance of seeing celebrities, during the TV production season from August to roughly December. Motion pictures shoot year-round; film sets are likely to be closed to tours, but more scenes are shot outside in the summer, and the actors tend to walk around the lot more in warm weather. But really it comes down to luck; who you see depends on what shows happen to be shooting and who walks over to the commissary when you are there.

LOS ANGELES CENTER STUDIOS
1201 West 5th Street
Los Angeles, CA 90017
☎ 213-534-3000

This is a new studio in downtown Los Angeles; they have never done formal tours, but Pete Brosnan of the studio's Public Relations department tells us they are willing to do tours for small private groups. You should take advantage of this, especially if you are staying right downtown, because you will be among the first to see the inside workings of this very active studio. Since they are new in the business they just may let you see more actual shooting than the more established studios do, but there are no guarantees. Phone the studio and ask for Pete Brosnan's office. They would prefer groups of five to 10, no more than that; if you are fewer than five, ask your hotel concierge if he can put a couple of additional people with you. But don't be surprised if your concierge has not heard of this studio yet.

▇ FILM GLOSSARY

Two Shot – A camera shot of two people close together from the waist up.

★★ PARAMOUNT PICTURES

5555 Melrose Avenue
Hollywood
☎ 323-956-1777
www.paramount.com

No more than 15 people are permitted at a time on the two-hour stroll around the lot. You will get a historical overview and learn how movies are made as you visit the various departments at this working studio. You will also be taken to several sound stages; whether you see scenes being filmed depends what is in production at the time. After the tour you might want to go into the commissary, which is open from 7am-3pm. There is a cafeteria for a quick bite, or a dining room that serves French-American cuisine and is a nice place for lunch (reservations are required; ☎ 323-456-8399). Tours start at the main gate every half-hour from 9am-2pm. Call for reservations. The cost is $15; no one under 10 is allowed. Parking is available across Melrose at a public parking lot.

Paramount also hosts an annual **Children's Festival of the Arts** each August, which gives the whole family an opportunity to go visit the lot. The festival is sponsored by the Hollywood Arts Council and the Junior Arts Center and includes music and dance performances and arts workshops. For more information, call ☎ 323-871-ARTS or check online at www.hollywoodartscouncil.org.

★ SONY STUDIOS
10202 West Washington Boulevard
Culver City
☎ 323-520-TOUR

Sony owns the old MGM lot, so this is one of the real historic gems, and there's a lot to see. A two-hour walking tour visits the sound stages so you can see whatever sets are up at the time, but no actual shooting. You will see the paint shop, the wardrobe department... all the inner workings. Tours are given Monday-Friday, at 9:30 and 11am, noon, and 3pm; phone for a reservation. The cost is $20; children 12 years and older allowed. The studio takes up all the land from Washington Boulevard to Culver Boulevard, and Overland to Madison avenues. Go to Madison at the east end of the lot between Washington and Culver, and park underneath the Sony Pictures Plaza Building – it's the big sloping glass building across from the studio. Walk across Madison to the gate.

The Sony Studios Tour ends at the studio gift shop.

20TH CENTURY FOX
10201 West Pico Boulevard
Century City
☎ 310-369-1000

The studio previously had a very good tour that took only a handful of people at a time on an electric cart; it was canceled after September 11, 2001. At this writing they had not yet reinstated the tours, but there is always a chance they will eventually. Give 'em a call.

★ UNIVERSAL STUDIOS
100 Universal City Plaza
☎ 818-622-3801
www.universalstudios.com

Universal's tour is different than those at other studios in that it is combined with a theme park that rivals Disneyland in popularity. The tour is conducted on large, 50-passenger trams with TV screens that show celebrities in a film montage sharing their experiences on the lot; there is also a live narrator. The tour shows you where and how various pictures were shot. You can also see any show and take any of the rides in the theme park. The rides and attractions are, of course, based on Universal pictures: *Back*

The Movies & More

to the Future, *The Mummy*, *Jurassic Park*, *E.T.*, etc. Admission is $43 for ages 10 and older; $33 for ages three to nine; $37 for seniors age 60 and older. The VIP Tour includes a customized trek around the studio, with no more than 15 visitors at a time on a smaller tram; guests see the inside of more sound stages and sets in greater comfort. Price is $125 per person. Parking is $7 for cars and motorcycles, $10 for RVs.

★ WARNER BROS.
4000 Warner Boulevard
Burbank
☎ 818-954-1744

While you're in the Warner Bros. prop department, look for the chandeliers from Rick's in Casablanca.

They call this the VIP Tour, and it is. They take no more than 12 people at a time, and you'll see whatever is happening, not displays and stunts put on just for the tourists. If a lot of films and TV episodes are being shot when you are here, you are that much more likely to see filming and stars. You are sure to see the New York Street set and some of the other permanent sets, and some sound studios, whether films are being shot there or not, plus the prop department, construction workshops and wherever there is activity going on.

Most of the tour is on a golf cart type of vehicle, but there is some walking so they advise wearing comfortable shoes. The two-hour tours start every half-hour from 9am-4pm, Monday-Friday. The cost is $32; no one under eight years of age is allowed. There is free parking by the Tour Office; enter by Gate 4 at Hollywood Way and Olive Avenue.

To get here from Hollywood, take the Hollywood Freeway (101) or Cahuenga Boulevard to Barham Boulevard, right past Warner Bros. Studio to Olive Avenue, which turns right. A block ahead is Gate 4, the "Hollywood Way Gate." If you are coming via the Ventura Freeway (134), phone for directions.

Going On Location

Look! There's the old man from Scene 24!
— Graham Chapman (King Arthur),
Monty Python and the Holy Grail

If you would like to see the process of filming, the easiest way is to watch as it occurs on locations around the area. Fortunately, much filming is done on the streets; when the shoot is at an interior location you'll find yourself looking at nothing but a lot of trucks parked outside. The Hollywood Film Office, which coordinates film permits for most of Hollywood and Los Angeles, no longer gives out filming information for security reasons, but the smaller cities in the LA area also have film permitting offices, and some will be happy to tell you where filming is going on in their area.

If you see a bunch of white trucks and trailers parked along the street, you are almost sure to catch a film crew on a location shoot. There may also be an open-sided commissary tent. To find the action, look around for cardboard signs tacked to telephone poles, hand-printed with something like "Charlie" or "Flash" and an arrow; this will often point the way to crew parking for a shoot. Sometimes you will see small film units shooting on the street; some producers making movies on the cheap avoid permit fees by shooting fast, ready to pack up the camera and leave in a hurry if necessary. You can watch them, and the process is the same as it would be for a big film costing a hundred million dollars; there are simply fewer people and less expensive equipment around. And no stars.

The Movies & More

FILM GLOSSARY

Mise en scène – The scene captured by the camera, the composition, or the staging.

Film Office Contact Information

Beverly Hills Film Office, Bonita Miller, ☎ 310-285-2438. Beverly Hills is very protective of residents' privacy so they will not divulge filming locations in residential areas, but they have a weekly calendar of filming in commercial areas. Phone and they will fax it to you.

Culver City Film Permit Office, ☎ 310-253-6212. They can give you times, locations and name of the film shooting, but only 48 hours in advance of shooting, sometimes only 24 hours. Phone and ask for the officer in charge of film permits.

Sometimes the name attached to a picture at the time of production is a working title and will be changed before release.

Malibu Film Permit Office, ☎ 805-495-7521. About 1,000 days of filming per year is done in Malibu. Most of it is on the beaches, where it is easy to watch.

Santa Monica Public Works, Film Permits, ☎ 310-458-8737. The office requires three days' notice from the film studios who want to shoot in Santa Monica. Phone and they can tell you date, time, location of shooting and the name of a current film project. The office is open Monday-Thursday, 7:30am-5:30pm; Friday, 8am-5pm; closed every other Friday.

West Hollywood Film Permit Office, ☎ 323-848-6489, e-mail wehofilm@weho.org. They will be happy to tell you when and where all shoots are going on.

For the rest of LA County, contact the **Entertainment Industry Development Corp.**, 7083 Hollywood Blvd., 5th Floor, ☎ 323-957-1000, Los Angeles, www.eidc.com; open Monday-Friday, 8am-6pm. The EIDC, popularly known as the Film Permit Office, issues a "shoot sheet" every weekday morning with details about each film that is shooting on location. Since September 11, 2001 the sheet has been available only to those in the film industry, but there is talk of making it public again. We suggest you phone or check the Web site to find out the current status.

Be In A Movie

Audience Associates rounds up anywhere from 200 to 15,000 "spectators" for big mob scenes. These are not extras, who are provided with costumes and told what to do, but just live bodies, mostly people who want to go on the lot or on location for a day and watch a movie being shot. For instance, in the wrestling scene from *Man on the Moon*, which was filmed in the Olympic Auditorium in downtown LA, most of the people in the seats were out-of-town visitors. Other recent films using spectators were *Rat Race*, *Spiderman* and *Little Nicky*. There's no pay, but meals are provided and there is a place to sign up for Central Casting in case you would like to become a real card-carrying extra. Phone ☎ 323-653-4105, or www.beinamovie.com.

TV Show Tickets

You can see specific shows as they are put on film by writing ahead of time and requesting tickets, or you can pick them up in Hollywood. There is no charge for tickets. For popular shows, like *The Tonight Show*, writing ahead is a good idea. Age limits vary from one show to another; on *Wheel of Fortune* no one under eight is allowed; on *Jeopardy* no one under 10; for *The Tonight Show* it is 16; on most shows you must be 18; and for a few even 20. If this would be a problem for your family, ask ahead of time. The prime production season runs from August through March, and most television shows are on hiatus during the summer months. If you will be here during the off-season, check for pilots that may be filming. Once you have

The Movies & More

tickets, get to the studio early. Many shows hand out more tickets than the studio can accommodate. No cameras, camera bags, recording devices, cell phones or backpacks are allowed into a taping. Other than that, enjoy!

▤ FILM TRIVIA

The modern practice of shooting a variety or comedy show before an audience was common in early television, Carl Laemmle, who created Universal Pictures, charged the public 25¢ to watch the making of silent pictures from specially built bleachers back in 1915.

Contact the Studios

CBS TELEVISION CENTER
7800 Beverly Boulevard (at Fairfax)
Los Angeles, CA 90036
☎ 323-575-2458

Currently you can get tickets here for the long-running *The Price is Right*. The box office is open Monday-Friday, 9am-5pm. The show is taped Monday-Wednesday, three out of four weeks each month, but the schedule often changes. Write for tickets or pick up at the CBS ticket window, which opens at 9am. If you wish to be a contestant, arrive early in the morning with two forms of ID and verification of your Social Security number.

NBC
3000 West Alameda Avenue
Burbank, CA 91523
☎ 818-840-3537, recorded; 818-840-3538, ticket office

For *The Tonight Show*, which is what most people visiting NBC want tickets for, write early and enclose a SASE. You can get up to four tickets by mail. You may also pick up tickets in person, but only for that day; the ticket office opens at 8am, Monday-Friday. Only two tickets are given out per person. The show is taped at 5pm and you should be in line by 4pm; actual admission is first-come, first-served. You must be 16 or older. You can also get tickets for other programs at NBC.

PARAMOUNT GUEST RELATIONS
Paramount Visitor Center
5555 Melrose Avenue
Hollywood, CA 90038
☎ 323-956-5575 (recorded)

Reservations can be made five days before a show is taped. Contact them the day of the show between 9am and noon to confirm your reservation, and arrive at the studio one hour prior to taping. The Paramount Visitors Center is open Monday-Friday, 9am-2pm.

▪ FILM GLOSSARY

Gel – A piece of acetate placed in front of a studio light to change its color.

Be In The Audience

The shows listed below have been running for quite a while, and seem likely to be on the air for some time to come. They tape regularly throughout the year, often several times a week. Taping days are subject to change, so call ahead to confirm. Show tickets are also often handed out in front of Grauman's Chinese Theatre on Hollywood Boulevard and a few steps south of Windward Avenue on Ocean Front Walk in Venice. There are no reservations attached to these tickets, they are strictly seats-available, so get to the studio early.

◆ *I've Got A Secret* – Sunset-Gower Studios, minimum age 16. Tapes Tuesday-Thursday, three times a day, at 10:30am, 2:30pm and 6pm. Call ☎ 323-653-4105 for reservations.

◆ *Jeopardy* – Sony Studios, 10202 West Washington Boulevard, Culver City, CA 90232. Show tapes Tuesday and Wednesday, 1pm and 4pm. Tickets by mail or call ☎ 323-280-8856.

The Movies & More

◆ *Politically Incorrect* – CBS Television Center, 7800 Beverly Boulevard, Los Angeles, CA 90036. Minimum age 18. Tapes Tuesday and Thursday, 6:30pm; arrive by 5pm. Call ☎ 323-852-2655 for tickets.

◆ *Wheel of Fortune* – Sony Studios, 10202 West Washington Boulevard. Minimum age eight. Show tapes Thursday-Friday, 2pm and 5pm. For tickets, write to: Wheel of Fortune Tickets, PO Box 3763, Hollywood, CA 90028. To be a contestant, call ☎ 323-520-5555. For show information, ☎ 800-482-9840.

There are a few companies in the business of getting warm bodies to fill all the seats in those taping studios. Each of these is involved with a number of TV shows, which change as old ones (and many new ones) are canceled and even newer ones come along. Call or look at their Web sites to see who they represent right now.

AUDIENCE ASSOCIATES
7471 Melrose Avenue
Hollywood, CA 90046
☎ 323-467-4697
www.freeTVtickets.com

These people have been in business a long time and always represent a bunch of shows. They have been handing out tickets to *Just Shoot Me*, *The Price is Right* and *Hollywood Squares* for years, as well as for *Wheel of Fortune* and *Jeopardy*; to be a contestant for these you only have to be in the audience. It is best to contact them in advance because the tickets you receive are for specific reserved seats, not for standby. For *The Tonight Show*, you can get tix either at NBC or from Audience Associates, and they often run out. You can also get tickets from Audience Associates at their Web site. If you order by phone you will need a fax number to receive confirmation. If you order by mail, include a self-addressed stamped envelope.

AUDIENCE UNLIMITED
100 Universal City Plaza
Building 4250
Universal City, CA 91608
☎ 818-753-3470
www.TVtickets.com

AU usually hands out tickets for around 30 shows at 10 different studios. Right now they represent shows at CBS Studio City, Disney, Sony, 20th Century Fox, Universal and Warner Bros. You can order tickets up to 30 days in advance; the sooner you order the better your chances of getting in on the date you prefer. Ask for maps and directions to all the shows. If you contact them by mail, enclose a self-addressed stamped envelope.

Awards Ceremonies

C'mon, Oscar, let's you and me get drunk!
– Bette Davis, grabbing her award for *The Star*

The **Academy Awards** ceremony is the big one, the one that it seems everyone in the world sees. Unfortunately, ordinary people, non-Academy members, cannot get in to see The Oscars in person. But there are some awards ceremonies that allow the public in, some with stars, tuxedos, fine dining and the whole nine yards. Top off your visit to Hollywood with something to remember; watch the limos roll up and the stars get out while the cameras flash.

February

★★ PROFESSIONAL DANCERS SOCIETY
☎ 310-285-1411

The annual Gypsy Awards luncheon is given for and by the great dancers of the film industry. The 2002 ceremony honored June Haver and Gregory Hines and featured a dance tribute to Busby Berkeley. The luncheon is usually held at the Beverly Hilton Hotel. The public may attend; tickets are $125.

The Movies & More

March

DIRECTORS GUILD OF AMERICA AWARDS
☎ 310-289-2000
www.dga.org

You must be a guest of a DGA member to attend their annual black-tie dinner and awards presentation, which is held at the Century Plaza Hotel in Century City.

▪ FILM GLOSSARY

Directors Guild of America – The Directors' union, the DGA negotiates working conditions and minimum pay for directors and ADs (assistant directors).

★★ ACADEMY OF MOTION PICTURE ARTS & SCIENCES
Kodak Theatre
Hollywood & Highland
☎ 310-247-3020
www.oscars.org

The Academy Awards ceremonies are always held on a Sunday in late March.

The Oscars are being handed out in a new, permanent theater after a lifetime of moving from place to place. The Kodak Theatre, after several rows are taken out for camera movement, has only 3,300 seats for the audience. There is always a bigger demand within the industry than there are seats, so there are obviously none left over for the public. Bleachers are set up on Hollywood Boulevard to witness the stars' arrivals. There are fewer spaces available, and new security arrangements call for early applications for seats and background checks. If you are interested, check the Academy Web site.

★★ SCREEN ACTORS GUILD
☎ 323-549-6707
www.sagawards.org

Non-members of SAG may attend this black-tie dinner and ceremony as guests of members, but each member can bring only one guest. The event is held at the Shrine Auditorium, south of downtown on Jefferson Boulevard close to USC. Of the three guild awards ceremonies (actors, directors and writers), this is the one with lots of stars in attendance. The general public can see them coming and going out front in all their finery.

WRITERS GUILD OF AMERICA

7000 West 3rd Street
Los Angeles 90048
☎ 323-782-4569, fax 323-782-4801
www.wga.org

This black-tie event has been held in the International Ballroom at the Beverly Hilton Hotel in Beverly Hills for many years, usually on the first weekend in March. Unlike the other guild awards ceremonies, non-members can attend on their own or as guests of members. The ticket price is $125, which includes dinner and the awards presentation. In the past the evening also included what was often one of the funniest floor shows in town, usually with a few stars sprinkled in among the cast members. The show has not been included in the last several years, but there is talk of reviving the tradition, so one can hope.

June

★★ TONY AWARDS PARTY
☎ 323-933-9266, ext. 54

This event is held in early June in conjunction with the presentation of the Tony Awards in New York; party attendees watch the awards presentation via a live television feed. In 2001 the party was held at Santa Monica's Museum of Flying. Lots of stars attend for cocktails, dinner and the live telecast, plus an auction and the presentation of the Julie Harris Lifetime Achievement Award. Public invited, $175.

August

★★ HOLLYWOOD MOVIE AWARDS
Hollywood Film Festival
433 North Camden Drive, Suite 600
Beverly Hills, CA 90210
☎ 310-288-1882
www.hollywoodawards.com

This black-tie dinner and awards presentation is held the last night of the Hollywood Film Festival, usually at the Beverly Hilton Hotel. There are lots of stars to rub shoulders with. Presentations include awards for Hollywood Movie, Actor and Actress of the Year, and Outstanding Achievements. This event is not televised. In 2001 the guests and presenters included Jacqueline Bisset, Sandra Bullock, Cameron Diaz, Harrison Ford, Sally Kellerman, Charlize Theron and director Robert Wise. The ticket price is $250 per person, and they sell out fast, so reserve early.

September

★★ ACADEMY OF TELEVISION ARTS & SCIENCES
5220 Lankershim Boulevard
North Hollywood, CA 91601
☎ 818-754-2800
www.emmys.org

The public can attend the Emmy award presentations, but tickets are expensive. The big night, always in mid-September and usually at the Shrine Auditorium downtown, is a two-part event: the awards ceremony, and the following dinner and Governor's Ball. Tickets to the award ceremony do *not* get you into the dinner, dancing and rubbing elbows that follows, which is only for members.

The awards presentation itself is a black-tie event, and tickets are generally $200, $300 and $400 for the third, second and first balconies respectively. Occasionally a few orchestra seats are available to the public. Contact the Academy; they will send you an invitation, which needs an

RSVP and payment. If you are not going to be inside, there are bleachers outside to watch the arriving celebs.

★★ SOCIETY OF SINGERS
8242 West 3rd Street, Suite 250
Los Angeles, CA 90048
☎ 323-651-1696
www.singers.org

The annual ELLA Award Dinner at the Beverly Hilton Hotel is a very show-biz affair. In 2001 the honoree was Julie Andrews, and the tab was $400 for dinner and a high-powered show that featured Dick Van Dyke, Michael Feinstein, Audra McDonald, Richard Crenna, Robert Goulet, James Garner, Robert Loggia, Carol Burnett, Andy Williams and a chorus of 50 voices. You do not have to know anyone to attend, just contact the Society to get current information. Past recipients of the award include Ella Fitzgerald, Frank Sinatra, Peggy Lee, Lena Horne, and Tony Bennett.

Film Festivals

First actor, to audience: "Well, that's all the time we have for our movie. We hope you found it entertaining, whimsical and yet relevant, with an underlying revisionist conceit that belied the film's emotional attachments to the subject matter."
Second actor: "I just hope you didn't think it sucked."
– Mike Myers and Dana Carvey, *Wayne's World*

Not so long ago, people around here used to say, "How come there are film festivals all over the world and none here in the world's cinema capital?" They certainly do not say that anymore. All of these festivals are open to the public, entirely or in part.

The Movies & More

February

AMERICAN FILM MARKET
Loews Santa Monica Beach Hotel
1700 Ocean Avenue
Santa Monica
☎ 310-446-1000
www.afma.com

This is a film festival in a different sense: it is an international movie distribution market, where thousands of people in the film industry flock together. Half of those attending are hoping to sell new films they have made, and the rest are there to buy distribution rights for various markets around the world. Rooms are not available at the hotel during the event, as they are turned into hundreds of offices where deals are made. The films are screened at theaters up and down Santa Monica's 3rd Street Promenade; some of the screenings are open to the public.

There are usually 75 to 100 films shown during the event. Because the Market is a clearinghouse for independently produced films from all over the world, films have not previously screened, so you never know quite what to expect. Phone or look on the Web site for the schedule and location of screenings. The best part is the cost – it's free.

★ TIP

A survey of those attending the American Film Market revealed that many deals are made over food, and the favorite places for deal-making while wining and dining were Il Fornaio, Ocean Avenue Seafood and Chinois on Main.

THE PAN AFRICAN FILM FESTIVAL
Magic Johnson Theatres
3650 Martin Luther King Boulevard
☎ 213-896-8221
www.paff.org

This two-week-long event is dedicated to independent films from Africa and the African diaspora, and presents over 150 movies from more than 30 countries. The festival includes the Spoken Word Fest; several evenings of poetry, performance art and music; and a one-day Children's Fest. The Magic Johnson Theatres are in the Baldwin Hills Crenshaw Plaza; from downtown take the Santa Monica Freeway (I-10) or Wilshire Boulevard west to Crenshaw Boulevard and go south. Call for ticket information; the theater has plenty of parking.

March

★★ DOCUFEST
International Documentary Association
☎ 213-534-3600
www.documentary.org

You can be one of the few people in the country, or the world, to see every one of the documentary films nominated for the Academy Awards. And you can have a chance to meet and have weighty discussions with the filmmakers. The festival takes place the last Saturday before the Oscars are handed out, and generally runs 10am-midnight. Tickets are usually $5 and $7 per program; all-day passes run $15 and $20. Some years the event is held at the Directors Guild Theatre, but call or check the Web site for current information.

ROY ROGERS AND DALE EVANS
WESTERN FILM FESTIVAL
Victorville, CA
☎ 760-240-3330

This two-day festival of Western films and TV shows from the 1940s and '50s commemorates the lives and careers of the shows' stars. Proceeds benefit the Happy Trails Children's Foundation. One-day passes run $6-$15; family admission is $30. Two-day passes are $10-$20, with family admission of $45. Victorville is on the high desert about 60 miles northeast of Los Angeles, off I-15 (take I-10 east to Rancho Cucamonga, where you pick up I-15).

★★ INTERNATIONAL FAMILY FILM FESTIVAL

PO Box 801507
Santa Clarita, CA 91380-1507
☎ 661-257-3131
www.sciff.org

The week-long event features family movies, industry panels, workshops and readings of original screenplays. Films containing gratuitous violence, nudity or four-letter words are not included. One of the big events is the closing gala, at which well-known film industry people are honored. Screenings are usually at the Edwards Cinema at the Valencia Town Center, just off I-5. From LA, head north on the Hollywood, San Diego or Golden State freeway, any of which will connect to I-5.

May

ASIAN PACIFIC FILM & VIDEO FESTIVAL

Visual Communications
120 Judge John Aiso Street, Basement Level
Los Angeles, CA 90012
☎ 213-680-4462, fax 213-687-4848
www.vconline.org

This week-long festival features a wide variety of films from countries in Asia and the Pacific, which are rarely seen in the US. There is also a series of seminars with prominent filmmakers held at the Directors Guild of America. Films are screened at various locations, including the DGA Theatre, the Village at Ed Gould Plaza in Hollywood, the Japanese-American National Museum and Japan America Theatre in Little Tokyo downtown. Phone for schedule and ticket information.

July

OUTFEST – LOS ANGELES
GAY & LESBIAN FILM FESTIVAL
3470 Wilshire Blvd, Suite 1022
Los Angeles, CA 90010
☎ 213-480-7088
www.outfest.org

This is the largest film festival in Southern California.
The opening gala is a very glamorous and grand event; in
2001 it was held at the Orpheum on Broadway, downtown.
Screenings are held at various theaters and venues on the
west side of town. There are also screenings all year long
on Wednesday nights (and occasionally on Fridays), at the
Remberg Theatre at The Village, 1125 N. McCadden Place,
Gould Plaza, in Hollywood. Shows usually begin at 7:30pm;
tickets are $7 for adults; $6 for students and seniors. For
ticket information, call ☎ 213-480-7090.

*Guest of
honor at
Outfest's
opening night
gala in 2001
was (gasp!)
Tammy Faye
Bakker.*

August

HOLLYWOOD FILM FESTIVAL
433 North Camden Drive, Suite 600
Beverly Hills, CA 90210
☎ 310-288-1882
www.hollywoodfestival.com

Lots of networking goes on at this week-long fest. Many of
the panel discussions are held at the Hollywood Roosevelt;
most films are screened at Paramount Studios and at Ra-
leigh Studio across Melrose Avenue.

WORLD ANIMATION CELEBRATION
30101 Agoura Court, Suite 110
Agoura Hills, CA 91301
☎ 818-575-9615
www.wacfest.com

Last year the festival received 800 entries from 65 countries and screened more than 100 animated commercials,
public-service announcements, and short- and feature-
length films. Participants usually stay at the Hollywood

*The World
Animation
Celebration
is the biggest
animation
festival in
North Amer-
ica.*

The Movies & More

Roosevelt Hotel; most showings are at the Egyptian Theatre.

AFI INTERNATIONAL FILM FESTIVAL
American Film Institute
☎ 323-856-7707
www.afifest.com

This festival presents features, shorts and documentaries, some domestic, but concentrating on international works. A Latino Cinema Series is held at Hollywood Boulevard theaters as part of the festival. All screenings are open to the public; tickets for premiers and galas, such as the opening and closing screenings, usually cost $75-$100; for Filmmaker Tributes, $20; and for regular films, $8.50-$9. Call or check the Web site for schedule and information.

Organized Tours

There are tours for every taste, from the highlights of all of Los Angeles to the arcane bits of Hollywood history. You can get on a bus with 40 strangers to drive by the homes of stars, or have a personally guided tour for just two of you of clubs where only the merengue is danced. Here are some tours that have been around for quite a while and have it down pat. Reservations highly recommended.

CASABLANCA TOURS
Hollywood Roosevelt Hotel
7000 Hollywood Boulevard
Cabana 10
Hollywood, CA 90028
☎ 323-461-0156, 800-49TOUR1
www.casablancatours.com

Casablanca has several tours available, including Los Angeles City; movie stars' homes; the beaches; a nighttime tour; etc. Price for two-hour movie stars' homes tour is $29 for adults, $19 for children; for a longer, four-hour tour, $42/$25; a city tour is $44/$28. The bus will pick guests up at hotels in Hollywood, Universal City and Studio City, otherwise tours start at the Hollywood Roosevelt Hotel on Hollywood Boulevard.

L.A. NIGHTHAWKS
PO Box 7642
Santa Monica, CA 90406
☎ 310-392-1500

Owner Charles Andrews, who used to write about music for the magazines, knows the clubs as they come and go. He gives personalized nightlife tours and tailors your tour to your own tastes; if you want to see intimate comedy, hear the best jazz and finish by dancing to a merengue beat, all in one night, that is just what you will get. Parties of up to eight go by limo, larger groups by luxury bus. Prices range from $195 to $350 per person, depending on the length of the tour and the number of passengers. All tours feature champagne in the stretch limo, roses for the ladies and all cover charges.

L.A. TOURS
3314 South La Cienega Blvd.
Los Angeles 90036
☎ 323-993-0093, 800-286-8752, fax 323-993-0090
www.la-tours.com

This company runs tours of the city from downtown to Beverly Hills; tours of movie stars' homes, beaches and shopping; and evening tours. Most start early or mid-morning; some have afternoon departure times. The two-hour tour of movie stars' homes is $29 for adults, $19 for children; an all day tour is $58/$46. Reservations are required; phone L.A. Tours or see your hotel concierge. Foreign language tours should be arranged well in advance.

STARLINE TOURS OF HOLLYWOOD
6541 Hollywood Boulevard
Hollywood, CA 90028
☎ 323-463-8333, 800-959-3131
www.starlinetours.com

Starline has a narrated, one-hour trolley tour of Hollywood that leaves every hour from Grauman's Chinese

Theatre on Hollywood Boulevard ($16 for adults, $12 for children). They also offer numerous other tours, including one of movie stars' homes and a grand tour of downtown Los Angeles and Hollywood. Tours take from one hour to all day and range in cost from $16 up to $85.

THE NEXT STAGE
PO Box 1065
Pasadena, CA 91102
☎ 626-577-7880
e-mail nextstagetours@aol.com

This special company offers unusual tours, such as an all-night Insomniac Tour of Los Angeles, or an Ups and Downs Tour via escalators and elevators from downtown to the sea. Other tours include Culinary Arts; a yummy Chocolate Covered Los Angeles; Fountains of Los Angeles; Secret Gardens; Downtown Treasures; and Los Angeles Arts and Artists. Tours range from $25 to $75.

VIP TOURS
9830 Bellanca Avenue
Los Angeles, CA 90045
☎ 310-641-8114
www.viptoursandcharters.com

VIP gives tours of Los Angeles, Hollywood, Beverly Hills, Venice, and movie stars' homes. Tours run from 4½ to 6½ hours; the one of stars' homes (4½ hours) is $46 for adults, $30 for children; others priced accordingly. Call for reservations.

▤ FILM GLOSSARY

Match Cut – A cut between two shots with similar actions or compositions, such as between a man falling off a building to a leaf falling into the water.

Places of Special Interest

For Western Movie Lovers

The Western movie was not born in Hollywood. In fact, *The Great Train Robbery* was shot in New Jersey in 1903. A few years later, Bronco Billy Anderson, the first major Western star, began making films in Niles, a small town in Northern California. But in 1913 Cecil B. De Mille shot the first full-length Western, *The Squaw Man*, in Hollywood, and eventually the great majority of Westerns were filmed in Southern California. Some of the places most connected to Western movies are still here and can be visited by the public.

The film version of The Squaw Man *was based on a popular New York stage play of the same name.*

Autry Museum of Western Heritage. This museum has a collection covering the history of Western movies, plus much more about the real Old West; see pages 168 and 575.

Paramount Ranch. Located in the Santa Monica Mountains National Recreation Area, the ranch has been used for decades as a shooting location; it is reached from either Malibu or the San Fernando Valley. Paramount Pictures bought 2,400 acres of the old Rancho Las Virgenes for use as a "movie ranch" in 1927, and possibly thousands of films and TV episodes have been shot here since then, including *Dr. Quinn, Medicine Woman*, which was filmed here from 1991 to 1998. Although the ranch has the typical Southern California mountain chaparral and live oaks, it became colonial Massachusetts for *The Maid of Salem* (Claudette Colbert), 13th-century China for *The Adventures of Marco Polo* (Frederic March), a South Seas island in *Ebb Tide* and, of course, hundreds of western locations. After Paramount sold the ranch it continued to be used as a movie location. In the early days of filmed TV, *The Cisco Kid* and *Dick Powell's Zane Grey Theatre* were shot here. The tradition continued even after the National Park Service took over in 1980.

To get here, take Ventura Freeway (101) west, out past Las Virgenes/Malibu Canyon Road; turn left and go south about a quarter-mile to Cornell Road; go left and continue for less than two miles to the park entrance. The ranch is

The Movies & More

Bicycles are permitted on trails at Paramount Ranch but must yield to hikers and horseback riders. Hikers yield to horseback riders.

open daily, sunrise to sunset, year-round; admission is free. There are several hiking trails throughout the ranch. For more information, contact the National Park Service Office in Agoura Hills; ☎ 805-370-2301.

Roy Rogers-Dale Evans Museum. The first thing to catch your eye will be the statue of Trigger outside. Inside is a wide-ranging look at the cowboy star's career and that of his wife and screen partner, Dale. 15650 Seneca Road, Victorville, CA 92392; ☎ 760-243-4547 (taped information), 760-243-4548 (a live person), www.royrogers.com. The museum is open daily, from 9am-5pm, but it's best to get there by 3 or 3:30pm to have time to see everything. Admission is $8 for adults; $7 for seniors 65+ and teens 13-16; and $5 for children six-12; under six free. Call for directions.

Santa Clarita Cowboy Poetry & Music Festival. This is an annual event, usually held on a weekend in late March or early April. Activities are held at various locales, including the William S. Hart Ranch and Gene Autry's old Melody Ranch Motion Picture Studio, which is normally closed to the public. Admission is $10 in advance; $15 at the gate. Call for directions, ☎ 661-286-4021, 800-305-0755, or www.santa-clarita.com/cp.

Will Rogers State Historic Park. The vaudeville star-humorist-movie star moved to his Pacific Palisades ranch in 1928. The house is filled with memorabilia of his wide-ranging careers and is maintained much as it was when he lived there. There are several walks and hiking trails on the ranch property. The park is open daily, sunrise to sunset; tours of the ranch house are given hourly on the half-hour, from 10:30am-4:30pm. $3 for parking. The facility is located at 1501 Will Rogers State Park Road, Pacific Palisades, ☎ 310-454-8212; see pages 317-319 for more information.

The bearskin rug in William S. Hart's ranchhouse living room was a gift from Will Rogers.

William S. Hart Park and Museum. Hart, who played authentic cowboys as opposed to the later singing cowboys, was a big star in the 1920s, on a par with Charlie Chaplin. His ranch in Newhall and its Spanish-Colonial ranch house, La Loma de los Vientos, were bequeathed to LA County for the use of the public free of charge. To see it is to visit the early days of Hollywood when Westerns were the most popular films. 24151 San Fernando Road, Newhall, ☎ 661-259-0855 (park), 661-254-4584 (museum). The facility is open daily, sunrise to sunset; tours of the ranch house are given every 30 minutes, Wednesday-Friday, 10am-12:30pm; Saturday and Sunday, 11am-3:30pm; admission is free. Newhall is in the northwest corner of the San Fernando Valley off I-5; phone for directions.

Where Stars Are Buried

His mother has been dead and buried in Green Lawn Cemetery for the past ten years.

– Referring to Norman Bates' mommy, Psycho

Clark Gable and Carole Lombard are interred side by side in Forest Lawn-Glendale's private Great Mausoleum.

The cemeteries in most cities are places where the only living people you ever see – except the gardener – are an occasional relative or two wandering among the grave markers. In Hollywood it's different. Here, you are likely to run across tour groups following guides from headstone to headstone. Because, of course, buried here are stars!

If you visit any of these cemeteries you might run into **Hollywood Underground**, a group that meets once a month at a different cemetery to look for new stars' graves and revisit some older Hollywood legends. They can be contacted through several Web sites (see page 572).

★ FOREST LAWN MEMORIAL PARK, GLENDALE
712 South, Glendale Avenue
☎ 800-204-3131

This is the more famous of the Forest Lawn sites, the one Evelyn Waugh was referring to in his 1948 novella *The Loved One* satirizing Hollywood's commercialization of death. Those buried here include Gracie Allen, Theda Bara, Humphrey Bogart, Clara Bow, Francis X. Bushman, Jack Carson, Nat Cole, Russ Columbo (a singer who predated Bing Crosby; he had a great voice, and was wildly popular), Dorothy Dandridge, Sammy Davis Jr., Walt Disney, the Dolly Sisters, Marie Dressler, W.C. Fields, Larry Fine (one of the Three Stooges), Errol Flynn, Sid Grauman, Jean Harlow, Jean Hersholt, Alan Ladd, Jeanette MacDonald, Aimee Semple McPherson (the evangelist), Chico Marx, Gummo Marx, Tom Mix, Alexander Pantages (of the Pantages Theatre in Hollywood), Mary Pickford, David O. Selznick, Casey Stengel, Jimmy Stewart, Irving

Jack Paar referred to Forest Lawn, Glendale as "Disneyland for shut-ins."

The Movies & More

Thalberg and Spencer Tracy. The park is open to visitors daily; in summer, hours are 8am-6pm; in winter, 8am-5pm.

A HAUNTING TIP

Clifton Webb is thought to haunt the Abbey of the Psalms at Hollywood Forever. Strange lights and sounds have been reported at night, including a glowing presence that walks one of the foyers. Webb is best remembered for the *Mr. Belvedere* films and for the 1944 film *Laura*.

★ FOREST LAWN MEMORIAL PARK
HOLLYWOOD HILLS
6300 Forest Lawn Drive
☎ 800-204-3131

There was quite a furor when this cemetery was created because it was carved out of Griffith Park. After all, Colonel Griffith had deeded the land to the city to be used as a park for the people of Los Angeles and nothing else. Yet, 100 years later, Forest Lawn took over a couple of the park's hills and filled them with graves (Forest Lawn doesn't like to use the term "cemetery"; they are "Memorial Parks").

As we remember, a compliant Los Angeles City Council passed a law that once a body (any body) was interred somewhere, that ground could never be used for anything but a cemetery. Those trying to keep Griffith Park intact tried to block the new law, but the moment it went into effect at 12:01am, Forest Lawn buried a couple of unclaimed paupers on that land, and it has been a Memorial Park ever since. Now the paupers can rest easy, knowing they are in the company of quite a few stars. Among them are Lucille Ball, Clyde Beatty (the "Bring 'em Back Alive" lion tamer), Scatman Crothers, Bette Davis, Dan Duryea, Bobby Fuller ('60s rocker, *I Fought the Law*, who was murdered), Rex Ingram ("De Lawd" in *The Green Pastures*), Buster Keaton, Ernie Kovacs, Stan Laurel, Charles Laughton, Liberace, Ozzie Nelson, Freddie Prinze and Jack Webb. Bonny Lee Bakley, the slain wife of actor Robert Blake, was buried here in 2001. Forest Lawn Hollywood

Hills, across the Los Angeles river from Burbank and Disney Studios, is open daily; in summer, the hours are 8am-6pm; in winter, 8am-5pm.

★ HILLSIDE MEMORIAL PARK
6001 West Centinela Avenue
Baldwin Hills
☎ 310-641-0707

Al Jolson (1886-1950) had a 40-year career that took him from the stage to recording to film. He was at one time the biggest star on Broadway and the most popular recording artist in America and, in 1927, he made film history in *The Jazz Singer*, the first full-length film with sound. Look for the **Al Jolson Memorial**. Visit Hillside Memorial Park's **Mausoleum**, the burial place of Jack Benny, Ben Blue, Eddie Cantor, Jeff Chandler, David Janssen, George Jessel and Dick Shawn. In the **Courts of the Book** are Selma Diamond (staff writer for Sid Caesar's *Show of Shows*, and actress, *Night Court*), Lorne Greene and Dinah Shore. And in the **Garden of Memories** are Sorrell Booke (*Dukes of Hazzard*); Mickey Cohen (bootlegger, gangster); Percy Faith (band leader); Arthur Freed (songwriter and Oscar-winning producer, who did *Singin' in the Rain*, *An American in Paris, Gigi)*; Moe Howard (The Three Stooges); and Harry Richman (1895-1972, vaudeville song and dance man, *Puttin' on the Ritz*).

Visit Hillside's **Mount of Olives** where you will see the graves of Vic Morrow (*Combat*); Jerry Rubin (Yippie co-founder, one of the Chicago Seven); and Dan Seymour (*Casablanca, Key Largo*). Also buried at Hillside Memorial Park are Isadore "Friz" Freleng, who won five Academy Awards for animation (with Warner Bros.), including *The Pink Panther*; Sam Lerner, who wrote musical scores for Hitchcock films; and Hal March of *The Burns and Allen Show* and *The $64,000 Question*.

Hillside is open 8am-5pm; closed Saturdays and Jewish holidays. The San Diego Freeway (405), the Marina Freeway (90), Sepulveda Boulevard and Centinela Boulevard all intersect at Fox Hills, and Hillside is just east of Sepulveda.

The Movies & More

A FRIEND TO THE END...

When Adrian Scott (producer of *Crossfire* and a member of the Hollywood Ten) and Joan Scott (a screenwriter) were blacklisted, they decided to rent their house in the San Fernando Valley so they could move to England to work. Mickey Cohen showed up as a tenant. He was a perfect gentleman, and was impressed to meet the Scotts; he thought of them as fellow rebels being persecuted by the government. The Scotts eventually returned to Hollywood. Years later, when Adrian died, we went to the memorial service at the Unitarian Church on 6th Street. We met Mickey Cohen there, who showed up in a black car with his chauffeur and bodyguard: a friend to the end.

★ HOLLYWOOD FOREVER

6000 Santa Monica Boulevard
Hollywood
☎ 323-469-1181

Hollywood Forever encourages picnicking on the grounds with plenty of benches and shade trees.

If you see a reference to Hollywood Memorial Park, this is the place, and that book you are reading is old. This cemetery has had a close connection to the movies for a long time, since 1901; on the other side of the back wall of the grounds is Paramount Studios. In fact, there are more dead movie stars here than any other place in the world.

There are no regularly scheduled tours, but if a staff member is available they will lead a tour of stars' graves, so it is worthwhile to ask. And there is something here that you will find nowhere else. Look for a slab of stone, called a Memorial Kiosk, with a screen set in it. A touch brings forth a video archive of biographies, which may include everything from simple photos to voices, pictures and music documenting the lives of some of those buried here.

Crypt No. 1205 in the Cathedral Mausoleum at Hollywood Forever contains the remains of Rudolph Valentino.

There are three kiosks on the grounds, as well as a small Forever Theatre where you can view screen bios. All of the information contained in the archives can be downloaded from www.forevernetwork.com.

Here you will find the burial places of Mel Blanc, Louis Calhern, Harry Cohn (fabled head of Columbia Studio), Marion Davies, Cecil B. De Mille, Nelson Eddy, Douglas Fairbanks Sr., Peter Finch, Victor Fleming (director of *The Wizard of Oz* and *Gone With the Wind*), Griffith J. Griffith (donor of Griffith Park), John Huston, Jesse Lasky, Peter Lorre, Jayne Mansfield, Adolph Menjou, Paul Muni, Tyrone Power, Edward G. Robinson, Bugsy Siegel (subject of *Bugsy*), Carl Switzer ("Alfalfa," *Our Gang* comedies), Norma Talmadge, Rudolph Valentino, Clifton Webb and H.H. Wilcox (founder of Hollywood). The office has a map with locations of stars' graves for $5, and there is a directory, with all listed, for $10. Hollywood Forever is open daily, 8:30am-5pm.

Mel Blanc's stone is inscribed, "That's all, folks."

TIMES CHANGE

In 1952, Hattie McDaniel, who won a Best Supporting Actress Oscar for her role as Mammy in *Gone With the Wind*, was not allowed to be buried at Hollywood Cemetery – African-Americans were not buried along with whites then. The new owners of the cemetery, now called Hollywood Forever, have tried to make up for that; they dedicated a memorial to the actress on the 47th anniversary of her funeral. The four-foot-tall memorial is by a lake near the graves of Marion Davies, Douglas Fairbanks and Tyrone Power.

The "whites only" policy affected Asians as well. Keye Luke, a well-known Chinese-American actor (*Charlie Chan*), was denied permission to bury his mother in Forest Lawn. Those policies would be unthinkable now.

The Movies & More

★ HOLY CROSS CEMETERY
5835 West Slauson Avenue
Culver City
☎ 310-670-7697

At Holy Cross Cemetery you will find the graves of Charles Boyer, Bing Crosby, John Candy, Joan Davis, Jimmy Durante, Rita Hayworth, Spike Jones, Mario Lanza, Bela

Lugosi, Louella Parsons, Rosalind Russell, Sharon Tate and Lawrence Welk.

Holy Cross is open daily, 8am-5pm, and is near Hillside. The Marina Freeway (90) dead-ends on Slauson just east of the San Diego Freeway (405); to reach Holy Cross, go a few blocks east of there, and turn right onto Slauson; the cemetery is on the left.

HELPFUL WEB SITES

◆ **www.graveconcerns.com** is where you will find *The Original Map to the Stars' Bones* by Steve Orkin, member of Hollywood Underground.

◆ **www.beneathlosangeles.com** features photos of stars' memorials by Steve Goldstein, member of Hollywood Underground.

◆ **www.findagrave.com** – here you can locate graves by name, claim to fame, place, and other specifics.

◆ **www.hollywood-underground.com** – this site also has information about graves of celebrities.

★ MOUNT SINAI MEMORIAL PARK
5950 Forest Lawn Drive
☎ 323-469-6000

This is where you will find Irwin Allen (screenwriter/producer/director, *Voyage to the Bottom of the Sea*), Lee J. Cobb, Cass Elliott, Totie Fields and Phil Silvers, among others. Mount Sinai is next door to Forest Lawn Memorial Park Hollywood Hills; it is open Sunday-Friday, 8:30am-5pm.

★ WESTWOOD VILLAGE MEMORIAL PARK

1218 Glendon Avenue
Westwood
☎ 310-474-1579
www.seeing-stars.com/maps/piercebrosmap.shtml

Westwood is our favorite cemetery; it is small, beautiful, right in town so you do not have to drive far, and you are in such good company. Among those buried here are Eve Arden, Lew Ayres, Jim Backus, Richard Basehart, Fanny Brice, Les Brown, Sebastian Cabot, Sammy Cahn, Truman Capote, John Cassavetes, Richard Conte, Will and Ariel Durant, Brian Keith, Stan Kenton, Burt Lancaster, Oscar Levant, Dean Martin, Walter Matthau, Marilyn Monroe, Lloyd Nolan, Donna Reed, Buddy Rich, George C. Scott, Dorothy Stratten, Mel Torme, Harry Warren, Cornel Wilde, Natalie Wood and Darryl Zanuck. The cemetery is open daily, 8am-5pm. Glendon Avenue is the first street east of Westwood Boulevard; the cemetery is one block south of Wilshire.

☞ DID YOU KNOW?

Joe DiMaggio paid for a rose to be kept next to Marilyn Monroe's crypt "forever." But he discontinued it when he learned that fans were stealing his flowers. The money is now donated to charity.

★ WOODLAWN CEMETERY
CITY OF SANTA MONICA CEMETERY

1847 14th Street
Santa Monica
☎ 310-450-0781

Woodlawn has tall gothic headstones dating back to the 1800s, marking the graves of many of the city's founding fathers and mothers. It was originally the family graveyard of the Machados clan, who held the land grant to Rancho Boca de Santa Monica; there are over 50 members of that family here. Abbot Kinney, creator of Venice, and his family are here, as well as Leo Carrillo, Vernon Duke

The Movies & More

(composer for films, including *April in Paris* and *I Can't Get Started*, and the musical *Cabin in the Sky*), William Haines (1920s silent film star) and E.C. Segar (cartoonist, creator of Popeye).

LIVING ON IN FILMS

Angeles Abbey Memorial Park in Compton has no movie stars resting there, but it may have been seen by more people than those that are heavily populated with celebrities. In 1923 the founder of the cemetery sent two architects to India; when they returned they built a miniature Taj Mahal in a Compton field as a mausoleum with room for 1,000 crypts.

Ever since then, film companies have been shooting here, the background standing in for locales in the Middle East or South Asia. *The Untouchables*, *JAG* and countless movies and television series set in Cairo, Kuwait or Calcutta have used Angeles Abbey.

 Resources

Recommended Reading

For children, we recommend *City of Angels: In and Around Los Angeles*, Julie Jaskol & Brian Lewis, illustrated by Elisa Kleven, Dutton Books, 1999. The slender hardcover book has a few good paragraphs of text alongside each big, colorful illustration. Kids will learn about Hollywood, Chinatown, Olvera Street, Santa Monica and Venice, in a format designed to make them eager to see all this and more.

Los Angeles A to Z: An Encyclopedia of the City and County, Leonard & Dale Pitt, University of California Press, Berkeley, 1997. They are not kidding about encyclopedia; this is perhaps more than you will ever want to know about LA.

Los Angeles Survival Guide (How to relocate and find everything you need to survive in Los Angeles), Curt Northrup, Arkobaleno Press, LA, 1992. In case this visit to Hollywood has so disoriented someone that they decide to move here, this is the book for them. A bit dated, but still has lots of practical information.

Santa Monica Bay: Paradise by the Sea, Fred E. Basten, Hennessey & Ingals, 2001. This big coffee-table book, full of wonderful old photos, offers a pictorial history of Santa Monica, Venice, Marina del Rey, Ocean Park, Pacific Palisades, Topanga and Malibu, but it is overwhelmingly about Santa Monica and Ocean Park (a part of SM), with sections about Venice.

Stairway Walks in Los Angeles, Adah Bakalinsky and Larry Gordon, Wilderness Press, Berkeley, 1990. The authors (Gordon is an assistant editor at the *Los Angeles Times*) found 200 public stairways around town and concentrated on 18 of the most historic and interesting stair streets in the city's hillside neighborhoods. "A lot coincide with the early development of Hollywood. The stairways tended to lead down to mass-transit points. People were able to ride the Red Cars home and walk up the hills." This book offers fascinating views of old Hollywood hillside living.

Libraries & Archives

★ MARGARET HERRICK LIBRARY
ACADEMY OF MOTION PICTURE
ARTS & SCIENCES
333 South La Cienega Boulevard
☎ 310-247-3020

The Herrick Library contains books, clippings, posters and screenplays documenting the history of film (see page 271).

The Movies & More

★ AUTRY MUSEUM OF WESTERN HERITAGE RESEARCH CENTER
4700 Western Heritage Way
Griffith Park
☎ 313-667-2000

This museum has books, photos, posters about the real and the film West; see pages 168 and 565 for details.

FRANCES HOWARD GOLDWYN HOLLYWOOD PUBLIC LIBRARY
1623 North Ivar Avenue
Hollywood
☎ 323-856-8260

The Goldwyn Library has a large collection of books on movies and Hollywood; it is located a half-block south of Hollywood Boulevard, one block west of Vine Street. Open Monday-Thursday, 10am-8pm; Friday and Saturday, until 6pm; Sunday, 1-5pm.

SCHOOL OF CINEMA-TELEVISION LIBRARY
Doheny Memorial Library
University of Southern California (USC)
3550 Trousdale Parkway
☎ 213-740-2924

This library, with its collection of books, periodicals, stills and personal papers on the subject of film and television, is just south of downtown Los Angeles. You cannot park on campus, so find a spot along Jefferson or Hoover avenues and walk. There are signs to guide you around campus; find Tommy Trojan Square and the Bogart Auditorium, and the library is across the way.

UCLA FILM & TELEVISION ARCHIVES
Research & Studies Center
Powell Library, Room 46
UCLA Campus, Westwood
☎ 310-206-5388
www.cinema.ucla.edu

Parking on side streets around UCLA is restricted almost exclusively to residents.

These awesome archives contain 220,000 film and television programs and over 27 million feet of Hearst newsreel footage; all are available for viewing by those working on research projects. See the Web site for film screenings open to the public. Archives are open Monday-Friday, 9am-5pm. As you enter the campus, pay the $6 parking fee and ask for the Powell Library.

JAMES R. WEBB MEMORIAL LIBRARY
Writers Guild of America
7000 West 3rd Street
Los Angeles, CA 90048
☎ 323-782-4544
www.wga.org

The focus here is entirely on writing and writers for screen, television and radio. The general public is welcome to use the facilities, but materials can not be checked out. Open Monday-Friday, 10am-5pm. The WGA building is the large one on the corner of Fairfax Boulevard, kitty-corner from the Farmers' Market.

UCLA MUSIC LIBRARY SPECIAL COLLECTIONS
UCLA Campus
Westwood
☎ 310-825-4882
www.library.ucla.edu/libraries/music

The UCLA Special Collections includes books and scores from popular, theater, film and television music. We have found the staff here very helpful and friendly. Open Monday-Thursday, 8am-10pm; Friday, 8am-5pm; Saturday, 9am-5pm; and Sunday, 1-10pm. The phone is answered on weekdays only, 10am-4pm. From Westwood Village, go along the east side of the campus on Hilgard Avenue to Westholm; turn left into parking lot #2 ($6 to park). Ask for directions there.

CHARLES E. YOUNG RESEARCH LIBRARY
UCLA Library Dept. of Special Collections
Westwood
☎ 310-825-4988
www.library.ucla.edu/libraries/special/scweb/

Books, screenplays, and all sorts of printed material are in the Young Library's excellent collection, open Monday-Saturday, 10am-5pm. The library is adjacent to the Sculpture Garden and Bunche Hall; parking lot #5 off Hilgard Avenue is closest ($6). Ask at the lot for a map of the campus.

> ### ▬ FILM GLOSSARY
>
> **Cyclorama** – A painted or blown-up photographic background, usually curved and designed to blend in with the studio floor.

Script Registration

We know that a large percentage of the people arriving in Hollywood have a story idea for a screenplay or teleplay tucked away somewhere. Most people are afraid to share their ideas for fear they will be stolen. What writers in Hollywood do to protect themselves is to register their story ideas with the **Writers Guild of America** (WGA). Anyone can register a story idea, whether it is a screenplay, teleplay or a radio script, as long as it is on paper; once your story idea is registered the Guild will go to court for you, if necessary. WGA is located at 7000 West 3rd Street, Los Angeles 90048 (corner of 3rd and Fairfax, across from the Farmers' Market), ☎ 323-782-4540, fax 323-782-4803. You'll need to bring one copy on 8½x11-inch paper, with your legal name and Social Security number. The cost to register your work is $20 for non-members. The WGA office is open Monday-Friday, 9:30am-5:30pm. Registration can also be done by mail.

Writers as Speakers

Writers Bloc presents screenwriters and international novelists, non-fiction writers and poets in a year-round series at the Writers Guild Theatre, 135 Doheny Drive, Beverly Hills. Admission to the event is usually $15 for non-WGA members. For information on the upcoming schedule call ☎ 310-335-0917, or check online at www.writersblocpresents.com.

Index

www.hunterpublishing.com

Hunter's full range of travel guides to all corners of the globe is featured on our exciting Web site. You'll find guidebooks to suit every type of traveler, no matter what their budget, lifestyle, or idea of fun. Full descriptions are given for each book, along with reviewers' comments and a cover image. Books may be purchased on-line using a credit card via our secure transaction system. All on-line orders receive a 20% discount.

Adventure Guides – There are now over 40 titles in this series, covering destinations such as Costa Rica, the Yucatán, the Cayman Islands, Alaska Highway, and Florida's West Coast. Adventure Guides are tailor-made for the active traveler, with a focus on hiking, biking, canoeing, horseback riding, trekking, skiing, watersports, and all other kinds of fun.

Alive Guides – This ever-popular line of guides takes a unique look at the best each destination offers: fine dining, jazz clubs, first-class hotels and resorts. In-margin icons direct the reader at a glance. Top-sellers include *Aruba, Bonaire & Curaçao, Cancún & Cozumel*; *Martinique & Guadeloupe*; *Miami & The Florida Keys*; and *St. Martin & St. Barts*.

Our ***Hunter-Rivages Hotels of Character & Charm*** books are top sellers, with titles covering France, Spain, Italy, Paris and Portugal. Originating in Paris, they set the standard for excellence with their fabulous color photos, superb maps and candid descriptions of the most remarkable hotels of Europe.

Hunter's ***Romantic Weekends*** guidebooks provide a series of escapes for couples of all ages and lifestyles. Unlike most "romantic" travel books, ours cover more than just charming hotels and delightful dining venues, featuring fun activities for couples of all ages and lifestyles. Use these guides to plan a trip that you and your partner will remember forever!

One-of-a-kind travel books available from Hunter include *Best Dives of the Caribbean*; *The Jewish Travel Guide*; *Golf Resorts*; *Cruising Alaska*; *Desert Dancing* and many more.

The
Regency
Season

DANGEROUS
DUKES

CAROLE MORTIMER

MILLS &
BOON

Published in Great Britain 2017
By Mills & Boon, an imprint of HarperCollins*Publishers*
1 London Bridge Street, London, SE1 9GF

THE REGENCY SEASON: DANGEROUS DUKES © 2017
Harlequin Books S.A.

Marcus Wilding: Duke of Pleasure © 2014 Carole Mortimer
Zachary Black: Duke of Debauchery © 2014 Carole Mortimer
Darian Hunter: Duke of Desire © 2014 Carole Mortimer

ISBN: 978-0-263-93146-4

52-0817

MARCUS WILDING: DUKE OF PLEASURE

The Regency Season

DANGEROUS DUKES

August 2017

SHAMEFUL SECRETS

September 2017

BLACKMAILED BRIDES

October 2017

RUINED REPUTATIONS

November 2017

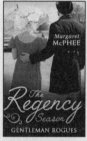

GENTLEMAN ROGUES

December 2017

PASSIONATE PROMISES

January 2018

SCANDALOUS AWAKENING

February 2018

CONVENIENT MARRIAGES

March 2018

WICKED RAKES

April 2018

HIDDEN DESIRES

May 2018

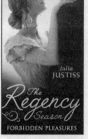

FORBIDDEN PLEASURES

June 2018

DECADENT DUKES

July 2018

Peter, my forever hero.

Carole Mortimer was born in England, the youngest of three children. She began writing in 1978, and has now written more than 200 books. Carole has six sons: Matthew, Joshua, Timothy, Michael, David and Peter. She says, "I'm happily married to Peter Sr; we're best friends, as well as lovers, which is probably the best recipe for a successful relationship. We live in a lovely part of England."

Chapter One

February 1815
Worthing House, London

'Forgive me, Lady Armitage, but for a brief moment I was sure I heard you request that I tutor you in the art of making love to and with a man before you take a lover!'

Julianna remained unmoved by the hard and derisive smile that accompanied Marcus Wilding's drawled dismissal of such a notion ever being possible. 'There is nothing wrong with your hearing, Your Grace. Except perhaps for me to add that I made a statement of intent, rather than a request,' she added with the same determination she knew to be evident in the sharp tilt of her chin.

The Duke of Worthing's brows rose up beneath the rakish fall of his ebony hair as he now regarded her with icy and pale green eyes through narrowed lids. "'A statement of intent'?'

Julianna was not fooled for a moment by the mildness of the duke's tone, or the relaxed way in which his long and elegant length lay sprawled in the chair opposite her own in the blue salon of his London home. She was only too aware that this particular gentleman was at his most threatening when he appeared to be at his most reasonable.

He and her own brother, and three of their closest friends, were not known in society as The Dangerous Dukes because of their pleasing and easygoing natures. Nor were they named such solely on the basis of their reputation on the battlefield. Their exploits in the bedchamber were equally as scandalous. Enough so that most of society's marriage-minded mamas knew better than to allow their daughters anywhere near the rakish bachelors. And Julianna had good reason to suspect Marcus Wilding was the most dangerous of them all.

Not that she cared a whit about his reputation; remarrying was the very last thing on her mind where Worthing, or any other gentleman, was concerned.

Nevertheless, she was still glad that she had refused to relinquish her black cloak to the duke's butler on her arrival. That garment was succeeding not only in covering her completely from shoulders to ankles, but also in hiding the trembling of her gloved hands beneath its voluminous folds. Her pale grey bonnet, unfortunately, only concealed the vibrant red of her hair, and not the pallor of the face beneath its brim.

A face that Julianna now forced to appear calm and composed as she looked across at Marcus with unflinching dark grey eyes. He had been a friend of her brother, Christian, and so she knew this gentleman well enough to know he was perfectly capable of exploiting any sign of weakness. 'A statement of intent,' she confirmed evenly.

'Indeed.' He continued to look at her with those pale green eyes between dark lashes that were wickedly long and thick, his face having the grace and beauty of a fallen angel—or was that devil? 'Might one ask why, having been a married lady and now a widowed one, and so yes, perfectly at liberty to take a lover rather than remarry, if that is your choice—'

'It is,' she stated firmly.

He nodded. 'And do you have any specific gentleman in mind to become this…lover?'

'Not as yet, no.'

He frowned. 'Then my question must be why

have you chosen to come to me, and invited me to be the one to undertake the scandalous enterprise of becoming your sexual instructor?'

Julianna was caught off-guard by the mild query in his tone. Indeed, she had been prepared for Worthing's scorn rather than the easy tolerance he now displayed. This man was one of the most eligible gentlemen in England, and she had, as Worthing had already stated, been a wife and was now a widow, both of which had taken their toll on her appearance as well as her spirit.

She had been a young lady of only eighteen summers on her wedding day four years ago, her heart full of optimism for what the future might hold. But three years of that cold marriage to the adulterous Lord John Armitage and almost a year of widowhood following his death, had resulted in Julianna vowing not to remarry when her year of widowhood came to an end in just two weeks' time. No, better by far to take a lover, she had decided. One of her own choosing and on her own terms.

As such, who better to tutor her in the art of lovemaking than the gentleman reputed to be the most accomplished lover in England?

It had seemed the perfect solution to Julianna, until she now found herself face-to-face with the man. Seated only feet away from the dangerously mesmerizing Duke of Worthing, she now had serious cause to doubt the wisdom of her actions.

For not only was Worthing an accomplished lover, but also he was, at age two and thirty, surely the handsomest gentleman of the ton, with his dark and overlong curls arranged into a rakishly careless style on his brow and about his ears and nape. Long, dark lashes surrounded eyes of palest green, sculptured cheekbones framed an aristocratic nose and his mouth—oh lord, that wicked mouth was far and away his most dangerous feature, his lips both full and seductive.

Added to all of that, it was obvious that the width of Worthing's shoulders, his narrow waist, and his muscled thighs and long legs in a black evening jacket, grey waistcoat, snowy white linen, and black breeches owed nothing to the expertise of his tailor and boot-maker, and everything to the hours she knew he spent with his closest friends in both the boxing ring and at sword practice.

Nor had Worthing shown even the slightest interest in her since her marriage to John Armitage, other than the necessary politeness shown to her as the young sister of his friend.

'Surely my choice is obvious, when your

prowess in the bedchamber is legendary?' she said, trying to appear uninterested.

Those dark brows rose a second time. 'Indeed?'

'Oh yes,' Julianna confirmed coolly.

'Your husband did not…introduce you to sexual pleasure?'

Julianna's mouth tightened even as she felt the warmth of humiliation colour her cheeks. 'My husband was too busy occupying the beds of other, more experienced women to spare but the minimum of his valuable time in occupying mine, and then only in an effort to secure his heir. A task at which he obviously failed.' She straightened determinedly at the mention of her childless state. 'I have accepted that love and happiness in marriage is the exception rather than the rule. But hopefully a lover is a different matter. As such, before embarking on such an enterprise, I fully intend to learn to give and receive physical pleasure to the best of my abilities.'

Whether he was meant to do so or not, Marcus heard a wealth of pain beneath the bitterness of that statement. And humiliation. And it was his opinion that no woman should ever be made to suffer either of those things at the hands of a man. Especially to the point that she would be intent on taking a lover at the end of her year of mourning rather than so much as considering the idea of marrying again.

Julianna had been but five years old, and something of a hellion, the first time Marcus had been invited to spend several weeks of the summer holidays at the home of his friend Christian Seaton, the two boys having met at Eton two years earlier. There had been five new boys in the cavernous hallways of Eton that day almost twenty years ago, and surprisingly each of them heir to a dukedom, an unusual occurrence which had resulted in a lifelong bond of friendship.

Christian's parents, the previous Duke and Duchess of Sutherland, were indulgent and loving parents, but also often absent ones, leaving their two children in the care of the servants at their country seat during the summer months. And so it had been during most of the times Marcus and the other three boys stayed at Sutherland Park during the next ten years or so, visits when Christian's little sister had insisted upon following the boys as well as joining in on every adventure, from climbing trees to fishing. She hadn't cared if she suffered a scraped knee or a dunking in the stream, as long as she could be with them rather than in the nursery with her nanny.

Looking at her now, Marcus could see that the

hellion, whilst not exactly tamed, was at least subdued beneath her widow's weeds. But he was only too aware of the slenderness hidden beneath that voluptuous cloak, her face a beautiful ivory cameo beneath her grey bonnet—her pale cheeks slightly hollow, adding emphasis to the magnificent grey of her eyes, which sat above full, unsmiling lips.

It was not difficult to realize that her unhappy marriage to Armitage was the cause of these changes in Julianna. An unhappiness that Marcus had guessed at before, having once overheard a private conversation at a gambling club, when Armitage had quietly boasted to his disreputable group of companions of his preferences in the bedchamber. But the past could not be changed, no matter how Marcus might have wished it so, and he could not help but feel responsible for some of her unhappiness.

Marcus had spoken to no one four years ago of the feelings he had for his oldest and closest friend Christian's sister Julianna. Or the blow Marcus had suffered upon learning, after his return to England following yet another bloody battle against Napoleon's army, of her marriage to Lord John Armitage some weeks earlier.

Marcus had continued to suffer the inner demons of hell during the years that followed, just thinking of Julianna in the arms, the bed, of another man, especially when that man was the adulterous and perverted Armitage.

Now, with only a few weeks of her widowhood left to pass, Marcus had fully intended to approach Julianna, as he should have done four years ago, with a marriage proposal of his own.

Never in Marcus's wildest dreams, in his wildest fantasies—and some of them had been very wild indeed!—had Marcus ever expected to arrive home after a long night's gambling to be informed that Julianna was awaiting his presence in the blue salon, unaccompanied by so much as a maid. Or to hear now that she had come to him with a proposal of her own, not of love and marriage, but for him to become her sexual instructor for the benefit of her future lovers.

Chapter Two

Marcus rose to his feet, moving restlessly across the room to stand beside the fire, but feeling none of its warmth as he stared down at the leaping flames, and wondered how best to proceed with this delicate situation.

From what he already knew of Julianna's marriage, and the little she had revealed today, it was clear that she was now cynical toward even the idea of remarrying, and that a quest for the knowledge of physical pleasure, so far denied her, was her only reason for approaching him. The only reason she would ever have contemplated coming to Marcus at all.

Marcus found himself seriously considering becoming her sexual instructor, tutoring Julianna in all the ways of pleasuring a man as well as herself. But he had no intention of letting another man ever become recipient of that knowledge—something he didn't believe she was ready to hear. Yet.

Was he capable of doing that? Was he strong enough? Could he remain aloof enough, removed enough, in order to instruct Julianna in the art of lovemaking, in the hopes that she might love him as he had loved her for so long?

He didn't have any other choice, when just the thought of Julianna presenting some other man with the same proposition made him feel sick to his stomach, as well as violently disposed to that nameless, faceless other man.

Julianna had no idea what thoughts were going through Worthing's handsome head as he stared down at the flickering flames of the fire, but she did not think they could be pleasant ones from the bleakness of his expression. His eyes remained a pale and icy green, lips thin, jaw tense.

She rose abruptly to her just over five feet in height, a proud tilt to her chin. 'Perhaps I made a mistake in coming to you—'

'Then why did you?' Worthing straightened as he looked at her with those unreadable eyes. 'What possible reason did you have for thinking you might be able to persuade me into becoming your sexual tutor?'

The length of Julianna's throat moved as she

swallowed before answering him. 'I thought—
I have known you for many years… You are a
friend of my brother!'

'Reason enough not to approach me rather
than the reverse, I should have thought,' Worthing rasped harshly.

'Perhaps,' she allowed. 'But I believed that
connection might, at least, ensure your silence
on the matter should you choose to refuse.'

'And are you not afraid, if I do refuse your
request, that I might relay the details of this
conversation back to your brother, Christian, at
least?'

'No.'

Those green eyes narrowed at her certainty.
'Why not?'

She gave a shrug of her shoulders beneath
her cloak.

'Because if you did, I should then have to
inform Lord Standish exactly where, and with
whom, his wife spent the night before their wedding four years ago.'

Marcus stilled at the obvious threat beneath
her statement. A threat he may well have deserved if he had not come to his senses in time.

It was the same night he had learnt of Julianna's marriage to Armitage, and Marcus had been
heartsick and ever so slightly drunk. Enough

so that he had initially been receptive to Emily Proctor's proposition that they make love before she married the elderly Randolph Standish the following day.

To his credit, Marcus had put a stop to things and managed not to totally disgrace himself, but it was especially ironic that Julianna was now attempting to use his behaviour that night against him, behaviour brought about by his desire for her.

He raised dark brows. 'And might I inquire how you could possibly know where, and with whom, Lady Standish spent the night before her wedding?'

Julianna gave a triumphantly scornful smile. 'Because she told me so, of course.'

Marcus eyed her dubiously. 'She did?'

'Oh yes.' Julianna nodded with satisfaction. 'Men are not the only ones to boast of their sexual conquests, you know,' she assured him mockingly. 'And I have it on Emily Standish's knowledgeable authority that you more than live up to your reputation of being "the most accomplished lover in all of England".'

If the deceitful Emily Standish had been within Marcus's reach at that moment then he believed he would have enjoyed nothing more than to strangle the woman with his bare hands. Except...

It would seem that Emily Standish's personal, if unknowledgeable, recommendation, along with his reputation as a lover, was the reason Julianna had chosen to come to him now.

He clenched his jaw. 'And why should you assume it would bother me if you were to go to Standish with this information?'

Julianna gave a challenging smile. 'Because I know that you and Christian have recently entered into a business partnership with him.'

Marcus frowned. 'Oh?'

'Yes.' She nodded confidently. 'Something to do with shipping, if you doubt my knowledge.'

Marcus had no reason to doubt her word. He did, however, curse Christian for discussing business matters with his sister.

'I am sure, under the circumstances, you would rather avoid the scandal that your having bedded Standish's wife before he did might cause,' Julianna added triumphantly at his continued silence.

That Julianna would dare to use such knowledge against him, without so much as asking him if it were true, filled Marcus with a cold anger. It was true that Julianna could have no idea that Emily Standish had lied, but even so, Marcus believed Julianna deserved to be punished, if only a little, for not so much as asking him if it were the truth, and for having attempted to blackmail him into acquiescing to her request. 'Remove your cloak,' he instructed softly.

Julianna gave a nervous blink of her long lashes as she eyed Marcus warily, sweeping the moistness of her tongue across the stiffness of her lips before speaking. 'Why?'

'So that I might gaze upon your physical attributes before making my decision.'

'I do not see that it is at all necessary for me to—'

'How do you expect me to be able to instruct you in how to pleasure a man if I do not find you physically attractive enough to be able to attain an erection for you to pleasure?' Marcus pointed out testily.

Julianna felt the blaze of colour in her cheeks as she once again acknowledged that she had not thought this situation through properly before coming to the duke's home so early in the morning. That nowhere in those plans had she considered the…the intimacy of having Marcus Wilding talk to her of such things, let alone— let alone…

'I only wish for you to instruct me, not— not—' She drew in a deep breath. 'It is my intention the instruction shall take a verbal form rather than a physical one.'

'And it is my "intention" it shall not,' Marcus assured her dryly, hands clenched at his sides as he resisted the impulse to put Julianna across his knee, before throwing her gown up to her waist and administering several slaps to her bottom until those rounded cheeks glowed a delicious red.

The thoughts of which caused his cock to engorge instantly and pulse hotly inside his breeches—making a mockery of his suggestion that he may not find Julianna attractive enough to attain an erection.

Everything about her aroused him, from the rich red-gold of her hair to the beauty of her face dominated by those full and sensuous lips, the creamy swell of her breasts to the slenderness of her waist and the fiery thatch of curls that he was sure protected those other equally as full and sensuous lips between her thighs.

And she dared…she dared come to him and attempt to blackmail him into teaching her of physical pleasure. 'Take off your cloak,' he repeated uncompromisingly.

Julianna's fingers trembled slightly as she reached up to her throat and unfastened her cloak before easing it from her shoulders to stand before him in her plain grey silk gown.

'Place it upon the chair,' Marcus instructed gruffly, waiting until she had done so before adding, 'And now take off that ugly bonnet and release your hair.'

Once again, Julianna faltered, this time in the act of placing her bonnet on the chair beside her cloak. 'Release my hair?'

His mouth twisted derisively. 'Your first lesson shall be to learn that a gentleman considers the only reason for a woman to pin up her hair to be so that same man might enjoy the pleasure of watching her unpin it.'

She gave a puzzled shake of her head. 'I do not recall my husband ever—'

'The inadequacies of your dead husband have no place here and now between the two of us!' Marcus Wilding's eyes glittered in warning.

'But—'

'If I agree to your request then here, in my home, there will be only the two of us, Julianna,' he continued determinedly. 'No past, no future, only the now.'

'The now?'

'Indeed.' His mouth twisted as she remained as still as a statue. 'Lovemaking is a feast for all the senses, Julianna. First sight, then scent,

followed by taste and sound, and lastly touch. I
have decided we shall begin today with sight,
after which we shall add another sense with
each successive day that follows. I have already
seen that you are beautiful enough, curvaceous
enough, your breasts full enough, to have caught
the imagination of your lover. Now that lover
would have you release your hair for his delectation.'

The trembling that had begun in Julianna's
fingers now coursed through the whole of her
body, sensitizing her skin. Her breasts felt full
and heavy, the red berries at their tips becoming engorged against the fabric of her gown. The
place between her thighs was hot and aching,
as she knew herself to be the complete and intense focus of Marcus's green gaze. A determined gaze that did not ask but *demanded* that
she obey him.

Chapter Three

Her hands dropped back to her sides in protest of that demand. 'It was not my intention for our lessons to begin today.'

Marcus gave a humourless smile as he saw the nervousness in those deep grey eyes, despite that determined tilt to her stubborn little chin. 'The sooner we begin then the sooner this will be over, yes?'

A frown marred her ivory brow. 'I did not come prepared to—to begin our lessons today.'

'The most enjoyable and exciting lovemaking has nothing to do with being "prepared,"' Marcus dismissed her impatiently. 'The passion, desire, between a man and a woman should always be spontaneous. This is not your marriage bed, Julianna,' he continued as she made no move to comply with his instruction. 'There will be no snuffing of the candle, a rustle of the sheets, and then a hasty rutting between your thighs for the two of us.'

Julianna's face paled with shock, at both the bluntness of his speech and how accurate his description was of those humiliating occasions when John had deigned to visit her bed, before just as hastily leaving again. Occasions when Julianna had been left feeling both soiled and used as she'd risen quickly and attempted to wash away all trace of John's invasion, before stripping and remaking her bed with clean sheets and then crawling back beneath them to cry herself to sleep.

Marcus instantly had cause to regret the force of his anger as he saw the way Julianna's face had paled, proving that the scorn he had cast upon her marriage bed was correct. And if that was so then it was no wonder that Julianna wished to learn if there was a more tender side to lovemaking.

But it was a tenderness that Marcus knew he was in no mood to give her today.

'Why did you never tell your brother of your husband's brutality?' Marcus had no doubts that Christian would have taken action if he had known the full extent of Armitage's cruelty to his beloved sister.

She gave a humourless smile. 'Tell my brother

what, exactly? That John had only pretended to love me before we were married? That he wanted me only because of my name, and my wealth and position as the sister of a duke? That, and for me to give him his heir?' She gave a scathing shake of her head. 'There are dozens, hundreds of such marriages like that in society, so what right did I have to complain once I learned that mine was to be no different from so many others?'

She was right, of course; society married for prestige and fortune rather than love. So it was, so it had always been, with the very rare exception of a love match. Marcus's own parents had married because of their names and fortune, and then been lucky enough to fall in love with each other after they were married. In marrying Armitage, Julianna had not been so lucky.

'He did not beat me, was never cruel to me in public,' Julianna continued flatly. 'He did not deny me my friends, gave me a generous allowance—'

'Of your own money!'

'And the law decreed that money become his upon our marriage,' she reminded Marcus with a sigh.

'Then it is a law which should be changed!'

'Perhaps you and my brother might turn your attention to it when you are not both too busy with other business?' she returned sharply. 'As the law stands, a woman's money becomes the property of her husband upon their marriage. As does the woman herself.' She shrugged slender shoulders. 'I had a husband, beautiful homes both here and in the country, servants to care for my every need, what more can a woman ask for from marriage than that?'

Marcus believed a woman could, *should*, also ask for tenderness, pleasure, laughter, love from her husband. Damn it, if only Julianna had married *him* four years ago.

But she had not married him, Marcus reminded himself heavily. Would she have done so if he had offered for her before going off to continue the fight against Napoleon? Would she have flowered, blossomed, become all she could be beneath the shower of love and lovemaking he had wished to bestow upon her following the evening when he had danced with her at Almack's on her eighteenth birthday and realized that the little hellion had grown into a beautiful and desirable woman? A beautiful and desirable woman he wanted for his own.

Marcus would never know the answer to that, because he had not offered for her, had believed he was being gallant by keeping his distance from her, from not declaring himself. Once the war with Napoleon was over, and he was sure he would not as quickly make a widow of her as a wife, there would be time enough for him to go to Julianna and tell her how he felt about her. Instead of this, when he returned to London just months later it was to find Julianna married to another.

And the Julianna who had come to him today was not the same Julianna he had fallen in love with four years ago. That Julianna had still believed in loving and being loved. It was now up to Marcus to show Julianna that tenderness and pleasure did exist, and he had to hope that when he had done so the laughter and the love might follow.

It was a foolish hope, no doubt, but it was better than the past four years he had suffered having no hope at all where she was concerned.

Marcus straightened abruptly. 'Very well, Julianna, I will agree to become your sexual tutor.' He almost smiled as he saw her brief look of triumph quickly replaced by uncertainty of exactly what she was embarking upon. 'We will begin your first tutelage here tomorrow morning at six o'clock. You cannot be seen arriving or leaving here any later than that,' he advised as her beautiful grey eyes widened. 'In fact, you cannot be seen arriving unaccompanied, or leaving my home again, at any time of the day or night, as you have today. Not without causing scandal. Which I am sure you have no wish to do?' He arched dark brows.

No, of course Julianna did not wish to be involved in any sort of scandal, least of all with the dangerous Duke of Worthing. Indeed, she was no longer certain that she wished to come to his home again at all!

It had seemed such a practical solution to her dilemma when she'd come up with this outrageous scheme. A scheme she had believed to have been forced upon her, by the baying of the eligible gentlemen simply waiting for her time of mourning to be over so that they might pursue her. But here and now, in the presence of the disturbing—the dangerous?—Marcus Wilding, she no longer felt as confident in having chosen him, of all men, as the man to instruct her in sexual knowledge.

Oh she had no doubts that this man would more than live up to his reputation as 'the most accomplished lover in England'; it was her own ability to withstand Marcus's mesmerizing attraction, the man himself, that she now doubted.

Her deceased husband may have cared nothing for her pleasure in their marriage bed, but that did not mean Julianna had never experienced, never felt, the emotions of lust and desire. And she had felt them all for the man now standing across the room from her.

As a young child she had hero-worshipped Marcus Wilding, and as a young lady newly entering her teen years, she'd had what was commonly called a 'crush' on her brother's closest friend.

That crush had deepened into lustful thoughts once Julianna had been introduced into society, and was able to gaze upon the wickedly handsome Marcus several times a week as they attended the same social functions.

On the occasion of her eighteenth birthday Marcus had gone so far as to invite her to stand up for the first waltz of the evening with him at Almack's. That he had no doubt done so at the behest of her brother, in order to ensure her success in society, had made absolutely no difference to the love that had burgeoned in her heart for him that evening. Or the desire that had heated Julianna's body the moment the handsome duke had taken her in his arms, that heat deepening, intensifying, as he held her, his chest and those long elegant legs brushing temptingly against hers as they danced together.

Just a few minutes in Marcus Wilding's company today had shown Julianna that she still felt at least that unrequited desire for him. Her breasts were so full and aching beneath the bodice of her gown, the nipples sensitively engorged, and there was that uncomfortable heat between her thighs.

Sight.

Marcus had told her that it was the first sense to awaken in sexual desire, and these past few minutes of gazing upon his wicked handsomeness had been enough to show her how true that claim was.

Just to look at this man's face was enough to cause Julianna's fingers to itch with the desire to touch the rakish curls that fell dark and thick onto his brow and curled so temptingly about his ears. And the pale, knowing glitter of his eyes as he looked at her was enough to cause a trembling deep within her.

As for Marcus's mouth—no man should ever have been blessed with such a decadently sinful mouth; he had lips she could all too easily imagine feasting on her body, caressing her skin along with those long and elegant hands.

'Time is passing, Julianna, and I still require an answer. Will you return here tomorrow morning to begin your lessons, yes or no?' he pressed.

Yes or no….

Chapter Four

'Ah, I am pleased to see you have acted upon the instructions I gave before you left yesterday morning and have worn something less funereal for me to gaze upon, for our second encounter,' Marcus murmured with satisfaction at six o'clock the following morning once his butler, having brought Julianna to him, had removed himself and closed the door behind him.

Julianna had thought long and hard about returning to Worthing House today, and in the end had only done so because she refused to suffer the mockery she knew would be in those pale green eyes the next time they met if she did not.

And she was now more than a little unnerved at finding herself alone with Marcus in the confines of what was obviously his private study. Even more so by the fact that Marcus's hair was slightly damp from where he must have bathed earlier, that he wore no jacket or cravat over or above his waistcoat, and that his white shirt was unfastened at the throat as he sat behind the heavy leather-topped desk.

As Marcus had informed her yesterday, sight was usually the first of the senses to be pleased by a lover. Julianna had no doubts of that as she found it hard to do so much as breathe, totally unable to look away from the temptation of that open V as it revealed the silkiness of dark curls that no doubt covered the whole of Marcus's chest. And lower.

'Do you like what you see?'

It took every ounce of willpower that she possessed for Julianna to slowly drag the heaviness of her gaze back up to meet Marcus's piercing green eyes, to sweep the moisture of her tongue across lips gone dry before answering him. 'You should have had your butler inform me on my arrival if the time is inconvenient for you, after all.'

Dark brows rose. 'The time is perfectly convenient for me.'

'I—but—you have not finished dressing after bathing.' It was nervousness that made Julianna point out the obvious.

'Deliberately so, for your own delectation,' he assured her huskily. 'I thought you said yesterday that you also wished for your own senses to be aroused, as much as the man's? Does the informality of my clothing arouse you, Julianna? Answer me, pet,' he ordered as she remained silent.

'I—yes!' She had been married to John for three long years, and never in all that time had she seen her husband without so much as his jacket during their waking hours, and he had always worn a nightshirt fastened tightly at his throat on those increasingly rare occasions he had briefly visited her darkened bedchamber, before returning instantly to his own adjoining room once he had spilt his seed.

To now find herself gazing upon Marcus's muscled shoulders and chest, covered only by that thin layer of the finest linen and silk waistcoat, with those tantalizing glimpses of the olive skin at his throat, was—

Julianna took a step back as Marcus rose to his towering and suddenly predatory height behind the desk. He stepped around it to stand before her, causing her to arch her throat as she tilted her head back to look up into the sinfully handsome face just inches above her own.

Marcus had been aware of the trembling of Julianna's body and the tightness of her clenched hands the moment she entered his study wearing a gown of pale russet, the colour a perfect foil for the richness of the red-gold curls secured loosely upon her bared head. A trembling that testified to her nervousness, despite the challenge in those deep grey eyes that spoke to her stubborn determination not to turn tail and run.

He felt gratified for that stubborn determination, knowing it was, in all probability, the only thing that had brought Julianna back to him. She had certainly looked less than sure she would return yesterday morning once he had issued his list of dos and don'ts for their meeting this morning. Do not wear those widow's weeds in my presence again, do not wear the unnecessary—and damned annoying—corset beneath your gown, soften the style of your hair, and so it went on, until Marcus felt sure that Julianna had been tempted to tell him to go to the devil with his instructions.

Instead, she had clamped her lips together before departing Worthing House as anonymously as she had arrived, that black cloak once again covering her from head to toe as she stepped into the equally anonymous carriage.

But here she was, after all, Marcus's cock instantly leaping to attention as he gazed upon that red-gold hair loosely secured at her crown. Unless he was mistaken, and he was sure he was not, she was wearing no corset beneath the becoming russet gown that revealed the swell of the tops of her ivory breasts. Their proximity also allowed Marcus to detect the faint and tantalizing smell of roses upon that luminescent flesh.

'I—is your study not a strange place in which to—to carry out our second meeting?' Julianna now asked nervously.

Marcus smiled slightly. 'The location of lovemaking, even the danger of discovery, can often be an arousing introduction to the act. Do you not find it more exciting being here, in my study, an obviously masculine room that you would normally never have reason to enter?'

She did, Julianna acknowledged wonderingly. There was something so—so forbidden about being in Marcus's study with him, the only furniture being that huge mahogany desk and the chair behind it, and an ornate Japanese screen beside the bay window. How delicious it was to imagine sitting upon Marcus's thighs as he sat in the chair, or having him drape her across the width of that desk—

'You do.' Marcus nodded his satisfaction as he obviously saw the flush to Julianna's cheeks and the fevered glitter in the grey of her eyes.

'Yes,' she breathed softly, forcing herself to remain unmoving as Marcus lifted one long and elegant hand to begin removing the pins from her hair, the wideness of her gaze fixed upon his bared throat. She could see the way Marcus's pulse leapt as he removed the last pin and the cascade of her hair fell loosely onto her shoulders and down the length of her spine.

Marcus certainly seemed to enjoy the sight of a woman's unbound hair, his expression completely distracted as he gazed appreciatively at the silky length of her curls. 'I believe I shall one day very soon enjoy the painful anticipation of having the feel of this silky flame draped across the bareness of my thighs.'

Julianna's breath caught in her throat as she tried to imagine under what circumstances her hair might come into contact with Marcus's bared thighs. Was Marcus saying—was he implying that? Surely there was no reason for her hair to ever be anywhere near the vicinity of his...

'Have I succeeded in shocking you, Julianna?' he asked as he heard the softness of her gasp.

Her gaze flew up to meet his. 'I was merely wondering, considering, attempting to imagine—' She broke off awkwardly.

'If one is to truly enjoy lovemaking then not a single inch of a lover's body should remain untouched, uncaressed, by the other,' Marcus explained throatily. 'Every single inch, Julianna.'

Julianna felt completely flustered now as she

imagined touching, fondling, caressing the most intimate parts of Marcus's body. As she thought of exactly where her mouth might be for the silkiness of her hair to lie caressingly across his thighs.

'You said your anticipation would be "painful,"' she said abruptly. 'Why should such thoughts cause you pain?'

'It would pain a certain part of my anatomy,' he corrected softly. 'A part of my anatomy that has been erect with that same anticipation since the moment you walked into my study today,' he added as she continued to look up at him blankly.

Julianna's gaze dropped instantly to the front of his pantaloons, her cheeks aflame with heat as she saw the long length of that erection beneath the material. Marcus gripped her chin and tilted her face up, leaving Julianna no choice but to look into those pale green eyes glittering down at her with such displeasure. His cheekbones were taut, his mouth a thin angry line. 'Whatever you may have suffered at the hands of the man who had no right to call himself any woman's husband, it will not be any part of what the two of us will share together. Do you understand me, Julianna?' he pressed gruffly.

She did understand. In that instant, looking up into those beautiful pale green eyes, Julianna understood exactly what Marcus was offering her. Gifting her. It was the gift of appreciation. For her own femininity. For her beauty. And perhaps even tenderness, for her inexperience. Gifts never bestowed upon her by the man who had been her husband for three long years.

Julianna straightened her shoulders, and she stood several inches taller as she looked up unflinchingly into Marcus's eyes before answering him. 'I understand, Marcus.'

He continued to look down at her searchingly for several long seconds before giving a satisfied nod of his head. 'Good.'

'I—do you intend to kiss me?' she prompted as he made no effort to release her.

Marcus drew in a sharp breath even as he felt a nerve pulse in his tightly clenched jaw. 'Touch does not enter into your instruction for several more days yet.'

'But did you not say that lovemaking should always be spontaneous?'

He smiled inwardly as he heard the teasing beneath her challenge. 'I have also heard it said that anticipation is good for the soul!' he drawled self-derisively.

'But painful,' Julianna reminded, the definite light of mischief now in the dark grey of her eyes as she looked up at him.

It was teasing and mischief that gratified Marcus, as he acknowledged he had not seen that playful light in her eyes for some time now, and realized how much he had missed it. How much he had missed Julianna the hellion.

And how much he wished to do exactly as she challenged and kiss her. A capitulation guaranteed to reveal to her that it was in fact the pupil who controlled the tutor.

A knowledge he could not yet give her.

Marcus released her abruptly before stepping back to resume his seat behind the mahogany desk. 'I believe that to be enough instruction for today.' Any more of this and he was seriously in danger of revealing how his love for her ruled him.

'But I have been here but a few minutes—'

'I have said today's lesson is over!'

Just when Julianna had felt herself on the precipice of a discovery, she knew herself dismissed. Quite what that discovery might have been she had no idea, only that she had felt something in the gentling of Marcus's fingers against her chin, seen an elusive something in his eyes, some nuance of emotion she had not quite been able to grasp before a shutter had come down over his gaze, and Marcus had abruptly released her before moving away and dismissing her.

An elusive something that Julianna, aware of this man in every particle of her being, longed to see and to feel again.

Chapter Five

She hesitated. 'Shall I return tomorrow morning at the same time?'

Marcus looked down the length of his nose at her. 'That is our agreement, is it not?'

'And tomorrow is smell?' Julianna wrinkled her nose delicately at the thought of what form that smell might take.

Marcus's tension eased slightly and he gave a grin as he leaned back in his chair to watch as Julianna refastened her hair in preparation for leaving. 'Somehow I do not believe we are thinking of the same thing at all.'

'Smell is smell, surely?' she dismissed as she straightened.

'One might imagine so.' Marcus nodded slowly, eyes hooded by heavy lids. 'Have you ever smelt yourself, Julianna?'

Her eyes widened indignantly. 'I will have

you know that I bathe at least once a day, some-times twice!'

'I am gratified to hear it,' he drawled, all too aware of how many of the ton chose to try to hide their unwashed bodies beneath strong perfumes. *Try*. Because they never quite succeeded. 'That is not the sort of smell I am referring to, Julianna. Everyone has a subtle, natural perfume, one that a lover inevitably finds themselves drawn to.'

Such as lemon and sandalwood, and clean healthy male, and an underlying musk Julianna was sure was all Marcus, and which had drawn her to him when he had stood so close to her just a few minutes ago.

'Your own perfume is that of roses, with an underlying scent of desirable woman—' He broke off as Julianna's cheeks flushed a fiery red. 'You know, of course, of the fluid a man emits during lovemaking? Obviously you do,' Marcus answered his own question grimly. 'But have you never smelt the perfume of your own unique arousal? Touched, and perhaps breathed in the scent of the arousal which dampens your thighs?'

Julianna was too shocked now to even gasp. 'Certainly not!' But she had, Julianna acknowl-edged wonderingly, as she recalled the dampness she had noticed when she'd returned home yesterday after being with Marcus, something she had never ever experienced in John's company, in bed or out of it.

Because she was aroused? Because just looking at Marcus, smelling that lemon and sandalwood she would now always associate with him, and discussing such intimacies with him, had caused a desire she'd never experienced before? If that was so, then what would happen if he should touch her with that same intimacy?

'Sound,' Marcus murmured appreciatively.

Oh dear Lord, had she really just groaned out loud just thinking of having Marcus's hands upon her? She had, Julianna acknowledged restlessly, knowing she had given a low and husky groan of longing as heat flared between her thighs.

She gave an agitated shake of her head. 'You are right, it grows late and I should leave.'

And, much as he might wish it otherwise, for the moment Marcus knew he must let her go.

But his thoughts were grim as he recalled the look of disgust on Julianna's face moments ago, when he'd talked of the result of a man's arousal. Even worse, her pained expression, her surprise, her curiosity, when he'd talked of a woman's physical reaction to lovemaking made it evident that she had never experienced that arousal with John Armitage.

Damn it, had the man shown no consideration at all for Julianna's innocence? Was it really possible, that even on their wedding night, Armitage had taken Julianna's virginity without caressing her, reassuring her, loving her, without giving her any preparation at all? That the other man—damn and blast Armitage to hell!—had just parted her thighs, climbed on top of her, taken his own pleasure, and then left her shaken and disillusioned? And that each subsequent taking had been equally as inconsiderate and brutal?

The possibility of that having been the case filled Marcus with a blaze of hot fury, and caused his eyes to gleam with unholy vengeance toward a man who was no longer accessible to him.

'Yes, you should go now, Julianna,' Marcus agreed as he rang for his butler; and she must go now, quickly, if she was not to bear witness to Marcus punching his fist through one of the walls of his own study.

The last thing he wished to do was frighten Julianna with the force of his present turmoil of emotions. Emotions that he needed time, and space, in order to control. An hour or two in the boxing ring might suffice to cool the blast of fury he felt toward the deceased Armitage. No doubt Christian would be only too happy to spar with him. And it would also allow Marcus to question his friend as to what he had known of his sister's marriage, and why he had done nothing to stop her suffering.

Julianna hesitated. 'Tomorrow is smell, the day after, taste?'

'You seem in something of a hurry to complete our lessons' he mocked.

'I am merely...curious.'

'Then yes, the day after tomorrow we shall build upon the sight and smell we will explore more deeply tomorrow. Taste, but also sound—I do not believe it will be possible for either of us to have one without the other, Julianna,' Marcus drawled as she frowned. 'I certainly doubt I will be able to taste your flesh without also making murmurs of appreciation.'

Julianna's eyes widened, her pulse pounding loudly, palms becoming damp, at the thought of Marcus 'tasting' her flesh. As she would taste his?

Her gaze was drawn immediately to the flesh visible at his throat, to that tantalizing glimpse of the start of the black hair that no doubt covered his entire chest. What would it feel like to touch that hard and bared flesh, to allow her fingertips to caress and learn the dark contours of his body, not just of that magnificent chest but lower as well?

'Exactly,' Marcus murmured with satisfaction as Julianna gave a second, breathy groan, a groan to which his cock instantly leapt in response. A loss of control that was unprecedented. 'Be prepared for a deepening of intimacy as we add each successive sense upon the other, Julianna,' he warned huskily, still far from sure he would be able to retain control once it came to tasting her.

It was going to be absolute torture for him to taste that bared ivory flesh, with his tongue as well as his lips, and for her to taste him in the same way. So much so that Marcus was not sure he would be able to stop himself from taking that ultimate step of possessing her completely. Something Marcus had promised himself he would not—could not—do unless it was clearly what Julianna wanted too.

She may have asked—demanded—that he teach her, tutor her, in an appreciation of the pleasures of the flesh, but she had not specified whether or not there would be a natural conclusion to all of that lovemaking.

'Do you have any dos and don'ts for tomorrow, Marcus?'

His gaze felt heavy with desire as it was drawn back to Julianna's face. She stood across the room looking so vulnerable, and yet so proudly courageous, too. He wished to do nothing more at that moment than go to her and beg her to stay.

Instead, aware that he had to be patient, to tempt and cajole Julianna into loving him, he remained seated behind his desk, his expression deliberately impassive. 'Do not wear drawers tomorrow, Julianna,' he instructed coolly. 'Leaving your thighs naked will aid in my enjoyment,' he added as her face paled slightly, making those dark grey eyes seem larger than ever.

Her throat moved as she swallowed before answering him. 'I—I thought touch was for the day after?'

'It is my intention for *you* to touch yourself there,' he stated evenly. 'How else can you fully appreciate the unique scent of your own arousal unless you bathe your fingers in it?'

'I—is that really necessary?'

'Unless you would prefer that I be the one to touch you?' Marcus questioned boldly.

Even the suggestion of that caused Julianna's alarm to deepen, as she once again acknowledged the hornet's nest of emotions and embarrassment she appeared to have opened up for herself by blackmailing Marcus into tutoring her.

Unless he was just deliberately punishing her for having blackmailed him in the first place?

'And will you also leave off your own undergarments and touch yourself, Marcus?' she challenged.

A nerve pulsed in his tightly clenched jaw. 'Yes.'

So much for Julianna's childish attempt to beat this man at his own game; she should have known better! 'Very well.' She nodded, that nod turning to a curtsey as Marcus's butler opened the door beside her. 'Until tomorrow, Your Grace,' she drawled before following the butler out into the cavernous hallway of Worthing House.

Marcus waited only long enough for Wilkins to close the door behind himself and Julianna before standing up and punching his first through the Japanese screen beside the window.

Chapter Six

'What have you done to your hand, Marcus?'

Exactly what Christian had asked him when the two men met at Jackson's Boxing Salon yesterday afternoon, when Marcus had also refused any suggestion that the bandage upon his hand prevented him from participating in the sport. Indeed, his turmoil of emotions had still been such that he had felt no pain at all from his bruised hand as he'd bested Christian over the agreed three rounds.

Marcus had removed the bandage earlier for his morning meeting with Julianna, but there was still a certain amount of obvious bruising to his knuckles from his dispute yesterday with the Japanese screen. 'I assure you, my opponent looks much worse than I do,' he dismissed unconcernedly, the broken screen having been removed from his study and replaced by a rich, red velvet chaise, which Marcus had yesterday instructed servants to bring in here from his own private parlour.

'I dined with my brother yesterday evening,' Julianna came back accusingly. 'By which time his bruised eye had gone several shades of purple!'

'Oh?' Christian had not reacted yesterday to Marcus's discreet questioning in regard to Julianna's marriage, but could that only have been for Marcus's benefit? Had Christian saved his own questions for his sister for later that evening?

'We always dine together on Tuesday evenings,' Julianna immediately answered the unspoken question dismissively as she moved farther into his study. Her gown was emerald green today, and perfectly complimented her ivory skin and red-gold curls.

'Did you do as I instructed and leave off your drawers?' he asked harshly.

The aching hardness of his arousal, which seemed to have been with Marcus constantly for these past two days and nights, and which now surged up thick and heavy beneath his pantaloons without the benefit of his own restricting drawers, gave an increasingly familiar throb of appreciation for even the idea of Julianna being almost naked beneath her gown.

'I did. And you?'

'Yes.'

Julianna felt that now-familiar heat course through her body just thinking of what lay beneath the fine material of his pantaloons. Marcus's gaze was just as intent upon her, as if he might see through her gown to her nakedness beneath.

A nakedness Julianna had been completely aware of since dressing earlier, her lack of drawers resulting in a sensitivity between her thighs, and a total awareness of the silky abrasion of her chemise against that bared flesh.

A sensitivity that had deepened the moment she'd entered the study and looked at Marcus, and seen that today he had dispensed with his waistcoat as well as his jacket and cravat, enabling her to fully appreciate the muscled width of his shoulders in the loosely flowing white shirt. The fastening at his throat was once again laid bare, revealing even more of his olive-skinned chest than it had yesterday.

Would he dispense with the shirt, too, by tomorrow, the day they were to explore taste and sound together? For surely they would not be able to do so if they both remained fully dressed.

But she was moving ahead of herself again, had yet to get through the ordeal of today's lesson. For an ordeal it must surely be, if Marcus intended to go through with his instruction of having her touch herself. As she had touched herself yesterday evening after bathing.

Julianna had gazed at herself often in a mirror before her marriage to John Armitage, youthfully pleased with the image reflected back at her, and hoping that her husband would be pleased, too, once she was married. The years of being John's wife, of his complete indifference to her body or physical pleasure, had resulted in Julianna slowly but surely avoiding looking at her nakedness in a mirror again.

Until yesterday evening.

Marcus's arousal that morning had shown an appreciation for her body as well as her looks, and had caused Julianna to feel curious enough to see for herself what it was he had found to appreciate.

The reflection in the mirror had shown she was far more slender than she had been at eighteen, but that slenderness only served to emphasize the fullness of sloping breasts tipped with rosy nipples, her waist dipping inwards, with red-gold curls nestled between curvaceous thighs.

Julianna had skimmed her hands along those red-gold curls and up the slenderness of her waist before cupping beneath the fullness of her sensitive breasts. Her eyes had widened at the sensitivity of the rosy nipples at their tips, her knees almost buckling beneath her when she touched them out of curiosity and felt the pleasure of that caress course through the whole of her body before it settled intensely between her thighs. A pleasure Julianna had then touched wonderingly with her fingertips, trembling as she briefly felt the sensitive folds beneath and breathed in her own musky perfume.

Just the thought of having to do that again today, in front of Marcus this time, was enough to weaken her knees all over again.

'Shall we begin?' she prompted. 'I have an appointment with the dressmaker later this morning, the last fitting for the new gowns necessary for my return into society next month following my year of mourning.'

Marcus scowled at thoughts of the man she had supposedly been in mourning for, and at the idea of other gentlemen very soon being able to fully appreciate Julianna's alluring beauty in a no-doubt delicious array of coloured gowns. Men, he knew, would be intent upon winning Julianna for their own.

He stood up abruptly. 'Take down your hair and then we shall sit on the chaise together.'

Julianna turned in surprise to look at the red velvet chaise in the window. 'Was there not a beautiful Japanese screen here yesterday?' she asked uncertainly as she removed the pins from her hair and allowed it to fall silkily about her shoulders.

'It was damaged,' Marcus dismissed.

'That is a pity.'

'Yes,' he acknowledged as he took her hand in his uninjured one to accompany her over to the chaise, waiting until she was primly seated upon its edge, her back defensively straight, before lowering his long length to sit beside her, their thighs almost touching.

Almost.

Because, much as it physically pained him to be in this continuous state of arousal, Marcus was enjoying these private times with Julianna too much to wish them over too soon. He intended to use every advantage he had, in the short time she had allotted to him, not only to instruct her in an appreciation of the pleasures of the flesh but also to try to captivate Julianna himself.

He lowered his head toward her throat, breathing deeply. 'Your perfume is of roses again today,' he murmured huskily. 'And something else,' he added curiously.

Julianna trembled slightly even as she felt the bloom of warmth in her cheeks as she easily guessed that other perfume to be the arousal deepening between her thighs. An arousal she knew was caused not only by Marcus's close proximity but also by thoughts of having to touch herself in front of him.

'Julianna?' Marcus prompted huskily as he saw the fevered glitter that had appeared in those dark grey eyes.

She avoided meeting his gaze. 'I—could we please hurry? As I said, I have another appointment. Marcus?' she said sharply as he placed a hand beneath her chin and turned her flushed face toward his.

'Something has happened.' Marcus looked down at her searchingly, noting those fevered eyes, the flush to her cheeks, the redness of her pouting lips. 'Tell me, Julianna.' His hands lightly grasped the tops of her arms as he refused to allow her to turn away from him. 'Tell me, damn it!' He shook her slightly.

'I—I cannot!' she said on a sob, head bowed. 'I—it is too shameful. Too embarrassing! I should not have—I cannot say it!' she gasped on another sob.

What on earth?

Marcus stilled as he contemplated those over-bright eyes for several more seconds, the flush to her cheeks, the pouting and aroused lips, and the way the fullness of the tops of her breasts pressed up and over her gown, as if bursting to be free. 'Ah,' he finally murmured with satisfaction. 'Perhaps part of our lesson today is superfluous?'

She raised startled eyes. 'What?'

Marcus smiled slightly. 'Tell me, Julianna, did you perhaps touch between your thighs last night, breathe in the perfume of your arousal, as I had suggested you would do for me today?'

'No!' Her face paled slightly as she pushed against his chest in an attempt to pull away, breathing heavily as she failed to free herself. 'I—yes! Yes, I—I touched myself!' she admitted as she glared up at him heatedly, challengingly. 'It was your fault!' she continued defensively. 'All your talk of arousal and... Yesterday evening, after I had bathed, I looked at myself in a mirror, at my nakedness, and then—then I touched my breasts, and the moisture you spoke of gathered between my thighs, and...and...'

'And?' Marcus encouraged her.

'And I am ashamed of what I did! So

ashamed!' She broke off with a wail as she collapsed against his chest and cried in earnest.

Marcus took her into his arms, allowing her tears. While he stroked the length of her spine, he enjoyed the sensation of having Julianna cling to him, of knowing that he had been responsible for Julianna's arousal yesterday evening. 'And did you like it, pet?'

'Too much!' She trembled at the admission.

'One can never like physical pleasure too much, Julianna,' Marcus chuckled huskily.

'No?' She sounded uncertain.

'No,' he assured her softly. 'Did you breathe in your own unique perfume?'

'Yes!'

'And did that arouse you even more? Enough so that you stroked yourself there?'

'S-stroked myself?' Her voice was muffled against his chest, but he could hear her shock nevertheless.

'Did your pleasure increase as you touched yourself? Did you climax?'

'Yes. Yes. I don't—' She burrowed her hot face closer against his chest. 'No, I do not think I climaxed.'

Marcus chuckled again. 'You would remember it if you had. Are you wet now, Julianna? The truth now,' he warned as he felt her hesitation.

Julianna groaned softly in her throat as she felt her desire grow just talking to Marcus in this way, having him so close to her, breathing in the warmth of lemon and sandalwood that was so uniquely him. 'Are you not shocked?' She frowned as she looked up to find him looking at her with curiosity rather than condemnation. 'Disgusted, at least, at my having behaved so—so shamefully?'

He gave a shake of his head. 'I believe I feel pride more than anything, in knowing that our short time together has broken down your previous inhibitions so readily. I am not in the least shocked or disgusted by your behaviour, Julianna,' he assured her huskily. 'Rather, I should like to have been there, to have been allowed to watch you.'

She blinked. 'You would?'

He nodded. 'It would have aroused me to do so.'

'Sight…' she breathed softly, wonderingly.

'Yes. That you now know some of the pleasure of your own body is a natural process, pet,' he explained as she still frowned her uncertainty. 'And a necessary one, too, if you are to help guide a partner into also learning what pleases you.'

It was all too much for Julianna to take in.

Far too much, after the things she had already revealed to Marcus today, and when her body trembled and ached with heated arousal just being close to him in this way, able to feel his hard strength beneath her cheek and against her sensitive breasts, to breathe him in.

'You said my—my actions yesterday only rendered part of our lesson today superfluous?' she reminded softly.

He nodded. 'You have still to learn of a man's...musk.'

Julianna's gaze instantly moved lower, the lengthy throb so clearly visible between Marcus's thighs telling her of his arousal. 'Now?' she breathed softly. Curiously. Eagerly.

Marcus released her to lean back against the chaise, giving her easier access to the buttons fastening the sides of his pantaloons. 'Right now,' he said throatily.

Chapter Seven

Marcus's erection surged up thick and long, and his heart began to beat a loud and wild tattoo in his chest as Julianna's hands moved tentatively, and then more surely, to unfasten the buttons of his pantaloons.

And again he worried that, after wanting her, desiring her, loving her for so long, he wouldn't be able to retain control over the increasingly desperate need he felt to make love to her completely.

The last thing Marcus wanted to do was hurt Julianna, frighten her with the depth of the passion he felt for her, as that bastard Armitage had so obviously hurt and frightened her in their marriage with his coldness and brutality.

'Marcus?'

Damn it, he could see by the uncertainty of Julianna's expression, as she hesitated about folding down the flap of his pantaloons that would bare him to her completely, that she was already doubting the wisdom of her actions, that if he did not do something, say something soon to alleviate that uncertainty, she might cut and run. Perhaps, this time, forever.

Her next words confirmed it. 'If you would rather we put an end to our bargain now, I believe I have learnt enough to—'

'I have no intention of putting an end to our bargain!' he bit out, instantly regretting that hardness as he saw the way in which she flinched. 'We made an agreement, Julianna,' he reminded evenly. 'And I am not about to renege on that. I hesitate only because—I know you have been married, Julianna, but the things you have said of that marriage have not... Have you even seen a man naked?'

'Not John, certainly.' She raised her chin determinedly at the enormity of her admission, at what it must tell Marcus of that loveless marriage. 'But I saw my brother, Christian, in his drawers often when we swam together as children—'

'I said a man, Julianna. Nor was I referring to his chest,' Marcus added dryly.

Colour blazed in her cheeks. 'I—then no, no, I have never seen a man naked.'

Marcus breathed deeply. 'Or aroused?'

'No.' Her eyes were now wide grey pools of anticipation.

'But you would like to?'

'I—' She moistened her lips with that little pink tip of her tongue.

A tongue Marcus longed, ached, to feel against his aroused flesh. Just to think of it, imagine it, was enough to cause his cock to throb.

'Yes,' she breathed softly. 'I believe I should very much like to see *you* aroused, Marcus….'

His breath left him in a shaky sigh of relief. 'Then do so, Julianna,' he encouraged. 'Fold back the flap of my pantaloons and look your fill,' he invited gruffly.

Julianna's breath caught in her throat as she slowly did as he instructed. Her eyes widened as she looked at the length of his arousal, which jutted up thick and strong from the thatch of dark curls between his thighs, engorged veins running along the length of the pulsing shaft, the bulbous tip glistening with moisture.

She found it impossible to look away from the beauty and the power of Marcus's arousal. 'I—will you touch it or shall I?' she breathed longingly.

'You do it,' he encouraged hoarsely, hands clenching into fists at his sides.

It was not exactly what they had decided upon yesterday, but Julianna was only too eager to reach out and touch that burgeoning length, instantly surprised by how silky the skin over that hard and pulsing flesh was, only vaguely aware of the way Marcus's breath hitched in his throat as she wrapped the fingers of both hands around his length, a length that seemed to grow even longer and thicker in her encircling fingers. A bead of moisture escaped from the slit at the top, before it was joined by another, and then another, until it dribbled down that length to dampen the back of her hand.

Fascinated, Julianna was too enthralled to feel embarrassed by this depth of intimacy as she brought that hand beneath her nose, breathing in deeply, the scent a pleasing and arousing mixture of earthiness and an underlying sweetness. Was this the 'musk' Marcus had spoken of?

'It is the lubrication that is needed, along with your own, in order to make penetration easier,' Marcus murmured gruffly.

And not the painful business it had always been with John, Julianna instantly recognized. Because her husband had not taken the time to prepare her. Even on their wedding night he had just climbed into bed beside her, pushed up her night rail and pushed himself inside her, rip-ping through the thin barrier of her virginity, and eventually grunting his release, before leaving her.

A cold and painful introduction to the marriage bed.

And John's member had been nowhere near as—as long as Marcus's, or as thick, meaning it would surely take more than just their mutual arousal in order for Marcus to penetrate her without causing that same pain.

But Marcus had not expressed a wish to penetrate her. By showing her these things, teaching her, he was merely fulfilling his part of the blackmail she had practiced upon him, nothing more. This blatant evidence of his arousal was how any man would react to having a young woman fondling him so intimately.

Julianna released him abruptly before sitting back, only to stare down in fascination as that hard shaft pulsed eagerly upward while more liquid escaped the glistening bulbous tip.

'He is asking for more,' Marcus drawled ruefully, reluctantly refastened his pantaloons as he realized, as far as Julianna was concerned, this particular 'lesson' was over and he would have to deal with the results of that lesson himself once Julianna had gone.

'"He"?' Julianna echoed curiously.

Marcus nodded. 'Most men refer to their genitalia as a separate entity—probably because it has a will, a determination, completely separate from the logic of a man's brain!'

Which meant it was only Marcus's cock that had just reacted to her touch, Julianna accepted heavily, not Marcus himself. No doubt it could penetrate her, too, take its pleasure, and feel none of the regret in the act the man—Marcus—most assuredly would. Because, she reminded herself fiercely, Marcus was only doing these things, allowing these intimacies, because she had forced him into it. He did not care for her personally, had no real interest in making love to her. And he was probably longing to be rid of both her and her ridiculous demand to be taught how to make love to a man.

Julianna, on the other hand, had realized these past few days how much she desired Marcus in particular.

Not just desired him but loved him.

Had she always loved him?

Certainly since the night of her eighteenth birthday, when he had danced the waltz with her at Almack's, flirted with her, flattered her, before returning to his regiment just days later to resume fighting against Napoleon's army. Julianna had mooned about for weeks afterwards, foolishly hoping that night had meant something to Marcus, too. That he might have fallen in love with her.

Foolish, foolish hopes that had ended in heartbreak and hurt pride once she'd learnt that Marcus had rejoined his regiment without so much as speaking with her again. It was that same injured pride that had caused her to then accept Lord John Armitage's marriage proposal; at least there was a man who wanted her, she had consoled herself. Her brother had been home on leave recovering from an injury at the time, and it had seemed the ideal thing for her to marry before he had to return to his regiment.

It was only now, during these past few days of being with Marcus so intimately, that Julianna had realized her insistence on an immediate wedding four years ago had been because she had hated the thought of Marcus returning to England and perhaps guessing that she was pining away with unrequited love for him.

She had hoped by marrying John that she would get over her love for Marcus. Instead, she had merely buried her love for him in the deep recesses of her heart. She had never loved John—how could she when it had been Marcus, the man who had unknowingly held her heart in his elegant hands, whom she loved?

Whom she still loved.

What a fool she had been not to recognize this before now!

Because Marcus must surely despise her now, after she had blackmailed him into sharing such shocking intimacies with her these past three days, in order to prepare her for a future with other men.

Chapter Eight

'Julianna?' Marcus prompted with increasing unease for her silence and the faraway look in those grey, unfocused eyes.

He didn't feel the least reassured as she stood up abruptly before crossing the room to stand beside the fireplace, the soft curtain of her hair hiding her face as she turned away from him. 'I should never... This is wrong. I was wrong to force you to do this,' she added firmly, shoulders stiff above the rigidity of her spine. 'I apologize for—for... You should know I would never have gone to Lord Standish and told him of your—your involvement with his wife, before their marriage.'

'I am gratified to hear it,' he murmured softly.

Tears glistened in those beautiful grey eyes as she lifted her head to face him, her cheeks pale. 'I sincerely apologize, Marcus, beg your forgiveness for having forced you—' She gave a shake of her head, her hair like a living flame as it flowed down about her shoulders and over the swell of her breasts. 'I can only hope that my scandalous behaviour these past three days has not in any way affected your long-standing friendship with my brother.'

'Not in the least,' Marcus reassured her gruffly, wary of what she was going to say next.

'But your poor hand—'

'My "poor hand", as you call it, was injured before Christian and I sparred together in the boxing ring yesterday,' he assured her.

Her gaze sharpened. 'It was?'

'Yes.' Marcus stood up, realizing that it was Julianna's intention to call an end to their arrangement, and that the time for prevarication was over. 'I put my fist through the Japanese screen after you left me yesterday, hence it becoming "damaged".'

Her eyes widened. 'Accidentally?'

'No,' he answered her honestly. 'After our conversation yesterday I could not bear the thought—' He broke off, choosing his next words carefully. 'I was angry, furiously so, at thoughts of how you must have suffered all those years at Armitage's hands.'

'It was not all John's fault—'

'Yes, it was, damn it!' he bit out fiercely.

'No,' she insisted quietly. 'I did not love him any more than he loved me. I... Perhaps if I had—'

'John Armitage preferred the company of whores to that of a wife, and the looser their morals the better!' Marcus bit out grimly, having no intention of allowing Julianna to take the blame for her unhappy marriage. 'His tastes were... unusual.'

Her brows rose. 'In what way?'

'I would rather not—'

'In what way, Marcus?' Juliana persisted firmly.

'In the way of his preferring to—to share his bed with more than one person.' He scowled darkly.

Her face grew even paler. 'I don't understand.'

Marcus drew in a deep, controlling breath. 'Man, or woman, Armitage had no preference as to which as long as it added to his entertainment.' His gaze sharpened. 'He did not ever ask you to—'

'No,' Julianna assured hastily, feeling ill as she thought of those increasingly rare nights when John had come to her bed—perhaps straight from the arms of his lovers? Perhaps he had even needed that stimulation before he was able to come to her bed at all.

Her nausea deepened at the thought. 'And I had thought his lack of interest in me to be because I was…because I was not desirable.'

Marcus almost laughed at such a nonsensical notion. Almost. Because he could see from Julianna's pained expression, and the shadows in her eyes, how she had suffered because of Armitage's indifference to her. 'You were, and still are, a lady, Julianna, and a very desirable one. And Armitage's sexual preferences were founded in the gutter.'

She blinked. 'H—How do you know these things?'

'I overheard him talking one night in a gaming club almost four years ago, not long after you were married,' Marcus revealed reluctantly. 'He was bragging of his sexual preferences. I— it disgusted me to the point that I—' He broke off abruptly, hands clenched at his sides at the memory—the shameful memory—of what else had almost happened that night.

'I—that is—almost four years ago, you say?' Julianna realized softly. 'Is it possible you heard this conversation the night before Emily Proctor was to marry Lord Standish?'

Marcus stilled. 'Perhaps…'

'Was it?' Julianna persisted determinedly.

'Yes!' A nerve pulsed in his tightly clenched jaw.

She looked up at him searchingly. 'Marcus?'

He turned away to walk across and stare sightlessly out of his study window, unable to withstand that penetrating gaze a moment longer. 'You should know, I did not...agree to our arrangement these past few days because you blackmailed me, Julianna.'

Julianna stared at the uncompromising set of Marcus's shoulders, the stiffness of his spine beneath the flowing white shirt, wondering if she had misunderstood him, if it were not merely wishful thinking on her part that she thought he might care for her.

Whatever the outcome of this conversation, Julianna knew that there were things between them that needed to be said, and that if they were not said now they might never be.

Her pride dictated that she not open herself up for the same rejection she had suffered in her marriage. At the same time, the memory of the difficulties she had placed herself in the last time she let pride dictate her actions mocked that reluctance. There must be truth between the two of them now, even if that truth resulted in her humiliation. Surely, after these past three days, she owed Marcus that much, at least.

She drew in a deep breath before speaking softly. 'And I have realized these past few days that I did not blackmail you, and only you, because of a sudden need for sexual knowledge.'

Marcus turned slowly, eyes searching the pale calm of Julianna's face. 'Then why did you?' he finally asked.

She smiled ruefully. 'Forgive me, but even I had not realized my true reasons until a few minutes ago.' She closed her eyes briefly as she gave a shake of her head. 'Do you even remember that night all those years ago when you danced a waltz with me at Almack's?'

He nodded. 'It was the night of your eighteenth birthday. You looked... you were so beautiful that night, Julianna, that just to look at you took my breath away.'

'I fell in love that night,' she revealed softly.

He scowled. 'With Armitage? I do not remember seeing you with him—'

'*You* were the one I fell in love with that night, Marcus,' Julianna corrected him softly, having no intention, after the things she had learnt today, of so much as mentioning her deceased husband's name ever again. He was the past, and it was only the future that concerned her now. With or without Marcus in it.

She could never love another as she now realized she loved Marcus, as she had always loved him, but if he did not want her then she would at least know that she had told him of the feelings she had for him, before she had to leave him to find what future she could without him.

She straightened her shoulders determinedly as she looked steadily across the room at Marcus. 'I loved you then, I have loved you every day since, and I love you still. I say this not because I expect you to be able to say the same to me,' she added hurriedly as Marcus looked stunned by her words. 'But because I have wronged you these past three days, have made demands upon you which must have shocked and dismayed you—'

'Did you listen to anything I said to you earlier, Julianna?' Marcus demanded impatiently as he quickly crossed the room to her side, coming to a halt just inches in front of her as he looked down at her. 'I am neither shocked nor dismayed. And I only allowed you to believe you had blackmailed me into teaching you of lovemaking, when in reality I never laid so much as a finger on Emily Proctor.'

Julianna started. 'She lied?'

'She lied.' He nodded as he reached down to take both of Julianna's hands in his. 'I could not—I did not want her. Not even when the woman I really wanted, the woman I ached for, wanted, was in love with, was denied to me. *You* were denied to me, Julianna,' he revealed.

She gasped softly, wonderingly. 'Me?'

'You,' he repeated firmly. 'I fell in love with you the night of your eighteenth birthday, possibly even before that, but that was the night I realized my true feelings for you. But in my arrogance I believed it best that I wait until the war with Napoleon was over before coming to you and declaring my love for you, that it was unfair to you to do otherwise, when I might make you a widow so soon after becoming a bride. You married Armitage in my absence.' He gave a humourless smile at the irony of events.

Julianna could barely breathe as she listened to Marcus telling her of how he had realized his love for her on the very same night she had acknowledged to herself the deep love she felt for him. 'I believed, when you went back to war without seeing me again, that you did not want me, and that I would never become a bride at all if I did not accept John's offer when it was made. But all the time, all these years, it was you I loved, Marcus. You I wanted to be with. As I want to be with you now. Fully and completely,' she added breathlessly. 'As your lover—'

'As my wife,' he insisted.

Julianna looked up at him in shock. 'You wish to marry me?'

'More than anything! I know you were un-happy in marriage the first time, that you have decided not to marry again, but I assure you marriage to me would not be like that. Not ever! I love you, Julianna.' Marcus swept her into his arms. 'I will always love you.'

'And I love you!' she assured him fervently as she clung to him. 'Make love with me, Mar-cus, please? Here, or in your bedchamber, I do not care where, as long as you allow me to make love with you as I have long wished to do. As you have so pleasurably taught me to do,' she added huskily.

Marcus moved back slightly to look down at her wordlessly for several long seconds be-fore laughing happily at the unwavering love he saw shining in those beautiful grey eyes. 'Then I choose the privacy of my bedchamber.' He swung her up completely into his arms, paus-ing only long enough to allow her to open the door. 'In the knowledge that I will always love you, Julianna,' he told her throatily.

'Let us show each other our love.' Julianna glowed up at Marcus as she allowed him to carry her up the stairs.

To heaven.

Chapter Nine

'Sight,' Julianna murmured longingly just minutes later as she looked at the muscled contours of Marcus's bared chest.

'Sight,' he echoed huskily. Both of them were naked as they stood so close but not quite touching, having quickly undressed each other, their clothes scattered on the floor about them.

'Scent.' Julianna laid her cheek against that perfect chest as she breathed in the lemon and sandalwood, the musk that was so uniquely Marcus.

'Scent.' Marcus nuzzled against the delicate curve of her throat, breathing in her essence before slowly, oh-so-slowly, dropping to his knees in front of her. 'Scent,' he repeated hoarsely as he buried his face gently against the silky red-gold curls between her thighs.

Julianna's breath hitched in her throat as she

looked down at him. 'Taste?' she murmured curiously.

Marcus looked up at her, still concerned about shocking her, frightening her, with the depth of his need for her, and was instantly reassured by the longing in Julianna's eyes and the fevered flush to her cheeks. 'Taste,' he groaned achingly as he now nudged her thighs gently apart, his hands on her hips to steady her as he moved closer.

Julianna gasped, her hands moving quickly to grasp Marcus's shoulders as she felt the first pleasurably rasping caress of his tongue against her sensitized flesh.

The repeated rasp of that marauding tongue, the suckling of her centre between surprisingly soft lips, the gentle bite of teeth, was pleasure such as Julianna had never known, never realized existed. That wicked tongue moved lower still, thrusting into her heat at the same time the soft pad of Marcus's thumb caressed the hardened nubbin above.

'And sound,' Marcus murmured with satisfaction as Julianna groaned with each prolonged thrust of his tongue.

'It is too much, Marcus!' she gasped long minutes later, fingers gripping his shoulders tightly as he felt her nubbin pulsing against his thumb, as evidence of her rapidly approaching climax.

'It can never be too much between the two of us, Julianna. Never!' he said raggedly, filled with the taste of her, the scent of her arousal as he laid siege to that ripe nubbin. He suckled deeply, again and again, as she mewled softly, desperately, and he knew she was poised on the edge of her release. His cock surged to bursting as he thrust a finger into her moist and welcoming sheath in the same rhythm in which he suckled her deeper, harder, into the heat of his mouth.

Julianna had never known that such pleasure as this existed. She wanted it to go on forever, though at the same time as she knew she was beyond control. Pleasure washed over her in ever-deepening waves as she moved her hips instinctively into Marcus's complete possession. Until that pleasure soared free and all-consuming, wave after wave of earth-shattering pleasure exploding into a kaleidoscope of colour beneath her closed lids as she clung on to Marcus's shoulders, her only point of contact with the earth.

Marcus closed his arms about Julianna as she crumpled and fell to her knees in front of him. Her breath a rasping sob, she lay weakly against his chest. Marcus was full to bursting with the satisfaction of knowing he had been the one to give her this first taste of pleasure. And that there was more, so much more for them to explore.

Together.

It still seemed like something of a dream to him, an unexpected but oh-so-welcome dream, that Julianna loved him, as he loved her, and he vowed then and there to tell her so every day for the rest of their lives together.

She roused slightly in his arms to look up at him with satiated dark eyes. 'My turn to taste you,' she murmured longingly as she shifted out of his arms to kneel in front of him. 'Ah,' she murmured knowingly as her hair lay as a fiery caress across Marcus's thighs.

Marcus's breath caught at the back of his throat as her fingers closed possessively about his rock-hard arousal before she lowered her head and flicked the rasp of her tongue across the glistening tip. 'Dear God!' he groaned weakly as the pleasure surged through him, proving that, as he had suspected, the pupil had no more need of the teacher.

Julianna had never tasted anything as intoxicating as Marcus. She continued to lick his shaft from base to tip before daring to part her lips and draw that bulbous tip completely into her mouth, drawing, suckling on him in the way he had her just minutes ago, moving one of her hands to cup the sac beneath, and emboldened by the increased raggedness of Marcus's breathing, which told her how much that pleasured him.

'No more, Julianna!' Marcus finally gasped as he pulled her gently away. He wanted nothing more than for her to continue that pleasurable suction with her hot little mouth, and the increasingly daring caress of her fingers, but he was also aware of the outcome if she did. He wanted to be buried inside Julianna when he came. Deep, deep inside her.

She looked up at him with dark, aroused eyes as she licked her lips. 'You taste delicious.'

'As do you,' he said gruffly as he stood to lift her up into his arms and carry her over to the bed. He laid her there before he settled above and between her parted thighs, his weight on his elbows. 'Will you allow me inside you now, darling Julianna?'

'I long for it!' she breathed, her hands caressing his back.

'I do not ever want to hurt you—'

'You couldn't,' she said with certainty. 'I know without a doubt that you never could.'

As Marcus had hoped, their previous lovemaking had more than prepared Julianna, her sheath hot and so very moist. Even so, he took care with her, easing his cock inside her an inch at a time, until he filled her completely. He stilled above her, allowing her time to adjust to the fullness as he cupped a hand either side of her flushed and satiated face and looked down at her beautiful smile. 'I love you so very much, Julianna. Will you please make me the happiest man alive and become my wife?'

'Oh yes, Marcus.' Her eyes glowed as she smiled up at him brightly, trustingly. 'Yes, yes, a thousand times yes!'

'Thank God,' he murmured thankfully as he claimed her mouth with his and they both became lost—and, at the same time, found—in their mutual pleasure and love for each other.

* * * * *

ZACHARY BLACK: DUKE OF DEBAUCHERY

To all of you, thank you for reading my books.

Chapter One

Late February, 1815, outside White's Club, London.

'What the—?' Zachary Black, the Duke of Hawksmere, came to an abrupt halt as he climbed into his carriage and noticed the shadowy figure already seated on the far side. The lantern inside was turned down low, preventing him from seeing if it was a man or woman who sat back in the shadows. 'Lamb?' He turned to look accusingly at his groom, silver eyes glittering in the soft glow of the flickering lamp.

The middle-aged man straightened to attention. 'She said as 'ow you was expecting 'er, your Grace,' he offered questioningly.

His intruder was a woman then, Zachary processed grimly. But certainly not one he had been expecting.

Unless…

He had just spent the evening and part of the night at his club with his four closest friends celebrating the forthcoming nuptials of one of them, Marcus Wilding, the Duke of Worthing, and his ladylove, Lady Julianna Armitage. Their wedding was due to take place later on today.

Zachary had briefly toyed with the idea of marriage himself the previous year, a decision forced upon him by the circumstances of his father's will. But his attempt to secure a wife had gone so disastrously wrong he was reluctant to repeat the experience. However, his cynicism did not prevent him from wishing Worthing well in the venture. Indeed, he had done so until almost dawn.

Which now caused Zachary to wonder if perhaps the woman in his carriage was a part of those wedding celebrations? Possibly a gift from Worthing? And perhaps each of Zachary's other three close friends would all find a similar present awaiting them in their own carriages?

Maybe so, but Zachary intended to remain cautious until convinced otherwise. The war with Napoleon might be over, and the Corsican currently incarcerated on Elba, but these were still dangerous times, and finding an unknown woman waiting for him in his carriage was certainly reason enough for him to stay on his guard.

'Hawksmere House, Lamb,' he instructed tersely as he climbed fully into the carriage and the door closed behind him. He took a seat across from the mysterious woman, placing his hat on the seat beside him as the carriage moved forward.

Zachary's sight had now adjusted enough to the gloom for him to note that the woman wore a black veil, one that covered her from her bonneted head to her booted toe. Such an effective covering prevented Zachary from being able to tell if she was old or young, fat or thin.

Deliberately so?

No doubt.

Zachary maintained his silence. This woman had sought him out, and therefore it was incumbent upon her to state her reasons for having done so.

To state whether she was friend or foe.

Georgianna's heart was beating wildly in her chest as she looked across the carriage at the silently watchful Zachary Black, the Duke of Hawksmere. A man, should he discover her identity, who had every reason to dislike her intensely. And rumour had it that the hard and cynical Zachary Black was a dangerous man when he disliked, intensely or otherwise.

Georgianna repressed a shiver as she straightened her spine before greeting him huskily, 'Your Grace.'

'Madam.' He gave a terse inclination of his head, his fashionably overlong hair appearing the blue-black of a raven's wing in the dimmed lighting. His silver eyes were narrowed in his aquiline face; his brows were dark over those pale and shimmering eyes. He had sharp blades for cheekbones above an uncompromising and sculptured mouth and stern jaw.

Georgianna's gaze was drawn down inexorably to the spot just beneath that arrogant jaw, to the livid scar visible above the white of his shirt collar. A wound so long and straight that it almost looked as if someone had attempted to cut his throat. Which had no doubt been the intention of the Frenchman wielding the sabre which had been responsible for the injury.

She repressed another shiver as she hastily returned her gaze to the dark and saturnine face above it. 'I realise my presence in your coach might be considered as an...an unorthodox way of approaching you.'

'That would surely depend upon your reason for being here,' he drawled softly.

Georgianna's gloved hands were clenched tightly together beneath the concealing shroud of her black veil. 'There is... I have important news I need to... to impart to someone I believe is an acquaintance of yours.'

The man seated opposite her in the carriage did not appear to move, his expression remaining as mockingly indifferent as ever, yet Georgianna nevertheless sensed a sudden, watchful tension beneath that indifference.

'Indeed?' he murmured dismissively.

'Yes.'

He raised those dark brows. 'Then I may assume you did not intrude upon my carriage with the intention of sharing my bed for what is left of the night?'

'Certainly not!' Georgianna pressed back in shock against the comfortably upholstered seat.

He continued to look at her with those narrowed and merciless silver eyes for several long seconds. 'Pity,' he finally drawled. 'A satisfying tumble would have been a fitting end to what has already been a most enjoyable evening. Pray tell, then, what is this important news you so urgently need me to impart to an acquaintance of mine? So important, it would seem, that you wilfully used subterfuge and lies with which to enter my carriage, rather than call upon my home during the daylight hours?' he prompted mockingly.

Now that she was face-to-face with Zachary Black, albeit with her own face obscured beneath the black veil, Georgianna was asking herself the same question.

At two and thirty, the arrogantly disdainful Duke of Hawksmere was a man she believed few would ever approach readily.

Admittedly, his prowess on the battlefield, with both sword and pistol, was legendary. His prowess in the bedchamber equally so. But he was also a gentleman rumoured to deal with both in the same cold and ruthless manner.

A coldness and ruthlessness, as Georgianna knew better than most, said to be frighteningly decisive.

So much so that she had no doubt that were he to identify her he would not hesitate to halt the carriage and toss her unceremoniously out into the street.

That he might still do so, of course.

She drew in a deep breath. 'It is rumoured, or more precisely I have reason to believe you have certain… connections? In government?'

Zachary remained lazily slouched on the plushly upholstered seat of his ducal carriage, his expression of mockery and boredom unchanging. But inwardly he was instantly on the alert, not caring for the way in which this woman had hesitated before questioning his connections.

It implied that she had some knowledge of his having worked as an agent for the Crown this past four years. Information which was certainly not public knowledge. Indeed, his endeavours in that area would be of little use if it were.

He gave a dismissive shrug. 'I have many acquaintances in the House, if that is what you are referring to.'

'We both know it is not.'

'Indeed?' Damn it, who was this woman?

A younger woman, from the light and breathless sound of her voice, and possibly unmarried if her shocked reaction to the suggestion she was here to share his bed was any indication. She also appeared educated from her accent and manner of speaking, although that veil still prevented him from knowing as to whether she was fair or dark, fat or thin.

Or what she knew of his connections in government.

'Yes,' she asserted firmly.

'I am afraid that you have me at something of a disadvantage, madam. While you claim to know a lot about me, I do not even know your identity,' Zachary dismissed coldly.

Georgianna doubted that the arrogantly assured Zachary Black had ever been at a disadvantage in his privileged life. Nor was he under one now, for this was his carriage, and their conversation one over which he ultimately held power. As he always held power over all who were allowed, or dared to, enter his privileged world.

A power, a proximity, that she frankly found overwhelming.

She had forgotten—chosen to forget?—that the duke was so immediate, and his personality so overwhelming, that he seemed to possess the very air about him. Air perfumed with the smell of good cigars and brandy, no doubt from the evening he had just spent at his club with his friends. There was an underlying hint of the sharp tang of lemons and an earthy, insidious aroma she could only assume to be that of the man himself.

Allowing her personal nervousness and dislike of the man to bedevil her now, after all she had gone through, was not going to help Georgianna's cause in the slightest.

'It is not necessary for you to know who I am for you to arrange for me to meet with one of those gentlemen,' she continued determinedly.

'That is for me to decide, surely?' The duke leisurely picked a speck of lint from the sleeve of his black evening jacket before he looked up and pinned her once again with those coldly glittering eyes. 'And why come to me on the matter? Why not simply make an appointment and impart this knowledge to one of those gentleman yourself?'

Georgianna's gaze lowered. 'Because I very much doubt any of them would agree to meet with a mere woman. Not without the recommendation of some-one such as yourself.'

'You underestimate the influence of your own sex, madam,' Hawksmere drawled derisively.

'Do I?' Somehow Georgianna doubted that.

She had been barely nineteen ten months ago when her own father had accepted on her behalf the offer of marriage she had received from an influential and titled gentleman, all without giving any consideration as to whether or not Georgianna would be happy in such a marriage.

Her now-deceased father, she reminded herself dully, having learnt upon her return to England just yesterday that her father had died nine months ago, and in doing so making a nonsense of the anger she had felt towards him in regard to that betrothal.

'I believe so, yes,' Hawksmere dismissed harshly. 'Either way, I am not in the habit of listening to news imparted to me by unknown women—most espe-cially one who feels it necessary to lie her way into my presence—let alone recommending that anyone else should do so.'

Georgianna had expected this distrust and cyni-cism from a man whom she knew allowed very few people into his inner circle of intimates—the four friends from his schooldays, also dukes, being the exception. Those same four friends with whom she knew he had just spent the evening and most of the night.

'Who I am does not have any bearing on the veracity of the information I wish to impart,' she maintained stubbornly.

'In your opinion.'

'In the opinion of any patriot.'

Zachary Black raised a mocking brow at her vehemence. 'A patriot of what, madam?'

'Of England, of course.' Georgianna glared beneath the veil.

'Ah, yes, England,' he drawled drily. 'I trust you will forgive my ignorance, but I had thought England to currently be at peace? That we had held celebrations in honour of that peace just this past summer?'

'That is the very reason—' Georgianna broke off her outburst in order to draw in a deep and controlling breath. Being anything less than in control in this particular gentleman's company was not wise when he was more like than not to take advantage of it. 'I can trust in your discretion, I hope?'

He raised those mocking brows. 'Should that not have been something you ascertained before you decided to invade the privacy of my carriage?'

Yes, it should, and Georgianna had believed that she had done so; she would not have approached the Duke of Hawksmere if she had not known he was exactly the gentleman she needed to speak with initially.

And yet, alone with him now in his carriage, and presented with the perfect, and wholly private, opportunity in which to convince him into speaking on her behalf, she found herself hesitating.

To the country at large the Duke of Hawksmere was nothing less than a war hero. He'd fought bravely and long in Wellington's army and had been severely wounded for his trouble. That he had also worked secretly for the Crown was not so widely known, but just as heroic. It was Georgianna's personal dislike of the man which now caused her hesitation.

Alone with Hawksmere in his carriage, so totally overwhelmed by the sheer presence of the man, Georgianna could not help but be aware that he was also a man known for his ruthlessness.

Once again she straightened her shoulders as if for battle. 'You may pretend and posture all you like, your Grace, but I have no doubt that, once we have spoken a little longer, you will choose to speak on my behalf.'

Zachary would admit to being somewhat intrigued and not just by the information this young woman so urgently wished to impart. It was the woman herself who also interested him. Her voice might be young and educated, but it had also sounded slightly naïve when she stated her impassioned loyalty to England. Her claimed loyalty to England?

And Zachary still wondered what she looked like beneath that concealing veil.

Was she fair or dark? Beautiful or plain? Slender or rounded?

Zachary now found himself curious to know the answer to all of those questions. To see this young woman, if only so that he could look upon her face and judge for himself as to whether she spoke truthfully or otherwise. These last four years of working secretly for the Crown had shown him only too well not to trust anyone but his closest friends. How easily this could be an elaborate trap, a way of piquing his interest, before this mystery woman proceeded to feed the English government false information.

And his interest was most assuredly piqued.

To the extent that he no longer felt the least effect from the wine and brandy he had enjoyed with his friends earlier on.

So much so that he had no intentions of allowing this young woman to leave his carriage without first ascertaining exactly who she was and how she came to know things about him she should not have known.

He glanced out of the window to see that dawn was just starting to break over London's rooftops.

'Then might I suggest…' he turned back to the young woman, just able to discern the pale oval of her face beneath that veil now '…as we will reach my home in just a few minutes, that now might be as good a time as any for you to confide at least a little of that information?'

Her hands twisted together beneath that veil. 'I— It concerns the movements of a…a notable personage, currently residing on an island in the Mediterranean.'

It took every ounce of Zachary's considerable self-control not to react to this statement. Not to show, by so much as the twitch of an eyelid, that her information might be of interest him.

Who in hell was this woman?

And what exactly did she know?

He turned once again to look out of the window, as if bored by the conversation. 'As far as I am aware I do not have any acquaintances currently residing on a Mediterranean island.'

'I did not say he was a personal acquaintance of yours—'

'Then I cannot see what possible interest any of this can be to me,' Zachary cut her off harshly; even mentioning that the noble personage in question was a he could be dangerous.

Having chosen his servants himself, Zachary trusted them implicitly. But that did not mean he wished to test that trust by allowing any of them to overhear the details of his conversation with this woman and her implication that he was an agent for the Crown.

A young woman whose eyes now glittered across the width of the carriage at him from beneath that veil. Dark eyes. Brown or possibly a deep blue, he could not tell.

'I assure you, it will be of great interest to...'

'You have run out of time, I am afraid.' Zachary returned her gaze coldly as the carriage came to a stop outside Hawksmere House. 'Perhaps you would care to come inside and finish the conversation there?'

Said the spider to the fly, Georgianna mentally added as she gave another shiver of apprehension. Being alone in this man's carriage with him had been more than a test for her nerves. Entering Zachary Black's home with him would push her well beyond her limits of daring.

Although many might think otherwise, she acknowledged heavily, knowing her reputation was beyond repair as far as society was concerned. And most assuredly so in Hawksmere's cold and condemning gaze.

What would he say or do if he were to learn exactly who she was? Would he shun her, as all of society now shunned her? Or would he exact the revenge she had long been waiting for? That Sword of Damocles which she had felt balanced above her head for so many months now.

Zachary Black, with his reputation as the coldly ruthless Duke of Hawksmere, was not an enemy any sane person would voluntarily wish upon themselves.

And yet Georgianna had done so.

And done so willingly at the time, in the belief that she had no other choice in the matter. It had only been in the months since that she'd had time to reflect, as well as deeply regret, her previous actions. To appreciate exactly what manner of man it was she had chosen to make her mortal enemy.

After just a few minutes spent in the company of Hawksmere, and being made totally aware of the dangerous edge beneath his smooth urbanity, was enough to confirm that he was the type of man who would never forget a slight or an insult.

And Georgianna had insulted him most grievously.

'I think not, thank you,' she now answered him coolly.

'I really wish you had answered differently.'

Georgianna was not fooled for a moment into thinking that Hawksmere's words of regret were because he was still under the misapprehension she was a lady of the night and he wished to bed her. His tone had been too unemotional, too calmly conversational, for that to be true.

She pressed back against the shadows of the carriage as the groom opened the door and the duke rose to his feet before stepping down on to the cobbled road, placing his hat upon his head before turning to hold out a hand to her.

'Our conversation is far from over,' he murmured pointedly as she made no attempt to take that hand.

'If you will just agree to speak to—speak on my behalf, your Grace,' she corrected as he frowned darkly, 'then I will return in a day or so for your answer. For now I choose to wait here a few minutes longer, before quietly leaving. I believe it preferable if we were not seen leaving the Hawksmere ducal carriage together.'

He raised one dark and mocking brow as he turned from dismissing the listening groom. 'Are you perhaps under the misapprehension that your preferences are of any interest to me?'

'On the contrary, I am sure they are not.' Georgianna continued to press back into the shadows. 'I was thinking of your own reputation rather than my own.'

Hawksmere gave a humourless smile. 'I am informed by my closest friends that my reputation is that of a gambler and an irredeemable rake.'

And Georgianna now believed that to be a reputation this man had deliberately fostered, as a way of diverting attention from the fact that he worked secretly as a spy for the Crown.

Oh, he was also undoubtedly both a gambler and a womaniser. He had more than enough funds to accommodate a liking for the former and both the arrogance and dangerous attraction to ensure he could satisfy the latter. He could surely have any woman who might come to the attention of those piercing silver eyes.

Well, almost any woman, Georgianna reminded herself, knowing that one woman, at least, had escaped the attentions of both that silver gaze and the man himself.

'No doubt you are,' she conceded softly. 'I would nevertheless still prefer to remain in the carriage until you are safely inside the house.'

Zachary was not a man known for his patience. Or his forbearance. Or, indeed, any of those admirable qualities that made certain gentlemen of the *ton* so acceptable to both the young débutantes and their marriage-minded mamas. The opposite, in fact; he and his four closest friends had earned the sobriquet The Dangerous Dukes amongst the *ton* this past ten years or more, and one of the reasons for that had been because they were none of them amiable or obliging. Or in the least interested in marrying any of those irritatingly twittering young women who appeared year after boring year on the marriage mart.

Zachary's brief flirtation with the idea of marriage had been out of necessity rather than inclination, his father's will demanding that he be married and have an heir by the time he reached the age of thirty-five, or forfeit the bulk of the Hawksmere fortune. The scandalous end to that betrothal meant that Zachary had delayed repeating the experience as yet. Although, now aged two and thirty, he appreciated that his time was assuredly running out, and he would soon be forced to once again take his pick of the Season's beauties.

Worthing was to marry later on today, of course, but as he was to marry the younger sister of another of The Dangerous Dukes, it did not signify; the beautiful Julianna Armitage was neither twittering nor irritating.

So far in their acquaintance, Zachary had not found the earnest young woman behind the black veil to be either of those things either, though.

'You consider I am in some danger, then?' he enquired mildly. 'From yourself, perhaps?'

'Certainly not,' she gasped. 'I assure you, I did not come here to cause you any more harm—' She broke off abruptly even as she seemed to cringe even further back against the carriage seat.

'More harm?' Zachary's eyes narrowed even as he leant forward until his shoulders filled the doorway of the carriage, his gaze searching on that veiled figure. 'Who are you?' he prompted harshly.

'I am no one, your Grace.'

'On the contrary, you are most certainly someone.' He reached into the ever-lightening gloom of the carriage to grasp one of her arms before pulling her along the seat towards him. A soft and slender arm that answered at least one of his earlier questions; the young woman beneath the veil was slender, very much so.

'Let me go.' She struggled against his hold, her gloved hand moving up in an effort to try to prise his fingers from about her arm. 'You must release me, your Grace.' There was now a distressed sob in her voice as her attempts failed to secure her release.

'I think not,' Zachary said slowly.

It had never been his intention to just allow this young woman to leave. Not since she had mentioned having information on Bonaparte, not by name but by implication.

Besides which, his curiosity to know more about this woman had only deepened with her comment about inflicting more harm.

The implication surely being that she had caused him some personal harm in the past?

If that was the case, then Zachary intended to know exactly who she was and in what way she might have caused him harm.

To that end he leant inside the carriage and pulled her easily towards him, until she fell forward across his shoulder despite her struggles.

'What are you doing?'

'I should have thought that was obvious.' Zachary backed out of the carriage before straightening to heft his feather-light burden more comfortably on to his shoulder, his arm tight about the backs of the young woman's thighs. He shot the curiously observing Lamb a grimly satisfied grin as he stood beside the horses' heads, holding the reins to keep them steady. 'The lady has expressed a fancy to pretend she is being kidnapped by a lusty pirate and carried off to his lair.'

Georgianna gave an indignant squeak at the deliberate and mortifying fabrication, before turning appealingly to the stoic-faced groom. 'Do not believe a word of it,' she pleaded desperately, the blood having rushed to her head and now causing her to feel slightly dizzy. 'I am certainly being kidnapped, but not by any lusty pirate.'

'Quiet, wench.' The Duke of Hawksmere gave her a hearty slap on her backside to accompany the piratical instruction. 'Wish me luck with my plundering, Lamb,' he added drily, 'for I am certain I shall need it.'

'Not you, your Grace.' The groom grinned his enjoyment of the entertainment. 'Women are much like feisty mares and I've never known of one of 'em as you couldn't tame to the bridle.'

Georgianna's cheeks were aflame with colour, her light-headedness giving the whole situation a dream-like quality. One in which she felt like the spectator at a theatre farce.

What other explanation could there possibly be for the way she now dangled over one of the wide and muscled shoulders of Zachary Black, the dangerous Duke of Hawksmere?

To now be jostled and bounced as he carried her up the steps of his town house, through the open doorway, before taking the three-pronged and lit candelabrum from the surprised and haughty-faced butler into his other hand?

The duke continued on through the entrance hall before taking the steps two at a time as he carried Georgianna easily up the wide staircase to the bed-chambers above.

Chapter Two

'Remove the veil.' Zachary looked down grimly at the young woman he had just seconds ago dropped unceremoniously on top of the covers on his four-poster bed. The lit candelabrum he had placed on the bedside table allowed him to see the way her petticoat and the skirt of her black gown rode up and revealed slender and shapely ankles. Catching him looking, she hastily pulled the garments down again. Unfortunately that concealing veil had remained irritatingly in place. 'Now,' he ordered uncompromisingly.

Georgianna looked up warily through her long lashes at her towering adversary as she scrabbled further up the bed, as far away from the ominously threatening Duke of Hawksmere as it was possible for her to be. 'I have no intentions of removing my veil.'

'Are you in mourning?'

Was she? Her father had certainly died in the past year, but even so that was not her reason for wearing the veil.

'If you have to think about it, then obviously not,' the duke dismissed coldly. 'Remove the veil. Now. Before I lose what little patience I have left,' he added warningly.

Georgianna's response to Hawksmere's danger-ously soft voice was to sit up straighter in the lush pile of snowy white pillows at the head of the four-poster bed. 'You cannot treat me in this high-handed manner.'

'No?' His tone was low and menacing. 'I do not see anyone rushing to your rescue.'

Her cheeks flamed with heat as she continued to look at him from beneath lowered lashes. 'That is because you told your groom… Because your ser-vants now think…'

'That I am continuing to play my part in your erotic fantasy and am now ravishing you?' Hawks-mere completed derisively.

'Yes.'

The duke gave a grimly satisfied smile. 'And can you tell me truthfully that you have never had such a fantasy? That you have never dreamed,' he added, sensually soft, 'of a swashbuckling pirate carrying you off to his ship before having his wicked way with you?'

Of course Georgianna had once had such fanta-sies. What young and romantic girl had not dreamed of being carried off and ravished by a wicked pirate, or perhaps a dashing knight, who would then fall in-stantly in love with her and keep her for ever?

But she was now twenty years of age and felt much

older than that in her heart. Nor did she have any faith left in romance and love. She knew only too well that the reality did not match up to the fantasy, that the wicked pirate or the dashing knight invariably had feet of clay.

'Those are the daydreams of silly young girls who do not know any better,' she dismissed flatly.

'And you do?'

'Oh, yes,' she assured with feeling.

Hawksmere's lids lay heavy over his eyes as he smiled down at her mockingly. 'In that case, might I suggest you stop behaving like the ridiculous heroine in a lurid novel and remove your veil?'

Georgianna did not see that she had any choice in the matter when the duke was so much bigger than she was and could so obviously force her to his will if he so chose. And his mocking assertions earlier as to his reason for bringing her to his bedchamber meant she could not expect to receive any assistance from Hawksmere's servants, either.

She had, Georgianna now realised, placed herself completely at the duke's mercy.

And those cold silver eyes, and the uncompromising set of his arrogant jaw, confirmed that this man gave no quarter, to man or woman.

She slowly raised her shaking hands to where the pins held the veil in place. 'You will not like what you see,' she warned as she slowly began to remove those pins.

Hawksmere raised dark brows. 'Are you disfigured in some way? From the pox, perhaps?'

'No.' She sighed as she placed the pins on the night table beside the candelabrum of three flickering candles.

'Ugly, then?' he dismissed uninterestedly. 'Something my bedchamber has certainly not seen before.'

And such a richly ornate bedchamber it was, too, and entirely fitting for a duke as wealthy and powerful as Hawksmere. The curtains at the windows and about the four-poster bed were of a rich blue velvet and the furniture was heavy and dark and at the height of fashion. A thick, predominantly blue Aubusson carpet almost entirely covered the floor while a cheery fire burned in the large, ornate fireplace.

The room was almost as magnificent as the duke himself, attired as he was in tailored evening clothes of black jacket and breeches, and waistcoat of fine silver brocade, his linen snowy white, a diamond pin glinting in the neckcloth at his throat.

The same magnificent duke whose mistresses were rumoured to be some of the most beautiful women in the land.

'I am neither ugly nor beautiful, I am merely a woman.' Georgianna's hands trembled even more as she began to remove the concealing black veil.

'Then I fail to see what it is you believe I shall dis—' Zachary stopped talking as the veil came off completely and he was able to look at the woman's face for the first time.

She had lied to him because she was most certainly beautiful. Very much so. Her hair was raven-black beneath her bonnet, equally black and shapely above eyes hidden by the lowering of the longest, darkest lashes he had ever seen, her nose short and straight. Best of all was her magnificent mouth, the lips full and pouting, and surely meant for a man to kiss and devour? And other, much more carnal delights.

That was Zachary's first thought. His second was something else entirely as he eyed that pale face, that delicious mouth, in frowning concentration. 'Do I know you?'

Georgianna almost choked over the hysterical laughter that rose in her throat, at having Zachary Black, of all men, ask if he knew her.

If he knew her?

Not only was it highly insulting to have him look at her with such quizzical half recognition, but it also made a complete mockery of her having bothered to wear the black veil as a disguise in the first place; she had fully expected this man to take one look at her and remember exactly how, and why, he knew her.

'Perhaps if you were to cast your mind back to last April, your Grace, it might help to jolt your memory?' she prompted sarcastically.

'Last April?' Zachary's lids narrowed as he studied her more closely. 'Take off your bonnet,' he ordered harshly.

Her brows lowered as she looked up at him for the first time without that concealing veil and revealing deep blue eyes, the colour of violets in springtime.

Unforgettably beautiful eyes, even if the rest of this woman's appearance, apart from that tempting mouth, had changed beyond all recognition.

If this young woman was indeed whom Zachary suspected she might be, then the last time he had seen her she had been plump as a pigeon and stood only an inch or two over five feet in height. She'd rosy, rounded cheeks, ample breasts spilling over the top of her gown, and curvaceous hips a man would enjoy grasping on to as he parted those plump thighs and thrust deep inside her.

She now appeared so slender that a puff of wind might blow her away. Indeed, Zachary knew from carrying her up the stairs that she weighed no more than a child of ten. Her skin was very pale against the black gown buttoned up to her throat, her breasts small, waist and thighs slender, as were the shapely calves and ankles he had glimpsed earlier.

She sighed. 'I am growing a little tired of your instructions, Hawksmere.'

'And I am beyond tired of your delay,' he returned angrily.

'Perhaps if you were to consider using the word please occasionally, especially when addressing a woman, you might meet with more co-operation to your requests?' She reached up slender hands to untie the ribbon beneath her pointed chin.

Zachary's hands were now clenched so tightly into fists at his sides that he knew he was in danger of the short fingernails piercing the skin. 'I reserve such politeness for women who have not invaded my carriage by the use of falsehood and lies. Now, remove the damned bonnet.'

Georgianna knew from the violence in Hawksmere's tone that she had now pushed him to the limit of his patience. Perhaps beyond that limit, for those silver eyes glittered dangerously in that harshly handsome face, his hands clenching and unclenching at his sides as if he were resisting the urge to reach out and place them about her throat before squeezing tightly.

If he had finally recognised her, then she had no doubt that was exactly how he felt.

Georgianna glared up at him defiantly as she finally removed the offending bonnet, revealing thick, ebony curls secured at her crown, a shorter cluster of curls at her temple, and the slender nape of her neck.

'Well, well, well.' Hawksmere gave a predatory smile, that silver gaze remaining on Georgianna's face as he began to pace slowly at the foot of the bed. His sleek and muscled body seemed to flow with the dangerous grace of the predator he now resembled. 'If it is not Lady Georgianna Lancaster come to call. Or perhaps I should now be addressing you as Madame Rousseau?' he added scornfully.

Leaving Georgianna in no doubt that this man, Zachary Black, the arrogant Duke of Hawksmere, now knew exactly who she was.

She felt the colour leach from her cheeks, her heart once again beating erratically in her chest, as she saw how the duke's silver eyes glittered with a cold, remorseless, and utterly unforgiving anger.

An anger that turned to scathing satisfaction as he saw the answer to his question in her now-ravaged expression. 'So your gallant Frenchman did not marry you, after all, but merely settled for having you warm his bed,' he stated mockingly as he ceased his pacing and suddenly lowered his lean and muscled length into the chair beside the ornate fireplace, those devil's eyes never leaving Georgianna's deathly pale face for a moment.

An icy coldness settled in Georgianna's chest. Her limbs felt heavy with fatigue, her lips so numb she doubted she would be able to speak even if she tried.

But she did not try; she knew that she deserved whatever scorn Hawksmere now chose to shower upon her head.

However, being carried so unceremoniously up to the duke's bedchamber and forced to reveal her identity was not supposed to have happened.

She had intended to meet Hawksmere in the darkness of his carriage, under the guise of anonymity, making her request for him to arrange for her to speak to someone in government, before fading into shadowed obscurity as she awaited an answer to that request. Fully aware it was all she could expect from Hawksmere, following the events of ten months ago.

'And is your French gallant here in England with you?' Hawksmere now prompted softly.

Georgianna drew in a steadying breath. 'You must know that he is not.'

He raised dark brows. 'Must I?'

She blinked back the sting of tears in her eyes. 'Do not play cat-and-mouse games with me, your Grace, when I have no defences left with which to withstand your cruelty.'

Zachary felt cruel. More than cruel. Despite his

outward calm, he had an inner longing to punch something. Someone. To take out his anger, his frustration with this situation, on living, breathing flesh.

Oh, not Georgianna Lancaster's tender flesh, of course; he had never hit a woman in his life, and as deserved as the anger he felt towards her might be, he was not about to start now by so much as placing a finger upon that smooth alabaster skin.

For, unlikely as it might seem, it truly was her, Zachary acknowledged incredulously as he continued to study her through narrowed lids. And he could surely be forgiven for not having recognised her immediately, when she was so much paler and more slender than she had been a year ago. When those beautiful eyes no longer brimmed over with a love of life.

With love for her erstwhile French lover?

If that was true, then, she had got exactly what she deserved, Zachary dismissed coldly. Disillusionment. Betrayal.

Unless…

'When did it become obvious to you that your lover was not the French *émigré* he claimed to be when he came to take up residence in England, but was actually a spy sent here by Napoleon himself?' Zachary channelled his anger into biting words rather than physical retribution. 'That his name was not Duval at all, but Rousseau?'

She bowed her head. 'Not soon enough.' The tears spilt unchecked over those long dark lashes before falling down her pale and hollow cheeks.

Not soon enough.

Zachary knew exactly what that meant. 'Did he ever have any intention or marrying you, do you think?' he scorned. 'Or was it his plan all along to just use you to hide his true identity?'

'What a truly hateful man you are.' Georgianna buried her face in her hands as the hot tears fell in earnest, sobbing brokenly at the same time as she knew that she wholly deserved Hawksmere's anger and his scorn. His disgust.

For she truly was a disgrace. That romantic fool whom Hawksmere had described earlier.

A young and romantic fool who had believed André loved her, that they were running away together, eloping, in order to be married. That he'd acted as her saviour, rescuing her from the prospect of a loveless marriage. Only for her to discover, once they reached a chaotic Paris, the city still in turmoil following Napoleon's surrender, that her lover had never had any intentions of marrying her.

Something André had wasted no time in revealing once he was safely back in France. Their elopement, he had told her, had acted only as a foil; as a way of hiding his real reason for fleeing England so suddenly and returning to his native France.

Something she felt sure that Hawksmere, as a spy for the Crown, must surely now be aware of. Not because he had any interest in learning what had become of her, but because André and his fellow conspirators—Bonapartists—were men whom England needed to watch.

'How you personally feel towards me has no bearing on the importance of the information I have brought back with me from France,' she now assured the duke dully.

'France?'

'Yes.'

Hawksmere shrugged those wide shoulders, elbows on the arms of the chair in which he sat, his fingers steepled together in front of his devilishly handsome face.

'Information which must surely be tainted by the mere fact that your word is not to be trusted. That you might now be a spy yourself, come to give the English government false information on your lover's behalf.'

Geogianna's eyes widened at the accusation. 'I told you I am a loyal subject of England.'

'One who has willingly been living in France with her lover this past ten months.'

'I have not seen or spoken to André Rousseau for many of those months,' Georgianna denied heatedly.

At first she had been too ill to leave France; once recovered, there had been no money to enable her to leave, even if she had wanted to. Which in reality she had not, knowing herself to be unwelcome in England after disgracing her whole family, as well as herself, in the eyes of society.

A family she was sure must have disowned her completely following her elopement with André.

So, yes, she had remained in France, all the time keeping her ears and eyes open to the plots and plans that so abounded in the streets, the shops, and the taverns of the city. Plots to liberate Napoleon from the Mediterranean island of Elba, where he now reigned as emperor of just twelve thousand souls.

Which, she reminded herself determinedly, was the only reason why she would ever have deliberately sought the company of the Duke of Hawksmere.

'No?' The duke eyed her mockingly.

'I gave you my word.'

'And I, of all people, have good reason to doubt your every word, Georgianna.'

She sighed. 'Your distrust of me is understandable.'

'It is kind of you to say so,' Hawksmere drawled with obvious sarcasm.

A flush warmed her cheeks at the deserved rebuke. 'I am well aware that I wronged you.'

'You wronged and disgraced yourself, madam, not me.' Zachary stood up restlessly to stride over to the window and look out into the park below as he wondered if such a strange and ridiculous situation as this had ever existed before.

Here he was, the powerful Duke of Hawksmere, fêted and fawned upon by the elite of the *ton* and society as a whole, alone in his bedchamber with Lady Georgianna Lancaster, a woman who had behaved so disgracefully in the past that if it were publically known, he doubted society would ever open its doors to her again.

A young woman whom Zachary had good reason to believe would never enter his bedchamber, under any circumstances.

And she had not come willingly this time, either, he reminded himself, but she'd been carried up here, thrown over his shoulder with no more concern than if she had been a sack of coal, her indignant protests at his actions completely ignored.

Because Zachary had not known who she was at the time, could have no idea that it was Georgianna Lancaster hiding beneath that veil and bonnet.

And if he had?

Would he have behaved any differently if he had known of her identity?

That identity, her history and association with André Rousseau, would have made it impossible for Zachary to simply ignore her. Or the information she said she had come here to impart.

'I apologise for my past wrongs to you.'

'I have absolutely no interest in your apologies, Georgianna, in the past or now,' Zachary assured her scathingly as he turned back to face her, his cool expression masking the shock he once again felt at the changes these past ten months had wrought in her.

Georgianna Lancaster's face was now ghostly pale rather than rosy as a freshly picked apple. Her violet eyes now dark and haunted, her alabaster skin stretching tautly over the delicacy of the bones at her cheeks and throat and her figure wraith-thin.

Because, as she claimed, she had been seduced, before then being abandoned by her French lover?

Or because of the nervousness of possibly days or weeks spent considering the enormity of the deception she was about to practise on her lover's behalf?

Zachary was wary and cynical enough to know that the rift that apparently now existed between Georgianna Lancaster and André Rousseau could all just be a ruse. And that she might have only returned to England to carry out her lover's instructions of passing along false information to the English government.

Until Georgianna revealed the full details of that information, Zachary had no way of knowing what was true and what was not.

Georgianna raised her chin, determined that Zachary Black should hear her out. Whether he wished it or not. The cold mockery in those glittering silver eyes, which now looked down at her so disdainfully, conveyed that he did not.

Her own eyes lowered so that she no longer had to look at that disdain. 'I have information.'

'Well?' he prompted hardly as she hesitated.

'It is Bonaparte's intention to leave Elba shortly and return to France as emperor.'

He shrugged wide shoulders. 'There have been rumours of his escaping Elba since he was first exiled there.'

'Oh,' Georgianna murmured flatly before rallying. 'But this time it is true.'

'So you say.'

Her eyes widened in alarm at the boredom of his tone. 'You have to believe me.'

'My dear Lady Georgianna, I do not have to do anything where you are concerned,' the duke assured softly as he crossed the bedchamber on stealthy feet, until he once again stood beside the bed on which she still sat. 'What were your lover's instructions regarding what you should do next, I wonder?' he prompted conversationally as he sat down on the bed beside her. 'If met with resistance from me, were you to then attempt to seduce me in order to gain my trust?'

Georgianna could only stare at him with wide and apprehensive eyes as he now sat so dangerously close to her his muscled thighs were just inches from her own. Close enough she could feel the heat of his immense body, smell the clean scent of lemon and sandalwood and that hint of the brandy and cigars he had enjoyed during the hours spent at his club earlier tonight.

So close that she could now see the black circle that rimmed those silver irises looking down at her so disdainfully. She noted the tautness of the flesh across aristocratic cheekbones. The top one of those sculptured lips curled back with the haughty disgust he so obviously felt towards her. That livid scar upon his throat a warning to all of how dangerous this gentleman could be.

As if to confirm that danger he gave a slow and sensuous smile.

'Feel free to begin any time you wish, Georgianna.'

Her alarm deepened at the cold mockery she saw in those hard silver eyes looking at her so contemptuously. 'I have no intention of attempting to seduce you.'

'No?' he drawled. 'Pity. It might at least have

proved amusing to see just how much your French lover has taught you this past year.'

'I told you, I have not so much as spoken to André in months.'

'And I am expected to believe that claim?' the duke drawled. 'To accept your word?' His jaw tightened, a nerve pulsing beside that livid scar at his throat. 'I am to accept the word of a woman whom I am only too well aware does not know the meaning of the word honour, let alone trust?'

Georgianna flinched at the icy dismissal of his tone. 'I was very young and foolish when you knew me last.'

'It was only ten months ago,' he cut in harshly. 'Am I now to accept that you have changed so much in that short time? That your word can now be trusted? The word of a woman who did not hesitate to cause disgrace to her family and herself just months ago in her desperation to elope with her French lover?'

Each deserved and hurtful word was like a whip lashing across Georgianna's flesh. Her eyes flooded anew with stinging tears, her body quivering at the landing of each successive and precise blow to her sensitised flesh.

She gave a weary shake of her head, unheeding of the tears still falling hotly down her cheeks. 'I am asking you to accept that the information I bring is completely removed from my own behaviour. That it is most urgent, even imperative, that you believe me when I tell you it is Bonaparte's intention to leave Elba soon and take up arms once again.'

'When, precisely?'

Her gaze dropped from meeting his. 'If you could arrange for me to speak with someone…'

'You do not trust me with this information?' He raised incredulous brows.

'Forgive me, but I have learnt this past ten months not to trust anyone completely,' she answered dully.

Zachary studied her between narrowed lids, hardening his heart to the tears that still lay upon those pale and hollowed cheeks. He reminded himself that this was the woman who had thought nothing of deceiving her own father, and the man who was to have been her husband, in order to run away with the Frenchman who was her younger brother's tutor.

It might be true that she had not seen André Rousseau for some months. Just as it might also be true that Georgianna Lancaster's unmarried state meant that she had reason to regret ever having eloped with the Frenchman in the first place.

But it might be just as true that this was all just a ruse and that she had been sent here by that lover to deceive and mislead the English government.

If the first of those things was true, then it was of no personal concern to Zachary; the woman had made her choices and must now live with them. No, it was the little information Georgianna Lancaster had already imparted, in regard to Napoleon's intention to soon leave Elba, which interested him.

For no matter what he might have said to Georgianna Lancaster, no rumour of Napoleon leaving Elba was ever ignored.

His nostrils flared.

'And I have no intention of so much as telling anyone of your presence back in England until I am satisfied you have told me all that you know.'

'Please.'

'Poor, bewildered Georgianna,' Zachary mocked the pained expression on her beautiful face as he slowly lifted his hand to gather up one of her tears on to his fingertip, looking down curiously at that tear before allowing it to fall to the carpeted floor at his feet as his gaze returned to her face. 'Did you really imagine it would be so easy to convince me of your sincerity? That I would listen to your information, be so concerned by it that I would then immediately arrange for you to speak to someone in the government?'

She swallowed. 'You must.'

'I have already told you I must do nothing where you are concerned, Georgianna,' Zachary thundered before quickly regaining control of his temper. A control he lost rarely, if ever. Testament, no doubt, to the anger he still harboured towards this woman. 'What have you really been doing these past ten months, I wonder?' he mused grimly.

She blinked. 'I told you, after André— Once I learnt he had merely been using me, I had no choice but to leave him.'

Zachary was fully aware that her violet gaze could no longer meet his own. A sure sign that she was lying? 'And what did you do then?' he prompted. 'How did you continue to live in France, Georgianna, with no money and, as you claim, no lover's bed to warm you?'

'It is not just a claim.'

'I am afraid that it is.'

Georgianna looked up at the duke apprehensively, not fooled for a moment by the calm evenness of his tone. 'What do you mean?'

He returned her gaze contemptuously. 'I mean that you have made a mistake in claiming Rousseau would ever have allowed you to leave him.'

Georgianna ran the tip of her tongue across suddenly dry lips before speaking huskily. 'Why do you say that?'

He gave a derisive laugh. 'My dear Georgianna, if you really were just the foolish romantic you claim to be, then once your usefulness to Rousseau was at an end he would have had no choice but to kill you for what you already knew about him, rather than simply allowing you to leave.'

She drew her breath in sharply, the colour draining from her cheeks even as she felt the burning in her chest and temple, a painful reminder that André had attempted to do exactly that.

She still cringed at the numbing disillusionment, the cruel and frightening way in which she had discovered André had never cared for her, but had merely been using her. And the shock, the devastation of learning that André intended to rid himself of the nuisance of her by taking her out of the city before killing her.

That he had not succeeded in doing so had been more by chance than deliberate intent.

And Georgianna had the scars, physical as well as emotional, to prove it.

Zachary remained unmoved by the haunted expression on Georgianna Lancaster's suddenly deathly pale face. Her elopement with André Rousseau, the mystery of where she had been and what she had been doing this past ten months, were all more than enough reason for him to distrust every word that came out of her delectable mouth.

And he did still consider it a delectably sensual mouth, he conceded regretfully. The sort of mouth that he had once imagined doing wild and wonderful things to his body—

Zachary stood up abruptly. 'Fortunately, the decision as to the truth, or otherwise, of the information you wish to impart, does not rest with me.'

'Then with whom?'

Zachary looked down at her grimly. 'There are others—less gentle than myself—who will decide the matter.'

'I do not understand.'

'You will, Georgianna.' Zachary hardened his heart to the increased bewilderment in those violet-coloured eyes. 'Have no doubt, you most certainly will.'

She stared up at him with fearful eyes. 'You cannot mean to— You are saying I shall be tortured, in order to ascertain whether or not I am telling the truth?'

'The English government does not resort to torture, Georgianna.' Zachary bared his teeth in a hard and mocking smile. 'Not openly, at least,' he added softly.

'You are trying to frighten me,' she accused emotionally.

'Am I succeeding?' he taunted.

'You must know that you are.' Her slender fingers tightly gripped one of the downy pillows.

'Poor Georgianna,' Zachary drawled mockingly. 'Are you even aware of your father's death?' he prompted sharply.

'Yes. I learnt of it yesterday when I returned to England.' Her lashes lowered. 'I— Do you have any news of Jeffrey?'

'He is well, I believe. Inheriting the title put paid to Cambridge, of course,' he drawled dismissively. 'But he fares well with his new responsibilities as Earl of Malvern, with the aid of his guardian.'

'Who on earth…?'

'I am sure your belated concern for your brother is all well and good, Georgianna,' Zachary continued dismissively, 'but it will not succeed in deflecting me, and others, from the suspicion that you might also now be a spy for Napoleon.' He gave a mocking shake of his head. 'And to think, just ten months ago the situation was all so very different. That if you had not run away, then all of this might now be yours.'

All of this, Georgianna knew, being the Hawksmere houses and estates, the title of duchess, and the Duke of Hawksmere himself as her husband.

All of which would most assuredly have been hers,

if she had continued with the betrothal her father had accepted on her behalf and married Zachary Black, the aloof and enigmatic Duke of Hawksmere.

It was every young girl's dream, of course, to receive an offer of marriage from a duke, to become his duchess, revered and looked up to by society.

It might also have been Georgianna's dream, too, if her father had once consulted her and not instead roused her stubbornness by accepting Hawksmere's offer without so much as discussing it with her.

If she had truly believed she could bear to be married to such a cold and arrogant man as Hawksmere, a man she had no doubt did not love her.

If she, stupid romantic fool that she had been, had not already believed herself to be madly in love with another man, a penniless tutor, whose situation in life had appealed to her young and too-innocent heart. The man she had believed to be in love with her.

As opposed to this man, Zachary Black, the icily composed Duke of Hawksmere, whom she knew had not loved her, but had only offered for her because she was the eminently suitable, and malleable, nineteen-year-old daughter of the Earl of Malvern.

Chapter Three

Georgianna had been flattered but terrified when her father first came to her and proudly told her of the offer of marriage he had received, and already accepted, on her behalf, from the wealthy and powerful Duke of Hawksmere.

Until that moment Hawksmere had been a gentleman Georgianna had never so much as spoken to and seen only rarely, and then only from a distance, at several of the *ton*'s entertainments during the past two Seasons. The toplofty gentleman had much preferred his clubs, and the company of his close friends, to the bustle and formality of society's much tamer entertainments.

But even viewed from a distance, Hawksmere had seemed intimidating to her, and aged one and thirty years to her nineteen, their twelve years' difference was so obvious in experience as well as age.

His demeanour was always one of icy disdain as he habitually looked down his arrogant nose at the crush of guests assembled at those entertainments. And the terrible scar visible upon the duke's throat had caused Georgianna to tremble every time she so much as glanced at it, as she imagined the raw savagery that must have been behind such an injury.

The very idea of her ever becoming the wife of such a haughtily cold and frightening gentleman had filled her young and romantic heart with fear. Especially so when the two of them had not so much as spoken a word to each other. Indeed, the only possible reason Georgianna could think of for the proposal was that, as the only daughter of the Earl of Malvern, Hawksmere must consider her a suitable candidate to provide his future heirs.

The dukedom aside, even the thoughts of the intimacy necessary to provide those heirs with such a terrifying man as Hawksmere had been enough to cause Georgianna's heart to pound fearfully in her chest.

Besides which, she was already in love and had been so for several months. With André Duval, the handsome and charming blond-haired, blue-eyed French *émigré* her father had taken pity on and brought into their home, so that he might help to prepare her younger brothe,r Jeffrey, for his entry into Cambridge.

That same handsome and charming blond-haired, blue-eyed Frenchman who just weeks later had so unemotionally taken her out to a wood outside Paris with the intention of killing her.

Tears of humiliation now burned Georgianna's

eyes as she looked up at Hawksmere. 'As I said, I was very young and very foolish,' she said dully.

'And now you are so much older and wiser,' Hawksmere taunted.

'Yes.' Georgianna's eyes flashed darkly. This man could have no idea of how much older and wiser she was, how much even a loveless marriage to him would have been preferable to the fate that had befallen her.

He eyed her pityingly. 'I trust you will forgive me when I say I do not believe you?'

'I very much doubt that you have ever needed anyone's forgiveness, least of all mine, to do just as you please.' She sighed as she moved to the edge of the bed before standing up. 'Very well, Hawksmere. Arrange to take me to your torturers now and let us put an end to this.'

Looking at her from between narrowed lids, Zachary could not help but feel a certain grudging admiration for the calmness of Georgianna Lancaster's demeanour and the slender dignity of her stance. A dignity so at odds with the frivolously young and plumply desirable Georgianna Lancaster of just ten short months ago.

Zachary had not been consciously looking for his future wife the evening he attended the Duchess of St Albans' ball, only making that brief appearance because the duchess had been a friend of his deceased mother. He had thought only to while away an hour or so out of politeness to that lady before making his excuses and departing for somewhere he could enjoy some more sensual entertainments.

Indeed, he had been about to do exactly that when Georgianna Lancaster had chanced to dance by in the arms of some young rake. Even then it had been her eyes which first drew his attention.

Eyes whose colour Zachary had never seen before. Long-lashed and violet-coloured eyes, laughing up merrily into the face of the gentleman twirling her about the ballroom.

It had taken several more minutes for Zachary's hooded gaze to move lower, for his body to respond, to harden, at sight of those delectably pouting and sensual lips, the swell of full and creamy breasts above her gown and curvaceous, childbearing hips.

To say that his arousal at her abundance of femininity had come as something of a surprise to him was understating the matter.

Normally he did not so much as glance at any of the young débutantes paraded into society every Season, having long ago decided they were all prattling flirts who sought only a titled and wealthy husband, none of them having so much as a sensible thought in their giddy heads.

Georgianna Lancaster did not look any less giddy than her peers, but at least his manhood had sprung to attention at sight of her, a necessary function if one was in need of an heir, and, he had decided, the daughter of the Earl of Malvern would do as the mother of that heir as well as any.

He had even convinced himself that her youth was an asset rather than the burden an older, more demanding woman might become. He would be able to mould Georgianna to his ways; he could wed her and bed her, enjoy that lusciously ripe body to the full whilst he impregnated her, before then leaving her to enjoy her role as the Duchess of Hawksmere, and so allowing him to return to the more sophisticated entertainments he preferred.

Or so Zachary had decided as he had looked upon Georgianna Lancaster that evening ten months ago.

What he had not considered at the time, or for some days after the announcement of their betrothal appeared in the newspapers, was that Georgianna Lancaster had not been the one to accept his offer of marriage. That, young as she was, she had a mind of her own. She had no intention of becoming the wife of a man, even a duke, she neither knew nor loved.

Or so she'd stated in the letter she had left behind for her father to read after she had eloped with her French lover, and which Malvern had reluctantly shared with Zachary when he had demanded the older man do so.

Zachary's mouth thinned as he remembered the days following Georgianna's elopement with her French lover.

The formal withdrawal of the betrothal in the newspapers so soon after it had been announced.

The condolences he had received from his uncles and aunts.

Most humiliating of all, perhaps, had been the knowing looks of the *ton*, all of them aware that Zachary Black, the haughty Duke of Hawksmere, having finally chosen his future duchess, had then just days later been forced to retract the announcement when that future bride had withdrawn from the betrothal.

Or so the story had been related to society at large. Very few people were made privy to the knowledge of Georgianna's elopement with the young and handsome French tutor.

Certainly none knew that it had been discovered, after the elopement, that the French tutor was not who he'd claimed to be, but was in fact a spy.

As Georgianna Lancaster was herself now also a spy, at the behest of her French lover?

She certainly knew far too much of Zachary's private business, of his connections, to be the complete innocent she claimed to be.

'Your Grace?'

Zachary's eyes narrowed as he returned his attention to the here and now. 'If only it were as simple as that, Georgianna,' he bit out scathingly. 'Unfortunately, there are several aspects of your story which the two of us will need to discuss in more detail.'

'Such as?'

'Such as why you chose to come to me, of all people, with this fantastical tale.'

'It is not fantastical or a tale.'

'Why me, Georgianna?' he persisted.

Her lashes lowered over violet eyes. 'I—I can see no harm in my admitting that it was André who informed me that you had long been acting as a spy for the Crown.'

Zachary gave a humourless smile to cover the inner jolt her words had given him; if Rousseau knew of the work he carried out in secret for England, then surely it followed that others must also? 'Could you not have found more stimulating pillow talk?' he said scornfully.

Georgianna's cheeks coloured at the insult even as she straightened the narrowness of her shoulders determinedly. 'He taunted me with the knowledge when he...when he...'

'Yes?'

She raised her pointed little chin. 'When he admitted that he had never been in love with me.' Her lashes lowered, her voice husky. 'When he told me that he had deliberately seduced me, then used our elopement as a way of leaving England. That there were now some who suspected his real reason for being in England.'

Zachary nodded abruptly. 'He had only just been put under more intense investigation at the time of your elopement.' And if Rousseau now knew of Zachary's own secret work for the Crown, then his usefulness in that capacity had surely come to an end?

'How disappointing for you,' he drawled dismissively in order to cover his inner disquiet.

Violet eyes flashed rebelliously. 'Do not dare to mock me, your Grace.'

All humour faded as Zachary's mouth thinned in displeasure. 'Your behaviour these past ten months dictates that I shall now dare to treat you in whatever manner I please, madam.'

The fight went out of Georgianna as quickly as it had flared to life. She bowed her head, totally shamed at the truth of the duke's words. She had behaved like a fool ten months ago. A stupid and naïve fool who had fallen completely for André's charm.

A charm that had completely deserted him the night he had taunted her, mocked her, for having run away with him, a spy for Napoleon. When the man to whom she was betrothed, the man she had run away from, was in fact the honourable one and more of a hero to England than any but a select few knew.

'That still does not explain how you knew where I should be this evening.'

Georgianna raised her head wearily, too tired now to do any more than answer Zachary Black's questions. 'I returned to England by ship yesterday.'

'Does your brother know you are returned?' he prompted sharply.

'No one but you knows.' She gave a sad shake of her head. 'It would have been most unfair to burden Jeffrey with that knowledge.' Much as she might long to see her brother again, to know if he at least was able to forgive her for her past recklessness, he was still but nineteen years of age, and newly become the Earl of Malvern, with all of the responsibilities that title entailed. He did not need to be burdened with the knowledge of the return to England of his disgraced sister, too.

'Obviously you did not feel a need to treat me with the same consideration,' Hawksmere rasped disdainfully.

She winced. 'I have explained why you are different. Why I had no choice but to seek you out and speak with you.'

'But not how you knew where I should be this evening,' he reminded grimly.

'I made it my business to keep a watch of your comings and goings as soon as I arrived in London yesterday, in an effort to speak with you alone. This evening, spent at your club, to celebrate the nuptials of your friend, offered me the opportunity I needed.'

Hawksmere gave a dismissive shake of his head. 'I should have known if you had been following me.'

'Obviously you did not.'

Which was worrisome, Zachary acknowledged with a frown. It implied a complacency on his part now they were no longer at war, a laziness, if he had failed to realise he was being so closely watched.

He straightened. 'This has all been very interesting, I am sure, but I have several other things that require my attention this morning, not to forget a wedding to attend this afternoon. So I am afraid I cannot waste any more time on this particular conversation just now.'

She nodded. 'I am staying at lodgings in Duke Street—perhaps you can send word to me there once you are have decided what to do?'

'Oh, no, Georgianna, I am afraid that will not do at all,' Zachary drawled drily, grateful for the approximate knowledge of where she was staying in London. And that no one but he was aware of her presence back in England.

She stilled warily. 'What do you mean?'

'I mean that, for the moment, I cannot allow you to leave this bedchamber.'

She gasped. 'You cannot keep me a prisoner here.'

He eyed her mockingly. 'Can I not?'

'No.'

'And, pray tell, who is to stop me?'

Her hands clenched at her sides. 'You are attempting to frighten me again.'

'And succeeding?' Zachary prompted mildly.

'Not in the least.' Georgianna clamped her lips stubbornly together as she refused to show any fear at Hawksmere's threats.

As she refused to ever show fear again, of anything, or anyone, after the way she had suffered at Rousseau's hands.

Which did not mean that Georgianna was not inwardly quaking at the icy determination so clearly shown in Hawksmere's expression.

She repressed a shiver at how, just ten months ago, she had so narrowly escaped becoming the wife of this cold and ruthless gentleman. A man, Georgianna had no doubt, who would have settled her in one of his ducal homes following the wedding and then repeatedly bedded her, until she had filled his nursery with his heir and his spare. After which, like many of the gentlemen of the *ton*, he would no doubt have abandoned her to find her own entertainments, whilst he returned to the life he had enjoyed before their marriage.

Such, Georgianna knew, was the life of many wives in society. A loveless and boring existence.

A life she had hoped to escape when she had eloped with André.

Only to then find she had placed herself in an even more dire position than becoming Hawksmere's unloved duchess.

Did she regret her elopement of ten months ago?

Of course she did.

If she could live that time over again, she would have remained in England with her family.

And become the wife of Zachary Black, the Duke of Hawksmere instead?

Never!

Despite all that Georgianna had endured these past months, despite all that she might still have to endure, she did not have a single regret in regards to refusing to become the wife of the Duke of Hawksmere.

She would never marry at all now, of course. How could she, when her reputation was now such that no gentleman would ever consider making her his wife? And to lie about her past, to pose as a widow, perhaps, in order to marry a lower-born gentleman, was a deceit she refused to practise on any man, or any children born into that marriage.

No, Georgianna had accepted that she would spend the rest of her life alone. As she fully deserved to do, when her impetuous actions of ten months ago had resulted in such shame and scandal.

'Do not look so sad, Georgianna.' The duke deliberately chose to misunderstand the reason for that sadness as he crossed the bedchamber on predatory soft steps, until he now stood just inches away from her. 'I may be busy for the rest of the day, but I shall return later this evening. And when I do—' those glittering silver eyes held her mesmerised as he slowly raised a hand and allowed the hardness of his knuckles to graze softly over the warmth of her cheek '—I am sure we shall be able to think of several ways in which to keep you entertained, during your incarceration in my bedchamber.'

Georgianna gasped as she heard the intent beneath that softly sensuous voice. Just as she now flinched as the hardness of those knuckles travelled the length of her throat before moving lower, lingering to caress the swell of her breasts through the material of her gown.

Leaving her in absolutely no doubt as to what those entertainments might be.

Her cheeks burned with humiliated colour as she pulled back from those caressing knuckles. 'I may have fallen from decency in society's eyes, Hawksmere, but I assure you I have absolutely no intention of becoming your plaything.'

The duke eyed her derisively. 'The arousal of your breasts, from just the merest touch of my knuckles, tells a different story,' he drawled mockingly as he glanced pointedly downwards.

Georgianna's startled gaze followed the direction of his mocking gaze, her face paling as she saw what Hawksmere so obviously saw; those rosy berries that tipped her breasts were now swollen and full, and could clearly be seen outlined against the soft material of her gown buttoned up to her throat.

Because they were aroused?

By Hawksmere?

Impossible.

Oh, he was handsome enough to set any woman's heart beating faster. But it was a dangerous attraction, a challenge those silver eyes proclaimed no one woman would ever be able to satisfy.

Too much of a challenge, it was rumoured, for any woman, high- or low-born, married or unmarried, to resist sharing the duke's bed once he had expressed an interest.

But Georgianna was not one of those weak and susceptible women. How could she be, when she found Hawksmere no less intimidating now than she had ten months ago?

Except...

There was no denying the physical evidence of her breasts having become aroused by his lightest of touches.

Not with desire but fear, Georgianna instantly assured herself.

Because Hawksmere had just threatened to keep her here, a prisoner in his bedchamber, for as long as he chose to do so.

She straightened her spine. 'You cannot keep me here against my will,' she repeated firmly.

'I can do anything I wish with you, Georgianna,' Zachary murmured with satisfaction, mocking her response, her undeniable arousal at his caress.

An arousal which Zachary knew no woman could fabricate or control.

As he had been unable to control his own arousal

as he had lightly caressed the engorged tip of her breast.

Despite her having run away from marrying him ten months ago, Zachary could not deny that he still physically desired this woman. In his bed, beneath him, to be buried to the hilt between her thighs.

Try as he might, Zachary had found no explanation for that sudden clench of desire when he had looked at Georgianna Lancaster ten months ago, and he had none now, either. It was enough to know that it still existed.

A weakness, in the current circumstances, best kept to himself.

He stepped back abruptly. 'As I said, I have other things to occupy me this morning, but I will go downstairs now and arrange a breakfast for you, and then I advise that you get some sleep.'

'I am not hungry, nor shall I sleep.'

Zachary's eyes narrowed on her critically, noting the hollows in the paleness of her cheeks, her slenderness beneath the unbecoming black gown. 'You are grown too slender.'

'I said I am not hungry.' Those violet-coloured eyes flashed again in warning.

Another show of temper Zachary did not care for in the least, as he stepped deliberately closer to her, so close that he could see the way the pupils of her eyes expanded as she now looked up at him apprehensively.

'Nevertheless, you will eat all of the breakfast I have brought up to you.'

She maintained her ground even as a nerve pulsed rapidly at her throat, no doubt as evidence of her inner nervousness. 'And I have said I shall not.'

Once again Zachary felt that grudging admiration for her stubbornness; not too many people dared to stand against him, least of all women. She was a very young woman at that, and one who did not as yet appear to fully appreciate the danger she had placed herself in by choosing to step back into his life.

He gave a slow and deliberate smile. 'I advise you not to defy me, Georgianna.'

She eyed him rebelliously. 'Why should I not?'

He gave a nonchalant shrug as he murmured softly, 'Because I shall win and you will lose.'

Georgianna repressed another shiver of apprehension as she heard the arrogant certainty in his voice. As she acknowledged that, through her own stupidity this time, Hawksmere now had her completely at his mercy. She was his prisoner, to do with as he wished.

Hawksmere smiled confidently as he seemed to guess at least some of her thoughts. 'I shall be locking you in here in my absence, of course, and taking the key with me. And I advise that you not bother giving yourself a sore throat, or knuckles, by screaming or shouting, or banging on the door for my servants to release you whilst I am gone,' he added derisively. 'I shall make sure to inform them, before I depart, that it is all part of the erotic play between the two of us, and that the more you ask to be set free the more you desire to stay here and await my return.'

'You truly are a monster.' Georgianna's cheeks burned with humiliated colour.

He shrugged. 'I have never made any pretence of being anything else.'

The implication being, Georgianna knew, that she was the one who had practised deceit, when she'd lied to her family and her betrothed in order to run away with André.

And that Hawksmere believed she was lying to him even now.

Except she was not. And Hawksmere's decision to keep her locked up here, and his threats, did not change the fact that time was more the enemy than this arrogant duke. 'You will speak to someone this morning on my behalf?'

Hawksmere's mouth thinned into an uncompromising line. 'I have no plans to do so until the two of us have spoken again, no.'

'But you must,' Georgianna gasped desperately. 'Napoleon...'

'Enough, Georgianna,' Hawksmere rasped his impatience with her persistence as he grasped her arms, his silver eyes as cold as ice as he looked down the length of his arrogant nose at her. 'I have not had the opportunity to sleep, either, this past night, and my patience is now at an end.'

'But...'

'I said enough, Georgianna,' he thundered.

Tears blurred her vision. 'You have every right to be angry with me, to despise me for my having ended our betrothal in the way that I did.' She gave a weary shake of her head. 'Take your revenge upon me any way you please. I do not care what you do to me, as long as you take my warnings seriously.'

'And if it is my wish to claim your body, for your having run from me, from our betrothal, ten months ago?' he taunted softly.

She shook her head. 'As long as you also listen to me in regards to Napoleon.'

'One more mention of that man's name and more pressing responsibilities be damned, I shall be forced to begin that punishment now!' the duke warned darkly. 'Now that I think about it, it might be best if I were to request that you remove your gown,' he mused hardly. 'You will be less likely to attempt an escape if you are half-naked.'

'I will not take off my gown.' Georgianna pulled out of his grasp to move quickly away from him, her hands held up defensively in front of her rapidly rising and falling chest.

Zachary studied her through narrowed lids as he noted the wild panic in those beautiful violet-coloured eyes. Much like a deer the moment it realised it was caught in the sights of the hunter's gun.

All because he had asked her to remove her gown?

Surely a woman who had shared one man's bed for the past ten months would not be quite so averse to the idea of another man seeing her naked?

Unless…

'Did he hurt you?' Zachary scowled darkly.

That violet gaze sharpened. 'What?'

His mouth thinned. 'Did Rousseau hurt you?'

'Of course he hurt me! How could he not, when he used me to make good his escape?'

'That is not the type of hurt I am referring to, Georgianna.' Zachary took several steps towards her, coming to a halt as Georgianna shadowed those steps by moving back, until she was now pressed up against one of the velvet curtains hanging at the window. 'I have no intentions of harming you, Georgianna.'

She gave a choked and bitter laugh. 'You have just threatened to take away my gown.'

'And that is all I have threatened.'

She gave a shudder. 'It is enough!'

Zachary's eyes narrowed. 'Some men like to give pain to their bed partner during lovemaking, as a way of heightening their own arousal.'

She gasped. 'Do you?' Pale and slender fingers now tightly clasped at the throat of that unbecoming black gown as she stared at him with dark and shadowed eyes.

'No, I most certainly do not,' Zachary assured grimly. 'But I am beginning to suspect that Rousseau did. Do you perhaps share his perversion?'

'No!'

'I am glad to hear it.' Zachary's eyes narrowed. 'But has he left lasting marks upon your body you would not wish another man to see?' he added harshly, surprised at how violent it made him feel to think of there being so much as a single bruise administered to that alabaster skin, let alone any lasting reminder of the man Rousseau.

Georgianna breathed shallowly, not sure she understood all that Zachary Black was saying to her. Not sure she wanted to understand.

Surely lovemaking was exactly that? An expression of the love a couple felt for one another? Or if not love, then at least a tenderness, a caring, for the other's welfare?

What the duke was describing, the deliberate inflicting of pain, did not sound as if it could be any of those things.

And yet Georgianna did indeed bear scars, and ones inflicted upon her by André Rousseau. Not the visible scars to which Hawksmere seemed to refer, of course, but they were damning none the less. A testament to the scorn, the total uninterest in which André had held the impressionable young girl who had forsaken all for her love of him.

'I can see that he did.' Hawksmere obviously took her silence to be her answer, his expression grimmer than ever. 'And you still love such a man?' he added disgustedly.

'No.' Georgianna choked in protest; how could she possibly love a man who had treated her as André had?

To her everlasting shame, Georgianna was no longer sure she had ever really loved André, or whether she had not just been in love with love itself.

A year ago she had been so young and idealistic, had believed in love and romance. And the handsome and penniless Frenchman employed by her father had seemed so much more romantic, so much easier to love than the intimidating and distant Duke of Hawksmere. To the extent that Georgianna had woven all of her dreams about the golden-haired and romantic Frenchman in order to run away from marrying the dangerous duke.

Reality had proven to be so much less than those silly, romantic dreams.

Not that she believed Hawksmere to be any less dangerous now than she had previously. The opposite, after the things he had said and done to her today.

But she certainly had no romantic dreams left in regard to André Rousseau, either, or indeed any other man.

Hawksmere's top lip curled up in distaste, silver eyes a pale glitter between narrowed lids. 'Again, this is something we will have to discuss further upon my return. No doubt we shall have the opportunity to discuss many things during the hours we spend here in my bedchamber together,' he added pleasantly.

'How long do you intend to keep me here?' Georgianna stared at him disbelievingly.

'As long as it takes to get to the truth,' Zachary assured uninterestedly.

She gave a desperate shake of her head. 'Have you not listened to a word I have said? Do you not understand the urgency of the things I have told you?'

He eyed her mockingly. 'I have listened to the little you decided to share with me, yes.'

'What will it take to convince you of my sincerity?'

'More than you have already told me, obviously,' Zachary drawled drily, brows raised questioningly.

A frown creased Georgianna's forehead as she obviously fought an inner battle as to how much more she intended revealing to him.

Finally she gave a defeated sigh. 'Napoleon is to leave Elba before the end of this month.'

'And you come to me with this story now?' He raised sceptical brows. 'With the end of the month just days away?'

'I did not—' Georgianna gave an impatient shake of her head as she accepted that to Hawksmere this was still just a 'story'. 'I only learnt of the plan nine days ago and I could not immediately get passage from France. I...' Her gaze lowered. 'André has men placed at all of the ports, watching and waiting for anyone who might wish to betray Napoleon.'

'And yet here you are,' Hawksmere drawled disbelievingly.

She nodded. 'But I had to bide my time and make good my escape when the chance came for me to join a large family travelling together. I was all the time fearful that someone might recognise me. Am I boring you, your Grace?' she prompted sharply as the duke gave a yawn.

'As it happens, yes, you are.' He nodded unapologetically.

'But...'

'I really am uninterested in listening to any more buts or arguments just now, Georgianna,' he rasped harshly.

Georgianna looked up searchingly into his hard and implacable face. Noting the cold glitter of his silver eyes. The tautness of the skin across sculptured cheekbones. The sneering curl of his top lip.

The determined set of his arrogant and unyielding jaw.

She knew in that moment that all of her efforts of appeal for Zachary Black's help had been a waste of her time.

That this man despised her so utterly he would never believe a single word she said to him.

Chapter Four

Zachary was irritable and tired by the time he returned home several hours later, his morning having proved to be a frustrating one.

Not least because the man he had wished to speak with, the man to whom he had reported this past four years, was unavailable, and likely to be so for the next few days, as his deputy had informed Zachary. It happened, of course, but it was frustrating, nevertheless.

He had duly passed along the relevant information to the deputy, of course, but even so he still felt a sense of dissatisfaction.

It was true that there had been dozens of rumours of plots and plans to liberate the Corsican from Elba these past months and each and every one of them had necessarily to be investigated.

What if Georgianna were telling the truth and Napoleon really did mean to leave Elba before the month's end and return to the shores of France? Possibly as emperor? That would not suit Louis or England.

Zachary had also requested to look at the file they had accumulated on André Rousseau these past months, hoping it might shed some light upon Georgianna Lancaster's own movement. There had been no sightings of her in Rousseau's company for some months. No sightings of her at all, it seemed, since a week or so after she and Rousseau had arrived in Paris together.

A curiosity in itself.

Where had Georgianna been all this time? And what had she been doing? For that matter, if she had not been with Rousseau, then where had she come by the information regarding Napoleon?

For the moment Zachary's instructions were clear; he was to continue to keep Georgianna Lancaster imprisoned in his home and continue questioning her until such time as he was notified otherwise.

For all that Zachary had earlier today taunted Georgianna with the possibility of her continued incarceration, he was not best pleased at receiving orders to do exactly that.

And one of the main reasons for that was Georgianna herself.

The previous year she had been an inexperienced and idealistic young girl, that plump and desirable pigeon that Zachary had decided to marry, bed and subsequently mould into being his undemanding duchess.

Just a few minutes in her company earlier this morning and Zachary knew that Georgianna's ten months in France had wrought more changes in her than just the physical ones.

That bright-eyed young girl, eager for life, was no more. And in her place was a coolly dignified, capable and stubborn woman. One who had lived in Paris, by all accounts, completely alone for some months, before arranging her own passage back to England. Who had then managed to follow him without his knowledge, until such time as she was able to speak with him privately. Moreover, Georgianna had shown him that very morning she was not a woman who intended to ever be cowed, by him, or anyone else.

If anything, that air of dignity, her independence and intelligence, appealed to and aroused Zachary even more than that naïve young woman he had intended to make his wife.

And whatever else Georgianna might claim to be now, she had eloped with André Rousseau ten months ago. She had been the Frenchman's lover for a number of weeks, if not months, before and following that elopement.

For Zachary to feel desire and admiration for such a woman, a woman he had every reason to distrust, was not only rash on his part, but it could also be dangerous.

Zachary drew in a deep breath as he came to a halt outside the door to his bedchamber, noting there was no sound coming from within. He had questioned his butler on his arrival, and been informed that all had been silent above stairs all morning. Georgianna had obviously taken Zachary's advice to heart and refrained from screaming, or banging on the door, demanding to be set free.

And perhaps that had just been a ploy and she was even now poised behind the silence of that door, candelabrum in hand, ready to knock Zachary senseless before making good her escape?

His smile was grim as he quietly unlocked the door to his bedchamber. He entered softly and saw the room was in semi-darkness, the curtains pulled halfway across the two picture windows, nevertheless allowing him to see that the breakfast tray still sat on the table near the door where he had placed it earlier.

The untouched breakfast tray.

A single glance was enough to show him that none of the food on the plates had been eaten. Only the dregs left in the bottom of the delicate china cup to show that Georgianna had drunk her tea at least.

The half-drawn curtains allowed the weak February sunshine to shaft across the room to where Georgianna lay asleep on top of his bed. She was still dressed in that unbecoming black gown. The curling ebony hair had been loosened, however, and now flowed thick and silky over the pillows behind her and across her breasts down to her tiny waist.

Zachary put down the bag he carried to cross softly to the bedside and look down at her. Her face appeared as a beautiful pale oval in the weak light. Long lashes fanned silkily against ivory cheeks as she continued to sleep, her rosy and sensual lips slightly parted as she breathed softly and evenly.

A deceptive picture of innocence, if not beauty.

So she might once have looked in their marriage bed, Zachary acknowledged with annoyance as his traitorous body stirred, hardened, as he continued to look down at her. And he had no doubt that until a year ago she had been an innocent, those violet-coloured eyes full of joy, of the expectations of life, rather than swirling with dark shadows as they had been earlier today.

Feeling any sort of empathy, sympathy, for this woman would be a mistake on his part. Most especially when he still questioned her real motives for seeking him out.

Zachary's mouth thinned as he turned away impatiently and walked determinedly from the bedside with the intention of pulling the curtains completely across the windows. He had no time to rest himself—he had Wilding's wedding to attend—but Georgianna might as well continue to sleep peacefully.

Zachary was in need of a bath and a change of clothes after his own sleepless night, before he then attended the wedding in just a few hours.

'Leave them. Please.'

Zachary gave a start at the sound of Georgianna's voice. A voice that sounded as if it were underlined with panic. Or possibly fear? Simply because he had been about to draw the last of the curtains fully across the windows to shut out the daylight?

He turned to see that Georgianna had moved up on to her elbows, those ebony curls falling past her shoulders and cascading back on to the pillows behind her.

Her face was still that ghostly oval, her eyes so

dark they appeared almost purple as she looked across at him pleadingly. 'Please,' she beseeched earnestly.

'What is it, Georgianna?' Zachary prompted sharply as he crossed, frowning, to her side.

Her breasts quickly rose and fell. 'I—I am afraid of... I do not like complete dark.' She sat up abruptly to curl her arms defensively about her drawn-up knees, looking for all the world like that frightened deer of earlier.

'What foolishness is this, Georgianna?' Zachary chided impatiently. 'If you think to appeal to my softer side with exhibitions of feminine—'

'How could I possibly do that, when we both know you do not have a softer side for me to appeal to!' she came back sharply as she moved swiftly to the side of the bed before standing up and crossing to the window on stockinged feet. There she pulled back the curtains to allow in the full daylight. 'And I assure you I speak only the truth.' Her hands, no longer hidden in those black lace gloves, were clasped tightly together in front of her, the knuckles white as she looked up at him. 'I do not like to be in the complete dark. Ever.' Her lips firmed as she raised her chin in challenge.

Zachary ignored Georgianna's insult as he continued to study her through narrowed lids. Her face was ashen, but that could be because she had not slept for long enough, nor had she eaten the breakfast he had had brought to her.

No, it was those tightly clasped hands, and the defiance in her stance, which now convinced Zachary that she was sincere in her dislike, even fear, of the complete dark.

'And why is that?' he prompted softly.

Georgianna swallowed, hating that she had shown any sign of weakness in front of Zachary Black, the mocking Duke of Hawksmere. She hated him for dwelling on that weakness, whereas before she had merely feared him.

Nor did she have any intention of telling this hateful man of the head injury she had suffered and which, for two weeks, had left her blind. For that short time she had been caught in eternal darkness, afraid that she would never be able to see again.

It had been fear unlike anything Georgianna had ever known before, including the bleakness of those hours after André had attempted to murder her, leaving her body in the woods for the wild animals to devour.

She accepted she had wronged Zachary Black in the past and had apologised for it, but surely, surely she did not have to now reveal all of her humiliations so that he might taunt her further?

She hoped to keep some dignity.

'How did you get that?' she demanded sharply, eyes wide as she saw and recognised her travelling bag sitting on the floor just inside the door of the bedchamber.

Hawksmere gave it a cursory glance before turning back with a dismissive shrug. 'It was collected from your lodgings this morning, of course.'

'I— But— How did you know where…? I told you

earlier the name of the street where I had taken lodgings,' Georgianna confirmed heavily.

'You did, yes.' Zachary gave a hard smile of satisfaction. It had not taken long at all for one of his footmen to be sent to Duke Street to discover in which lodging Georgianna was staying. 'It was not too difficult to guess that the Anna Smith, who arrived in London yesterday, was in fact Georgianna Lancaster,' he added coolly as she seemed to have been struck momentarily dumb. 'And the two small portraits on the dressing table of your mother and father together, and another of your brother, confirmed it was so.'

Those violet eyes rose quickly to meet his. 'You went to Mrs Jenkins's house yourself?'

He shrugged. 'I did not think you would appreciate having one of my footmen pawing through your more personal items.'

She bristled. 'Obviously you did not hesitate to do so yourself.'

'Obviously not.' Zachary gave a mocking nod. 'We may have fought a war with France, but I have always considered that they do make the most sensual of ladies' undergarments.'

Two spots of colour appeared in the paleness of Georgianna's cheeks. 'And no doubt you have seen enough of them to be an expert on the subject?'

'No doubt.' Zachary's mouth quirked in amusement. 'Is it not a little late for you to be exhibiting such maidenly outrage, Georgianna?' he added hardly.

He was right. Of course he was right, Georgianna

acknowledged heavily. She knew she had forfeited any right to feel outrage, maidenly or otherwise, in Hawksmere's eyes, as well as those of all decent society, the moment she left her home in the middle of the night and eloped with André.

Except, unbelievable as it would undoubtedly be for others to learn, she was still a maiden...

She and André had spent the first night and day of their elopement travelling by coach to the port where they intended to board the boat bound for France, their intention being to marry there rather than linger overlong in England. And André had explained, once they reached that port, that they stood more chance of remaining undetected if they travelled as brother as sister. A logic for which Georgianna had been exceedingly grateful.

Not least because, by that time, she had begun to doubt the wisdom of her actions.

It had all seemed so romantic, so exciting, when she and André made their plans to elope together in the middle of the night. But the long hours spent in the coach together, the rattling and jostling too severe to allow sleep or even rest, and fraying both their tempers and patience, had enabled Georgianna to see André as rather less than the romantic hero she had thought him to be.

To realise that, by running away with André in the middle of the night, she had cut herself off completely from her family, from society, in a scandal so shocking she would never be able to return.

The respite of travelling on the boat together as

brother and sister had been something of a balm to her already frayed nerves.

To accept that she was no longer as sure that she wished to become André's wife at all.

Considering the nightmare that had followed, it was perhaps as well she had already begun to have those doubts.

She drew herself up to her full height of just over five feet as she now met Hawksmere's gaze unflinchingly. 'I trust you are not expecting me to thank you for something that was unnecessary in the first place?'

'Oh, it was very necessary, Georgianna,' he corrected harshly. 'As I informed you earlier, you are to remain here for the next few days. And I thought you might feel more comfortable if you had your own things with you.'

Georgianna's head ached from having awoken so suddenly, in response to Hawksmere shutting out the daylight. The same response, panic and fear, she always felt now at finding herself in complete darkness.

Nevertheless, headache or no, she could not allow Hawksmere's words to go unchallenged. 'We both know your only concern was to allay Mrs Jenkins's suspicions when I did not return there later today. No doubt she was suitably impressed at the presence of the illustrious Duke of Hawksmere in her modest home?'

He gave that derisive smile. 'No doubt.'

Georgianna gave a disgusted shake of her head.

'You really do mean to keep me a prisoner here, then?'

His jaw tightened. 'For the moment, yes.'

She sighed. 'An occurrence which I can see does not suit you any more than it does me.'

He shrugged his wide shoulders. 'It would seem that neither one of us has a choice in the matter. But there is a bright side to all of this, Georgianna,' he added softly as he crossed the bedchamber with those soft and predatory steps. 'Just think, you did not have to marry me in order to share my bedchamber.'

Georgianna refused to be intimidated as Hawksmere now stood just inches away from her. So close, in fact, that she could see every detail of the livid scar upon his throat, as well as the dark stubble on his jaw, evidence that he had not yet had time to shave today. Indeed, his evening clothes from the night before showed that he had not so much as taken the time to change his clothes yet this morning.

Because, despite his scepticism towards her earlier, he had believed enough of what she told him to not waste any time in sharing that information?

Georgianna certainly hoped that was the case.

She could bear any amount of Hawksmere's mockery, as well as his scorn and disgust, if at the same time he helped to thwart this latest plot to liberate Napoleon from Elba.

She gave a humourless smile. 'We must all be grateful for small mercies, your Grace.'

Zachary's bark of laughter was completely spontaneous. A genuine appreciation of Georgianna's continued feistiness, despite the direness of the situation in which she now found herself.

And not much succeeded in amusing Zachary any more.

As an only child, he had inherited the Hawksmere title eleven years ago, upon the death of both his parents in a carriage accident. The years that followed had been lonely as well as busy ones, mainly filled with the responsibilities of his title, and fighting against Napoleon, in open battle, and secretly as an agent for the Crown.

Those same years had shown him that women, young and old, thin or plump, fair or dark, single or married, were willing to do almost anything for the attentions of a duke. This had resulted in a jading, a cynicism within him, beyond Zachary's control.

It appeared Georgianna Lancaster was the exception.

Not only had she chosen to run away from becoming his duchess ten months ago, but even now she continued to defy and challenge him in ways that no other woman ever had.

'I believe I prefer you feisty and defiant, Georgianna, rather than the naïve ninny you were ten months ago,' Zachary murmured appreciatively as he looked down searchingly into the pale face she held up to challenge him. The arching of her slender neck allowed those ebony curls to fall silkily down the length of her spine to her pert little bottom.

'A naïve ninny you nevertheless intended to make your wife,' she reminded scathingly.

He shrugged. 'I believed you to be a malleable ninny then.'

Her brows rose. 'And now?'

Zachary gave a slow and appreciative smile. 'Now I believe this added fire makes you more appealing than I might otherwise have expected.'

Georgianna shuddered, keeping a watchful eye on Hawksmere as she instinctively took a step back from him. She was wary of the way in which his eyes now glittered down at her so intently, almost as if a white light had been ignited in those silver depths. Georgianna was unsure of precisely what that flame might mean, but she did know that she no longer wished to stand quite so close to him.

Hawksmere took that same step forward before raising his hand to gently cup one side of her face, the soft pad of his thumb moving in a soft caress across her parted lips. 'There is nowhere you would be able to run this time, Georgianna, that I would not find you.'

Her heart was beating rapidly in her chest: at Hawksmere's threats, his proximity, and the effects of that caressing thumb against her lips. A sensuous caress, much as Georgianna might wish it otherwise, which caused a heat to course through her whole body, leaving her skin feeling flushed and tight and her breasts swelling uncomfortably beneath her gown.

Because, as Hawksmere had claimed earlier, she was aroused by his touch?

How could that possibly be, when she disliked this

man, when she had run from him, from the very idea of becoming his wife, less than a year ago?

Perhaps it was just that she had been alone, and lonely, for so very long? Too long without the gentle touch of another? Since she had been held by another? Looked at with warmth, if not affection?

Except the warmth in Hawksmere's gaze was so clearly predatory rather than affectionate.

Georgianna pulled back sharply from the mesmerising effect of that silver gaze. 'I have no intentions of running anywhere,' she assured him decisively. At least, not until this matter of Napoleon's liberation was settled. 'Did you go to your superior this morning and report my information?'

Zachary continued to look down at Georgianna for several long moments more. His response to her was undeniable. To her beauty, her proximity, to having touched and caressed those soft and pouting lips. Totally undeniable, when his erection pressed so insistently against the front of his breeches.

'And what business is it of yours whether I did or I did not?' He arched a challenging brow.

'But...' she blinked her bewilderment '...I am the one responsible for giving you that information.'

He nodded abruptly. 'All the more reason for it to be mistrusted, surely? What did you expect, Georgianna?' he taunted as she looked pained. 'Did you think that by returning to England, by twittering about some ridiculous plot of how Napoleon intends to leave Elba before the end of the month, that all would be forgiven? That you would be a heroine, and could then return to your family, to society?' he prompted cruelly.

Those striking eyes became misty with unshed tears. 'I am well aware there can be no forgiveness, in any quarter, for the way I have behaved,' she spoke so softly Zachary could barely hear her, as her tears fell unchecked down the paleness of her cheeks.

Zachary felt instant regret for his deliberate cruelty. Whatever this woman might have done to him personally in the past, there was an undeniable vulnerability about her now, an aloneness, that Zachary knew he could relate to.

He breathed deeply through his nose. 'Perhaps that situation is not quite so bleak as you think it is.'

She tilted her head curiously. 'What do you mean?'

He owed this woman nothing except his contempt and distrust, Zachary reminded himself impatiently. Certainly not absolution for her deeds of ten months ago.

And yet...

He was not a deliberately cruel man, no matter what others might say or think to the contrary. He considered their past association.

Could Georgianna really be blamed for what had happened in their past? She was a young girl of only nineteen who'd feared, to the extent of running away from marriage to a man who had not even troubled himself in getting to know her before offering for her. He'd been a man who had not even spoken to her before making that offer. And once made, she'd had that offer accepted by her father without knowing a thing about it—or him.

Much as it galled him, Zachary knew he must accept some of the blame for the way in which Georgianna had run away back then.

But not for what had happened since that time, or the possible depth of her continued involvement with Rousseau.

He hardened his heart against the idea of telling Georgianna of the way in which he and her father had, between them, managed to salvage her reputation at least, if not their own embarrassment.

'A place can always be found in a gentleman's life for a beautiful woman,' he rasped insultingly.

Her throat moved as she swallowed. 'As his mistress, you mean?'

Zachary bared his teeth in a humourless smile. 'But of course.'

'I believe I should rather become an old maid,' she answered with quiet dignity.

'Do not make your decision based on your experience with Rousseau, Georgianna,' he advised coldly. 'Being the mistress of a gentleman would not be like it was with him. You would have a house of your own. Servants. An elegant carriage. A generous allowance, for clothing and such.'

Her chin rose. 'You, of course, would know of such things.'

In actual fact, Zachary had no personal knowledge of such an arrangement. He had never been enamoured enough of any of the women he had bedded in the past to have so much as ever considered making any his permanent mistress.

What sort of mistress would Georgianna make? The depths to those violet-coloured eyes, the sensual pout of her lips, and the uncontrollable response of her breasts to his lightest touch, all spoke of a passionate nature. Of a woman who was more than capable of meeting his physical demands with an equal fire.

And that she was untrustworthy?

Perhaps that might even add to the excitement, the danger, of such an arrangement?

He was a fool for even considering taking Georgianna Lancaster as a mistress, when there was no question that she had been mistress to Rousseau. Might still be so, for all Zachary knew of that situation.

'Not recently, no,' he answered bitingly. 'Which means the position is currently available, if you are interested in applying?' He raised goading brows.

Georgianna drew herself up proudly. 'So that you might insult me by refusing, no doubt?'

'No doubt.'

She gave a shake of her head. 'I am not, nor will I ever be, interested in such a role, in your life or any other man's.'

Zachary gave a hard smile. 'It is the only one still available to you.'

'I said I am not interested,' she repeated firmly.

'Then I will see that the bedchamber adjoining this one is prepared for your use. Yes, I too appreciate the irony of having you now occupy the bedchamber intended for my duchess,' he drawled as Georgianna's eyes widened. 'But it would seem that for the moment, at least, I am to have little choice in the matter.'

'You have the choice of releasing me—you just refuse to take it,' Georgianna pointed out sharply.

'I do, yes.' The duke gave a haughty inclination of his head. 'But I do not intend to keep you prisoner all the time, Georgianna. When I return later this evening you will join me downstairs for dinner. And I wish you to wear the lilac gown I brought from your lodgings rather than the black.'

'I will not be told by you what I shall do or what I shall wear.'

'You will if you do not wish to find yourself face first over my knee, with your skirts thrown up to your waist, whilst I thrash your bare bottom a rosy red for daring to disobey!' Hawksmere assured harshly.

Georgianna gasped at the crudeness of the threat. A threat she knew this man to be more than capable of carrying out. 'You are a barbarian, sir.'

He bared his teeth in a smile. 'All men are barbarians at heart, my lady.'

Georgianna repressed a shudder as the conversation brought back the painful memory of the violence she had suffered at André's hands. A violence she would not have believed possible of the once gentle man she had thought she knew and loved. A violence which had left her both blind and fighting for her life.

Again she wondered if Hawksmere would believe her, trust that she only spoke the truth, if she were to tell him of that terrible night when André had tried to kill her. When he thought he had killed her. It was only luck, and the arrival of a local farmer who had heard the shots being fired and feared for his livestock, that had ensured she had not died that night.

'What are you thinking about?' Hawksmere demanded shrewdly.

Would he believe her if she were to show him the scars her body carried from that night?

They were undoubtedly the scars left by a bullet wound, but there was no guarantee, even if Georgianna were to bare her flesh, that Hawksmere would any more believe it was André Rousseau himself who had inflicted them than the duke believed the information she had brought to him regarding Bonaparte's intended escape from Elba.

Georgianna had little in her life now except the small amount of pride left to her. She feared she might lose that, too, if Hawksmere were to both ridicule and scorn, and to disbelieve the physical scars she bore as proof of André Rousseau's complete disregard for her.

Hatred was far too strong a word to use to describe the calculated way in which André had come to the conclusion that she had outlived her purpose. He had been completely unemotional that night in the woods before he shot her, having assured her it was not a personal action, rather it was that he had no more use for her.

She could not bear to now have Zachary Black, the scornful Duke of Hawksmere, prod and poke at the even deeper wound that had been inflicted that night upon her heart and soul.

She raised her chin. 'I do not care for your threats.'

'No?'

'No!'

He shrugged wide shoulders. 'Then do as I say and wear the lilac gown for dinner this evening.'

'I am not hungry.'

'You will eat, Georgianna,' Hawksmere bit out determinedly. 'As I also have to eat. And I have no intentions of looking across my dinner table at the unpleasant sight of a scarecrow in a black mourning gown.'

She drew in a sharp breath. 'You are exceedingly cruel.'

'I am, yes,' he acknowledged unapologetically. 'Perhaps if you had eaten your breakfast, as I instructed you to do…' He shrugged. 'But you did not, so there it is.'

'I told you then, I was not hungry.'

'And I distinctly recall telling you that you are too thin,' he countered forcefully. 'You look as if a stray breath of wind might blow you away. It is a fact that most gentlemen prefer a little meat on their women.'

'It is not my intention to be attractive to any gentleman.'

'Then you have succeeded. Admirably so, in fact,' Hawksmere added grimly.

'And most especially to you,' she concluded fiercely.

'Most especially me?' he repeated softly, dark brows raised speculatively.

'Yes.' Her cheeks were flushed.

Hawksmere gave a slow smile. 'Then I am sorry

to inform you that I do not appear to find the loss of your curves to have affected my own physical ardour in the slightest.'

'And I am sorry to inform you that I am not in the least interested in a single one of your likes or dislikes,' she replied heatedly.

'I believe you made that more than obvious when you broke our betrothal to elope with another man.'

Georgianna blinked at the harshness of his tone. As if he might actually have cared about her ten months ago?

But of course he had cared, she reminded herself heavily. Oh, not about her, but he most certainly cared about the blow she had dealt him by running away with André. But it was Hawksmere's pride which had been injured, not his heart. Because he had no heart to injure?

He drew in an impatient breath. 'I do not have the time to discuss this any further just now, Georgianna. I have a wedding to get to.' He eyed her irritably. 'If you were to stop being so damned difficult, then I might arrange for a bath to be brought up to you later this afternoon. You would like that, would you not?'

Georgianna had no interest in dining with this cold and insulting man, no interest in eating, nor being in Hawksmere's company any more than she had to be.

But if agreeing to wear the lilac gown, and sitting down to dinner with him this evening, also ensured she was allowed the luxury of a bath, then perhaps it would not be so bad? She might even find the chance to escape this house some time during the evening.

'You obviously know something of a woman's weaknesses, your Grace.'

He gave another of those humourless smiles. 'You have the honour of being one of the women from whom I have learnt that particular lesson, Georgianna.'

Her gaze dropped from meeting his at the obvious reference to her elopement with André. 'Very well, I will wear the lilac gown and sit down to dinner with you,' she conceded quietly. 'But I warn you again, I have little appetite.'

Her breath caught in her throat at the intensity of Hawksmere's gaze as he now crossed the distance between them on stealthy feet, her heart fluttering wildly in her chest as she refused to give ground when he came to a halt in front of her.

He smiled slightly at her defiance as he raised his hand and once again cupped the side of her face. He ran the soft pad of his thumb across the swell of her bottom lip. 'Not to worry, Georgianna, I believe I can find appetite enough for the both of us this evening,' he promised gruffly, his gaze continuing to hold hers for several long seconds, before he abruptly lowered his head to sweep the firmness of his lips across hers. 'So soft,' he murmured appreciatively, his breath warm as those lips now trailed caressingly across the paleness of her cheek to her earlobe, teeth gently biting.

Georgianna was too stunned by the unexpected intimacy to be able to move, could barely breathe, as her heart pounded erratically in her chest.

Hawksmere raised his head to look down at her for several long seconds, silver eyes glittering, before he straightened abruptly and turned on his heel to cross the room and depart, followed seconds later by the sound of the door locking behind him.

Leaving Georgianna in a state of complete emotional turmoil.

Chapter Five

'You see how much pleasanter it is when you do as I ask, Georgianna?' Zachary mocked several hours later as he pulled back a chair for her to sit down at the dinner table before taking his place in the chair beside her.

He had left instructions that he and Georgianna would be dining together in the smaller, more intimate dining room. A fire crackled merrily in the hearth, and two three-pronged candelabra illuminated the crystal glassware and silver cutlery. A bowl of pale pink roses had also been placed in the centre of the small round table.

To her credit, Georgianna had been ready and waiting for Zachary when he'd unlocked the door and entered the bedchamber adjoining his own, her expression one of cool composure as she stood in the middle of the room.

The darkness of her hair was smooth and shining and once again secured at her crown, with those tantalising bunches of curls at her temples and nape. The lilac gown had darkened her eyes to that deep violet. Her face was a pale ivory, her lips a full and rosy pout against that pallor.

Zachary shifted uncomfortably now as he realised he was once again aroused by the sight and scent of her.

No other woman had ever physically aroused him as easily as this one appeared to.

Zachary's gaze narrowed on her critically as she smiled her thanks up at Hinds as he poured wine into her glass. What was it about this woman in particular that she managed to hold him in a constant state of arousal?

She was undoubtedly a beautiful young woman, her hair so dark and silky, and her delicately lovely face dominated by those violet-coloured eyes. And the lilac gown was certainly an improvement on that unbecoming black. But even so the style of the new gown still left a lot to be desired. It was not particularly fashionable, with its high neckline buttoned all the way up to her throat, revealing none of the tempting swell of her breasts as so many other women did nowadays, some of them to a degree of indecency.

Zachary had seen, and bedded, many beautiful women in his lifetime and all had been more fashionable and some more beautiful than Georgianna. So why was it that she affected him in a physical way he appeared to have absolutely no control over?

He should not have kissed her earlier, of course. Certainly should not have enjoyed the softness of her lips quite so much as he had, to the point that he had almost said to hell with attending Worthing's wedding and carried Georgianna back to the bed instead. It was not a pleasant realisation for a man who had always put duty, and the well-being of his close friends, first.

'I should have worn the lilac gown this evening in any case.'

It took Zachary several moments to pull out of the bleakness of his thoughts and realise that Georgianna was now answering his own earlier comment. Defiantly. Challengingly.

And there he had it.

This was the way in which Georgianna differed to every other woman Zachary had ever met. Because no man, or woman, had ever dared to defy or challenge the will of the Duke of Hawksmere.

That plump pigeon of ten months ago had undoubtedly feared him, as much as she had feared becoming his wife, but this Georgianna gave the impression that she feared nothing and no one. Except...

'Have you always disliked being in complete dark?'

Georgianna had not been expecting the question. Although perhaps she should have done; Hawksmere was a man who liked to disarm his adversaries rather than put them at their ease. As he had just done by unexpectedly mentioning her fear of darkness.

As he had disarmed her a short time ago, when he had unlocked and entered her bedchamber through the door which adjoined that room to his own. Looking every inch the handsome and highly eligible Duke of Hawksmere, dressed in impeccably tailored black evening clothes and snowy-white linen, his fashionably overlong hair a damp and ebony sheen about that saturnine face. A face dominated by those piercing silver eyes.

As sitting beside him now at the dinner table, the warmth of his thigh almost touching her own, was also disarming her.

Only because he had unexpectedly kissed her earlier, she reassured herself impatiently. A totally unwelcome kiss.

A kiss she had nevertheless been unable to forget in the hours that followed.

Instead of the suppressed violence she might have expected, Hawksmere's kiss had been gentle, searching, as if seeking a response from her rather than demanding one.

And all these hours since Georgianna had questioned if in fact she had responded.

It had been such a fleeting kiss, a mere brushing of Hawksmere's lips against her own, and Georgianna had been so surprised by it that she had no memory of whether or not she had returned the pressure of those firm lips. She certainly hoped not, but still she could not be sure.

She turned to him with cool eyes. 'I have been wondering about that wound to your throat, and the possibility it was inflicted by another female who was equally as unwilling to become your duchess?'

And there he had it again, Zachary acknowledged,

as he began to smile and then to chuckle openly; not only did Georgianna challenge him, but she also had the ability to make him laugh, at himself as much as others. 'There have been no others females, unwilling or otherwise, whom I have asked to become my duchess.' He finally sobered enough to answer her.

'You surprise me.'

He gave a mocking inclination of his head. 'My only unsatisfactory venture into contemplating the married state has made me wary of repeating the experience.'

'Then your wound really was, as it is rumoured, inflicted by a French sabre?' She was barely able to suppress a shiver.

Zachary's humour faded, his expression darkening as he ran his fingertips along the six-inch length of the scar. It had been with him for so long now that he rarely thought about it any more. Or the effect it might have upon others. Upon Georgianna. 'You find it repulsive?'

'I find the idea of the violence behind it repulsive, yes,' she answered him carefully.

'Indeed?' he rasped.

'I did not mean you any insult,' Georgianna assured hastily. 'I—I am sure we all have our scars to bear, some more openly than others.' Her gaze moved to the fireplace as she picked up her glass and took a sip of her wine.

'Do you?' Zachary continued to study her profile through narrowed lids.

She straightened her spine but continued to look

towards the fireplace rather than at him. 'Of course. How can I not after the events of this past year?'

'Tell me where you have been these past nine months, Georgianna?' he prompted softly.

She gave a start—a guilty one?—as she now looked down at the food in front of her, as if seeing it for the first time. 'Should we not eat our soup before it becomes cold?'

'By all means.' Zachary nodded. 'But there is no reason why we cannot continue talking as we eat,' he added once Georgianna had raised the spoon to her lips. A spoon that shook precariously as her hand began to tremble, until she placed it carefully back beside the soup bowl. 'What are you hiding, Georgianna?' Zachary demanded sharply as he saw that nervousness.

'Nothing.'

'Do not lie to me, Georgianna.'

She drew in a ragged breath as she now looked down at the tablecloth. 'I am not hiding anything. Or rather, I am hiding, but it is not from a what but a who,' she continued so softly it was difficult for Zachary to hear her.

'Who?'

Her eyes closed. 'Rousseau, of course.'

'Why?'

She gave another involuntary shudder. 'Because I fear what he would do if he were to ever find me again.'

Zachary had absolutely no doubt that Georgianna's fear was real. He could feel it in the tension of the air surrounding them. As he could see it, in the trembling of Georgianna's body and the quivering of her lips. 'What do you have to fear from that, Georgianna?' he prompted gruffly.

'What do you care?' She turned on him fiercely, two spots of angry colour in her cheeks. 'You have not believed a single word I have said to you so far today, so why should you think I might now bare my soul to you? Just so that you might have the pleasure of ridiculing me again?'

She had a point, Zachary conceded impatiently. But could she not see how difficult it was for him to believe the things she had told him, a woman who had eloped with a known French spy?

Except it had not been confirmed that Rousseau was a spy when Georgianna eloped with him, that certain knowledge only having come later, he reminded himself.

'This conversation is not at all conducive to our digestion.' She gave a weary shake of her head. 'Perhaps it would be best if you were to lock me back in the bedchamber.'

'You have to eat, Georgianna, or you will starve yourself to death.' Zachary scowled.

Her laugh sounded bitter. 'I am harder to kill than you might imagine!'

He was taken aback by the vehemence of her tone. 'What?'

'How went your friend's wedding today?' Once again she avoided answering his question.

The whole conversation of this past half an hour

had resembled that of a sword fight, Zachary realised irritably. He would thrust. Georgianna would parry. Georgianna would thrust. He would then parry. It was frustrating, to say the least.

But her question as to how Worthing's wedding had proceeded earlier today brought forth memories of the love and pride that shone in Worthing's face as he turned to watch his beautiful bride walk down the aisle towards him. Of that same love and pride shining in Julianna's eyes as she walked without hesitation to join her handsome bridegroom at the altar, before they spoke their vows to each other. Declaring loudly and clearly, sincerely, to love and to cherish each other from this day forward.

A bittersweet reminder to Zachary that he could never hope to have that love and devotion bestowed upon him.

And bringing into sharp contrast the wedding which should have taken place the previous year. Between a bridegroom who was only marrying because he was in need of a wife to provide his heir and to retain his fortune. And the young and romantic woman who had feared her bridegroom so much she had eloped with another man.

Zachary looked at that young woman now, once again acknowledging that he was partly, if not wholly, to blame for Georgianna having run away from her family and her home.

And for the things that had happened to her since.

Whatever they might be.

Whatever they might be?

He drew his breath in sharply. 'I believe I owe you an apology, Georgianna.'

She gave him a startled glance. 'I don't…?'

'For the manner of my proposal to you last year,' Zachary continued grimly. 'Worthing's wedding today made me see that I was unfair to you then. That I should never have spoken to your father regarding a marriage between you and I before we knew each other better.'

'We did not know each other at all!'

He nodded. 'And for that I apologise.'

Georgianna stared up at him wordlessly for several seconds, those violet-coloured eyes searching his face. 'Do not be kind to me, Zachary, please,' she finally choked out. 'I believe I can bear anything but your kindness.' She stood up to cross the room on slippered feet, coming to a halt beside the fireplace, her head bowed, revealing the vulnerable arch of her nape.

Zachary rose more slowly to his feet, more inwardly pleased than he cared to contemplate, at hearing Georgianna use his name for the first time.

He crossed the room silently until he stood just behind her, not quite touching, but enough to feel the warmth of her body just inches away. 'My actions then were selfish and totally without thought for how you might have felt in regard to marrying me. For that I am deeply sorry.' His apology still sounded awkward. As evidence, perhaps, that it did not come easily to him?

As it did not. Zachary was unable to remember the

last time he had apologised to anyone for anything he had said or done.

Georgianna's shoulders moved as she sobbed quietly. 'It does not matter any more, Zachary.'

He reached out to lightly grasp the tops of her arms. 'It does matter if it forced you into unnecessary anger towards your father and consequently into a course of action you might otherwise not have taken—' He broke off as the door opened quietly and Hinds stood uncertainly in the doorway. 'I will ring when I need you.' Zachary dismissed him grimly, waiting until the butler had left again before resuming the conversation. 'Is that what happened, Georgianna? Was it my selfishness that pushed you into taking the step of defying your father, leaving your family, and eloping with Rousseau?'

'What does it matter?' She shook her head. 'What is done cannot now be undone.'

'Georgianna.' His hands slid down the length of her arms until he clasped the bareness of both her hands in his. 'What the—?' Zachary turned her to face him before looking down to where he held her hands palms up in both of his, noting how red and roughened the skin was, with several calluses at the base of her fingers on both hands.

Georgianna almost laughed at the shocked expression on Hawksmere's face as he looked down at her work-worn hands. Except it was no laughing matter. 'They are not as pretty as they once were, are they?' She grimaced, knowing her hands were no longer those of a pampered and cosseted lady.

Zachary ran his thumbs across the calluses. 'How did this happen?'

Georgianna had learnt this past few dangerous months that it was best, whenever possible, to keep to the truth as much as possible. Far less chance of making a mistake that way. 'After André had... After he made it clear he did not want me any more, I left Paris for a while.' She raised her chin determinedly as she pulled her hands from his. 'I was lucky enough to be taken in by a kindly farmer and his wife.'

'And they obviously used you like a workhorse.' Hawksmere scowled his displeasure.

'Not at all.' Georgianna smiled slightly. 'I did work for them, of course; I could not accept their hospitality without repaying them in some small way. But it was never hard labour, just—just milking cows and feeding chickens and such. And Madame Bernard taught me how to cook. Stews, mainly. I think because...' Georgianna drew in a breath. 'They had a daughter, but she had married the year before and gone off with her soldier husband. I think they were pleased to have a young woman about the place again. In any case, they allowed me to stay with them for almost two months, after which time I decided I should return to Paris.'

'Why, when you were so obviously safe and with people who cared for you?'

She shrugged. 'I decided that I was behaving the coward by hiding away in the countryside and might be of more help to England if I were to return to the city and keep my ears and eyes open to the plots and intrigues that so abounded there. I found a job working in a tavern.'

'A tavern!' Hawksmere repeated, obviously more shocked than ever.

'In the kitchen, preparing food, rather than the tavern itself,' Georgianna assured ruefully. 'The lady who owned the tavern assured me I was not...was not buxom enough to work in the tavern itself.'

The duke raised dark brows. 'You are thinner than you were, certainly, but that does not detract... Never mind,' he said dismissively. 'I suppose this is another of those occasions when we must be grateful for small mercies?'

Georgianna smiled slightly. 'Indeed.'

'The name of this tavern?' he prompted sharply.

Georgianna had no doubt that, as she had suspected might be the case, Hawksmere would make it his business to check as to the truth of what she was now telling him. That he would not simply take her word for any of it. So, yes, better by far that she had kept to the truth as much as was possible.

Her gaze met the duke's unflinchingly. 'It was the Fleur de Lis.'

'And?' Hawksmere stilled as he looked down at her between narrowed lids. 'Surely that is the name of the tavern owned by...'

'Helene Rousseau, the sister of André Rousseau,' Georgianna confirmed evenly as she turned away to once again stare down at the fire. 'I did not go there as Georgianna Lancaster, of course, but assumed the identity of Francine Poitier, the married daughter of the farmer and his wife.' Again, she had kept to the truth as much as possible when she returned to Paris, knowing that if her identity were to be checked by Helene Rousseau, that the other woman would learn that the Bernards' did indeed have a married daughter called Francine.

Zachary released her hands to step back, not sure if he dared believe this fantastical tale. But he wanted to. Oh, yes, he found that he dearly wanted to believe it.

But, in truth, it seemed too much to accept that the young and flirtatious Georgianna Lancaster, that indulged and plump pigeon, the daughter of the Earl of Malvern, could possibly have worked as a labourer on a farm for several months, and then in the Paris tavern owned by Helene Rousseau, albeit in the kitchen. 'And how did you manage that?' he prompted in perfect French.

'I managed it very well, thank you,' Georgianna replied just as fluently. 'My father was unaware of it, of course...' she grimaced ruefully as she reverted back to English '...but during the winter months we spent at Malvern Hall before I...before I left, I had attended all of Jeffrey's French lessons with him.'

Zachary's mouth twisted humourlessly. 'No doubt drawn more by the charming and handsome Frenchman teaching the subject, than an interest in the language itself.'

'No doubt,' she conceded quietly. 'But, as you now hear, I did learn it.'

'That must have made it doubly choking for you

when the duke who offered for you was neither charming nor handsome,' he rasped harshly.

Georgianna's eyes widened incredulously. Hawksmere could not be serious, could he?

Oh, he definitely lacked the charm, was too forthright and forceful to ever be called charming, but as any woman of the *ton* would be only too happy to confirm, he was most certainly handsome. And it was a handsomeness that would cause most women to willingly overlook his lack of charm.

Even Georgianna admitted to having been taken with his dark and dangerous good looks during her first two Seasons. Indeed, he was a man it was impossible for any woman, young or old, to ignore. His arrogant bearing was always shown to advantage in his perfectly tailored clothes and she had never been able to decide whether his face was that of a fallen angel or a devil. André had possessed the face and golden hair of an angel, of course, but as Georgianna knew to her cost, he was most certainly a devil.

Whereas Zachary Black had long been considered the catch of any Season.

It had been the fact that Georgianna had been the unlikely one to 'catch' him which had come as such an unpleasant shock to her ten months ago.

Gazing at such a handsome and unobtainable duke from afar was one thing—being informed he was to become her future husband was something else completely. Even the thoughts of becoming the wife of such a cynical and experienced gentleman had thrown

Georgianna into a turmoil of doubt and fears. Mainly fears, she now realised.

What could a young girl of nineteen know of being married to a jaded gentleman of one and thirty? How would she even know what to talk to him about, let alone perform any of her other wifely duties? Georgianna had shied away from even thinking of the two of them in bed together, she plump and inexperienced, he as sleek and beautiful as a Greek god, with a legendary number of women known to have shared his bed.

Nor did she understand why he had chosen her at all, when he had never so much as even spoken or danced with her. The reason had become obvious, of course, and Hawksmere had confirmed it earlier today when he admitted he had believed her to be young enough, malleable enough, to make him an undemanding duchess.

She clasped her hands tightly together as she forced her gaze to meet his. 'So there you have the answer to your earlier question. Working in Helene Rousseau's tavern was inadvertently the way in which I gathered the information I gave you earlier.'

Impossible as it seemed, Zachary had already guessed that might be the case. Although he still had to question whether the delivery of that information had been deliberate or accidental. 'And why did you find it so difficult to confide that to me earlier?'

She drew in a deep breath. 'Because I feared you would not believe me.'

He raised dark brows. 'But you no longer fear that might be the case?'

She grimaced. 'Whether I do or I do not is no longer relevant—having now lost my liberty, I consider I have nothing else left to lose, and everything to gain, by confiding all to you.'

His eyes narrowed. 'And you expect me to believe that Helene Rousseau confided in you, a young woman she had employed to work in her kitchen?'

'Of course I do not.' Georgianna gave him an impatient glance for the derision in his tone. 'The truth is that I eavesdropped on the conversation in which Napoleon's liberation from Elba was discussed.'

'Eavesdropped how?'

'I quickly realised that a group of men, including André, met upstairs in a room of the tavern several times a week. And I discovered, quite by accident, that a convenient knothole in the floor of that room allowed their conversation to be overheard in the storeroom directly below.'

'You will have to forgive my scepticism, Georgianna.'

'Will I?' she retorted sharply.

Zachary grimaced. 'The Rousseaus, both brother and sister, have been watched constantly since it was discovered that André Duval was actually André Rousseau, a known spy for Bonaparte.'

'I am gratified to hear it,' she responded tartly. 'Indeed, it is a pity his duplicity was not discovered earlier, as it might then have saved me from considerable heartache.'

And Zachary was not in the least gratified to hear that Rousseau's treatment of her had succeeded in breaking Georgianna's heart. 'You speak now of having a fear of meeting Rousseau again; how is it that you did not fear meeting him again at his sister's tavern?'

She shook her head. 'He was present at all of those meetings, but ordinarily he had no reason to ever enter the kitchen.'

'Even so, you were taking a huge risk, Georgianna.'

'Have you never heard that it is easier to hide in full view than it is to run away and attempt to hide?' She sighed heavily.

It was a ploy Zachary had used several times himself these past four troubled years. 'I have, yes.'

'Besides, you only have to look at me now...' Georgianna glanced down ruefully at her slenderness '...to see I am nothing like the girl I once was.'

Because she was no longer a girl but a woman, Zachary conceded grimly. Beautiful, intelligent, confident, capable, but most of all, in spite of everything, utterly desirable.

And nothing Georgianna had told him this evening had lessened the pounding of the relentless desire Zachary had felt for her since meeting her again. Was it only a matter of hours ago? It seemed as if he had been in this state of constant arousal for days rather than just hours.

He gave a shake of his head in an attempt to clear his head, at least, of that desire; his body was another matter entirely. 'You understand I shall need time to confirm this new information?'

She held herself up proudly as she nodded. 'I expected nothing less.'

Zachary gave an inward groan at the way the straightening of Georgianna's spine had now pushed her breasts up against the soft material of the lilac gown. They were full and pert breasts, the nipples resembling ripe berries. As her waist would be slender, her hips gently curving, with a tempting triangle of dark curls hiding the succulent fruit between her...

'Zachary?'

'Say my name again,' he encouraged gruffly.

Georgianna blinked, taken aback by this sudden change of subject.

More than taken aback when she realised Hawksmere was now standing so close to her she could once again feel the heat of his body through the material of her gown.

Her heart began to pound rapidly in her chest as she found herself unable to look away from the fierce intensity of those mesmerising silver eyes.

Chapter Six

'Zachary, I do not...'

'Yes,' he murmured with satisfaction, his eyes glittering down at her intently as he stepped even closer to her, his thighs almost touching hers as he raised a hand to cup one of her cheeks. 'Say it again, Georgianna,' he encouraged huskily as his thumb moved caressingly across her lower lip.

She flicked her tongue out with the intention of moistening her suddenly dry lips, quickly withdrawing it again as she inadvertently caught the edge of Zachary's thumb, instantly able to taste the tangy salty sweetness of his skin. 'Zachary,' she protested weakly.

His thumb was a rousing caress in the tiny indentation in the centre of the fullness of her bottom lip. 'Are you wearing the white silk drawers tonight, Georgianna? The ones with the little lilac bows?'

Georgianna was so lost in the burning heat of that silver gaze that it took several seconds for her to realise exactly what Zachary had said. Her cheeks blushed a fiery red as she acknowledged the intimacy of his question. 'How did you know about...? You were responsible for packing my things earlier,' she said, remembering in embarrassed consternation.

He gave a feral grin. 'And I have been imagining you wearing those drawers ever since.'

Georgianna breathed shallowly. Zachary's close proximity, and that caressing thumb against her lip, made it difficult for her to think, let alone breathe.

'And the matching camisole,' he continued softly, his breath a warm caress as he lowered his head, his lips a light caress against the warmth of her throat. 'Are you wearing them both tonight, Georgianna?'

His feather-light kisses burned an arousing path down the length of her throat to the sensitive hollows beneath. Georgianna was barely breathing at all now, her hands moving up to grasp his muscled shoulders even as she arched her neck into that sensuous caress. 'Zachary, you have to stop,' she attempted half-heartedly.

'Why must I?' His hands moved down to her hips, moulding the softness of her curves against his much harder ones as his tongue dipped moistly and then withdrew from those hollows at the base of her throat, sending shivers of pleasure down the length of her spine. 'We are neither of us is involved with anyone else. Are we?'

'No.' The heat coursed through her body, tightening her breasts under her gown and camisole, warming between her thighs beneath her drawers, only the soft sighs of their ragged breathing now to charge the air. It made it impossible for Georgianna to think of a single reason why Zachary should stop.

That Zachary was equally affected was apparent by his ragged breathing and the throbbing length of his desire as his thighs pressed along the welcoming softness of her abdomen.

'Are you wearing them, Georgianna?' he pressed gruffly.

'I am, yes,' she confirmed softly, her legs feeling so weak now she was sure that if she were not clinging to the firmness of Zachary's shoulders she might find herself sinking down on to the carpeted floor at his feet.

She truly felt in danger of doing exactly that, as Zachary continued to lick and taste the length of her throat even as one of his hands slowly skimmed along the length of her hip and waist before cupping beneath the firm fullness of her breast. Her nipple instantly responded, swelling, engorging beneath the thin material of her gown and camisole in reaction to that caressing heat.

This was madness.

Complete madness.

And yet Georgianna had no strength to stop it. No will to pull away from Zachary. From the pleasure created by his lips and hands. From the closeness of him. From feeling wanted, held, for the first time in months.

And that was all this was, Georgianna told herself firmly. A need, an ache, to feel wanted and to be held. 'Have you forgotten I might be a spy?' She sought desperately for a return to sanity.

Zachary raised his head to look at her with mercurial grey eyes. There was a flush to the hardness of his cheeks and the darkness of his hair was dishevelled. 'I have forgotten nothing, Georgianna,' he assured huskily. 'If anything, I find that edge of danger only makes you more intriguing. Besides which, if you are a spy, then you are currently an imprisoned one. My imprisoned spy.' He smiled his satisfaction with that fact.

Georgianna drew her breath in sharply as she once again felt the soft pad of his thumb caress across the hardened tip of her breast.

'Perhaps that was my plan all along?' She tried to fight the sensations currently bombarding her senses: pleasure, arousal, heat. 'Has it not occurred to you that maybe my plan is to stab you at the dinner table with a knife from your own ducal-silver dinner service?' she persisted breathlessly even as she found it impossible not to arch once again into that marauding mouth as it continued to plunder the sensitive column of her throat.

'No.' Zachary smiled against the fluttering wildness of the pulse in her throat. He might have become slightly blasé this past few months, but he was nevertheless positive his self-defence skills were still as sharp. 'Because I very much doubt you will find the opportunity. Or, if you did, that my strength would not far outweigh your own.'

'Then perhaps it is my intention to hide one of the

knives and take it back upstairs with me, so that I can stab you later, while you sleep?' There was now an edge of desperation to Georgianna's voice; she simply couldn't allow this to continue.

Zachary deftly released the first button at the throat of her gown. 'Then I will have to ensure that the door between our two bedchambers remains locked at night.'

'I do not believe you are taking me seriously.'

'When I am holding you in my arms and about to kiss you? No, you may be assured I am not taking your threats seriously at all, Georgianna,' he acknowledged gruffly.

'Zachary!'

'Georgianna,' he chided gently as he released the second button and revealed the top of the silky smooth skin above the swell of her breasts.

'I cannot… This is not—' She broke off abruptly as Zachary claimed her mouth with his and silenced her protest.

She tasted as delicious as she smelt, of honey and roses, and everything that was so sweetly, temptingly Georgianna.

Zachary groaned low in his throat as he deepened the kiss, his hands sliding down the length of her spine to cup the sweet curve of her bottom and pull her closer against him, the length of his arousal nestling into the heated welcome of her abdomen.

Georgianna could not think, could only continue to cling to the strength of Zachary's shoulders as the firmness of his mouth now claimed, devoured, her own.

She felt dizzy, light-headed, as her body burned, a heated dampness moistening between her thighs as Zachary cupped the rounded globes of her bottom and held her firmly into and against him. Her breasts were crushed to the hardness of Zachary's muscled chest, the length of his erection pounding, pulsing, to the same rhythm as his heart beating so erratically against hers as his hands now roamed restlessly up the length of her spine.

A need, a want, a desire Georgianna became totally lost in. Until she felt the warmth of one of Zachary's hands against the bare skin at her throat and then lower still as he cupped the bareness of her breast beneath the material of her gown.

Her emotions immediately turned to one of panic as she realised that Zachary must have unfastened all the buttons down the front of her gown as they kissed, the material now gaping wide and revealing everything.

She wrenched her mouth from beneath his, both her hands moving up to push him aside as she pulled the sides of her gaping gown back over her chest, before glaring up at him accusingly. 'You will stop this immediately!'

His eyes narrowed to silver slits, that flush still to his cheeks and his hair dishevelled on his brow. 'Why?'

'Because I cannot allow this. It is…' Georgianna gave a shake of her head, feeling as if she were floundering, much like a fish newly hooked on the line and brought to shore. A fact Zachary was wholly aware of, if the mocking challenge in those silver eyes was any indication. And she had no doubt that it was. 'Because I do not want you,' she spat out determinedly as she hastily refastened the buttons on her gown.

'All evidence to the contrary, my dear Georgianna.' Zachary's insolent gaze moved slowly over her flushed face, slightly swollen lips, and then down the length of her throat and chest to where her nipples still pushed against the fabric of her gown.

Geogianna's lips firmed as she determinedly refused to follow the direction of that insolent gaze. 'That is purely a physical reaction to a man's touch. Any man's touch,' she added defiantly as he appeared satisfied at the admission. 'I assure you, my intellect tells me something else completely.'

'Intellect has very little to do with physical arousal,' he allowed disgustedly, all humour now gone. 'If it did, then I should not find myself in the least aroused by you, either.'

Georgianna flinched inwardly at the deliberate insult. 'Then we are in agreement on the subject, because my head tells me I should not allow a man such as you to take liberties.'

'A man such as me?'

She met his gaze defiantly. 'A libertine who is not to be trusted.'

Humour lit Zachary's eyes as he stepped back to regard her through narrowed lids. Admiration, too, because Georgianna Lancaster was, without a doubt, now a woman he could admire. Oh, not for her political beliefs, if indeed she should turn out to be a Trojan Horse for Rousseau's cause, but most definitely for the courage she had shown in the face of her present dilemma.

She was a woman who believed herself disgraced in English society. A woman who had nevertheless returned to England, only to now find herself a prisoner of the very gentleman she had once been betrothed to. Her suggestion earlier that it might have been deliberate on her part was, Zachary was sure, completely untrue; Georgianna had been far too genuinely shocked and outraged at finding herself incarcerated in his home for it to have been her intention all along.

And this, taking advantage of Georgianna, making love to her, when she was a prisoner in his home, was not a gentlemanly thing for him to do.

Georgianna's past behaviour might render her undeserving of such consideration on his part, but that did not mean he had to lose all honour.

Most especially when he still had no idea, as yet, as to whether or not Georgianna was merely Rousseau's minion, sent to England, to Zachary, at the other man's bidding.

The fact that she was now repelling his advances was, perhaps, a mark in her favour; a devious and manipulative woman would surely have used his obvious attraction to her own advantage?

Georgianna Lancaster was more than just a fully mature woman now, Zachary acknowledged, she was also an intriguing one. One who appealed to him on several levels. In her character. Intellectually. And certainly physically.

Which was all the more reason for him to keep his distance, at least until after he had confirmed, one way or the other, as to whether or not she was telling him the truth.

And if her information should prove correct, then he might no longer be given a choice about keeping his distance, because Georgianna would want nothing more to do with him after the way he had treated her whilst holding her prisoner.

His mouth twisted mockingly. 'It takes one to know one, my dear Georgianna.'

Georgianna gasped, her face paling at what she knew to be another deliberately delivered insult and a direct reference to her scandalous behaviour the previous year. 'I believe I will go back upstairs to my room now.'

'You have not eaten any dinner.'

'I am not hungry.'

The duke's lips firmed with his displeasure. 'It is no wonder you are now thin as a stick, if you do not eat.'

Georgianna refused, absolutely refused, to spill the heat of tears that now blurred her vision. 'You did not seem to have any complaints a few minutes ago, your Grace,' she reminded stiffly.

He shrugged wide shoulders. 'Thankfully the size of your breasts does not seem to have suffered in the process.'

Colour now burned Georgianna's cheeks. 'You are truly insufferable.'

He raised dark brows. 'Was that ever in any doubt?'

'Obviously not.' She blinked back those tears as she lowered her lashes before turning away, no longer willing to even look at that triumphantly mocking face. 'If you would care to act the turnkey again, I am more than ready to return to my room.'

Zachary cursed himself for feeling every kind of monster as he gazed upon the stiff slenderness of Georgianna's back and the vulnerability of her exposed nape, knowing he could not give in to the impulse he felt to take her back into his arms and apologise for having deliberately insulted her.

For having hurt her?

Her eyes had looked awash with tears again before she lowered those long, protective lashes, as if his cutting words really had injured her feelings.

Damn it, how long could it take to confirm or deny Georgianna's information? Zachary wondered impatiently. How much longer did he have to wait before he…?

Before he what? Exactly what difference was it going to make to Zachary's dealings with Georgianna once he did know the truth?

Georgianna might have responded to him a short time ago, but she also so obviously despised him, and herself, for that response. He could not see anything, even the unlikely confirmation of her information being true, ever changing that.

'Very well.' Zachary nodded abruptly, having no

appetite himself now. For dinner, at least. 'But a dinner tray will be brought up to your room.'

Her head remained bowed as she nodded. 'Thank you.'

'And you will eat its contents,' he added sternly.

Humour glinted in her eyes as she looked across at him. 'Must I remind you that your dictates to me so far have not proved in the least successful?'

No, Zachary needed no reminding of Georgianna's wilfulness. Or of his own response to those displays of stubbornness. 'That is because you are contrary in the extreme.'

'That being the case, perhaps you should have instructed me not to eat the food on the dinner tray rather than to eat it?'

'That would be a useless exercise now that we have discussed the possibility,' Zachary dismissed impatiently. 'Eat, or do not eat,' he advised wearily. 'Personally, I grew bored with the subject some minutes ago.'

As Georgianna had no doubt he was bored with having her in his home. With her. And who could blame him? It was so obviously not his choice, but had been foisted upon him by his superior. As she had been foisted on him.

Zachary could not really be blamed for having tried to lighten that burden by entertaining himself in making love to her. A woman whose intimate association with another man put her well beyond the need for either respect or maidenly consideration from the top-lofty Duke of Hawksmere.

She straightened her shoulders. 'Then I will relieve you of the necessity of suffering any more boredom by removing myself from your presence, so allowing you to go out and seek more entertaining and exciting company.'

Frustration surged inside Zachary as he eyed her impatiently, knowing he did not find Georgianna in the least boring. Indeed, she continued to intrigue and entertain him in a way he could not remember feeling with any other woman. Nor could he recall ever being anywhere near as 'excited' by another woman, as he had been just from kissing and caressing Georgianna.

He gave a mocking inclination of his head. 'That is very considerate of you.'

'I thought so, too,' she riposted drily.

Georgianna's sense of humour so appealed to his own that Zachary knew if he did not have a care he would find himself laughing once again, a move guaranteed to completely nullify the distance that he had deliberately put between them this past few minutes. It was a distance Zachary knew he desperately needed to maintain if he were to continue to keep the upper hand with this particular woman. If, indeed, he still had it. If he had ever had it?

Georgianna's flight from a marriage to him ten months ago would seem to imply, that even as the flirtatious and slightly immature Lady Georgianna Lancaster, she had possessed a wilfulness that had been strong enough to at least ensure the unwanted marriage did not take place. The Georgianna who had returned from France was even more determined to defy, and alternately beguile, him at every turn.

Zachary held himself stiffly. 'Luckily I do not need your permission to do anything I wish, or go anywhere I please, whereas the same obviously cannot be said of you.' He eyed her challengingly.

Rebellion glowed in those violet-coloured eyes. 'The bedchamber you have allocated for my use is far superior to my lodgings at Mrs Jenkins's house. It also has the added advantage of being given to me completely free of charge.'

Experience, so far in their reacquaintance, had served to show Zachary that it was doubtful he would ever manage to have the last word in a conversation with this particular woman. 'That could change at any moment,' he drawled challengingly in an attempt to do so.

Her chin rose stubbornly as she met that challenge. 'Your threats grow as wearisome to me as my company has become boring to you.'

The smile refused to be denied this time as Zachary gave a weary, defeated shake of his head. His lack of sleep the night before was certainly taking its toll on him now. A disadvantage Georgianna obviously did not suffer from. 'I do believe your tenacity of will has worn me down for this evening, Georgianna.'

'I am glad to hear it,' she replied pertly. 'Now, if you will excuse me? I really would prefer to return to my room.'

And Zachary, much as he might prefer to go out for the rest of the evening, well away from the temptation of knowing Georgianna was in the bedchamber adjoining his own, now knew himself to be so tired, from lack of sleep and the exhaustion of constantly crossing verbal swords with Georgianna, that he wanted nothing more than to go to his own bedchamber and sleep like the dead for a dozen hours or more.

He nodded abruptly. 'I will arrange for Hinds to bring you up a tray of food shortly.'

She arched one dark brow. 'Do you not intend to lock me in again first?'

He smiled slightly. 'I believe Hinds may find it rather difficult to deliver your tray if the door is locked.'

'And if I should attempt to escape in the meantime?'

Zachary took two predatory steps forward, coming to a halt just inches in front of Georgianna and forcing her to tilt her head back in order to look up at him.

'If you were to escape, Georgianna, then I should then have the pleasure of tracking you down,' he told her softly. 'And when I had, you may be assured I should extract the necessary revenge for your having dared to defy me.'

Georgianna repressed a shiver of apprehension as she saw the raw intensity of emotion glittering in the hard depths of Zachary's eyes. Challenge. Confidence. Amusement.

It was the latter emotion that caused her to straighten resentfully. 'You would have to find me first. Something I believe you were not too successful in doing ten months ago,' she added with deliberate sweetness.

His lids narrowed about those silver eyes. 'Perhaps that is because I did not bother to look too hard for my obviously reluctant bride?'

Colour warmed her cheeks. 'As you had never so much as bothered even speaking to her, I am not surprised. Indeed, as I have already told you, my only surprise is that you haven't found my replacement and married since.'

Zachary looked down at her coldly, only too well aware that his time for marrying, and producing an heir, was ticking by faster than he would have wished. 'Perhaps that is because I have decided to be more cautious in my second attempt at matrimony.'

'How sad to know you were the second choice for the Duke of Hawksmere's duchess!' she retorted tartly.

He drew in a sharp breath. 'My wife will not be my second choice, but the correct one. Which you, most assuredly, were not.'

The colour deepened in Georgianna's cheeks. 'Then it appears we may both be thankful for having escaped such an ill-matched union.'

'Indeed, we can,' Zachary bit out harshly.

They stared each other down for several more long seconds before Georgianna turned sharply on her heel and walked hastily from the room.

Much as he might wish to, Zachary did not trouble himself in following her, knowing he was in no mood at the moment to deal with her gently. Besides, he had meant it when he said he would very much enjoy the pleasure of recapturing her, and extracting payment, if she should try to escape Hawksmere House.

And him.

Chapter Seven

'It is past time you woke up, Georgianna.'

Georgianna roused slowly from the deepness of her slumbers at the sound of that intruding voice. She'd been sleeping so deeply, lost in a most wonderful dream. A dream where she had felt both safe and warm, something she had not been for so very long.

'Georgianna!'

She frowned as the impatient voice rallied her for a second time. She was so very reluctant to relinquish those feelings of safety after months of fear and the nervousness of discovery.

'If you do not open your eyes in the next few seconds, Georgianna, then you will leave me with no choice but to throw this jug of cold water over you.'

It really was Hawksmere talking to her, she realised with a groan.

For surely only Zachary Black, the forceful Duke of Hawksmere, could be so very demanding? So impatient for her to obey his every instruction, he threatened to douse her in water?

She forced her lids to open before going up on her elbows to seek his exact location in the half gloom of the bedchamber. 'What? That was deliberately cruel.' She glowered across the room at the duke as she saw he stood beside where he had just thrown back the curtains fully in order to let in the brightness of the morning's sunshine.

He gave a hard and unapologetic smile. 'But no doubt preferable to the dousing in cold water. Of course, the water for washing was not cold when it was delivered to your room three hours ago,' he added scathingly. 'But it most certainly will be now.'

Three hours ago? 'What time is it?' Georgianna pushed the silky curtain of her hair over her shoulders.

Hawksmere strode impatiently to the bedside, revealing he was already dressed for the day, in a dark grey superfine, silver brocade waistcoat over white linen, with pale grey pantaloons and brown-topped Hessians. 'After eleven.'

Georgianna blinked up at him. After eleven o'clock in the morning? Then she had must have slept for a dozen hours or more after eating a little of the food from the tray that Hinds had delivered to her room last evening. How could she have slept for so long? It had been weeks, months, since she had been able to sleep so deeply.

She recalled her dream. The safety and the warmth she had felt cocooning her. Implying she felt safe in

Hawksmere's home? With Hawksmere just feet away in the adjoining bedchamber? The same gentleman who had threatened and imprisoned her? Impossible!

And yet...

Georgianna could not deny that she had felt that sense of safety and warmth as she awoke, as if nothing and no one could harm her whilst she was in Hawksmere House.

A feeling she had no intentions of sharing with Hawksmere himself.

'Obviously you slept well,' he added mockingly. 'No doubt you will claim it was the sleep of the innocent.'

Georgianna frowned at his harshness, checking that her nightgown was securely fastened up to her throat before sitting up in the bed to glare accusingly at her tormentor. 'You should have woken me earlier if my sleeping late displeases you.'

He raised dark brows. 'I do not believe that is included in my duties, as your gaoler.'

'Then perhaps in future it should be,' she snapped irritably.

Hawksmere frowned grimly. 'I have had other things to occupy me this morning, other than troubling myself to wake you from your lazy slumbers.'

Georgianna almost laughed at his words; there had been no lazy slumbers for her since she'd left England for France the previous year!

The time she had spent with André had been rife with tension and the days had started early on the Barnards' farm. The tavern had been even worse, with late nights cooking food followed by early mornings spent cleaning in readiness for the next influx of customers.

All so very unlike her previous pampered and privileged life as the only daughter of the Earl of Malvern.

She looked up at Hawksmere searchingly now, immediately noting the grimness about his eyes and the firmness of his mouth. His expression was altogether one of harshness this morning, rather than the lazy mockery he had shown towards her yesterday evening. His movements were restless as he turned away from the bed and began to pace the bedchamber.

'What other things have occupied you this morning?' she prompted warily.

Zachary shot her an impatient glance, not sure how much he should reveal to Georgianna, how much he needed to reveal to her, when the information delivered to him earlier this morning was not confirmed, only suspected at this point in time. When his instructions were still to keep her a prisoner here.

He drew in a controlling breath. 'I shall be leaving London later today and I am uncertain when I shall return.'

'You are leaving London?' she echoed sharply. 'To go where?'

Zachary had known that Georgianna was too intelligent, had grown too unconventional in her ways, to accept his statement without suspicion or question, as most women in society would have done. To most women a gentleman's activities outside their home were his own affair and definitely not to be questioned too deeply. Not so with the forthright Georgianna, unfortunately.

He glowered down at her, wishing she did not look quite so delectable this morning, her face soft and flushed from sleep, that silky dark hair once again loose about her shoulders and down her spine. The white cotton nightgown also did little to hide the fact that she was naked beneath it, her breasts jutting out firm and tempting against its voluptuous folds.

'What will you do with me while you are away?' she added slowly.

Zachary scowled. 'You will remain here, of course.'

Her eyes widened. 'You intend leaving me a prisoner in this bedchamber indefinitely?'

'I see no alternative.' Much as he might wish it were otherwise. And the thought of keeping Georgianna cooped up in this bedchamber was not a pleasant one. Especially when he had no idea how long her incarceration would last. Or when he would return to England.

'Where are you going, Zachary?' she demanded sharply. 'Tell me,' she insisted determinedly as his mouth thinned.

He sighed his impatience as he once again wished for a less intelligent and astute woman than Georgianna. 'As you are to remain incarcerated here, I can see no harm in your knowing that rumours have reached our shores that Napoleon is on the move.'

'I knew it!' Georgianna announced, her face aglow with triumph as she threw back the bedcovers before climbing out of the bed and revealing that her nightgown covered her from her throat down to her slender ankles.

Or it attempted to do so, because Zachary could clearly make out the shadowy outline of the rosy tips to the fullness of her breasts, as well as the dark shadow of the curls nestled so seductively between her thighs.

He gave an inward groan as his own body instantly reacted to those tantalising glimpses of the shadowy outline of Georgianna's body, his arousal hardening to pulsing need inside his pantaloons.

'Did I not tell you it would be so, Zachary?' she continued excitedly, her face glowing with that excitement as she paced quickly to one of the windows, unknowingly allowing the sun, as it shone through the glass, to instantly turn her nightgown diaphanous.

Zachary closed his eyes briefly in order to shut out the sight of Georgianna's slender nakedness so clearly outlined through the white material. A brief visual respite that made absolutely no difference to the engorging of his erection as it continued to pulse, to lengthen and thicken, with impatient need.

He gave a shake of his head as he opened his lids to look across at her guardedly. 'Has no one ever told you it is most unattractive to say *I told you so* in that triumphant manner?'

'Hah to that.' Georgianna was too excited at being proved right to behave in the least ladylike about it, despite Hawksmere's rebuke. 'I was right, Zachary, and you were wrong, and you may mock all you like, but…' She stilled, excitement dying as she took in the full import of Hawksmere's statement. 'He is already on the move, you say?'

The duke gave a haughty inclination of his head. 'So it is reported, yes.'

'Then I was too late to be of help, after all.' Georgianna groaned, shoulders slumping in defeat. 'I delayed too long and arrived too late, Zachary.' She buried her face in her hands. 'Too late.'

Zachary was instantly torn between the need to go to Georgianna and comfort her by taking her into his arms, and the certain knowledge that if he did so he would be unable to stop himself from making love to her again. Last night had been a tortuous hell for him after he and Georgianna had parted so ignominiously. Knowing Georgianna was in the adjoining bedchamber, that silky ebony hair no doubt once again loose about her shoulders and breasts, and wearing nothing more than one of the two white nightgowns he had packed into her bag earlier in the day at her lodgings, had played havoc with his efforts to find rest, let alone sleep.

So much so that he had quickly worked himself up into a fine temper, his annoyance with both Georgianna, and his own weakness in desiring her, making it impossible for him to relax.

He had finally given up all attempt of sleeping just before two o'clock in the morning. He'd thrown back the bedcovers to get out of bed and pull on his brocade robe over his nakedness before pacing about his bedchamber instead. All the time aware, so totally aware, that Georgianna was just a door-width away from satisfying the lust that coursed so hotly through his body.

A lust Zachary could not, dare not, allow to rule him, when he still distrusted the woman responsible for that emotion.

Only to then realise, when Georgianna had slept in so late this morning, that while he had been suffering the torments of the damned the night before, she had been perfectly at peace in the adjoining bedchamber, sleeping like the dead—or innocent?—and so totally unaware of his own tormented longings.

His visitor earlier this morning, bearing news of Napoleon's possible flight from Elba, had done nothing to improve the already short fuse on his overstretched temper. To so much as touch her now would be insanity on his part.

Oh, to hell with his caution, Zachary dismissed as he took the two long strides that brought him to her side, before reaching out to take her in his arms. He wanted this woman, to kiss her, to caress her, and God knew when he would have the opportunity to do so again.

She was so very slight, in both height and stature. Her head rested against his chest just beneath his chin. So slender, it was almost like holding a child in his arms.

Almost.

Because it was a certainty that Georgianna did not bring out even a spark of paternal instinct in him.

'I should not have delayed my departure from France for so long.' Her voice was muffled against his chest, her breath a warm caress through the thin material of his shirt. 'Should not have been so cautious, so worried, that I might be discovered attempting to leave. And now Napoleon will return to France and— My God—' she lifted her head to look up at Zachary searchingly, her face paling as realisation dawned '—that is where you are going, is it not?'

It so happened that that was exactly where Zachary was going.

But he was not allowed to discuss his mission. Even with the woman who was responsible for bringing him the news that it was Napoleon's intention to leave Elba. If, as was suspected, the Corsican had not already done so.

Zachary gave a mocking smile. 'I had not realised you had such a vivid imagination, Georgianna.'

'Do not even attempt to treat me like the foolish young girl I once was, Zachary,' Georgianna warned fiercely.

His expression was grim. 'Oh, I assure you, I am only too well aware that you are no longer that young innocent, Georgianna, foolish or otherwise.'

'Then do not... Umph!' The last came out as a protesting squeak as Zachary silenced her by claiming her mouth with his own, his arms like steel bands about her waist as he held her so tightly to him her body was melded close against his own.

Georgianna fought against the confinement of those arms as she also tried to wrench her mouth from beneath his. All to no avail, as Zachary merely tightened his arms and deepened the kiss by parting her lips beneath his with the invasion of his tongue into the moist heat of her mouth.

His marauding tongue that explored every sensitive and heated contour of her mouth, before stilling her as that tongue stroked against her own in a slow and sensuous caress, claiming, possessing, and sending rivulets of pleasurable heat coursing through the whole of Georgianna's body.

She had never... No one had ever made her feel like this before.

The sheer carnality of Zachary's kiss was beyond anything Georgianna had ever experienced before, beyond anything she had ever imagined, and she had no defences against it.

No defence against Zachary as he continued to plunder and claim her mouth even as he lifted her up into his arms and carried her across the room to lay her down upon the bed before joining her there. He draped one of his legs across her thighs to keep her in place beside him as he continued to kiss and taste her even while one of his hands began to roam restlessly along the length of her body.

Her neck arched as Zachary broke that kiss to explore the column of her throat. She gasped as his hand cupped beneath her breast, instantly seeking out the sensitive berry at its tip, caressing, stroking and causing a tingling ache that spread like wildfire from her nipple down to between her dampening thighs.

Nevertheless, she knew she must seek some semblance of sanity, to put an end to the madness that had so rapidly overtaken them. 'Zachary.'

'Do not deny the desire that exists between us, Georgianna.' He raised his head to look at her, his eyes glittering fiercely, a flush across the sharp blades of his cheekbones, his lips thinned.

As evidence that his own desire for her angered him rather than pleased him?

No doubt it did, when Zachary had every reason to believe she had been André Rousseau's lover.

'I will allow you to think of nothing and no one else whilst you are in my arms, Georgianna,' he warned harshly, as he seemed to guess some of her thoughts. 'And I fully intend to have you before I leave,' he continued determinedly as he rose above and then over her, pushing her nightgown up her thighs as he settled between her legs. 'All of you.'

She swallowed at the lustful violence she now saw in the fierceness of Zachary's gaze. A violence of emotion that threatened to overwhelm completely Zachary's previous cautions where she was concerned.

Georgianna ran the moistness of her tongue across the dryness of her lips. 'You will only regret it.'

'As you warned me yesterday I should regret having insisted you remove your veil?' he retorted harshly as he slid slowly down the length of her body, able to smell the sweet lure of her arousal once he was comfortably settled between her thighs.

'Yes.'

'And I did regret it. I regret it still. But it seems that regret does little to change the fact that I also desire you.' Zachary gave a shake of his head, his endurance, and his patience, pushed beyond his control after his second sleepless night in succession. Because of this woman. Because of the desire he felt for her. A desire he had every intention of satisfying before he left England later today.

'Please, Zachary.'

'Oh, I intend to please you, Georgianna.' He looked down as his hands moved up her thighs, pushing her nightgown up to her waist, revealing smooth, ivory skin and the dark thatch of curls nestled between her thighs. 'And by pleasing you I also intend to please myself,' he promised darkly, even as his fingers parted those curls to reveal the lushness of her rosy red folds with the little nubbin peeking out temptingly from beneath the hood above. 'Open your legs wider and let me in, Georgianna,' he encouraged gruffly.

'I cannot.'

'You can.' Zachary moved even lower, the width of his shoulders pushing her thighs further apart, and allowing the heat of his gaze to feast on the slickness of her folds. So deep and rosy coloured, the lips there already swollen, moist, with Georgianna's own arousal. 'You are so beautiful, Georgianna,' he murmured as his thumbs moved to part those folds, revealing the moist and welcoming centre. 'Like a flower unfurling petals touched by the morning dew.'

Georgianna was not sure which mortified her the most, the suddenness of this intimacy, or her unmistakable arousal. Certainly she could not deny she was aroused, but at the same time she felt embarrassed by that response. At having a man, any man, look at and touch her so intimately. To have Zachary look and touch where she had never even looked or touched herself.

'I had not taken you for a poet, Hawksmere.'

'You and this lush bounty make me one,' he assured gruffly as his fingers lightly caressed the delicacy of her skin.

'I...'

Georgianna's protest died in her throat, her back arching off the bed at the first pleasurable sweep of the heat of Zachary's moist tongue against that very private place, before he commenced a slow and sensuous licking of those sensitive folds. He greedily lapped up the moisture now flowing between her thighs.

'I do not...' Georgianna halted with a gasp as the pleasure became so intense it threatened to totally overwhelm her.

Zachary felt the deepening of Georgianna's response as his tongue now probed beneath the hood above her folds, seeking out that erect nubbin, lathing and then sucking it fully into his mouth as he felt it pulsing against his tongue as evidence of her rapidly approaching climax.

His senses were filled with the taste and smell of her, like the sweetest of nectars, and just as addictive. 'Yes, Georgianna,' he encouraged hotly as she now arched up into the stroking of his tongue. 'Find your rhythm, love. Move with me. Into me. Yes,' he muttered fiercely as she found that rhythm with the undulating arching of her hips.

He slipped a finger between the slickness of her folds, stroking the edge, before sliding slowly inside, groaning low in his throat as he added a second finger and felt her muscles tighten about him. Imagining, craving, those same muscles tightening snugly about his erection in exactly the same way they gripped his fingers.

But first he intended to pleasure Georgianna, to obliterate from her memory any other lover she had ever known.

He continued that slow thrusting with his fingers even as he lowered his head and his tongue once again stroked the erect nubbin above, suckling it into his mouth before closing his teeth gently about it.

Georgianna gasped and then cried out as the pleasure rose up to an unbearable height before crashing, streaking through her in hot, burning flames, threatening to consume her with their intensity. Wave after wave of mindless, all-consuming pleasure, tossing her higher, and then higher still as Zachary continued to stroke and thrust her to a second, even more exquisitely powerful climax with the merciless strokes of his tongue. Her body contracting as he continued to thrust his fingers deep inside that flooding heat.

'No more. Please, Zachary,' she finally cried out weakly, so sensitive now that every touch, every stroke threatened to send her over the edge of falling into yet another exquisite climax.

'Why not?' Zachary's eyes were dark as he raised his head to look up at her, his cheeks flushed.

Georgianna felt the heat burn her cheeks as she saw how glistening wet his lips were, and realised it had to be from the copious flowing of her juices. 'I had not realised... I did not know. Do men enjoy doing that?'

'I do,' Zachary assured gruffly, pleased beyond measure that he was obviously the first man to have introduced Georgianna to this intimacy. 'You taste divine, Georgianna,' he added huskily as he licked the juices from his lips and had the pleasure of watching her cheeks blush an even deeper red.

'And I—' He broke off with a scowl as a knock sounded on the door of the bedchamber. 'What is it?' He turned to direct that scowl towards that closed door.

'The Duke of Wolfingham is awaiting your presence down in the blue salon, your Grace,' Hinds informed him stiffly through the closed door.

Damn it. Zachary had completely forgotten that Wolfingham was joining him here this morning.

Forgotten everything but his need to make love to Georgianna.

Chapter Eight

Georgianna washed, and dressed herself in the black gown, then arranged her hair neatly at her crown in record time after Zachary left her bedchamber. She was determined that when, and if, the duke should return, her appearance would at least be respectable.

The only thing she now considered 'respectable' about herself.

She had no idea what had happened with Hawksmere just now. One minute they had been talking, and the next…

Oh, dear lord, the next.

Just thinking about Zachary possessing her with his mouth was enough to make Georgianna quiver with embarrassment.

Or possibly remembered pleasure?

Unimagined, indescribable, out-of-this-world pleasure.

She had not known such intimacies, such pleasure, as that existed.

The attentions of Zachary's mouth, tongue and fingers had been centred between her thighs, but the pleasure had been felt everywhere. Radiating out from between her and consuming her every sensation, as it coursed, burned through her torso and throat, and into all of her limbs to the very ends of her fingers and her toes. And not just once, but twice! That pleasure building again, carrying her along on a tide of sensation. By the time Hinds had knocked on the door of her bedchamber...

Hinds!

What must he think? What conclusion could the butler have come to, in respect of the time his employer had spent in Georgianna's bedchamber this morning?

Considering the reason Zachary had informed his household staff for her being here at all, no doubt the butler had drawn the correct conclusion regarding their activities this morning.

Georgianna was genuinely shocked at her own behaviour. Mortified. She had no idea how she was going to face Zachary again when he had looked at her and touched her so intimately.

However, this personal mortification paled into insignificance in the face of Napoleon's move from Elba.

If it was true, and if Napoleon should indeed return to the shores of France, then there was sure to be another war. England and her allies could not just sit back and allow the Corsican to retake the French crown for his own. And if, when, that happened, more Englishmen would die.

And to think, Georgianna might have prevented it if she had been more courageous. If she had not wasted so much time seeking safe and undetected passage for herself from France.

Zachary might be one of the ones to die.

Sooner rather than later if, as she suspected, he was leaving for France later today.

If Napoleon should make it back to France in the next few days, as he was bound to do, then the next few weeks, as he marched towards Paris, would be dangerous indeed. Having lived there for the past few months, Georgianna knew, perhaps better than most, that the people of France were not all enamoured of having their king returned to them. And that many, given the choice, would far rather that Napoleon return as their emperor.

The thought of Zachary deliberately placing himself in the midst of that turmoil was a frightening one.

Georgianna shied away from admitting why she found the idea of Zachary in danger so disturbing. Shied away from facing that truth. Even to herself.

She should hate Zachary Black. For having imprisoned her here. For disbelieving the things she had told him about André, as well as Napoleon's plans to leave Elba. Most certainly for the liberties he had taken with her this morning.

And yet she found she could not bring herself to hate Zachary. Certainly not enough to wish him ill. To wish him dead.

Surely she had not come to care for him this past day or so? To feel something, some nameless, softening of emotion, for the very man she had run away from marrying in the first place?

What other explanation was there for her response to him such a short time ago?

It would be worse than ironic if that should be the case.

'What are you thinking about so intently?'

Georgianna spun sharply to face the man standing in the doorway of the bedchamber. The same gentleman, who now occupied so much of her thoughts.

Her face was instantly ablaze with embarrassed colour, as she found her gaze drawn to those beautifully sculptured lips. Lips, that such a short time ago, had been kissing and suckling her intimately.

'I was merely wondering exactly when you intended leaving for France, so that I might know when I will, most thankfully, be relieved of your company,' she replied tartly, her gaze now meeting his boldly.

Zachary gave a slow and mocking smile at that now-familiar sharpness; ridiculous of him to have expected that their earlier intimacies might have in any way softened Georgianna's feelings towards him.

The fact that she had once again dressed in the unbecoming black gown in his absence was evidence enough, surely, that she regretted those intimacies?

At the same time as Zachary acknowledged he now had no choice but to believe that the information Georgianna had given him about Napoleon's movements was, in fact, the truth.

As had been her claim not to have seen Rousseau for many months?

The intelligence report that Zachary had read on Rousseau would seem to indicate that also was true.

Which, taken to its logical conclusion, must also mean that Georgianna had indeed parted from Rousseau only a week or so after arriving in France, and that she had then worked on a farm for several months, before going to back to Paris to work as a kitchen maid in Helene Rousseau's tavern.

Zachary found himself scowling at the thought of this beautiful young woman wandering alone about the French countryside, let alone returning to Paris to work in such a lowly tavern as the Fleur de Lis, leaving herself prey to any and all of that inn's patrons.

'Never mind my own plans for now, what on earth did you think you were doing by remaining in France once Rousseau had finished with you, and so putting yourself in danger for so many months?' He scowled his displeasure.

Oh, yes, André had certainly finished with her, she reflected bitterly. Indeed, as far as she was aware he still believed he had finished her off completely and that her stripped and bleached bones now lay scattered about a forest outside Paris.

She gave an uninterested shrug. 'Why not stay, when I had nothing to return to in England?'

'Your father was still alive then, and your brother...'

'A father and a brother who had quite rightly disowned me,' she responded tautly.

The duke scowled.

'Why did the Duke of Wolfingham need to speak with you so urgently?' she prompted shrewdly.

Zachary raised dark brows. 'I do not recall Hinds indicating that Wolfingham's visit was urgent in nature.'

'I assumed, from the haste with which you left earlier... Silly me.' Georgianna gave a discomforted grimace. 'No doubt the urgency was for you to leave my bedchamber, rather than your need to rush to Wolfingham.'

'And yet here I am, back again,' he drawled.

'Only because you had not finished our earlier conversation, I am sure.' Georgianna turned away to walk over to one of the windows. 'You cannot seriously intend to leave me a prisoner here whilst you go to France?'

'I do not believe I have ever confirmed my intention of going to France.'

'But we both know that you are.' Georgianna glanced back at him as he did not deny it a second time. 'And you would have admitted it was so earlier if we had not been...' Her face flushed fiery red as she remembered the reason for their earlier distraction.

'No, I would not, Georgianna, and for the simple reason I do not consider my immediate plans to be any of your concern,' Zachary bit out harshly.

Georgianna recoiled at the disdain underlying his dismissal. It was as if he had physically struck her. As if, despite everything, Zachary still distrusted her.

She turned stiffly to face him. 'Nevertheless, you

cannot expect me to continue to remain here whilst you are away.'

'And yet that is exactly what I expect.' Hawksmere eyed her challengingly.

'And if I should choose to make my presence here a difficult one?'

'Then do so by all means. It will make no difference to the outcome.' Zachary was no happier than Georgianna about the arrangement, and as such, his patience had worn beyond thin on the subject.

She raised haughty brows. 'You may be lord and master of all you survey in your own world, Zachary, but I assure you, you are not my lord or master, in this world or any other.'

No, because if he were, Zachary would have put her over his knee by now and spanked her obstinate little bottom into obedience. As it was, he was so angry with her, not just for her stubbornness now, but because he now knew she had deliberately placed herself in danger these past months. So angry that he might still be driven to that action, if Georgianna didn't cease arguing with him at every turn.

Not that he had really expected their earlier intimacy to have changed that stubbornness in any way. Georgianna had shown him only too clearly that this wilfulness was part and parcel of who she was. Or, at least, who she had become.

No doubt those weeks and months she had spent alone in France, fearing for her safety, for her life, were in part responsible for her present independence of nature.

The truth was, after the information Zachary had received this morning, he now believed the things Georgianna had told him about the time she had spent in France. And knowing that she had wilfully chosen to put herself in harm's way by working at the tavern of Helene Rousseau was enough to turn the blood cold in Zachary's veins. Anything might have happened to her; a young and beautiful woman, so obviously alone and without male protection.

As perhaps anything had?

His eyes narrowed. 'Where did you live while working in the kitchen of Helene Rousseau's tavern?'

Georgianna eyed Hawksmere warily as she heard the steely edge beneath the softness of his tone. 'I do not see that is any of your concern.'

'Answer the question, damn you.' He strode forcefully across the room.

She blinked up at him as he now stood just inches in front of her. 'I was given a room in the attic.'

'You lived on the premises?'

She nodded. 'So I was about to tell you, if you had let me finish.'

He drew in a slow and deliberate breath. 'You, Lady Georgianna Lancaster, daughter, and now sister of the Earl of Malvern, lived in the attic of a common French tavern?'

Georgianna had no idea why Hawksmere was so obviously angry on the subject. Living in the attic of the Fleur de Lis paled into insignificance when she considered the other dangers she had faced during those months in France. 'Mademoiselle Rousseau allowed me to stay there as part of my payment.'

'So that you might entertain men there?'

Georgianna gasped in shock. ' Of course not! How dare you imply—?' She broke off as Hawksmere took a painful grasp of the tops of her arms, his face tight with anger as he towered over her.

'I was employed as a kitchen maid, not a whore, Hawksmere.'

'I very much doubt that the men who frequented the tavern were capable of making that distinction.' he said scornfully.

She frowned. 'You are obviously more familiar with the practises of such places than I.'

His hands tightened painfully as he shook her. 'It is not a question of what I am familiar with.'

'Is it not?' Georgianna challenged scathingly. 'I worked in the kitchen of the tavern, Hawksmere,' she maintained firmly. 'And that is all I did.' She looked up at him defiantly.

Zachary looked down at her searchingly, seeing the challenge glittering in those violet-coloured eyes, the unmistakable pride in the tilt of her chin, indignation in the stiffness of her body. As proof of her innocence? In regard to the months she had spent working at the tavern, perhaps; the weeks she had spent as Rousseau's mistress were a different matter entirely.

'What more is it going to take for you to trust me, Zachary?' She looked up at him with pained eyes. 'You now have information that confirms Napoleon is to leave Elba, if he has not already done so. What more do you need from me to be convinced that I have told you nothing but the truth since we met again yesterday?'

His jaw tightened. 'You have yet to tell me how you escaped from Rousseau once your association was over.'

Her gaze avoided meeting his. 'Is that really necessary?'

'It is if you truly wish for me to trust you.'

She moistened dry lips. 'And if I tell you, will you then consider allowing me to leave this house at the same time you do?'

'To go where?'

'Anywhere I am not a prisoner.'

'I will consider the idea, yes,' he bit out tautly.

'That is not good enough.'

'It is all the concession I am willing to make at this point.'

Georgianna stared up at Hawksmere's hard and unyielding expression, his eyes that glittering remorseless silver. As evidence that he would not relent without that last irrefutable proof from her as to her innocence.

She had hoped to spare herself this final humiliation, but saw now that it was not to be, that the time for such prevarication was now at an end.

'Release my arms, if you please,' she instructed softly.

Zachary looked down at her searchingly for several long seconds before his fingers slowly loosened, his hands dropping back to his sides as he took a step back.

Georgianna averted her gaze from meeting his own, her hands shaking as she raised them to the neckline of her black gown, fingers fumbling as she began to unfasten the tiny buttons.

'Georgianna, I do not have the time now to finish what we started earlier,' Hawksmere dismissed impatiently. 'Nor will you succeed in distracting me by attempting to seduce me,' he added scathingly.

'You are arrogance personified.' Georgianna's fingers paused on the buttons of her gown as she gave him a pitying glance. 'I have absolutely no intentions of distracting or attempting to seduce you.'

He raised dark brows. 'Then why are you unfastening your gown?'

She sighed heavily. 'Because it is the only way I know of to show you how I escaped from Rousseau.'

'I do not see how the unfastening of your gown will help convince me of anything.'

'Will you please cease your sarcasm for just a few moments, Hawksmere?' Georgianna's voice shook with emotion, her vision blurred by unshed tears as she looked up at him. 'I cannot——' She bit her bottom lip as she gave a shake of her head. 'I believe if I have to suffer another one of your insults then I might begin to scream and never stop.'

Zachary could see that by the strained expression on Georgianna's face. Her eyes were a dark purple and shimmering with tears, her cheeks pale and hollow, all the colour seeming to have drained even from the fullness of her lips. She was seriously distressed. Enough to scream? He believed so, yes.

'In that case, please continue,' he invited in a bored voice as he moved to slowly lower his length comfortably down on to the chair placed in front of the dressing table.

Her eyes narrowed as she glared across at him. 'I only intend to unfasten a few buttons of my gown, Hawksmere, not provide a striptease show with you as the audience.'

'That is a pity,' he drawled as he crossed one elegant leg over the other.

Georgianna closed her eyes briefly in an attempt to dig deep inside herself for the courage needed for her to continue along this course.

Not an easy feat when Hawksmere continued to treat her with such disdain. Nor was there any guarantee, having literally bared her scarred soul to him, that he would dispense once and for all with the distrust with which he continued to treat her.

But she had to at least try.

Her fingers trembled even more than before as she recommenced unfastening the buttons down the bodice of her gown, causing her to fumble several times before the last button was finally unfastened.

She hesitated, holding the two sides of her gown together, as she forced herself to look across at Hawksmere. 'Please attempt to hold your derision and scorn at bay, if only for a few minutes, if you please, Hawksmere.' Her voice shook with emotion.

Zachary frowned as he looked across at her searchingly, having no idea what it was that Georgianna was hiding from him. He was nevertheless aware that, whatever it was, it affected her deeply. 'Show me,' he encouraged gruffly, shoulders tensed.

Georgianna kept her eyes closed, her lips clamped firmly together, as she slowly parted the two sides of her gown before her fingers pulled down the soft material of her camisole, fully exposing her breasts to him.

It was impossible for Zachary to hold back his sharply indrawn breath as he saw the discoloured and livid scar between the swell of Georgianna's breasts for the first time.

Even from across the room he could see that the redness of the puckered and scarred skin now exposed to him was recent and several inches around. It was the same type of wound and scarring he had unfortunately seen many times during his years of battle against Napoleon's armies.

His gaze moved sharply back up to the pallor of Georgianna's face. Her eyes were once again open as she looked back at him with a flat and unemotional expression. He moistened lips that had gone suddenly dry.

'Is that…?'

'The result of a bullet wound?' Georgianna finished dully. 'Yes, it is.'

Zachary stood up, too restless, too disturbed by what he was seeing to remain seated for a moment longer. He crossed the room in long strides before gently pushing her fingers out of the way so that he might better see the livid red scar. 'How is it you did not die from such a wound?'

She gave an emotionally choked laugh. 'As it was so obviously intended that I should?'

'Yes.'

'How typical of you, Hawksmere, to cut straight to the point.' She looked up at him coldly. 'It was pure chance that I did not die, that the force of the bullet was deflected slightly by the locket I wore about my neck at the time.'

Zachary gave a dazed shake of his head, unable to stop looking at the terrible scarring that had been inflicted on Georgianna's otherwise beautiful and flawless skin. He was unable to stop himself from imagining a bullet entering Georgianna's smoothly perfect flesh, and the agony she must have suffered as it ripped through that delicate tissue, no doubt taking her down. Miraculously the locket prevented it from actually killing her.

He looked up, eyes narrowed. 'Who did this to you?'

Her smile turned humourless. 'Ah, and now comes the intelligence beneath the scorn and derision.'

'Georgianna.'

'Have you seen enough that I might refasten my gown now?' she challenged tensely.

His jaw clenched tightly as he demanded again, 'Who did this to you?'

Her eyes hardened to glittering violet jewels. 'Who do you imagine did it to me?' She refastened her gown without waiting for his permission. 'Who was it that you yourself said could not allow me to live once I had left him?'

'Rousseau,' he breathed softly.

'Exactly. Rousseau,' she confirmed flatly. 'Have you seen enough yet to believe me, Hawksmere?' she challenged tautly. 'Or would another scar help to finally convince you that everything I have told you is the truth?' She lifted a hand to move back the cluster of curls gathered on her left temple, revealing a long scar where a second bullet appeared to have grazed and broken her skin without actually penetrating it. 'This one was to be the coup de grâce, I believe. Unfortunately for André it was dark that night and I must have turned my head away at the last moment, because the second bullet only succeeded in rendering me unconscious rather than killing me outright.'

A single bullet to the heart and another to the head.

'An assassin's method,' Zachary acknowledged gruffly.

'Because André killed me,' Georgianna confirmed emotionally. 'Or, at least, he believed that he had when he left me for dead in that deserted forest just outside Paris,' she continued flatly. 'Which is where Monsieur Bernard, having heard the two shots and fearing for his livestock, found me unconscious and took me back to his farm.'

'The doctor?'

'The Bernards dare not call in a doctor, because they had no way of knowing who had inflicted such injuries. And, being unconscious, I could not tell them, either.' She smiled ruefully. 'Madame Bernard removed the bullet herself, then she sewed the wound back up as best she could. It could have been worse, I suppose, and *monsieur* might have lived alone and so been the one to attempt to sew the wound.'

'For pity's sake, be silent a moment, Georgianna.' Zachary choked as he finally found the breath to speak.

'Why?' she challenged. 'Did I not tell you yesterday that we all carry scars, some more visibly than others? Or does it sicken you to see such imperfection? It sickened me at the time. Although, in truth, I did not see the scars for some weeks,' she continued conversationally. 'I remained unconscious for several days afterwards and delirious for the better part of a week or more,' she explained flatly as Zachary looked at her sharply. 'And then, finally, when I did awaken it was to discover that I was blind, Zachary. Completely and utterly blind.' She raised her chin as she looked at him in defiant challenge.

'Dear God.'

'Yes.'

Zachary closed his eyes momentarily. 'That is the reason you do not like full dark.' It was a statement rather than a question.

'Yes. The blindness lasted only a couple of weeks, but it was the longest fortnight of my life, as I lay there wondering if I should ever see again. Do you believe me yet, Zachary?' she continued tauntingly. 'Or do you require further proof? If so, I am afraid I have none.'

'Stop it, Georgianna. For pity's sake.'

'Pity?' she echoed bitterly. 'And why should I pity you, Hawksmere? You were not the stupid fool who believed she was eloping with the man she believed herself in love with and whom she believed loved her, only to discover that she had been nothing more to him than a useful pawn. A pawn who was totally dispensable once he was safely returned to his native France and fellow conspirators.'

Zachary gave a dazed shake of his head. 'I meant only that you have had months to grow accustomed to this, Georgianna. I have had only a few minutes. Rousseau truly believes he has succeeded in assassinating you?'

'Oh, yes.'

'That is why you did not fear his looking for you after you had left him? Because he believed you already dead?'

She nodded abruptly. 'And my body then eaten by scavenging animals, yes.'

Now Zachary did feel sickened. But not by Georgianna's scars. Never that.

How could he ever be sickened by those, when they were the scars of the war she had been forced to fight alone, and in a country not her own? Indeed, it was the same evidence of war which he carried upon his own throat.

Georgianna might well have died, but for the kindness of a French farmer and his wife. And she had then placed herself in danger by working in a French tavern for months, followed by days of fearing being discovered at any moment as she waited at the dockside to return to England, so that she might bring back the information she had overheard of Napoleon's intention of leaving Elba.

There had been no father to defend her.

No brother to cherish her.

No husband to protect her.

Chapter Nine

'I demand to know where you are taking me,' Georgianna insisted even as she accepted Hawksmere's hand to aid her in climbing inside the ducal carriage.

Hawksmere waited until she was seated before climbing in behind her and sitting on the seat opposite as the door was closed. His expression was as grimly forbidding as it had been this past hour, since he had informed her she would be leaving Hawksmere House at the same time as he. 'Somewhere you will be safe.' He turned away to look out of the carriage window as it moved forward.

Georgianna had no idea what to expect from Hawksmere after her revelations to him earlier in the bedchamber. She had waited nervously as he went exceedingly quiet, restlessly pacing the room, so deep in thought he seemed almost to have forgotten she was there. Zachary had then come to an abrupt halt and instructed her to repack her bag and be ready to leave within the hour, before he had then departed her bedchamber.

There had been very little for Georgianna to repack. The things she had originally taken with her to France had all, apart from what she had carried in her reticule, been left behind when André took her to the forest outside Paris with the intention of killing her.

The Bernards had later provided her with a couple of worn gowns left behind by their daughter when she went off to marry her French soldier. And Georgianna had added two more gowns to that meagre wardrobe with the wages she'd earned at the tavern. She was wearing one of the only two sets of undergarments she possessed. As she had last night worn one of her only two nightgowns. Otherwise she had no other possessions.

Consequently she had spent most of that hour sitting in a chair beside the window, worrying about what Hawksmere intended to do with her now. As his final words had implied, he intended doing something.

'Is there such a place?' she prompted softly now.

Zachary turned back to look at her, his expression unreadable beneath the brim of his beaver hat as he answered her. 'I believe so, yes.'

Georgianna gave a pained frown. 'Is it your intention to foist me off on to one or other of your close friends? Perhaps that was the reason for Wolfingham's visit to you this morning?' she asked heavily.

Zachary now had cause to regret many things in his life. The nature of his marriage proposal to Georgianna Lancaster certainly being one of them. But the cruelty of his distrust of her these past two days, in light of the things she had revealed to him this morning, the terrible scars he had seen upon her body, and no doubt a reflection of the scars she also carried inside her, by far and away exceeded any previous regrets.

And Georgianna was as yet unaware of the worst of the cruelties of which he was guilty.

Once she did know then her disgust with him, her hatred of him, would no doubt be complete.

Zachary had consulted with no one on the decision, the change of plans, he had made in regards to what he should do with Georgianna when he left for France. He took full responsibility for that decision. And he challenged anyone to question him on it. If they dared.

As far as he was concerned, Georgianna had suffered enough. For her *naïveté* in regard to love, for her youthful belief and trust in a man who had used her and then attempted to kill her. Damn it, as far as Rousseau was concerned, he had killed her.

As Zachary now wished to kill Rousseau.

His hands clenched on his thighs with the need he felt to encircle the other man's throat and squeeze until no more air could enter Rousseau's lungs. To make him suffer, as Georgianna had surely suffered. First, by her humiliation in the man's duplicity. Then by being shot and left for dead. Regaining consciousness days later, only to find she was blind and in terrible pain. And then the months spent in Paris after that, and still fearing for her life. The latter because of her loyalty to England. A loyalty Zachary had distrusted and mocked her for, again to the point of cruelty.

Zachary was heartily ashamed of his harsh behaviour towards Georgianna these past two days. For having disbelieved her. For taunting her. And for then having made love to her, as if she were no better than that whore she had earlier denied being.

He could only try to make amends for those wrongs and hope that Georgianna might one day be able to forgive him.

And Rousseau deserved to die for his treatment of her.

Zachary intended seeing that it happened. Before too many days had passed, if he had his way. And he would. Because, in his eyes, Rousseau was no more than a rabid dog in need of being put down. Not for his loyalty to Napoleon, but for using an innocent, such as Georgianna had once been, to achieve his ends. For attempting and believing he had killed her when she was of no further use to him.

None of which helped to ease the burden of what Zachary now had to reveal to Georgianna, before then watching the hatred and contempt that would burn in those beautiful violet-coloured eyes towards him.

He drew in a long, controlling breath. 'I am taking you to your brother at Malvern House.'

Georgianna sat forward with a start, her face paling beneath her black bonnet. 'You cannot.' Her eyes were wide in her distress. 'Zachary, how can you be so cruel as to humiliate me further, by having my own brother turn away from me? I told you the truth earlier. I showed you.'

'There will be no humiliation, Georgianna.' Zachary sat forward on his own seat to reach out and grasp both of her tiny gloved hands in his, knowing it was possibly the last time she would allow him such familiarity. 'There will be no humiliation for you, Georgianna, and your brother will not turn away from you,' he assured evenly, 'because there was no scandal.'

She stilled at the same time as she blinked rapidly to hold back the tears now glistening in her eyes. 'I do not understand,' she finally murmured huskily.

And Zachary had no wish to tell her when he knew it would result in those beautiful eyes hardening with hatred for him. But his behaviour towards Georgianna this past two days allowed for no mercy being given on his own behalf. He deserved no forgiveness from her, no mercy. For any of the things he had said and done to her.

He released her hands to sit back against his seat as he looked across at her between narrowed lids. 'The notification of the ending of our betrothal appeared in the newspapers only a week after it was announced.'

Guilt coloured her cheeks. 'I expected no other.'

'That announcement stated,' Zachary continued firmly, 'that Lady Georgianna Rose Lancaster had decided, after all, against marrying Zachary Richard Edward Black, the Duke of Hawksmere.'

'But that is not what happened!'

'It also stated that it was your intention to retire to

the Malvern country estate for the remainder of the Season,' Zachary completed determinedly.

Georgianna now looked at him with wide, disbelieving eyes.

'Your father died in a riding accident only a month later,' Zachary continued evenly, 'at which time it was decided between your brother Jeffrey and myself that he would announce that you both intended to remain secluded at Malvern Hall for your time of mourning.'

She swallowed. 'What are you saying?'

Zachary drew in a deep breath before answering softly. 'That there was no scandal. As is acceptable, you were the one to end our betrothal and since then it is believed you have been living quietly at Malvern Hall with your brother.'

'How can this be?' Georgianna gave a dazed shake of her head.

The duke moved restlessly. 'Your father, brother and I discussed it after it was discovered you had eloped with Duval, or Rousseau, as he was later discovered to be. It was your family's hope that you would be found and returned before—well, before any harm might be done to your reputation and without any but the close family, and myself, being the wiser for it.'

Georgianna's cheeks became even more flushed in acknowledgement of the harm to which Hawksmere referred. 'And you agreed with this decision?'

Hawksmere's mouth tightened. 'Yes.'

'Because such an announcement lessened your own humiliation?'

His mouth thinned. 'No doubt that was part of it,' he allowed drily. 'But I hope I also thought of you, and your family, in that decision. I am not a vindictive man, Georgianna,' he assured evenly as she now looked at him blankly. 'No matter the impression I may have given to the contrary these past two days,' he acknowledged heavily.

Georgianna did not believe Hawksmere's behaviour to have been particularly vindictive towards her. She knew that she had fully deserved his anger, for her having eloped with another man so soon after the announcement of their own betrothal, causing him embarrassment. As she also deserved the distrust Zachary felt in regard to her return, when he knew that the man she had eloped with was actually a spy for Napoleon.

But this? Having allowed her to continue to think, these past two days, that she was unforgiven by her father and a pariah to her brother, the only family she had left in the world, as well as ostracised in society, was another matter entirely.

She frowned. 'Does no one in society know of my elopement with André?'

Hawksmere shrugged. 'A few may have guessed at the truth of the matter, but none knows for certain.'

'Then I am not shamed? Or ostracised?'

'No.'

'And does my brother know I shall be returning to him today?'

'I sent him a note earlier informing him so and

have received confirmation back from him, yes,' Hawksmere added softly.

'And does he welcome me back, despite knowing of my past behaviour?'

'He holds Rousseau completely responsible for past events.'

'Then I may return to my brother, my home, into society, without fear of rejection?'

A nerve pulsed in the tightness of Hawksmere's jaw. 'Yes.'

'And you have known this since we met again yesterday, known how much it pains me to think of my father's disappointment in me, to be estranged from Jeffrey? And yet you have continued to let me believe...' Georgianna did not even take the time to consider her next action, merely reacted, eyes glittering angrily as she lifted her hand and stuck Hawksmere across one hard and arrogant cheek.

Zachary had seen the angry spark in Georgianna's eyes, had noted the lifting of her gloved hand and guessed her intent. He'd made no attempt to avoid the painful slap she administered to the side of his face. Knowing he deserved it. That he deserved so much more than a single slap.

So, yes, let Georgianna slap him. Again and again, if that was her wish. Zachary would neither protest nor attempt to stop her.

'You are truly despicable!' Georgianna now glared across the width of the carriage at him. 'A despicable, unprincipled bastard! Oh, yes, Hawksmere,' she declared scornfully as he raised surprised dark brows.

'I assure you, I heard far worse than that during my months of working in Helene Rousseau's tavern. And you—you deserve to hear every one of those words for the way in which you have deceived me.' She blinked back the tears as they now blurred her vision of the arrogantly superior face across from her own.

'Perhaps we should take them as having already been said?' Zachary excused himself gruffly.

She gave an impatient shake of her head, her hands clenched together. 'I have spent months in despair of ever being able to see or speak to my brother again. Of ever seeing my home again. Of knowing that all in English society shunned me. This past few days of believing I would never be able to visit my father's graveside and beg his forgiveness. A despair which you might have spared me, if you had a mind to do so. If you had a heart with which to do so. Which you so obviously do not,' she added coldly.

Zachary had no defence against Georgianna's accusations. He knew he was guilty of everything she now accused him of. Except perhaps the latter.

It was true he had offered for Lady Georgianna Lancaster ten months ago because he needed a wife and an heir before his thirty-fifth birthday. It was true also that he had been more annoyed than concerned at the inconvenience when she had eloped with another man. As he had no doubt also agreed with Malvern's solution to that problem, as a way of saving himself deeper humiliation, as much as he had Georgianna's reputation.

But he had not really known Georgianna at that

time. Had seen only that plump pigeon, whom he'd decided would make him a suitable and undemanding wife, and a mother for his heirs.

The Georgianna with whom he had spent so many hours these past two days was not only a beautiful woman, but one for whom he knew he had felt a grudging admiration even before she had revealed the extent of the scars she bore, as evidence of Rousseau's betrayal of her.

She was also a woman for whom Zachary felt desire every time he so much as looked at her.

Even now, with her looking across at him with such contempt, Zachary was aware that his body pulsed with that same desire beneath his pantaloons.

Perhaps not as proof that he did indeed possess a heart, but enough so that Zachary knew he felt regret for the wide chasm that now yawned between the two of them. Fuelled by the dislike and contempt Georgianna now felt towards him.

His expression was grim as he nodded abruptly. 'I deserve each and every one of your accusations.'

She eyed him scathingly. 'That was never in any doubt.'

'No.'

Georgianna frowned her frustration with the calmness of Hawksmere's acceptance of her anger. What she really wanted was for him to mock or taunt her, as he usually did, so that she might have the satisfaction of slapping him again.

At the same time she felt as if a heavy weight had been lifted from her shoulders. She could see her brother Jeffrey again. Could go to Malvern Hall and visit her father's graveside and offer him her apologies for her behaviour the previous year. Could return to Malvern House if she wished. Take part in the upcoming Season, too, if that was what she decided to do.

Not that she intended telling Hawksmere of any of the lightness and elation she felt; his contemptuous behaviour towards her this past two days did not deserve to be forgiven, or forgotten, so easily.

At the same time as Georgianna knew she could never forget his lovemaking of earlier this morning.

Having believed her to have been André's mistress for several weeks, at least, Georgianna might have expected Zachary to show contempt for her during their lovemaking. Instead he had been poetical in his appreciation of her body. Giving, even gentle, in his caresses, as he introduced her to a pleasure she had never imagined, let alone experienced.

But beneath all of that appreciation and gentleness Zachary had been keeping the secret that she was not in disgrace, after all, Georgianna reminded herself, impatient with the softening of her emotions towards him. Which surely must make him every inch that bastard she had just called him?

'Again, I owe you my heartfelt apologies, Georgianna.'

She looked sharply across at him, unsure what he was apologising for. For not telling her before now that she was not in disgrace in society? Or for the intimacies of this morning?

Zachary sighed heavily as Georgianna made no

response to his apology. 'Except, of course, I do not possess a heart,' he acknowledged evenly. 'In which case, I will instead offer you my sincerest apologies. For having wronged you and hurt you these past two days.'

Deliberately. And without remorse. Each word was like the lash of the whip across the flesh on his back.

Georgianna looked across at him uncertainly. 'And is that supposed to excuse your behaviour?'

'No,' Zachary answered heavily.

'To make you feel better, perhaps?' she added scornfully.

He gave a humourless smile. 'If it was, then I assure you it has failed miserably.'

She raised haughty brows. 'I trust you will understand when I say that I am glad of that?'

How could he have ever thought this young woman was just a plump and malleable pigeon to be taken to the altar, impregnated, and then left forgotten and languishing on one of his country estates?

Even without her terrible experiences of this past year, he very much doubted that Georgianna would ever have been that malleable wife he had deliberately sought, and expected. If he had taken the time and trouble to get to know her, then he would have realised she possessed far too much spirit, was too emotional, to have ever settled for just being his ignored duchess and the mother of his heirs.

A spirit that was now denied him for ever.

Georgianna, quite rightly, would never forgive him for having deceived her. For deliberately allowing her to think she was still in disgrace. For imprisoning her. For making love to her.

'I understand, and completely accept, the anger you feel towards me.' He nodded abruptly just as the carriage drew to a halt outside Malvern House. 'Would you like me to come in with you or would you prefer to reconcile with your brother alone?'

Georgianna felt extremely nervous now that they had actually arrived at Malvern House, the same house she had always lived in whilst in London. The house where her brother Jeffrey now awaited her.

Her brother would be nineteen now and already he had been the Earl of Malvern this past nine months. Without benefit of even his sister to support him, with only that guardian, an elderly friend of her father's, to guide and help him.

'Georgianna!'

She was given no more time for those regrets, or the insecurity of wondering if Jeffrey really would be pleased by her return, as the carriage door was flung open and her brother himself hurtled inside the carriage before pulling her into his arms.

Georgianna gave a sob as she clung to Jeffrey, totally overwhelmed by the eagerness of his greeting, and being with someone she loved and who obviously still loved her. It had been so long since anyone had held her so tenderly, so unconditionally. Hawksmere's lovemaking did not count when she knew his motive had been revenge for her past misdemeanours towards him.

Zachary felt the unaccustomed sting of tears in his

own eyes as he witnessed the emotional reunion between brother and sister. Jeffrey with his usual youthful enthusiasm, Georgianna crying with joy as she clung to the younger brother she obviously adored and had missed so much.

A reunion that Zachary could have allowed her much sooner than this, if he'd had a mind to do so.

Georgianna might never forgive him for that, but Zachary knew he would never forgive himself, either. Or for any of his behaviour towards her these past two days.

Behaviour for which he would happily have got down on his knees and begged for forgiveness if he had thought it would do any good!

He raised a hand to the cheek that still stung from where Georgianna had slapped him just minutes ago. A vehemently delivered slap he had fully deserved.

As he deserved the tearfully accusing gaze she now gave him over her brother's shoulder.

Jeffrey was the one to finally pull back as he continued to beam down at his sister. Their colouring was similar, both were dark haired and blue eyed. 'Perhaps we should take this reunion into the house? Join us, Hawksmere?' Jeffrey prompted lightly as he glanced at Zachary.

Zachary saw the flash of resentment in Georgianna's eyes as she remained tucked beneath her brother's protective arm. 'I think not, thank you, Jeffrey. I have several other things in need of my attention this morning.' He excused himself.

The younger man frowned his disappointment. 'I thought you might at least come in for a few minutes?'

Zachary bit back his impatience. 'As I said, I have other things to do today.'

'I am sure we have taken up enough of Hawksmere's valuable time, Jeffrey,' Georgianna exclaimed without so much as a glance in the duke's direction.

'I did not think.' Jeffrey grimaced. 'Of course you are busy. But perhaps you would like to join us for dinner later this evening?'

'Jeffrey.'

'That will not be possible, I am afraid,' Hawksmere drawled over Georgianna's alarmed protest.

She blinked. 'His Grace is leaving.'

'For my country estate later today.' Once again the duke rudely spoke over Georgianna, his eyes flashing a reproving silver as he gave her a pointed glare. Evidence that Jeffrey was not one of the people privileged to know of Hawksmere's activities for the Crown.

Georgianna felt the warmth of that rebuke in her cheeks as she lowered her gaze. 'Of course.'

'Thank you for returning my sister to me.' Jeffrey grinned his pleasure at the older man as he held Georgianna close to his side.

Hawksmere nodded abruptly. 'I believe you will find that it was Georgianna who has returned herself to us all.'

She looked up at him sharply, searching that hard and arrogant face for some indication of Hawksmere's signature sarcasm and finding none. Instead he gazed across at her guardedly, as if unwilling to reveal his emotions. Which, no doubt, he was.

She straightened before speaking formally. 'I trust you will have a safe journey, your Grace.'

'As do I,' he drawled before turning to Jeffrey. 'I will be in touch when I return to town, Malvern.'

'We shall look forward to it, shall we not, Georgianna?' Jeffrey beamed enthusiastically.

'Of course,' Georgianna concurred softly, purposefully not looking at Hawksmere, knowing she would see only mockery for her there, both of them aware that if they never saw each other again it would be too soon for either of them.

And yet...

Once Georgianna had alighted from the carriage and begun slowly walking up the steps to Malvern House beside her brother, she was aware of a feeling of discomfort as she heard Hawksmere's carriage move on down the cobbled street. Of feeling slightly bereft at not knowing when, or if, she would see ever him again.

She was angry with him, yes, as her slap to his cheek had demonstrated. But what if he did not return from France? She was not angry enough, did not dislike him enough, to never wish to see him again.

Georgianna came to a halt on the top step into Malvern House before turning to gaze after Hawksmere's carriage, catching a brief glimpse of his profile inside the carriage as it turned the corner before disappearing from view.

'Are you well, Georgianna?'

She turned to find Jeffrey looking down at her with concern, his eyes bluer than her violet-coloured ones, his boyish face having grown handsome, chiselled, this past year. No doubt from his added responsibilities as Earl of Malvern. 'I am very happy to be home, thank you, Jeffrey,' she assured him warmly.

'You looked a little wistful for a moment. We shall see Hawksmere again very soon, I am sure,' he added reassuringly. 'He has become a regular visitor at Malvern House these past few months.'

'He has?' Georgianna looked up at her brother curiously as the two of them entered the house together, warmly accepting the butler's beam of pleasure and kind words at seeing her returned to Malvern House.

Jeffrey nodded. 'I have found his guidance invaluable these past months.'

'But what of your guardian? I would have thought that he would have been your mentor rather than Hawksmere?' Georgianna handed Carter her bonnet and gloves.

'Perhaps we should discuss this in the library,' Jeffrey requested before turning to the butler. 'Lady Georgianna and I would like hot chocolate and crumpets beside the fire, if you please, Carter.'

Georgianna's heart melted at the reminder of the way in which she and Jeffrey had passed many an afternoon together in the schoolroom when they were younger. 'Oh, yes, please, Carter.' She squeezed her brother's arm as they walked companionably to the library. 'It is so good to be back with you, Jeffrey,' she spoke emotionally once they were seated opposite each other beside the warmth of the fire.

Her brother sat forward, looking quite the dandy in his blue superfine and high-collared shirt. 'And you will tell me all about your adventures in a minute,' he promised. 'But first, did Hawksmere not talk to you of our guardian?'

'He mentioned that you have one,' Georgianna answered carefully, not sure of exactly what Zachary had told Jeffrey in his note in regard to when, how and why she had returned to England.

'We both have one, the same one, until we are both one and twenty,' Jeffrey corrected ruefully.

Georgianna's eyes widened. 'But...' She had a guardian? After all she had been through this past ten months, the independence, the decisions she had been forced to make for herself, she now had to suffer having a guardian until her birthday in three months' time? 'Who is it?' she demanded as a terrible foreboding began to wash over her.

Jeffrey grinned. 'Hawksmere, of course.'

That was the very answer Georgianna had begun to suspect, and dread.

Chapter Ten

'Would you care to tell me exactly what we are still doing in Paris, Zachary, when our mission was to sound out public feeling here, in regard to Napoleon's imminent arrival in Paris, before returning to England with our report?'

Zachary did not so much as glance at his companion as he kept his narrowed gaze levelled upon the establishment across the street from where the two of them stood, dressed as middle-class citizens of Paris.

'Do you remember Bully Harrison from Eton?'

There was a slight pause. 'How could I forget him, when he took such pleasure in beating the younger boys at every opportunity?' Wolfingham confirmed impatiently, green eyes hard. 'I also remember you taking an even greater delight in giving him a beating of your own, as a warning for him to instantly cease those unpleasant activities. Which he did. But I do not see what Harrison has to do with us being here in Paris.'

'There is an even worse bully inside that establishment.' Zachary nodded in the direction of the Fleur de Lis tavern across the street. 'A monster who took delight in hurting a woman.'

'Ah.'

'Indeed,' Zachary confirmed grimly.

'A woman of your acquaintance?'

'Yes.'

'Is she—? Did he hurt her very badly?'

Zachary's jaw tensed. 'He lied to her. Seduced her. For his own selfish reasons. And, when she was of no further use to him, he shot her. Twice. Once in the chest and then in the head.'

'Assassin!' Wolfingham hissed.

Zachary nodded. 'Miraculously she did not die. But she now lives in daily fear of the monster discovering his failure. Of him seeking her out and completing the assassination.'

Wolfingham glanced across at the tavern. 'And he is in there now?'

'I saw him enter a short time ago, with half-a-dozen cohorts.' Zachary nodded.

'Knife or pistol?'

'I believe I told you that he shot her.'

'I enquired as to whether you intend to use knife or pistol?'

Zachary's brow cleared slightly as he turned to look appreciatively at one of his closest friends. 'I apologise for underestimating you, Wolfingham,' he drawled ruefully. 'And I shall use my pistol. I believe I should like him to know what it is like to stare down the barrel of a gun and know you are about to breathe your last,' he added with grim satisfaction as he thought of how Georgianna must have suffered the night Rousseau attempted to kill her. And he wasn't just thinking of her physical wounds, but the emotional ones he doubted would ever completely heal.

There was little enough he could do to make amends for the emotional wounds he had inflicted on her since, but dispatching Rousseau was certainly a start.

'I should warn you, though, I have reason to believe the man may recognise me,' Zachary warned, unconsciously touching the definitive scar upon his throat.

Wolfingham nodded. 'What would you like me to do in order to divert his cohorts?'

Zachary gave a hard grin. 'Succinct and to the point—I have always liked that about you.'

'A man who would treat a woman in such a despicable way does not deserve to live.'

A sentiment exactly matched by Zachary's feelings on the matter.

Georgianna paced restlessly up and down the yellow salon at Malvern House, totally unaware of the luxuriously appointed room she had so enjoyed choosing the décor and furnishings for just two short years ago.

Those two years might just as well have been twenty.

Because she was not that same person who had

once so painstakingly pored over swatches of materials for curtains and furnishings for weeks on end, voicing a complaint when the material on one of the chairs proved to be the merest shade darker than its twin.

It all seemed so unimportant now, so petty. As had the ordering of the new gowns Jeffrey had insisted upon, in preparation for their return to society, when it was discovered that all of last year's gowns were far too big for her now-slender figure.

A society with its rules and strictures upon behaviour and speech, which she had so long believed she wished to be part of again, but now found totally stifling.

As she did the fact that those calls and entertainments continued, as if Napoleon and his ever-increasing army were not even now marching doggedly and triumphantly towards Paris.

Indeed, the majority of the *ton* seemed far more interested in the fact that Lady Georgianna Lancaster was returned to town, inciting an avalanche of calls and invitations from those of the *ton* who had already returned in preparation for the full Season.

Polite calls and invitations, which had nevertheless possessed an underlying curiosity to know as to how she had spent the past year. Georgianna had answered all of those queries with the same reply Jeffrey had given at the time of her disappearance; she had spent her time quietly at Malvern Hall, initially following the breaking of her betrothal, and then in mourning for the death of their father.

As Hawksmere had said, some might suspect otherwise, but none dared question the word of either the Duke of Hawksmere or the new Earl of Malvern.

Hawksmere.

As might be expected, there had been neither sight nor sound of Zachary Black and Georgianna could only presume, having heard nothing to the contrary, that silence must mean he was still in France. Perhaps he was even now witnessing Napoleon's triumphant march towards Paris.

If not, then he would no doubt have made a point of calling upon his two wards before now.

Georgianna had far from forgiven Hawksmere for that deception!

As no doubt Hawksmere, in his turn, did not believe he had any need to explain himself to anyone, least of all the two young people who were now under his guardianship.

Georgianna could only wonder what on earth had possessed her father to choose such a man as guardian to his young son and daughter, most especially when that daughter had eloped in order to escape marriage to that same gentleman.

Which was perhaps answer enough as to why Hawksmere had been chosen. As he already knew of the scandal behind the breaking of their betrothal, making him their guardian had meant there would be no need for Georgianna's absence to be explained to a third party after her father's death.

Which did not make the unpleasant fact of being under the guardianship of Hawksmere, of all men, for another three months, any more acceptable to Georgianna.

Something she intended informing him of at the earliest opportunity.

In the meantime, Georgianna was returned to her family, to her home. She already had a whole new wardrobe of gowns, deliberately designed to hide the unsightly scar upon her chest, in which she could receive guests, as well as drive out in the family carriage in the afternoons. She and Jeffrey had also spent some time in deciding which social invitations they could or should accept, when their year of mourning was not quite at an end.

And it all seemed so pointless to Georgianna. So uninspiring. So unexciting after her months of freedom from those strictures.

Oh, she could not deny that they had been terrifying, uncertain months, too. Days and nights when she had feared for her very life. Which was perhaps one of the reasons she was so restless and bored by the tedium of her life now?

And the other reason?

Again that was down to Hawksmere.

Angry as she was with him—furious, in fact—Georgianna could not deny that everything seemed so much duller, flatter, without Hawksmere's arrogantly powerful presence.

Which was utterly ridiculous on her part, when she should be relishing that dullness after so many months spent in fear and torment.

A fear and torment that was not over and never

could be whilst the danger of André Rousseau lurked so ominously in the shadows of her life.

'Is it time for hot chocolate and crumpets beside the fire again?'

Georgianna turned with a smile as her brother quickly crossed the room to kiss her warmly upon the cheek.

'What makes you say that?'

Jeffrey looked down at her quizzically. 'You looked very forlorn and wistful when I entered the room.'

Forlorn and wistful?

Because of her thoughts of Hawksmere?

No, of course it had not been because of thoughts of Hawksmere; she had been thinking of André, not Zachary, when Jeffrey entered the salon. 'I believe I am still adjusting to being back in England and society,' she excused lightly.

'But you are pleased to be, surely?' he cajoled.

Barely a year separated them in age and Jeffrey had certainly matured exponentially during his months as the Earl of Malvern under Hawksmere's guidance. But still Georgianna felt so much older than her brother now, in her emotions as well as her interests.

Not that she could explain to Jeffrey without fear of revealing too much of her experiences over the past year.

They had necessarily talked of her elopement, her parting from André, her months of working, though she had not revealed exactly where she had worked, only that it was in a kitchen, to earn the money for her boat passage back to England. Not once during their conversations had Georgianna told Jeffrey the complete truth about the months she had spent in France. How could she, when that truth was so horrible, so demeaning, so frightening?

It was a truth which only Hawksmere knew for certain.

Such was her brother's obvious admiration and liking for the older man, and oblivious of their guardian's work for the Crown, Jeffrey had so far not questioned why she had chosen to go to Hawksmere, of all people, immediately upon returning to England. Nor had Georgianna chosen to enlighten her brother as to the exact day of her return, or that she had been kept a prisoner in Hawksmere's home for two days and nights.

She might be angry with Zachary, resentful even, but it served no purpose for her to confide in her brother, when he obviously admired Hawksmere so. The older man was to be his guardian for some time to come. Also, it could endanger the work Zachary even now carried out for the Crown.

'Of course.' She gave her brother a brightly reassuring smile. 'I am merely finding it strange, after so many months away.'

'In that case, a dinner party is exactly what is required.' Her brother moved to the fireplace to warm his hands, the darkness of his hair appearing blue-black in the firelight.

'A dinner party?' Georgianna's pulse jumped in nervousness, her heart leaping in her chest, as she joined Jeffrey beside the fire. 'But I thought tomorrow evening at Lady Colchester's musical soirée was to be our first appearance back into society?' Individual calls by members of society was one thing, as was riding in her carriage in the afternoons, but Georgianna was dreading having that society staring at her *en masse* and wondering if any of the rumours that so abounded about her were true.

'I should have said a dinner party *en famille*,' Jeffrey corrected cheerfully. 'Hawksmere has sent word he is returned from the country and wishes the two of us to join him at Hawksmere House for dinner this evening.'

Hawksmere?

Georgianna moved to sit down abruptly on the chair beside the fireplace, her knees feeling suddenly weak at the knowledge that Zachary was returned from France. And safely, too, if he was inviting the two of them to join him for dinner this evening.

'You have seen him?' she prompted huskily.

'He sent for me this afternoon.' Jeffrey nodded.

But not her, Georgianna realised. Because she would be his ward for only a matter of months more? Or because he had no wish to see her again? Including her in this evening's dinner invitation was, after all, what Jeffrey would have expected of their guardian.

'Hawksmere is hardly family, Jeffrey,' she remonstrated stiffly.

'As good as,' he dismissed unconcernedly, seeming completely unaware of Georgianna's reaction to the news of Hawksmere's invitation.

Georgianna had not realised until that moment how worried she had been about Zachary's safe return from France.

A concern she was starting to fear might be based on something other than the anger she bore towards him, for once again having omitted to tell her the full truth.

'It really was not necessary for you to include me in this dinner invitation, Hawksmere!'

Zachary found himself smiling for the first time in days as Georgianna attacked him with her acerbic tongue the moment she entered the blue salon of his home on her brother's arm, rather than offering the expected polite greeting.

'And how gratified you must be to know that there is only the matter of three months before you will be relieved of my guardianship,' he continued haughtily even as she sketched him a polite curtsy.

'Georgianna?' Jeffrey looked nonplussed by his sister's sharpness towards their guardian.

Zachary, on the other hand, found himself highly entertained. 'The history between your sister and me necessarily means that we are still working on acquiring an acceptable politeness between the two of us, Jeffrey,' he excused to the younger man, even as he stepped forward to take Georgianna's gloved hand in his, his own gaze meeting her glittering violet one as he raised that hand to his lips. 'You are looking exceptionally lovely this evening, Georgianna,' he drawled as he straightened before slowly relinquishing her hand.

She did indeed look very beautiful, the darkness of her hair fashionably styled so as to conceal the scar at her temple. Her fashionable gown was the same violet colour as her eyes, with a swathe of lace artfully fashioned across the top of her bosom, so concealing the scar Zachary knew she also bore there.

'I am sure there is no need for false politeness between the two of us in the privacy of your home, Hawksmere,' she dismissed offhandedly as she moved away, at the same time reminding Zachary, at least, that he had not felt the need for this same politeness the last time she had been in his home. 'Jeffrey cannot help but be aware of the reason for our strained relationship.'

Zachary raised dark brows. 'I had hoped we had come to a different understanding of each other since your return?'

Those violet coloured eyes flashed darkly. 'Only in as much as I believe that we have come to an acceptance of our hearty dislike of each other.'

'Georgianna!'

'Do not be alarmed, Jeffrey.' Once again Zachary soothed his younger ward's shock at his sister's rudeness. 'Georgianna and I understand each other perfectly. Do we not, Georgianna?' The hardness of his tone was a warning for her to temper her anger and dislike of him. Her behaviour was not only alarming her brother, but also implied that they knew each other far better than their previously known acquaintance might imply.

Which they obviously did.

Zachary had thought of Georgianna often these past two weeks, whilst he was away in France. More often than he might have wished, if truth be known, and not just because of his dealings with Rousseau.

Georgianna had only been a prisoner in his home for a matter of thirty-six hours, but they had been intensely intimate hours. Hours, when Zachary came to know Georgianna rather better than he had ever known any woman. Hours, when he had come to admire her, for her spirit and determination. Hours, when he had come to like, even appreciate, her outspokenness and the way that she refused to be cowed by anything he did or said to her. Hours, when he had come to desire her more than any woman of his acquaintance.

As he desired her still, Zachary acknowledged as he studied her through narrowed lids.

Georgianna appeared less strained than she had been two weeks ago, the lines smoothed from her forehead and beside her eyes and mouth, and there was a becoming colour in the smoothness of her cheeks and full, pouting lips. But she still looked too slender in that violet-coloured gown. Perhaps more so, her unadorned neck and throat appearing delicately vulnerable, as did the slenderness of her arms.

And Zachary's desire to possess all that loveliness was almost painful.

Damn it, it was painful.

His body throbbed with desire for her even more after their two weeks apart.

'Yes, Hawksmere, I believe we do indeed understand each other. Perfectly.' She lifted her chin in challenge.

Zachary very much doubted that Georgianna's understanding of that statement was the same as his own. Because, without the strictures Jeffrey's presence necessarily put on his behaviour, Zachary very much doubted he would be able to control the desire he now felt to make love to Georgianna again.

And not just physically. He ached to possess all of her. Her spirit. Determination. Her outspokenness. Along with her often sarcastic sense of humour, the latter more often than not at his own expense.

Georgianna had shown him this evening, with just a few brief words, that she disliked him as much now as she ever had.

Which was no doubt a fitting punishment for his having proposed marriage to her so shabbily the previous year. And Zachary knew he had again treated her abominably when she returned from France so unexpectedly.

Was it any wonder that she now disliked him so intensely?

Or that he, having thought about her so much, remembering over and over again making love to her, touching her, kissing her, bringing her to completion, desired her more now than he had two weeks ago?

'Are you ill, Hawksmere?' she now taunted mockingly. 'You have gone exceedingly quiet for someone who I believed always had an answer for everything.'

'I say, Georgianna...' cautioned Jeffrey.

Zachary held his hand up to prevent Jeffrey from continuing to chastise his sister on his behalf. 'I do not believe I as yet have the answer to you, dearest Georgianna,' he assured softly.

Georgianna felt the burn of colour in her cheeks, knowing she had brought Hawksmere's taunt upon herself by her challenging and rude behaviour. Except she could not seem to behave in any other way when in his company, her hackles rising, defences instantly up, as she verbally attacked him. Before she was attacked herself?

Maybe so, but she certainly did not appreciate his sarcasm in addressing her as 'dearest Georgianna', when they both knew she was here on sufferance only. Because it would have appeared odd to Jeffrey if his sister had not been included in the dinner invitation from their guardian. A guardianship, in regard to herself, that Georgianna had no doubt Zachary found tiresome, to say the least.

'It is a woman's prerogative to remain something of a mystery to a gentleman, is it not?' she dismissed airily, very aware that this man knew her far better than any other, physically as well as emotionally.

Challenging Zachary the moment the two of them met again had been Georgianna's only way of dealing with those memories of their previous intimacy, her only defence against the rush of emotions and the memories, which had threatened to overwhelm her the moment she looked at him. Of him kissing her, caressing her, pleasuring her, with those sculptured lips and large, and wholly seductive, hands!

There was no denying that Zachary looked very handsome this evening, in his black evening clothes and snowy white linen. His hair had grown longer this past two weeks and now curled silkily about his ears and nape. He appeared slightly thinner in the face, too, no doubt from the weeks he had spent in the turmoil of France, bringing into stark relief his handsome features.

Just to look at him caused Georgianna's heart to beat faster and the palms of her hands to dampen inside her lace gloves.

'So it is,' he drawled in answer to her comment as Hinds appeared discreetly in the doorway. 'Shall we go into dinner now?' He offered Georgianna his arm.

Georgianna hesitated at the offered intimacy, having no desire to touch Zachary, to be made so totally aware of him, and of those memories that had haunted, and so bedevilled, her these past two weeks.

Nevertheless, she forced herself to show no emotion as she placed her gloved hand upon his arm and walked beside him to the dining room.

The same intimate dining room in which she and Zachary had dined alone together two weeks ago.

Chapter Eleven

'I'm sure you will have received many visitors and invitations now that you are returned to society?'

'Hawksmere, I give you permission to cease all attempts at this strained politeness between the two of us for the time my brother is out of the room,' Georgianna dismissed impatiently, Jeffrey having excused himself on a call of nature just a few short minutes ago.

Zachary smiled at her customary straightforwardness. Georgianna was right: their efforts at maintaining that imposed social politeness, because of Jeffrey's presence, had become more and more difficult as dinner progressed, to the point that even the boyishly enthusiastic Jeffrey had seemed to become uncomfortable in their company.

'I am far more interested in knowing how things progress in France than in the two of us being socially polite to each other,' Georgianna prompted interestedly as she sat forward eagerly.

Zachary gave a guarded shrug. 'As you say, they progress. At least, Napoleon does,' he added grimly.

She gave a soft gasp. 'And do you believe he will be successful in his endeavour?'

Zachary did not bother in so much as attempting to dismiss Georgianna's concerns. She was far too intelligent to be fobbed off. Besides which, the months she had spent in France had given her an insight into the turmoil which had once again beset that country. 'I do not believe I am breaking any confidences by revealing that his army grows bigger by the day and that he will soon enter Paris itself.'

'And the king?'

'I believe Louis is preparing to flee.'

Georgianna's cheeks grew pale. 'Then there will most certainly be another war.'

'Undoubtedly.'

She flicked him a glance beneath long silky dark lashes. 'You will be a part of that war?'

'Most certainly.' Zachary gave her a mocking grin. 'Just think, Georgianna, I might even manage to get myself killed, and in doing so relieve you of the burden of suffering both my guardianship as well as my company.'

Georgianna frowned across at him darkly. 'You are being unfair by inferring that I have ever wished you dead, Hawksmere.'

'Just consigned to Hades.'

'Well, yes, there is that.' A beguiling dimple appeared in her cheek as she smiled genuinely for what seemed to be the first time this evening. 'A little singeing by those hellish fires, at the very least, might succeed in stripping you of some of your irritating arrogance.'

Zachary found himself chuckling. 'I do believe I have missed both you and your insults, Georgianna.'

She raised dark brows. 'Somehow I doubt that very much!'

Then she would be wrong, Zachary acknowledged. Georgianna was a woman with whom he now spoke almost as freely, and on similar subjects, as he did his closest male friends. Something he had not believed possible with any woman in society.

It had long been his experience that the women of society preferred not to know of the more unpleasant facts of life, their main topics of conversation seeming to be fashions, gossip, and the managing of their household and family. Georgianna's experiences this past year had taken her far beyond being interested in such trivialities.

Reminding Zachary only too forcibly that there was something he needed, rather than wished, to discuss with her in private.

'You will not allow Jeffrey to fight?' Georgianna looked at him anxiously now.

Zachary frowned. 'He is a man grown, Georgianna.'

'And you are his guardian.' Her eyes glittered a deep, emotional violet.

'And, no doubt, you will never forgive me if something should happen to him.' It was a statement rather than a question.

'And I doubt my forgiveness is of the least interest, or importance, to you.'

'You might be surprised,' Zachary murmured softly before sighing as Georgianna continued to look at him expectantly. 'I make no promises, but I will see what can be done to prevent Jeffrey from rushing headlong into the coming war,' he added grimly.

She sighed. 'He admires you tremendously, you know.'

'Unlike his sister,' Zachary drawled drily.

She gave him a brief glance. 'It is not a question of not admiring you, Hawksmere. Indeed, I admire your endeavours on behalf of the Crown enormously.'

'That is something, I suppose,' he drawled.

'The rest of your personality leaves a lot to be desired, of course,' she added caustically, 'but one cannot have everything.'

'As usual, the sword thrust in the velvet glove.'

Georgianna eyed him mockingly. 'At least I am consistent.'

'Oh, you are most certainly that, Georgianna,' Zachary allowed before sobering. 'Is it convenient for you to come here tomorrow afternoon?'

'Why?' She eyed him warily now.

He grimaced. 'I would prefer to discuss that with you tomorrow.'

And Georgianna would prefer to know now what that discussion was to be about.

Unfortunately, Jeffrey chose that moment to return to the dining room, so putting an end to their own conversation as they all began to talk instead of the invitations they had accepted for the coming season.

'Thank you, Hinds.' Georgianna smiled politely at the butler as he showed her into the blue salon of Hawksmere House the following afternoon.

After she had spent the night, and all of this morning, fretting and worrying as to what it was Hawksmere could possibly wish to discuss with her today in private.

Hawksmere himself had his back turned towards her as he stood in front of one of the large bay windows, looking out of into the garden beyond. He turned the moment the door closed as evidence of his butler's departure.

'I did not think, when I asked you to come here.' He frowned darkly. 'You do at least have a maid with you, I hope?'

Georgianna nodded. 'She is waiting out in the hallway.'

'Would you care for refreshment?' the duke offered politely. 'Tea, perhaps?'

She eyed him scathingly. 'The only time I have been in this house, apart from that surreal dinner with Jeffrey yesterday evening, was as your prisoner, so, no, I do not require the nicety of tea, thank you, Hawksmere.'

'The time for social politeness between the two of us really is over then, hmm?' he guessed drily.

'I am not sure it ever began.'

Once again Zachary found himself chuckling at

Georgianna's honesty. 'Let us at least sit down,' he invited ruefully.

'You consider I might feel a need to do so, once you have spoken with me?' she murmured concernedly as she moved to perch demurely on the edge of one of the armchairs.

Zachary had debated with himself long and hard as to what he should tell Georgianna about Rousseau. And still he had no real answer, only knew that she needed to know that the other man no longer posed a threat, to her liberty or her life.

She looked so lovely today, dressed in a gown of pale silver, the darkness of her curls peeping out from beneath the matching bonnet, her face youthfully flushed by the freshness of the breeze outside, that Zachary baulked at even introducing the subject of her previous lover.

Her previous lover?

Well, yes, because the intimacies the two of them had shared two weeks ago meant that Zachary had certainly been Georgianna's most recent lover.

And now that he was alone with her once again, he found that the last thing he wished to do was talk of Rousseau.

'Have you thought of me at all this past two weeks, Georgianna?' he found himself prompting huskily.

She blinked at the unexpectedness of his question. 'Politely or impolitely?'

'Oh, impolitely, I am sure,' he allowed with another laugh.

'Then, yes, I do believe I have thought about you. Often,' she added pointedly.

Zachary smiled ruefully. 'And were all these impolite thoughts unpleasant ones?'

Georgianna was uncertain where Zachary was going with this line of questioning. They were two people who had once been betrothed to each other and now found themselves thrust into a situation not of their choosing. She very much doubted that Zachary had wished to become her guardian, any more than she now wished him to be. And that was without the awkwardness of the intimacies which had taken place between the two of them two weeks ago. That certainly made for a very strained relationship between the two of them.

To a degree that Georgianna had found herself wondering many times since how such a thing could ever have happened between two people who could not even claim a liking for each other?

And then she remembered the touch of Zachary's hands upon her, his lips, his tongue, and she knew exactly how such a thing had occurred between them. They were a man and a woman, who had been forced into a situation of close proximity. Factor in Zachary's feelings of anger towards her for past wrongs, then making love to her, ensuring that she enjoyed having him make love to her, and those intimacies had become inevitable.

Her own response to them she found harder to explain.

'Unpleasant enough,' she answered him sharply as she stood up restlessly. 'Now...?'

'I thought of you, too, whilst I was away, Georgianna.'

She stilled, once again eyeing him warily. 'Oh, yes?'

Zachary nodded, his expression intense. 'They were not unpleasant thoughts at all.'

Georgianna's heart began to beat loudly in her chest, her cheeks suddenly warm. 'You surprise me.'

'Do I?' He crossed the room silently until he stood only inches away, looking down at her. 'Does it really surprise you that I remember our time together here so vividly and so pleasantly, Georgianna?' he repeated huskily.

It did, yes. Hawksmere had not earned his reputation, as one of the five Dangerous Dukes, solely on his war record. No, his exploits in the bedchamber were also lauded by the ladies of England and much envied by the gentlemen. Georgianna did not imagine that someone as inexperienced as herself would have been in the least memorable amongst the dozens of beauties who were reputed to have shared a bed with Hawksmere.

As she had done. However briefly.

Her legs trembled slightly, hands clasped tightly together, as she looked up at him. 'It would surprise me very much,' she answered stiltedly.

'And yet?'

'I really would rather not talk about that particular subject, Hawksmere.' She had meant the words to come out as a set-down, but instead they sounded wistful and yearning.

Yearning?

Could it be that she secretly wanted there to be a repeat of the events, the intimacies, they had shared that morning in the bedchamber above them?

That would be madness on her part.

Georgianna's thoughts were broken off abruptly, indeed, her mind went a complete blank, as Zachary took her in his arms and claimed her lips firmly with his own.

The passion and desire were instantaneous, as Zachary's arms tightened about her even as his mouth devoured hers hungrily. It was all that Georgianna could do to remain on her feet, by clutching tightly to the tops of his muscled arms as she returned the heat of those kisses.

Zachary broke the kiss to graze his lips against the softness of Georgianna's cheek. 'I have thought this past two weeks—' he kissed her earlobe '—of doing this again.' He tasted the delicate column of her neck. 'Constantly.' His tongue sought out the hollows at the base of her throat, the creamy softness of the tops of her breasts through the silver lace. 'And none of those thoughts matched up to this reality,' he acknowledged gruffly, his body throbbing and achingly engorged. 'God, how I want you, Georgianna!'

She gasped. 'Zachary, we cannot. We must not.'

'I must,' he rasped fiercely as he lifted her up in his arms and carried her over to the chaise. He lay her down on its softness and sat down beside her, his gaze holding hers as he untied her bonnet before removing it completely.

'You have the most beautiful hair, Georgianna, so soft and silky.' He removed the pins as he spoke, before gazing down at her appreciatively as he loosened those curls about her shoulders.

'Zachary,'

'And your skin is like the finest ivory.' His gaze followed the path of his hand as it trailed down the column of her throat to the swell of her breasts. 'So pale and so soft to the touch.' He pushed the lace aside to reveal the scar between her breasts. A scar Zachary did not find any more repellent than she appeared to find the one upon his own throat. No, he considered this scar to be Georgianna's own, very private, war wound.

A sign, a remembrance, of the battle she had fought, and won, and which now only he and she had knowledge of.

'You can have no idea how much I have thought of making love to you again, Georgianna,' he groaned achingly.

Georgianna thought, from the intensity of his kisses and the fire now gleaming, burning, in the silver depths of his eyes as he slowly lowered his head, that she might hazard a guess.

And the thought that this man, that Zachary, wanted her so deeply he had thought of her even whilst he was away in the turmoil of France, filled her with an elation, a happiness Georgianna had not even known she secretly longed for.

She gasped as she felt the warmth of his lips against the scar on her chest. 'Zachary, don't.'

'Let me, Georgianna.' He breathed hotly against her even as his lips continued to kiss every inch of that scarred flesh.

'It is unsightly.' It took every effort of will Georgianna possessed to stop herself from pulling that lace back over the disfiguring scar on her chest, her jaw tight, her hands clenched at her sides.

'No more so than my own scar. Does that repulse you?'

'How could it, when it is evidence of your bravery?' she assured unhesitatingly.

He looked up at her darkly. 'As your own scar is a part of the brave and beautiful woman that you are. One who has suffered and yet survived.'

'I barely survived, Zachary,' she reminded weakly.

'And you are all the braver and stronger for it.'

Was she braver and stronger? Stronger, certainly, but she did not think herself braver. She still suffered nightmares in her bed at night. Dreamt constantly of that night in the woods. The pain, both emotional and physical, that she had suffered. The terror of waking up blind and in so much pain. The months afterwards when she had continued to fear for her life.

Of still suffering from that same fear.

Georgianna's limbs turned to water, all other thoughts fleeing her mind, her hands moving up to entwine her fingers in the darkness of Zachary's hair as he unfastened the buttons at the front of her gown and she felt the warmth of his lips against the bare swell of her breast.

She cried out achingly as his lips parted and he took the aroused and aching tip of that breast into the heat of his mouth, before suckling, gently at first, and then more deeply, hungrily. She arched up into him, instinctively seeking, wanting more, receiving more as Zachary's hand cupped beneath her other breast and he began to roll and squeeze the second nipple to the same arousing rhythm.

The sensations were overwhelming. An all-consuming heat and a glorious pleasure that radiated out from her breasts and coursed through the rest of her body, her nipples both hard and aching, the folds between her thighs swelling and moistening, the muscles deep inside her contracting and squeezing hungrily.

And it was a selfish need.

'Zachary?' She breathed weakly as she felt his hand trailing along her calf, pushing up her gown to above her knees and then higher still, until she felt the warm brush of air against those heated and swollen folds between her thighs.

'Allow me to pleasure you again, Georgianna,' he groaned, his breath a hot caress against the dampness of her nipple. 'Grant me that, at least.'

'But what of your own pleasure?' She knew very little about men, but she knew enough to know that Zachary's erection was both hard and demanding as it pressed, pulsed, against her hip.

'I am happy in the knowledge that I please you, Georgianna.'

'No.'

'I am not pleasing you?' Zachary pulled back slightly, his expression one of concern. 'Did I hurt you? Was I too rough with you just now?'

Delicate colour warmed her cheeks. 'I did not say that.'

'Then what?'

'Zachary...' Her gaze could no longer meet his, aware as she was of the fact that the top of her gown still gaped open, revealing the fullness of her breasts. The bare fullness of her breasts. 'Pleasure is surely to be given as well as received?'

'Yes.'

Georgianna moistened stiff lips. 'Then of course I should like to give you pleasure, too. If you will teach me, show me, what pleases you,' she added uncomfortably, knowing that she was far less experienced, make that lacking in experience at all, than all those other women Zachary was reputed to have made love with.

Zachary looked down at her searchingly. It had been his experience in the past that there was no *of course* about it, when it came to a man's pleasure during lovemaking. Whores were one thing and would do what they were asked for with the giving of coin. Wives, he had heard, preferred the act to be without embellishment and over with as quickly as was possible for the begetting of an heir. Other women in society, those married women who took a lover once the heir and spare had been provided, usually considered it enough that they were giving carte blanche with their body and, as such, had no interest in what she might do to please the man in her bed.

Obviously Georgianna was different from all those other women, being neither whore, nor wife, nor a married woman in society looking for a lover. As he could only assume she also meant she wanted him to show her, to teach her, what best pleased him in particular, rather than…

No, he refused to think of Georgianna's relationship with Rousseau now. He would not allow anything or anyone else to intrude upon their stolen time together. 'Are you sure you wish to pleasure me, Georgianna?' he prompted huskily.

She flickered a glance up at him before looking down again.

'It seems only fair I should do so, after—after you gave to me so unselfishly when—when we were last together.' The colour flooded her cheeks once again.

'That did not answer my question.'

Because Georgianna had no idea how to answer his question! She knew nothing of lovemaking, be it man or woman. She only knew, from these times with Zachary, that she could not be a selfish lover, that she wished to please Zachary as he had pleased her. As her own achingly aroused body said she now must.

'What would you be willing to do to give me pleasure, Georgianna?' he prompted huskily at her silence.

'Whatever you wished me to do.'

'Anything?'

She swallowed at the intensity of his silver gaze fixed unblinkingly on her blushing face. 'I believe so, yes.'

He smiled ruefully. 'Words are easily spoken, Georgianna.'

'Then I shall answer in deeds rather than words.' She sat up before sliding down to the base of the chaise to swing her feet on to the floor, before standing up and turning to face Zachary.

His eyes widened in surprise as she put her hands on his shoulders and pushed him down on to his back on the chaise before sitting beside him; obviously Hawksmere was not a man used to a woman taking charge in the bedchamber. Or in this case, the blue salon of his London home.

Georgianna was not a woman used to taking charge in lovemaking, either, but in this case it seemed completely desirable.

Besides, she had not spent all of her time in the kitchen, or the storeroom, at Helene Rousseau's tavern. She had occasionally ventured out to help serve behind the bar if they were especially busy; some of the surprising acts she had witnessed between the male and female customers when she did so had made her blush to the roots of her hair. There had been one act in particular that the gentlemen had seemed to enjoy very much.

If Georgianna only had the courage to now put into practise all that she had witnessed.

'I believe I should like to kiss you as you once kissed me.' She licked her lips in anticipation.

'Georgianna?'

She glanced up enquiringly from where she had already unfastened the buttons on Zachary's pantaloons and was now in the process of untying his drawers. The bulge beneath the linen, stretching and tightening that material, was making that task more difficult than it ought to be and was certainly causing a lack of sexual prowess on her part.

'What are you doing?' He looked pained as she at last managed to unfasten his drawers and reached inside to withdraw the pulsing and throbbing hard length beneath.

Georgianna's fingers stilled as she looked down at him uncertainly. 'You do not like it?'

'Oh, I most assuredly do like it, Georgianna!' he breathed shakily. 'I am just— Are you sure you wish— Do you know what you are doing?'

Colour burned her cheeks. 'I am sure I shall not be as experienced as some of your other ladies, but…'

'That is not at all what I meant,' he grated from between gritted teeth, his fingers having curled about the slenderness of her wrists to halt her movements. 'And I have said there will be no talk between the two of us of any others. I merely wanted to know if you are sure this is what you want. What you would enjoy.'

She glanced down at the thick length of his arousal as she slowly curled her fingers about it, the skin feeling surprisingly soft as velvet.

Georgianna swiped her tongue over her lips. 'It

most certainly appears to be what a certain part of you wants,' she murmured with satisfaction at Zachary's obvious response to her touch.

Zachary could not deny that. Had no desire to deny it. Indeed, just seconds ago he had feared he might spill at the first touch of the softness of Georgianna's fingers closing about him.

He had managed to hold, thank goodness, but he could not deny that his instinct was still to thrust into those encircling fingers, to bid her grip him tighter, stroke him faster, harder, as they worked together towards his release.

'I merely want you to be sure—' Zachary broke off with a strangled groan of pleasure as Georgianna lowered her head, her long hair falling in a soft caress against his thighs as she licked the silken tip. A long and rasping lick that caused him to arch up off the chaise.

'You like that.' She repeated that slow and agonisingly pleasurable rasp.

Liked it? Zachary had thought of this woman constantly this past two weeks, had imagined time and time again making love to her again, pleasuring her again. And in none of those imaginings had he thought of Georgianna pleasuring him, as she was now doing with each slow and delicious swipe of her tongue, the pleasure so intense he could already feel the start of his climax in the tightening, drawing up of his balls.

His gaze dropped to her bared breasts visible through the silky curtain of her hair as they jutted free of her unfastened gown as she bent over him. He wanted to hold them. To caress and squeeze them.

As he came and came!

'Come up here, Georgia,' he groaned urgently even as he lifted her up and over him so that she now had a leg either side of his thighs on the chaise. He pushed her dress up to her hips before lowering her down on top of him, not penetrating her, but arching into her in a slow rhythm as her moist and heated folds rubbed caressingly along the sensitised length of his erection.

'Zachary.'

'Do not worry I shall put you at risk, Georgianna,' he assured gruffly, eyes feeling hot and fevered. 'I merely wish to feel your heat upon me. Oh, that feels so damned good!' The hardness of his length moved easily against the slickness of her juices. 'So, so good!' He reached up to cup and squeeze her breasts, to caress and flick his fingernails against those jutting and sensitive nipples.

Georgianna clutched on to Zachary's chest for support, her head feeling dizzy with her own pleasure as Zachary continued to arch and thrust beneath her, even as he caressed and pinched her engorged and sensitive nipples to the exact same rhythm as the hard length of his erection rubbed against her folds and that sensitive nubbin above.

'Harder, Georgia. Faster. Harder again,' he urged, his eyes glittering, a flush to the hardness of his cheeks. 'Come with me, Georgia. Now!' he urged fiercely, sculptured lips parted as his hips surged up in the most powerful thrust of all.

Georgianna had no time to think about what he meant by that as her own pleasure ripped through and over her as the heated jets of Zachary's release pounded against her own sensitive nubbin, prolonging that pleasure until she screamed his name as he now hoarsely shouted hers.

Chapter Twelve

'Georgia?' she questioned Zachary as she lay on the chaise in his arms in the aftermath of their love-making. She felt physically sated and still inwardly moved at the way in which Zachary had kissed that unsightly scar upon her chest.

'You do not like it?' He played absently with the long strands of her loosened ebony hair as he turned to look at her.

No one had ever shortened her name in quite that way before now. Jeffrey often called her Georgie when they were alone together, in remembrance of their time together in the nursery. Her father, when he was alive, had occasionally addressed her affectionately as Anna, which had been her mother's name. But she could not recall her name ever being shortened to Georgia before now, no.

Before Zachary.

And she did like it. Coming from this man, she

found she liked that familiarity. A lot. That she liked, even loved, Zachary a lot, too.

She had no idea when the liking, the admiration, for the strong and determined man that he was, had happened, let alone whether or not she loved all of him. Or how it could possibly have happened, if that was the case.

Zachary had more or less kidnapped her, then kept her a prisoner in his home.

He had ridiculed and insulted her.

And then he had made love to her.

Which was when the liking had begun, Georgianna now realised.

Because when Zachary made love to her he forgot to insult and ridicule her. To dislike her. Most of all, he was a generous and fulfilling lover. Oh, that first time might have begun as a punishment for her, for daring to elope with another man when she was betrothed to him. But Zachary's generosity of nature, his own physical enjoyment of her, had quickly overcome that emotion.

And today, despite knowing of that disfiguring scar, he truly had made love to her, had kissed and caressed that scar as if it were something to admire rather than be disgusted by.

As Georgianna had made love to him?

She shied away from so much as thinking of that emotion in connection to Zachary Black, the Duke of Hawksmere—the very same man whom she had once shied away from marrying—knowing that to love him would lead to even more heartbreak than had her ill-fated and humiliating elopement with André Rousseau.

'I do not dislike it,' she answered Zachary non-committally, only to look up at him quizzically as he began to chuckle softly. 'What is it?'

'I laugh because, as usual, your thoughts and emotions remain a mystery to me, Georgia.' He gazed down at her indulgently.

She frowned her puzzlement. 'I do not mean them to be.'

'Any more than I believe just now to have been my finest hour.' He had sobered slightly, a teasing smile now curving those sculptured lips.

'I do not understand?' Everything had seemed more than satisfactory to Georgianna. Very much so. 'Did I do something wrong?' she prompted anxiously.

'Lord, no.' He groaned his reassurance. 'If you had done anything more right, then I believe I might now be lying here dead from a heart attack.'

She blushed at his effusive praise for her lovemaking. 'Then I still do not understand.'

Zachary could see that she really had no idea what he was talking about. Had Rousseau been such a uninterested and unsatisfactory lover that even Zachary's hasty lovemaking just now was preferable? Hasty, because his thoughts of Georgianna these past two weeks had caused him to hope, to anticipate, the worshipping of every inch of her delectable and responsive body. To kiss and caress her. To give her pleasure again and again.

Instead Georgianna had taken control of the situation, of him, and made love to him in a way that had surpassed all and any of his fantasies of being with her again.

He grimaced. 'We might have expected our love-making to last for longer than a few minutes,' he explained gruffly. 'I had expected my own control to last for longer than a few minutes,' he added ruefully. 'I wanted it to be enjoyable for you, too.'

'How could you ever imagine it was not enjoyable for me, too, when I cried out my pleasure?' Her cheeks blushed a becoming rose.

'Because I know it could have been better.' He caressed that blush upon her cheeks. 'I could have been better. Instead, I was as out of control as a callow youth being touched by a woman for the first time.' Indeed, he had been lost the moment he had felt the soft fullness of Georgianna's lips upon him, and the soft rasp of her tongue as she licked and tasted him; at that moment he'd had no more control than the night he had lost his virginity fifteen years ago.

'What was your finest hour?' Georgianna now prompted almost warily.

Zachary knew she was questioning him about his previous physical experiences. Unnecessarily, as it happened, because enjoyable as those past encounters might have been, none of them had affected him in the way that making love to and with Georgianna did. And that was without his having as yet fully made love to her, because he had yet to bury himself in the heat and lushness of her.

Even this, their closeness now as they cuddled in

each other's arms in the aftermath of that lovemaking, was an unusual occurrence for Zachary. Usually he could not vacate a woman's bed quickly enough once the deed was done.

This closeness with Georgianna was one he cherished rather than wished to avoid.

At the same time he knew that he must now put an end to that closeness. That he had yet to tell Georgianna of his encounter with Rousseau in Paris.

And he had no idea how she would react, what she would say, once she knew her previous lover was now dead.

Admittedly, Rousseau had treated her abominably, had seduced her, deceived her, betrayed her, before believing he had killed her.

But love, the emotions of a woman's heart, were not things Zachary was familiar with, either. Despite all that Rousseau had done to her, Georgianna might still feel some vestige of that emotion for the other man. Knowing that Zachary had been instrumental in his demise might shatter this unique, and highly enjoyable, time between the two of them.

Did he want to risk that, put an end to this time of harmony between the two of them, for the sake of honesty?

No.

But if he chose not to, then how could he ever reassure Georgianna that she no longer had anything to fear from Rousseau? Or expect Georgianna's forgiveness, when she eventually learnt, as she surely must, that he had kept this information from her and for such selfish reasons?

No, he could not keep Rousseau's death to himself. He knew he must share that news with Georgianna.

Even at the risk of bringing an end to the fragile intimacy that now existed between the two of them.

Reluctantly he pulled his arms from around her, removing his handkerchief from his pocket and gently mopping up the worst of the evidence of their love-making, before standing up to turn away and refasten his clothing. He ran agitated hands through the tousled length of his hair as he contemplated how to begin this next conversation.

'Zachary?' Georgianna eyed him uncertainly as she slowly sat up, continuing to look at him even as she absently refastened the buttons on the front of her gown. Her hair was beyond repair at this moment, the pins scattered about the floor from when Zachary had released it earlier.

The lover of just moments ago was gone. Zachary's expression was guarded when he turned back to face her and flatly announced. 'Georgianna, there is no other way for me to tell you this. My dear, Rousseau is dead.'

She felt the colour leach from her cheeks even as she swayed slightly where she sat, unable to believe, to process the enormity of what Zachary was saying to her.

André was dead?

How was such a thing even possible?

André was still a young man, aged only seven and twenty, and in the best of health when she had last seen him just weeks ago, so his death could not possibly have been through natural causes.

Her gaze sharpened on Zachary, his own eyes, as he met her horrified gaze, a pale and glittering silver in his harshly forbidding face. 'You killed him.' It was not a question, but a statement.

Zachary's expression was grim. 'Unfortunately I did not have that particular honour.'

'But you were responsible for ordering his death?' She could see the answer to that accusation in the tightening of Zachary's jaw and the arrogant challenge now in those eyes, as he looked down at her through narrowed lids.

Zachary had instructed André should be killed.

The question was, why had he done so?

Because the other man had been shown to be Napoleon's spy and in part responsible for the Corsican's escape from Elba?

Or because of a reason more personal to Zachary, in that the other man had taken something of his, had taken Georgianna, when he eloped with her?

She somehow doubted very much it had anything to do with the other man hurting and having attempted to kill Georgianna after they had arrived in France.

The first of those reasons, at least, would be honourable. To have someone killed out of a sense of personal vengeance would not.

She looked up at Zachary searchingly, but could read nothing from the harshness of his expression, could only see the challenge in the set of his shoulders beneath his superfine and his stance: legs slightly parted as he stood on booted feet, his hands clasped together behind the broadness of his back.

Leaving Georgianna in absolutely no doubt that whatever his reason for having André dispatched, Zachary did not feel a moment's remorse over it.

And nor should Georgianna.

But, no matter how cruel and deceitful as André had been, murderously so, and despite the freedom from future fear his death now gave her, Georgianna still could not find cause for celebration. Not for André's demise, nor the fact that Zachary was tacitly admitting to being the one responsible for ordering that death, if not the reason for it.

His mouth twisted derisively now. 'I had expected a happier response from you upon hearing this news?' he drawled mockingly.

Georgianna drew in a ragged breath before speaking. 'Why did you wait until now to tell me?'

'Sorry?' Zachary frowned darkly at the question.

Georgianna lifted her shoulders. 'Why did you wait, until after we had made love, to tell me?'

'It was not a conscious decision.'

'Are you sure of that?' she scorned. 'Could it be that the delay was because you knew I would not wish, or have the inclination, to make love with you once I knew?' she guessed shrewdly.

He gave a shake of his head. 'Georgianna—'

'Why did you do it, Zachary?' Georgianna pushed determinedly, deciding she could not think of Zachary's duplicity now. That she would think of it later. Much later.

'I do not recall admitting that I am the one responsible for Rousseau's death.' He arched arrogant dark brows over those now arctic-grey eyes.

No, he had not. And yet, still, Georgianna knew instinctively that he was. That the Zachary standing before her now, every inch one of the cold and remote Dangerous Dukes, was more than capable of killing if called upon to do so. That he had no doubt killed many men during his years as an agent for the Crown. And lived with the consequences of those deaths without regret or remorse.

But having André Rousseau killed was different to those other deaths. For one thing, they were not yet again at war with Napoleon. And no matter how much Zachary might have assured himself it was necessary to have André killed, it could not change the fact that he had also despised the other man on a very personal level. To the point of seeking out the other man and personally seeing to his demise?

Whatever Zachary's reasons for having dispatched André, Georgianna found she was not as capable as he of placing the events of her life into neatly labelled boxes. She needed time, and solitude, in which to come to terms with what she knew was Zachary's involvement in André's death. 'Were you there when he died?' She looked at Zachary searchingly.

His jaw was tightly clenched. 'Yes. Damn it, Georgianna, the man was a spy against England.'

'And I remind you we are no longer at war with France!'

'We very soon will be again.' A nerve pulsed in that tightly clenched jaw. 'Have you forgotten that just last night you asked that I do all that I can to prevent Jeffrey from becoming embroiled in that war?'

'Do not turn this conversation around on me in that way, Zachary,' she warned through clenched jaw as she stood up abruptly before collecting up her bonnet and gloves. Zachary's words confirmed that at least part of his reasoning for having André killed was because the other man had spied upon England.

Selfishly, perhaps, had she secretly wished that it might have been out of defence of her? She might, with time, have forgiven that. Because it might also have meant that Zachary had perhaps come to care for her as she cared for him.

But the thought that Zachary could have ruthlessly ordered the other man be killed, because of a personal slight against himself, as much as because he was considered to be an enemy of England, was a side of Zachary, that cold and dispassionate side, from which she had run just eleven short months ago.

And from which she must run away again now.

'Where are you going?' Zachary demanded as he watched Georgianna walk to the door of the salon without saying so much as another word to him, her hair a bewitching dark waterfall of curls down the slenderness of her defensively straight spine.

He had half expected this might be Georgianna's

reaction to the news of Rousseau's death. Expected it, but hoped that it would not be so.

Because, he had also hoped, prayed, that she had no softer feelings left inside her for the other man after the abominable way he had treated her. For having attempted to kill her.

Georgianna's reaction now to the news of Rousseau's death, and her obvious disgust with Zachary for what she believed to have been his part in it, now showed him how wrong he had been to harbour even the smallest hope in that regard.

Stupidly, naïvely, because of the warmth of her responses to him earlier, Zachary had harboured another hope, a dream, that all of her softer feelings were now reserved for him.

He had been wrong not to have told her of Rousseau's death immediately—he accepted that now. But he had wanted to hold her in his arms once more at least before he did so, and once he held her in his arms, he'd had no thought for anything else!

An omission for which Georgianna obviously now despised him, as much as she was so obviously distressed at Rousseau's death. She was disgusted, too, with Zachary for what she perceived to be his part in that death.

Because, despite his intentions, he really could not claim to be the one who had delivered the death blow to Rousseau.

Oh, he and Wolfingham had faultlessly carried out their plan for Wolfingham to engage Rousseau and his cohorts when they eventually emerged from his sister's tavern in the early hours of the morning. They had selected Wolfingham because he was unknown to Rousseau, as Zachary was not.

His friend had been the one to weave drunkenly past the inn at the exact moment the group emerged, deliberately knocking into one of them without apology and instantly receiving an aggressively challenging response. At which point Wolfingham had delivered the first punch.

In the mêlée and confusion that followed, Zachary was supposed to emerge from his own shadowed hiding place, to separate Rousseau from his cohorts, before taking him somewhere far quieter than the street, so that the other man might learn exactly the reason he was about to die.

All had gone according to that plan until Rousseau had pulled a gun from within his coat, his obvious intention to dispatch Wolfingham. At which point Wolfingham had no choice but to defend himself. There had been a shot fired as Zachary landed several blows on the other fellows in his efforts to reach his friend's side, but within seconds of the gun being fired, it seemed, the majority of the men had scattered, instantly becoming lost to various parts of the city and leaving behind the two men who lay still upon the ground, their life's blood glistening on the cobbles beneath them.

Rousseau and Wolfingham.

Zachary's own heart had ceased beating in his chest as he rushed to his friend's side and had only started again once he had roused Wolfingham and had satisfied himself that his friend's gunshot wound to the shoulder was nasty, but thankfully did not appear to be life-threatening.

Rousseau had been less fortunate, blood pumping from the artery in his slit throat, his eyes already starting to take on that opaque appearance of one about to die. Nevertheless, he had managed to focus enough to recognise Zachary, a mocking smile curving his lips. 'Hawksmere. I should have known. You are too late, I am afraid—your betrothed is dead,' he managed to taunt gruffly.

Zachary's breath left him in a hiss. 'Is she?' he taunted back angrily. 'I assure you that when I last saw Georgianna, just days ago, she still breathed, and walked, and talked. Mainly she talked of how much she hates you for your failed effort to kill her in a forest outside this very city.'

Surprised blond brows rose above those rapidly glazing blue eyes. 'She still lives?' he croaked, the blood still pumping from his slit throat.

'Oh, yes, despite your intentions for it to be otherwise, Georgianna most assuredly still lives,' Zachary had replied grimly. 'And loves.

'And hates. She also told us a pretty tale about your own involvement with the Corsican's recent departure from Elba.'

The other man gave a gurgling laugh as some of the blood gathered in the back of his throat. 'Georgianna ever saw herself as the heroine.'

'She is a heroine, you bast—'

'*Vive Napoleon,*' Rousseau murmured with his last

breath, those blue eyes wide as he stared lifelessly up into the darkness of the starlit sky above.

Zachary had left him where he lay in his own blood as he hurried back to Wolfingham's side, putting a supporting arm about his friend as they made good their own escape. The two of them hid at the dockside until it was time for them to board their ship and set sail back to England that same night.

The satisfaction of being able to tell Rousseau, before he died, that Georgianna still lived became a hollow victory as Zachary now saw the way Georgianna looked across the room at him with emotionless eyes.

'I am leaving, of course,' she answered his earlier question flatly. 'I presume informing me of André's death was the reason you wished to speak with me today?' She arched cool brows.

There was such a coolness about her, a distance, that frustrated Zachary intensely. Had he been wrong, misread the situation completely, and Georgianna did indeed still have feelings for the man who had once been her lover?

'You should know I have absolutely no regrets concerning Rousseau's death,' he assured through gritted teeth. Wolfingham had no cause for regrets in the matter, either, had merely been defending himself when Rousseau met his end. If Rousseau had not died, then Wolfingham assuredly would have, and that was totally unacceptable to Zachary. 'A friend of mine was also grievously wounded that night.'

Georgianna frowned slightly. 'Wolfingham?'

'Yes.'

'But he lives still?'

'No thanks to your friend Rousseau.'

'He was never my friend.' Her eyes glittered, with the fierceness of her anger as well as unshed tears. 'I must go.'

'Georgianna!'

She gave a fierce shake of her head. 'We have nothing left to talk about, Hawksmere.'

Addressing him as Hawksmere was indication enough of how Georgianna now felt towards him, the cold dismissal in her tone only adding to that obvious disdain.

And pride, though a cold bedfellow, was preferable to Zachary having his further pleas for her understanding rejected out of hand. 'I will see you again this evening, when I accompany you and Jeffrey to Lady Colchester's musical soirée.'

Georgianna gave a shake of her head. 'I am not sure I feel well enough to attend.'

'You most certainly will attend, Georgianna.' Zachary grated harshly. 'Not only will you attend, but you will also give every appearance of enjoyment in the enterprise. In appearing at my side, along with Jeffrey, as my two wards.'

She raised her chin in challenge. 'I am sure you know me well enough by now, Hawksmere, to know that I shall not be bullied into doing anything I do not wish to do, by you or anyone else.'

His jaw tightened, eyes glittering dangerously. 'Nevertheless, it was planned for this evening to be your first appearance back into society, following your period of mourning. As such, as your guardian, I must insist that you accompany Jeffrey and me.'

She looked across at him searchingly, knowing by the coldness in Zachary's eyes, the bleakness of his expression and the nerve pulsing in the tightness of his jaw, that he meant exactly what he said. Nor could she deny the importance of her appearance at Lady Colchester's tonight, following what many in society believed to have been the ending of her engagement to Hawksmere and her term of mourning her father. 'We shall see,' she finally answered noncommittally.

This young woman would surely be the death of him, Zachary acknowledged impatiently. Either that, or he might go quietly and completely insane.

How could it be that just a few moments ago the two of them had been so enjoyably making love together, as close as any two people could be—certainly as close as Zachary had been to any woman—and now they were as distant as they had been ten months ago? More so, for then Zachary had not really known what it was to be close to Georgianna, had never so much as even spoken to her; now he knew exactly what, and who, he would be losing when she walked out of his life for a second time.

The woman he had come to admire above all others.

Georgianna.

Georgia.

Chapter Thirteen

'I do believe you are alarming our poor hostess with the darkness of your scowls, Zachary,' an amused voice drawled beside him as Zachary stood near one of the windows in Lady Colchester's music room during a break in the entertainments.

His eyes widened as he turned to look at Wolfingham. 'Should you be out and about when you are still recovering from a bullet wound to your shoulder?'

'It would look decidedly odd if I were absent from society for any length of time. Besides which, needs must, I am afraid.' Wolfingham gave a grimace.

'Oh?'

His friend nodded abruptly. 'I do not suppose you have seen anything of my little brother this evening?'

Zachary's brows rose. 'Should I have done?' As far as he was aware, young Lord Anthony Hunter had been fortunate enough not to have put in even a nominal appearance at Lady Colchester's musical soirée.

Not unless he had arrived and left before Zachary and his party arrived.

'Obviously not,' Wolfingham uttered disgustedly. 'Is there a problem?'

'If there is, then it is for me to deal with,' his friend dismissed briskly. 'What were you scowling at so intently just now?' Wolfingham glanced across the room in the direction Zachary had been scowling earlier. 'Who is the honeypot attracting all the bees?'

Zachary did not at all appreciate hearing Georgianna described as a honeypot. Even if that was exactly what she had been from the moment they arrived at Lady Colchester's home several hours ago.

Georgianna was resplendent in a gown of purple silk, a strip of lace styled discreetly across the tops of her breasts, and so concealing that damning scar, with a matching purple feather adorning the darkness of her curls.

They had barely had time to greet their hostess before the first of the handsome young bucks began to flock about them. Most of them acquaintances of her brother, Jeffrey, eager to be re-introduced to his beautiful sister. But there had been some older gentlemen, too. Single gentlemen, of Zachary's own age and older, attracted no doubt by the air of untouchable remoteness with which Georgianna appeared to have steeled herself in order to endure appearing at this evening's entertainment.

A remoteness, which had thawed throughout the evening until, as now, she appeared to be enjoying the attentions of so many handsome gentlemen. The wariness had slowly faded from her gaze, a becoming blush now adorning her cheeks, and those two familiar dimples having appeared in those same cheeks when she smiled, at what were no doubt flattering and flirtatious comments being made to and about her.

And for the whole of this time Zachary had wished for nothing more than to dismiss the attentions of every single one of those handsome and fawning gentlemen, before whisking Georgianna away somewhere they could be private together.

So, yes, Wolfingham's description of his having been scowling minutes ago—enough so as to have warned off the approach of all and any who were not closely acquainted with him, who were very few— was no doubt an accurate one.

'My ward, Lady Georgianna Lancaster,' he now supplied.

Wolfingham continued to look at Georgianna consideringly. 'This is the same young woman to whom you were so briefly betrothed last year?'

'Yes.'

The other man's brows rose. 'She appears to be much changed from a year ago.'

Zachary's mouth tightened at the reasons for those changes, in both Georgianna's appearance and demeanour. 'She is, yes.'

Wolfingham turned to look at him through narrowed lids. 'I was not just referring to the more obvious changes in her appearance.'

A nerve pulsed in Zachary's jaw, knowing that his friend was able to detect the air of remoteness, and the sophistication, which had been so lacking in Georgianna just a year ago. 'No.'

'Zachary.'

'I would prefer not to discuss my ward any further,' he warned harshly. 'Even with you.'

Wolfingham continued to study him for several long seconds before nodding slowly. 'If you will just answer one more question?'

Zachary scowled his irritation. 'Which is?'

'Does she know that Rousseau is dead?'

'Yes, she knows.' Zachary did not attempt to pretend to misunderstand Wolfingham, knew that his friend had guessed, correctly, that Georgianna Lancaster was the woman whom Rousseau had treated so despicably. The reason the other man had to die.

'You like her?' Wolfingham guessed astutely.

Zachary's jaw clenched at the understatement. 'I do.'

'Enough to consider renewing your betrothal?'

His jaw clenched. 'There is absolutely no chance of that ever happening.'

'None?'

The nerve in his jaw pulsed even more rapidly. 'None whatsoever.'

'Time is passing, Zachary, and the condition in your father's will that states you must marry and produce an heir before your thirty-fifth birthday remains just as pressing,' Wolfingham reminded softly.

'And Georgianna is the last woman who would ever accept a—another—marriage proposal from me.' Zachary grimaced. 'Indeed, I believe Georgianna despises me more now than she did a year ago.'

Wolfingham sighed heavily. 'Life can be complicated at times, can it not?'

'Very,' Zachary grated.

His friend nodded. 'If you will excuse me, I believe I must continue to search for my own complication.'

Zachary frowned. 'Is Anthony in trouble?'

'Only with me,' Wolfingham assured darkly.

'If you should need any assistance in the matter...'

Wolfingham nodded distractedly. 'For the moment just be grateful you do not have a sibling for whom you are guardian.'

Zachary had very much regretted not having siblings when he was very young, but since meeting his four close friends at school he had not felt that same need, those four gentlemen more than filling that gap in his life. As they had all been there for him when he'd lost his parents when he was a child.

As they all remained there for each other as adults. 'Anthony is not in any danger?' He studied Wolfingham closely.

His friend's mouth thinned. 'Again, only from me. No doubt you have a similar headache, since becoming guardian to the two Lancaster siblings?'

Zachary glanced across at Georgianna once again, eyes glittering as he saw her batting her fan playfully in order to ward off the attentions of one of her more ardent suitors. 'If you will excuse me.' He didn't wait for his friend to reply before marching purposefully across the length of Lady Colchester's music room.

'I believe you are crowding the lady, Adams!' He glared down the length of his nose at the younger man.

Georgianna raised her open fan to hide her surprise as Hawksmere took up a protective stance at her side, his expression grimly forbidding as he glared at the gentlemen surrounding her.

Not that she did not appreciate Zachary having joined her; the gentlemen were becoming more and more persistent in their attentions, several of them currently vying for the honour of dancing the first set with her at the Countess of Evesham's ball tomorrow evening. A ball Georgianna was not sure she wished to attend any more than she had wished to attend this soirée.

This evening had been every bit the ordeal Georgianna had thought it might be.

Being with Hawksmere again had proved to be every bit of the ordeal she had imagined it might be!

It seemed incredible to her that she and Hawksmere had allowed themselves more than once to become embroiled in a situation of deep intimacy. An intensity of intimacy that made her blush with embarrassment every time she so much as thought about it.

And, to her shame, she had been unable to stop herself from thinking about it ever since she and Hawksmere had parted earlier today. Of how he had felt beneath the touch of her hands and lips. How he had tasted.

It had not helped that Zachary had looked, and continued to look, every inch the arrogantly handsome Duke of Hawksmere when he arrived at Malvern House earlier this evening. His muscled physique was shown to advantage in his black evening clothes and snowy white linen, the darkness of his hair arranged in tousled disarray as it curled over his ears and nape and about the sculptured perfection of his face.

Georgianna's heart had skipped several beats when she'd first gazed at him earlier this evening, a reaction she'd been quick to hide as she'd turned to thank her brother as he held out his arm to her in readiness for their departure.

She had deliberately seated herself beside Jeffrey in Hawksmere's carriage, very aware of, and avoiding meeting, the steadiness of Hawksmere's gaze as he sat directly across from her. She had kept her face averted as she looked out the window beside her, pretending an interest in the busy London evening streets.

Only to then find herself accompanied protectively by Jeffrey on one side and Hawksmere on the other, as they had entered Lady Colchester's London home together.

A closeness that had allowed her to feel the warmth emanating from Hawksmere's body through the silk of her gown, to smell his familiar smell of sandalwood and citrus, along with expensive cigars and just a hint of brandy upon his breath.

The latter in evidence, perhaps, that Hawksmere had felt in need of some restorative himself, in order to be able to get through the evening ahead?

Somehow Georgianna doubted that Hawksmere had ever needed a restorative, of any kind, to get through anything.

Nevertheless, Georgianna had felt grateful that the interest and conversation of Jeffrey's friends had separated her from Hawksmere, both before and during this break in the entertainments. His close proximity as they had sat together listening to several of the young ladies perform on their various musical instruments, had disturbed Georgianna on a level she had found distinctly uncomfortable. She still had no idea how she felt about Hawksmere's involvement with André's premature death.

That she no longer had anything to fear, in regard to André ever finding her again, was a relief beyond measure. Nor, having had time to adjust to André's demise, did she find she felt the least regret. How could she regret it, when she had lived in fear of discovery by him these past months? No, it was Hawksmere's involvement in the other man's death which still unsettled her.

Frightened her?

No, she was not frightened by the thought of such violence. She was sure that most men, and women, were capable of committing murder if pushed to the extreme. That she had been more than capable, given the weapon to do so, of killing André herself that night in the woods outside Paris, when he had tried to end her life.

But if she had succeeded in killing André, then it would have been an act of desperation on her part, of self-survival, rather than the cold-blooded murder she suspected his death to have been.

'If you gentlemen will excuse us?' Zachary's narrowed gaze precluded there being any objections to his announcement as he took a firm hold of Georgianna's arm to walk purposefully across to the other side of the room, well out of earshot of Lady Colchester's other guests. A frown darkened his brow as he now looked down at Georgianna through narrowed lids.

'You are hurting my arm, Hawksmere.' She gazed up at him steadily, pointedly, while all the time keeping a smile of politeness upon her lips for the benefit of their audience. The curious glances in their direction by the ladies present were surreptitious, but there nonetheless. No doubt due to the fact that the two of them had once been betrothed to be married. To each other.

Zachary lessened his grip, but refused to release her completely, at the same time as his own expression remained one of bland politeness. No doubt also for the benefit of their audience. 'I realise I am not your favourite person, Georgianna, but I do not think that ignoring me is in any way going to help quell the gossip, as this evening was predisposed to do, regarding our past broken betrothal,' he muttered impatiently.

Zachary believed he was not her favourite person?

Georgianna's feelings in regard to Hawksmere were now in such confusion that she no longer had any idea what she felt towards him. Despite the fact that he only had to touch her, it seemed, for her to melt into his arms.

Surely her reaction could be termed as being merely a physical response to a handsome and desirable gentleman?

Merely?

Her responses to Zachary were above and beyond anything Georgianna had ever experienced in her life before him. Not even that imagined love for André had filled her with such longings, such desires, as she felt when Zachary took her in his arms and kissed and caressed her.

Longings, and a desire, she had no right to feel for a man who would never be—could never be anything more to her than her reluctant guardian. And even that tenuous connection would very soon cease to exist.

Her chin rose defensively now. 'Is it not enough that I am here, as you instructed me to be? I do not recall your having said I had to enjoy or like it?' she added pointedly.

Zachary drew in an impatient breath. 'You appeared to be enjoying the attentions of those other gentlemen just a few minutes ago.'

Georgianna arched a brow. 'Was that not what I was supposed to do?'

As far as Zachary was concerned? No, it was not. In fact, he found he did not enjoy having any other gentleman within ten feet of Georgianna.

His jaw tightened. 'I do not think it a particularly good idea for you to encourage a repeat of society's past belief in your reputation as being something of a flirt.'

Her eyes widened with indignation. 'You— I— You are insulting, sir!'

Deliberately so, Zachary acknowledged heavily. And knowing he was not endearing himself to Georgianna in the slightest by acting the part of the jealous lover.

Even if he knew that's exactly how he felt.

He had hated every moment of watching Georgianna being flattered and admired by those other gentlemen this evening. Had wanted nothing more than to sweep her up in his arms and carry her off to a place no other man could look at her, let alone flatter and charm her into possibly falling in love with him.

Quite what Zachary was going to do about the heat of his own emotions in regard to Georgianna he had no idea, when she now gave every impression of disliking him intensely.

Was he, as her guardian, to be forced to stand silently by whilst some other man charmed and flattered her into falling in love with him?

Would he then have to welcome that suitor into his own home, when that gentleman came to ask his permission for seeking Georgianna's hand in marriage?

Impossible.

Just the thought of it was enough to cause Zachary's hand to clench into a fist at his side. He would not, could not, allow it. 'Are you ready to leave this insipid entertainment?' he prompted harshly.

Violet-coloured eyes widened in the pallor of

Georgianna's face. 'If you have somewhere else you wish to go, then I am sure Jeffrey is more than capable of acting as my chaperon for the rest of the evening.'

'The only somewhere else I wish us both to go is far away from here!' Zachary bit out harshly, only to draw in a long and calming breath as Georgianna's face became even paler at his vehemence. 'I believe we need to talk further, Georgianna,' he added softly.

Her brows rose. 'About what, exactly?'

'In private.' A nerve pulse in his tightly clenched jaw. If he did not find himself alone with Georgianna in the next few minutes then he was afraid he was going to do something that would cause them both embarrassment. Not that he cared on his own behalf, but Georgianna was likely to be less forgiving if he caused a scene on her very first evening back into society.

And a Georgianna who felt angry and resentful towards him was not what he wished for at all.

Georgianna eyed Zachary warily, not sure that she wished to be anywhere private with him, when he was in his current mood of unpredictability. Not that he had ever been in the least predictable to her, but there was such an air of tension about him this evening she felt even more wary of him than she had in the past.

'To what purpose?' she persisted guardedly.

A nerve pulsed in his throat. 'Does it matter?'

'Yes, of course it matters,' Georgianna answered irritably. 'As you have already pointed out, this is my first venture back into society, and my leaving with you now, halfway through the entertainments, would seem… It would look improper,' she concluded lamely.

It was possible to hear Hawksmere's teeth grinding together. 'Then let it.'

Georgianna's eyes widened in alarm. 'Can it be that you are foxed, Hawksmere? I seem to recall I thought I could smell brandy upon your breath when you arrived at Malvern House earlier this evening.'

'I am most assuredly not foxed, nor do I have any intentions of being so,' he bit out harshly. 'I am merely expressing a wish for the two of us to leave this hellish torture and go somewhere where we might talk privately together.'

Her brows rose. 'I do not recall your having been so eager, or particularly interested, in anything I had to say to you in the past.' She felt no qualms in reminding him that he had not so much as had a conversation with her before offering her marriage mere months ago. Or of his distrust of her, and of the information she'd wished to impart to him, when she'd first returned to England just weeks ago.

Was it really only three weeks since she had secretly returned to England? So much had happened in that time it seemed so much longer.

Zachary knew that he well deserved Georgianna's criticism. But he wished to remedy those wrongs now. He wanted to make amends for his past arrogance and thoughtlessness. If Georgianna would only allow it.

'I freely acknowledge that I have behaved appallingly towards you in the past, Georgianna.'

'How gracious of you to admit it!'

Zachary closed his eyes briefly as he heard the sarcasm underlying Georgianna's tone. As he inwardly fought to hold on to what little temper he had left. 'I am asking, politely, that you now leave this place with me, Georgianna, in order that we might talk together in calmness and—'

'This hellish place?' she interrupted tauntingly.

It had been hellish for him to have to sit at Georgianna's side and listen to the often painful musical efforts of half a dozen twittering young women, all of them hoping to impress the gentlemen present with their questionable talents. A so-called entertainment which Zachary would never have bothered himself to suffer through in the past and had only done so this evening as an open support of Georgianna's return to society.

But enough was enough, as far as Zachary was concerned; he simply could not sit through another minute of either of those painful entertainments, or Georgianna's coolly distant presence, as she sat silent and unmoving beside him. Nor could he witness further demonstration of the attentions of other men.

'Do not pretend you have the least interest in listening to any more of this unholy caterwauling,' he muttered disgustedly.

Georgianna quickly caught her top lip between her teeth in an effort to hold back her humour at Hawksmere's characteristic, and totally familiar, rudeness. A rudeness she far more readily understood than the intensity of emotions which seemed to be bubbling beneath the surface of Hawksmere's present mood of restless impatience.

'That is very ungentlemanly of you, Hawksmere,' she murmured reprovingly.

'The truth often is,' he came back unrepentantly.

The truth.

What was the truth of her feelings for Hawksmere? Did she loathe him or love him? She had once loathed him with a passion, enough so as to have eloped with another man, rather than become his wife. Her responses to Zachary since her return to England, the way she trembled even now just at his close proximity, said she no longer felt the least loathing for him, that her emotions now moved in another direction entirely.

Towards love?

For Hawksmere?

If that was truly what she felt for him then she must still be as stupidly naïve as she had been in the past. Certainly more so even than she had been eleven months ago, when she had believed herself to be in love with and loved by André!

Until now she had believed that to have been her defining moment of *naïveté*, but it was as nothing compared to the self-inflicted torture if she had indeed allowed herself to fall in love with Zachary Black. There could be nothing but pain and disillusionment from loving a man such as he. A man so cynical, so indifferent to the emotion of love, he had thought nothing of tying himself for life to, of marrying, a young woman he had not so much as had an interest in speaking privately to or with before offering for her.

And yet he was expressing a wish to talk privately with that same young woman now.

Perhaps so, but it was no doubt only because she had brought an abrupt end to their conversation earlier regarding André's death. A subject about which Georgianna had no desire to hear, or learn, any more than she already did. André was dead, by whatever means, and she did not need to know, could not bear to know, any more on the subject.

She straightened her spine determinedly. 'I am afraid it is not possible for me to leave just yet, your Grace.' She ignored the way Hawksmere's mouth tightened at her deliberate formality. 'My friend Charlotte Reynolds is about to play the pianoforte in the second half of the entertainments and I have already promised her I will stay long enough to listen.'

Zachary snorted his frustration with this development. 'And our own conversation?'

She shrugged uninterestedly. 'Will just have to wait.'

Zachary did not want to wait. Did not want to share Georgianna for another minute longer. With her friends. Her brother. Or the dozen or so eager young bucks watching them so curiously from across the room. No doubt all waiting for the moment they could pounce upon Georgianna again. If there was any pouncing to be done, then Zachary wished it to be only by him!

What he really wanted to do was to once again

make Georgianna a prisoner in his bedchamber. To keep her there, making love to and with her, until she did not have the strength to even think of leaving him again.

It was a side of himself Zachary did not recognise. A side of himself which he was uncertain he wished to recognise.

His mouth thinned. 'You are refusing to leave with me?'

'I believe I must, yes.' Georgianna gave him an impatient glance as his scowl of displeasure deepened. 'You are acting very strangely this evening, Hawksmere.'

No doubt. He felt very strange, too. Felt most uncomfortable with the uncharacteristic emotions churning inside him. There was most certainly impatience at their surroundings. That restlessness to be alone with Georgianna. The desire to make love to her again. And that interminable, unacceptable jealousy of the other men, just waiting for the opportunity to fawn over and flatter her.

What did it all mean? This turmoil of emotions, this possessiveness he now felt towards Georgianna?

Until he knew the answer to those questions, perhaps he should not talk privately with Georgianna, after all, but instead go to his club? Perhaps with the intention of imbibing too much brandy? If only as a means of dulling this turmoil of unfathomable emotions that held him so tightly in its grip.

He removed his hand from the top of Georgianna's

arm as he stepped back to bow formally. 'I will wish you a goodnight, then, Georgianna.'

Georgianna blinked her surprise at the abruptness of Zachary's sudden capitulation to her refusal to leave with him, when just seconds ago he had seemed equally as determined that she would do so.

Would she ever understand this man?

Probably not, she conceded wearily. 'Goodnight, your Grace.'

She bowed her head as she curtsied just as formally.

'Georgianna.'

She glanced up at Hawksmere from beneath lowered lashes as she slowly straightened. 'Yes?'

A nerve pulsed in his tightly clenched jaw, his face pale, a fevered glitter in the paleness of his silver eyes as the words seems forced out of him rather than given willingly. 'Never mind,' he muttered, his gaze no longer meeting hers. 'I wish you joy for the rest of your evening.' He gave another curt bow. 'If you will excuse me? I will inform Jeffrey of my early departure.'

She nodded. 'Your Grace.'

Zachary had never felt such heaviness in his chest before as he now felt walking away from Georgianna in search of Jeffrey Lancaster. He felt strangely as if he were leaving a part of himself behind. A very vital part. Almost as if he might never see Georgianna again after this evening. Which was ridiculous, when he was to be her guardian for another three months at least.

'I believe you and I need to talk privately, Hawksmere.'

Zachary turned at the harsh sound of his younger ward's voice, eyes narrowing as he took in the angry expression on Jeffrey Lancaster's youthfully handsome face.

'Is there a problem, Jeffrey?' he prompted warily, wondering if Jeffrey had witnessed the tension just now between his sister and Zachary.

The younger man's face flushed with displeasure. 'I did not mean— It was not done intentionally— I had thought to join you and Wolfingham earlier and…I inadvertently overheard part of your conversation,' he bit out accusingly.

And, as Zachary so clearly recalled, any part of his private conversation with Wolfingham would be considered damning to a third party. Most particularly Wolfingham having spoken of the conditions of Zachary's father's will, as being the reason for his betrothal and intended marriage to Jeffrey's sister eleven months ago.

Chapter Fourteen

Zachary slouched down in the chair beside the fireplace at his club as he stared down morosely into the bottom of his empty glass. A glass which seemed to have been emptied of brandy far too often these past few hours.

The club was much quieter than it had been when he arrived here after leaving Lady Colchester's musical soirée, the group of gentlemen who had been playing cards upon his arrival, having long departed. In fact, the club seemed to have emptied almost completely now that Zachary took the trouble to take stock of his surroundings. Something he had certainly not noticed before now, lost in the darkness of his own thoughts as he had been, and still was.

He continued to frown as he filled his glass again from the decanter on the table beside him. The alcohol dulled his senses, if it had not settled the confusion of his thoughts.

Of one thing he was absolutely certain, however: Georgianna now hated him.

And what reason had Zachary provided for her not to feel that way?

He had not so much as given a thought to Georgianna's feelings when he made his offer of marriage to her father eleven months ago. Had thought only of his own needs then and assumed that Georgianna would be flattered by the offer, and more than content just to become a duchess, as most young women of his acquaintance would have been.

Zachary had not realised, had not known then, that Georgianna was not like other young women and had a definite mind of her own in regard to what she wanted for her future. And duke or not, a loveless marriage to Zachary Black had certainly not been what she had wanted.

Zachary was not the man she had wanted, either.

And he was still not the man she wanted in her life.

To a degree that Georgianna did not just scorn him, but now heartily disliked him.

Why that should disturb him, hurt him, quite so much as it did was still something of a mystery to him.

Zachary had always lived his life exactly as he pleased, answerable to no one since his parents died. He did not understand why Georgianna's good opinion should now be of more importance to him than anything or anyone else.

He gave a shake of his head in an effort to clear his mind. But, damn it, what did it mean, when thoughts of a certain woman haunted his every waking moment? When just to look at her caused a tightness in his chest? When her unique perfume alone succeeded in arousing him?

When wanting Georgianna, desiring her, now consumed him utterly?

It was thoughts of their explosive and satisfying lovemaking which had made Zachary's torment this evening all the deeper. Far better that he had never known the softness of Georgianna's lips against his flesh, the caress of her hands upon his body. How he wished he'd never touched the silkiness of her own skin and enjoyed her own unique taste. Better that than to suffer the torment of remembering the way in which Georgianna had withdrawn from him after he had informed her of Rousseau's death.

The shock upon her face yesterday, when he had informed her of that death, her obvious disgust at his own involvement in Rousseau's demise, her coldness towards him since, was proof enough, surely, that she still had feelings for the other man?

And that she would never feel any of those softer feelings in regard to Zachary.

Even more so, now that Malvern had overheard part of Zachary's conversation with Wolfingham earlier this evening. The damning part: when Zachary had discussed the conditions of his father's will and the reason he had offered for Georgianna at all the previous year.

A disclosure that had been the truth then, even if it was not now, and which Zachary had not felt it was within his power to ask Jeffrey to keep from telling his sister.

Even though that truth would no doubt damn him for ever in Georgianna's eyes.

Bastard.

Cold, unfeeling, arrogant, impossible, selfish, selfish bastard!

Georgianna's ire towards Zachary was so intense this evening she did not feel in the least guilty about her repeated use of that unpleasant word inside her head, even as she had danced and flirted with all of the gentlemen at the Countess of Evesham's ball.

As she now muttered several other, stronger, French epithets she had in her vocabulary, as she edged her way round the ballroom of the Countess of Evesham's London home towards the open French doors and the solitude of the terrace beyond.

How could Hawksmere have done such a thing?

To any woman?

To her?

Her conversation with Jeffrey the evening before had revealed that she had been wholly correct in her previous assumptions concerning Hawksmere having calculated intentions when he'd offered marriage to her eleven months ago.

Indeed, it was worse than she had thought, because the offer had been made only so that Hawksmere might attain a wife and impregnate her, and so ensure that his heir was born before his thirty-fifth birthday. And all so that he might inherit all of his father's estate rather than a portion of it.

Poor Jeffrey was most disillusioned with the man he had previously so looked up to and admired.

To Georgianna it explained so much of Zachary's behaviour eleven months ago, of course. The reason he had offered marriage at all to a woman he did not even know and so obviously did not care to know. Followed by his anger that she had then chosen to elope with another man rather than marry him. And his distrust and punishment of her for that misdeed upon her return to England.

No doubt it also explained the penchant Hawksmere had for making love to her. As an example to her, no doubt, as a lesson to her never to cross a duke.

And Hawksmere had dared to be angry with her when they met again? To punish her?

How she despised him now.

Hated him.

Wished him consigned to the devil.

'Where are you going?'

Georgianna came to an abrupt halt, unable to keep the surprised expression from her face as she now turned to see the man who so occupied her thoughts.

Primarily because Hawksmere was not supposed to be at the Countess of Evesham's ball at all this evening. He had sent a note to Malvern House late this afternoon to inform Georgianna and Jeffrey that he would not be attending. He had offered no explanation, but had ended the brief note by wishing them both a pleasant evening.

That he was now standing before her, after all, caused Georgianna's heart to flutter erratically in her chest as she gazed up at him from beneath the fan of her lowered lashes.

He looked magnificent, of course, in his black evening clothes and snowy white linen, a diamond pin glittering amongst the intricate folds of his cravat, his fashionably tousled hair appearing as dark as a raven's wing in the bright candlelit ballroom.

And yet beneath that magnificence Georgianna noted the lines of strain around Zachary's eyes and etched beside the firm line of his mouth, the skin stretched tautly across the pallor of his chiselled cheeks. His mouth was set grimly, eyes glittering that intense silver as he continued to look down at her intently.

She moistened her lips before answering. 'I was going outside on to the terrace to take the air.'

He nodded abruptly. 'Then I will join you.' He took a firm hold of her elbow before cutting a determined swathe through the other guests towards the doors leading outside.

A determination none present dare question and leaving Georgianna no choice but to accompany him.

She was not sure she wished to be alone on the terrace with Zachary, or anywhere else.

Her conversation with Jeffrey the evening before, the confirmation of Hawksmere's perfidy, had cut into her almost with a pain of the same terrible intensity as when André had shot her. Starkly revealing, to Georgianna at least, that she had been using the anger she felt towards Zachary as a defence to hide what she really felt for him.

Love.

How it had happened, why it had happened, she had absolutely no idea, but during the events of the past year she had promised herself, if she survived, that she would never deceive or lie to herself again. And somehow, in these past three weeks, she had managed to fall in love.

She was in love, deeply and irrevocably, with Zachary Black, the emotionally aloof and coldly arrogant Duke of Hawksmere.

The same man who, it now transpired, had only offered for her the previous year because of his father's will. A man who had made it more than obvious, now as then, that he did not believe in love, let alone have any intention of so much as pretending to ever have felt that emotion in regard to Georgianna.

She glanced across at him now as he stood beside her in the moonlight, her expression guarded. 'Your note said that you would not be attending the ball this evening.'

Zachary gave a humourless smile. 'Obviously it is not only a lady's prerogative to change her mind.' In truth, he had regretted sending the note to Malvern and his sister almost the moment it had left his house earlier today, meaning, as it surely did, that he would now have no opportunity in which to see Georgianna today.

At the time of writing the note, Zachary had been feeling decidedly under the weather, his head fit to burst from the copious amount of brandy he had consumed the night before. Even the thought of attending the tedium of a ball increased the pounding inside his head.

Until Hinds, with his usual foresight, had provided Zachary with one of his cure-alls and, in doing so, managed to alleviate that pounding headache to a more manageable level. At which time Zachary had deeply regretted having ever informed Jeffrey and Georgianna that he would not be attending the ball with them this evening, after all.

'I do not think it altogether proper for the two of us to be out here alone together.'

Zachary scowled. 'I am your guardian.'

'And that distinction surely covers a multitude of sins!' she came back sharply.

One of those sins surely being Zachary having made love to her. 'Georgianna...'

'Could we please not argue again tonight, Zachary?' she requested wearily. 'I fear I am not feeling strong enough to deal with our usual thrust and parry this evening.'

Zachary looked at her searchingly, easily noting the pallor of her cheeks. 'Are you feeling unwell?' He swallowed. 'Perhaps because you are mourning Rousseau's death?'

'No!' Georgianna assured vehemently.

The duke looked puzzled. 'And yet it so obviously distressed you when I informed you of his demise yesterday afternoon.'

She moistened dry lips. 'I am, of course, sorry to

hear of the death of any man or woman, but I cannot in all conscience say I am sorry that André is no longer here to torment or frighten me.'

'But you blame me still for instigating that death.'

She had never blamed him for André's death, only questioned the reasoning behind it. But to reveal that to Zachary now must surely also reveal the depth of her own feelings for him.

A depth of feeling he so obviously did not return, nor would he ever do so.

In the circumstances, it was humiliating enough, surely, that she had now realised she had fallen in love with the man she'd once so passionately despised. Surely she did not need for Zachary to be made aware of her humiliation, too?

'Georgianna?' he prompted softly now.

She gave a dismissive shake of her head as she avoided looking into that searching silver gaze. 'I blame no one for André's death but André himself.'

He let out a shaky breath. 'I wish I could believe that was true.'

'You may be assured that it is. I was shocked to learn of his death, nothing more. But I believe I must go back inside now,' she added quickly as she realised he was about to question her further on the subject. 'It is somewhat colder out here than I had realised.'

'Here, take my jacket.' Zachary began to shrug his shoulders out of the close-fitting garment.

'No.' Georgianna had taken a horrified step backwards at the suggestion. She was already completely physically aware of Zachary, of his closeness, his warmth, his tempting masculinity, without being surrounded by the warmth and smell of him, too, as she would be if he were to now place his jacket about her shoulders. 'I really must go back inside.' She took another step back.

Zachary sighed heavily, as he obviously saw her efforts to put yet more distance between them. 'If it is not Rousseau causing you to now flinch away from me, then I can only presume— Jeffrey lost no time last night in informing you of the conditions of my father's will, I take it?' A nerve pulsed in his tightly clenched jaw.

Her chin rose. 'No.'

He nodded. 'There is no excuse for the selfishness of my actions last year. I deeply regret— I am sorry for— Damn it, would you perhaps consider forgiving me if I were to get down on my knees and beg?' he grated harshly, eyes glittering fiercely in the moonlight.

Exactly what was Zachary asking forgiveness for?

For that cold and cynical offer of marriage he had made for her last year?

For his distrust and mistreatment of her when she'd returned to England three weeks ago?

For having made love to her so exquisitely that just to be near him again now made her tremble with that knowledge?

For being complicit in, if not personally responsible, for André's death?

For having made her fall in love with him?

Georgianna had already forgiven Zachary for

those other things, but the love she now felt for him, a love she knew he would never return, was like a painful barb in her chest. And would, she believed, remain so for the rest of her life.

It was not Zachary's fault she had fallen in love with him, of course, but...

To have Zachary get down on his knees in front of her for any reason? To hear him beg for her forgiveness?

No.

Never!

It was unthinkable in such an aristocratic and proud man.

In the man she now realised she loved with all her heart.

'No,' she answered decisively. 'Can you not see how impossible it all is, Zachary?' she added forcefully as he scowled darkly. 'That apologies between us now are— That on their own they are not enough?'

Zachary had nothing else to offer Georgianna but his sincere contrition for any and all of his past misdeeds to her. A contrition Georgianna now made it obvious she neither wanted nor wished to hear. It was as he had suspected: Georgianna could never forgive him. For any of his actions, in the past, or now.

He had thought long and hard today on his confusion of thoughts at his club the previous night. On what that confusion of feelings, he now felt towards Georgianna, might mean.

The answer had been so shocking that he had sat alone in his study for hours after the truth had hit him squarely between the eyes, totally stunned, at the re-alisation that he had fallen in love with Georgianna.

He had come here this evening in the hope that if Georgianna would at least allow him to apologise, if he could perhaps persuade her into not hating him, that he could then be content with his lot in life. That he could then accept the little she was prepared to give him, as his ward, and perhaps even as his friend.

Instead he now found he could not. That he wanted so much more from Georgianna than her forgive-ness, or her lukewarm friendship. That he wanted all or nothing.

And this conversation with Georgianna told him it was to be nothing.

He straightened abruptly. 'It only remains for me to bid you goodnight, then, Georgianna.'

She raised startled lids. 'You are leaving?'

Zachary nodded stiffly. 'My only reason for com-ing here this evening was to talk to you. To ask your forgiveness. To see if— In the hope that—' His jaw tightened as he broke off abruptly.

He had been completely serious in his offer to Georgianna just now, had been fully prepared to get down on his knees and beg her forgiveness for his past actions, if it would in any way help to change how Georgianna now felt towards him. If he could ask for her friendship, at least. Her definitive reply had assured him there was no hope even of that.

Better by far, then, that he should now withdraw and leave Georgianna to enjoy the rest of the evening, to allow her to blossom and glow under the attentions of the other gentlemen present. One of whom she would no doubt one day fall in love with and marry.

'I do apologise, Georgianna.' He held himself stiffly, unable to so much as think of Georgianna being married to another man. 'For all and every wrong I have ever done you. And now, pray be assured, I will not bother you again on this, or any other subject you find so unpleasant.' He bowed formally before turning on his heel and abruptly leaving the terrace.

Zachary had spoken with such finality that Georgianna could not mistake his words for anything other than what they were. An end to any hope of there ever being so much as a friendship between the two of them.

'Georgie?'

She was totally unaware of the tears falling down her cheeks as she turned to see that her brother, Jeffrey, had now stepped outside on to the terrace. 'Did you hear any of that?' she asked dully.

'Most of it, I believe,' Jeffrey admitted as he crossed the terrace to her side before taking both of her hands in his. He looked down at her searchingly. 'I saw your expression as the two of you left the ballroom together and I was concerned enough to stand guard at the doors, so that I might be close enough to be of assistance if you should have need of me. Your conversation was not at all what I had imagined. Georgie, am I right in thinking you have fallen in love with Hawksmere?'

'Yes.' Georgianna made no attempt to deny it.

Her brother nodded. 'And he obviously has feelings for you.'

'Desire is not enough on its own, Jeffrey,' she assured heavily.

'Are you so certain that is all that Hawksmere feels for you?'

She smiled sadly. 'I am sure you heard Zachary say goodbye to me just now? Not necessarily in words, but in the cold formality of his manner?'

'I heard him saying a reluctant goodbye to you, yes. Georgie—' Jeffrey frowned '—you are much changed since your return from France. You have suffered through so much, more than I know, I am sure. And yet you have survived. More than survived. You have grown into a beautiful and independent woman. More forthright in your manner. Less patient of society's strictures and more determined where your own wishes are concerned.'

'Yes.' Again Georgianna did not attempt to deny it; she had indeed become all of those things these past months.

Her brother nodded. 'I have no idea how you and Hawksmere can have become so close in such a short time, but I am young still, Georgie, though I am far from stupid,' he reproved gently as she would have spoken. 'And there is most certainly something between the two of you. An emotion so strong, so intense, that it is possible to feel the tension in the air whenever the two of you are in a room together.'

Her cheeks warmed. 'As I said, desire alone is not enough.'

'I do not believe Hawksmere came here this evening with any intention of making love to you, Georgie,' her brother reasoned softly. 'I heard enough of your conversation to know that he wished only to talk to you. To offer to get down on his knees and beg for your forgiveness, for any and all of his past misdeeds to you, if necessary. Can you not give him some credit for that, at least, Georgie? Some understanding of what it must have cost him, such a proud man, to have offered to do such a thing? And to question why he would have made such a self-demeaning offer of apology to you at all?'

She sighed deeply. 'Who is to know why Hawksmere does anything?'

'You know, Georgia,' Jeffrey chided. 'You know Hawksmere better than anyone, I believe. Is it not time you searched your own heart? That you forgo a little of your own pride? Talk with him again, before the distance between you becomes too wide to ever be crossed,' he urged softly.

Georgianna did not need to search her own heart to know that she was in love with Zachary.

Could she dare to hope, to believe, that his actions tonight implied he might love her in return?

'What do you have to lose, Georgie?' Jeffrey cajoled.

Nothing. She had absolutely nothing left to lose when it came to loving Zachary.

Chapter Fifteen

'Good evening, Hinds.' Georgianna handed her bonnet and cloak to the surprised butler as she stepped past him into the cavernous hallway of Hawksmere House. 'Is his Grace at home?'

The butler looked more than a little flustered by having her arrive at his employer's home at eleven o'clock in the evening. 'He returned some minutes ago and has retired to his study.'

'Which is where?' She gazed pointedly at the half dozen doors leading off the entrance hall.

'The second door on the right. But…'

'Thank you.' Georgianna gave the butler a brightly dismissive smile, determined to go through with her decision to speak with Zachary again. 'Perhaps you might bring through a decanter of brandy?' Bravado had brought her thus far—she did not intend to let it desert her now.

'His Grace has just this minute instructed I do so,

my lady.' Hind's brows were still raised in astonishment at her commanding behaviour.

Understandably so, when she considered the butler was fully aware that she had once been held here as Hawksmere's prisoner.

Although she did feel slightly heartened by the fact that Zachary had obviously felt in need of a restorative brandy—or two—upon his return home. 'I will not delay you from your duties any longer then, Hinds.'

'What on earth is going on, Hinds?' Hawksmere came to an abrupt halt in the now-open doorway of his study, his expression one of stunned disbelief as he gazed across at her.

'Georgianna?'

'Hawksmere.' She managed to greet him with the same brightness as she had addressed the butler seconds ago, determined not to lose her nerve now that she found herself face to face with Zachary.

As Jeffrey had gently chided earlier, the situation between herself and Zachary had come to a breaking point, with no going back, only forward. Wherever that might take her. Consequently, Georgianna had nothing left to lose now but her pride. And where Zachary was concerned, she found that she now had none. How could she have, when she knew he had cast aside his own pride earlier this evening, by offering to get down on his knees and beg her forgiveness.

'The brandy, Hinds, if you please?' she reminded, sending Hinds scurrying down the hallway.

Zachary was dressed far less formally than he had

been earlier this evening, having removed his jacket and cravat, leaving him dressed only in his waistcoat over the snowy white shirt open at the throat and black pantaloons, which clearly showed the lean perfection of his muscled legs and thighs.

He looked delicious, Georgianna decided, good enough to eat, in fact. The heated colour warmed her cheeks as she recalled that she had already tasted and devoured Zachary, when the two of them made love together yesterday afternoon.

She held Zachary's wary gaze unwaveringly as she softly crossed the hallway to join him. 'May I come in?' she beseeched huskily, her heart beating erratically in her chest as he made no effort to stand aside and allow her entry into his study.

Zachary's hand tightened on the doorframe, where he had reached out to steady himself in his complete surprise at seeing Georgianna standing in the entrance hall of his London home. 'Is Jeffrey with you?'

'Jeffrey knows that I am here, because he put me into our carriage himself. Otherwise, I am quite alone,' she dismissed huskily.

A scowl darkened Zachary's brow. 'That was most improper of you.'

She gazed up at him quizzically. 'As you stated earlier, we are well past that point.'

Maybe so, but Zachary's concern was on Georgianna's behalf, rather than his own. His own reputation was such that her visiting him alone would only add to his reputation as being something of a rake, whereas Georgianna's still bore a question mark, as far as society was concerned.

'Why are you here, Georgianna?' he prompted warily.

'You would rather I had not come?'

He would far rather Georgianna stayed and never left. Ever again. But, as their earlier conversation had seemed to confirm that was not even a possibility, he could not help but question as to the reason why Georgianna had left the Countess of Evesham's ball only minutes after he had done so himself. With the intent, it seemed, of following him here. With her brother's full consent and co-operation, by the sound of it.

His mouth tightened disapprovingly. 'Jeffrey should have known better than to allow it.'

'Jeffrey overheard part of our own conversation on the terrace earlier.'

'I can see I shall have to have words with that young man regarding his habit of eavesdropping on private conversations.' Zachary scowled.

Georgianna shook her head. 'He is far more mature and sensible than either of us have given him credit for,' she assured drily. 'But would you rather I left again, Zachary?' She looked up at him searchingly.

He drew a deep breath into his starved lungs as he realised he had forgotten to breathe. He allowed himself to indulge his senses where Georgianna was concerned, gazing upon her obvious beauty and the dewy perfection of her skin, that begged to be touched and tasted, and now breathing in her unique perfume—

something floral as well as the unique and feminine warmth that was all Georgianna.

'I would rather you had not come here at all,' he maintained harshly, still making no effort to step aside and allow her entry to his study. It was his last bastion of defence, a place where he did not have any visible memories of being with Georgianna. Unlike his bedchamber upstairs. And the bedchamber adjoining that one. And the blue salon.

Her chin rose determinedly. 'I wished to continue our earlier conversation.'

His jaw tightened. 'And I believe we said then all that needs be said to each other.'

Georgianna looked up at Zachary searchingly, as she easily noted his unkempt appearance. His hair was tousled, as if he had run his agitated fingers through it several times since returning home. The lines beside his eyes and mouth seemed deeper, his mouth set in a thin and uncompromising line, and there was a dark shadow upon his jaw, where he was obviously in need of a second shave of the day.

Altogether, he looked nothing like the suave and sophisticated gentleman who had arrived at the Countess of Evesham's ball earlier this evening.

Because of the unsatisfactory outcome earlier of that conversation with her?

That was what Georgianna was here to find out. And, having made that decision, she had no intentions of leaving here tonight until she had done so.

'You know, Zachary, we both have scars that are visible to the eye if one cares to look for them.' Her gaze softened as she reached up to gently touch the livid scar upon his throat, stubbornly maintaining that touch even when he would have flinched away. 'But I, for one, have other scars, ones deep inside me, that are not at all visible to the naked eye.' She smiled sadly. 'They are the scars left by my unhappy experience at André's hands. Of uncertainty. Of questioning my self-worth.'

'The devil they are.'

Georgianna nodded as Zachary scowled his displeasure at her admission. 'Those scars make it difficult for me to believe that any man, any gentleman, could ever, would ever, want to be with me after— Zachary?' she questioned sharply as he reached up to curl his fingers about her wrist before pulling her inside his candlelit study and closing the door firmly behind them. His eyes were a dark, unfathomable grey as he gazed down at her hungrily before his arms moved about her and he lowered his head to crush her lips beneath his own.

It would have been so easy to lose herself in that kiss. For Georgianna to give in completely to the arousal which instantly thrummed through her body. To feel gratified, to revel, in this proof that Zachary still desired her, at least.

But she could not. Dared not. Because she knew it would be all too easy to give in to those desires and for the two of them not to talk at all. And they needed the truth between the two of them, before, or if, there was to be any more lovemaking.

Georgianna wrenched her mouth from beneath

Zachary's even as she pushed against his chest to free herself.

His arms fell reluctantly away as he stepped back, his heavy lidded gaze now guarded. 'I trust that answers your question as to whether or not you are wanted by me?'

She drew in a shaky breath, even more determined, after Zachary's show of passion, to say all the things she knew needed to be said between them. 'I made a mistake last year, Zachary, one for which so many people have suffered.'

'You most of all,' he pointed out gruffly.

She sighed equally as shakily. 'I really was so very young, and even more foolish. I am ashamed to say that at the time I saw it all as a grand adventure, with no real thought for what the long-term consequences of my actions might be.'

'Except to escape being married to me,' Zachary reminded drily.

'Yes.' Georgianna's gaze now avoided meeting his, as she began to pace the rug before the warmth of the fireplace. 'And now I have so many things to thank you for, Zachary.'

His eyes widened. 'What on earth...?'

'I am so grateful for your own efforts, last year and now, to maintain my reputation in society,' she continued determinedly. 'So thankful that Jeffrey has had you to help him through these trying months since our father died. And...' she looked up at him helplessly '...and, yes, I am more gratified than I have cared to admit, until now, that you have helped rid the world of a monster such as André Rousseau.' That last admission was against everything she had been brought up to believe in regard to the sanctity of human life.

It was also, Georgianna now accepted, a large part of why she had been so angry with Zachary when he had informed her of André's death. Because, having lived in fear of discovery by André these past few months, she had wanted him to be dead. Wished him so. And she had inwardly rejoiced yesterday when Zachary had told her André was indeed dead.

It was a reaction, a rejoicing, of which she had felt heartily ashamed.

But that shame and anger were directed towards herself, not Zachary. 'I was ashamed to admit it until now,' she admitted huskily.

'But you loved him. Love him still, damn it.'

Her eyes widened. 'I most certainly do not. I...' She paused, chewing briefly on her bottom lip before continuing. 'I fear I have been less than honest, with myself, and with you, on that matter.'

Zachary gave a grimace. 'Your reaction yesterday, your distress, were evidence enough of how you felt. That you still had feelings for the man,' he added harshly.

'No,' Georgianna denied vehemently. 'Never that. Never,' she repeated with a shudder of revulsion. 'The truth of the matter is—I realised some time ago— Zachary, I do not believe I was ever truly in love with André.' She gave a pained grimace at the admission. 'I was very naïve, flattered by his attentions and desperate to escape a loveless marriage and, I now know, in love with love rather than André himself.'

Zachary stared at her searchingly for long, tense moments, before turning abruptly to cross the room and seat himself behind his imposing mahogany desk. That she had not loved Rousseau after all was no reason to suppose, to hope, she would ever love him.

'I am gratified to you—' he nodded '—for allowing me to know that Rousseau's death has not succeeded in breaking your heart, as I previously believed it to have done.'

Georgianna could hear the *but* in his voice.

But the admission made no difference to the outcome of their own conversation, perhaps?

Whether or not that was true, Georgianna had no intentions of leaving here tonight without there being complete honesty between herself and Zachary. After which, fate, or rather Zachary, could do with her what it would. 'Are you not interested to know how it is I came to be certain I was never in love with André?'

His mouth twisted wryly. 'No doubt it is difficult to continue to love a man whom you knew had attempted to kill you.'

'Indeed.' She nodded ruefully. 'Almost as difficult, in fact, as finding you have fallen in love with the very same gentleman whose hand in marriage you had once shunned so cruelly.'

Zachary rose sharply to his feet. 'Georgianna?' His eyes glittered as he gazed across at her uncertainly.

Her heart was now beating so erratically, so loudly in her chest, she felt sure that Zachary could not help but be aware of it, too, despite the distance between them. 'It is the truth, Zachary.' She forced herself to forge ahead, to not retreat or back down, now that she had come so far. 'Since I returned to England you have shown me a side of yourself I did not know existed. That I did not even dare dream existed. On the outside you are so very much the cool and arrogant Duke of Hawksmere, so very much in control. But inwardly there is a kindness to you, one which you try to hide, but which shines through anyway.'

'And you reached this conclusion by my having locked you in my bedchamber? By my making love to you at every opportunity?' He raised incredulous brows.

'I reached that conclusion by knowing that you could have been so much harsher with me, after the way I had behaved in the past. By knowing that you were complicit in protecting my reputation, despite that behaviour. By your overwhelming kindness to Jeffrey these past months. And by the realisation this evening, the certainty,' she declared determinedly as he would have spoken, 'that your reasons for seeing André dispatched were not, as I had supposed, because of loyalty to England, or because of a personal grudge you held against him, for having dared to elope with your future bride.'

'Dear God, you thought that of me?'

Colour warmed the paleness of her cheeks. 'I am ashamed to say it occurred to me those might be your reasons.'

'I did it because of you, Georgianna. Because

André had attempted to kill you.' Zachary's hands were clenched at his side.

It was as Georgianna had thought earlier when he'd pleaded with her so emotionally.

'Just leave it on the side table there,' Zachary instructed his butler harshly as the man entered after the briefest of knocks, holding aloft the tray with the decanter and glasses. 'And in future, would you please knock and wait before entering any room in which Lady Georgianna and I are alone together?' he added, his gaze remaining intent upon Georgianna.

'Certainly, your Grace.' The butler placed the tray upon the side table. 'Will that be all, your Grace?'

Zachary barely resisted the impulse to tell the man to go to the devil, wishing to be alone again with Georgianna, to continue their conversation. To hear her repeat that she had fallen in love with him.

Something he hardly dared to believe.

'You may retire for the night, Hinds,' Zachary dismissed distractedly. 'And thank you.'

His butler gave him another startled glance before gathering himself and leaving the room. As evidence perhaps that Zachary's temper had been less than pleasant this past few days?

As no doubt it had, caught up in the pained whirlpool of his uncertainty in his own emotions, as he had surely been.

'Is that not a strange request to make of your butler, when there is no reason to suppose that the two of us might ever be alone together in a room in this house again?' Georgianna queried huskily.

Zachary stepped out from behind his desk. 'There is every reason to suppose it, Georgianna.' He strode purposefully towards her before grasping both of her hands in his. 'Believe me, when I tell you, that these past three weeks I have come to love and admire you beyond anything and anyone else in this world.'

'Zachary?' she choked out emotionally.

'Georgia, will you please, I beg of you, consent to becoming my wife?'

Georgianna stared up at him wonderingly, sure Zachary could not truly have told her that he loved her, too. That he had begged her to marry him?

His hands tightened about hers as he obviously mistook her silence for hesitation. 'And not because of any ridiculous clause in my father's will, either. Indeed, if you require it as proof of the sincerity of my feelings for you, I will give away half of the Hawksmere fortune to my cousin Rufus forthwith, as my father's will decrees if I do not have an heir by my thirty fifth birthday. Anything, if you will consent to become my wife immediately.'

Georgianna's mouth felt very dry, and after its wild pounding earlier she was sure her heart had now ceased to beat altogether. 'Is your cousin in need of half the Hawksmere fortune?'

'Thanks to Rufus's business acumen, he is already one of the richest men in London.' Zachary bared his teeth in a brief smile before just as quickly sobering. 'Nevertheless, I will happily give him the money, if it will ensure that you believe I am sincere in my declaration of love for you. If you will only consent to become my wife as soon as it can be arranged?'

Georgianna had no idea what she had expected the outcome of her visit here this evening to be, but she knew she had certainly never expected it to be the complete and utter happiness of hearing Hawksmere declare his love for her and his asking her to marry him.

Her vision was blurred by those tears of happiness. 'You truly love me?'

'To the point of madness,' Zachary assured fervently. 'Indeed, I believe I have been half-insane with the emotion these past few days.' The intensity of his gaze held her. 'I love you so very much, Georgianna Rose Lancaster.'

'As I love you, Zachary Richard Edward Black,' she answered him huskily. 'Completely. And always.'

His face lit up. 'Then put all of the past behind us and consent to marry me.'

She swallowed. 'Are you absolutely sure that is what you want, Zachary? My reappearance in society is still tenuous.'

'What are you suggesting, Georgianna?' Zachary demanded. 'That I should make you my mistress rather than marry you? That I should hide you away somewhere?'

'I am something of a novelty in society just now, Zachary, but if anyone should ever learn of my elopement with André…'

'They will not discover it,' Zachary announced arrogantly. 'And even if they did, none would dare to question the reputation of the Duchess of Hawksmere.'

It was a name, a title, when used in connection to herself, that had once filled Georgianna with such dread. Now it only filled her with a happiness that threatened to overwhelm her. 'I am so in love with you, Zachary. So very, very much, my darling. And if you are serious in your proposal of marriage...?'

'I will accept nothing less,' he assured firmly.

She glowed up at him. 'Then I believe I should much prefer that you keep the Hawksmere fortune intact for our children, when they are born.'

'Georgianna?' Zachary had almost been afraid to hope, to dream, that Georgianna would ever accept his proposal. 'You truly will consent to become my wife?' His fingers tightened painfully about hers. 'You will marry me as soon as a special licence can be arranged?'

She nodded happily. 'And Jeffrey shall give me away and one of your friends, Wolfingham, perhaps, shall stand up with you. Oh, yes, I will marry you, Zachary. Yes, yes, please, yes.' She launched herself into his arms as his mouth swooped down to once again claim hers.

'You were very brave to come here alone this evening, my love,' Zachary murmured admiringly some time later, Georgianna's head resting on his chest as the two of them lay on the chaise in his study together. He played with her curls, having once again released her hair so that it cascaded loosely down her back.

She laughed softly, contentedly, the two of them having professed their love for each other over and over again this past hour or more. 'To confront the fierce lion in his den?'

'To have completely tamed the lion in his den,' Zachary corrected with humour. 'Indeed, I find I am so much in love with you I very much doubt I shall ever be able to deny you anything in future, love.'

Georgianna hesitated, knowing that there was still one thing that she had not confessed to her beloved. The last confession.

When she first returned to England she had been too angry at Hawksmere's incarceration of her, to talk of such things, and since then there had been no right time, no opportunity, for her to do so.

'What is it, Georgia?' Zachary sat up slightly as he sensed her sudden tension. His hands gently cupped either side of her face as he looked down at her searchingly. 'Tell me, my love.'

She chewed on her bottom lip. 'I— It is only— A lady should not talk of such things,' she choked out emotionally.

'Now you are seriously worrying me, love.' Zachary frowned. 'We have talked about so much this past hour. The past, the now, our future together. What on earth is there that still bothers you so much that you look as if you are about to cry?'

Georgianna felt as if she were about to cry. It was all too embarrassing. Too humiliating.

Her gaze dropped from his as she moistened her

lips with the tip of her tongue. 'When I eloped with André...'

'I thought we had agreed earlier that we would not discuss that ever again,' Zachary reminded with chiding gentleness.

'Just this one thing, Zachary,' she pleaded. 'It is important, if we are to be married.'

'We are most certainly going to be married and sooner rather than later.' Zachary had never been as happy as he had felt this past hour of knowing that Georgianna loved him, that she had consented to marry him. He could not bear it if that happiness—if a lifetime with Georgianna as his wife, should ever be snatched away from him.

'Whatever you have yet to tell me, never doubt my love for you, Georgianna. Never. Do you understand?' He held her tightly against him. 'Be assured, nothing you have to say, now or in the future, will ever change that,' he added with certainty.

Georgianna looked up at him wonderingly, moved beyond measure at the knowledge that Zachary loved her so deeply, so unconditionally. The same deep intensity of emotion with which she now loved him. 'It is nothing bad, my love,' she assured huskily as she reached up to stroke his cheek. 'Only embarrassing for me to speak of,' she conceded ruefully.

'I grow more intrigued by the moment, my love.' He eyed her quizzically.

'Where to start?' Georgianna pulled out of his arms before standing up and turning away slightly, her hands clasped tightly together in front of her.

'When I eloped with André—allow me to finish, my love, please!' she begged as Zachary made a noise of protest. 'We spent several uncomfortable days being jostled about in the coach together on the way to the seaport. We passed the sea journey as brother and sister in separate cabins. And once we reached Paris…' She gave a shake of her head. 'You are well aware of what transpired within days of our reaching the French capital.'

Zachary's narrowed gaze remained intently on Georgianna as he slowly stood up to move softly to her side, reaching down to lift her chin so that he might gaze down directly, searchingly, into the frankness of those violet-coloured eyes. 'Are you saying…?' He drew in a sharp breath, hardly daring to believe.

'I am saying that André and I had never shared any more than a few chaste kisses before we eloped and that he did not so much as kiss me during the whole of our journey to France.'

'Georgianna?'

She swallowed. 'The intensity, depth, of our own lovemaking was—is, the first I have ever known.'

'Can it be? Are you a virgin still, Georgianna?' Zachary prompted tensely.

The colour deepened in her cheeks as she nodded. 'I could not bear to tell you before now.' She grasped tightly to the front of his waistcoat as she gazed up at him imploringly. 'The Zachary I met on my return to England would have enjoyed tormenting me with that knowledge. Would have mocked and taunted me as to André's disinterest in me. Would have—'

'Hush, my love.' Zachary placed a silencing fingertip against her lips, his heart having swelled almost to bursting point in his chest.

He had long ago accepted that Georgianna had been Rousseau's lover and it had made no difference to the deep love and admiration, respect, that he now felt for her. But to now realise, to know, that Georgianna had never, would never, belong to any other man but him?

It was a priceless gift. A gift beyond anything Zachary might ever have imagined.

'I took such liberties with you.' He groaned, disgusted with himself. 'I was far too rough in my lovemaking. Too advanced in the things I did to you and demanded from you in return.'

'I loved the way you made love to me, Zachary, and so enjoyed making love to you,' she admitted shyly. 'Indeed, I cannot wait to repeat it.'

'That will not happen until after we are married,' he assured her determinedly.

She chuckled throatily. 'Can it be that Zachary Black, the arrogant and haughty Duke of Hawksmere, has now become prim and respectable?'

'You may take it that Zachary Black, the arrogant and haughty Duke of Hawksmere,' he repeated huskily, 'intends to cherish and love, to make love to, Georgianna Rose Black, Duchess of Hawksmere, and only Georgianna Rose Black, Duchess of Hawksmere, for the rest of their lives together.'

It was so much more, so indescribably, wonderfully, ecstatically more than Georgianna Rose Lancaster, soon to be Black, could ever have hoped or dreamed of.

* * * * *

Don't miss the next book in
Carole Mortimer's dazzling
DANGEROUS DUKES *duet:*
DARIAN HUNTER: DUKE OF DESIRE

DARIAN
HUNTER:
DUKE OF DESIRE

My good friend, Susan Stephens.
What fun we have on our travels!

Prologue

March 1815—White's Club, London

'You wanted to speak to me?'

Having been perusing today's newspaper, whilst seated in an otherwise deserted private room of his club, Darian Hunter, the Duke of Wolfingham, now continued reading to the end of the article before folding the broadsheet neatly into four and placing it down on the low table beside him. He then glanced up at the fashionably dressed young gentleman who had addressed him so aggressively. 'And a good afternoon to you, too, Anthony,' he greeted his younger brother calmly.

Anthony eyed him impatiently. 'Do not come the haughty duke with me, Darian! Most especially when I know it is you who wished to speak with me rather than the other way about. You have left messages for me all over town,' he reminded as Darian raised dark brows questioningly. 'I presumed the matter must be of some urgency?'

'Is that why it has taken you those same two days to respond to those messages?' Darian was not fooled for a moment by his brother's bluster. He knew that his brother always went on the attack when he knew he was in the wrong, but was refusing to admit it.

'I have better things to do with my time than seek out the more often than not elusive Duke of Wolfingham—even if he does happen to be my big brother as well as my guardian. The latter for only another three months, I thank heavens!'

'Oh, do sit down, Anthony,' Darian snapped. 'You are making the place look untidy.'

Anthony gave a wicked grin at having obviously succeeded in irritating Darian as he threw himself down into the chair opposite. He was dressed in the height of fashion as usual, in his jacket of royal blue, with a bright blue-and-green paisley-patterned waistcoat beneath and buff-coloured pantaloons, his dark hair rakishly overlong and falling across his brow. 'When did you get back to town?'

'Two days ago, obviously,' Darian drawled.

'And you immediately sought me out?' Anthony raised mocking brows. 'I am flattered, brother.'

'Don't be,' he advised pointedly.

His brother now raised his gaze heavenwards. 'What have I done to annoy you this time? Overspent at my tailor's? Gambled at the cards a little too heavily?'

'If only it was your usual irresponsible behaviour

then I should not have needed to speak with you at all, but merely dealt with the matter as I always do,' Darian drawled in a bored voice. 'I am sure we are both well aware of why it is I wished to speak with you, Anthony,' he added softly.

'Not the slightest idea.' The fact that Anthony shifted uncomfortably, his gaze now avoiding meeting Darian's as a slight flush coloured his cheeks, instantly gave lie to the claim.

Darian gave a humourless smile. 'Do not force me to mention the lady by name.'

Anthony narrowed eyes as emerald green as Darian's own, the two of them very alike in colouring and looks, and so obviously brothers, in spite of the eight years' difference in their ages; Darian aged two and thirty to his brother's four and twenty. 'If you are referring to the actress with whom I had a liaison last month, then I do not even recall her name—'

'I am not.'

Anthony gave an exaggerated stretch of his shoulders. 'Then give me a clue, brother, because I have absolutely no idea what—or possibly who?—you might be referring to.'

Darian's mouth firmed at his brother's determination not to make this an easy conversation. For either of them. 'It has been brought to my attention that you have been seen in the company of a certain lady, more often than is socially acceptable.'

Anthony stilled. 'Indeed?'

Darian nodded. 'And while it is perfectly acceptable for you to discreetly indulge in a gentleman's diversions, this particular lady could never be considered as being in the least discreet. Indeed, she is—'

'Have a care, Darian,' Anthony warned softly.

'Her associations, past and present, mean she is not a woman with whom it is acceptable for a gentleman of your standing to indulge in these diversions,' Darian maintained determinedly. 'You—' He broke off as Anthony sprang lightly to his feet, hands clenched into fists at his sides as he glared down at Darian. 'I have not finished—'

'In regard to this particular lady, I assure you that you have indeed finished,' Anthony said fiercely. 'And might I say that you have a damned nerve, daring to lecture me about my behaviour, when you have only just returned from spending almost two weeks in the company of whatever doxy it was who had so taken your fancy you might have disappeared off the edge of the earth! Or perhaps it is that you consider a duke is allowed to live by different standards than us mere mortals?'

Darian lowered heavy lids as he flicked an imaginary speck of lint from the sleeve of his jacket, at the same time avoiding meeting his brother's accusing gaze.

Not because he had just spent almost two weeks with his latest doxy. 'Latest doxy'? Darian could not even remember the last time he had spent any length of time in a woman's company, let alone her bed.

No, the reason for his avoidance of Anthony's probing gaze was because he had not been in a woman's company at all, but had spent almost two weeks across the sea in France, acting secretly as an agent for the Crown.

Almost two weeks when he and his good friend Zachary Black, the Duke of Hawksmere, had roamed the French countryside, and then Paris itself, as they endeavoured to gauge how the French people themselves felt about Napoleon's return, the emperor having recently escaped from Elba and currently on his way to the French capital.

Not even Darian's own brother was aware of the work he had undertaken for the Crown these past five years. Anthony certainly had no idea that Darian had suffered a bullet wound to the shoulder just days ago, a souvenir of this last foray into France. And that he was suffering with the pain and discomfort of that wound even now.

Something that had not improved his temper in the slightest. 'Perhaps you would care to lower your voice?'

'Why should I, when there is no one else here to hear us?' Anthony challenged as he looked about the otherwise empty room.

Darian sighed. 'I am well aware that this lady has certain attributes that you—most gentlemen!—might find diverting. But she is not a discreet woman. Far from it, if gossip is to be believed. People in society are starting to comment upon your marked attentions to her.'

'Then let them,' Anthony dismissed with bravado.

He sighed. 'It simply will not do, Anthony.'

'Says who? You?' his brother challenged, aggressive once again. 'I am almost five and twenty, Darian, not five. Nor,' he added darkly, 'do I appreciate your interference in this matter.'

'Even when I have your best interests at heart?'

'Not when I am in love with the lady, no.'

Darian held on to his temper with difficulty, having had no idea that his brother's affections had become engaged to such a degree. A physical diversion, if discreetly handled, was acceptable; a love affair most certainly was not. 'I am sure the lady has certain charms and experience, which you obviously find attractive. But it would be a mistake on your part to confuse lust with love.'

'How dare you?' Anthony challenged fiercely, his face having become a mottled and angry red. 'My intentions towards the lady are completely honourable!'

Then it was worse even than Darian had feared. 'By all means continue to bed her then, Anthony, if that is your wish. All I am asking is that you at least try to make less of the association when the two of you are in public.'

'Continue to—' Anthony looked as if he might now explode with the depth of his fury. 'I have not laid so much as an indelicate finger upon the lady. Nor do I intend to do so until after I have made her my wife.'

Now it was Darian's turn to stand up, his shock at this announcement too great to be contained. 'You cannot even think of making such a woman your wife!'

'Such a woman? You damned hypocritical prig!'

Anthony glared at him, eyes glittering darkly. 'You return from who knows where, after spending days, almost two weeks, in some woman's bed, and you have the nerve to tell me how I might conduct my own life. Whom I may or may not marry! Well, I shall have none of it, Darian,' he dismissed heatedly. 'In just a few more weeks I shall have control of my own life and my own fortune, and when I do I shall marry whom, and when, I damn well please.'

Darian gave an impatient shake of his head. 'This particular woman is—'

'A darling. An angel.' His brother's voice rose angrily. 'And it is as well you have chosen not to so much as say her name, because your conversation today shows you are not fit to do so.'

Darian winced. From all that he had heard of the lady, she was neither a darling nor an angel. Far from it.

Nor did he have any intentions of allowing his brother to marry such a woman.

And if Anthony could not be made to see sense, then the lady must...

Chapter One

***

Two days later—the ballroom of Carlisle House, London

'Would you care to repeat your remark, Wolfingham, for I fear the music and loud chatter must have prevented me from hearing you correctly the first time?'

Darian did not need to look down, into the face of the woman with whom he was dancing, to know Mariah Beecham, widowed Countess of Carlisle, *had* heard him correctly the first time; her displeasure was more than obvious, in both the frosty tone of her voice and the stiffness of her elegantly clad body.

'I doubt that very much, madam,' he drawled just as icily, as the two of them continued to smile for the benefit of any watching them as they moved about the dance floor, in perfect sequence with the other couples dancing. 'Nevertheless, I will gladly repeat my statement, in that it is my wish that you immediately cease to encourage my brother in this ridiculous infatuation he seems to have developed for you.'

'The implication being that you believe me to have been deliberately encouraging those attentions in the first place?' His hostess for the evening arched one haughty blonde brow over eyes of an exquisite and unusual shade of turquoise blue.

A colour that Darian had previously only associated with the Mediterranean Sea, on a clear summer's day.

Darian had long been aware of this lady's presence in society, of course, first as the Earl of Carlisle's much younger wife and, for these past five years, as that deceased gentleman's very wealthy and scandalous widow.

But this was the first occasion upon which Darian had spent any length of time in her company. Having done so, he now perfectly understood his younger brother's infatuation with the countess; she was, without doubt, a woman of unparalleled beauty.

Her hair was the gold of ripened corn, her complexion as pale and smooth as alabaster; a creamy brow, softly curving cheeks, her neck long, with elegantly plump shoulders shown to advantage by the low *décolletage* of her gown. Those unusual turquoise eyes were surrounded by thick dark lashes, her nose small and pert above generous—and sensual—lips and the ampleness of her breasts revealed above a silk gown of the same deep turquoise colour as her eyes.

No, Darian could not fault his brother's taste in women, for Mariah Beecham was a veritable diamond, in regard to both her beauty and those voluptuous breasts.

Unfortunately, she was also a widow aged four and thirty to Anthony's only four and twenty, and mother to a daughter of seventeen. Indeed her daughter, the Lady Christina Beecham, was newly out this Season, and so also present this evening. She also bore a startling physical resemblance to her mother.

The young Lady Christina Beecham did not, however, as yet have the same scandalous reputation as her mother.

It was that reputation that had prompted Darian's recent concerns in regard to his brother's future happiness and for him to have uncharacteristically decided to interfere in the association.

He would have understood if Anthony had merely wished to discreetly share the lady's bed for a few weeks, or possibly even months. He accepted that all young gentlemen indulged in these sexual diversions—indeed, he had done so himself for many years at that age—for their own enjoyment and in order to gain the physical experience considered necessary for the marriage bed.

Unfortunately, this lady could never be called discreet. And Anthony had made it more than plain, in their conversation two days ago, that he did not regard Mariah Beecham as his mere mistress.

As Anthony's older brother and only relation, Darian could not allow him to entertain such a ruinous marriage. As Anthony's guardian, for at least another few months and so still in control of Anthony's considerable fortune, Darian considered it to be nothing more than an unsuitable infatuation.

His efforts so far to dissuade Anthony from continuing in his pursuit of this woman had been to no avail; his brother could be as stubborn as Darian when he had decided on a course of action.

Consequently, Darian had been left with no choice but to approach and speak to the woman herself, and he had attended the countess's ball this evening for just that purpose. His forays into polite society had been rare these past few years.

He much preferred to spend his evenings at his private club, or gambling establishments, in the company of the four gentlemen who had been his closest friends since their schooldays together. The past ten years had seen the five of them become known collectively in society as The Dangerous Dukes. It was a reputation they had earned for their exploits in the bedchamber, albeit discreetly in recent years, as much as on the battlefield.

Confirmed bachelors all, Darian had recently watched as two of his close friends had succumbed to falling in love—one of them had already married, the second was well on his way to being so.

Much as he might deplore the distance a wife would necessarily put between himself and two of his closest friends, Darian considered the two ladies in question to be more than suitable as his friends' consorts, and had no doubt that both ladies were equally as smitten as his two friends and that the marriages would flourish.

Also, Worthing and Hawksmere were both gentlemen aged two and thirty, the same age as Darian himself, and so both old enough, he considered, to know their own minds, and hearts. His brother, Anthony, was so much younger, and as such Darian did not consider him old enough as yet to know enough of life, let alone the true meaning of love for any woman.

Most especially, he knew Anthony could have no previous experience with a woman of Mariah Beecham's age and reputation. Nor had it helped to quell Darian's disquiet over the association that, when he had arrived here earlier this evening, his first sighting of his younger brother had been as he danced with the countess, a besotted smile upon his youthfully handsome face!

That she now felt just as strongly opposed as Anthony did to Darian's interference in the friendship was in no doubt as he looked down into those cold and challenging turquoise eyes.

It was a long time since Mariah had allowed anyone to anger her to the degree Darian Hunter had just succeeded in doing. Not since her husband, Martin, had been alive, in fact. But Darian Hunter, the arrogantly superior Duke of Wolfingham, had undoubtedly succeeded in annoying her intensely.

How dared this man come into her home and chastise her in this way? As if she were no more than a rebellious and impressionable young girl for him to reprove and reproach for her actions?

Actions of which she was, in this particular instance, completely innocent.

Mariah had, of course, been aware of Anthony Hunter's youthful attentions to her during these past few weeks. Attentions that she had neither encouraged nor discouraged. The former, because Anthony could never be any more to her than an entertaining boy, and the latter, because she had not wanted to hurt those youthful feelings.

All of which she would happily have assured his arrogant duke of a brother, if Wolfingham had not been so determined to be unpleasant to her from the moment they began dancing together.

She should have known that Darian Hunter, a gentleman known for his contempt of all polite social occasions, would have an ulterior motive when he had accepted the invitation to her ball. That he had also claimed a dance with her was unheard of; the duke's usual preference was to stand on the edge of society, looking coldly down his haughty nose at them all.

So much for that particular social feather in her cap! For Mariah now knew that Darian Hunter's only reason for attending her ball, for asking her to dance, had been with the intention of being unpleasant to her.

If only he was not so devilishly handsome, Mariah might have found it in her heart to forgive him. After all, his concern for the welfare of his younger brother and ward was commendable; Mariah also felt that same protectiveness in regard to her daughter, Christina.

And Wolfingham's arrogant handsomeness was

of a kind that no woman could remain completely immune to it. Not even a woman as jaded as herself.

That she knew she was not immune rankled and irritated Mariah more than any of the insulting things Wolfingham had just said to her.

The duke was excessively tall, at least a foot taller than her own five feet, his overlong hair as black as night and inclined to curl slightly on his brow and about his ears. His face—emerald-green eyes fringed by thick dark lashes, a long patrician nose, sharp blades for cheekbones, with sculptured lips that might have graced a Michelangelo statue, along with a strong and determined jaw—possessed a masculine beauty that was undeniably arresting.

The width of his shoulders, and broad and powerfully muscled chest, were all also shown to advantage in his perfectly tailored, black evening clothes. As were his lean and muscled thighs, and the long length of his legs and calves.

Wolfingham was, in fact, everything that Mariah, while acknowledging his male splendour, recoiled from and disliked in a man.

'I was not implying anything, madam.' Those sculptured lips now turned back contemptuously. 'Merely stating a fact.'

Mariah eyed him coldly. 'Indeed?'

Wolfingham nodded tersely. 'I know, for example, that my brother has attended every one of the same excessive amount of entertainments as you have these past three weeks or more. That he then rarely leaves your side for longer than a few minutes. That he calls at your home at least three, sometimes four, times a week and that he stays well beyond the time of any of your other callers. And that, in turn, you—'

'You are having me watched?' Mariah gasped, so disturbed at the thought she had almost stumbled in the dance.

'I am having my brother watched,' Wolfingham corrected grimly, his tightened grip upon her gloved hand having prevented her stumble. 'It is an unfortunate... coincidence that you have always happened to be wherever Anthony is and so your own movements have been afforded that same interest.'

It was truly insupportable that the haughtily contemptuous Duke of Wolfingham dared to so blatantly admit to having monitored those innocent meetings. Totally unacceptable on any level Mariah cared to consider and regardless of Wolfingham's reasons for having done so.

Lord Anthony Hunter was young, yes, but surely old enough to live his own life as he chose, without this excessive interference from his arrogant and disapproving older brother?

As for Mariah, she did not care in the least for having her personal life placed under such close scrutiny.

'Well, madam, what is your answer to be to my request?' Darian prompted impatiently, aware that the dance would soon come to an end and having no desire to waste any more of his evening than was absolutely necessary at the countess's ball. His shoulder, still healing from the recent bullet wound, was currently giving him an excessive amount of pain, following his exertions on the dance floor.

Mariah Beecham pulled her hand from his and stepped back and away from him as the dance came to an end. 'My answer is to make a request of my own, which is that *you* should leave my home forthwith!'

Darian's eyes widened in surprise before he was able to hide it; he had been the Marquis of Durham for all of his life, and the Duke of Wolfingham these past seven years, and as such no one talked to him in such a condescending manner as Mariah Beecham had just done.

He did not know whether to be irritated or amused that she should have done so now. 'And if I should choose not to?'

Her smile was again obviously for the benefit of anyone observing them, rather than genuinely meant, her gaze remaining icily cold as she took the arm he offered to lead her from the dance floor. 'In that case I will have no choice but to ask two of my footmen to forcibly remove you,' she answered with insincere sweetness as she removed her hand and turned to face him.

In contrast, Darian's own smile was perfectly sincere. Indeed, he could not remember being this amused and entertained, by anyone or anything, in a very long time. If ever! 'Are you certain two footmen would be sufficient to the task?' he drawled derisively.

An angry flush coloured those alabaster cheeks at his obvious mockery. 'I do not care how many footmen it takes, your Grace, as long as they are success-ful in removing you, and your insulting presence, from my home.' Her voluptuous breasts quickly rose and fell in her agitation.

'I believe I have only been stating the obvious, madam.' Darian arched a challenging brow.

'Which is that you consider me entirely unsuitable as a focus for your brother's infatuation?'

'I would go further, madam, and say that I find you entirely unsuitable to occupy any situation in my brother's life.' Darian's mouth thinned disapprovingly at the realisation that *he* now found himself in the po-sition of being attracted to this bewitching woman. A woman, he had discovered during the course of the past few minutes, totally unlike any other he had ever met.

Mariah Beecham was undoubtedly a dazzling beauty and it was impossible for a man's gaze not to admire the rise and fall of those voluptuous and creamy breasts. But he had discovered, as they danced together, that she was far more than just a beautiful face and a desirable body.

Her forthright manner, and her obvious contempt for him, was a refreshing change after the years of women simpering and flirting in his company, in a bid to secure his attention and in the hopes they might one day become his duchess.

Mariah Beecham was obviously a mature and sophisticated woman. A wealthy and independent woman more than capable of making her own deci-sions as well as bringing up her young daughter alone.

Moreover, the countess was a woman who made it perfectly clear that she would do it in exactly the way that *she* pleased.

That sophistication and independence of will was having the strangest effect upon Darian's libido. Indeed, he found himself becoming aroused by her to a degree that he acknowledged his shaft had risen, and was now painfully engorged, in response to the desire he was currently feeling towards her.

Which had not been his intention when he came here this evening. Darian's only *desire* had been to protect Anthony from the woman.

His jaw tightened. 'I will leave willingly, and gladly, madam, if you will first consent to cut my brother loose from your enthralment.'

Mariah's breath caught in her throat at this man's temerity in continuing to insult her after having come to her home for the sole purpose of upbraiding her, in regard to what he considered her encouragement of his brother's attentions to her. 'I believe you must address any such remarks to your brother, rather than to myself, Wolfingham.'

'Anthony is too besotted with you to listen to reason.'

'That would seem to imply that you have tried?' she taunted.

Wolfingham's mouth thinned at her mockery. 'I do not appreciate your humour on the subject, madam.'

Her eyes flashed. 'And I, sir, do not in the least appreciate the insulting manner in which you have chosen to address me this evening.'

'Then it would appear we are at an impasse,' he drawled coldly.

Mariah's eyes narrowed. 'If you will excuse me— Let go of my arm, Wolfingham.' Her warning was dangerously soft as she looked first at those long and elegant fingers currently wrapped about the top of her arm, before raising the coldness of her gaze to stare challengingly into the duke's grimly arrogant face.

Darian had not meant to so much as lay another finger upon Mariah Beecham, not when he was already far too physically aware of her. His action, of reaching out to clasp her arm, had been purely instinctive, a reaction to the fact that she obviously intended to walk away from him.

Something he found he did not like in the slightest.

'I believe we would be better continuing this conversation outside on the terrace,' he bit out grimly as he maintained his hold upon her arm long enough to cross the ballroom and step outside on to the deserted terrace.

He released her arm as abruptly as he had earlier grasped it, before placing both of his hands behind his back and clasping them together as he looked down the length of his nose at her.

'How dare you manhandle me in that way?' Mariah Beecham gasped her outrage at finding herself alone outside on the terrace with him.

'I believe you will find that I dare much in the protection of my impressionable younger brother, madam.' Darian looked down at her coldly. 'Most especially so when I have good reason to believe a woman such as yourself could never have any serious intentions with regard to a man as young and *inexperienced* as Anthony.'

'A woman such as me?' she repeated softly.

Darian nodded tersely. 'We must both be aware of your reputation, madam.'

She eyed him coldly. 'Must we?'

His gaze turned frosty at her tone. 'That reputation apart, you were married to a man at least twenty-five years your senior and now you are dallying with a man at least ten years younger than yourself.' Darian gave a shrug. 'Perhaps it is that you are afraid of entertaining the attentions of a man of your own age?'

Mariah knew that this man could have absolutely no idea of the unhappiness she had suffered during her years of marriage to the much older Martin Beecham; they had both taken great care, for their daughter, Christina's, sake, to ensure that society did not learn of their deep-felt dislike of each other.

As for her dallying with this man's younger brother? It was pure nonsense. The young Lord Anthony had certainly received no encouragement from her, in what Wolfingham now claimed was his brother's infatuation with her.

Truth be told, Mariah did not have a serious interest in any gentleman, her marriage to Martin having soured her towards spending too much time in the company of any man, let alone trusting her emotions, her heart, to one of them. In her opinion, all men were selfish and controlling. And she had no intentions of being controlled by anyone ever again.

Certainly not Wolfingham!

'A man such as yourself, you mean?' she taunted drily.

'I would appear to fit that criteria, yes,' he bit out harshly.

She gave a scornful smile. 'I believe you are still a year or two younger than I, Wolfingham. Nor, after this conversation, would I be foolish enough to ever believe any interest you showed in me, now or in the future, to be in the least sincere.'

Then she would be wrong, Darian acknowledged reluctantly. Because these past few minutes in her company had shown him he was very interested in Mariah Beecham. Intellectually as well as physically.

Not only was it an unwise interest on his part, but it was also a forbidden one, in light of Anthony's feelings for the woman. Darian could not be so disloyal to his brother as to try to win, and bed, the woman Anthony believed himself to be in love with.

'You would be perfectly correct to mistrust any such interest,' he conceded drily.

'Then if we have quite finished this conversation?' She arched haughty brows. 'It is rather chilly out here and I have other guests to attend to.'

'First I wish to know if it is your intention to continue seeing Anthony.'

'As it would appear he attends most, if not all, of the same entertainments as myself, I do not see how I can do otherwise.'

So much for his being a voice of reason, Darian derided himself impatiently. He seemed, in fact, to have only succeeded in making the situation worse, rather than better. By approaching Mariah Beecham and talking to her of his concern for Anthony, he appeared to have angered the lady into doing the opposite of what he asked.

Not only that, but he now seemed to have developed a physical desire for the woman himself!

She looked especially lovely in the moonlight, her hair having turned palest gold, her flawless skin pure ivory against the darker silk of her gown. As for her perfume! It was a mixture of flowers and some heady and exotic scent Darian could not quite place, but that seeped insidiously into his very pores, heightening his senses, so that he was aware only of the woman standing so proudly beautiful before him.

'Must we continue to argue about this, Mariah?' His voice lowered huskily even as he took a step forward.

Her gaze became guarded as she tilted her head further back in order to be able to look up at him. 'I have not given you permission to use my first name,' she bit out frostily. 'Nor am I aware of any argument between the two of us. You have made a request and I have discounted the very idea of there ever being any sort of alliance between your brother and myself. As far as I am concerned, that is an end to the subject.'

Darian drew in a deep breath. 'I do not see how it can be, when Anthony seems so set upon his pursuit of you.'

Mariah was not at all happy at the way Darian Hunter had moved so much closer to her. So close, in fact, that she felt as if her personal space had been invaded. And not in an altogether unpleasant way.

Her years of marriage to Martin had been extremely difficult ones, so much so that in the early years of their marriage she had preferred to remain secluded in the country. Maturity had brought with it a certain confidence, a knowledge, if you will, of her own powers as a woman, if not in regard to her husband, then at least towards the attentions shown to her by other gentlemen. With that confidence had come the art, the safety, of social flirtation, without the promise of there ever being anything more.

It was a veneer of sophistication that had stood her in good stead since Martin's death five years ago, when so many other gentlemen had decided that the now widowed and very wealthy Countess of Carlisle would make them an admirable wife.

As if Mariah would willingly forgo the newfound freedom and wealth that widowhood had given her, in order to become another man's wife and possession!

Oh, she knew well the reputation she had in society, of a woman who took as her lover any man she chose. Knew of it, because it was a reputation she had deliberately fostered; if Mariah Beecham was known only to take lovers, rather than having any intention of ever contemplating remarrying, then the fortune hunters, at least, were kept at bay.

Occasionally—as now!—a gentlemen would attempt to breach those walls she had placed about herself and her private life, but to date she had managed to thwart that interest without offence being taken on either side.

Even on such brief closer acquaintance, she knew that Darian Hunter, the powerful Duke of Wolfingham, was not a man to be gainsaid by flirtatious cajolery or, failing that, the cut direct.

And he was currently standing far too close to Mariah for her comfort.

'I have already told you that you must speak with your brother further on that subject, Wolfingham.' Mariah tilted her chin challengingly. 'Now if you would kindly step aside? As I have said, it is now my wish to return to my other guests.'

Instead of stepping away Darian took another step forward, at once assailed by the warmth of Mariah Beecham's closer proximity and the aroma of that exotic and unique perfume. 'And do you always get what you wish for, Mariah?' he prompted huskily.

The nerve fluttered, pulsed, in the slender length of her neck, as the only outward sign of her disquiet at his persistence. 'Rarely what I wish for,' she bit out tersely, 'but invariably what I want!'

'And what is it that you want now, I wonder?' Darian mused as he continued to breathe in, and be affected by, her heady perfume. 'Can it be that your air of uninterest and detachment is but a ruse? And that secretly, inwardly, you long for a man who will take the initiative, take control of the situation? To take control of you?'

'No!' the countess gasped, her face having paled in the moonlight.

His brow rose. 'Perhaps you protest too much?'

'I protest because it is how I genuinely feel,' she assured vehemently. 'I am no gentleman's plaything, to be controlled.'

'No?' One of Darian's hands moved up of its own volition, with the intention of cupping the smooth curve of her cheek.

'Do not touch me!' She flinched back, her eyes huge turquoise pools now in the pallor of her face.

Darian frowned at her vehemence. 'But I should very much like to touch you, Mariah.'

'I *said*, do not touch me!' Her expression was one of grim determination as she reached up and attempted to physically push Darian away from her.

It was now Darian's turn to gasp, to lose his breath completely, as one of her tiny hands connected with his recently injured and painfully aching shoulder, causing pain such as he had never known before to burst, to course hotly, piercingly, through the whole length and breadth of his body.

He clasped his shoulder as he staggered back, his knees in danger of buckling beneath him at the depth of that pain, black spots appearing in front of his eyes even as his vision began to blur and darken.

'Wolfingham? Tell me what is wrong.'

Mariah Beecham's voice seemed to come from a long distance away as the darkness about Darian first thickened, then became absolute.

Chapter Two

Darian felt totally disorientated as the waves of darkness began to lift and he slowly awakened.

Quite *where* it was he had awakened to, he had no idea, as he turned from where he lay on the bed to look about the unfamiliar bedchamber.

It was most certainly a feminine room, decorated in pale lavenders and creams, with delicate white furnishings and lavender brocade curtains at the windows and about the four-poster bed on which he currently reclined, the pillows and bedclothes beneath him of pale lilac satin and lace.

It was Darian's idea of a feminine hell!

Certainly he felt ridiculous lying amongst such frills and fancies. Nor did he remember how he came to be here in the first place.

He recalled attending the Countess of Carlisle's ball, dancing with her, and then that heated conversation with her on the terrace. Followed by the excruciating pain, and then—nothing. He remembered absolutely nothing of what had happened beyond that.

Either he was still at Mariah Beecham's home, which, considering their argument, he doubted very much, or he had gone on to a club or gaming hell, where he had drunk too much, before spending the night with some woman. Both would be uncharacteristic; Darian never drank too much when he was out and about in the evening, nor did he bed random women.

As such, neither of those explanations seemed likely for his current disorientation.

He struggled to sit up, with the intention of removing himself from his hellish surroundings. All to no avail, as he found it impossible to move his left arm.

Glancing down at the source of the problem, Darian realised that he was wearing only his pantaloons. His jacket, waistcoat, his shirt *and* his boots had all been removed and his left shoulder was now tightly strapped up in a white bandage, his arm immobilised in a sling across the bareness of his chest.

'And just what do you think you are doing?'

Darian, having finally managed to manoeuvre himself into a sitting position on the side of the bed, now turned sharply at the sound of that imperious voice, his eyes widening and then narrowing as Mariah Beecham stepped into the bedchamber and closed the door quietly behind her.

She was no longer dressed in the turquoise silk gown, but now wore a day-dress of sky blue, the style simpler, with just a touch of lace at the cap sleeves. Her hair was also less elaborately styled than at the ball, the blonde curls merely gathered up and secured at her crown and completely unadorned.

The reason for those changes in her appearance became apparent as she lightly crossed the room on slippered feet in order to pull back the lavender brocade curtains from across the windows, allowing the full light of day to shine into the bedchamber.

She turned to look across at him critically. 'You are looking a little better this morning, Wolfingham. The doctor advised last night that you are *not* to attempt to get out of bed for several days,' she continued firmly as Darian would have stood up. 'You had burst several of the stitches on the wound on your shoulder and it was also in need of cleansing before new stitches and a bandage could be applied,' she added reprovingly.

Darian knew his wounded shoulder had been paining him for several days now, but at this moment it throbbed and ached like the very devil!

'Something, the doctor assured me yesterday evening as he reapplied those stitches, that you must have been aware of for some time before last night?' the countess added sternly.

Of course Darian had been aware of it, but his brother's future, and this unsuitable alliance, had been of more importance to him than his own painful shoulder. Nor was it the state of his own health that was now his main concern.

The reason for *that* was the how and why he came to still be in Mariah Beecham's home on the morning following her ball, for he had no choice but to accept that was where he was.

Darian frowned as he recalled their unsatisfactory conversation on the terrace of Carlisle House the evening before. How he had been unable to resist moving closer to Mariah, drawn by her unique perfume and the temptation of the perfection of her skin in the moonlight.

He also had a vague memory of Mariah reaching up to physically push him away after he had ignored her instructions to step back from her. The pain that had followed that push had been excruciating. So intense that it had caused Darian's breath to cease and his knees to buckle as the waves of blackness engulfed him. After that he remembered nothing.

Did that mean he had remained unconscious for the whole of the previous night?

That he had spent that night in Mariah Beecham's home? Possibly in her own bedchamber?

If that was indeed the case, then Darian certainly had no memory of any of those events.

But neither did he recall having departed Carlisle House. Or having been attended by a doctor.

'You are currently in one of my guest bedchambers,' the countess supplied drily, as his horrified expression must have given away at least some of his thoughts. 'My daughter's choice rather than my own,' she continued with a rueful glance at their feminine surroundings.

Darian licked the dryness of his lips before speaking for the first time since he had awoken. 'Lady Christina knows I spent the night here?'

'Why, yes,' Mariah drawled, Wolfingham's obvious discomfort in his surroundings succeeding in dissipating some of her own irritation in having to accommodate him here for the night, following his faint the previous evening. 'There was nothing else to be done once you had fainted dead away on my terrace. What else would you have me call it, Wolfingham?' she added mockingly as he gave a grunt of protest.

He scowled his displeasure. 'I was obviously overcome with pain—to call it a faint makes me sound like a complete ninny.'

'It does rather.' She arched mocking brows. 'Very well, Wolfingham, when you were overcome with pain,' she conceded drily as he continued to glower. 'Whatever the cause, it left me with no choice but to have two of my footmen carry you up the servants' stairs, before placing you in one of the bedchambers and sending for the doctor—much as the temptation was for me to just leave you unconscious upon my terrace, apparently inebriated, for one of my other guests to find!' she added.

Green eyes narrowed. 'I suppose I should thank you for having resisted that particular temptation,' Wolfingham growled.

'I suppose you should, yes,' Mariah drawled dismissively. 'But I doubt you intend doing so?'

'Not at this moment, no,' Wolfingham bit out from between gritted teeth.

She gave a mocking shake of her head. 'Bad show,

Wolfingham, when at considerable inconvenience to myself, I have undoubtedly helped you to maintain your reputation as being the stern and soberly respectable Duke of Wolfingham.'

His brow lowered darkly. 'You have also put me in the position of now having to remove myself from your home, without detection by a third party, on the morning following your ball.'

'And so tarnishing that sterling reputation anyway,' she derided. 'Poor Wolfingham!'

He remained disgruntled. 'My reputation in society is one of sternness and sober respectability?'

'Oh, yes.' Mariah strolled across to where Wolfingham still sat on the side of the bed, the darkness of his hair, tousled and unkempt, succeeding in lessening his usual air of austerity and also taking years off his age of two, or possibly three, and thirty.

Nevertheless, it was far safer for Mariah to take in the tousled appearance of Wolfingham's hair than to allow her gaze to move any lower. To where the removal of his top clothes had rendered Darian Hunter naked from the waist up, apart from the bandage and sling the doctor had placed about his left shoulder and arm the night before.

And a very masculine and muscled chest it was, too, with a light dusting of dark hair, which deepened to a vee down the firm and muscled length of his stomach, before disappearing into the loosened waistband of his black evening trousers.

None of which Mariah was at all happy to realise she had taken note of! 'The doctor remarked that the original injury to your shoulder has all the appearance of being a bullet wound,' she said challengingly. 'And was possibly inflicted a week or so ago?'

'Six days ago, to be precise,' he conceded gruffly. 'I would now have your word that you will not discuss this with anyone else,' he added harshly.

Her eyebrows rose. 'And will you trust my word if it is given?'

'I will.' Darian had little choice in the matter but to trust to Mariah Beecham's discretion. Besides which, there might be plenty of gossip in society in regard to the countess, but he had never heard of her having discussed with anyone the gentlemen with whom she was known to have been intimately involved.

'Then you have it.' She nodded now. 'Nevertheless, I should be interested to learn how you came to receive such a wound. Unless England is already once again at war and I am unaware of it?' She arched mocking blonde brows.

Darian knew that for most women, this would have been her first question upon entering the bedchamber and finding her uninvited guest had finally awoken from his stupor!

But, as he had learnt yesterday evening, Mariah Beecham was not like most women. Indeed, he truly had no idea what manner of woman she was. Which only added to her mystique.

And attraction?

Yesterday evening Mariah Beecham had given the appearance of being the sophisticated and confident woman of society that she undoubtedly was.

Today, free of adornment or artifice, Mariah Beecham looked no older than her seventeen-year-old daughter.

Her figure was that of a mature woman, of course, but her face was smooth and unlined in the sunlight, her eyes a clear Mediterranean turquoise, despite her having hosted a ball the previous evening and no doubt having retired very late to her own bedchamber.

Darian felt that stirring of his arousal, which was rapidly becoming a familiar reaction to being in this woman's company, as he gazed upon her natural loveliness through narrowed lids. 'I fear that peace will not last for too much longer, now that Napoleon has returned to France and is currently reported to be on his way to Paris,' he rasped in an attempt to dampen his physical response to this woman.

'I do not interest myself in such boring things as politics and intrigue,' she drawled dismissively. 'Nor does any of that explain how you came to receive such a wound.' She continued to look at him pointedly, before a derisive smile slowly curved the fullness of her lips at his continued silence. 'Can it be that the cold and haughty Duke of Wolfingham has recently fought a duel? Over a woman? Surely not?' Mocking humour now gleamed in her eyes.

Darian had not cared for the disparaging way in which Mariah Beecham had earlier said his reputation was one of sober respectability. Or that she now referred to him as the cold and haughty Duke of Wolfingham. Nor did Darian like the implication that she doubted he had ever felt so emotional about any woman that he would have fought a duel over her.

Admittedly, he was, by nature, a private man. One who had long preferred his own company or that of his few close friends. But he'd had no idea, until now, that this privacy of nature had resulted in society, in Mariah Beecham, believing him to be sober—boring?—as well as cold and haughty—arrogant?

As the elder son of the sixth Duke of Wolfingham, and Marquis of Durham from birth, Darian had been brought up to know he would one day inherit the title of Duke from his father, along with the management of all the estates entailed with the title. An onerous and unenviable responsibility, which had become his at the age of only five and twenty; much earlier than might have been expected, but his father had been but sixty years of age when he died.

With the title of Duke and its other onerous responsibilities had also come the guardianship of his younger brother, Anthony.

All of these things had made it impossible for Darian to continue with the hedonistic pursuits he had previously enjoyed with his close friends and that, along with his soldiering, had hitherto occupied much of his time.

He had not realised until now that it had also rendered him as being thought stern and sober, as well as haughty. By society as a whole, it would appear, and by this woman in particular.

Nor did he care to be thought so now, for it made him sound as old as Methuselah and just as uninteresting! A circumstance Darian did not enjoy, when he considered his own undoubted physical response to Mariah Beecham.

His mouth tightened. 'I am sure you are as aware as I that the fighting of duels is forbidden.'

She arched blonde brows. 'And do you always follow the rules, Wolfingham?'

Darian gave a humourless smile. 'Your opinion of my reputation would seem to imply as much.'

'But we are all so much more than our reputations, are we not?' Mariah Beecham replied enigmatically.

'Do you include yourself in that statement?' Darian studied her through narrowed lids, taking note of that curling golden hair, the smoothness of her brow, those clear and untroubled blue eyes and the light blush that now coloured her alabaster cheeks, her lips both full and succulent.

A face that appeared utterly without guilt or guile.

Misleadingly so? Or could that air of innocence, so unusual in a woman of four and thirty, possibly be the real Mariah Beecham?

In view of this woman's reputation, Darian found that impossible to believe; the countess could no doubt add 'accomplished actress' to her list of other questionable attributes!

Mariah did not at all care for the way in which Wolfingham was now studying her so intently.

Having Wolfingham point out, the previous evening, that his younger brother had shown a marked interest in her these past weeks was irritating enough.

But to have the far too astute, and equally as intelligent, Darian Hunter, the Duke of Wolfingham, show an interest in her, for whatever reason, was not only disturbing, but could also be dangerous.

For Mariah was most certainly not all that her reputation implied. Indeed, she did not believe, after Wolfingham's revelations the night before regarding that reputation, that she was much of any of what society, or this man, believed her to be.

Deliberately so. For who would suspect that the scandalous Mariah Beecham, the widowed Countess of Carlisle, was also an agent for the Crown, and that she had been so these past seven years and more?

She had not set out for it to be so. She had become embroiled in the intrigues of the English court quite by accident, after discovering that her own husband was a traitor to both his country and his king.

Having no idea what to do with that knowledge, it had taken Mariah some weeks to find a member of the government to whom she might pass along that information.

Only to discover that once she had done so the first time, there was no going back. That her position in society could, and did, open many doors, as it invited confidences from both ladies and gentlemen of the *ton*.

And so, from that time on Mariah had made a point of forming her friendships only with those ladies and gentlemen who might have knowledge that would be of benefit to, or was opposed to, the English monarchy or government.

She had been brought up in the knowledge that her parents' only expectation of her was that she become the wife of a titled gentleman, even if she did not love that gentleman. Her father was himself extremely wealthy, but not completely acceptable to all of society. Indeed, greater acquaintance with society had shown her that love was not a requirement of any of the *ton*'s marriages.

Her husband's only expectation of her had been that she bring a considerable portion of her father's fortune to their marriage, his own fortune having become depleted almost to extinction.

Mariah loved her daughter dearly and, because of that, had willingly sacrificed the years she had suffered of being thought of as just an adjunct of her husband, Lord Martin Beecham, the Earl of Carlisle.

Finding herself suddenly of use, her opinions of importance, had caused Mariah to relish the new role in her life.

As a consequence, the past seven years were the first ones where Mariah had felt useful and valued for herself alone.

She would be unable to continue along that path if anyone in society were to ever discover that she used her title and wealth only as a way in which she might work, and spy, for the Crown.

If the shrewd Darian Hunter, Duke of Wolfingham, were to ever discover her work as a spy for the Crown...

She forced a teasing smile to now curve her lips.

'Surely that is for me to know and for others to find out?'

Darian drew in a sharp breath at Mariah Beecham's huskily flirtatious tone, a quiver of awareness tingling down the length of his spine as his body responded.

At the same time, he sensed that Mariah's flirtation was somehow not genuine, but forced, although he had no idea why that should be.

Indeed, nothing about this woman, or her actions, was in the least clear to him. And until such time as it was, if it ever was, he would be well advised to remain wary in her company.

'Considering that you have refused my request to discourage my brother's interest in you,' he answered her briskly as he stood up, 'and the amount of times our paths have chanced to cross these past seven years or more, I very much doubt there will be any opportunity in future for me to know you any better than I do at this moment.'

'Do I detect a note of regret in your tone?' she taunted.

'Not in the least,' Darian dismissed harshly. 'I am more than ready to leave and so end our acquaintance.'

'Then you had best do so,' she drawled unconcernedly.

His eyes narrowed. 'Did you dismiss my carriage last night?'

The countess laughed huskily. 'Tempted as I was to do otherwise!' She nodded in confirmation. 'It might have been amusing to see how you would have explained that occurrence to any who cared to ask. But, of course, you are Wolfingham, one of The Dangerous Dukes,' she continued drily. 'And like your four friends, Wolfingham does not care to explain himself, to any man or woman!'

Darian's eyes narrowed. 'You do not have a very good opinion of me, do you?'

'Until yesterday evening I do not believe I held any opinion of you whatsoever,' she assured uninterestedly.

His breath caught in his throat at that dismissal; if he did not care to explain himself to man or woman then it was equally as true that same man or woman would never dare to question him, either! 'And now?'

'Now I know without a doubt that you are both arrogant and insulting.'

Darian winced at her dismissive tone, knowing that he had been both of those things in his dealings with this woman. 'If you would kindly send word to Wolfingham House, via one of your obviously capable footmen, and inform my butler that I have need of my carriage, I will then be able to remove my intrusive self from both your household and your presence!'

Mariah felt a sense of disquiet at the abruptness of Wolfingham's departure. 'I had not expected you to capitulate quite so easily, Wolfingham, in regard to my continuing friendship with your brother?' she mocked.

'I am not capitulating, merely withdrawing in order to rethink my strategy,' he assured drily.

'Ah.' Mariah nodded knowingly. 'I remind you that the doctor instructed that you were to remain abed for the next three days at least.'

Having now crossed to where his clothes lay draped over the bedroom chair, Wolfingham turned to look at her with those narrowed green eyes.

Green eyes surrounded by the longest, thickest, darkest lashes Mariah had seen on any man.

Indeed, Darian Hunter was a man of startling and masculine good looks; the nakedness of his back was exceedingly broad and muscled for a man who supposedly ran his estates from the comfort of his home here in London. As were his arms and the flatness of his abdomen, his legs also appearing long and muscled in those black evening trousers. Even his feet, *sans* his boots, bore a long and elegant appearance.

And Mariah could not remember the last time she had noticed the masculine beauty of any man, fully clothed or otherwise!

Perhaps when she had been Christina's age, and on the brink of womanhood, she might have allowed her head to be turned a time or two by a handsome gentleman, but certainly not at any time since. The very nature of her marriage to Martin Beecham had meant there had never been any further inclination on her part to indulge in those girlish infatuations.

But Mariah could not deny, to herself at least, that she had noticed, and been aware of, every muscle and sinew of Darian Hunter's muscular torso these past few minutes. And also been affected by it, as the slight fluttering of her pulse, the warmth in her cheeks and the aching fullness of her breasts all testified.

And she did not want to feel any of those things for any man!

Warning her that Darian Hunter more than lived up to his dangerous reputation, not only to her continued work for the Crown, but also to Mariah's own peace of mind.

'Nor shall I once I am returned to it,' Darian now answered the countess huskily, aware of the sudden, sexual, tension in the heavy stillness of the bedchamber. 'As for my brother, if all else fails, then I fear Anthony must learn of the vagaries of women in the way that all men do—the hard way!' he added derisively.

'Now you are being deliberately insulting again, Wolfingham, not just to me, but all women.' An angry flush now coloured Mariah Beecham's cheeks.

A blush that only succeeded in enhancing her beauty; her eyes glittered that deep turquoise, her cheeks glowing, her lips having become a deep and rosy red.

A very kissable deep and rosy red...

'That was not my intention,' Darian dismissed softly.

'No?'

'I believe my remark was more specific than that,' he assured huskily, holding Mariah's gaze as he slowly crossed to where she stood so stiff and challenging in the middle of the bedchamber. 'Might I ask for your assistance in dressing? I realise it is usual for a man to ask a woman for help to *un*dress,' he added drily as Mariah's brows rose in obvious surprise at his request, 'but I am unable to pull my shirt on over my head on my own.'

Mariah accepted that Wolfingham's request for assistance was perfectly logical, given his injury, and yet she still baulked at the thought of performing such a task of intimacy for him.

She very much doubted that Wolfingham—or any in society!—would believe it if told, but Mariah had seen no man, other than her husband, even half-naked as Wolfingham now was. And Martin, twenty-five years her senior, had certainly never possessed the same muscular and disturbing physique Wolfingham now displayed so splendidly.

Her mouth firmed. 'I will send for one of my footmen to assist you.'

'There is no need for that, surely, when you are standing right here before me?' Darian murmured throatily, his good sense having once again deserted him as he was again assaulted by Mariah Beecham's unique and arousing perfume. An arousal he was finding it more and more difficult to control when in this woman's presence.

In view of Anthony's infatuation with Mariah Beecham, it would be unwise for Darian to allow his own attraction to her to develop into anything deeper than the physical discomfort it already was. Even if Mariah Beecham was herself agreeable to taking it any further, which he already knew that she was not.

On a logical level, Darian knew and accepted all of those things.

Unfortunately, his aroused and hardened body had a completely different opinion on the matter!

'If you please?' His gaze was intent upon her face now as he held out his shirt to her, allowing him to note the deepening of the blush that coloured her cheeks and the pulse throbbing at the base of her slender throat.

A surprising physical reaction, surely, coming from an experienced woman reputed to have indulged in many affairs, both during her marriage and since?

Darian's gaze narrowed searchingly as she stubbornly lifted her chin to meet his challenging gaze. She still made no effort to relieve him of his shirt. 'Unless, of course, you find the idea, and me, too repulsive…?'

It took every effort of Mariah's will to hold back the choked, slightly hysterical, laugh that threatened to burst from her throat, at the mere suggestion that any woman, that *she*, might find anything about Wolfingham in the least repulsive.

For the first time, in more years than she cared to remember, Mariah found herself wholly and completely physically aware of a man.

Of Darian Hunter, the arrogant and contemptuous Duke of Wolfingham, of all men.

Nevertheless, Mariah was aware. Of his reassuring height. His rakishly handsome good looks. And the lean and muscled strength of his body.

And she did not welcome the sensation.

She placed a disdainful curl on her lips. 'It is certainly true that I have always been…particular…as to which men I choose to be intimate with.'

'All evidence to the contrary, madam!'

Mariah drew her breath in sharply at the unexpected and contemptuously delivered insult, before just as quickly masking that response; the sophisticated and experienced Mariah Beecham—a public persona she had deliberately nurtured these past seven years—would laugh derisively in the face of such an insult.

Which was exactly what Mariah did now. 'I am flattered that you should have even taken the time to notice such things in regard to myself, Wolfingham.'

His nostrils flared. 'You take delight in your reputation?'

Did she?

Oh, yes!

It was Mariah's own personal joke on society, that they should all perceive her as being one thing and she knew herself to be something else entirely. Only her darling Christina, now seventeen, and currently enjoying her very first Season, had necessarily been informed of the true reason for Mariah's flirtatious behaviour in public. It was a risk to share that confidence with anyone, of course, but Mariah simply could not have borne for her darling daughter, the person she loved most in all the world, to ever believe the nonsense society gossiped about her.

'No doubt as much as you do your own,' Mariah now dismissed enigmatically.

Darian scowled as he recalled what this woman had described as being his reputation. 'Then that would be not at all.'

She smiled. 'Unfortunately, even you cannot dictate what society thinks of you.'

'Even I?'

'Why, yes, for you are the omnipotent Duke of Wolfingham, are you not?' she dismissed airily. 'Your shirt, if you please,' she instructed briskly, reaching out to take the item of clothing from him. Wolfingham continued to hold on to it, standing far too close to her while he did so.

Darian looked down at her intently, wishing he knew at least some of the thoughts going on inside that surprisingly intelligent head of hers. Before speaking with Mariah Beecham yesterday evening, Darian would have described her, had considered her, as nothing more than an empty-headed flirt, with little in her beautiful head but the pursuit of her own pleasure.

He still had no idea of what or who Mariah Beecham truly was, but an empty-headed flirt she certainly was not.

Rendering her flirtation with Anthony, a man fully ten years her junior, all the more puzzling.

'Mariah—' Darian broke off his husky query as there was the briefest of knocks on the door to the bedchamber before it was opened.

'Mama, I—' Lady Christina Beecham stopped what she had been about to say as she stood in the open doorway, eyes wide as she took in the apparent cameo of intimacy between her mother and their half-dressed guest.

Darian had certainly never been discovered in quite such a scene of apparent intimacy by the daughter of any woman, and he now found himself momentarily nonplussed as he searched his mind for something appropriate to say or do. He frowned down at Mariah Beecham as she looked up at him. She began to chuckle huskily, before that chuckle became a full-throated laugh of pure enjoyment.

At Darian's obvious expense…

Chapter Three

'I trust, Lady Christina, that you do not think too badly of me for the circumstances under which we last met?' Darian murmured politely as the two of them danced together at Lady Stockton's ball, fully a week after their first momentous meeting in a guest bedchamber at Carlisle House.

A week in which Darian had necessarily to spend most of his time in his own bed, recovering from the setback from his bullet wound. For much of that time he'd found his thoughts returning to that morning in Mariah Beecham's guest bedchamber.

Not that there had been a great deal for him to re-member and think about once Christina Beecham had appeared in the bedchamber so unexpectedly.

Mariah's amusement at the interruption had been short-lived, her movements having then become brisk and businesslike as she had helped Darian on with his shirt before excusing herself to go downstairs and see to the ordering of his carriage. The two ladies had left the bedchamber arm in arm together.

Darian had felt surprisingly weak after having completed dressing himself as best he could, sitting on the side of the bed to recover as he awaited the arrival of his carriage. Once arrived, his groom had then helped him down the stairs and into that carriage, necessitating that Darian's words of gratitude for the countess's assistance be brief.

Once returned to Wolfingham House, he had sent for his own physician, who'd agreed with his colleague's diagnosis, as he confined Darian to bed for the next three days at least, and rest thereafter for several more days, unless Darian wished to shuffle off his mortal coil completely.

Darian despised any form of weakness, in himself more than others, and that enforced time abed had not sat easily upon his shoulders, despite receiving several visits from his closest friends to help relieve the boredom. Anthony had also called upon him several times and been told that Darian was indisposed and not receiving visitors, which allowed Darian to at least avoid that particular confrontation until he was feeling more himself.

He had to trust that the countess would keep her promise in regard to discussing with others the bullet wound to his shoulder and the night he had necessarily spent in her home. But he had no doubt Mariah would have taken great delight in regaling Anthony with the details of Darian's efforts to persuade her to end their friendship.

Once he felt well enough, Darian had dictated a letter of gratitude to his secretary, to be delivered to the countess, carefully worded so as not to reveal the full extent of his indebtedness to her. He had received no acknowledgement or reply to that missive. As if Mariah Beecham, like himself, would prefer to continue as if that night had not taken place at all.

Consequently, this was the first occasion upon which Darian had been able to offer his apologies in person, to the younger of the two Beecham ladies at least, for the manner of his indisposition the week before.

Mariah Beecham had proved somewhat more elusive this evening than her daughter, always flirting or dancing away on the arm of some other gentleman whenever Darian had attempted to approach her. Christina Beecham had proved far less averse to his request that she dance a set with him. No doubt, unlike her mother before her, Christina Beecham was fully aware of the compliment being paid to her, as the Duke of Wolfingham did not, as a rule, dance at any of these occasions.

She looked up at him shyly now from between thick blonde lashes, her eyes the same beautiful turquoise colour as her mother's, her blonde-haired beauty also similar to that of the countess. 'Mama has already explained the situation to me, your Grace,' she now dismissed huskily.

Darian would be very interested to hear how Mariah had managed to do that, when he was not altogether sure how to explain the situation himself. *To* himself, as well as to others.

'Indeed,' he murmured noncommittally. 'She seems

to be fully occupied this evening.' Another glance about the ballroom had shown him that Mariah Beecham was no longer in the room.

Christina gave a smile of affection. 'Mama's time, and dance card, are always fully occupied at such entertainments as these, your Grace.'

Darian looked down searchingly at the younger of the Beecham ladies. 'And are you not bothered by having to witness the spectacle of seeing so many gentlemen flirting and leering at your mother's— Forgive me,' he bit out stiffly. 'That was unforgivably rude of me.' And, he realised, far too close to his feelings on the matter for his own comfort.

Mariah was wearing a red silk gown this evening, with a very low *décolletage* that revealed the full, ivory swell of the tops of her breasts. A fact Darian had noted several gentlemen taking advantage of as they talked or danced with her.

'Yes, it was,' Christina Beecham answered him with the same bluntness as her mother. 'But then, Mama had already warned me you are very forthright, in both your manner and speech,' she added pertly.

Darian found he did not care for being dismissed so scathingly. Nor did he believe Mariah had used a word so innocent as 'forthright' to describe his previous manner and conversations with her. 'I meant no disrespect to you,' he bit out tersely.

'Only to Mama,' she acknowledged drily. 'Mama has taught me that it is better not to pass comment on what one does not know.'

'Obviously my own mother was neglectful in that particular duty.'

'Obviously.'

Yes, this lady, for all she was very young, was proving to be just as capable of delivering a set-down as her mother!

Darian was also aware that his own reaction to those flirting and leering gentlemen was not one of impartiality, but rather one of complete partiality. Indeed, he had disliked intensely to have to stand by and witness those other gentlemen showing Mariah such marked attentions.

In truth, he had thought of Mariah Beecham far more than was wise this past week. Of her beauty. Her unique perfume. Of his own physical and uncontrollable response to the lush curves of her body.

And, quite frankly, he found the whole situation annoying. Distracting. *Unbearable.*

'My dance, I believe, Darian?'

Darian roused himself from those troubling thoughts to look about him almost dazedly; the music had stopped playing and the other couples had left the dance floor, as they now gave curious glances their way. All without Darian having been aware of any of it. His brother, Anthony, was also now standing beside him with eyebrows raised expectantly, as he waited for Darian to release Christina Beecham.

'Of course.' He straightened abruptly as his arms fell back to his sides and he stepped away from Lady Christina. 'I— Thank you,' he added with a belated bow towards the young lady.

Anthony continued to look at him frowningly, eyes narrowed speculatively as he took his brother's place at Christina Beecham's side. 'Are you quite well again now, Darian?'

'Quite, thank you.' Darian nodded abruptly.

'In that case I will call upon you tomorrow,' Anthony stated firmly, his expression challenging, telling Darian that the conversation between the two of them might have been delayed for this past week, whilst he was feeling unwell, but it was not to be avoided altogether!

'Very well.' Darian gave another distracted nod as he once again glanced about the ballroom to see that the three of them were still the focus of more than one group of gossiping people.

'Your Grace?'

'Lady Christina?' Darian turned, one brow raised enquiringly.

A sparkle of humour now brightened those eyes, so like her mother's. 'I believe Mama to have accepted Lord Maystone's invitation to accompany him into the next room to partake of refreshment.'

Had he made his interest in Mariah's whereabouts so obvious that even her daughter was aware of it?

And what the deuce was Mariah doing in Maystone's company, a gentleman Darian had reason to know rather better than might be socially apparent?

Aged in his late fifties, and a widower for more than twenty years, Aubrey Maystone was nevertheless still a handsome man, with his head of silver hair and chiselled features. Nor had his trimness gone to obesity, as had happened to so many of his peers.

He was also Darian's contact at the Foreign Office in regard to his work for the Crown.

Whatever the reason for Aubrey Maystone's interest in Mariah, Darian had no intentions of wasting any more of his own time this evening in an effort to secure the opportunity in which to converse with her again.

He took care to avoid his brother's no-doubt accusing gaze as he gave Lady Christina a rueful smile. 'Thank you.' He gave another bow before turning to cross the ballroom in long and determined strides as he went in search of the refreshment room.

And Mariah Beecham.

'I believe you have accepted an invitation to attend Lord and Lady Nicholses' house party in Kent this weekend?' Lord Maystone nodded his acquaintance to Mrs Moore, as she stood across the room, even as he continued his softly spoken conversation with Mariah.

'I have, yes.' Mariah eyed him curiously. 'Will you also be attending?'

'Good heavens, no!' Maystone turned to give her his full attention, a look of distaste upon his lined but handsome face. 'Subjecting myself to a single tedious evening of socialising in a week is quite enough for me. I assure you, I have no intentions of suffering through a weekend of it.'

'Poor Aubrey.' Mariah chuckled sympathetically,

placing a conciliatory hand briefly on his arm as she sobered. 'Do you have a special reason for asking whether or not I am to attend this particular weekend party?' Aubrey Maystone had long been her contact for the work she did for the Crown.

'I have reason to believe— Ah, Wolfingham.' Aubrey turned to greet the younger man warmly. 'Just the man! The countess is as polite as she is beautiful, but nevertheless I believe her to be in need of far younger company than my own.'

Mariah was relieved she had her back turned towards Darian Hunter, so he would not mistake the colour in her cheeks for anything other than what it was: annoyance at the way in which he had seemed to dog her every step this evening.

Lady Stockton had obviously been as surprised as her guests when the Duke of Wolfingham, a man who rarely attended any of the entertainments of the *ton*, but who had now attended two in as many weeks, had arrived at her home earlier this evening. A surprise that had lasted for only a few seconds, as that lady hastily crossed the room to welcome her illustrious guest.

Mariah's reaction to seeing Wolfingham again had been less enthusiastic. She wondered what he was doing here.

Indeed, she had gone out of her way not to show any reaction at all, but rather to ignore him completely.

Not an easy task, when it seemed that every time she had turned round this evening Wolfingham had been standing there behind her, looking very dark and handsome in his impeccable evening clothes, the darkness of his hair rakishly dishevelled.

Nor did Mariah believe his appearance now, in the refreshment room, to be coincidental, either.

No doubt, whilst forced to convalesce, in order to recover completely from his injury, the duke had also had time to rethink his decision not to leave his younger brother's fate to chance—or Mariah's caprice or whimsy.

Whatever the reasoning behind Wolfingham's dogged persistence this evening, Mariah was more than a little weary of reassuring him that she had absolutely no romantic interest, nor would she ever have, in his brother, Anthony.

'Not at all, Aubrey.' She gave Maystone a warm smile as she now linked her arm with his. 'Indeed, you are so handsome and distinguished that you put all younger men to shame,' she added before turning to look up at Wolfingham now that she felt reassured her cheeks were no longer flushed.

Darian's lips twitched and he held back a smile as he met Mariah Beecham's challenging gaze, recognising her remark for exactly what it was: an insult to him rather than just a compliment to Aubrey Maystone.

Although the warmth of familiarity between the two of them did seem to imply a deeper acquaintance than just a socially polite one.

To the degree that Maystone might be Mariah's current lover? If that was so, then it made a nonsense of Darian's request that she cease her friendship with the far more youthful and inexperienced Anthony.

The possibility of that being true also brought a scowl to Darian's brow. 'Lady Beecham.' He bowed formally as it was the first occasion upon which the two of them had actually spoken this evening; Mariah's avoidance of him had been absolute. 'May-stone.' Darian's nod to the older man was terse.

'Wolfingham.' There was a mischievous twinkle in the older man's eyes, as if he had guessed Darian's thoughts and was amused by them. 'Have you come to steal Mariah away from me for a dance, or are you going to join us in some refreshment?'

'Well, I am certainly not here for refreshment.' Darian made no effort to hide his distaste as he eyed the glasses in their hands. 'I have heard it said that Lady Stockton is parsimonious with the brandy in her punch.'

'Surely it is not necessary to become inebriated in order to enjoy oneself?' Mariah drawled mockingly.

'Not at all.' Darian observed her between narrowed lids. 'But if I wished to drink something as innocuous as fruit juice then I should request fruit juice.' Standing so close to Mariah, he was once again aware of her unique perfume, the lightness of spring flowers and that deeper, more exotic perfume, which he now recognised as being jasmine. It was a heady and arousing combination.

'How true.' Maystone's dismissive laugh broke the tension that had been steadily rising between Darian and Mariah. 'It seems I must forgo your delightful company for now, my dear.' He placed his glass down on the table and raised Mariah's gloved hand to his lips before releasing it. 'And allow a younger man to steal you away from me for a dance.'

Mariah frowned as she answered coolly, 'To my knowledge, his Grace has not had the foresight to request a dance with me this evening. As such, I am afraid my dance card is completely full.'

'Well, there you have it, Wolfingham.' Maystone turned towards him with a grin. 'You will have to be much quicker off the mark in future, if you are to secure a dance with our delightful Mariah,' he teased jovially.

Darian's frustration with his own increasing arousal, as well as Mariah's avoidance of him, was now such that he could barely keep the impatience from his tone and he knew the frown had deepened on his brow. 'A pity, of course, Lady Beecham,' he drawled coldly. 'But as consolation I have just enjoyed the pleasure of dancing with your lovely daughter, Lady Christina. A delightful young woman and a credit to both you and her father.'

Mariah looked up sharply at Wolfingham, easily noting the mocking challenge in his deep green eyes as he returned her gaze unblinkingly. No doubt because he was fully aware of the fact that she would prefer that he stay well away from her young and impressionable daughter.

Oh, Christina had accepted readily enough Mariah's explanations as to Wolfingham's indisposition the previous week having been the reason for his having to remain at Carlisle House overnight. But beneath that acceptance there had been an underlying girlish excitement, a curiosity, about the arrogantly handsome and illustrious Duke of Wolfingham. The last thing Mariah wished was for Christina to develop a crush on the man.

Not that she thought Wolfingham was in the least serious in his attentions to Christina; rather Mariah believed his intention had merely been to annoy her. If so, he had succeeded!

The less she, and Christina, had to do with Darian Hunter, the dangerous Duke of Wolfingham, the better Mariah would like it. Her lifestyle was such, most especially her work for the Crown, that she did not wish to have such an astutely disturbing gentleman as Wolfingham taking an interest in it, or her.

'I believe the music and dancing have now stopped for supper, your Grace.' Mariah had noted the influx of people into the room and strolling towards the supper tables. 'It appears to be raining outside, so perhaps you might care to accompany me for a stroll in the West Gallery?' At which time she intended to warn him to stay away from her daughter!

Darian was not particularly proud of himself for having used Lady Christina Beecham as a means of securing Mariah's company, but neither was he about to apologise for it. Not when it had succeeded in accomplishing his aim, which was to talk with Mariah again. In private.

Although he wasn't sure that being alone with Mariah was an entirely good idea, given his painful state of arousal.

'You will stay away from my daughter!' Mariah barely waited until the two of them had entered the long and deserted picture gallery, lit by a dozen candles or more, before removing her hand from Wolfingham's arm and glaring up at him, her cheeks hot with temper in the candlelight.

'Will I?' he came back with infuriating calm, dark brows raised in equally as mild query.

'Yes—when it is not a serious interest, but merely a means of punishing me.'

'That is not very flattering to Lady Christina.'

'But true.'

'Is it?' he returned mildly.

'What do you want from me, Wolfingham?' Mariah looked up at him in exasperation. 'A public declaration of my uninterest in your brother? Would that appease you? Reassure you?'

He gave a humourless smile. 'It would most certainly not appease or reassure Anthony.' His mouth tightened. 'Nor would it do anything for my own future relationship with him, if you were to tell him that I had been instrumental in bringing about the sudden end to your friendship.'

Mariah drew in a deep breath through her nose. 'Perhaps you should have thought of that before you chose to so arrogantly interfere in his life a week ago?'

'What is your relationship with Maystone?'

Mariah was momentarily disconcerted by this sudden change of topic. As she was meant to be?

She and Aubrey Maystone preferred to keep the true nature of their relationship private and as such it was rare for them to pass any time together in public. Indeed, they would not have done so this evening if Aubrey had not expressed a wish to speak with her urgently. A conversation that had been cut short by the arrival of Darian Hunter.

But the manner of the public acquaintance between Mariah and Lord Maystone was such that Wolfingham could not possibly have guessed that there was a deeper, more private, connection between the two of them. Could he?

Mariah was quickly learning that it would not be wise on her part, or anyone else's, to underestimate the intelligence or astuteness of Darian Hunter.

'My acquaintance with Lord Maystone is a long-standing one,' she answered frostily. 'Come about because he was once a friend of my late husband.'

'And is that all he is to you?'

'What are you accusing me of now, Wolfingham?' Her tone was impatiently exasperated, deliberately so. 'Do you imagine that I am currently enjoying a relationship with Lord Maystone, as well as your brother? Would that not make my bed very overcrowded?' she added scathingly. 'And what business would it be of yours, even if that were the case? I am a widow and they are both unattached gentlemen, so there is no prior claim to hinder the existence of either relationship.' She gave a dismissive shrug.

A nerve pulsed in the duke's tightly clenched jaw. 'Except a moral one.'

'You are a fine one to preach to me of morals, Wolfingham, when you are currently sporting the bullet wound you received whilst fighting a duel over some woman!' Her eyes flashed in the candlelight.

Darian glowered his frustration down at her, wanting to deny the accusation, but knowing that to do so would then bring the real cause of that wound back into question. A question he would not, could not, answer.

Having no answer, he decided to act instead.

Although that was possibly an exaggeration on his part, when his arms seemed to have moved of their own volition as they encircled Mariah's waist and he pulled her in close against the hardness of his body.

Her exotic perfume immediately filled all of his senses as his head swooped down to capture her lips with his own. Soft and delectable lips that had parted with surprise, so allowing for further intimacy as Darian's tongue swept lightly across her lips before plunging into the heated warmth beneath.

She felt so slender in his arms, the fullness of her breasts crushed against his chest, her lips and mouth tasting of honey. A silky-soft sweetness and heat that drew Darian in even closer, as he attempted to claim, to possess, that heat as his own. To claim, to possess, Mariah as his own.

Mariah had been totally unprepared for Wolfingham taking her into his arms, let alone having him kiss her. So unprepared, that for several stunned seconds she found herself responding to that kiss as her hands moved up to cling to the lapels of the duke's evening coat, her body crushed, aligned with Wolfingham's, as his mouth continued to plunder and claim her own. Making her fully aware not only of the hardness of his chest, but also the long length of his arousal pressing against the warmth of her abdomen.

She allowed herself to feel a brief moment of triumph, at the knowledge, this physical evidence, that Darian Hunter, the coldly arrogant Duke of Wolfingham, was aroused by her. From holding her in his arms. From kissing her.

Those brief moments of triumph were quickly followed by ones of panic and a desperate need to free herself. A move she attempted to instigate as she now pushed against that hard and muscled chest even as she wrenched her mouth out from beneath that sensually punishing kiss. 'Release me immediately, Wolfingham!'

Her eyes now gleamed up at him in the candlelight, her chest quickly rising and falling as she breathed heavily, having managed to put several inches between the hardness of his body and her own, but failing to release herself completely.

'You are taking your protection of your brother too far, sir,' she added fiercely as her hands against his chest kept him at a distance but he still made no effort to remove the steel band of his arms from about her waist.

A nerve pulsed in the tightness of his jaw. 'This has nothing to do with my brother.'

'It has everything to do with him.'

Darian was breathing heavily, unable to reason clearly as he looked down at Mariah, his mind and senses too full of her to form a coherent thought, other than the taste of her on his own lips and tongue. The feel of her soft curves against his much harder ones. The smell of her causing his body to throb and pound with need.

A need that the pallor of Mariah's face in the candlelight, and over-bright turquoise eyes, said she did not reciprocate.

He gave a pained frown. 'What did you think would happen when you invited me to join you alone here in the gallery, Mariah?'

'Not this!' Her breasts quickly rose and fell in rhythm with her agitated breathing as she continued to hold him at arm's length. 'Never this!'

Darian's frown deepened to one of concern as he heard the underlying sob in her voice. 'Mariah—'

'I believe the lady has expressed a wish to be set free, Darian!'

Darian's head whipped round at the sound of his brother's harshly reproving voice, a scowl darkening his brow as he saw Anthony watching them from the shadowed doorway into the gallery, the expression on his brother's face one of disgust as well as fury.

A disgust and fury Darian fully deserved, given the circumstances, of Mariah's obvious distress and the feelings Anthony had previously expressed for the woman Darian now held in his arms.

Feelings that Darian had totally forgotten about in his need to claim Mariah's lips for his own.

His arms fell heavily back to his sides as he stepped back and away from her, only to then reach out a hand to steady Mariah as she appeared to stumble.

'Do not touch me!' she lashed out verbally even as she pulled free of his grasp, twin spots of fevered colour now high in her cheeks as she turned away. 'Accompany me back to Lady Stockton's ballroom, if you please, Lord Anthony,' she requested stiffly as she left Darian's side to walk quickly down the gallery to take the arm his brother so gallantly offered her.

Anthony paused to give Darian a warning glance over the top of Mariah's averted head. 'I have changed my mind, Darian, and we will now talk again later tonight, rather than tomorrow morning.'

Darian recognised those words for exactly what they were: a threat, not a promise.

Chapter Four

Darian found himself seated beside the fire at his club the following afternoon, after partaking of luncheon with two of his closest friends; Christian Seaton, the Duke of Sutherland, and Griffin Stone, the Duke of Rotherham.

'You are saying the countess refused to see you when you called at Carlisle House this morning?' Sutherland prompted lightly.

Darian scowled into the depths of his brandy glass. 'Her butler claimed she was indisposed and not receiving visitors.'

'Women do tend to suffer these indelicacies, you know.' Rotherham nodded dismissively.

The scowl remained on Darian's brow as he looked across the fireplace at his friend slumped in the chair opposite. 'So you think the indisposition might be genuine, rather than an excuse not to see me in particular?'

'Well, I would not go quite so far as to say that,' Rotherham drawled. 'From what you told us over luncheon, you did make rather a cake of yourself, you know, throwing out accusations and insults in that overbearing manner of yours!'

Darian gave a wince. 'Thank you so much for your reassurances, Griff.' After Anthony's promised late visit to Wolfingham House the night before, Darian had every reason to know he had indeed made a cake of himself where Mariah Beecham was concerned and certainly did not need Rotherham to tell him as much.

The need to apologise to Mariah was the very reason Darian had attempted to call upon her this morning. Only to be sent away by her butler without so much as a glimpse of the lady, let alone be allowed to give the apology owed to her.

'Think nothing of it, old boy.' Rotherham grinned across at him unabashedly.

'Beautiful woman, the countess,' Sutherland murmured appreciatively as he relaxed in a third chair.

'Oh, yes!' Rotherham nodded.

Darian eyed the two men sharply. 'Have either of you...?' He could not quite bring himself to say the words; the thought that Sutherland or Rotherham might have been Mariah's lover was enough to blacken his mood even more than it already was.

'Never had the pleasure.' Sutherland sighed his obvious disappointment.

'Unfortunately not.' Rotherham looked equally as wistful.

Darian found himself breathing a little easier at knowing that two of his friends, at least, had never been one of Mariah Beecham's lovers. Even if rumour suggested that plenty of other gentlemen had!

'I suppose there is always the possibility the countess was not actually *at* home when you called this morning?' Sutherland quirked a brow. 'You did say she was rather pally with Maystone yesterday evening, so perhaps she went home with him? Just a thought.' He shrugged dismissively as Darian's scowl deepened.

'The idea did occur to me.' Of course it had occurred to him that Mariah might have spent the night elsewhere than her London home.

Until he had remembered that Mariah had accompanied her young daughter to the Stockton ball and so was hardly likely to have abandoned that young lady in favour of going home with a lover.

Of course Mariah could have gone out again once she had returned Lady Christina to Carlisle House.

He shifted restlessly, aware that he was taking far too much of an interest in front of his two friends, who along with himself were the last of the bachelor Dangerous Dukes, in what Mariah Beecham did or did not do.

'Do you have hopes in that direction yourself?' Sutherland now arched a curious brow.

Did he?

Darian had been unable to sleep last night for thinking of Mariah, of holding her in his arms and kissing her.

Of his desire for her!

A desire he had neither sought nor wanted.

Because every objection he had given Anthony for his brother to bring an end to his involvement with Mariah Beecham—apart from the difference in their ages—also applied to Darian himself. An association, any association on his part with the notorious Mariah Beecham, was unacceptable.

A realisation that seemed not to make a bit of difference to the desire Darian felt for her and that had so disturbed his sleep the night before.

Oh, it was perfectly acceptable for Darian to take a mistress if he so chose, even if he had never chosen to do so before now. But Mariah Beecham, a woman whose private life was gossiped and speculated about constantly, was not suitable even for that role in the public *or* private life of the Duke of Wolfingham.

His continuing work for the Crown had caused Darian to long ago make a conscious decision not to bring any unnecessary attention to his private life. And any liaison with Mariah Beecham would necessarily become public and ultimately throw him front and centre of the same gossip that always surrounded her. Gossip Darian wished to avoid, even if Mariah had been willing to enter into such a relationship with him.

Which Darian had every reason to believe, to *know*—more so than ever, after his clarifying conversation with Anthony the night before—she was not!

So Darian had told himself again and again, as he lay in his bed unable to sleep the previous night.

Today, with the disappointment of not being able to see and speak with Mariah this morning, as he had fully intended that he would, he was not so sure on the matter.

'Of course not,' he answered Sutherland sharply. 'I am merely aware that I owe the woman an apology and I am anxious to get it over and done with.'

'Protesting a little too strongly, do you think, Sutherland?' Griffin Stone turned to prompt the other man drily.

'More than a little, I would say,' Sutherland drawled as they both turned to look at Darian, brows raised over mocking eyes.

Darian withstood that look with a censorious one of his own, having every intention of making his apologies to Mariah Beecham before returning to their previous relationship—that of complete indifference to each other.

Something Darian very much doubted was going to happen, on his part at least, when he was shown into the gold salon of Mariah's home late the following morning and his rebellious body responded immediately.

He had wisely sent her a note late yesterday afternoon, requesting she supply a suitable time for him to call upon her today, rather than run the risk of calling and being turned away for a second time.

Mariah looked ethereally beautiful this morning, in a fashionable gown of the palest lemon, her blonde curls a golden halo about the pale delicacy of her face and throat.

A pallor that implied that perhaps Mariah's claim, of being indisposed yesterday, had indeed been genuine?

'Are you feeling any better today?' Darian prompted gruffly as he crossed the room to where she now stood, taking the gloved hand she raised to him in formal greeting.

'Such politeness, Wolfingham. Indeed, I should hardly recognise you,' Mariah taunted drily as she deftly removed her hand from his before resuming her seat, the gold brocade sofa a perfect foil for her golden loveliness. Deliberately so?

His mouth thinned. 'Could we perhaps at least attempt a modicum of politeness between the two of us, rather than begin to argue immediately after we see each other again?'

'I do not believe it is a question of us arguing, Wolfingham. We simply do not like each other!'

He drew in a sharp breath, knowing that for his part that claim was untrue, that he liked—indeed, he *desired*—Mariah Beecham far more than was comfortable.

Mariah studied Wolfingham from beneath lowered lashes as he made no reply to her taunt.

It had been her dearest wish never to find herself alone with this gentleman again. She had only agreed to this morning's meeting because she knew he was not a man she could continue to avoid indefinitely, if he had decided it should be otherwise. Her claim of being indisposed yesterday, as a way of avoiding Wolfingham when he called, had not been all fabrication; Mariah had stayed in her bed late yesterday morning, her head aching after suffering a restless and sleepless night.

Because she had not been able to stop thinking of Darian Hunter. Or his having kissed her.

Or remembering that she had responded.

A response that was so unprecedented, and had troubled Mariah so deeply, that she had found it impossible to sleep these past two nights for thinking of it.

A response she had since assured herself would not happen again.

Could not happen again!

So it was entirely frustrating for her to acknowledge her awareness of how arrogantly handsome Wolfingham looked this morning, dressed in a dark green superfine and buff-and-green-striped waistcoat, his linen snowy white, buff-coloured pantaloons moulded to the muscular length of his long thighs above his brown-topped black Hessians. His hair was in its usual fashionable disarray about his sharply etched features.

As she also noted the pallor to those sharply etched features and the dark shadows beneath his deep green eyes. As evidence, perhaps, that Wolfingham had not rested any better than she had herself these past two nights?

Although she doubted it was for the same reasons.

Against all the odds—her dislike of Wolfingham and the years of her unhappy marriage to Martin— for the first time in her life Mariah had found herself actually enjoying being held in a man's arms two nights ago.

Even more surprising was the realisation of how she had *responded* to that depth of passion Wolfingham had ignited in her.

Her marriage to Martin had been completely without love and affection from the onset, on either side, and equally as without passion. Indeed, for the first ten years of their marriage, the two of them had spent very little time even living in the same house, Mariah languishing in the country with their daughter, while Martin preferred to spend most of the year living in London. At best they had been polite strangers to each other on the rare occasions they did meet, for the sake of their daughter, and more often than not they had ignored each other completely.

That had changed slightly seven years ago, when Mariah began to spend the Season in London, Martin necessarily having to accompany her to at least some of those social engagements. But even so, those occasions had only been for appearances' sake, and they had continued to retain their separate bedchambers, and for the most part live their separate lives, on the occasions they were forced to reside in the same house together.

So, it had been all the more surprising to Mariah that she had not only responded to, but enjoyed being held in Darian Hunter's arms and being kissed by him, the night of Lady Stockton's ball. Not only an unprecedented response, but an unwanted one as well, and ensuring that Mariah was all the more determined it would not occur for a second time.

'Did you have something in particular you wished to discuss with me when you called upon me yesterday morning, then sent a note requesting a convenient time you might call again today? Or is it as I suspected and you merely wish to add to the insults you invariably make when we meet?'

Darian's breath left him in a hiss at this deliberate challenge; at least when he was breathing out his senses were not being invaded by Mariah Beecham's heady and arousing perfume.

Darian had once again been aware of that perfume the moment he stepped into the salon. Indeed, he believed he now knew that unique aroma so well he would be able to pick Mariah Beecham out of a roomful of veiled and heavily robed women, just by the smell of that heady perfume alone.

Seeing Mariah again this morning, being with her again, his senses once again invaded by her beauty and aroused by that heady perfume, made a complete nonsense of his denials of yesterday to Rotherham and Sutherland, in regard to his not having the slightest interest in pursuing a relationship with Mariah Beecham.

He might not *want* to feel this desire for her, but he did feel it nonetheless.

'Oh, do stop scowling, Wolfingham, for it is giving me a headache,' Mariah snapped at his continued silence. 'I am sure there are many women who might find all this brooding intensity attractive, but I am not one of them.' She wrinkled her nose in disgust. 'Personally, such behaviour has always filled me with a burning desire to administer a weighty smack to the cheek of the gentleman in question.'

The situation in which Darian currently found himself did not at all call for any sign of levity on his part. Consequently he did try very hard not to give in to the laughter that threatened to burst forth.

To no avail, unfortunately; his amusement was such that it refused to be denied and he found himself chuckling with husky appreciation for Mariah's obviously heartfelt sentiments.

'You are incorrigible, madam,' he admonished once he had regained his breath enough to speak.

'I, sir, merely remain unimpressed by any gentleman's angst,' Mariah returned disparagingly.

'But more so when that gentleman is me,' Wolfingham acknowledged drily.

'Yes.' She did not even attempt to deny it as she gave an impatient shake of her head. 'It was *you* who asked if you might call upon me today, Wolfingham, so I ask once again that you state your business and then leave. I find maintaining even this level of politeness between the two of us to be taxing in the extreme.'

Darian knew he fully deserved Mariah's lack of enjoyment of his company. He had made so many mistakes in their short acquaintance, it seemed. Too many for her to forgive him? Easily, if at all.

He drew in a deep breath. 'I needed to speak

with you again because it appears that I owe you an apology, Mariah.'

Her eyes widened in obvious surprise. 'Indeed?'

His jaw grated he held it so tightly clenched. 'Yes.'

'For what, pray? You have made far too many insults, to me and about me, for me to ever be able to pick out a specific one for which you might apologise.'

Darian bristled. 'Such as?'

'The disgusting thoughts you so obviously held two evenings ago, with regard to my friendship with Aubrey Maystone, for one.'

Ah. Yes. Well, there was that, of course…

He shifted uncomfortably. 'It was a natural conclusion to have come to, surely, given the circumstances of the ease of the friendship between the two of you?'

'Only if your mind was already in the gutter, as yours so often appears to be where I am concerned!' Her eyes flashed.

Darian could not deny that he had thought the worst of Mariah before he had even met her, hence his initial alarm regarding Anthony's involvement with her. But in his defence Mariah Beecham's reputation in society was such that surely, at the time, he could have formed no other opinion, in regard to Anthony's obvious and public attentions to her.

At the time.

Darian knew differently now, of course. Which was the very reason he had been so determined to speak with Mariah these past two days. So that he might apologise and, hopefully, discuss the matter with her further.

'It was doubly insulting, when you had already accused me of being involved in an affair with your younger brother,' she now accused coldly.

And now, Darian recognised heavily, was the perfect opportunity in which to make that apology and inform her of his mistake.

He grimaced. 'I have had the opportunity to speak with Anthony again, since the two of us parted so badly at the Stockton ball.' He ignored her scathing snort; she knew as well as he did that it had been Anthony's parting remark—promise—that had caused the two brothers to talk again later that very same night. 'And it would seem—it would seem—'

Darian was not accustomed to apologising for his actions, to anyone, and yet in this particular instance he knew he had no choice; he had seriously wronged Mariah and now he must apologise for it.

He sighed. 'My brother has now made it more than clear to me that his affections lie elsewhere than yourself.'

'Hah!' Those turquoise-blue eyes gleamed across at him with triumphant satisfaction. 'Did I not tell you that you were mistaken in your accusations?'

'It is very unbecoming in a woman to say "I told you so" in that gleeful manner, Mariah.' Darian scowled, still more than a little irritated with himself for having initially jumped to the wrong conclusion where his brother's affections were concerned, and even more so for having then acted upon those conclusions by insulting Mariah to such a degree he now owed her an apology.

He was equally as irritated that by doing so he had now placed himself in the position of being the one to tell Mariah the truth of that situation.

'Not when that woman has been proved right and you have been proved wrong.' she came back tartly.

Darian chose his words carefully. 'I was only half-wrong—'

'How can a person, even the illustrious and arrogant Duke of Wolfingham, be half-wrong?' she scorned. 'Admit it, Wolfingham. In this matter you were completely and utterly in the wrong.'

'No, I was not.' Darian sighed deeply, choosing to ignore the scathing comment in regard to himself; no doubt Mariah would have more, far stronger insults to hurl at him before this conversation was over. 'I was merely mistaken as to which of the Beecham ladies held Anthony's affections and consequently, the reason for his polite and public attentions to you.'

He also had absolutely no idea how Mariah was going to react upon learning that Anthony was paying court to her young daughter, Christina, rather than to herself. Even if he only took into consideration Mariah's feelings towards *him*, Anthony's despicable and insulting older brother, then Darian was sure that it could not be in a favourable way.

Any more than were his own feelings on the matter. Admittedly, he could not help but feel a certain amount of relief at having learnt that Anthony was not besotted with Mariah Beecham, after all. For the reasons he had previously stated.

But also on a personal level.

Unwanted as his own desire for Mariah might be, Darian nevertheless felt a certain relief at knowing he was not harbouring a desire for the same woman for whom he had believed his brother had serious intentions.

As for the real object of his brother's affections…

Admittedly the seventeen-year-old Lady Christina Beecham was more acceptable as a wife for Anthony than her mother could ever have been. But, in Darian's opinion, only marginally so. Christina Beecham could not escape the fact that she was the daughter of a woman with a notorious and scandalous reputation.

A woman with a notorious and scandalous reputation who, he realised belatedly, for the moment seemed to have been struck uncharacteristically dumb. At having learnt that his brother, Anthony's, romantic inclinations were directed towards her young daughter rather than herself?

Mariah drew a harsh breath into her starved lungs as she realised she had forgotten to do so these past few seconds. 'Forgive me, but I— Am I to understand that your brother, Lord Anthony Hunter, a gentleman aged almost five and twenty, believes himself to be in love with—that he has serious intentions towards my seventeen-year-old daughter?'

Wolfingham gave a terse nod of his head. 'That is exactly what I am saying, yes. I have no reason to believe that your daughter returns Anthony's feelings.' His eyes narrowed. 'But perhaps you do?'

'Not as such, no.'

'You seem unduly concerned?'

'She is seventeen years of age, Wolfingham. At the very least Christina will have been flattered by the attentions of an eligible and sophisticated gentleman such as your brother,' Mariah answered distractedly as she now recalled all those occasions these past few weeks when Lord Anthony Hunter had been included in the group of admirers surrounding herself and Christina.

As she also remembered the polite attentions the young Lord Anthony had paid to her and the visits he had made to Carlisle House—and that Wolfingham had mistaken for a romantic interest in Mariah—in an effort, no doubt, to ingratiate himself into Mariah's good opinion.

And Christina's youthful heart?

The more Mariah considered the matter, the more she believed that her daughter could not help but be aware of Anthony Hunter's romantic interest in her.

Having spent much of Christina's early years closeted alone together in the country, Mariah believed she and Christina were closer than most mothers and daughters of the *ton*. But Christina was fully grown now—or believed that she was!—and Mariah now realised that those childhood confidences had become fewer and fewer during these past few weeks spent together in London.

Perhaps because Christina harboured a secret passion for her handsome admirer?

A secret passion that, because of her age, she knew Mariah could not, and would not, approve of?

Oh, she had been unable to deny Christina her first Season; her daughter was seventeen, after all. But Mariah had not launched Christina into society with any intentions of seeing her young daughter engaged to be married within weeks of her having made that appearance.

As she herself had been.

Mariah gave a determined shake of her head. 'Whether she does or does not, it will not do, Wolfingham.'

He arched dark brows. 'You would refuse Anthony's suit?'

'Her uncle, the earl, is her male guardian, but I will strongly advise against it, yes.'

'Why would you?' Having been so set against the match himself, Darian now felt contrarily defensive on his brother's behalf. Anthony might be young, and occasionally irresponsible, but none could doubt his eligibility in the marriage mart. 'Lady Christina is seventeen years of age—'

'And so far too young to fall in love, or consider taking on the duties of marriage!' Mariah scorned.

'Surely she is the same age as you must have been when you married?'

'We were not discussing me!' Those turquoise-coloured eyes now glittered fiercely across the room at him.

Wolfingham's gaze became quizzical at her vehemence. 'I thought an advantageous marriage was the whole purpose of a young lady making her debut in society?'

'That is a typically male assessment of the situation.'

He arched a dark brow. 'Then perhaps it is that you consider that having a daughter married to be ageing to yourself?'

'Do not be any more ridiculous than you have already been, Wolfingham!' Mariah stood up agitatedly. 'My reservations have absolutely nothing to do with myself and everything to do with Christina. She is far too young to know her own mind in such matters.'

'She seemed a prepossessing young lady when I danced with her the other evening.'

'So she is.' Mariah nodded her impatience. 'And no doubt I will one day, in the distant future, be happy to dance at her wedding. But not now, when Christina has only been out for a matter of weeks, rather than years. Nor do I have any reason to believe that you would approve of an alliance between your brother and my daughter?' She looked up at him challengingly.

No, of course Darian did not approve of it and he had voiced his reservations regarding the match to his brother when the two of them had spoken so frankly together two evenings ago. A disapproval that Darian knew had once again fallen on deaf ears; Anthony was bound and determined in his pursuit of Christina Beecham.

A determination that was obviously to now be thwarted by that young lady's mother.

Again, Darian found himself playing devil's advocate. 'I still fail to see, apart from your daughter's youth, what your own objections can be to the match. Anthony will come into his own fortune on the occasion of his twenty-fifth birthday in just a few months' time. He is the grandson, the son and now the brother of a duke—'

'I am fully aware of who Lord Anthony is and of his family connections,' Mariah assured him dismissively.

'And the fact that the severe and sober Duke of Wolfingham is his brother is no doubt part of the reason for your own objections to the match?' Darian surmised drily.

'Do not even pretend to be insulted, Wolfingham, when you know full well your feelings on this matter entirely match my own.' Mariah sighed her impatience.

'I repeat, why are they?'

Mariah drew in a deep and controlling breath, knowing she was overreacting to this situation, allowing her own unhappy marriage at the age of seventeen, the same age as her daughter was now, to colour her judgement. And in front of the astute and intelligent Darian Hunter, of all people. 'Of course I wish for Christina's future happiness. Just not yet. She is so young and has not yet had chance to enjoy even her first Season.'

'Is it only because he is my younger brother?' he guessed shrewdly.

Mariah gave a determined shake of her head. 'I also have no doubt that, if Christina were ever to become your brother's wife, you would make her life, as your sister-in-law, nothing but a misery.'

He stiffened. 'You are insulting, madam, to believe I would ever treat any woman so shabbily.'

'You would treat any daughter of *mine* more than shabbily,' she insisted. 'And I do not want that for Christina. She deserves so much more than that.' So much more than Mariah had suffered herself as Martin's wife, unloved by her husband and disapproved of and ignored by his family for her more humble beginnings. 'No.' She shuddered at the thought of Christina suffering the same fate. 'If Lord Anthony should ask, I will not ever give my blessing to such a match.'

Darian frowned darkly. 'And what of your daughter's feelings on the matter? Have you considered that perhaps she might return Anthony's affections? If not now, then at some future date?'

'It is perhaps a possibility that she may one day *believe* she returns those feelings,' Mariah allowed grudgingly. 'But at seventeen she is too young to know her own heart and mind.'

'As you yourself were at the same age?'

She stiffened. 'Again, we were not talking about me.'

'Then perhaps we should be.'

'No, we will not,' Mariah informed Wolfingham coldly. 'Not now, nor at any time in the future.'

Darian studied Mariah intently, knowing by the stubborn set of her mouth, and those flashing turquoise eyes, that she would not be moved on the subject of her own marriage.

And so adding to the mystery that Mariah Beecham had become to him.

A mystery that had already occupied far too much of his time and thoughts these past ten days.

He gave a grimace. 'Have you considered how your husband might have felt regarding an alliance between his daughter and the Hunter family?'

Her chin rose. 'I had no interest in my husband's opinions whilst he was alive and I certainly have none now that he is dead.'

Because, as he had begun to suspect, like so many marriages of the *ton*, the Beecham marriage had been one of convenience rather than a love match? A question of marrying wealth to a title? The wealth of Mariah's father matched to Beecham's title as the Earl of Carlisle?

Darian's own parents had married under similar circumstances, but they had been two of the lucky ones, in that they had come to feel a deep love and respect for each other, ensuring that their two sons had grown up in a family filled with that same love and respect.

The fact that Mariah had only been seventeen to Beecham's two and forty when their marriage took place, and the rumours of her numerous affairs since, would seem to imply she might not have been so fortunate.

'That is a very enlightening comment,' he said slowly.

'Is it?' Mariah returned scathingly. 'I doubt I am the first woman to admit to having felt a lack of love for the man who was her husband.'

'Your words implied a lack of respect, too.'

Those eyes flashed again. 'Respect has to be earned. It is not just given.'

'And Carlisle did not earn yours?'

'The feeling was mutual, I assure you.'

'And yet the two of you had a daughter together.'

A cold shiver ran down the length of Mariah's spine as she remembered the night of Christina's conception. A painful and frightening experience for Mariah and a triumphant one for Martin.

Her gaze now avoided Wolfingham's probing green one. 'I believe it is time you left.'

'Mariah—'

'*Now*, Wolfingham!' Before Mariah broke down completely. Something she dared not do, in front of the one man who had already somehow managed to get through the barrier Mariah had long ago placed about both her emotions and the memories of the past. For fear they might destroy her utterly.

Darian had no idea what would have happened next. Whether he would have acceded to Mariah's request for him to leave, or whether he would have followed his own instincts and instead taken Mariah in his arms and comforted her. This talk of her marriage to Carlisle seemed to have shaken her cool self-confidence in a way nothing else had.

Instead, their privacy was interrupted as the butler entered the room bearing a card upon a silver tray, which he proceeded to present to Mariah.

She picked up the card and quickly read it, before tucking it into the pocket of her gown as she spoke to her butler. 'Please show his Lordship into my private parlour, Fuller,' she instructed briskly. 'And then return here and show his Grace out.' Her gaze was challenging as she turned and waited for the butler to leave before looking across the room at Darian.

Darian breathed out his frustration, both with what was obviously Mariah's dismissal of him and a burning curiosity to know the identity of the man the dismissed butler was even now escorting to Mariah's private parlour.

Which was utterly ridiculous of him.

He had lived for two and thirty years without having the slightest interest in Mariah Beecham, or any of her friendships, and for him to now feel disgruntled, even jealous, of this other man was ludicrous on his part.

And yet Darian could not deny that was exactly how he now felt.

Just as he knew Mariah was equally as determined that her two male visitors would not meet each other.

'I believe I am perfectly capable of showing myself out, Mariah,' Darian informed her harshly.

She blinked. 'Fuller will return in just a moment.'

'And I am ready to depart now.'

'But—'

'Good day to you, Mariah.' Darian bowed to her stiffly before crossing the room and stepping out into the cavernous hallway, only to come to an abrupt halt as he saw the identity of Mariah's caller.

'Wolfingham!' Lord Aubrey Maystone turned at the bottom of the staircase to greet him enthusiastically; eyes alight with pleasure as he strode forward to shake Darian warmly by the hand. 'How fortuitous this is, for you are just the man I wanted to see.'

Darian failed to see how that was possible, when Maystone could not have had any idea that Darian would be at Mariah Beecham's home this morning.

Or could he?

As Darian knew only too well, from working so closely with the older man for so many years, Maystone was deceptively wily. A man capable of weaving webs within webs and all without losing sight of a single thread of those intricate weavings.

Although Darian seriously doubted that the other man's role as spymaster was his reason for calling upon Mariah this morning.

Indeed, Mariah's instruction, for Maystone to be taken to her private parlour, left only one conclusion in regard to Maystone's presence here this morning: that the older man was indeed the man Mariah was currently intimately involved with and his joviality was now merely a politeness in front of Mariah's butler.

Chapter Five

Mariah had hurriedly followed Wolfingham out into the entrance hall and had arrived just in time to witness Aubrey Maystone warmly greeting and shaking the younger man by the hand. Much, she noted ruefully, to Darian Hunter's stony-faced displeasure.

No doubt because Wolfingham had now deduced, despite her denials to the contrary, that she was indeed involved in an affair with Aubrey Maystone.

Just as she was sure that Aubrey Mayston's real reason for calling upon her so unexpectedly this morning was sure to be a matter of some delicacy and no doubt related to her work for the Crown.

In which case, the arrogantly disapproving Darian Hunter would just have to continue to think what he would regarding her relationship with the older man. As, it seemed, he always chose to think the worst of her.

'Aubrey!' She greeted the older man with a warm smile as she crossed the hallway to link her arm with his and allowed him to kiss her lightly on the cheek. 'His Grace was just leaving.' She turned to look at Wolfingham with coldly challenging eyes.

'I would prefer him to remain, my dear.'

To Mariah's surprise it was Aubrey Maystone who answered her softly, rather than the harsh response she had fully expected from Wolfingham regarding her obvious dismissal of him. A frown marred her brow as she turned to give the older man a puzzled glance.

Maystone raised his brows pointedly towards her hovering butler before answering her. 'Might I suggest you consider ordering us all some refreshment?'

'Er—of course.' Mariah was more than a little disconcerted. 'Bring tea and brandy, if you please, Fuller,' she instructed distractedly before the three of them turned to enter the gold salon. Mariah was still totally at a loss to understand why Aubrey Maystone should have deliberately delayed Wolfingham's departure.

'What is this all about, Maystone?' Darian Hunter felt no hesitation in expressing his own impatience with the older man's request, as he restlessly paced the length of the room once the three of them were alone together with the door closed behind them. A disdainful smile curled his top lip. 'I trust we are not about to engage in a proprietary claim of ownership on your part, in response to your having discovered my having paid the countess a visit this morning?'

'Wolfingham!' the older man snapped reprovingly.

Mariah also gasped at Wolfingham's deliberate

insult. 'I am not a hunting dog, nor a piece of horse-flesh, Wolfingham, to be *owned* by any man!'

In truth, it had not been Darian's intention to insult Mariah. He had merely meant to challenge the older man for what he perceived must be Maystone's displeasure at finding Darian in the home of his mistress.

Darian had not *meant* to insult Mariah, but he could see by the stiff way that she now held herself, the fierce glitter in her eyes and the two spots of angry colour that had appeared in her otherwise pale cheeks, that was exactly what he had done. 'I meant you no disrespect—'

'Did you not?' she scorned.

Had he?

Darian frowned as he realised that *he* was the one who felt displeased and unsettled, both at the other man's arrival and the unmistakable familiarity that he knew existed between Maystone and Mariah.

It was obvious, from the warmth of Mariah's tone and manner whenever she spoke to the older man, that she liked and approved of Aubrey Maystone. Just as it was equally as obvious, from the coldness of her tone and manner whenever she addressed Darian, that she disliked and disapproved of *him* intensely.

And he, Darian acknowledged heavily, had done little in their acquaintance so far to dispel or temper those feelings of dislike. The opposite, in fact. 'I sincerely apologise if I spoke out of turn.' He bowed stiffly to Mariah before turning to the older man. 'Perhaps, if you have something you wish to say to me, Maystone, it might be better if we arrange another time and place in which to have that conversation?'

'I trust you are not considering engaging in *another* duel, Wolfingham?' Mariah Beecham scorned.

'Another duel?' Lord Maystone looked confused.

'A misunderstanding on Lady Beecham's part,' Darian dismissed coolly; Aubrey Maystone was one of the few people who knew in exactly what manner Darian had received the bullet wound to his shoulder. 'If you will send word when it is convenient for me to call upon you, Maystone?'

'I was perfectly serious when I said it was fortuitous that you happened to be here this morning.' The older man eyed him impatiently.

Darian studied the older man through narrowed lids, noting the hard glitter to Maystone's eyes and the lines of strain etched beside his nose and mouth. Evidence that the other man's mood was not as cheerfully relaxed as it had appeared to be when he had arrived? 'What could you possibly have to discuss with me if not my visit this morning to Mar—Lady Beecham?'

Mariah was wondering the same thing, as she also wondered why Aubrey Maystone had called at her home at all; as a precaution, the two of them had never met at Aubrey's offices in the Foreign Office or here in her home, but chose instead to pass information on to each other whenever Aubrey arranged for them to meet socially. The fact that Aubrey had chosen to call on her here this morning must mean that he had something of a serious nature to import.

Although that still did not explain why it was he wished Wolfingham to remain.

'That will be all, thank you, Fuller.' Mariah smiled at the butler once he had straightened from placing the tray bearing the tea and brandy on the low coffee table. 'I am not at home to any more callers this morning,' she added, waiting until her butler had left the room and closed the door behind him before turning back to Aubrey Maystone. 'What—'

'I shall begin this conversation,' Maystone spoke firmly, 'by first stating that it is necessary that I now inform both of you of the other's involvement in certain matters of secrecy and delicacy to the Crown.'

Mariah was so stunned by Aubrey's announcement that she instantly sank down weakly into one of the armchairs, before she even dared to look up and see that Wolfingham's expression was one of equal shock—proof that he was just as stunned as she was at being so bluntly outed as an agent for the Crown, by the very man who acted as her—no, their?—spymaster?

Mariah was more than shocked; she was having great difficulty believing Aubrey Maystone's announcement in regard to the haughtily disapproving and condescending Duke of Wolfingham.

The man Mariah knew society believed to be both sober and stern.

A man she personally knew to be arrogant and unpleasant, as well as insulting.

That same gentleman worked secretly, as she did, for the Crown?

It seemed barely possible it could be true, yet it must be so if Aubrey Maystone said that it was.

The puzzle was why Aubrey Maystone had now revealed something that had, in Mariah's case, remained a secret to all but her daughter for seven years.

A sentiment, a confidence, that Wolfingham echoed, if the glittering green of his eyes was any indication. 'What do you mean by talking so frankly, Maystone?'

'Recent developments have made it necessary, Darian,' the older man excused heavily as he gave a dismissive wave of his hand. 'And I also suggest that the two of you get over your shock as quickly as possible, so that we might then proceed.'

Darian *was* shocked by Maystone's unexpected announcement, too much so to be able to hide the emotion.

And it was a knowledge, in regard to Mariah Beecham, that instantly posed a dozen other questions in Darian's mind.

Such as how long had Mariah been engaged in such dangerous and secret work for the Crown?

And why had she?

When did she?

Where?

And how?

It was perhaps the answer to that last question that interested Darian the most.

For surely there was only one way in which a woman in society might go about gaining secret information?

'It would seem, Aubrey, that Wolfingham is too

busy drawing his own conclusions as to the methods I might utilise—flirtation, teasing, *seduction*—in order to be able to garner that information, to be able to proceed at the moment,' Mariah drawled coldly, for once Wolfingham's thoughts having been crystal clear to her. Unpleasantly so!

He scowled. 'I was merely—'

'I am well aware of what you were *merely thinking*, Wolfingham,' she snapped disgustedly.

His jaw tightened. 'Do not presume to know the thoughts in my head, madam—'

'Enough,' the older man interrupted wearily. 'We do not have time for petty arguments this morning.'

Those green eyes turned as hard as the emeralds they resembled as Wolfingham turned his attention back to the other man. 'Then perhaps you might state what it is we do need to talk about so urgently that you have deliberately chosen to put both myself and Lady Beecham in a position of personal vulnerability?'

'Only to each other.'

'Exactly!' Wolfingham scowled darkly.

Maystone grimaced. 'It was necessary, Darian.'

'As I said, I would be interested to know why.'

'Plots and treason, Wolfingham,' Maystone stated emphatically.

'There is always talk of plots and treason,' Wolfingham dismissed scathingly.

'This time it is different.' The older man frowned darkly. 'Perhaps you will better understand the situation if I tell you that in the past week plots to assassinate the tsar and the Austrian emperor have been discovered and the assassins dealt with. That such a plot, despite all our efforts to make it otherwise, still exists in regard to our own Prince Regent.'

'Good lord!' Wolfingham slowly lowered his body down into one of the armchairs, his face pale.

Maystone nodded. 'Five days ago two people, a tutor and a footman, attached to and working in the households of two prominent politicians, were taken in for questioning on the matter. My own private secretary was taken into custody late last night,' Maystone continued grimly. 'And he is even now being questioned as to the part he has played in the plot to assassinate the Regent himself.'

'How is such a thing possible?' Mariah breathed faintly, her hand shaking as she lifted it to her mouth.

Maystone gave Darian a telling glance. 'I am sure *you*, at least, will better understand the seriousness of this threat if I say that your old friend Rousseau was involved?'

Both men were well aware that the Frenchman was no friend of Darian's. Indeed, Rousseau was responsible for the bullet wound in Darian's shoulder. As Darian was responsible for having brought the other man's life to a swift and sudden end.

He gave a shake of his head. 'He left England and returned to France almost a year ago.'

'But not before he had set up a network of his own spies and assassins amongst the households of some of the leading members of the English government,' Maystone rasped disgustedly. 'All set in place and ready to act when or if Napoleon departed Elba and attempted to return to France as emperor, which, as we all know, he is currently doing. At which time the heads of the allied countries were to be eliminated, an act designed to throw the governments of the alliance into chaos.'

Darian lay his head back against the chair and closed his eyes, better understanding the reason for Maystone's agitation now. Such a plot as the other man was outlining could have had, might still have, a devastating effect on the shaky alliance formed against Napoleon.

Especially so, as Napoleon was even now marching triumphantly towards Paris, an army of hundreds of thousands at his back. And all without, as Napoleon had claimed it would be, a shot being fired.

'How was it even possible for a Frenchman to do such a thing?' Mariah frowned.

Maystone gave a humourless grimace. 'Because he worked and lived in England for a year under the guise of tutor to a son of a member of the aristocracy. Jeffrey Lancaster, the future heir and now the Earl of Malvern, to be exact.'

'You are referring to the French tutor the Lancaster chit eloped with last year?' Mariah gasped. 'Does it surprise you, knowing what you do now, that I have made a point of knowing these things?' she added dismissively as Wolfingham gave her a frowning glance.

'That "Lancaster chit" is now the Duchess of Hawksmere and the wife of a close friend of mine!' he reminded stiffly.

'She was also the lover of this man, André Rousseau, for several months, if I am to understand this situation correctly,' Mariah maintained stubbornly.

'Situations are not always as they appear.'

'As I once reminded you,' Mariah said pointedly 'You—'

'Could we please concentrate on the subject at hand?' Maystone interrupted irritably, before sighing heavily. 'Yes, my dear Mariah, for the sake of clarity, I can confirm that you are quite correct in believing that André Rousseau was tutor to young Jeffrey Lancaster for a year and also the same man who persuaded Lancaster's sister Georgianna into eloping with him. I would like to add in her defence,' he continued firmly, 'that she was also responsible for bringing us information vital to our government just weeks ago. Information that also resulted in Rousseau's death in Paris just fifteen days ago.'

'Fifteen days ago?' Mariah did a quick calculation in her head as she recalled that it had been nine days ago that Wolfingham had told her he had been shot 'six days ago, to be precise'.

It did not take a genius to add nine and six together and come up with the correct answer.

She slowly turned to look at Wolfingham, knowing by the challenging glitter in those emerald-green eyes as he returned her gaze, that her calculations were correct.

Wolfingham had killed André Rousseau in Paris fifteen days ago.

And in doing so he had received a bullet wound to his shoulder.

She had no doubt now that Darian Hunter, the haughty Duke of Wolfingham, was not only a spy for the Crown, as she was, but that he had also travelled to France in the past three weeks, in the midst of the turmoil of the Corsican's escape and return to France, and succeeded in killing the man who was a known spy for Napoleon.

As Wolfingham had killed others, in the past, who had threatened the security of the Crown?

It was both shocking and a little daunting to realise there was so much more to the Duke of Wolfingham than the disdain he chose to show outwardly and those flashes of passion he had so ably demonstrated to Mariah privately.

So much so that Mariah now viewed him with new and wary eyes. She had already considered her unwanted physical response to Darian Hunter to be a risk to her peace of mind, but this new information, on exactly what sort of a man the Duke of Wolfingham really was, now caused Mariah to consider him as being completely dangerous.

Indeed, he reminded her of a stalking predator, a wolf, hiding behind a mask of stern urbanity.

Proof indeed that he had more than earned his place as being thought of as one of the five Dangerous Dukes.

'If we could return to the more immediate problem of this plot to assassinate the Regent?' Lord Maystone prompted drily as he obviously saw this silent battle of wills between Mariah and Wolfingham.

Mariah found it hard to breathe, let alone break

away from that glittering green gaze, feeling as if she were a butterfly stuck on the end of a pin and with no way of escape.

She began to breathe again only when Darian Hunter, after giving her a hard and mocking smile, turned his attention back to Aubrey Maystone.

'I am presuming that your own private secretary's involvement with Rousseau will also have exposed the names of the network of people who work for you?' Wolfingham prompted astutely.

Mariah's eyes widened in alarm as she saw the truth of that statement in the heavy mantle of responsibility that instantly settled on Aubrey Maystone's slumped and aged shoulders.

'Almost all.' The older man nodded. 'We had our first inkling of that exposure, of course, when Rousseau revealed to Georgianna Lancaster that he knew of Hawksmere's work for the Crown.'

Darian nodded grimly, that information having meant that Hawksmere could no longer play an active role in Maystone's network of spies. Perhaps it was as well, now that Hawksmere was a married man, but even so...

'I am also presuming, as you wished to speak with both of us this morning, that perhaps Lady Beecham and myself have so far not been exposed?'

'That is so, yes,' Maystone confirmed tightly. 'I do not keep written records of my agents, as you know, but of the twelve in my network, only the two of you have never had reason to call at the Foreign Office or my home.'

'And would not the fact that you have chosen to call at the countess's home this morning have succeeded in alerting any now watching you to the possibility that she—'

'I am not completely without the resource of stealth myself, Wolfingham,' the older man snapped impatiently. 'I left my home by the servants' entrance, hired a hackney cab to bring me to within two streets of this house and walked the rest of the way. All whilst keeping watch for any who might be taking any undue interest in my movements.'

'I apologise.' Darian gave a rueful inclination of his head.

'Apology accepted.' Maystone nodded briskly. 'Could we now return to the subject of these assassins and their infernal plots?'

Darian sank back into his armchair. 'I presume you are now about to tell us what part you expect the two of us to play in foiling this plot?'

Mariah had been aware of the sharpness and acuity of Wolfingham's intelligence, but she had also learnt a wary respect for his astuteness these past few minutes as the two gentlemen talked and knew, by the irritation in Aubrey Maystone's face, that the Duke's words had once again hit their mark.

'What could the two of us possibly do that you have not already done yourself?' she prompted guardedly; positively the last thing she wished for was to spend any more time in Darian Hunter's company than she needed to.

Aubrey Maystone seemed completely unaware of

her reservations as his next words instantly trampled that wish. 'Mariah has already told me that she has accepted her invitation to go to Lord and Lady Nicholses' house party in Kent this weekend. I now wish for you to accompany her, Wolfingham.'

'But—'

'I am aware it is not your usual choice of entertainment, Wolfingham,' the older man acknowledged drily. 'But in this instance it is too dangerous for Mariah to attend alone.'

'Then why attend at all?' she questioned sharply, her heart having leapt in alarm just at the thought of spending a weekend in the company of the judgemental Darian Hunter. He despised her utterly already, enjoyed thinking the worst of her, without the added humiliation of knowing he was watching her with those cold green eyes as she moved about flirtatiously at one of Clara Nichols's licentious weekend house parties. 'It will be no hardship to me to send my apologies to Clara Nichols.'

'That is the last thing I wish you to do, my dear,' Aubrey Maystone assured gently, before launching into an explanation of exactly why the two of them must attend the Nicholses' house party together.

'And to think that you once told me that such things as politics and intrigue bored you,' Wolfingham drawled mockingly.

Lord Maystone, having stated his business, had now departed as abruptly as he had arrived, after stating that he would now leave the two of them alone together, so that they might discuss and consider his request, before giving him their answer later on today.

A request, as far as Mariah was concerned, that was so outrageous as to be unthinkable.

And yet...

She had never said no to anything that Aubrey Maystone had asked of her in the past and she could not bear to think of doing so now, either.

Except for the fact that this time it involved Wolfingham, a man she had serious reason to be wary of.

Her gaze flickered across to where Wolfingham now lounged in the armchair opposite her own, both the pot of tea and the decanter of brandy now empty, after almost an hour of intense discussion. 'I believe you also allowed me to continue to think that you came by your bullet wound by engaging in a duel rather than disposing of André Rousseau?'

'How delicately you put it, my dear Mariah!' Wolfingham drawled. 'But I also have reason to believe that you have greatly enjoyed tormenting *me* with the possibility of it coming about because of some tragic love affair?' He arched a mocking brow.

Yes, Mariah had indeed enjoyed taunting the haughtily disapproving Duke of Wolfingham with the possibility of his having fought a duel over a woman.

Only to now know that he had come by his bullet wound after days of secretly scouting the French countryside for information to bring back to the English government. Followed by a hand-to-hand fight in which the other man—the Frenchman André Rousseau, a spy for Napoleon, both here in England and in France—had died and Darian Hunter had been shot.

'It would seem that we have both had something to hide,' Wolfingham bit out abruptly. 'The question is, what do we do now in regard to Maystone's audacious request of the two of us?'

It *was* outrageous, Mariah acknowledged with a pained wince. Worse than outrageous, as it involved herself and Darian Hunter giving every appearance, in public at least, of being intimately involved with each other. An affair they were to use as their cover when, if, the two of them agreed to attend the house party at Lord and Lady Nicholses' house in Kent this following weekend.

Because the Nicholses had, apparently, been named in the plot against the Prince.

The Nicholses were notorious for giving licentious house parties once or twice a Season. Parties at which the Prince Regent, usually resident in a house nearby, always made an appearance on the Saturday evening of the masked ball, although Aubrey Maystone and other members of the government had succeeded in persuading the Regent into not attending this one.

The Prince Regent particularly enjoyed making an appearance at such parties as these, occasions not designed for the attendance of the young debutantes and their marriage-minded mamas, but for the older, more sophisticated members of the *ton*, where their *risqué* behaviour would not be frowned upon.

Mariah would never dream of allowing Christina to attend, for example. Having accepted her own invitation, Mariah had instantly made arrangements for her young daughter to spend the weekend at the home of her friend Diana Gilbert. Diana's mother, Lady Gilbert, intended to chaperon her own daughter and Christina to a musical soirée on Friday evening and then a ball on Saturday evening, followed by church on Sunday morning, and Mariah would return in the evening.

Mariah had always made a point of attending the Nicholses' weekend parties, when inhibitions became relaxed and information was more freely given.

A lowering of inhibitions that Mariah now accepted could—and according to Aubrey Maystone's information, had—equally have been used to Lord or Lady Nicholses' advantage.

Aubrey Maystone's suggestion was that, the danger being high, Wolfingham would now accompany Mariah into Kent, posing as her lover. Explaining that it would not be unexpected, when the two of them had been seen talking and dancing together several times this past week or so, and apparently giving rise to a certain amount of gossip and speculation concerning whether or not there might be a relationship between the two of them.

Mariah could not claim to have heard any of that unwelcome gossip herself, but then she could not expect to have done, when that gossip was about her.

It would be an easy step, Maystone had assured, for the two of them to attend the house party together and so confirm the gossip and speculation.

But it was a pretence that Mariah, despite those two occasions in which Wolfingham had held her in his arms or kissed her, would not have believed the austere and disdainful Duke of Wolfingham to be capable of.

Before today…

Mariah had no doubts now that Wolfingham had indeed chosen to hide his real self behind the guise of that cold and disdainful duke, because she now suspected—*knew*—that behind that haughty exterior was a man of deep passions.

Deep and unrelenting passions that terrified her at the same time as they caused a wild fluttering inside her.

She straightened determinedly. 'You do understand that, if I should agree to do this in order to flush out the traitors, the public liaison between the two of us would be for appearances' sake only? That there would be no actual intimacy?'

Her eyes widened as Wolfingham gave a rueful chuckle, the signs of that humour, in the warmth of his green eyes and the soft curve of chiselled lips, instantly lessening his veneer of austerity and making him appear years younger than his age.

'You do have a certain way with words, Mariah.' Darian gave a wry shake of his head. 'And I assure you, I never doubted for a moment that our liaison,' he drily echoed her own words, 'would be for appearances' sake only.' He sobered. '*If* we should agree to go forward with Maystone's proposal,' he added harshly, 'which neither of us has yet done.'

Mariah did not see how either of them had any real choice in the matter, if the perpetrators of this plot to assassinate the Prince Regent were to be arrested.

Chapter Six

'What have you done with Lady Christina this weekend?' Darian prompted as he and Mariah travelled into Kent on Friday evening in the warmth of his lamplit coach. His valet and Mariah's maid, along with their luggage, had already travelled into Kent in a second coach sent on ahead earlier today.

Cool turquoise eyes turned to look at him across the width of the coach. Mariah looked cosily warm in a travelling cloak, bonnet and muff for her hands of that same vibrant turquoise colour. 'She is staying with friends.'

'And do you trust that my younger brother will not take advantage of your absence?' Darian had sent a note informing his brother that he would be away in the country this weekend, but not with whom; he fully expected to hear of his brother's displeasure if or when Anthony learnt that Darian had spent the weekend in the company of the mother of the young lady about whom he had serious intentions.

'I trust my daughter not to allow any gentleman to take advantage of my absence.' Mariah had chosen not to speak to Christina regarding Anthony Hunter in particular, believing that to do so would only cause her independent-minded young daughter's attention to fixate on the gentleman. But a casual conversation between mother and daughter had confirmed that Christina did not have serious feelings for any of the young gentlemen who flocked to her side on every social occasion.

Wolfingham nodded. 'And Lady Nichols was receptive to my accompanying you?'

Mariah gave a dismissive snort. 'What society hostess would not be receptive to counting the elusive Duke of Wolfingham amongst her guests?'

'The Countess of Carlisle?' Darian arched a mocking brow.

'True,' that countess drawled dismissively before turning away to look out of the window into the dark of the night.

This was the first time that Darian had seen Mariah since they had informed Maystone of their decision to attend the Nicholses' weekend house party together, their arrangements having then been made through an exchange of terse notes.

A terseness that obviously still existed between the two of them now that they were together again.

Darian straightened on his side of the coach. 'And how successful do you think we shall be at this ruse of an affair between the two of us, when you cannot even bring yourself to look at me for longer than a few seconds?'

Mariah closed her eyes briefly behind the brim of her bonnet before gathering herself to once again look coolly across the carriage at Wolfingham. 'We have not arrived at Eton Park yet, your Grace.'

Darian Hunter gave a mocking shake of his head. 'It is then that I am to expect that the woman who now calls me your Grace so condescendingly will suddenly turn into my adoring lover?'

Mariah firmly repressed the shiver that ran the length of her spine—she did not care to search too deeply as to whether it was a shudder of revulsion or a quiver of anticipation!—at the mere suggestion of herself and this forcefully powerful man ever really becoming lovers.

Wolfingham was just so *immediate*. So overpoweringly male. Just so—so *Wolfingham* that he would totally possess any woman brave enough to attempt to match herself against the passions that Mariah now knew, without a doubt, burned so fiercely behind that mask of stern disapproval.

Even seated in the confines of this coach with him Mariah was aware of that fire smouldering, burning, beneath his outwardly relaxed, even bored, countenance.

'I will never be any man's adoring lover, Wolfingham,' she scorned—or any man's lover at all! 'And I will only be your *pretend* lover for this one weekend,' she assured firmly. 'I believe that you will also find my acting skills are more than sufficient as to be convincing once we are in the company of others.' How could they not be, when for years she had managed, in public at least, to look as if she found pleasure in being at her husband's side?

'And might I enquire as to where and how you might have attained and honed these acting skills?' Wolfingham arched a sceptical brow.

'Perhaps you should turn your attention to your own performance rather than worrying about mine?' she challenged sharply rather than answer his question.

Darian noted that the asperity, which usually edged Mariah's tone whenever she spoke to him, had now returned. It was an improvement on her earlier cool uninterest, but only barely!

He settled more comfortably against the plush cushions of the seat. 'I do not recall ever having received any complaints in the past regarding my performance,' he drawled mockingly.

A flush now coloured Mariah's cheeks, of either embarrassment or anger—though Darian would guess at it being the latter; there was no reason for Mariah to feel embarrassment discussing such a subject when she had been a married lady for many years and so familiar with her husband's performance. And that of the other gentlemen who had shared her bed during and after her marriage!

A thought that did not give Darian any pleasure whatsoever.

He eyed her with frustration from behind lowered lids. Indeed, it had been long days—and nights—of frustrations since the morning he had called at her home and they had been joined by Aubrey Maystone.

Not least because Mariah had proved so elusive on the occasions Darian had asked for the two of them to meet in person since that time, so that they might discuss how they were to proceed this weekend. Requests Mariah had consistently refused, on the excuse of having far too many other engagements, and the arrangements to be made for their weekend away in Kent, to be able to fit a visit from him into that busy schedule.

Darian's suggestion that, as her lover, he was *supposed* to be visiting her had been met with a wall of silence on Mariah's part. A silence that had not been broken until he had called at her home to collect her earlier this evening.

Another frustration had been Maystone's inability to persuade any of the three men, now being held and questioned, into giving them more information regarding one or both of the Nicholses' involvement in this plot against the Prince.

Thankfully, Maystone and other members of the government had succeeded in continuing to convince the Prince Regent that it was for the best that he not attend even the Nicholses' masked ball on Saturday evening.

Instead, Aubrey Maystone and several of his agents would take up residence at Winterton Manor for the weekend, just five miles away from Eton Park, and await word from Darian and Mariah as to the Nicholses' reaction to the note the Prince Regent would have delivered to them at Eton Park at precisely five o'clock on Saturday afternoon, explaining his absence. Five o'clock had been chosen deliberately, when all would be gathered for tea, so that Mariah and Darian might observe Lord and Lady Nicholses' reaction to the news, and also what followed. If anything.

It was the thought of being thrust into the midst of this weekend of licentiousness that had become yet another thorn in Darian's side, when he would normally avoid such events like the plague. Not because, as Mariah was so fond of telling him, he was too proper and austere to attend, but simply because he preferred to perform acts of intimacy without an audience. *All* acts of intimacy.

Such as the numerous acts of intimacy he had imagined engaging in with Mariah, the moment he had retired to his bed these past three nights.

Resulting in him rising early each morning following a restless night's sleep, in order to take a cold bath, before joining one or other of his friends at the boxing saloon and so allowing him to dispel some of his frustration in the boxing ring.

All of which Darian doubted would be a possible outlet for all of his restless energy during this weekend spent in Kent at Mariah's side.

No, he fully expected to be put through even worse torture whilst in the Nicholses' home. Especially since, as was usual at these types of unrestrained weekends of entertainment, his bedchamber would no doubt tactfully adjoin Mariah's own.

Having already spent several hours in the coach

with Mariah, that exotic and erotic perfume once again invading his senses, Darian was unsure whether or not he would be able to withstand the nightly temptation of opening the door that connected his bedchamber to hers.

'Do you always wear the same perfume?'

Mariah looked sharply across at Wolfingham, surprised by the sudden, and harshly spoken, change of subject, but also searching for some sign of criticism. As usual his expression proved too enigmatic for her to decipher.

Her chin rose. 'You do not like it?'

'It is unusual,' he answered noncommittally.

Mariah laughed softly. 'That does not answer my question, Wolfingham.'

'Darian.'

She blinked. 'I beg your pardon?'

'So far we have progressed from having you address me as your Grace to the more familiar Wolfingham. I thought now might be as good a time as any for you to begin calling me Darian.'

'Did you?' Mariah returned with the coolness that had become her only defence against the fire of emotions she now knew burned behind those cold green eyes. Emotions that surprisingly sparked something similar within her own fast-beating heart.

Wolfingham now shrugged those exceptionally wide shoulders, shown to such advantage in the black fitted superfine, as was the flatness of his stomach beneath a grey waistcoat and snowy white linen, his pantaloons also black, his legs long and sprawling as he relaxed back against his side of the carriage. 'I believe most couples, in a situation such as ours is supposed to be, address each other by their given names rather than their titles.'

'You believe?' Mariah gave a taunting smile. 'Do you not know for certain?'

Darian's mouth thinned at what he knew to be her deliberate mockery. 'The ladies I have bedded in the past have not usually had the privilege of a title,' he drawled dismissively and had the satisfaction of seeing that blush once again colour Mariah's cheeks. 'But I have no particular aversion to addressing you at all times as Countess, if that is the game you like to play?' His brief moment of satisfaction quickly faded as he saw the smile instantly waver and then disappear from those beautiful red lips, her gaze equally as uncertain. He rose abruptly to his feet. 'Mariah—'

'Stay on your own side of the carriage, Wolfingham.' She held up a hand to ward him off from his obvious intention of crossing the carriage to sit on the seat beside her.

Darian froze even as he studied her face intently, noting the shadows beneath those beautiful eyes and the way the colour had now deserted her cheeks, leaving her pale and delicate. At thoughts of his moving closer to her? 'Are you sure you wish to go ahead with this charade, Mariah?' he finally prompted gently.

She smiled tightly. 'Who else will do it if we do not?'

He had no answer to that argument, knowing as he did, as Mariah did, that time was not their friend.

That Napoleon, having been joined by the defector Marshal Ney, and his army ever increasing, was now fast approaching Paris. There were already riots in the capitol in support of their emperor's return and King Louis was preparing to flee. If something were to now happen to England's Prince Regent, it was guaranteed to throw the allies into total disarray, so allowing Napoleon's return to the capitol to be a double-edged triumph.

Darian sank back down on to his seat, but remained sitting forward so that he might reach out and take both Mariah's hands from inside her muff, frowning as he felt the way that her fingers trembled as he held them in his own. 'There is nothing for you to be frightened of, Mariah,' he assured gruffly. 'I promise I will do my utmost to ensure that no harm shall come to you this weekend.'

Mariah held back the hysterical laugh that threatened to burst forth at the obvious sincerity of Darian's promise of allowing no harm to come to her—when the person she now feared the most was *him*.

Oh, not him exactly, but her responses to him certainly. Responses, of heat and desire, that did not seem to have dissipated or lessened in these past three days of not seeing him, as she had hoped that they might.

Responses that she had believed herself to be incapable of feeling towards any man.

Until Wolfingham.

Just a few minutes of being back in his company and Mariah had known that she was still aware of everything about him. The dark and glossy thickness of his hair. Those beautiful emerald-green eyes. The stark and chiselled handsomeness of his features. The strength of his muscled body.

The gentleness of the long and sensitive hands that now held her hands so lightly, but securely, within his own.

Hands that Mariah could only too easily imagine moving, exploring her body, lighting a fire wherever they touched, giving pleasure wherever they caressed. And what did she know of the pleasure of her body at any man's hands?

Nothing, came the blunt and unequivocal answer.

If she really were a normal widow, the woman of experience Wolfingham believed her to be, then she would know. Just as she would take every advantage of their weekend together to explore this attraction she felt for him.

Except Mariah was not normal, as a widow or a woman.

Christina had been conceived on the one and only occasion Martin had— No, Mariah could never think of what he had done to her that night as making love! It had been force and pain, and humiliation for her, nothing more and nothing less.

Their marriage had been nothing but a sham from the beginning, Martin spending most of his nights in the bed of his mistress, the same woman who acted as housekeeper in their London home, and had done so for twenty years or more before Mariah and Martin were married.

Many wives might have resented having her husband's mistress actually living in one of their homes, but Mariah had felt only gratitude; whilst Martin's nights were occupied with Mrs Smith then he would not think of coming to her bed. She had dismissed Mrs Smith after Martin's death, of course, for Christina's sake as well as her own, but Mariah's gratitude to that lady had been such that she had provided the other woman with a large enough pension for her to live comfortably for the rest of her life.

What would Wolfingham—a man who believed her to have been an adulteress in her marriage and to have had a multitude of lovers during her five years of widowhood—what would such a man think if he were to learn that Mariah had had but a single night of carnal knowledge in her life and that one occasion had been the most horrible, degrading, painful—

'Where have you gone, Mariah?' Darian had not liked the way in which her expression had grown distant, turned inwards, her thoughts giving a shadow to the depths of those beautiful eyes. He liked it even less when she had given an obvious shudder just now of what seemed like revulsion...

Because she did genuinely fear the coming events at the Nicholses' home?

Or because she felt revulsion for the idea of even that *pretence* of an intimate relationship with him?

Unfortunately, Darian had no answer to that question.

She roused herself with effort, purposefully pulling her hands from his as she straightened, a bright and meaningless smile now curving those ruby-red lips, a smile that did nothing to take away the shadows in her eyes. 'Why, I am right here in the carriage with you, Wolfingham,' she assured him with unmistakable brittleness. 'And I do believe we are now on the driveway approaching Eton Park,' she added with obvious relief.

Darian leant back abruptly against the cushions, knowing that their brief moment of tenderness was over. If it had ever really begun on Mariah's part.

His expression was grim as he turned to look out of the window to view the brightly lit house in the distance. He inwardly cursed himself for being a fool. He might have spent the past days and nights thinking of, desiring, Mariah, might even have anticipated being with her again, but she had shown him time and time again that she did not feel that same desire towards him.

He gave a shake of his head as he once again turned his own thoughts to the business of the weekend ahead. 'What sort of entertainments might I expect to endure this evening?'

Mariah shrugged. 'The full entertainments will not begin until tomorrow, obviously, but after dinner this evening I expect there will be cards and dancing.'

Darian grimaced. 'Sounds boringly normal to me.'

She chuckled huskily. 'I assure you there is nothing "normal" about cards and dancing in the Nicholses' home!'

Darian eyed her speculatively. 'Meaning?'

A small, secretive smile hovered at the corners of her mouth. 'You will see soon enough!'

Darian disliked the sound of that. As he disliked feeling as if he were at a disadvantage, as he surely was where such weekends as this were concerned.

And meaning that he would have to look to Mariah for guidance as to the correct way for him to behave.

But first, it seemed, he had to endure the simpering and coquettish Lady Clara Nichols as she gushingly welcomed him to her home, whilst her husband showed Mariah similar attentions. Attentions, he noted with satisfaction, that she laughed off quite easily.

Darian was not so successful where Lady Clara was concerned, as she proudly introduced them to the rest of the company still assembled in the drawing room after tea: several lords, an earl, half a dozen Members of Parliament, some with their wives, but most not. There were also a dozen or so other female members of the *ton*, a titled lady or two, several Honourables, three well-known actresses and an opera singer, and all without the escort of their husbands.

Lady Clara then insisted, her arm firmly linked with Darian's, on personally accompanying them up the stairs to show them to their bedchambers.

Darian felt quite sickened by her attentions by the time that lady finally took herself off to rejoin her other guests and no doubt indulge in gossip about the duke and the countess.

His top lip curled with distaste the moment the door of the bedchamber had closed behind his simpering hostess. 'There is something particularly sickening about a lady of possibly forty years giggling like a schoolgirl.'

Mariah chuckled, no doubt at the look of disgust on his face, as she untied her bonnet and threw it down on to her bed. 'How very ungrateful of you, Darian, when I do believe, from their situation of being at the front of the house and the opulence of these bedchambers, that Clara and Richard must have moved out of their own bedchambers in order to accommodate the two of us.'

As expected, the two of them had been given adjoining bedchambers, the door between those rooms having been left pointedly open, and no doubt the reason Darian had been subjected to Clara Nichols's girlishly suggestive giggles when she reminded them that dinner would be served in a little over two hours. No doubt she expected the two of them to indulge in some love play before that time.

Darian's room was acceptable, but Mariah's— Clara Nichols's own bedchamber?—was a ghastly nightmare of pink and cream lace and flounces. 'How will you ever be able to sleep in such an explosion of pink?' He grimaced as he stood in the doorway between their two rooms.

Mariah gave a dismissive shrug. 'I shall simply blow out the candles and then I shall not be able to see it.'

Darian admired the picture of grace and beauty Mariah made in the candle and firelight as she stood in the middle of that ghastly pink room. A veritable vision in turquoise and cream, her hair appearing like spun gold, colour now warming her cheeks.

His blood stirred and he felt that tingling at the base of his spine and between his thighs, the rising and thickening of his erection, as he imagined how much more lovely Mariah would look without any clothes on at all.

Would the curls between her thighs be that same gold or possibly a shade darker?

Would her nipples be the same ruby red as her lips?

And would the folds between her thighs—

'If you would not mind, Darian?' Mariah's voice softly interrupted his erotic musings. 'My maid will be here shortly to help me bathe and dress for dinner, as no doubt will your own valet. Oh, and, Darian…?' she added as he gave a terse bow of acceptance before turning to leave, waiting until he had slowly turned back to her before speaking again. 'Close the door on your way out, please.'

His jaw tightened at the dismissal as he stepped through the doorway and closed the door behind him, knowing he needed the privacy in order to take care of the need throbbing through his body, before he dared to rejoin Mariah!

'You are not intending to appear in that gown in public!'

Mariah turned from where she had been gazing at her reflection in the mirror as she put the last of the pearl clips into her hair, to now look at Wolfingham as he once again stood in the open doorway between their two bedchambers. His appearance was as resplendent as usual in black evening clothes and snowy white linen, an ebony sheen to his hair, his features once again as hard as granite.

It was the look of horror on those hard features, as he gazed back at her unblinkingly, that now brought a wry smile to her lips. 'You do not like it?'

Like it? Darian had never seen a gown like it before! Well, not outside the walls of a brothel, at least.

The gown left Mariah's shoulders bare except for two tiny ribbon straps and was made of some diaphanous cream material, lined with the sheerest of lace. It clearly revealed the bare outline of the curvaceous body beneath and darkening at the apex between Mariah's thighs—revealing the nakedness of the darker curls covering her mound.

As for the bodice of the gown! It was almost nonexistent, just that cream diaphanous material covering the fullness of Mariah's breasts, the nipples plump berries and clearly showing through as being as ruby red as her lips—that ruby colour aided by rouge, if he was not mistaken.

His traitorous body had surged back into full attention the moment he looked at the reflection of those plump nipples in the mirror, and imagined Mariah applying that rouge to those succulent berries. 'I see that a certain part of you does, at least.' Mariah looked pointedly at the unmistakable evidence of his arousal.

Darian did not in the least enjoy feeling like a callow youth taking his first look at a naked woman.

Except Mariah was not naked.

Perhaps he would not have reacted so strongly if she had been!

Of course he would, Darian instantly chastised himself. It was only that there was something so provocative about the tantalising glimpses of those slender and obviously naked curves as Mariah moved across the room to collect her gloves from the bed, giving just the hint of those golden curls nestling between her thighs. And her breasts were magnificent; creamy, full and plump, with those red and succulent rouged nipples just begging to be tasted and suckled.

Darian wanted nothing more at that moment than to lay Mariah down upon the bed before taking those berries into his mouth and sucking and tasting their plumpness until he was sated.

If he ever was!

As for the shadow of those darker golden curls and the promise of what lay hidden between her thighs—

Darian imagined lowering her gently down on to the bed and pushing her gown up her thighs so that he might explore every silken inch of that hidden treasure. To caress the plumpness of her folds. Taste and suck the tiny nubbin above—

Beads of perspiration broke out on Darian's forehead as he fought an inward battle not to give in to the urge to cross the room and take Mariah in his arms, to fulfil every single one of the fantasies that had been slowly driving him insane and that he now found impossible to stop.

'I am ready to go downstairs and join the other guests, if you are?'

It took every effort of his indomitable will to pull Darian back from the brink of giving in to his desires, his voice harsh as he answered her. 'Do you have a shawl or something you can wear about your shoulders?' The thought of other men ogling Mariah's almost naked breasts, and that tantalising outline of her naked curves beneath her gown, was enough to make him clench his fists violently.

Mariah gave a bell-like laugh as she collected up a fan from her dressing table rather than a shawl. 'You will see, Darian, my gown is quite modest in comparison with the gowns some of the other ladies will be wearing this evening.'

He had no interest in what the other ladies were wearing this evening; they could all walk around stark naked for all Darian cared. But if he caught one single gentleman in the act of ogling Mariah— He was behaving more than ridiculously, Darian recognised self-disgustedly, when he had no more right to approve or disapprove of other gentlemen ogling Mariah, tonight or any other night, than—than the Prince Regent did!

Although he had no doubt that the Prince Regent, if he had been one of the guests this evening, would have taken great delight in enjoying Mariah's appearance. The man might be plumper and more dissipated than he had been in his youth, but he still had charm enough to seduce the ladies.

Whereas Darian's charm, what little he did possess—and no doubt Mariah would say he possessed none!—seemed to have completely deserted him for the moment.

'Darian?' Mariah prompted again lightly.

He gathered himself to straighten determinedly before crossing the room to hold out his arm to her, feeling much as he had when he had necessarily to prepare himself before a battle.

And unsure whether that battle this evening would be with his own wayward emotions, or with the other gentlemen present.

Chapter Seven

Mariah was enjoying herself.

Actually enjoying herself, when normally she would simply have gone through the motions of doing so at this sort of entertainment, flirting and laughing with the gentlemen whilst at the same time keeping them in line—and their groping hands firmly at bay—with a delicately aimed flick of her fan.

And the reason she was enjoying herself was standing broodingly at her side now that all the guests had retired to the drawing room following dinner, giving every appearance of a dark and avenging angel, ready to swoop down on any who might even think of crossing over the invisible line he had drawn about the two of them since they had sat down to dinner earlier.

The dark and avenging angel Darian Hunter, the Duke of Wolfingham.

As she had warned Wolfingham before coming down the stairs earlier, most of the other ladies were dressed much more daringly than she was this evening. Indeed, there was a plethora of completely bared breasts visible about the drawing room as the gentlemen, and many of the ladies, completely against the normal rules of polite society, enjoyed an after-dinner brandy together. Most of the gowns were without the benefit of that layer of lace that covered Mariah's breasts and several of the gowns were made of a totally transparent and gauzy material that left absolutely nothing to the imagination.

And for all the notice Wolfingham had taken— was still taking!—of any of those erotically displayed ladies, they might as well have been wearing sackcloth.

It was a refreshing change for Mariah to be in the presence of a gentleman whose gaze was not constantly wandering to the half-naked bodies of other women.

Just as Wolfingham's glowering and tight-lipped disapproval of the approach of both the ladies and the gentlemen present this evening had kept everyone but their hostess from attempting to interrupt their privacy. Wolfingham had wasted no time in dispatching that lady, too, with a few choice and tersely spoken words.

Instead, he had centred all of his attention on Mariah as they ate the sumptuously prepared dinner served to them earlier, his conversation exclusive, and occasionally feeding her the odd delicacy of food from his own plate, as a way, no doubt, of giving further illusion to their intimacy.

Mariah had blushed like a schoolgirl the first time

Darian behaved so unexpectedly, that blush having deepened as he centred his hawklike gaze upon her lips when she finally leant forward to take the food from his fork. She had been better prepared the second time it had happened, but still felt unaccountably hot at the way his green gaze stared so intently at her lips.

And throughout all of it Darian had seemed completely unaware of the sexual play going on about them.

The assembled company had been slightly restrained to begin with, all obviously aware of having the imposing Duke of Wolfingham within their midst, but several glasses of wine later, along with Wolfingham's apparent distraction with Mariah, and those inhibitions had quickly fallen away.

Several of the gentlemen had openly caressed and tweaked bared breasts, and one gentleman had even crawled beneath the table for several minutes, the expression of rapture on the flushed face of the actress seated next to him, followed by her breathy and noisy gasps of pleasure as she climaxed, clearly showing where that gentleman was lavishing his attentions.

Mariah had glanced away as if bored as the gentleman crawled back up into his seat, his mouth moist and lips swollen, the expression on his flushed face becoming one of equal rapture as that lady returned the favour, by unbuttoning his pantaloons and openly stroking him until he, too, reached a completion.

It was a disgusting and embarrassing display, and one that Mariah had been forced to witness at least a dozen times during these past seven years of spying for the Crown.

And one that tonight had caused a flush of heat to course through Mariah's own veins and an unaccustomed tingling and warmth to spread between her thighs.

A heat and tingling that she had preferred not to question too deeply.

'Say no, Darian,' she warned Wolfingham softly now as she shook her own head at Clara Nichols as the other woman moved about the room gathering up the people who wished to play cards.

Darian gave a terse shake of his own head to their poutingly disappointed hostess before moving to stand slightly in front of Mariah, the broadness of his back and shoulders blocking her from the view of the majority of the other guests in the room. 'Why?' he returned as softly.

Mariah looked up at him beneath lowered lashes. 'Because I doubt you will like the forfeit if you lose. Do you ever lose?'

Darian raised one dark brow. 'At cards?'

'At anything!'

Well, he was certainly losing his battle tonight in regard to the desire he felt for Mariah.

Dinner with the Nicholses' guests had been a disgusting display of body parts and licentious behaviour, which he had found distinctly untitillating and which had actually turned his stomach on several occasions. Several sexual acts had actually occurred at the dinner table, made all the more incongruous by the fact that they were all seated about a formal dining table in an equally formal dining room and were being waited upon by the Nicholses' placid-faced butler and footmen.

He had noticed several gentlemen eyeing Mariah covetously when they first sat down at the dinner table. Glances he had frowned darkly upon. Those glances had then turned towards Darian, envious in some cases and actually belligerent in one or two others.

Because none of those gentlemen had been numbered amongst Mariah's lovers? Darian hoped it was so.

He had soon forgotten all but Mariah, as he shut out the presence and behaviour of the people around them and concentrated all of his attentions on her.

He had enjoyed talking with her, their conversations intelligent and witty. He had also fed her sweetmeats on occasion, initially as a way of publically demonstrating the intimacy of their relationship, but continuing to do so time and time again as his shaft hardened as he watched her lips encircle his fork and imagined how those soft and full lips would feel encircling him in the same sensuous way. He had almost come undone completely when she had once run her tongue along her bottom lip as she licked away an excess of cream from a bonbon he had just fed her.

'Very rarely,' he answered her drily now. 'What exactly is it that you forfeit here for losing at cards?'

'Watch.' She turned to where two tables had now been set up with four card players on each, two gentleman and two ladies on one and three gentlemen and one lady on the other.

'Good gracious.' Darian gave a shudder just seconds later as Clara Nichols, obviously the loser of the first hand of cards, instantly stood up to remove her gown, resuming her seat dressed only in silk drawers and pale stockings held up by two pink—what other colour would the woman choose!—garters, her breasts hanging down like two giant udders. 'There should be a law against such an unpleasant display.' Darian's mouth twisted with distaste.

'No doubt there is outside of the privacy of one's home.' Mariah smiled up at him impishly. 'And some gentlemen find such full breasts...erotic.'

'I cannot see how they could!'

'Watch,' she encouraged again, just in time for Darian to glance across the room and see a prominent member of the government—prominent in more ways than one at this precise moment!—lying back upon Lady Clara's bare thighs and placing his head beneath one of her pendulous breasts before sucking the nipple heartily into his mouth.

'He looks like a giant baby taking suck from its mother!' Darian muttered with disgust.

'I believe that is Lord Edgewood's little fetish, yes.' Mariah nodded. 'And many women's breasts become less pert as we age, especially when we have borne children,' she added with a playful tap of her fan on his shoulder.

Whether intended or not—and Darian suspected not, in his particular case—the movement drew attention to her own perfectly formed and jiggling breasts, beautifully pert rouge-tipped breasts that peeped out at him temptingly from beneath that thin barrier of lace. 'I am pleased to note your own have not suffered from a similar malaise,' he murmured gruffly.

Mariah's breath caught in her throat, her eyes widening in alarm, as she realised she had actually been *flirting* with Darian Hunter, the imposing and disapproving Duke of Wolfingham, these past few minutes. Openly, coquettishly, *flirting*.

'I believe I have seen quite enough for one evening,' Wolfingham now muttered harshly as he turned away as one of the gentlemen on the second card table, a short and overly plump member of the aristocracy, stood up to remove his trousers, revealing his small and glistening manhood sticking out from the opening of his smallclothes. 'Shall we retire?' He held out his arm to Mariah, a nerve pulsing in the hardness of his cheek.

She raised teasing brows as she rested her gloved hand lightly upon his arm and allowed him to accompany her from the room, aware of several pairs of eyes following their abrupt departure. 'You do realise that everyone will assume we are going upstairs for the sole purpose of making love together?' she teased drily as Wolfingham took a lighted candle from the butler before they ascended the staircase together.

'Let them think it!' Darian doubted he had ever actually made love to any woman. Had sex with, yes, but never made love with or to.

But this evening—*that* had been nothing more than

several hours of a sickening display of unrestrained debauchery and was beyond enduring for even another moment.

He gave a shudder as they came to a halt as they reached the top of the staircase. 'I do believe that just the memory of that image of Clara Nichols's pendulous breasts will make it difficult for me ever to be able to become aroused again, let alone have sexual relations with a woman. I dread to think what outrageous entertainments they will think of for the masked ball tomorrow evening!'

Mariah cursed the blush that had warmed her cheeks as Wolfingham talked so frankly of his arousal. She was a widow aged four and thirty, had been a married woman for twelve of those years. And Wolfingham, along with many others, believed her to have first been an adulteress, then a mistress several times over these past five years. Women as sophisticated and experienced as Mariah Beecham was reputed to be did not blush like a schoolgirl when a man talked of his arousal.

'This is just a small house party—the majority of the guests will arrive tomorrow evening just for the ball,' she dismissed lightly. 'This evening's guests will no doubt sleep most of the day away after tonight's excesses.'

'One blessing, I suppose,' he muttered.

Mariah nodded. 'I am afraid the wearing of masks tomorrow evening allows for even more licentious behaviour than you have witnessed this evening. Also, the Nicholses' smaller and private ballroom is…well, perhaps I should leave that as a surprise for you for tomorrow evening.'

He gave another shudder. 'I would rather you did not!'

Mariah was about to answer him when there came the sound of loud shouts and whistles of approval from down the stairs. 'I do believe another lady or gentleman has just been divested of another article of clothing.'

Wolfingham looked frostily down the long length of his nose. 'In that case I see little reason to celebrate.' He drew in a deep breath. 'Please tell me that you have never— Assure me that none of those *gentlemen* have ever—'

'No,' Mariah assured him hastily, the warmth deepening in her cheeks.

Those green eyes narrowed. 'None of them?'

Mariah's jaw tightened. 'No.'

'There is a God, after all!' he rasped with feeling as he took hold of her arm, the candle in his other hand lighting their way as they began walking down the hallway to their bedchambers.

Mariah eyed him quizzically. 'I fail to see why it should matter to you one way or the other.'

'It matters!' he ground out between clenched teeth.

'As I said, I do not see why. This, what is supposed to be between the two of us, is merely play—' The breath was knocked from Mariah's lungs as she suddenly found herself thrust up against the wall, the candle placed on a small side table as an ominous-looking Wolfingham towered over her. He had placed his hands on the wall either side of her head, making her a prisoner of both his encircling arms and the lean and muscled strength of his body. 'Darian...?' She looked up at him uncertainly between long, thick lashes.

Darian was breathing deeply, in an effort to retain his control. He had already been enraged, just at the thought of Mariah having ever been intimate with any of the other men present this weekend—he refused to think of any of those men again as ever being *gentlemen*! But being dismissed by Mariah, as if he were of no more importance to her, that he was no better than any of them, was beyond endurance.

His nostrils flared as he looked down at her between hooded lids, his senses aflame, flooded, *filled*, with both the sight of her and the increasing smell of that insidious and arousing perfume.

Her eyes were a deep and drowning turquoise, her skin creamy smooth, with that becoming blush to her cheeks. Her parted lips were so plump and tempting! The bareness of her shoulders made him ache to touch them, the hollows of her throat begging further investigation, with his lips and tongue. And her breasts moved, swelled enticingly beneath that thin lace barrier, as she breathed shallowly.

And all the time Darian gazed down at her hungrily, the very air about them seeming to have stilled, the intensity of that erotic perfume having deepened and swelled, engulfing him, *enslaving* him and threatening to destroy his last shreds of resistance.

Why had her perfume deepened now? How was it possible?

'Mariah, do you stroke your perfume across and between your breasts and between your thighs?' he prompted gruffly.

'Darian!' she gasped breathlessly.

'Do you?' he pressed raggedly.

'I— Yes. Yes!' she confirmed achingly.

And telling Darian that, for the perfume to have become stronger, Mariah's body heat must have deepened, and so increasing the perfume escaping from those secret, hot places.

He closed his eyes briefly, hoping it might aid him in holding on to his fast-slipping control. But closing his eyes only intensified his sensitivity to her perfume. He slowly opened half-raised lids, his heated gaze immediately homing in on the soft pout of Mariah's parted lips. Lips he had been longing to taste again since she climbed into his carriage earlier today.

An ache he found he could no longer resist as he held her gaze with his own, his arms on the wall beside her keeping his body from touching hers, as he slowly lowered his head to run his lips lightly across her slightly parted ones.

They were soft and hesitant beneath his own, tasting of sweetmeats and brandy as he ran his tongue gently along and between them, running lightly across the ridge of her teeth, stroking along the moist length of her own tongue, before retreating to start the caress all over again, their ragged breathing becoming hot and humid between them.

Mariah had never been kissed so gently before, so slowly and so *erotically*, her pulse leaping, and her heart beating loudly beneath breasts that had become swollen and sensitised, just the gentle brush of that lace across them causing her nipples to harden and ache as they became engorged and swollen almost to the point of pain. Just as she was aware of a similar swelling, heat, between her thighs.

Her neck arched as Darian's lips now travelled across her cheek, teeth nibbling her earlobe before moving lower still. Her hands moved out to grasp Darian's shoulders as she felt his lips against her throat, gently sucking on that flesh, tongue lathing moistly to ease the pain before moving lower still, the brush of that hot and moist tongue now dipping into the deep and sensitive hollows at the base of her arched throat.

'Darian!' Mariah was so beset with new and unfamiliar emotions that she had no idea whether her gasp was one of protest for him to stop, or a plea for him to continue.

The response and heat of her body felt so strange to her. Not an unpleasant strange—far from it! She had never felt such pleasure before, or this deep and yearning ache she had to press closer against Darian's body, to rub herself against him, in an effort— a plea—to find relief for this hot and burning need, both in her breasts and between her thighs.

She groaned low in her throat, her knees threatening to buckle beneath her as Darian's lips and stroking tongue now explored the tops of her creamy breasts.

Sighing her pleasure as she at last felt the heavy weight of Darian's thighs against her own as he leant inwards to prevent her fall, allowing her to feel his own long and engorged arousal pressed against her softness—and giving instant lie to his earlier claim!

Mariah should have felt trapped, should have felt awash with the usual panic she suffered whenever a man attempted to touch or kiss her. That need she always felt to escape. To free herself.

And yet she felt none of that with Darian, wanted only to press herself closer still, to rub herself over and against him, anything to be able to somehow alleviate the burning ache in her breasts and between her thighs.

'Darian!' Mariah gave a helpless gasp as she felt the moist stroke of his tongue across her bared nipple, the first indication she had that he had pulled down that delicate lace barrier and bared her breasts.

That stroke of his tongue was quickly followed by the hot and deliberate brush of his breath over the sensitised tip. The stroking of his tongue again, followed by that soft breath, her nipple standing erect and begging for more as he moved to lavish that same attention to its twin.

It was pleasure like nothing Mariah had ever known before, had never guessed existed.

'After you for a taste, if you don't mind, Wolfingham?'

Mariah had frozen at the first sound of that intrusive voice. She now turned her head quickly, her gaze stricken as she saw Lord Richard Nichols standing just feet away down the hallway, his face flushed with arousal, eyes fevered as he gazed unabashedly at Mariah's completely bared breasts.

That fevered gaze remained fixed lasciviously on her bared breasts as he took a step forward. 'I've long wanted a taste of this particular beauty.'

Mariah was barely aware of Wolfingham moving, aware only of the loss of his heat pressed against her as he strode ominously down the hallway towards the other man, allowing her time to pull the lace quickly back in place before looking up again as she heard Richard Nichols's squeak of protest and seeing that Darian now had the older man pressed up against the wall of the hallway, Nichols's feet dangling as he was held several inches above the floor by Wolfingham's hand about his throat. Darian's expression was one of cold fury as he looked at the other man.

'I do mind, as it happens, Nichols!' he grated harshly. 'In fact, I would mind very much if I were ever to learn that you had come within six feet of touching Mariah.'

'But—'

'Do I make myself clear?'

'Very—very clear.' The other man appeared to be having trouble breathing, let alone speaking. 'L-leave off, do, Wolfingham!' Nichols choked out, his hand about the younger man's wrist as he struggled to free himself.

Darian gazed contemptuously at Richard Nichols for several long seconds more, his gaze glacial as he conveyed a stronger, more silent threat to the older man. One of violence and retribution such as Nichols had never seen before.

'Darian?'

He was so angry, so filled with a need to shake the older man like a rag doll, like the insufferable cur that he was, that for several long moments Darian could think of nothing but the desire he felt to beat this man to within an inch of his life. He was so angry that he could not respond to Mariah's pleading.

'Darian, please!'

He heard the sob in Mariah's voice this time, causing him to break his murderous gaze away from Nichols in order to turn and look at her. She looked so pale, so tiny and vulnerable, in the softness of the candlelight, her shadowed gaze holding his with that same pleading he had detected in her voice.

His expression softened slightly as he continued to look at her. 'Do not worry, Mariah, I do not intend to kill Nichols. Not this time,' he added harshly as he turned back to look challengingly at the other man.

His reassurance did nothing to alleviate Nichols's obvious panic, the other man's face having become an unpleasant puce colour—much like the unpleasant colour of his wife's bedchamber!—his pale eyes bulging.

Perhaps because Darian still had his hand about his throat!

Darian gave a disgusted snort as he removed his hand before taking a step back, uncaring as the other man lost his balance and almost fell to his knees as he dropped those several inches back down to the floor.

'I advise that you stay away from Mariah in future, if you know what is good for you.'

Richard Nichols had his hand raised to his bruised throat, his expression one of belligerent irritation. 'You only had to say no, old chap. There's no need for—for such violence. There is plenty to go round—' He broke off as he obviously saw the savagery of Darian's expression. 'I— Well— Yes. I think I will go and rejoin my other guests down the stairs.'

At any other time Mariah might have found amusement in seeing the indignity of the obnoxious Richard Nichols scuttling hastily down the hallway before quickly turning the corner and disappearing in the direction of the staircase.

Here and now, the older man having stood witness to the heated lovemaking between Mariah and Darian—and who knew how long he had stood observing the two of them before he spoke up!—Mariah was too upset to be able to find any amusement in the situation.

Instead, she felt humiliated and sickened, the pleasure of that lovemaking becoming as degrading as the rest of this evening's events had been. She shuddered just thinking of Richard Nichols having lasciviously watched as Darian suckled and pleasured her breasts. Having heard her gasps and moans as the heat coursed through her body. It was— Her gaze sharpened on Wolfingham as she realised he had made no move since he had stepped back after releasing Nichols, those icy green eyes now narrowed in concentrated thought. 'What is it, Darian?' she prompted abruptly.

He drew in a deep breath before answering her distractedly. 'What was Nichols doing wandering about up here in the first place when the entertainment is downstairs?'

She gave a dismissive shrug. 'Perhaps he came to collect something?'

'Or perhaps he came up here for another reason entirely!' Darian rasped as he turned and strode determinedly down the hallway towards her, collecting up the candle and taking a firm grasp of her arm before continuing on his way to their bedchambers.

'Darian?' Mariah was totally at a loss to know what was bothering him as he stepped aside and waited for her to enter her bedchamber ahead of him, before following her inside and closing the door firmly behind him. Because something most assuredly was.

For herself, she could imagine nothing more humiliating than the two of them, their lovemaking, now being the amusing topic of conversation down the stairs, when no doubt Richard Nichols would skip over his cowardly response to Wolfingham's violent reaction, but enlarge and embellish what he had observed, for the lascivious pleasure of his listeners. It was—

'What are you doing?' She frowned as she watched Darian now moving about her bedchamber, lighting several more candles before he commenced prowling about the room. His expression was grim as he moved several paintings aside before moving on to examine the four-poster bed, stepping up on to the pink bed-spread to examine the top and back of it. 'Darian?'

Angry colour stood out in the hardness of his cheeks when he finally stepped down from the bed, a nerve pulsing in his tightly clenched jaw. 'There are peepholes, through several of the paintings and the frame at the back of the bed, all neatly disguised so that none would know if not aware of them, but there nonetheless.'

'Peepholes?' Mariah repeated uncomprehendingly.

'You had no idea they were there?'

'I—' She gave a dazed shake of her head. 'I do not even know what they are.'

He grimaced. 'No doubt Nichols came up the stairs just now to check on which bedchamber we had gone into, yours or my own. His intention then being to go back down the stairs and invite his guests to come up here and observe the two of us together through those peepholes, no doubt accessed through a shallow passage between the walls.'

Mariah dropped weakly down on to the side of the bed and felt all the colour leach from her cheeks as she took in the full import of what Darian was saying to her.

A peep show. They were to have been nothing more than a—

'It did not happen, Mariah,' Darian soothed as he moved to sit on the bed beside her before taking her into his arms as she collapsed weakly against his chest; one look at the blank shock on Mariah's deathly white face had been enough to tell him that this was the first she had known of those strategically placed peepholes in the walls of Lady Nichols's bedchamber.

He felt ashamed now for having harboured even the briefest of doubts that Mariah might have been a willing participant in the entertainment the Nichols had now intended providing for their guests.

An understandable doubt, perhaps, in view of Mariah's reputation, but Darian now felt a heady relief at realising, from her collapse against him, that if they had made love together she would have been as innocently unaware of the people watching as he was.

A reputation Darian had already started to question earlier this evening and about which he now had serious doubts.

She had been at deep pains in his carriage earlier to ensure that he understood that any show of intimacy between the two of them was for show only.

The gown she wore this evening was positively virginal in comparison with the other ladies' attire.

Mariah had seemed relieved rather than disappointed when his glowering presence beside her had kept all other gentlemen at bay this evening.

She had been as disgusted as he by the sexual play they had witnessed during dinner and since.

Lastly, he would swear that her responses just now, to his kisses and the caress of his hands, lips and tongue, had been completely without guile or pretence.

As had her dismay when she realised that Richard Nichols had been watching them.

'It could have,' she choked now. 'It could have!'

Mariah pulled out of Wolfingham's arms before standing up abruptly, knowing, that if Richard Nichols had not played his hand too early, that she had been on the brink—the very brink!—of allowing her emotions to rule her head.

She had *wanted* Darian Hunter to make love to her.

She had *hungered* for it.

Had been so lost to the pleasure of his hands and mouth, of wanting that pleasure to continue, that she had almost been on the point of *begging* him to make love to her!

It was incomprehensible.

Unbelievable.

Unacceptable!

She did not find pleasure in a man's arms, in his closeness, in his lovemaking. She never had. She never would. How could she when the single memory of that act was of the violation of her body rather than pleasure?

When Martin Beecham, the man who had later become her husband, had forced himself upon her shortly before her seventeenth birthday.

A rape of her body and her soul of which Christina was the result, thus forcing Mariah into becoming Martin's wife.

Chapter Eight

'What is it, Mariah?' Darian questioned sharply as he stood up.

He made no move to touch her again; Mariah now looked so fragile, in her emotions as well as her body, that he feared she might crumple and fall at his feet if he attempted to place so much as a finger upon her.

'You can ask me that?' she choked out incredulously, those turquoise eyes glittering brightly in the pallor of her face. 'After learning that the two of us were to be nothing more than exhibits in the Nicholses' peep show?'

He grimaced. 'Only if we had proceeded to make love together. Which we have not.'

Mariah could no longer meet his gaze. 'That does nothing to change the fact— Oh! Do you think anyone could have been behind those walls earlier this evening?' she gasped, eyes wide as she twisted her gloved fingers together.

Darian shrugged. 'I doubt, with the responsibility

of his other guests, that Nichols would have found the time to come up the stairs and observe you dressing.'

'I was referring to our conversation, Darian! Did we say anything in this room earlier that might have— Do you seriously think that weasel Nichols might have *watched* me bathing and dressing earlier this evening?' Mariah's face had taken on a sickly green hue at the thought of it.

'As I recall, our conversation was perfectly innocuous earlier,' he reassured. 'I also think it more likely that Lady Nichols, after escorting us to our bedchambers, would have lingered upstairs to observe *me*!' Darian's mouth twisted with distaste for the very idea of having that pale blue gaze moving lasciviously over his naked body whilst he'd bathed and dressed earlier.

Mariah stilled. 'You believe there to be similar peepholes in your own bedchamber? In *all* the bedchambers?' she added aghast.

'After tonight I believe the master and mistress of this house to be capable of anything! After all, this is not the Nicholses' main country residence.' He shrugged. 'They do not bring their children here, for example, but leave them at their Norfolk estate with their nurse. Thank heavens for small mercies!'

Mariah thought of the other occasions when she had stayed in this house, totally unaware of the eyes that might have been secretly watching her. As she bathed. As she went about her *toilette*. As she stood completely naked before dressing.

She felt ill.

Unclean.

Violated!

As violated as she had been that night eighteen years ago when Martin had lured her into one of the private rooms at a ball they were both attending, locked the door behind them and then coldly and calculatedly assaulted her. Warning her after the event that no one would believe the word of the daughter of a minor landowner and merchant against an earl's, if she were to accuse him of the deed.

Mariah had been but sixteen years old and was too frightened, too devastated, felt too unclean, to dare take the risk of telling anyone what Martin Beecham, the Earl of Carlisle, had done to her.

Most especially so as he had also warned her that he would repeat the violation, again, and then again, until such time as she was with child. Not because he particularly wished for an heir, but so that she was forced into marrying him, thus bringing a good portion of her father's fortune into the marriage.

And it had all worked out perfectly for Martin, of course, because Mariah had become pregnant with that very first attempt. She had tried to tell her parents the truth then, but as promised, Martin had denied her accusation of his having forced her, claiming that she had been as eager as he for the coupling. He also insisted that she was merely frightened of the repercussions after the event, now that she found herself with child. Repercussions that would cease to exist when she accepted his offer of marriage.

Whether or not her parents had believed Mariah's

version of events had not mattered at this point, although she liked to think that they had; she was an only child and their relationship had always been a close one.

But whether they believed her or not, her mother and father had been left with no more choice in the matter than Mariah. She would have to accept the earl's offer of marriage. A babe born seven months after the wedding could be overlooked by society and very often was! But if Mariah refused to marry the father of her child—the more-than-willing father!—then she would be ruined and both she and her parents ostracised from society.

Faced with those choices there had been only one decision that Mariah could make.

Marriage to the very man who had raped her.

Her body might not have been violated tonight, but her privacy, her very person, had.

She was no longer a girl of sixteen, of course, too frightened to accuse the person responsible for that violation. But the reputation she had nurtured in society, as the sophisticated and flirtatious Countess of Carlisle, would most certainly be in danger if she were to now voice her complaints to her host and hostess.

As her obvious shock now had already placed that reputation in danger in regard to Darian Hunter, the astute and intelligent Duke of Wolfingham.

Mariah drew in a deep breath before straightening her shoulders and unclasping her fingers, her chin high as she turned to give Wolfingham a derisive smile. 'How unfortunate, for the Nichols, that you grew wise to their little scheme!'

Darian was relieved to see that some of the colour had now returned to Mariah's cheeks. Although he did not believe for a moment that she was as composed as she now wished to appear; her obvious shock a few minutes ago had most certainly been genuine.

A shock he might not have expected from one as promiscuous as Mariah Beecham was reputed to be.

He also wondered what thoughts had been going through her head just a few minutes ago. Whatever they were, they had brought a grey tinge to her already pale cheeks and haunted shadows to those beautiful eyes.

'Very unfortunate,' he echoed drily, prepared, for the moment, to accept that Mariah was determined to place those walls back about her emotions. This was not the time, and certainly not the place, to question her further on the subject.

But the very fact that she had not as yet upbraided him for their lovemaking earlier was surely evidence of her inner unease?

A lovemaking, and Mariah's response, that Darian knew was going to haunt and disturb his own rest tonight—again!

'Do you have any shawls or handkerchiefs with you? I could place them over the pictures and the head of the bed to ensure your privacy,' he explained at her questioning frown.

'Oh. Oh, yes, of course,' she breathed in obvious relief as she moved to open the wardrobe and look through the things on the shelves in there. 'Here.' She handed Darian several handkerchiefs and two shawls. 'Will they be enough to prevent anyone from at least seeing into this room?'

'Oh, yes.' Darian tied the two shawls securely to the paintings before moving on to do the same to the bed with the handkerchiefs. 'There.' He nodded his satisfaction as he stepped back.

'What of your own bedchamber?'

'I have some handkerchiefs of my own,' he dismissed.

'I— Then I will wish you a good night.'

He frowned. 'Mariah—'

'I believe we have provided enough of a display for our audience for one night, Wolfingham. Besides which, it is late and I am very tired.' She arched one pointed brow.

Darian knew himself well and truly dismissed, without either of them having made direct reference to their heated lovemaking earlier.

If Nichols had not interrupted them then Darian might not have left this bedchamber at all tonight.

But equally, if Nichols had not interrupted the two of them, allowing Darian the time to think of what the other man was doing there at all, then they might even now be providing entertainment for the other guests.

Not that Darian was the prude Mariah had once thought him. Far from it. He had spent his share of time in gaming hells and the houses of the *demi-monde*, and knew full well the games played in such establishments. But that play was at the consent of both parties, not the intrusion, the violation, tonight's game would have been to the privacy of their love-making. He did not perform for the entertainment of strangers.

'Very well, Mariah.' He nodded as he strode across the room to bend down and kiss her lightly upon her brow. 'I wish you a good night,' he added huskily as he looked down at her intently.

Mariah felt flustered by Darian's close proximity, coming so soon after this shocking discovery of the peepholes in her bedchamber.

So soon after she had felt those strange and wonderful sensations as he made love to her earlier out in the hallway.

Sensations Mariah could still feel, in the tingling fullness of her breasts and the swollen dampness between her thighs.

And so reminiscent of those sensations she had felt when he'd kissed her at Lady Stockton's ball.

Was it possible, after all these years of feeling nothing, that her body was actually awakening to sexual arousal?

A sexual arousal caused solely and completely by Darian Hunter, the Duke of Wolfingham?

And felt only for him?

Mariah stepped back abruptly, too alarmed by even the possibility of that being true to be able to suffer his close proximity a moment longer. 'Goodnight, Wolfingham,' she stated firmly.

Darian studied her from between narrowed lids for several seconds longer, knowing from the determined set of Mariah's mouth and chin that she considered this conversation over.

He gave a terse nod. 'If you should need me, you know where I am.'

Her brows rose. 'You are suggesting that I might possibly be overcome with lust for you in the middle of the night?'

Darian grimaced at her scathingly derisive tone. 'I am suggesting that I noticed there is no key in the lock to this bedchamber. We could place a chair beneath the door handle,' he suggested as he saw the alarmed look Mariah gave in the direction of the door.

'Yes! Yes, please do,' she confirmed more coolly. 'Thank you,' she added softly, eyes downcast, as Darian saw to the placing of that chair.

Darian sighed his frustration as he looked at her bent head for several seconds more. Not sexual frustration—that seemed to be with him constantly whenever he was with Mariah. And when he was not!

No, his frustration now was due to another reason entirely.

With Mariah he so often felt as if he took one step forward and then was forced, by circumstances, into taking two steps back. As now. Their lovemaking had been beyond enjoyable. Darian could not remember ever having been aroused quite so quickly, or so strongly, by any other woman. And he knew, from the obvious responses of her body, her breathless sighs of pleasure, that Mariah had been just as aroused. And yet now she was dismissing him as if that closeness had never happened.

It was beyond frustrating; it was infuriating.

Mariah was a woman of four and thirty, had been a married woman for twelve of those years, and as such she could not be unaware of how much he had wanted to make love to and with her a short time ago. Or that she returned that desire for him to make love to and with her. And yet she behaved now as if that desire had never happened.

Was that only because of the unpleasantness of the circumstances here at Eton Park?

Or because, beneath that desire, she disliked him still?

Darian breathed out his frustration with the situation. 'Goodnight, Mariah,' he repeated harshly before turning on his heel and leaving the room abruptly, firmly closing the door adjoining their two bedchambers behind him.

Mariah sank back down on to the side of the bed the moment Darian closed the door between their rooms, her thoughts in turmoil. Not because, unpleasant as it was, of the knowledge of those intrusive peepholes in the walls of her bedchamber. Nor was she overly concerned as to what might or might not transpire tomorrow, after the Regent's note of apology had been delivered.

No, the reason for the present disquiet of her emotions was all due to Darian Hunter and the desire she could no longer deny, to herself at least, that she felt for him.

And him alone.

* * *

'Would you care to go for a ride, or perhaps a walk, in the fresh air this morning, Mariah?' Darian suggested as he looked across the breakfast table at her.

A breakfast table at which only the two of them sat, the other guests, as Mariah had suggested might be the case, either still asleep after their late night, or choosing to break their fast in the privacy of their bedchambers.

Darian had been awake shortly after seven o'clock, earlier than was usual for him, but as he had expected, he had passed another restless night and, once fully awake, could not bear to stay abed any longer. He had known, from the sounds and soft conversation he could hear in the adjoining room, that Mariah was also awake and talking to her maid.

He had found several peepholes in his own bedchamber the night before and used his handkerchiefs accordingly, but they had both agreed the coverings should come down during the day, if only so that the Nicholses did not realise they both knew of the peepholes.

If the Nicholses' butler—he had introduced himself as Benson, when Mariah had enquired—was surprised to see any of the guests appearing in the breakfast room a little after eight o'clock in the morning, then the blandness of his expression did not show it. He remained as stoically impassive as he had yesterday evening, as he served the Nicholses' guests dinner.

It did not help Darian's peace of mind that Mariah

looked beautiful and untroubled this morning, in a russet-coloured silk morning gown, her golden hair swept up and secured at her crown, with clusters of curls at her temple and nape.

She had also been coolly polite to him so far this morning, to the point of irritation.

As if their closeness last night had never happened.

As if Darian had not feasted upon her bared breasts.

As if she had not thoroughly enjoyed having him feast upon her bared breasts.

As if she was annoyed with him for having taken such liberties?

The temper that seemed to burn just below the surface of Darian's emotions whenever it came to Mariah once again raised its ugly head at her lack of response to his suggestion. 'Unless you would rather wait for some of the other guests to come down and perhaps join them?'

Mariah looked at Wolfingham beneath lowered lashes, having sensed that he was angry with her from the moment he knocked briskly on the door adjoining their two bedchambers earlier, then waited for her permission before entering. It had been her experience that Wolfingham did not wait for permission to do anything he pleased.

He looked very severe in his anger. Very much Wolfingham.

The darkness of his hair was brushed back severely from the harshness of his face. His eyes were a flinty, uncompromising green. And there were brackets of displeasure beside his nose and mouth. His movements were also brisk and impatient.

She raised cool brows. 'I shall be quite happy to seek my own entertainment this morning if you are too busy to accompany me on a walk.'

He speared her with that impatient green gaze across the width of the table. 'And what else could there possibly be here to keep me busy this morning?'

Mariah turned to smile at the butler as he lingered by the array of breakfast trays, in readiness for serving them more food. 'Could we possibly have some more coffee, Benson? Thank you.' She waited until the butler had left the room before turning back to Darian. 'If you wish to argue with me, might I suggest that you wait until after we have gone outside,' she hissed in warning.

His brows rose autocratically. 'Why should you imagine I might wish to argue with you?'

Mariah could think of only one reason for Darian's bad humour this morning: the same sexual frustration she had suffered last night!

She was not completely innocent in the ways of men, knew that a man's passion, once aroused, was apt to make him irritable if it was not assuaged; the housekeeper, Mrs Smith, had once taken a week's leave to visit her sick sister and Martin had been unbearable for the whole time she had been gone. To the point that Mariah had feared he might turn his attentions towards her in the other woman's absence. As a precaution against that possibility, Mariah had wisely taken herself off to the country for the rest of that week.

She could not avoid Darian Hunter's company by doing the same. Not for this weekend, at least.

Nor was she altogether sure she wished to.

She had lain awake in bed for hours after they had parted the night before, her body uncomfortably achy and needy. Her breasts had felt swollen, the tips seeming to tingle and burn, occasionally sending shards of pleasure coursing through her as they rubbed against the material of her night-rail. Between her thighs had felt uncomfortably hot and damp, despite her having used a washcloth before going to bed. And there had been an ache amongst the curls down there that had throbbed even harder when she pressed her thighs together, in an effort to dispel that unaccustomed heat.

For the first time in her life Mariah had suffered what she was sure must be sexual frustration.

And it was both frightening and exhilarating, to realise how attracted she had become to Darian Hunter in such a short space of time. How much she desired him. How much she desired to have him make love to and with her.

That realisation frightened her more than anything else!

She lowered her lashes in case that desire should now be reflected in her eyes. 'I know that you do, Darian,' she answered him quietly. 'And I am sorry for it—' She broke off as he stood up abruptly, his chair scraping back noisily on the polished wooden floor. 'Darian?'

His eyes glittered dangerously as he stood beside the table glowering down at her. 'Exactly what are you apologising for, Mariah?' he demanded exasperatedly.

She swallowed. 'I realise that last night—that it did not proceed, as you might have wished it to have done—'

'As *I* might have wished?' he repeated softly, dangerously so. 'Are you denying that your own wishes were exactly the same as my own?'

'I—'

'I advise caution with your answer, Mariah,' he warned softly, those green eyes glittering dangerously, a nerve pulsing in his clenched jaw. 'I am not some callow youth who does not *know* when a woman feels desire.'

Colour warmed Mariah's cheeks and she was unsure whether it was from embarrassment at the intimacy of their conversation, or jealousy, because Darian must have intimate knowledge of *other* women's desire to be so well informed. 'This is neither the time nor the place for—'

'Will it ever be, Mariah?' he bit out scathingly. 'Will you ever be willing to give yourself to me?'

Mariah drew her breath in sharply even as a bite of longing twisted almost painfully between her thighs. What would it be like to give herself to this man? Not just any man, but to Darian Hunter, the Duke of Wolfingham?

Nothing like that horrendous single experience with Martin, she was sure. Even in her limited experience, she knew Darian had already demonstrated that he was a generous and attentive lover, with more of an interest in ensuring his partner's pleasure than taking his own.

Could she give herself to this man? Could she let down her guard, her inhibitions, and open herself up to such intimacy? Such *vulnerability*?

She was starting to believe, that with Darian Hunter, she just might be able to do so…

She straightened her shoulders as she made her decision. 'Perhaps,' she allowed gruffly.

Darian's eyes widened as he barely heard Mariah's softly spoken reply. He had feared the worst minutes ago, as Mariah's eyes once again took on that look of distance, as if she were no longer quite here with him in this room, but somewhere else entirely. Lost in memories, perhaps? Some of them unpleasant ones, if he had read her expression correctly.

Of her husband? Or some other man she had been involved with during her marriage or since?

Darian's ire rose just at the thought of a man, any man, ever having hurt her, in any way.

'Mariah?' He sat down in the chair beside her before taking one of her hands in both of his. Instantly becoming aware of the trembling of her fingers beneath delicate lace gloves—evidence that those thoughts had indeed been unhappy ones? Whatever the reason, he felt heartened by the fact that she did not instantly pull her hand away from his.

'Do you think we could please get out of this oppressive house, if only for a few hours?'

She blinked long lashes. 'I ordered fresh coffee.'

'I am sure that Benson is an understanding fellow. He would have to be to suffer working for the Nicholses!' Darian grimaced.

'Ah, Benson.' The butler appeared in the room almost as if he had been cued to do so. 'The countess and I have decided to go for a walk in the grounds this morning—do you recommend any direction in particular?'

The butler poured fresh coffee into their cups as he answered, his face as expressionless as ever. 'I believe most of her ladyship's guests find Aphrodite's Temple of interest, your Grace.'

'Aphrodite's Temple?' Darian repeated doubtfully; if he remembered his Greek mythology correctly, from his years spent at Eton, Aphrodite had been the goddess of love, beauty and sexuality, but better known as being a goddess who indulged her own selfish sexual desires and lust.

Totally suited to the Nicholses' lifestyle, of course, but not necessarily Darian's own.

'It is Lady Nichols's name for it, your Grace.' Benson seemed to guess some of his thoughts, his expression still stoic and unrevealing. 'It is situated amongst the trees to the left of the lake at the back of the house.'

'Mariah?' Darian turned to prompt, aware that she had not taken part in the conversation as yet. But still Darian felt heartened by the fact that she had allowed her hand to remain in both of his.

She looked up at the butler. 'It sounds…intriguing, Benson.'

She dutifully picked up her cup with her other hand and drank some of the coffee.

The butler nodded. 'And it is always deserted during the day.'

Darian narrowed his eyes. 'But not in the evenings?'

'Not this evening, certainly, your Grace.'

To say Darian was intrigued would be putting it mildly. Although, bearing in mind the sexual games the Nicholses liked to play, he could well imagine that Aphrodite's Temple might prove a little too much for what he now believed to be Mariah's sensibilities. She was much more easily shocked than he might ever have imagined, or hoped for, before spending so much time in her company.

She had become, in fact, the most intriguing woman he had ever met. And was becoming more so rather than less, the more time he spent in her company. It was a certainty he had never been in the least bored when with her.

'Thank you, Benson.' Mariah smiled up at the butler warmly. 'Perhaps you might ask my maid to bring down my pelisse and bonnet from my bedchamber?'

'Of course, my lady.' He bowed.

The silence in the breakfast room seemed charged once the butler had left the two of them alone there. Almost as if the very air itself was waiting expectantly.

For what, Darian was unsure. He only knew that

he wanted to get out of this unpleasant and cloyingly decadent household, if only for a few hours. And that he wanted more than anything for Mariah to accompany him.

He stood up, retaining his hold upon her hand as he pulled her up beside him, so close he could almost feel the brush of her hair against his jaw, her perfume once again invading and capturing his senses. 'Ready?'

Mariah's heart leapt in her chest, as she knew instinctively that Darian was asking for more than if she was ready to go for their walk. That he was continuing their previous conversation rather than starting a new one.

Was she ready?

Was she prepared to take their relationship a step further?

To give in to the desires of her own body and engage in intimacy with Darian?

Could she do that?

Or would the memories of the past intrude once again and bring with them the fear and aversion that was all she had known as Martin's wife?

Mariah looked up at him searchingly, not at his handsomeness; that was all too apparent. No, she looked into his eyes, those clear, deep and unwavering green eyes. Eyes that spoke of a man of both honour and truth. A man capable of killing his enemy, if necessary, but totally incapable of physically hurting a woman, most especially one he desired. And Wolfingham did desire her, was making no effort to hide that fact as he steadily met and returned her searching gaze.

Was she ready?

Was it time for her to release her memories of the past, along with her inhibitions, and give in to these new, and at times uncomfortable, yearnings of her own body?

Was she ready to do that?

Chapter Nine

'Good gracious!' Darian winced up at the pale pink marble structure of what could only be described as a miniature copy of the Greek Parthenon he had visited whilst taking the Grand Tour ten years ago or more.

Nestled amongst the woodland to the left of the lake at Eton Park, exactly as Benson had said it would be, it had six small Doric-style marble columns fronting the building, with ten more along each side, and a domed cupola on the roof. And standing in pride of place before the huge wooden doors at its entrance was a nude statue, of what Darian could only assume was Aphrodite, cupping and stroking her own breast.

A nude statue that should not have been there, considering that, if Darian remembered his Greek mythology correctly, the Parthenon in Greece was dedicated to Athena, the virginal goddess of wisdom and philosophy.

'I can only assume that Lord and Lady Nicholses' knowledge of the Greek gods must be as lacking as their good taste,' Mariah drawled beside him, revealing that her own knowledge on the subject was not lacking at all.

Darian chuckled huskily. 'One does not need to make assumptions once they have seen this.'

Mariah's eyes danced merrily as she glanced up at him. 'It does err rather on the side of ostentatious.'

'That is one word for it!' Darian gave a disgusted shake of his head. 'I sincerely hope that Benson is not of the opinion that the two of us share his employers' bad taste!'

Mariah peered around the statue at the huge oak doors. 'What do you think is inside?'

'Even more lewd statues?'

'Perhaps,' she murmured distractedly as she moved forward to rest one gloved hand on the handle of the door. 'Shall we go inside and see?' she invited huskily.

Darian had to admit to feeling as if a heavy weight had been lifted from his shoulders since leaving the oppression of the Nicholses' household, having enjoyed being out in the fresh air with Mariah walking companionably beside him and wearing a pelisse and bonnet the same russet colour as her gown.

He was in no hurry to forgo that feeling of companionship by entering what he could only assume, in the knowledge of the Nicholses' tastes, and Benson's warning that it would not be empty this evening, was more than likely to be a place where the Nicholses continued their debauchery. 'I doubt it will be any more tasteful inside than out.' He grimaced.

Mariah turned the handle and pushed open the

door. 'We will not know— Oh!' She gave a gasp as she stepped inside. 'Oh, do come and look, Darian,' she encouraged breathlessly. 'It is— You will never believe what is in here!'

Darian found himself moving forward to join Mariah inside the temple, partially lured there at having her address him by his first name, something she rarely did voluntarily, but also out of the need to discover exactly what sort of debauchery had awaited her inside and rendered her so breathless.

Darian felt the difference in temperature as soon as he stepped inside—the cavernous marble building was filled with an inexplicable heat. Or perhaps not so inexplicable, as he breathed in the slightly sulphurous smell only thinly disguised by the scent of lavender and realised that the mixture of smells was emanating from the deep sunken bathing pool of water in the centre of the rose marble building.

Mariah's eyes were glowing with pleasure as she turned to look at him. 'I believe it is a natural hot spring!'

That was exactly what it appeared to be. Darian knew that there were a dozen or more of these natural hot springs in England and that society made a point of flocking to them, usually during the summer months, in order to drink or bathe in what they considered to be the health-giving waters.

But he had never before seen or even heard of there being a private hot spring such as this one obviously was...

He shrugged. 'We are close to Tunbridge Wells, so perhaps this is an offshoot of the one there?'

'It is wonderful!' Mariah drew off one of her gloves before stepping forward to crouch down and dip her fingers into the scented water. 'And it is lovely and warm!' she announced excitedly.

Darian was more than a little grateful for Mariah's distraction with the sunken bathing pool, once his gaze had skimmed over the rest of the interior of the marble building.

There were half a dozen tall candleholders about the cavernous room, fresh candles in them, no doubt in preparation for this evening's entertainments. And a dozen or more slightly raised platforms, each littered with sumptuous and brightly coloured silk cushions.

Darian gave a grimace, his gaze moving swiftly on, as he easily guessed the purpose for *those*.

The two-foot-high frieze on the walls was a plethora of painted scenes of the mythical gods engaged in acts of debauchery with man, woman and beast, as was the domed ceiling above them. But it was the five statues placed about the side of the pool that now caused him to draw his breath in sharply.

Each and every one of them was of Aphrodite, in all her naked glory, engaged in a variety of sexual acts so explicit that no imagination was necessary and causing Darian's mouth to set grimly.

It was so typical of the Nicholses that they had taken a thing of beauty and turned it into yet another scene for their own very questionable sexual tastes.

'Have you ever seen anything like it before, Darian?' Mariah was totally enthralled by the pool, her expression enrapt, as she moved her bare fingers backwards and forwards in the warmth of the water.

With its dozen or so steps down into the water it reminded Mariah of a painting she had once seen, of Queen Cleopatra bathing in such a pool filled with the ass's milk reputed to have preserved her wondrous beauty.

'No, I cannot say I have ever seen anything quite like this before,' Darian answered coolly.

She turned to look at him quizzically, noting the emerald glitter of his eyes and the slight flush to his cheeks, caused by the warmth of the temple. His mouth was pressed into a thin, uncompromising line. She straightened slowly. 'What is it?'

A nerve pulsed in his tightly clenched jaw. 'We should leave! And continue with our walk,' he added tersely as she looked confused by his vehemence.

Mariah blinked at the harshness of his tone. 'But it is so cosy and warm in here, and surely the perfect place for us to escape the company of the other guests until luncheon.' She had thought Darian had desired to be alone with *her* just a short time ago.

His shoulders were tensed beneath his perfectly tailored dark green superfine. 'I agree that the bathing pool is of interest.'

'But?'

He sighed his impatience. 'But the rest of the temple is far less so.'

Mariah had been so enthralled, so enchanted, at

the discovery of the beautiful sunken pool that she had not bothered to look at anything else in the room.

She did so now. And instantly felt the colour heat her own cheeks as she saw the erotic scenes painted on the walls and the ceiling above them. 'I am afraid this has ruined the surprise of the Nicholses' smaller ballroom—' Mariah drew in a sharp breath as she now saw the statues posed about the edge of the pool.

The naked goddess Aphrodite was cradling the head of an equally naked man, whose proportions were worthy of the name Adonis, as he suckled one of her breasts whilst the other hand cupped beneath its twin, thumb and finger in the act of pinching the turgid nipple.

The next was of Aphrodite sprawled upon a couch, the Adonis still at her breasts, her legs parted, a look of ecstasy upon her face as another man feasted on the bounty between her thighs.

Aphrodite reclining upon the same couch, one of the men now lying between her thighs, the hardness of his arousal poised at her entrance— Mariah's gaze moved quickly to the next statue, only to move quickly on again as she saw that Aphrodite was now posed on her hands and knees, her tongue licking her lips as a man stood behind her holding her hips in place, ready for him to enter her like a stallion covering a mare, whilst another man knelt in front of her, his hard arousal jutting forward—

Mariah ceased breathing altogether, her cheeks burning as her gaze hurriedly shifted to the last statue. She saw that the man behind Aphrodite had now buried himself to the hilt between her thighs, a smile now curving the fullness of her lips as she arched her throat, the huge erection of the second man in her mouth.

'You have never been in here before?' Wolfingham enquired harshly.

'I— No.' Mariah was too stunned still to be able to think straight. Or even attempt the sophisticated response that might have been expected of her! 'No, thank goodness,' she repeated irritably. 'I usually retire earlier than the other guests at these affairs and have never— I have never seen any of this before now.' She waved a dismissive hand, eyes downcast so that she did not have to actually look at those statues again.

Statues that should not have shocked the notorious Lady Mariah Beecham and would surely have amused the sophisticated Countess of Carlisle. And yet Mariah *was* shocked and far from amused.

She was also aware that her thoughts had taken flight as she imagined herself and Darian engaged in those intimacies.

His mouth on her breast.

His mouth feasting between her thighs.

His shaft buried to the hilt between those same thighs.

His entering her from behind with the fierceness of a stallion coupling with a mare.

Mariah's fingers encircling his hardness as she parted her own lips and took that swollen length into her mouth. She turned sharply on her heel, *knowing* her response should have been one of sophistication, and perhaps even boredom, at such an erotic display, but for the moment she was unable to even attempt to be either. 'You are right. We should leave.'

'Mariah?' Darian reached out and grasped her wrist as she would have brushed past him as she hurried to the door.

His gaze was searching on her flushed cheeks, and he drew in a sharp breath as she raised her lashes and he saw the fevered glitter in her eyes. An *aroused* and fevered glitter?

Mariah had presented him with one puzzle after another since the moment they'd first met, it seemed. One moment behaving every inch the sophisticated and notorious woman of society she was reputed to be. The next, as she appeared now, seeming to be as shocked as a girl barely out of the schoolroom, by this evidence of the excesses of the less reputable members of the *ton*.

The more time Darian spent in Mariah's company, the more of a mystery she became to him. And it was a mystery that Darian was fast becoming addicted to solving.

He had no wish for it to be that way. Had no wish to ever become so enthralled by one particular woman that he could think of nothing and no one else.

So enthralled that his every waking thought was of making love to and with her. As the pulsing and throbbing of his erection now testified he wished to do. With Mariah.

Perhaps if he made love with her, witnessed her

in the throes of sexual pleasure, saw that she was a flesh-and-blood woman with carnal needs that matched, or even exceeded, his own, then this hunger would go away?

His fingers tightened about her wrist. 'There is no reason for us to leave here just yet if you wish to remain.'

Mariah's heart leapt in her chest, the heat increasing in her cheeks, as she looked up and saw the burning intensity of Darian's gaze fixed so intently upon her lips. Lips that instantly tingled with the memory of his kisses from the evening before.

Lips that parted instinctively as Darian's gaze held hers captive as his head lowered towards her own.

It was as if the hours between their time together the previous evening and this morning had never happened; the desire was instant. Tongues duelled, hands caressed, their breathing sounding ragged in the silence of the temple as they kissed hungrily.

It was as if they could not get enough of each other. Could not get close enough.

Mariah could *feel* the evidence of Darian's desire pressing hot and heavy against her softness as the kiss continued, tongues tasting, teeth gently biting. She felt the pulse, the thrill, of that arousal, all the way from the top of her head to the tips of her toes. Her breasts swelled, ached painfully, against the bodice of her gown. She felt a gush of wetness between her thighs in response to that desire and she was aware of Darian groaning low in his throat as he now arched, ground that arousal, against and into her.

She felt her folds swell, become wet and slick, as Darian moved one of his hands down and in between them in order to cup her mound through her gown. His palm pressed against her, unerringly finding and putting rhythmic pressure upon the sensitive nubbin nestled amongst her curls, as his fingers curled to trace the delicate folds beneath. Teasing. Caressing.

Mariah wanted more, needed more, as she instinctively thrust up and into those caressing fingers, the pleasure building, growing unbearable as she arched her throat, head back, eyes widening— And instantly found herself looking up at those scenes of debauchery painted upon the ceiling!

It was as if a bucket of cold water had been thrown over her, dousing every measure of arousal and desire as Mariah wrenched her mouth from Darian's to draw in a deep and shaky breath at the same time as she pushed against Darian's chest and put herself at arm's length. 'I do not—' She gave a shake of her head. 'This place makes me feel…uncomfortable.'

Darian's eyes glittered down at her heatedly. 'Uncomfortable or aroused?'

Mariah's breath hitched in her throat and the trembling increased in her limbs. A trembling that Darian could not help but be aware of when his hands were still on her waist. 'A little of both,' she acknowledged gruffly.

She heard Darian draw in his own breath sharply before he answered her huskily, 'I feel the same way.'

Mariah glanced about them at the erotica depicted so graphically on the frieze on the walls and ceiling, and those explicitly erotic statues. And knowing that she could not—

'Not here, Darian. I could not bear to do this here—' She broke off with a shudder. 'I can only imagine the scenes of excess this room has witnessed during the Nicholses' weekend parties! And will no doubt witness again this very night.' She was so tense now that she flinched as one of Darian's hands moved up to cup her cheek before he gently lifted her face up towards his own.

Darian looked down at Mariah searchingly, once again struck by her beauty, at the same time as he recognised those familiar shadows in her eyes and the slight trembling of her lips.

As he also knew that the flush in her cheeks was partly due to the arousal the eroticism in this temple could not help but evoke.

Not completely because of him, or for him.

And it might be a matter of false pride on Darian's part, but when—*if*—he ever made love to Mariah completely, then *he* wished to be the only reason for her arousal.

He drew in a steadying breath before nodding abruptly and releasing her before stepping back. 'Then again I suggest we continue with our walk.'

Mariah was more than a little unsettled by the abruptness of Darian's acceptance of her withdrawal as she led the way out of the marble temple. Could it be that he had actually *wanted* to remain in the temple and indulge in those sexual fantasies depicted by the paintings and statues?

Sexual fantasies that still made the blood boil in her veins and her body ache for—for *Darian*.

Only for Darian.

She had never felt this attraction to any other man. Never felt this ache for a man's touch. Never wanted, hungered for, a physical closeness with any man. Never burned for the promise of pleasure his lips and hands had evoked.

Until Darian.

She looked up at him from beneath lowered lashes once they were outside again in the crisp March air. 'I apologise if my words of earlier led you to expect otherwise, Darian. But I simply could not bear the thought of us being together in such a place.' She gave a shudder of revulsion. 'It was—'

'Unpleasant at best and thoroughly disgusting at worst?' He nodded grimly. 'I thought so, too.'

'You did?'

'I did,' he rasped harshly. 'You may rest assured, I shall be having words with Benson on the subject once we have returned to the house,' he added grimly.

'You are not disappointed?'

A frown appeared between his eyes. 'Why should I be disappointed?'

'I gave the impression earlier—I all but implied— that we, the two of us, might—' She straightened her shoulders. 'I am aware that a man does not take sexual disappointment well.'

'From your husband?'

'No!' Mariah gasped in protest, only to quickly seek composure as she realised how telling her answer might have been. She strived to adopt a derisively dismissive smile. 'No man needs suffer sexual disappointment in regard to his own wife, when the law allows him to do with her whatever, and as often as he wills it.'

Wolfingham's eyes narrowed. 'Were you happy in your marriage, Mariah?'

She eyed him coolly. 'I believe I have already intimated to you, in a previous conversation, that I was not.'

'Ever?'

Her mouth tightened. 'No.'

Darian could read nothing from the stiffness of Mariah's expression. Or perhaps that stiffness was telling in itself.

'Was Carlisle cruel to you?' He found himself tensing as he waited for her answer.

Her chin rose proudly. 'Only if indifference can be called cruelty. And in the case of my husband, I did not consider it to be so.'

'His indifference? He did not love you?' Darian's gaze sharpened on the paleness of her face.

'No more than I loved him, no.'

'Then why marry him at all?' Darian frowned. 'Your daughter's age now intimates you yourself were barely out of the schoolroom when you married. That it was in all probability your first Season. Surely, as you informed me regarding your daughter, there was no hurry for you to accept the first offer of marriage made to you?' His mouth twisted harshly. 'Or perhaps you fancied yourself as being a countess?'

'No!' Her denial came out sharply this time, her eyes glittering as she looked up at him coldly. 'Sometimes—sometimes we cannot do as we wish but as we must,' she added tautly as Darian continued to look down at her beneath hooded lids.

'And you *must* needs marry Carlisle?'

'Yes!' she hissed vehemently.

Darian's gaze narrowed as he studied her intently, looking, searching for the answers he knew Mariah had not yet given him. That the closed expression on her face said she might never give him...

Part of Mariah's mystery was her unwillingness to discuss the past with him. Her past. A past that he was now sure had made her the coolly detached woman she so often was today.

A past that had also led to her being here with him now, acting as an agent for the Crown?

'Talk to me, Mariah. Help me to understand,' he invited gently. 'Explain why you felt you had to marry Carlisle when, as you have said, you did not love him, or he you, and you did not fancy yourself as becoming his countess. Was your family in financial difficulty? Did your father have debts owing to Carlisle directly? Help me to understand, Mariah,' he repeated gruffly.

'Why?'

'Because I *need* to!' he ground out harshly.

'Again, why?'

Darian forced all trace of anger from his voice and expression, already knowing that Mariah did not react well to either. 'Perhaps you might humour me by doing so?'

Her eyes flashed darkly. 'There was nothing in the least humorous about my marriage.'

He sighed. 'Perhaps I chose the wrong word. It would *please* me if you would do me the honour of confiding in me, Mariah,' he amended softly.

She looked at him searchingly for several long seconds, no doubt looking for sarcasm or mockery in his expression, but surely she would find only sincerity.

'Please, Mariah,' Darian encouraged again gently.

She breathed heavily. 'I married Carlisle for none of the reasons you have mentioned.' Her tone was still cold, uncompromising. 'My father was—still is, a very wealthy man. But Carlisle's coffers were bare and he required some of that wealth.' She shrugged. 'Enough to marry a woman he did not love and who did not love him. As might well be expected from such an ill-matched alliance, it was not a happy marriage. For either of us. And that is an end to it.'

Darian doubted that very much. 'And is that the reason you had affairs with other men? Why you now attend licentious weekend parties such as this one?'

'You are being deliberately insulting!' Her cheeks were flushed.

'I am trying to understand.' Darian drew in a deep and controlling breath as he saw the way in which Mariah drew back at his forcefulness. 'Can you not see, I am trying to understand *you*, Mariah,' he spoke more calmly, evenly, knowing his impatience would not endear him to Mariah, or encourage her in the confidences he wanted, needed, to hear from her.

'Why?' She eyed him challengingly. 'What should

it matter one way or another whether or not you understand me?'

Darian ground his teeth together. 'It matters to me.'

She smiled without humour. 'That is no answer at all.'

He sighed. 'Can you not see I am puzzled as to why any young and beautiful woman would marry a man she admits she did not love, who did not love her and who was so much older than herself? I could better understand it if Carlisle had been rich and you or your family had been in need. Or even if you fancied yourself as being Carlisle's countess. But you have denied any and all of those as being the reason for entering into a marriage that you admit to knowing would bring you no happiness. I can think of no other reason why—' Darian broke off abruptly, eyes widening as a third alternative began to take form and root in his mind.

A third alternative that would most certainly have required that Mariah *must* marry Carlisle.

Could that possibly be the answer to this puzzle?

Mariah admitted to being four and thirty, and her daughter, Christina, was now aged seventeen, which meant that Mariah could only have been sixteen when that daughter was conceived.

'You were with child when you married Carlisle,' he breathed softly, knowing he had guessed correctly as he saw every last vestige of colour leach from Mariah's already pale cheeks.

Mariah drew her breath sharply, wishing she could

deny it, yet at the same time she knew there was no point in her doing so.

Wolfingham had been intelligent enough, determined enough, to accurately guess as to the reason for her marriage to Martin. If she denied it now he would only need to ask any who had been part of society seventeen years ago to discover—to confirm—that the Earl and Countess of Carlisle's daughter had been born not quite seven months after their wedding had taken place.

Her chin rose challengingly. 'Yes, I was with child when Martin and I married.'

Those intelligent green eyes continued to look down at her, searching, probing, as if Wolfingham might pluck the answers to the rest of this mystery from inside her head.

Outwardly Mariah withstood the probe of that astute green gaze, her chin raised in challenge as her turquoise gaze returned his unflinchingly.

But inwardly she was far less secure in her emotions. In being able to withstand these probing questions, coming so soon after they had visited Aphrodite's Temple together. Not just because of those erotic and disturbing paintings and statues, but also because her body was still deeply aroused from Darian's kisses coming so soon after, and the manner in which he had touched her, aroused her, between her thighs.

An arousal, a desire for *more*, that she knew had already battered her shaky defences.

'How was such a thing possible?' Darian breathed softly.

Mariah gave a humourless laugh at the incongruity of the question. 'I believe Christina to have been conceived in the same manner in which all children are!'

Darian reached out to grasp the tops of her arms, relaxing his hold slightly as he instantly became aware of the way in which Mariah was trembling. 'You are avoiding answering the question directly, Mariah.'

Her gaze also avoided meeting his. 'No—'

'Yes,' he insisted gently. 'You did not love Carlisle. Your manner when you speak of him implies that you did not even like him. You have stated that he was indifferent to you and did not love you any more than you loved him. There have been no other children in your marriage. If those were the true circumstances—'

'I do not tell lies, Darian,' Mariah bit out tautly, her chin defensively high, while inside, much as she fought against it, she felt those walls about her emotions slowly but surely crumbling at her feet. 'I abhor it in others and will not allow it in or to myself.'

'Then why, young as you were, would you have given yourself to a man such as Carlisle—' Wolfingham broke off with a gasp, his cheeks taking on a shocking pallor. 'Carlisle took you against your will.' It was a statement, not a question.

It was too much. *Darian* was too much. And Mariah could no longer bear it. She could not look at him any longer!

'No.' Darian's hands tightened on Mariah's arms

as she would have pulled away from him, with the obvious intention of escaping. Of possibly returning to the house without him. 'No, Mariah,' he repeated softly, even as he released his grip to instead gather her into his arms as he cradled her close against him. 'We have come so far in this conversation, now we must finish it.'

'Why must we?' She held herself stiffly in his arms.

'Perhaps for your own sake?'

She gave a choked laugh. 'I already know the events of the past, Darian, I certainly do not need to talk of them in order to remember them with sickening clarity.'

'Please, Mariah,' Darian encouraged gruffly, holding back his need to know the truth as he sensed the emotions now raging within her.

He could sense her anger, certainly. Her pain. And perhaps still a little of the desire they had felt for each other earlier? Which, he realised ruefully, was perhaps the only reason that she had not already issued him one of her icy set-downs before marching back to the house. Alone.

Darian's arms tightened about Mariah. 'Was I right when I said that Carlisle took you against your will?'

She drew in a ragged breath. 'Yes.'

'Oh, Mariah,' he breathed out raggedly.

'Carlisle was— I told you, he was in need of funds,' she continued forcefully, as if to ward off any show of compassion from Darian. 'He knew, all of society knew, that my father was extremely wealthy.'

'And?' Darian encouraged gently.

She drew in a ragged breath. 'Can you not leave this alone?'

'No more than I can leave *you* alone,' he assured tautly.

Mariah sighed softly before answering him. 'The Season was only weeks old and Carlisle had danced with me several times at various balls. He could not have failed to know I did not—that I had no particular liking for him. Nor would I ever willingly accept a marriage proposal from him. No matter what his title,' she added ruefully.

Darian was now ashamed of himself for ever having suggested that might have been her motive for marrying a man so much older than herself. 'It was a natural, if insulting, assumption to have made.'

'Perhaps,' she allowed flatly before continuing. 'Carlisle was not a man to accept a refusal, most especially not from the daughter of a man he, and his family, considered as being so inferior to himself.'

'His family were cruel to you?' If that was so, then it explained Mariah's overprotectiveness towards her daughter's future husband and family.

'They considered me beneath them and treated me accordingly,' Mariah confirmed huskily, licking the dryness of her lips before speaking again. 'Knowing of my aversion, Carlisle lay in wait for me at one of those balls, trapped me alone in a room and—and then he— I will leave you to draw your own conclusion as to what happened next!' She shivered in Darian's arms.

'Mariah?' A black haze had passed in front of Darian's eyes at all that Mariah had not said. That she could not say. 'Why did your father not deal with him? Call him out? Expose him in society for the beast he was?'

'I did not— I dared not tell either of my parents what had happened.'

'Why not?' Darian scowled darkly.

Mariah shook her head. 'My father was very wealthy, but even so he was only a minor landowner, had made his money in trade and was only accepted into the fringes of society, as was I. Carlisle, on the other hand, might not have been rich, but his title made him extremely powerful in society. And if my father had challenged him, or Carlisle had called him out for making his accusations against him, I have absolutely no doubt as to which of them would have walked away.' She gave a shudder.

Nor did Darian; Martin Beecham had been known as an excellent shot and swordsman.

'Besides,' Mariah continued in that same flat voice, 'Carlisle had made it clear to me after—afterwards...' a little colour flared briefly in her cheeks before as quickly fading again '...that if I told my father what had happened, then he would deny my accusations, claim that it was just my own guilty conscience regarding our having acted on our desire for each other. And that the only outcome to my confession would be the one that he wanted anyway, our immediate betrothal and marriage. He also threatened—' She breathed shakily. 'He said he would do *that* again, and again, until I carried his child, so leaving me with no choice but to marry him.'

'The utter and complete bastard!' If Carlisle had been alive today then Darian knew that he would happily have thrust a sword or knife blade through the other man's cruel black heart, for what he had done to Mariah. Or put a bullet in that same warped and twisted heart.

Mariah pressed her face against Darian's chest, causing him to bend lower in order to hear her next words. 'When I discovered just weeks later that I was indeed expecting his child, I wanted to die, to run away. I even thought of ending my own life. And yet I could not do that either, not with the babe inside me. It would have been nothing less than murder. And my father, as Carlisle had predicted, once told of my condition could not refuse the earl's offer of marriage. Not without causing scandal and ruin for all of us. I was well and truly trapped. Into marrying a man I not only hated, but also had every reason to fear—' She broke off as a sob caught at the back of her throat.

Darian inwardly cursed himself for having forced the subject to the point that he had put Mariah through the pain of reliving those unhappy memories of her past.

The memory of the taking of what Darian was sure would have to have been her young and inexperienced body.

A body that now trembled almost uncontrollably against his own as Mariah battled to stop the tears from falling.

Darian had no doubt they were tears Mariah should have shed eighteen years ago. For the manner in which she had lost her innocence. For the babe, conceived in fear on Mariah's part and greed on Carlisle's.

For the twelve years of unhappiness she had spent as wife to the very man who had raped her.

Chapter Ten

Darian shifted slightly so that his arms were beneath Mariah's thighs and shoulders as he lifted her up and against his chest before striding across to sit down on one of the ledges along the outside of the temple. He settled Mariah comfortably on his thighs, her head, for the moment, resting against his shoulder.

Darian held on to her tightly. 'I believe it would be better if you now tell me all, Mariah, when you have already come so far.'

She gave a shake of her head. 'And I do not care to talk, or think, any more about those horrible memories.'

'The memories of when Carlisle raped you. What he did was the rape of an innocent, Mariah, nothing more, nothing less,' Darian insisted grimly as she stiffened in his arms.

'I am well aware of what it was.'

'After which, he then forced you into years of suffering an unhappy marriage with him, because of your daughter.' Darian could barely contain the violence he felt at learning of Carlisle's brutish behaviour. An impotent violence, in view of the fact that Carlisle was no longer alive to feel the lash of his tongue or the flash of his blade. Carlisle might have been an excellent swordsman, but Darian knew he was better.

'I may not have wanted the marriage, or Carlisle, but I have loved Christina since the day she was born,' Mariah instantly defended. 'She has always been the one shining light in my life.'

Darian nodded, only too well aware of the protectiveness she felt towards her daughter.

As he was also now aware of her reason for objecting so vehemently to the idea of Lady Christina marrying anyone at the age of only seventeen years. The same age as Mariah had been when she was forced to marry Carlisle.

'But there was no heir?' Darian prompted slowly.

'Carlisle did not— He had no interest in my producing his heir. He had a younger cousin he was perfectly happy should inherit the title. His only reason for marrying me was to attain a portion of my father's considerable fortune.'

'I have noted that marriage has a way of producing children, whether they are wanted or not,' Darian drawled ruefully.

'And I have already told you that Carlisle was completely indifferent to me as his wife.'

Darian looked down at Mariah with incredulous eyes. 'Are you saying— You cannot possibly mean—'

'What, Darian?' Mariah lifted her head to look up at him, her eyes dark and shadowed in the pallor of her face. 'I cannot possibly mean that my husband's uninterest in me was such that he did not share my bed, even once, after we were married?' Her smile was completely lacking in humour as she gave a shake of her head. 'Why can I not mean that, Darian, when it is the truth?'

A truth that Darian could not even begin to comprehend, when his own desire for Mariah was such that he found it difficult to sleep at night, to stop thinking about her day and night, of the ways in which he wished to make love with her. She had been Carlisle's *wife* for twelve years. Surely the other man could not have—

Mariah took advantage of his distraction to pull herself abruptly out of his arms before standing up and turning the paleness of her face away in profile, a shutter seeming to have come down over her emotions—no doubt because she deeply regretted having revealed them in the first place.

'Why should Carlisle have need of the attentions of his very young and very inexperienced wife,' she continued drily, 'when his mistress of over twenty years was the housekeeper of our London home?'

'Carlisle kept his mistress in your home after you were married?' Darian stood up slowly.

It was well known that many gentlemen of the *ton* kept a mistress after they were married. But never, ever, in the same house as their wife. It was not done.

It simply was not done. And yet, it appeared that that was exactly what Carlisle had done.

'In truth, I was grateful for Mrs Smith's existence.' Mariah shrugged dismissively as she briskly pulled her glove back on to the hand she had earlier dipped into the heated pool. 'And I was not made uncomfortable by the arrangement, visiting London rarely during the first ten years of our marriage. I much preferred to remain in the country with Christina.'

Darian breathed deeply. 'But something happened to change that? Did you and Carlisle perhaps reconcile?'

'There was nothing *to* reconcile.' She turned to frown at him. 'How could there be, when we had never been husband and wife in the true sense of the word?'

'But something did change.'

Mariah knew she had said too much already, revealed too much—more than she had ever told anyone else about the past and the reason for her marriage to Martin. The only thing she had not shared with Darian was Martin's treasonous behaviour. And the lie that was the rumour of her numerous affairs...

She had never confided as much to anyone about the past as she now had to Darian Hunter. Knew she had only been lulled into doing so this time because her emotions had already been disturbed by what she had seen and done in the temple. From her imaginings as to what it would be like to engage in those acts with Darian. Imaginings that had deepened, flourished, during the kiss that had followed.

And that momentary weakness had now cost her dearly.

Damn it, she had told him of Carlisle's brutality. Her forced marriage. She had *cried* in Wolfingham's arms. She, who never cried, preferring never to show any sign of weakness. To anyone.

And she did not intend to continue to do so now where Wolfingham was concerned, either. Had made a vow to herself long ago not to allow *anyone*, apart from Christina, to come so close to her, to know her so well, they were capable of hurting her. 'Do you still wish to continue with our walk, or has all this ridiculous emotion dampened not only your shirt but your enthusiasm for walking?' she prompted coolly.

That astute green gaze remained narrowed on her as Wolfingham stepped closer. 'There was nothing in the least ridiculous about your upset just now, Mariah.'

'And I believe it to have been an utterly ridiculous waste of time,' she insisted coldly, 'when the past, talking about it, changes nothing.'

'And what of the future, Mariah?' He stepped so close to her now that she could feel the warmth of his breath against her brow. 'What of *your* future?'

She gave a dismissive shrug. 'Once this weekend is over, I do not believe that to be any of your business.' Mariah clasped her hands together so that Darian could not see they were trembling still, evidence that her emotions were not as back under her control as she would have wished them to be. Her complete lack of control, just minutes ago, now made her feel vulnerable, in a way she found most disturbing.

Wolfingham raised his hands to cup both her cheeks before he tilted her face up so that he might look directly into her eyes. 'And what if I wish to make it my business?'

Wolfingham's gentleness was unbearable, before and again now, when Mariah knew her emotions, despite her denials to the contrary, remained ragged and torn. When her *defence* against Darian's gentleness remained ragged and torn.

'I am sure I am not the first woman to have been trapped into an unhappy marriage,' she said drily. 'Nor will I be the last. And as you say, I did become a countess because of it.'

'Do not attempt to make light of it, Mariah!' Wolfingham rasped harshly.

'How do you wish me to behave, Darian?' Her eyes flashed darkly as she looked up at him defiantly. 'I have wailed and railed, and now I wish to forget it. As I have forgotten it these past seventeen years.'

'Did you forget, Mariah?' He looked down at her searchingly. 'Did you ever really forget what that man did to you?'

Of course Mariah had never forgotten. She had not wanted to forget, was the woman she was today because of it.

Her chin rose. 'Enough so that I do not require, or need, your own or anyone's pity because of it.'

'Does this feel like pity to you?' Wolfingham had grasped one of her hands and placed it over the noticeable bulge in his pantaloons. 'Does it?' He pushed for an answer, his eyes glittering down at her darkly.

'And how long will that desire last, Wolfingham?' Mariah fell back on derision as her defence as she deliberately removed her hand at the same time as she returned his gaze mockingly. 'Until you have sated your lust between my thighs and then wish to move on to some other conquest? Possibly to a woman who is younger and less complicated!'

He gave a slow shake of his head. 'I find your complications intriguing and your age of four and thirty is unimportant to me.' A nerve pulsed in the tightness of his jaw. 'And I resent your assumption that my desire for you is a fleeting thing.'

'Perhaps I presume as much because it has been my experience that a man will say anything, promise anything, when he wishes to bed a certain woman.' She eyed him scornfully.

Darian frowned his frustration. He did not give a damn what Mariah's previous lovers had told her, or promised her, when *he* was the man now standing before her, telling her, physically *showing* her, how much he desired her. How much he desired to *be* with her.

A desire of such intensity that Darian had no doubt it would not abate for some time. If ever.

More than anything he wished to take Mariah to his bed. To gently kiss her, caress her, to *taste* her, to worship every satiny inch of her, and show her the depth of his desire for her. And then he wished to start all over again. And again. And then again. Again, and again, and again, until Mariah was left in absolutely no doubt as to the depth of his desire for her.

At the same time as he knew that this place, Eton Park, with its peepholes into the bedchambers and a temple worthy of the debauchery of the Roman Empire at the height of its power, and the guests to match, plus the Nicholses' intrigues, was not where he wished to lie with Mariah the first time. Not where he wished to make love with her, to worship her and her body, as she so deserved to be worshipped.

His hands fell back to his sides as he stepped back. 'Very well, we will continue with our walk for now. But we will talk on this subject again once we are back in London,' he added softly.

She arched a taunting brow. 'Not if I do not wish to do so.'

Darian's mouth quirked into an equally mocking smile. 'A word of advice, Mariah. I am not like any of your previous lovers. When you know me better, which you most assuredly will, I believe you will find that I am a man who *always* means what he says as well as *always* keeps his promises!'

Mariah masked her uneasiness as she fell into step beside him as he began to walk back in the direction of the lake, very much afraid that Darian Hunter was indeed a man who always meant what he said as well as kept all of his promises.

Afraid?

Oh, yes, Mariah was very much afraid, in spite of everything that had happened between them since they first met, that she desired Darian Hunter as much as he now claimed to desire her.

That she desired to know Darian in a way she had never desired any other man.

'Do try to smile, Darian, rather than scowl and glower in that dark and disapproving way,' Mariah advised lightly later that afternoon, viewing his reflection in the mirror after he had entered her bedchamber through the door adjoining their two rooms, after only the briefest of knocks. His appearance was elegantly foreboding in a black superfine, grey waistcoat and pantaloons. 'Else, once we arrive downstairs for tea, the other guests will think that the two of us have argued.' She looked at her own reflection in the mirror to give her already perfectly styled hair another pat, rather than continue to look at Darian's more disturbing reflection.

Everything about this man disturbed her.

The way he looked.

Her undeniable response to his touch.

The desire she was finding it more and more difficult to deny or control.

And the fact that she had confided so much of her past to him earlier today.

That breach in the barrier she had kept so firmly about her emotions for so many years disturbed Mariah most of all, so much so that she had spent the past four hours, since they parted downstairs after returning from their walk, attempting to shore up or replace that barrier.

Only to have taken but a single glance at Darian's reflection in the mirror as he strode forcefully into her bedchamber just now to know that those efforts, determined as they might have been, had been a complete waste of her time.

What was it about this man in particular that affected her so? Oh, he was handsome enough. Forceful enough. But he was far from the first handsome or forceful man to have expressed a desire to bed her. Desire she had found absolutely no difficulty in rejecting in the past.

No doubt because she had not felt a return of that desire for any of those other men.

The same desire that had so shaken and disturbed her earlier, to a degree that she had confided more of her past to this man than she had ever wished anyone to know.

The very same desire that made her feel so vulnerable whenever she was in his presence.

'I have absolutely no interest in what they do or do not think,' Darian answered her impatiently now, the scowl still dark upon his brow as he stepped further into the room.

Mariah turned slowly, a slight frown creasing her own brow now. 'Has something happened?'

Darian stared at her incredulously.

Had something happened?

As far as Darian's life was concerned, Mariah Beecham had happened.

So much so that just one look at her, when he entered her bedchamber just seconds ago and saw how beautiful she looked in an afternoon gown of the palest turquoise, her breasts a creamy and tempting swell, the very low and curved neckline of that gown revealing the tops of her nipples as being a deep rose, and he was forced to endure a hard and painful throb inside his pantaloons yet again.

At the same time he felt a ridiculous desire to cover up those beautiful breasts, so that no other man could look at or see any part of them. Or become aroused and tempted by looking at them, as he undoubtedly was.

A ridiculous reaction, when Mariah's coolness towards him this morning, once they had left the temple, and then completed their walk about the lake together in complete silence, had spoken only too clearly not only of her need to put a physical distance between them, but also of a return of that emotional one.

Darian had lingered in the hallway to have that promised word with Benson while Mariah went up the stairs alone. By the time he arrived up the stairs, the door to Mariah's bedchamber, and the door adjoining their two rooms, had both been firmly closed. He had known instinctively that Mariah meant them as a barrier between the two of them. One he crossed at his peril.

Because she had revealed too much about herself to him this morning? Because he now knew things about her life, her marriage to Carlisle, that perhaps no one else did?

Darian did not believe that Mariah was the type

of woman who would confide her deepest, darkest secrets easily. To anyone. And he knew from personal experience that Mariah's role as an agent for the Crown would also make it difficult for her to have close friends, male or female, for fear they might discover her secret.

The murderous rage Darian had felt earlier today, towards Martin Beecham, had not abated in the slightest in the hours that had passed since Darian and Mariah had parted so stiffly. Her husband had been an out-and-out bastard who had raped and terrified a young and inexperienced girl for the sole purpose of forcing his child and marriage on her, trampling all of the young girl's romantic dreams into the dust beneath his own greedy need for the bride's portion of her father's money.

Not only that, but Carlisle had doubly insulted Mariah by having his mistress in residence as housekeeper in one of the homes Mariah herself had necessarily to visit on occasion.

How did any woman survive that? But especially one as young and innocent as Mariah had been then?

Darian knew it would be difficult for a woman of any age to have survived such base and selfish cruelty.

Yet here Mariah stood before him, a lady in every sense of the word. So graciously beautiful, as well as being the most desirable woman he had ever known.

Nor was it any wonder, after all that she had suffered at Beecham's hands, that Mariah had turned to the comforting arms and desire of other men, both during and after her marriage.

Had any of those other men *made love* to her? Darian wondered as he continued to admire her beauty and poise. Truly made love to her? Showering Mariah with the gentleness, the care and consideration that was her due?

Or had they all without fail, as she had so scathingly scorned earlier, treated her as just another conquest in their bed? So that they might afterwards claim, to their male friends and associates, to have bedded the beautiful Countess of Carlisle?

'Darian?' Mariah prompted again, her expression having become wary at his continued silence.

Darian had spent most of the past four hours pacing his bedchamber and thinking of Mariah. Of all that she had told him of her past, at the same time as he now knew it was that past that had made her the woman she was today: cool, poised and determined to remain totally removed from emotional entanglements with any man.

It had brought Darian to the question that concerned him the most: how the two of them were to now proceed—or *if* Mariah would allow them to proceed at all.

For he had promised himself he would not use any type of force upon Mariah. That he might perhaps allow himself to cajole, tease and seduce her, but he would not, could not, ever use coercion or force of any kind.

'Nothing has happened.' He drew in a ragged

breath. 'I want— I need— No, I *ask*—' He broke off abruptly, only now appreciating how difficult it was going to be to keep the promise he had made to himself earlier, when just to look at Mariah again made his blood burn in his veins and his erection throb.

Mariah was now truly alarmed by Darian's behaviour. Of what might possibly have happened to put the arrogantly assured Duke of Wolfingham in such an obvious state of uncertainty. 'Yes?' she prompted tensely.

He straightened his shoulders, emerald gaze fixed intently upon her as he spoke abruptly. 'I would ask if you will allow me to kiss you before we go downstairs?'

Darian Hunter was a man Mariah had every reason to know was always and completely assured as to the rightness of his own actions.

As he had believed he was in the right two weeks ago, when he had warned her not to encourage his younger brother in his attentions to her.

As he had believed her friendship with Aubrey Maystone must be one based on intimacy.

As he believed her to be a woman who had indulged in many affairs, both during and after her marriage.

Wolfingham had believed he was in the right in all of those things.

Admittedly, he had already been proven wrong in two of those things, but the latter? Darian still believed in that legion of lovers Mariah was reputed to have had these past seven years, no doubt believed them to have been her comfort for the coldness of her marriage.

And yet he now asked if he might kiss her?

To say Mariah was flustered by Darian's request would be putting it mildly. Especially when she had every reason to know that the arrogantly self-assured Duke of Wolfingham never 'asked' permission to do anything, let alone asked permission to kiss *her*. The notorious and scandalous Mariah Beecham, Countess of Carlisle…

She attempted a sophisticated and dismissive laugh, hoping Wolfingham did not recognise it, as she certainly did, as sounding more nervous than assured. 'I thought we had agreed not to continue with that conversation until after we have returned to London.' She gave a pointed glance to where her shawls and handkerchiefs were once again draped over those peepholes into her bedchamber, in order to preserve her privacy, both while she'd bathed and changed her clothes earlier.

A nerve pulsed in his tightly clenched jaw. 'I find that my desire to at least touch you again cannot wait that long.'

His desire to touch her again!

It was Wolfingham's touch that had been her undoing from the beginning. Not just once, but so many times. On the terrace of her own home. In the guest bedchamber of her home, where he had necessarily to stay in order to recover after his collapse. In the gallery of Lady Stockton's home. And here. Here at

Eton Park she had allowed Darian to touch her more intimately than any other man had ever done before.

Mariah now feared her response to his touch.

Not because she thought Darian would ever physically hurt her—she was already sure he would never use force upon any woman. She had come to know him these past two weeks, knew he was not a man who showed his strength or power through physical dominance over others, but by the sheer force of his indomitable will.

No, she did not fear Darian would physically hurt her, as Carlisle had hurt and humiliated her, to such an extent she had never cared to repeat the experience.

Darian Hunter was capable of hurting her in a much different way.

She was not only aroused by him, felt desire for him, she also liked and admired him. His strength. His honesty. His family loyalty. His devotion to his country. He was, as she had learnt these past weeks, in all things an honourable man.

A man she might love.

And Mariah did not wish to love any man, even one as handsome and honourable as she now knew Darian Hunter, the Duke of Wolfingham, to be.

The independence of nature she so enjoyed now had been hard won, after years of living only half a life, hidden away in the country, and for the most part ignored by the husband she hated and despised. For the past seven years, since revealing Martin's treasonous behaviour to Aubrey Maystone, she had no longer had reason to fear Martin, or anything he might try to do to her. Aubrey Maystone had taken care of that.

For the first time in her life Mariah had done exactly as she pleased, her worthwhile work for the Crown enabling her to become a woman she could not only respect, but also like.

For her to fall in love, with any man, would, she believed, be to put all of that at risk.

To fall in love with Darian Hunter, the much respected and admired Duke of Wolfingham, would most certainly lead to heartbreak on the day he cast her aside and left her for another female who had caught his fancy.

Wolfingham might have a reputation in society as being severe and very proper, nor had there ever been any gossip as to his ever having taken a permanent mistress. But that did not mean there had not been other rumours, of his liaisons with several ladies of the *ton*, and the gaming hells and the houses of the *demi-monde* he had visited on the evenings he spent with the other Dangerous Dukes.

Dangerous.

Yes, where Mariah was concerned Darian Hunter more than lived up to his reputation as being dangerous. To her independence. To her untutored body. To her untouched heart.

And that she could not, dare not, allow.

'Goodness, Wolfingham, where on earth has all this politeness and solicitude come from?' she taunted him mockingly. 'If it is because of our conversation earlier today, then let me assure you that it is of no consequence.'

'No consequence?'

'Absolutely none,' she dismissed coolly in the face of his vehemence. 'It was too many years ago to be of any significance to the here and now. Nor, as I assured you earlier, do I have need of anyone's pity. Least of all your own,' she added with deliberate scorn.

'Least of all mine?' Wolfingham's eyes were steely now as he looked at her through narrowed lids.

'But of course.' Mariah returned that hard gaze with a challenging one of her own. 'You really are arrogance personified if you believed otherwise. In the circumstances I described to you earlier, a woman can either grow stronger from the experience or allow herself to be beaten down by it. I am certain that by now you know me well enough to have realised which one of those women I have become?' She arched haughty brows.

Oh, yes, Darian knew full well which one of those women best described Mariah. Her fortitude was only one of the reasons he admired and liked her so much. Desired her so much. A desire she was now at pains to inform him she wanted no part of.

To a degree she would not even give permission for him to so much as kiss or touch her again.

Was that avoidance not telling in itself?

Or was he simply grasping at straws, because he so much wished for Mariah to return his desire?

It was a question Darian intended to explore with

all thoroughness once they were well away from Eton Park.

He nodded. 'As it is almost five o'clock, might I suggest that we join the other guests downstairs for tea?'

A surprised blink of Mariah's long dark lashes was her only outward sign that she was surprised at his ease in accepting her refusal. 'But of course.' She nodded graciously as she collected up her fan before sweeping past him and preceding him out of the bedchamber.

Darian smiled grimly as he followed her out into the hallway before offering her his arm to escort her down the stairs.

Mariah might believe him to have been routed by her set-down, but if she had come to know him half as well as he now knew her, then she would very soon realise that his patience, in achieving his goals, was infinite.

And his most pressing goal, desire, was to make love with Mariah.

Chapter Eleven

'If one knows where to look, it is almost possible to see the bruises in the shape of fingerprints upon Lord Nichols's neck,' Mariah remarked conversationally a short time later before taking a sip of tea from her cup, as she and Wolfingham sat together on a *chaise* in the Nicholses' salon. Its placement by one of the windows allowed them to observe the other guests.

'He's lucky he still has a neck to bruise,' Wolfingham muttered, the ice in his gaze the only sign of his displeasure, as he gave every outward appearance of relaxation, lounging on the *chaise* beside her.

Mariah chuckled softly. 'I am not sure I ever thanked you properly for your gallantry last night.'

He turned to face her. 'No, I do not believe you did,' he drawled drily.

'Well, I do thank you.' Mariah was unnerved to once again find herself the focus of those piercing green eyes. 'These people really are an unpleasant lot, aren't they?' Her gaze now swept contemptuously over the other guests.

The men were drinking brandy instead of tea, with most of them already well on their way to being inebriated yet again. Including their host, as he occasionally cast a furtively nervous glance in Wolfingham's direction.

The women were once again wearing an assortment of gowns that would be more suited to a bordello or brothel. Not that Mariah had ever been in either establishment, but she could well imagine the state of *déshabillé* of the women who did.

Normally Mariah would have had no difficulty in maintaining a certain distance, from both the gentlemen's drinking and the ladies' state of undress, when attending one of these weekend parties. She had no doubt it was the challenge her coolness represented to the gentlemen that caused the *ton*'s hostesses to continue to include her in these weekend invitations. The gentlemen made no secret that they began each of these weekends with a wager on which one of them might succeed in bedding the Countess of Carlisle.

Yes, normally Mariah would not have the slightest difficulty maintaining that distance.

Wolfingham's presence, and Mariah's complete awareness of the lean and muscled length of his body as he lounged on the *chaise* beside her, had heightened her senses to such a degree, she now seemed to feel and view everything as if through a magnifying glass.

The way in which even the statuary and decor in this house seemed to be attuned to the debauchery that went on under its roof.

The gentlemen's red and bloated faces, and their avidly glittering eyes as they ogled the ladies' state of undress.

Those same ladies vying with each other, with more and more outrageous behaviour, in order to attract and hold the attention of the gentleman, or gentlemen, they had decided to bed.

The way in which Wolfingham's austere handsomeness, in the formal black of his clothing and snowy white linen, succeeded in putting him above any and all of the other gentlemen present.

Knowing that, *aware* of that, this weekend, and Mariah's forced association with Wolfingham, could not come to an end soon enough for her.

'Very,' Wolfingham now drawled disdainfully. 'I feel soiled just by being in the same room with them.'

Mariah arched a mocking brow. 'And yet you and the other Dangerous Dukes are rumoured to frequent brothels and the houses of the *demi-monde*.'

His eyes narrowed. 'I draw the line at brothels. And the ladies of the *demi-monde* do not pretend to be upstanding members of society.'

Mariah's curiosity was piqued by the fact that he had not denied frequenting *those* houses. 'Do you—'

'And what are you two whispering about together so secretly?'

Without either of them having been aware of it— Darian was sure that Mariah's attention had been as focused on him as his was on her—their hostess had crossed the room to join them and now stood looking down at them with coquettish curiosity. A lapse in concentration on their part, which Darian knew could have been very costly indeed, if they had chanced to be talking of their real reason for being here this weekend.

He stood up politely and instantly regretted doing so as his superior height gave him a clear view down the front of Clara Nichols's loose gown, as far as her navel—decidedly *not* an arousing sight. 'We were discussing the...merits of the temple in your garden, madam.'

Lady Nichols's rouged lips gave a knowing smile. 'So *that's* where the two of you have been all day.'

'This morning, at least.' Darian gave an acknowledging nod. 'Your butler was most helpful, this morning, in telling us of its existence.'

'Benson *has* turned out to be a treasure.' His hostess smiled fondly at the butler as he circulated amongst the guests, calmly refilling the gentlemen's brandy glasses with the same aplomb as he did the ladies' teacups, before withdrawing from the room with that same calm after one of the footmen had entered and drawn him aside to speak to him quietly. 'One is never quite sure, when one takes on new household staff, whether or not they are going to suit, but Benson did come personally recommended and he has more than lived up to it these past few months.' Lady Nichols turned to eye them speculatively. 'I trust you both enjoyed our little temple?'

'Most diverting,' Darian answered noncommittally, a glance at the clock on the mantelpiece revealing that it was just a few minutes after five o'clock, time for the Prince Regent's note to be delivered, for which he and Mariah had been patiently waiting these past twenty-four hours. And, hopefully, the reason Benson had been summoned from the room?

Well, the waiting had perhaps not been quite so patient, on Darian's part! Indeed, it had been unimaginable torture, having to suffer the company of such people and made all the worse by his increasing desire for Mariah. His only wish now was to have this charade over as soon as was possible, so that they might return to town and he could concentrate his considerable attention on seducing Mariah.

'You will have the opportunity to return there later on tonight, of course,' Lady Nichols continued to chatter. 'It is *so* romantic in the evenings.'

Darian almost choked on the sip of brandy he had been about to take, at the very idea of the erotica displayed in that temple ever being thought of as romantic. Certainly it appeared that Lady Nichols's idea of romance, and his own, differed greatly!

How long did it take Benson to collect the Prince's note of apology from the rider and return with it?

'We are both so looking forward to the masked ball this evening, Clara.' Mariah claimed their hostess's attention as Darian made no reply.

'And I trust that you will not remain quite so… exclusive…this evening, sir?' Lady Nichols gave Darian's arm a playful tap with her fan. 'There are many more ladies present who would welcome your attentions.'

Darian narrowed his gaze on her. 'Indeed.'

Where the hell was Benson with the Prince's note?

'Oh, yes.' Their hostess gave another of those tittering giggles, so incongruous in a woman who was aged in her forties, at the least. 'Indeed, the ladies have talked and speculated of nothing else since your arrival yesterday.'

'Indeed?' Darian repeated stiltedly, his hands clenching tensely into fists at his sides.

'Oh, my goodness, yes!' Lady Nichols looked up at him with what she no doubt thought was a winning smile, obviously having absolutely no idea how close Darian was to telling her to go to the devil and take her simpering flirtation with her! 'I myself would dearly love to—'

'I do believe Benson is trying to attract your attention, Clara,' Mariah put in hastily, having thankfully spotted the butler approaching them, a silver tray held aloft on one hand; the increasing coldness of Darian's expression, and those hands clenched at his sides, warned Mariah he was seriously in danger of telling Clara Nichols exactly how repugnant he found both her and her guests. Their reason for being here be damned!

'What *is* it, Benson?' Their hostess could barely contain her irritation at the interruption as she frowned at her butler.

'This was just delivered for you, madam.' Benson offered the silver tray. 'I took the liberty of asking the rider to wait, in case there is a reply,' he added helpfully.

Mariah could feel Darian's tension as the two of

them watched their hostess break the seal on the letter before quickly scanning its contents. Mariah actually held her breath as she waited for Clara Nichols's response, which for the moment appeared to be only a displeased frown.

'What is it, my dear?' Richard Nichols called out across the room.

A pout appeared on Clara Nichols's too-red lips. 'The Prince Regent is unable to attend the ball this evening, after all. Some urgent business requiring he return to town earlier than expected.'

There were several murmurs of 'too bad' and 'bad show' from the other guests, but it was Richard and Clara Nichols whom Mariah continued to study intently, as she knew that Darian did also.

'That is a pity.' Richard Nichols strolled over to join his wife before reading the note for himself. 'Oh well, can't be helped, old girl.' He patted his wife awkwardly on the shoulder. 'The country's needs must come first and all that.'

Lady Nichols continued to pout her disappointment. 'It really is too bad of him,' she snapped waspishly. 'I only invited Lady Henley on his instructions I should do so.'

'I am sure that there are plenty of other gentlemen present to keep that lady entertained. Hey, Wolfingham?' Richard Nichols attempted a conspiratorial and conciliatory smile at the haughty duke.

'You are welcome to do so, by all means, Nichols.' That smile was not returned as Darian looked coldly down the length of his nose at the older man. 'As I am sure I have made perfectly clear, I am happy in the company of Lady Beecham.'

'A man can have too much of a good thing, though, don't you think?' Nichols suggested slyly.

Wolfingham's jaw was tight. 'No, I most certainly do not think,' he bit out tautly, eyes glacial as he continued to look contemptuously at the other man.

A contempt, a danger, that Mariah knew the older man would be foolish to ignore. Most especially so when he still bore the bruises on his neck from the last time he had managed to infuriate Wolfingham.

She stood up to tuck her gloved hand into the crook of Darian's arm, administering a gentle squeeze of caution even as she turned to smile at Richard Nichols. 'I am afraid our…friendship…is relatively new, Lord Nichols, and Wolfingham is quite besotted still.' She felt the tension in Darian's arm beneath her fingertips as his response to such a ridiculous claim.

As it was indeed ridiculous to think of the haughty Duke of Wolfingham as ever being besotted with any woman, least of all the scandalous Countess of Carlisle!

'Well, can't blame a man for that.' Richard Nichols wisely backed down. 'Oh, do cheer up, Clara,' he turned to instruct his sulking wife impatiently. 'I am sure we shall manage quite well this evening without the Prince's presence. After all, we do have the elusive Duke of Wolfingham as one of our guests!'

'So he is.' Clara Nichols brightened before turning to the waiting butler. 'There is no reply, Benson.' She placed the note back on the tray. 'Could you see that this is put in my private parlour?' she added dismissively.

'Of course, milady.' The butler bowed politely before withdrawing.

Mariah frowned her puzzlement as she continued to study Richard and Clara Nichols; there did not seem to be any undue reaction to the Prince's note of apology, apart from Clara's obvious disappointment.

Clara Nichols now directed another of those coquettish smiles at Wolfingham. 'Where were we?'

'I believe that Mariah and I were about to return upstairs,' he bit out tautly.

'Again? So soon?' Clara Nichols gave Mariah an envious smile. 'My, he is a lusty one, isn't he, my dear?'

Mariah felt the warmth of colour enter her cheeks and dearly hoped that the other woman would see it as the burn of anticipation at being the recipient of Wolfingham's passion, rather than the embarrassment it really was. 'I am sure we are both very grateful to you for allowing us the privacy, in which to fully indulge ourselves, this weekend.' She curled her nails painfully, and quite deliberately, into Darian's tensed arm.

He moved his other hand to cover hers, squeezing with just enough pressure not to cause pain, but to administer a warning of his own. 'Very grateful,' he drawled drily.

'We appear to be completely superfluous here, my dear. Shall we return to the entertainment of our other guests?' Richard Nichols extended an arm politely to his wife. 'If you will both excuse us?' He bowed politely to Mariah and Wolfingham as the other couple moved away, Clara Nichols still twittering her disappointment over the Prince Regent as they did so.

Mariah waited only long enough for the Nicholses to be out of earshot before turning to Darian. 'Should we not wait here awhile longer before returning upstairs?'

'No.'

'But—'

'I believe we have seen all that we needed to see, Mariah,' he assured grimly.

'We have?'

He nodded tersely. 'Besides which, if I do not leave this company very soon, then I am afraid I might lose my temper completely.'

Mariah could see the truth of that claim in the dangerous glitter of his eyes and the nerve pulsing erratically in his tightly clenched jaw.

She held her head high as she accompanied him across the room, knowing they were being observed with interest as she heard the outbreak of whispering and laughter in the room behind them as they stepped out into the hallway. 'Must you always be so—so *obvious* as to our supposed intention of disappearing to make love together?' she hissed the moment they were out in the deserted entrance hall.

Darian was feeling murderous rather than obvious. How much longer must he endure this torture, of watching men like Nichols lusting after the woman he—the woman he—the woman he what? Exactly what was it that he felt towards Mariah?

Protective, certainly.

Proprietary.

Possessive.

To the extent he could quite cheerfully have taken on every man in that room who had so much as looked at Mariah sideways—which was all of them, damn it!

'You are missing the point, Mariah.'

'And it *appears* to me that you are enjoying yourself altogether too much at my expense!' she came back heatedly.

'Could we talk of this further once we reach your bedchamber?' he prompted softly as Benson appeared at the top of the stairs, no doubt after having delivered Lady Nichols's letter to her private parlour.

'May I get you anything, your Grace?' he offered politely as he reached the bottom of the staircase.

'No, thank you, Benson,' Darian answered distractedly, his hand firmly beneath Mariah's elbow as he pulled her up the stairs beside him.

'Darian?'

'You are missing the point, Mariah,' he repeated through gritted teeth as they reached the top of the staircase before turning into the hallway leading to their adjoining bedchambers.

'Which is?' she prompted as she opened the door to her room.

'The letter,' he reminded impatiently as he followed Mariah into her bedchamber. 'The response to the Prince's letter.' He closed the door firmly behind him.

All of Mariah's indignation fled as she realised

she had indeed allowed her embarrassment to distract her, that she was the one now guilty—however briefly!—of forgetting their reason for being at Eton Park at all this weekend. 'Apart from Clara's obvious disappointment as hostess that the Prince would not be gracing her ball tonight after all, there did not appear to be any response at all to his note,' she stated belatedly. 'No pointed looks, or conversation, with anyone else in the room. No one hastily leaving the room. There was no response whatsoever.'

'Exactly.' Wolfingham paced the room restlessly.

Mariah continued to frown. 'Does that mean Aubrey Maystone's information was wrong?'

'Maystone is never wrong,' he assured grimly.

'Then what happened just now?'

'Nothing. That is the problem.' Wolfingham looked grim.

Mariah chewed briefly on her bottom lip. 'Do you think that might be because someone suspects that we—'

'Came back upstairs to make love?' Wolfingham interrupted huskily. 'Oh, I think that was more than obvious, my love.'

Mariah blinked, momentarily confused at the sudden change in his tone. 'What—'

'I am sure that we have been more than obvious in our obsession to bed each other,' Wolfingham acknowledged indulgently. 'Indeed, I find I cannot wait another minute to undress you and make love with you,' he added gruffly, at the same time as the fierceness of his gaze now moved pointedly to the shawls and handkerchiefs Mariah had left in place over the peepholes about the bedchamber. 'Come over here, love,' he invited huskily.

A warning to Mariah that someone was standing behind one of the walls at this very minute, listening to their conversation?

And necessitating in their continuing with the act of lovers once again eager to be alone together, so that they could make love?

Oh, heavens!

She gave an abrupt nod of her head, in silent acknowledgement of their eavesdropper, as she crossed the room to Wolfingham's side. Her heart was pounding loudly in her chest, her pulse racing, as she wondered for how long, and how far, they would need to continue with their act of eager lovers.

At the same time she felt an inner yearning to satisfy, just a little, the desire she had discovered she felt for Darian.

All thoughts of anything else fled Darian's head as Mariah now stood in front of him, so close he could feel her breath brushing warmly against his throat as she moved up on tiptoe. 'Oh, yes, Mariah,' he groaned in approval—both of her quickness of mind, in realising they were not completely alone, *and* most certainly of the fact that her teeth were now nibbling in earnest on the sensitivity of his earlobe; surely an unnecessary embellishment to their act when they could be overheard, but not observed?

He turned his head slightly so that he could look into Mariah's eyes, the fullness of her parted lips now just inches beneath his own as their gazes clashed and held, both of them breathing softly, expectantly.

Darian took full advantage of Mariah's closeness as his arms moved about her waist to pull her in tightly against him, his gaze continuing to hold hers as his head lowered and he took fierce possession of those parted lips with his own.

Something Darian had wanted—*hungered for*—since they had parted so coolly after their walk earlier today.

So much so that there was no way to stop the avalanche of desire that now swept over and through him as he felt Mariah's lips part beneath his own, her arms about his waist.

Darian deepened the kiss, his tongue sweeping, tasting her parted lips, before plunging, thrusting into the moist heat beyond.

Mariah tasted of the honey cake she had eaten with her tea; sweet and utterly delicious. Combined with her exotic perfume, it was addictive.

Darian continued the depth of those kisses as, for the second time that day, he swept her up into his arms. Carrying Mariah across the room before placing her on top of the bedcovers and following her down. Settling his thighs between her parted ones, he took his weight on his elbows before cupping either side of her face with his hands and continuing to kiss her hungrily. Tasting, sipping, possessing!

Mariah gave a throaty groan as Darian's lips and tongue continued to claim her own. Even as his hands deftly removed the pins from her hair before loosening it on to the pillows beneath her, she moved her arms up over his shoulders as her fingers became entangled in the dark silkiness of his own hair.

She was filled with a yearning ache as the heat of Darian's arousal throbbed between her parted thighs. Pressing, shifting slowly against and into her, pleasure surging through her as that friction stroked against the throbbing nubbin between her now slick and swollen folds.

Darian broke the kiss, breathing heavily as moist lips now travelled the length of her throat. 'God, how I want you!' he groaned achingly. 'You are so beautiful, Mariah. So very beautiful.' One of his hands now moved caressingly, restlessly, beneath the curve of her breast, before pulling down that silken barrier to bare their fullness, his hand now cupping her breast in sacrifice to his questing lips and tongue.

'Darian!' Mariah's back arched off the bed as he claimed one aroused and sensitive nipple into the heat of his mouth, pleasure surging, filling her, as his tongue flicked against that hardened nub, teeth gently biting before he suckled deeply, drawing the whole of her nipple into the heat of his mouth.

Darian's mouth was heat and fire, pleasure beyond description. A pleasure that surged and intensified unbearably between Mariah's parted thighs, causing her to arch up against his hardness, in need of a greater friction as she searched, ached for the full promise of that pleasure.

'Yes!' she cried out as Darian shifted slightly to her side, his lips and tongue still drawing fiercely on her breast as his hand moved to push her gown up her thighs. Caressing, seeking, *finding* the opening in her drawers that allowed his fingers access to caress the slick moisture of her swollen folds, at the same time as the soft pad of his thumb stroked the throbbing nubbin above. 'Please, Darian! Yes!' Mariah was mindless with pleasure as she arched up into those caresses, wanting, needing, something *more*.

'Come for me, Mariah,' Darian encouraged throatily at the same time as first one finger, then two, entered the slickness of her core. 'Please come for me, Mariah!' He suckled hard on her nipple at the same time as those fingers now moved rhythmically, his thumb stroking, pressing down on that swollen nubbin above.

Pleasure, unlike anything Mariah had ever known, or imagined, now exploded between her thighs, her head thrashing from side to side on the pillows as that release coursed hotly, claiming the rest of her body in wave after wave of seemingly endless pleasure.

She was still lost to the wonder, the euphoria of that pleasure, as Darian gazed down at her darkly before sliding down the length of her body until he knelt between her parted thighs. Mariah offered no resistance as he slowly pushed her gown up to her waist before moving aside to allow for the removal of her drawers and bared her to his heated gaze as he parted her legs so that he might once again kneel between them.

'So pretty. Like a rose in bloom,' he murmured appreciatively as his fingers moved to part her swollen folds, allowing him to gaze his fill of her before he lay down between her thighs, his tongue a hot and pleasurable rasp against her highly sensitised and aroused flesh.

'Darian?' Mariah felt she should protest at such intimacy, but in truth she felt so satiated still, so lost in wonder as she felt the stirring of her arousal for a second time in as many minutes, that she could barely speak, let alone offer words of protest.

'Let me.' The coolness of his breath was sweet torture against her hot and aching flesh. 'You are so beautiful here, Mariah,' he groaned as he touched her gently. 'So beautiful!'

His lips and tongue caressed her at the same time as his hands moved up to cup her breasts. Mariah gazed down in wonder as those long fingers and thumbs tweaked and pinched her swollen nipples, at the same time as Darian's head was buried between her thighs, the sight of such intimacy enough to cause her to gasp anew.

'Again, Mariah,' he encouraged roughly. 'I want you to come for me again.'

Mariah felt captured, swept along in a relentless tide as a second wave of pleasure built higher deep inside her and then higher still. Higher and higher—

'Darian!' Her back arched to push her breasts into Darian's hands, encouraging, welcoming the pleasure-pain as he now squeezed and pinched her nipples to the same rhythm as her thighs moved into the stroking of his lips and tongue.

She gave a gasp, eyes wide with shock as pleasure even more intense than the first suddenly ripped through her.

This was what all the poets wrote about so ardently. What singers crooned about so achingly. What lovers so hungered for they were willing to throw away all caution and reputation in order to achieve it.

Mariah had never known, never guessed, that love-making, this wonderful feeling of completion, would be so all-consuming. So much so that nothing else mattered, the outside world, and everyone in it, ceasing to exist. Only Darian and Mariah remained at that moment.

'Oh, goodness.' She groaned weakly as she remembered that the two of them were not *all* that existed in the world, that they had a listening audience.

Darian raised his head to look at her, his face flushed, lips moist and slightly swollen from ministering to Mariah's pleasure. 'He or she left some time ago,' he assured gruffly, pulling her gown slightly down over her legs before he moved up the bed to lie down beside her.

Mariah looked at him anxiously. 'How do you know?'

'I heard the click of the door shutting as they left. I did not spend all my afternoon in my bedchamber, but explored those peepholes and passages' he explained as her eyes widened. 'I would never allow anyone to see or hear your pleasure but me, Mariah,' he assured softly as he lifted a hand to smooth back the hair at her temple.

Mariah felt grateful for Darian's reassurances,

even as she trembled at the full realisation of what had just happened between the two of them. What she had all but begged to happen, as she arched and thrust against the caress of Darian's mouth and hands.

She should feel mortification just thinking of those intimacies. Should feel embarrassment, if not horror, at her own wanton response and encouragement of those intimacies. Her complete lack of inhibition.

Mariah could feel none of those things.

Instead, for the first time in her life, Mariah felt totally fulfilled as a desirable woman. A desired and now totally satiated woman.

It was exhilarating.

Liberating, in a way Mariah had never imagined.

So much so that there was no room inside her for embarrassment or self-consciousness.

Darian Hunter, the austere and exacting Duke of Wolfingham, had just made thorough love to her. Had touched and caressed her more intimately than any other man had ever done. Than any other man had ever wanted to do. And he had not found her wanting.

Wolfingham had not found her wanting.

For so many years Mariah had wondered if it was because she was so undesirable that Martin had never wanted a normal marriage with her. Not that she had ever wanted a normal marriage with the man she had considered as being her rapist, but Martin's complete lack of interest in her physically, and for so many years, had certainly caused her to question her own desirability.

Oh, she had played her part well these past seven

years, had flirted and teased whichever gentlemen had needed to be flirted with and teased, in order for her to extract the information from them that she needed. But she had never felt like this with any of those other men, never *wanted* as she had wanted with Darian. Never felt even tempted with those other men, had known that she would just be another conquest to them.

In contrast, Darian had made love to her like a thirsty man in a desert, praising her all the while, telling her time and time again how beautiful she was to him. How much he desired her. How much he wanted and appreciated her body.

Gifting Mariah with that freedom, that liberation in her own sexuality that she had long believed dead inside her.

And in doing so Darian had given her pleasure unlike anything Mariah had ever known before.

A pleasure she now fully intended to gift back to him.

A seductive smile curved her lips as she recalled that look of bliss on the male statue's face as Aphrodite took his full and burgeoning length into her mouth.

Chapter Twelve

Darian did not believe he had ever seen anything as beautiful as Mariah looked at this moment; her loosened hair was a golden halo about her flushed face, her eyes soft and languid, her cheeks creamy smooth, her lips slightly swollen from their earlier kisses, her breasts still bared to the heat of his gaze. Perfectly rounded and pert breasts, tipped with ruby berries still puckered and reddened from his ministrations.

And beneath all that visual beauty was the smell of her pleasure and that tantalising and erotic perfume that Darian associated only with her.

The hardness of his shaft shifted, surged, as he continued to breathe in that perfume and gaze down at those perfect and desirable globes, as a painful reminder that his own arousal still needed to be dealt with. And sooner rather than later.

'You are very sure our eavesdropper has left?' Mariah murmured as she obviously felt that impatient movement of his arousal against her thigh. She sat up beside him to gaze down at that telling bulge in his pantaloons, her breasts still fully exposed to Darian's heated gaze, resulting in another fierce pulsing of his aching arousal.

Darian had been fully aware of Mariah's initial resistance to give in to the pleasure he offered, when she believed they had a listening audience. 'Very sure,' he confirmed gruffly.

'Then I believe it is now my turn to pleasure you.' Her fingers moved to unfasten the buttons of his pantaloons, the bared fullness of her breasts jiggling tantalisingly at the movement. 'I would not wish for anyone but me to see or hear your own pleasure, either…' she added softly.

'Mariah?' Darian placed one of his hands over both of hers as he looked up at her searchingly, wondering if she really meant what he thought she did.

He had bedded his first woman at the age of sixteen and there had been too many more women since then for him to remember all their faces, let alone their names. Several ladies of the *demi-monde* had also chosen to take him into their mouth and give him pleasure that way. Could Mariah really be suggesting she might do the same?

Just the idea of having Mariah placing those delectable and pouting lips about his shaft, of having her suck him into her mouth and all the way to the back of her throat, excited Darian to such a pitch he could barely contain it.

Mariah could see that she had momentarily surprised Darian with her intentions. Because, despite the licentiousness she had witnessed during this, and other weekend parties, most of the ladies of the *ton* were believed to be too delicate, too prim and proper, to be exposed to such acts as she had witnessed earlier today between those statues in Aphrodite's Temple?

Mariah's newly found pleasure and sexual liberation, her curiosity, was now such that she *must* know all. Whether or not she would be any good at this was another matter, but she fully intended to make up with enthusiasm what she lacked in experience.

Mariah looked down searchingly into Darian's face, noting the glitter to those dark green eyes as he looked back at her, the flush to his cheeks.

And knowing that her own eyes were probably just as fevered, her cheeks as flushed. In anticipation of freeing, of seeing, that enormous bulge inside Darian's pantaloons…

She had never seen that part of a man in the flesh, so to speak.

She had not seen Darian naked as yet, but even so a glance down at that telling bulge in his pantaloons told her he was so much bigger than Martin had been.

'Do not think of it, Mariah,' Darian rasped abruptly, his hand gentle on her cheek as he turned her averted face back towards him. 'The past has no place here between the two of us, Mariah,' he assured softly.

Mariah continued to look at him blankly for several long seconds, held captive by those memories, those awful, painful, disturbing memories.

'You shall be in charge here and now between the two of us, Mariah,' Darian assured her huskily. 'Or not. It is your choice to make. I assure you no one shall make you do anything you do not wish to do,' he promised gruffly as his hands dropped down to his sides. 'I am yours to do with exactly as you wish, Mariah. Or not,' he repeated gruffly.

'But—you have not found your own pleasure yet.' She frowned. 'Once aroused, I believed men to need that release more than a woman?'

Darian had to once again fight down his murderous feelings towards Martin Beecham. Because Mariah required his gentleness now, rather than a show of the anger he felt towards her dead husband. For having inflicted, over so many years of his indifference, such an uncertainty of her own sexuality, her desirability. A cruelty indeed to such a beautiful and courageous lady as he now knew Mariah to be.

Darian sat up slightly to run the soft pad of his thumb over the fullness of her bottom lip to take any sting from his next words. 'You do not have to do anything else, Mariah. I can return to my bedchamber and deal with my arousal myself,' he assured gently.

Her eyes widened. 'You are talking of— You would—'

'Yes.' He smiled at her reassuringly.

'You have done that before?'

'Many times. All young boys do it,' he dismissed without embarrassment as her eyes widened. 'Indeed, I believe it becomes their favourite pastime during adolescence.'

'But it has been many years since you were that age.'

Darian shrugged. 'A man's member tends to wake

up before him each morning. And without a wife to ease that arousal, it often becomes necessary for a man to take himself in hand.'

'I see,' she said slowly. 'And which would you prefer now, to feel your own hand or mine?'

Darian drew his breath in sharply at the candour of her question. 'Neither. I would prefer to have your mouth on me, Mariah,' he explained as she looked at him questioningly.

Delicate colour bloomed in her cheeks. 'As would I.'

Darian groaned low in his throat as he watched Mariah moisten her lips, as if in anticipation of the act. 'May I watch? It would enhance my own pleasure to do so, Mariah,' he explained as she gave him another of those curious glances.

Curious and slightly shy glances, which to Darian's mind did not sit well with the reputation of her being the scandalous and adulterous Countess of Carlisle.

The gossip of Mariah's adultery Darian could now understand, when her husband had been such an out-and-out and indifferent bastard to the needs of his own wife. That curiosity and shyness needed explaining—

All thoughts fled Darian's mind as Mariah moved up on her knees beside him so that she might place several pillows behind his head, her bared breasts jutting forward pertly as she moved, allowing her nipples to dangle, so swollen and tempting, just inches away from his rapidly moistening mouth.

'Give me just a taste of you first, Mariah!' he groaned achingly.

Mariah tilted her head as she looked down at Darian, easily noting that his fevered gaze was now transfixed on her bared breasts. She leant forward slightly in order to allow one of her nipples to touch his moist and parted lips, gasping slightly as he instantly suckled that fullness into his mouth, eyes closing, lashes resting darkly against his flushed cheeks, as his hand cupped beneath that breast as he drew hungrily on the nipple.

And allowing Mariah to learn another sexual revelation…

That a man could be just as vulnerable during lovemaking as a woman.

Perhaps more so, she realised, as she turned her head so that she might guide one of her hands to untie the ribbon on Darian's drawers, before turning back the folds of those drawers and finally exposing that impressive bulge.

Darian's shaft was incredibly long and thick as it jutted up from its nest of dark curls.

Mariah licked her lips. What would he taste like? Salty or sweet? And would—

'Darian!' She gave a sudden gasp as she felt a now familiar burn of pleasure growing, swelling, between her own thighs, Darian's mouth almost painful on her nipple as he suckled deeply, hungrily, teeth biting as his other hand alternately stroked and then squeezed its twin. 'Darian, I believe I am going to—'

'Come for me, Mariah!' he urged fiercely, both hands cupping her breasts now, squeezing and pinching her nipples as he gazed up into her flushed face.

'I—' She cried out her pleasure as another climax suddenly ripped through her body, the longest and strongest yet, as her empty sheath contracted and pulsed hungrily, again and again, the swollen nubbin above throbbing. 'I had no idea I could— That it could happen so—so spontaneously.' She rested her head weakly on Darian's shoulder.

It had never happened for Darian with any other woman before now. But as he now knew only too well, Mariah was indeed a woman unlike any other. And the fact that he had been able to give her such pleasure, just by touching her breasts, gave him more satisfaction than he could describe.

Not that he had time to dwell too long on those feelings of wonderment as Mariah now moved sinuously down the length of his body, her bared breasts briefly resting either side of his fiercely jutting erection before she moved to lie between his parted thighs and take him in hand.

'You are so wondrously big,' she murmured admiringly as she stroked the length of him. 'Your skin so velvety soft,' she added huskily before wrapping the fingers of both hands about the thickness of his engorged and throbbing length. 'And so wet.' The soft pad of her thumbs stroked over the tip of his shaft.

Darian felt his groin tighten as her fingers continued to caress him sensually. 'Mariah!' he groaned harshly, tensing, as he watched her little pink tongue flick out to taste the tip.

'Would you like me to stop?' Her glance up at him, from beneath her long lashes, was wickedly teasing.

'No!' Darian protested, groaning as he saw her smile widen, his head falling back on the pillows as he watched her continue to lick him, her tongue a sensuous rasp across his highly sensitised skin, her long golden hair cascading forward to drape sensuously across his thighs.

'You taste delicious,' she murmured appreciatively, her breath hot against his dampness.

'As do you,' he assured gruffly.

'Really? Let me see!' She moved quickly up the bed to lick her own juices from his parted lips. 'Mmm.' She nodded, her smile sensuous as she moved back down the bed to kneel between his thighs, before once again taking him in hand and holding him up as she parted her lips and took him into her mouth, her lips tight just beneath the tip and stretched tautly about his thickness.

Darian groaned, hips bucking, the second he was engulfed by the heat of Mariah's mouth, totally unable to stop himself from thrusting up rhythmically into that wet heat. His hands clenched into the bedclothes at his sides as he fought to hold off, to prolong the moment of his release.

An almost impossible task as he watched Mariah's head bob up and then down. Up and then down. Each time taking him deeper and then deeper still, her tongue swirling, dipping, as she rose up, before plunging him deeper on the downward stroke. Little by tortuous little, until he finally hit the back of her throat and she began to suck in earnest.

Finally, when Darian thought he might go insane

from the pleasure, she released him on the next upward stroke, eyes dark as she looked up at him at the same time as she moved one of her hands lower, caressing him tenderly. 'Come for me now, Darian,' she invited as her gaze held his at the same time as she parted her lips and slowly took him to the back of her throat.

Darian felt the tingling at the base of his spine, the painful tightening through his groin, and knew his climax was imminent. 'You must release me now, Mariah—'

Her own second and throaty 'Now!' vibrated down the length of him, sending Darian spiralling over the edge, totally unable to stop from coming as he became lost in the fiercest, most prolonged orgasm he had ever experienced in his life.

Mariah continued to suck on him greedily, cheeks hollowed, and she refused to release him until she had swallowed down all of Darian's salty-sweet release. Even then she could not resist licking the last few drops from the tip before sitting back on her heels to look up at him.

His dark hair was dishevelled, the dark curls lying damply tousled on his brow. Eyes glittered the colour of emeralds between sleepy half-closed lids, his cheeks were flushed, his lips parted. His body was completely relaxed and exposed to her as his erection lay half-hard still against the tautness of his stomach.

He was beautiful.

Completely satiated, wickedly decadent and utterly beautiful.

And she had done this. She, Mariah Elizabeth Beecham, Countess of Carlisle, had given Darian Hunter, the severe and oh-so-proper Duke of Wolfingham, that look of satiation.

A thrill of satisfaction rose up beneath Mariah's breasts, filling her chest to bursting, in the knowledge that she had succeeded in giving Darian the same pleasure he had given her.

'Come up here and lie beside me, Mariah, and let us both catch our breath,' he invited gruffly now as he opened his arms to her.

Mariah moved up the bed gladly before lying down at his side, her head resting on one broad shoulder, one of her arms draped across the muscled hardness of his stomach as he stroked the long tendrils of her hair. She had never felt so relaxed, never known such peace as this existed, as she glowed in the aftermath of their lovemaking.

This, this closeness, was what it should be like between a man and a woman. What she had been denied for so many years.

What she had denied *herself* for so many years, too afraid to risk this vulnerability with any man. A vulnerability that Mariah now knew applied to both the man and the woman; a man could not be any more vulnerable than when he allowed a woman to take that precious part of himself into her mouth and pleasure him. As she had been just as vulnerable when she'd allowed Darian to pleasure her in the same way.

Such intimacies required complete trust, from both the man and the woman.

As Mariah had learnt to trust Darian.

Not just with her body, but with the secrets of her past, as well as her work for the Crown. She had not told him all of her secrets, of course. Had not, for instance, confided that Martin had been a traitor to his country. Or revealed that that awful time with Martin had been her only physical experience with any man before today. But she had trusted Darian with so much more than that.

Had told him what had happened to her the night of Christina's conception.

Trusted him with the knowledge Aubrey Maystone had imparted, of the work she had carried out secretly for the Crown these past seven years.

Mariah believed she could trust Darian never to reveal those secrets to another living soul.

As she now trusted him with her life.

With her love?

Mariah tensed, barely breathing, as she considered what her feelings were for the man beside her. For Darian Hunter, the severe and sober Duke of Wolfingham.

She did trust him, yes. She also admired him. Truly believed he was a man she could trust with her life.

But with her love?

No!

Mariah dared not allow herself to fall in love with any man. It was too much of a vulnerability. Too much power—

'Mariah?' Darian could feel her sudden tension as

she lay so still beside him. 'What are you thinking about?' he prompted gently.

She made no answer for several long seconds before replying huskily, 'Do you think the person listening to us behind the wall might have been the assassin?'

'In all probability, yes,' he bit out grimly. 'Damn it, I shall have to send a note to Winterton Manor informing Aubrey Maystone of these most recent events.'

They both knew that the reason he had not already done so was because they had been too engrossed in each other, in the desire between them.

'I shall do so as soon as I have regained the strength to get out of bed and go down to the stables in search of my groom,' Darian added.

'Is it possible, as we were followed up the stairs, that perhaps we have not been as clever in our deception of being lovers as we had hoped to be?'

Darian did not believe for a moment any of this conversation had been the reason behind Mariah's sudden tension a few minutes ago; she had paused too long, considered her words for too long, before answering him. Nor was he insensitive to the fact that she seemed to be distancing herself from him once again, despite still being held in his arms, her half-naked body draped alongside his own, her hand resting warmly—trustingly?—on his chest.

At the same time he was aware of how tenuous still was the closeness between the two of them, despite the depths of the intimacies they had just shared.

That unless he wished to call Mariah a liar and risk alienating her even further, he had no choice but to accept this as her explanation for her sudden quiet.

For now...

'From the speed with which they left, once the two of us began to make love, I believe they can have no further doubt regarding the latter— Mariah?' he questioned again sharply as he felt her increase in tension. He turned on his side to look at her searchingly, easily noting the pallor of her cheeks, the shadows in those beautiful turquoise eyes, before she lowered her long, dark silky lashes and hid those shadows from his view. 'Do you regret what just happened between the two of us?'

She moistened her lips with the tip of her tongue— tasting him there, as Darian could still taste her on his own lips? The colour that suddenly warmed her cheeks, as she became aware of her movements, would seem to imply that she did.

'I accept it was necessary,' she answered him evenly now. 'If we were to successfully keep up this pretence that we are lovers.'

'It is no longer a pretence, Mariah!' Darian felt stung into snapping his frustration with her coolness. With the fact that they both knew there had been no need for the continuation of that pretence, once he had assured Mariah their eavesdropper had departed.

She swallowed, those long lashes still hiding the expression in her eyes. 'We have shared...certain intimacies. That does not make us lovers.'

'Then what does?' Darian scowled down at her

darkly. 'I will admit that this was far from the ideal place, or situation, for the two of us to have become lovers,' he continued impatiently, very aware that he had previously decided he could not allow such a thing to happen at Eton Park. But he could no more have resisted, denied himself the pleasure of making love to and with Mariah just now, than King Canute had been able to turn back the tide! 'But that does not change the fact that it is now exactly what the two of us are,' he added huskily.

Mariah drew in a ragged breath even as she gave a definitive shake of her head. 'I believe we have allowed the licentiousness and erotica at this place to colour our judgement. That once we return to town we shall both see how…ridiculous such a relationship would be between us.'

'Ridiculous?' Darian knew the frown had deepened on his brow.

'Of course.' She gave a dismissive laugh as she finally looked up at him, those eyes reflecting her derision. 'We have absolutely nothing in common outside of this current situation. No common interests, or friends. Indeed, in London you are every inch the austere and sober Duke of Wolfingham as I am the scandalous Countess of Carlisle.'

Having come to know Mariah better, Darian was now extremely sceptical about the latter.

'And this?' He reached out to grasp the tops of her arms. 'What was it that just happened between the two of us?'

'A very enjoyable but unrepeatable interlude,' she

dismissed drily. 'As I have said, I believe we have both allowed our forced alliance, along with the licentiousness of our surroundings, and the people here, to arouse and cloud our better judgement. Left to our own devices in town, the two of us would never have so much as spared each other an approving glance.'

Darian could not deny that his opinion of Mariah, before meeting her, had been far from favourable. Nor had that opinion changed once he *had* met and spoken to her, despite the unwanted and begrudging desire he had felt for her.

But sometime during these past few weeks his opinion of Mariah *had* changed. Dramatically. He now knew her to be a woman of great courage and fortitude. A woman who risked her own life and reputation, on a daily basis, in order to work secretly for the Crown. For that alone Darian might have admired and respected her.

But there was so much more to Mariah than that.

Darian now knew that she had also fought her own personal demons of the past and not just survived them, but had become a gracious lady of great dignity and personal independence.

Much like a soldier after a success in battle.

Truly, Darian believed Mariah to have as much courage, to be as heroic, as he or any of his four closest friends had been in their fight against tyranny, openly and secretly.

None of which changed the fact that Mariah was now rejecting, out of hand, the very idea of the two of them continuing any sort of relationship once they had returned to town.

A rejection, the challenge of her expression, as she met his gaze so fearlessly, he would do well to heed.

Darian had never been one to back down from any sort of fight. Least of all one that mattered to him as much as this one did. As much as continuing to see Mariah, to be with Mariah, now did.

But she was absolutely correct in one regard. This was not the time, or the place, for them to have this conversation. There was too much else at stake: a would-be assassin in this house they still had to identify and bring to justice.

As such, Darian would agree to delay the conversation between himself and Mariah.

For now.

Once they had left Eton Park and returned to town, he had every intention of pursuing a satisfactory conclusion to this conversation.

Of pursuing Mariah.

Chapter Thirteen

'Does our hostess seem less than composed to you this evening?' Darian murmured softly to Mariah, eyes narrowed as he observed a rather red-faced Clara Nichols across the crowded ballroom, as she issued low-voiced instructions to a somewhat panicked-looking young footman.

A small ballroom that, along with the hundred or so masked and indecently clothed guests laughing and talking too loudly, was every bit as outrageously decadent as Mariah had earlier warned him it would be.

The walls were all mirrors, reflecting back the dozens of candles illuminating the room, as well as the lurid and explicit frescoes painted on the ceiling above. Although to Darian's way of thinking, it was hard to decide which was worse, those erotic frescoes above, or the half-clothed guests milling about below.

He had certainly breathed a sigh of relief once he had realised that Mariah's gown, a delicate gold confection of some gossamer material to match the gold of her mask, was actually not as revealing as it at first appeared.

Her beautiful and creamy shoulders were completely bare, admittedly, but there was at least a bodice to the gown, albeit a sheer and delicate lace that did little to hide the fullness of her breasts and rouged nipples below. But the body of the gown was at least lined, with only the barest hint—literally!—of the silky limbs and blonde curls hidden beneath.

With things so unsettled between the two of them still, Darian did not believe he would have been able to hold on to his temper if he also had to cope with other gentlemen ogling Mariah's near nakedness!

'She does,' Mariah now answered him equally as softly. 'Perhaps I should stroll over and see what is amiss?'

Darian's first instinct was to say no, to keep Mariah safely beside him, rather than risk her moving through the crowded room, and the possible groping hands of the other gentlemen present, to where their hostess stood beside the doorway.

There was also a would-be assassin still somewhere in their midst.

Darian quickly repressed his overprotectiveness, knowing that Mariah would no more accept that than she had wished to listen to his conversation earlier, in regard to the continuation of their relationship once they were back in town. He had no doubt that she would especially baulk at any sign of possessiveness towards her on his part. Even if that was exactly how he felt!

Just the thought of any other man but himself so much as looking at Mariah with more than admiration was enough to cause his jaw to tighten and his back teeth to grind together.

'We shall both go,' he compromised as he held out his arm to her.

Mariah eyed Darian from behind her mask as she placed her gloved hand on his arm before allowing him to escort her across the crowded ballroom, knowing that the avidly covetous eyes of at least a dozen other women followed his progress.

He was, without a doubt, the most handsome and striking-looking gentleman in the room, formidably so.

Once again dressed all in black, accompanied by snowy white linen, the mask that covered the top half of Wolfingham's face was also a plain and unrelenting black, green eyes glinting warningly through the two eye-slits to ward off the approach of any of the other guests.

Mariah repressed a shiver at just how devilish Darian looked this evening. Dark and watchful. Cold and unrelenting.

Nothing at all like the warm and satiated man who had made love to her, and to whom she had made love, earlier this evening.

'Cold?' Darian turned to her solicitously as he obviously felt her shiver.

Mariah straightened determinedly; after all, she

was the one who had insisted there was nothing between them but the intimacy of the circumstances
under which they now found themselves. She was a
little disappointed, hurt, at how easily Darian had accepted her dismissal after making only a token protest, but that was for her to deal with, not him. Darian
had promised nothing and she had asked for nothing, which was how it should be. How it *must* be, if
she was to continue to maintain her emotional independence.

'Not at all.' She now gave him an over-bright smile.
'Did you manage to send your groom with a note to
Winterton Manor?' she prompted softly.

'Yes,' Wolfingham confirmed. 'Although he has
not returned as yet with Maystone's reply,' he added
grimly.

'Do you think that something might have happened to him along the way?' Mariah frowned; Aubrey had told them that Winterton Manor, where the
older man had waited these past twenty-four hours
or so, along with several other of his agents, until he
heard word from them, was only situated five miles
or so from Eton Park.

Darian frowned. 'We shall go out to the stables and
check for news of his return, once we have talked to
Clara Nichols.'

Mariah's brows rose. 'Surely there is no reason for
both of us to go?'

Perhaps not, but Darian still felt that reluctance to
leave Mariah's side. 'We shall both go, Mariah,' he
repeated uncompromisingly, returning the search-

ing glance Mariah gave him with one of cool determination.

Darian sensed an underlying air of tension in the Nicholses' ballroom this evening, one that smacked almost of desperation. As if someone in this room knew they were being hunted. And if anything amiss was about to happen, then Darian intended being at Mariah's side when and wherever it did.

'Very well.' Mariah finally nodded acquiescence, her eyes narrowing as they approached their flustered hostess and her obviously nervously trembling footman.

'Something definitely has Clara on the verge of a fit of the vapours,' she murmured softly to Darian, her voice rising as they reached Clara Nichols's side. 'Clara, darling, whatever is the matter?' She left Darian's side to link her arm companionably through the older woman's.

Lady Nichols dismissed the footman before answering. 'Oh, Mariah,' she wailed. 'Nothing this evening is going as it should, and— Oh! Good evening, your Grace,' she greeted hastily as she saw Darian was standing just behind Mariah.

'Can the countess and I be of any help?' he queried lightly, senses now on full alert, knowing it was most unusual for ladies of the *ton* to become so discomposed in front of their guests, no matter what the situation.

'Oh, no!' Clara Nichols looked horrified at the suggestion. 'No, thank you, Wolfingham,' she added with more calm. 'It was just a— There were several domestic matters in need of my attention. It is all settled now.'

Mariah somehow doubted that, from the hunted look still in Clara Nichols's pale and constantly shifting blue eyes. 'Could the capable Benson not have dealt with them?'

The older woman's mouth thinned, those angry spots returning to her cheeks. 'Benson is the main cause of the problem! Indeed, personal recommendation or not, I am seriously thinking of dismissing him the moment he returns.' Her eyes now glittered with her anger. 'The servants are all in disarray without his guidance.' She had obviously forgotten her earlier reassurances to the contrary, in her agitation. 'And I am sure that there are far more guests here this evening than were actually invited.' She looked askance at the very overcrowded ballroom.

'Indeed?' Wolfingham was narrow-eyed as he also glanced at the overabundance of masked guests.

'No doubt they had heard of the entertainments here and wished to be a part of it, whether invited or not,' Clara twittered coyly.

'No doubt,' Wolfingham drawled drily. 'When Benson returns from where?' he added softly.

Clara gave an impatient shake of her head. 'He has gone to be at the bedside of his sick father. Against my instructions, I might add,' she added agitatedly. 'When he asked earlier I refused him leave to go until tomorrow, but I learnt just minutes ago that he has gone this evening anyway!'

Mariah's breath caught in her throat as she turned to give Darian a wincing glance.

Stupid!

How could they both have been so utterly, utterly stupid?

Or, perhaps more accurately, how could she and Darian have allowed themselves to become so distracted, by their ever-deepening attraction to each other, as to totally miss what had been right in front of their noses this whole time?

Of course neither Richard nor Clara Nichols had reacted as had been expected to the news that the Prince would not be attending their masked ball this evening, after all. Why should they, when neither of them was the assassin or one of the conspirators, whom Mariah and Darian had been sent here to find, in the discovered attempt to assassinate the Prince Regent.

To date, all of the known network of arrested spies, set up by André Rousseau during the year he had spent working as a tutor in England, had been employees in the households of rich or politically powerful people. Servants of one kind or another who could move about at will without attracting attention. A private secretary. A tutor. A footman.

A *butler*...

Benson!

Benson had been Rousseau's spy in the Nicholses' household.

Benson, who had only been employed in the Nicholses' household for a matter of months.

Benson, who had proved to be such 'a treasure' since coming to work in the Nicholses' household.

Benson, who *had* been the only person to leave the Nicholses' sitting room after the Prince's note had been delivered and read.

Benson, who had carried that note up the stairs to Clara Nichols's private sitting room, before no doubt proceeding to read its contents!

Benson, his suspicions perhaps aroused, who had then followed Mariah and Darian back up the stairs, before entering that passageway behind the wall in Mariah's bedchamber, for the sole purpose of listening to their conversation?

Mariah knew by Darian's slight nod of acknowledgement, and the grimness of his expression, that he had already drawn those same conclusions.

As they both must now also be aware that Benson had already departed Eton Park, before either of them had been able to make that connection.

To go where, though, and for what purpose? Did Benson intend to go to London and somehow attempt to assassinate the Prince Regent still?

'You said that Benson came to you through personal recommendation?' Wolfingham, obviously one step ahead in his thinking than Mariah, now prompted their hostess shrewdly.

'Why, yes.' Clara Nichols looked slightly surprised by his interest, before then giving an affectionate smile. 'But, of course, I could not possibly be cross with dear Wedgy. I can only assume that Benson must have fooled him as to his reliability, in the same way that he has fooled all of us.'

'"Wedgy"?' Darian had little or no patience left for the woman's prattling, especially so when she obviously had absolutely no knowledge of just how *much*, and in what way, Benson had fooled them all.

His hostess continued to smile. 'Darling Wedgy. Lord William Edgewood,' she supplied irritably as Darian continued to glower down his aristocratic nose at her. 'But I have always called him Wedgy. William and Edgewood—Wedgy, do you see?'

Darian did indeed see. He saw exactly how the slightly rotund and jolly, and apparently innocuous, Lord Edgewood, a man he now recalled was also attached to the Foreign Office and so privy to certain information—such as the Prince Regent's social engagements!—might have conspired with others in an attempt to assassinate the Prince Regent.

'We have been friends since childhood, you see,' Clara continued to confide. 'More than friends in recent years, of course,' she added coyly, obviously in reference to the debauched display of that affection they had been forced to witness the evening before. 'But I have always considered that friends make the best lovers.'

'What colour mask is Wedgewood wearing this evening?' Darian could not even pretend to listen politely to this dreadful woman another moment longer.

Clara blinked at his obvious aggression. 'He is wearing the red mask of the devil.'

How appropriate! 'And have you seen him yet this evening?'

His hostess frowned as she nodded. 'Just before this latest crisis, as it happens.'

'Where?'

Clara frowned her irritation. 'Really, Wolfingham, you are being less than polite.'

'Where did you last see him, madam?' he demanded tautly.

She blinked pale lashes. 'He was talking to one of the musicians as they prepared their instruments before they commenced playing. Why, Mariah, what on earth is wrong with Wolfingham this evening?' She looked totally bewildered as the duke turned sharply on his highly polished heels to disappear into the melee of the crowded ballroom, without so much as a word of apology or explanation.

Mariah knew exactly what was wrong with Darian, and the reason for his having left so abruptly, and her heart began to beat a wild tattoo in her chest at the realisation that Darian had every intention of confronting Lord Edgewood. 'I will explain later.' She threw the words distractedly at Clara before herself hurrying off in Darian's wake.

Very aware that the assassin's plans for this weekend had been thwarted on two levels. First, by the arrival of the Prince Regent's note of apology. And second, by Benson's hurried departure.

Whether or not Lord Edgewood knew of the disappearance of his co-conspirator, *Mariah* certainly knew that a cornered animal was more likely to come out fighting, rather than cowering in the corner. And William Edgewood, once he became aware of Benson's defection, was obviously intelligent enough to realise he no longer had anything else to lose.

A single glance at the grimness of Darian's expression, before he left to go in search of the older man, had told her that the dangerous Duke of Wolfingham fully intended to confront the older man as being the traitor he so obviously was.

As Mariah was also aware that Darian had barely survived André Rousseau's bullet just weeks ago.

'A little caution, if you please, Wolfingham!'

Darian came to an abrupt halt to turn sharply in the middle of the ballroom, having easily recognised the softly spoken warning as coming from one of his closest friends, Christian Seaton, the Duke of Sutherland. And obviously also one of those uninvited guests Clara Nichols had referred to just minutes ago!

'These masks hide a multitude of sins.' Sutherland confirmed drily, dressed similarly to Darian, in dark clothing and a black mask, his eyes glinting violet through the eye-slits. 'Your groom arrived at Winterton Manor with your note and we arrived here just in time to stop and question the Nicholses' butler as he was attempting to leave,' he supplied economically. 'Rotherham and Maystone are here somewhere, too.'

'You know of Edgewood's involvement?'

'Oh, yes. Benson squeaked like a stuck pig once he knew the game was up. No doubt hoping to shift some of the blame!' The other man gave a grim smile.

'Griff and Maystone are watching him even as we speak.'

Darian nodded abruptly. 'Do we have a plan of extraction?'

'Maystone suggests— Good heavens, what is she doing?' Sutherland growled with a sudden start of surprise.

Darian tensed, very much afraid he knew exactly which 'she' his friend was referring to. 'Where?'

'The little fool!' Sutherland had now turned fully in order to look across the heads of the other guests in the direction of the musicians. 'Can you not keep your woman under control, Darian?' he demanded disgustedly as the two of them began to push their way towards where Mariah now stood in conversation with Lord William Edgewood.

'She is not my woman—' Darian broke off with a start as he realised that, yes, that was *exactly* what Mariah now was.

His woman.

The woman he wished to protect, with his own life if necessary.

The woman he admired and respected more than any other.

The woman he now realised meant more to him than any other woman ever had. Or ever would?

And at this moment *his woman* was deliberately endangering herself by engaging in conversation with the very man they both knew to have been one of the conspirators in the intended assassination of their beloved Regent.

His mouth thinned as he prompted again, 'Do we have a plan, Christian?'

'We did, yes,' the other man confirmed just as grimly. 'That may be a little more difficult now that— Where is she going now?' Sutherland demanded incredulously, both men coming to a halt and watching helplessly as Mariah, her hand companionably in the crook of Lord Edgewood's arm, now crossed to the French doors and strolled outside on to the terrace with him.

'Damn it to hell!' Darian had never felt so helpless in his life before as he did at that moment. Or so much like putting Mariah across his knee and administering a sound thrashing, for having endangered herself so deliberately. A thrashing, because of his earlier promise to himself never to cause Mariah any physical harm, that would have to take a verbal form. A verbal tongue-lashing he fully intended to carry out the moment the two of them were alone together again.

If they were ever alone together again.

'There is such an uncomfortable crush in there already,' Mariah remarked lightly as she stepped outside into the briskness of the March evening air beside William Edgewood.

He released his arm from her hold. 'You may drop the pretence now, Countess,' he dismissed scornfully.

'Pretence?' She gazed up at him guilelessly.

Edgewood gave a scathing snort. 'I am sure that we both know, with Wolfingham so obviously your lover, that you have absolutely no real interest in stepping outside into the moonlight with an old man like me.'

In truth, Mariah had not thought any further beyond the need she felt to prevent Darian from challenging the older man, as she had known he fully intended doing when he left her side so precipitously.

Outside, and alone on the terrace with William Edgewood—who appeared to have dropped all pretence of being that amiable fool everyone believed him to be and now looked at her with shrewdly calculating eyes—she now had time and opportunity to realise her mistake.

To realise that cornered animal had now turned its rabid attentions on to her.

She faced Edgewood unflinchingly as she decided to do exactly as he had suggested and cease all pretence. 'Your cohort has already fled.'

'So Clara unwittingly informed me a few minutes ago.' He nodded tersely.

Mariah nodded briskly. 'There is no way of escaping, nowhere you might go now where you will not be caught and held for trial as a traitor and attempted assassin.'

'Would not France be the practical choice?' he derided.

Mariah gave a pained frown. 'Why? Why would you turn traitor on your own country? On your Regent?' She had once asked Martin the same question.

'You can ask me that here, in the midst of this debauchery that has become England?' Edgewood scoffed. 'And with a Regent more licentious than the rest?'

And Martin's answer had been just the same.

'You are just as guilty of that licentiousness—'

'Necessarily so...' he nodded. '...if I was to fool others into not suspecting my real feelings on the matter. My mother was French, you know. I am half-French, and my loyalties lie there rather than— Ah, Wolfingham, I wondered how long it would take for you to follow your mistress!' Edgewood murmured derisively as he glanced over Mariah's shoulder. 'And I see you have brought several of your friends with you, too!'

Mariah turned sharply to look at where Darian— and several of his friends?—had now joined them outside on the terrace.

At least, she had fully intended to turn and look at them.

Instead, she found herself suddenly held as Lord Edgewood's prisoner, as he pulled her roughly in front of him and anchored her there, by placing an arm about her throat and pressing a pistol painfully against her temple.

A single glance at Darian showed his eyes to be glittering intently behind his mask in the moonlight, his displeasure, at the vulnerable position in which Mariah now found herself, clear for all to see as he glared at her furiously.

She quickly moved her gaze to the three masked gentlemen standing behind him, believing she recognised one of them as being the grey-haired Aubrey

Maystone, but the identity of the other two were hidden behind their masks. 'It would seem you are outnumbered, Lord Edgewood,' she remarked slightly huskily, the tightness of his arm about her throat preventing her from breathing properly.

'But I have the pistol,' he pointed out conversationally.

'We all have pistols, Edgewood,' Aubrey Maystone assured drily as those pistols now appeared in all the other gentlemen's hands.

Including Darian's, Mariah realised, wondering where on his person he could have kept it hidden until now.

Was she becoming slightly hysterical, in questioning something so trivial, when Lord Edgewood had a pistol pressed so painfully against her temple? Lord, she hoped not!

'But I also have the Countess of Carlisle,' Edgewood came back confidently. 'Eh, Wolfingham?' he added challengingly.

Darian was well aware of the fact that Edgewood now held a pistol against Mariah's temple. Could see all too clearly how the end of the barrel of that pistol was digging into her tender flesh. Hurting her.

'You are only making your situation worse, Edgewood.' Aubrey Maystone drew the other man's attention back to him.

'Could it possibly be any worse, when I am obviously already known as a conspirator and traitor against the Crown?' The other man eyed Maystone coldly.

Darian took advantage of Edgewood's distraction to inch his way slowly to the side and then forward, aided in his stealth of movement by Sutherland and Rotherham, as they both moved to flank Aubrey Maystone.

If Darian could just move a little further forward he might be able to—

'Stay exactly where you are, Wolfingham,' Edgewood warned harshly as he now pointed the pistol in Darian's direction.

It needed only that brief moment of Edgewood's distraction from Mariah for there to be a blur of movement at Darian's side as Sutherland dived downwards towards Edgewood's legs, at the same time as Rotherham leapt forward, with the obvious intention of wrestling the raised pistol from Edgewood's hand.

Leaving Darian to stand and watch as the scene played out before him.

Mariah was deafened as Lord Edgewood's pistol suddenly went off beside her ear, quickly followed by the report of another shot being fired, before she then felt herself toppling over as Lord Edgewood's legs were knocked from beneath him, pulling her down heavily on top of him. Her last vision was of a horrified Darian before she hit her head hard on the floor of the terrace and she knew no more.

Chapter Fourteen

'I trust you know that I am still very angry with you for behaving so recklessly, madam?'

Mariah was nestled comfortably against Darian's shoulder, held securely in his arms as they travelled back to London in his ducal coach several hours later. Despite the lateness of the hour neither one of them had wished to remain at Eton Park a moment longer than they had to, once the worst of the furore had died down.

Clara Nichols had been hysterical, of course, as had many of her female guests, at learning that her friend and lover Wedgy now lay dead upon the terrace at Eton Park, a bullet through his heart.

The gentlemen present had been more prosaic regarding the situation, readily accepting Aubrey Maystone's explanation of Lord Wedgewood having been caught in the act, by the Duke of Wolfingham, of forcing his attentions upon the Countess of Carlisle, before then being accidentally killed by his own pistol in the tussle that had followed. An act witnessed and confirmed by the Dukes of Sutherland and Rotherham.

It was far from an accurate account of the truth, of course, the fatal bullet having been fired by Aubrey Maystone himself. But none present had wished to challenge the word of men as powerful as Lord Maystone, and the Dukes of Wolfingham, Rotherham and Sutherland. And Clara Nichols had been too hysterical to question the fact that Lord Maystone, and the Dukes of Rotherham and Sutherland, had not even been invited to her masked ball.

No doubt the other woman would remember that fact once she had calmed down, but she had been far too busy enjoying being at the centre of the scandal, and the scandalous success of her masked ball, when Darian and Mariah had quietly taken their leave earlier.

The two of them had gone up the stairs to their rooms so that Mariah might change her bloodied clothes before departing, leaving Mariah's maid and Darian's valet to pack up their things before following tomorrow.

'Mariah, you are not to fall asleep until you have listened to what I have to say!' Darian gave her shoulders a shake to prevent that from happening. 'Do you have any idea how I felt when I looked down and saw you unconscious upon the floor and covered in blood?' he demanded harshly, his impatience barely contained. 'Do you even realise that my own heart stopped beating, when I thought Maystone had missed Edgewood and had shot you instead?'

Mariah was too tired, felt too safe in Darian's arms, to care about much of anything else at the moment. 'As you see, by my presence here, he did not and I was not.'

'Mariah!'

'Darian.' She moved slightly in his arms so that she might look up at him in the lamplight, noting the dark shadows in his magnificent green eyes, the grey tinge to his tightly etched face and clenched jaw. She reached up now to gently touch that clenched jaw. 'I am safe. We are both safe.' *Darian* was safe. Which, after all, had been Mariah's only intent earlier, when she hurried across the ballroom in order to reach William Edgewood's side ahead of Darian.

Her only *interest* had been to prevent Darian from challenging the other man and perhaps being hurt or killed in the process.

Because, she had realised, she was in love with him.

She loved, and was in love with, Darian Hunter, the Duke of Wolfingham.

And strangely that realisation no longer terrified her. The emotion was no longer something for her to fear. Nor did it make her less, as she had believed loving someone would, but somehow more.

Darian now repressed a shudder. 'He might have killed you.'

She smiled. 'But he did not.'

Darian looked down at Mariah searchingly, noting

the calmness of her expression and the tranquillity in those beautiful turquoise-coloured eyes.

While he was still a churning mass of emotions. Fear, for Mariah's life. Devastation, when he had believed her dead. Relief, when he had realised the blood on her gown was from Edgewood rather than her own. Elation, when she had opened her eyes minutes later and smiled at him.

Unfortunately, *all* those emotions had been followed by anger. That Mariah could have been so reckless as to have put herself in danger in the first place.

'What possessed you?' he demanded now. 'What on earth went through your mind when you deliberately placed yourself in a position of vulnerability by going outside alone on to the terrace with Edgewood?'

Her smile became rueful. 'I do not believe I was thinking much of anything at the time. It just seemed— It was the right thing for me to do, Darian.'

'It was the worst thing you could have done!' he contradicted explosively.

Her fingers rested lightly against the tautness of his cheek. 'Let us not discuss this any further just now, Darian. It is over. The Prince Regent is safe. The would-be assassins are all dead or in custody. Napoleon himself has been thwarted in his plan to devastate the alliance. It is all finally over, Darian.'

He tensed beneath those caressing fingers. '*We* are not over, Mariah!' His arms tightened about her. '*We* will never be over!'

She looked up at him quizzically. 'What do you mean?'

'Exactly as I say.' A nerve pulsed strongly in his clenched jaw. 'We have begun something this weekend, Mariah. Something good. Something wonderful. And I will not allow you to just calmly walk away from that. To walk away from *me!*'

Leaving Darian was the last thing that Mariah wanted to do. Indeed, she never wished to be apart from him ever again. Wished to spend her every waking moment with him, and her sleeping ones, too, for the rest of her life.

That was how much she had realised she loved Darian. More than life itself. More than any of the fears of love and intimacy that had plagued her for over half of her lifetime.

She looked up at him shyly beneath the sweep of her lashes. 'Did I say that I wished to walk away from you?'

'Well. No. But—' He looked nonplussed. 'It will not do, Mariah. I will not have you running all over London and putting yourself in danger as you have been doing these past few years. I will not countenance—' He broke off as she began to chuckle softly at his bluster, a dark scowl on his brow. 'I fail to see what is so funny, Mariah.'

'We are. The two of us.' She sobered as she saw that Darian was still bursting with anger. 'We are both so afraid to admit that we might care for or need anyone. In any way. Darian, I will not walk away from you once we are returned to London,' she assured him seriously. 'I will be yours for as long as you wish me to be,' she assured him huskily.

'You will?'

'I will,' she confirmed huskily. 'Of course there are still many things that need to be discussed between the two of us.' Her supposed affairs with other men being one of them. Her lack of experience in physical matters being another. 'But I am sure, once we have done so, that we will be able to come to some sort of arrangement, whereby the two of us—'

'Arrangement?' Darian repeated softly, dangerously. 'I am talking of the two of us marrying, Mariah, not forming an arrangement!'

The shock on Mariah's face at his pronouncement might have been amusing, if Darian were not so much in earnest. If he did not love this woman more than life itself. If he did not love, admire and respect Mariah more than he had realised it was possible to love, admire and respect any woman.

Except he did. Knew that he felt all of those things for Mariah. So much so that he really had thought his heart had stopped when he looked down at her earlier, covered in blood, and had thought her dead. His own life had ended, too, in those few brief moments. He had ceased to exist. Darian had ceased to live or breathe, in the belief that Mariah Beecham, Countess of Carlisle, and the woman he loved, no longer lived or breathed. All that had remained was a shell, a body, without emotions or feeling.

Until Mariah's eyes had fluttered open and she had looked up at him and smiled.

It was at that moment that Darian had decided that he was never going to let Mariah out of his sight ever again. Whatever he had to do, however long it took, he intended that Mariah would be his wife, his duchess, and at his side for the rest of their lives.

'I love you, Mariah,' he told her now, fiercely, his arms tightening about her. 'I love you and want to marry you. To spend the rest of my days and nights with you. I love you, Mariah,' he repeated determinedly. 'And however long it takes to convince you, I intend having you for my—'

'Yes.'

'—wife,' he concluded purposefully before his gaze sharpened as he realised what Mariah had said, if not why. 'Yes what?' he questioned guardedly.

'Yes, I will marry you, Darian!' She smiled up at him glowingly, tears now glistening in her eyes. 'I love you, too, my darling Darian. I love you!'

Darian continued to look down at her searchingly. Hardly daring to believe—to hope that—

'You love me? How can you possibly love me?' He frowned darkly. 'When I have been nothing but judgemental of you from the first. So disapproving. Scornful. Critical—'

'And kind, caring, protective and passionate,' Mariah spoke huskily. 'Would you prefer it if I did not love you, Darian?' she added teasingly as he still looked down at her in disbelief. 'I suppose I might try,' she continued conversationally. 'But it is so very difficult, when I believe you to be so much all of those things *I* mentioned in regard to how you are with me.

I could *try* not to love you but— Darian!' She gave a strangled cry as his mouth finally claimed hers, his arms gathering her in so close against him it felt as if he was trying to make her a part of himself.

And perhaps he was, because for the next several minutes there was nothing else between them but those passionate kisses interspersed with words of love and adoration.

'I intend that we shall be married as soon as is possible,' Darian finally warned as he continued to hold Mariah tightly in his arms, as if afraid, if he let her go, she might disappear in a puff of smoke. 'I believe the least we are owed, for helping to foil this plot against the Prince Regent, is the granting of a Special Licence. Unless, of course, you would prefer to have a big grand wedding, with all of the *ton* in attendance?' he added uncertainly as the idea occurred to him that Mariah had never really had a happy wedding day. 'I suppose I might be persuaded into waiting for a few weeks longer, as long as you will allow me to spend all of my days and nights before the wedding by your side.'

'A Special Licence sounds perfect,' Mariah assured him happily. 'I have already had the big white wedding attended by the *ton*,' she dismissed huskily. 'Neither it, nor that marriage, brought me any happiness.'

'Apart from Christina.'

She gave a shake of her head. 'I have always seen Christina as somehow being apart from that marriage.

As if she were only ever mine, to love and to cherish. Does that sound ridiculous, in the circumstances?'

Darian's arms tightened about her. 'Nothing you say ever sounds ridiculous to me. But I hope— I sincerely hope, would deem it an honour, if you would allow me to become another father to Christina once the two of us are married?'

Mariah's heart was already full to bursting with the love she felt for Darian, but in that moment she believed it truly overflowed with the emotion. 'I should like that very much,' she accepted emotionally. 'As, I am sure, would Christina. Martin was never a proper father to her anyway.' She frowned. 'He took as little interest in her as he did in me.'

'Carlisle was a fool.' Darian scowled. 'But his loss is my gain,' he dismissed firmly. 'I assure you that I intend telling and showing both of you, each and every day, how much you are both loved and cherished.'

'I know you will.' Mariah smiled up at him gratefully, before biting her bottom lip worriedly. 'There are still some things we need to discuss, before we make any more of these wonderful plans. Things you need to know about me—'

'No,' Darian bit out harshly.

'But—'

'I do not need to know anything more about you, Mariah, than that I love you and you love me. Nothing else matters but that,' he stated firmly.

'You have no idea how happy that makes me, Darian.' Mariah smiled tremulously. 'But these are things you really do need to know, if you are to become my husband.'

'I most assuredly am!'

'Then you *must* listen to me, Darian,' she insisted as he seemed about to deny her once again.

His jaw was tightly clenched. 'Not if you are about to tell me about the other men who have been in your life. I do not want to know, Mariah. They are unimportant, irrelevant—'

'Non-existent,' Mariah put in softly, although it inwardly thrilled her to hear Darian dismiss the existence of those lovers as being irrelevant to the two of them.

Darian's voice trailed off as he seemed to hear what she had just said, a frown between his eyes now as he looked down at her searchingly.

A searching look that Mariah returned with a steady gaze as she began to talk again. 'Seven years ago I discovered, quite by chance, that my husband was a traitor to the Crown. Let me tell all, before I lose my nerve, and then you may speak, Darian,' she pleaded as he would have interrupted once again.

'Very well.' Darian nodded slowly; in truth he was still completely stunned at Mariah's claim that she had taken no other lovers.

And so he listened. As Mariah told him of her husband's treachery to his country. Of how she had gone to London, and Aubrey Maystone, with the information. And how Aubrey Maystone had used that knowledge, and Mariah, to garner even more information from Carlisle during the last two years of that man's life. Of how she had continued her own work for the Crown for these seven years, and the sense of self and self-worth it had given her. The first she had known in her life, apart from being mother to Christina.

Darian was finally left speechless when Mariah confided in him that there had been no lovers in her life. That she had flirted, cajoled, teased information from certain gentlemen, but that she had never bedded a single one of them. That the rumour and speculation of scandal about her had grown over the years, because pride had dictated that none of those gentleman had ever wished to own to the fact that they had not been, nor ever would be, a lover to the Countess of Carlisle.

The conclusion this final revelation gave Darian was simply mind-numbing. 'Then that single, awful occasion with Carlisle, the evening Christina was conceived, was the only occasion—'

'Yes,' Mariah confirmed flatly.

'My darling!' Darian gave a pained groan. 'Then our own lovemaking—the things we did together—'

'Were utterly beautiful,' Mariah assured him firmly. 'You could not have been a more gentle, more caring, a more passionate lover, even if you had known the truth, Darian.'

Darian begged to differ. If he had known, if he had once guessed at Mariah's innocence in regard to physical love, then he would have taken things more slowly, more gently, been less physically demanding.

That Mariah had been able to respond so passionately as she had earlier today to his caresses, that she had attained her peak not once but three times, was a miracle!

Although Mariah's revelations did help to explain those puzzling moments of innocence he had sensed in her, those blushes that had seemed so out of character with the experienced siren she was reputed to be.

'I trust you are not having regrets about our lovemaking earlier today, Darian,' Mariah now teased him reprovingly. 'Because I am dearly hoping that we shall be continuing with my education, in that regard, as soon as we reach London. Christina is away until tomorrow evening,' she reminded huskily. 'And we shall have the house all to ourselves till then...'

Darian would like nothing more than to spend the night with Mariah, to make love to and with her for hours and hours without end. But he would also settle for just being in the same bed with her, of just holding her, as difficult as that might be, if she would rather wait until they were married for them to make love again.

'I would not be at all happy to wait,' Mariah answered decisively, Darian's first indication that he had spoken his reservations out loud. 'Darian, I am simply *dying* for us to make love again. I have so many years to make up for. So much I have missed. That I want to learn about and enjoy.' She curved her body seductively against his. 'You are not going to continue to deny me, are you, Darian?'

How could Darian ever deny this woman anything?

This woman whom he loved, and would always love, with every fibre of his being.

'Do you know what I thought after we had made love at Eton Park earlier today—yesterday now?' Mariah realised after a glance at the bedside clock revealed it was well after midnight, her fingers swirling in the darkness of the hair on Darian's naked chest as she leant up on her elbow beside him in the comfort of her dishevelled bed.

'Earlier today?' He arched his brows as he glanced down at their satiated and well-loved nakedness.

'Earlier today,' she insisted firmly. 'I thought, so this is what poets all write about, singers croon over and lovers will risk anything to possess. But I was wrong, Darian, because *this*, the absolute joy we have just found in each other's arms, is what poets write about, singers croon over and lovers will risk everything to possess!' Their lovemaking had been a revelation to Mariah.

She had never dreamed such pleasure existed, had never realised how wonderful it was to literally become a part of another person. To be joined to them, body, soul and heart.

To be joined to *Darian*, body, soul and heart.

'I love you, Darian,' she told him achingly, emotionally. 'I love you so very much, my darling.'

'As I love you.' His arms tightened about her once again. 'And I will love you for the rest of our lives together.'

'Promise?'

'Without a doubt. You?'

'Oh, yes!'

Mariah had absolutely no doubt it was a promise they would both cherish in their hearts and happily keep.

Epilogue

Two weeks later—Wolfingham House, London

'Was that a very despondent-looking Anthony I saw leaving just now?' Mariah prompted as she entered Darian's study.

'It was, yes.' Darian smiled as she walked across the room and straight into his welcoming arms.

She looked up at him quizzically. 'What on earth did you say to him to make him look so downhearted?'

His smile widened into a grin. 'As we had already discussed, I told him that my duchess and I had decided to give him permission to pay court to our daughter, Christina.'

After only a week of marriage, Mariah still felt a thrill in her chest at hearing herself referred to as Darian's duchess. For that was who she was now, Mariah Hunter, the Duchess of Wolfingham. How grand it sounded. And yet she knew she loved Darian so much, wanted to be with him so much, that she would have married him even if he had not been the top-lofty and wealthy Duke of Wolfingham.

Although she did not altogether trust that wicked grin upon her husband's face right now.

'If you told him that, why was Anthony looking less than happy?'

That wicked grin widened, green eyes glowing with laughter. 'Because I told him that not only does he have to win Christina's heart, but that as her stepfather, I will also expect him to prove himself as being sober and responsible, before we would agree to the match. And that even then we will not countenance there being a wedding until after Christina's eighteenth birthday.'

'What a wicked stepfather and brother you are, when you know full well that Christina has already admitted to us that she is smitten.' Mariah chuckled reprovingly.

'A little uncertainty will do my little brother good,' Darian dismissed unrepentantly, his arms now tightening about her waist as a different sort of wickedness now gleamed in his eyes. 'Have I told you yet this morning how beautiful you look?'

'About an hour ago, I believe.' She blushed as she remembered the *way* in which he had told her.

'Have I *shown* you yet this morning how beautiful you are to me?'

'Also about an hour ago,' Mariah answered shyly.

'And would my duchess be interested in my demonstrating the depths of those feelings for her again right this minute?'

Mariah felt the thrill in her chest at just how willing she was to allow Darian to do exactly that. A thrill of excitement that now coursed hotly through the whole of her body. 'I should like to demonstrate the depth of my feelings for you first,' she suggested huskily.

Darian chuckled softly. 'Then shall we retire to the ducal bedchamber?'

The ducal bedchamber that the two of them had shared every night before their wedding and again every night since, the two of them having decided there would be no separate bedchambers for them. Ever. That they would spend all of their nights, as well as all of their days, together.

Mariah had no idea what the future would bring. Another war to quell Napoleon was most certainly imminent. A wedding for her daughter and Anthony next year, she hoped. Perhaps a child or two of their own, for Darian and herself. A handsome boy who looked exactly like his father and a little girl, also with her father's dark hair and green eyes, so that their parents might spoil and pet them both. Mariah certainly hoped it would be so.

But she had no doubt whatsoever, that whatever the future might hold for the two of them, that they would face it together.

Always, and for ever, together…

* * * * *

Don't miss the next book in Carole Mortimer's dazzling DANGEROUS DUKES *series.*
Coming soon!